SHORT STORY INDEX

2011

AN INDEX TO STORIES IN COLLECTIONS AND PERIODICALS

Edited by

JOHN GREENFIELDT

IPSWICH, MASSACHUSETTS

H. W. WILSON
A Division of EBSCO Publishing, Inc.

2011

ISSN 0360-9774

Library of Congress Control Number 75-649762

Printed in the United States of America

CONTENTS

PREFACE

The present volume indexes 5,786 stories. Of these, 5,211 stories appeared in collections and 575 in periodicals. A total of 293 collections and 109 periodicals are included in this volume. The periodicals are those indexed in two other H.W. Wilson publications, *Readers' Guide to Periodical Literature* and *Humanities Index*.

As in previous volumes, the arrangement is by author, title, and subject in one alphabet. Stories in periodicals are indexed only by author and title. The author entry, which indicates the collection or periodical where the story can be found, is the fullest entry. A List of Collections Indexed and a Directory of Periodicals complete the volume. Further information about the content of entries is provided in the Directions for Use.

DIRECTIONS FOR USE

Part I of *Short Story Index*, the Author, Title, and Subject Index, is arranged in dictionary form with all entries in one alphabet. Part II is a List of Collections indexed. Part III is a Directory of Periodicals. The following directions apply to Part I.

Author entry

The author entry gives the name of the author and title of the story. For stories found in collections it also gives the title and editor of the collection. For stories found in periodicals it provides the periodical title, volume number, page numbers, and date.

Sample entry from a collection:

> **Card, Orson Scott**
> Jamaica
> The way of the wizard; edited by John Joseph
> Adams

The above example shows that the story by Orson Scott Card entitled "Jamaica" appeared in *The way of the wizard*, edited by John Joseph Adams. Further information about the book is given in the List of Collections Indexed.

Sample entry from a periodical:

> **Rash, Ron**
> The trusty
> *The New Yorker* v78 no14 p68-75 My 23 2011

The above example indicates that the story by Ron Rash entitled "The trusty" appeared in *The New Yorker*, volume 78, number 14, pages 68-75, in the May 23, 2011, issue. For fuller information about the periodical consult the Directory of Periodicals.

Title entry

Title entries are used to identify the author under whose name the story will be found. The first word (not an article) of each title is in boldface type.

Sample entries:

> The **obscure** bird. Royle, N.
> **Talk** is cheap. Ryman, G.

Subject entry

Stories found in collections are listed under subjects with which they deal in whole or in part. Subject entries are printed in capital letters, in boldface type. Consult the author entry for the title of the story collection.

Sample entry:

> **MARRIAGE PROPOSALS**
> Atkins, E. The wrong side of Mr. Right

SHORT STORY INDEX, 2011

PART I

Author, Title, and Subject Index

1.7 to Tennessee. Quatro, J.

1: Year of the Monkey. Yamashita, K. T.

4/18. Campbell, F.

12 Rounds. Sullins, J.

20 sculptures in one hour. Davis, L.

21x watch. Goodberg, D.

23. Sands, B.

23 Skidoo. O'Leary, P.

--30--. Barron, L.

55 miles to the gas pump. Proulx, A.

The 74th tale. Santlofer, J.

84 Avenue Foch. Ely, S.

1840: Venice: Tourist Destination [Excerpt from a short story, What the Moon Saw] Andersen, H. C.

1842: St. Petersburg: Nikolai Gogol on a labor of love [Excerpt from The Overcoat] Gogol, N.

1848: St. Petersburg: Fyodor Dostoevsky walks alone [Excerpt from a short story, White Nights] Dostoevsky, F.

1875: Hartford: Right ambition [Excerpt from The story of the good little boy] Twain, M.

1883: St. Petersburg: Lack of initiative [Excerpt from The Ninny] Chekhov, A. P.

1912. Goodberg, D.

1920: Prague: Senior management. Kafka, F.

1920: Prague: Urban Renewal [Excerpt from story, The City Coat of Arms] Kafka, F.

1922. King, S.

1929: the singular taffy puller. Jemisin, N. K.

1939: Paris: Iréne Nèmirovsky on the Quai d'Orleans. Némirovsky, I.

1943: a brief note pertaining to the absence of one olivaceous cormorant, stuffed. Swirsky, R.

1963. Slouka, M.

1963: the argument against Louis Pasteur. Lafferty, M.

1966. Shapiro, J.

1972: the lichenologist's visit. Sedia, E.

1984 1/2. Matheson, R.

1995: kneel. Evenson, B.

2000: Dr. Lambshead's dark room. Chambers, S. J.

2001: Port Ewen, NY: Packaging [Excerpt from Letter to a Funeral Parlor] Davis, L.

2003: the pea. Clairval, G.

$10,000 a year, easy. Vonnegut, K.

A

The **Aarne-Thompson** Classification Revue. Black, H.

The **abacus**. Somerville, P.

Abandoned. Goodberg, D.

ABANDONED CHILDREN
See also Orphans
Hall, T. M. Gravetending
Silver, M. The passenger
Thon, M. R. Heavenly creatures: for wandering children and their delinquent mother
Yoshimoto, B. A special boy

ABANDONED TOWNS See Extinct cities

ABANDONMENT OF FAMILY See Desertion and nonsupport

Abasiyanik, Sait Faik
Such a story
Tablet & pen; literary landscapes from the modern Middle East, a words without borders anthology; edited by Reza Asian.

Abbas, Ghulam
The room with the blue light
Tablet & pen; literary landscapes from the modern Middle East, a words without borders anthology; edited by Reza Asian.

Abbas, Luay Hamza
Spit Out What Is in Your Mouth
World Literature Today v85 no2 p19-21 Mr/Ap 2011

ABBESSES See Nuns

ABBEYS
See also Churches; Convent life; Monasticism and religious orders

Abbott, Lee K.
A great piece of elephant
Best of the West 2009; new stories from the wide side of the Missouri; edited by James Thomas and D. Seth Horton; foreword by Rick Bass.
Time and Fear and Somehow Love
The Georgia Review v65 no1 p14-29 Spr 2011

ABC antidote. Beah, I.

ABDUCTION See Kidnapping

Abdullah, Achmed
The soul of a turk
The Big book of adventure stories; edited and with a introduction by Otto Penzler; foreword by Douglas Preston.

Abercrombie, Joe
The fool jobs
The Best science fiction and fantasy of the year: volume five; edited by Jonathan Strahan.

ABNORMALITIES AND DEFORMITIES See Deformities; Dwarfs; Monsters

Aboard. Budnitz, J.

ABOLITIONISTS
See also Slavery

Abominable. Emshwiller, C.

The **abominable** child's tale. Emshwiller, C.

ABORIGINES, AUSTRALIAN *See* Australian aborigines

ABORTION
Bezmozgis, D. The train of their departure
Evans, D. Harvest
Harris, L. Mummy dust tea
Holt, E. Fem care
Leland, C. T. What it came to
Niedzviecki, H. Prenatal
Nutting, A. Teenager
Penkov, M. The letter
Price-Thompson, T. Brotherly love
Slesinger, T. Missis Flinders
Thon, M. R. Necessary angels
Treadway, J. Oregon

Aboulela, Leila
Missing Out
Granta no111 p7-24 Summ 2010

About All Dolls. Brown, R.
About Love. Francis, H. E.
About spring, Marwah and the feast. Khalaylah, A.
Above and below [Part of the Summer Fiction Issue] Groff, L.
Above the Imperial. Tafoya, D.

Abraham, Daniel
Baljour and Meriwether in the adventure of the emperor's vengeance
Steampunk II: steampunk reloaded; edited by Ann & Jeff VanderMeer.

Abraham, Pearl
Hasidic noir
Randisi, R. J. The Shamus winners: America's best private eye stories, volume II, 1996-2009; collected and introduced by Robert J. Randisi; founder, Private Eye Writers of America

Abrahamsen, Eric
(tr.) *See* Bi, Feiyu

Abridged version. Sands, B.
Absentminded. Davis, L.

Abu Lail, Sahar
A letter to a betrayer
Loud sounds from the Holy Land; short fiction by Palestinian women; edited and translated by Jamal Assadi with assistance from Martha Moody.
My neighbor is a whore!
Loud sounds from the Holy Land; short fiction by Palestinian women; edited and translated by Jamal Assadi with assistance from Martha Moody.
A stranger at the bus stop!
Loud sounds from the Holy Land; short fiction by Palestinian women; edited and translated by Jamal Assadi with assistance from Martha Moody.

ABUSE OF CHILDREN *See* Child abuse
ABUSED WIVES *See* Wife abuse
Abusing my interests. Sands, B.
Academician Sisoye's inaugural speech. Minevski, B.

ACADIANS
Louisiana
See Cajuns
Acceptance speech. Emshwiller, C.
The **accident**. Bill, F.
ACCIDENTAL DEATH *See* Accidents

ACCIDENTS
See also Airplane accidents; Drowning; Fires; Railroad accidents; Traffic accidents
Archer, J. Caste-off
Bill, F. The accident
Cardinale, J. The singularity
Davis, L. The bone
Doyle, R. Animals
Goodberg, D. Mercy blow
Gordimer, N. The moment before the gun went off
Ḥaqqī, Y. The first lesson
Heathcock, A. The staying freight
Holm, B. Q. The great actor
Johnston, B. A. Soldier of fortune
Laken, V. Separate kingdoms
Loory, B. The path
Lychack, W. Hawkins
Martel, Y. The moon above his head
Meyer, P. What you do out here, when you're alone
Nuila, R. Dog bites
O'Nan, S. Monsters
Pascoe, J. Paper
Ross, A. The suicide room
Sheinin, L. The hunting knife
Thon, M. R. First, body
Treadway, J. Dear Nicole
Trevor, W. The dressmaker's child

Accomplice to Memory. Zhang, Q. M.
An **account** in her name. Sterling, P.

ACCOUNTANTS
Ayau, K. J. At a loss for words
Eugenides, J. Great experiment

ACCULTURATION
See also Race relations
An **accurate** account. Dixon, S.

ACHILLES (LEGENDARY CHARACTER)
Lake, J. Achilles, sulking in his Buick
Achilles, sulking in his Buick. Lake, J.
The **acid** test. Kenyon, K.

Ackerman, Laura
(tr.) *See* Lercher, Lisa

Ackert, David and Rosenbaum, Benjamin
The king of the djinn
Sympathy for the devil; edited by Tim Pratt.

Ackley-McPhail, Danielle
The devil you don't
The stories (in) between; edited by Greg Schauer, Jeanne B. Benzel, and W. H. Horner.

Acknowledgment. Davis, L.
An **acolyte** of black spires. Harvey, R.

ACROBATS
See also Stunt men
Across the lake. Eisenberg, D.

ACTAEON (LEGENDARY CHARACTER)
Kushner, E. The children of Cadmus
Action at a distance. Cardinale, J.
Action Figure. Prince, A.
Activation. Martin, T. L.

ACTORS
See also Motion picture actors and actresses; Theater life
Berry, J. Twenty-eight scenes for neglected guests
Boland, J. C. Stand-in
Bowes, R. On the slide
Danishvar, S. The playhouse

ACTORS—*Continued*

Davis, L. The actors

Holm, B. Q. The great actor

Monzó, Q. Strategies

Nolan, W. F. Vampire dollars

Oliver, R. Baskervilles midgets

Parry, L. The vanishing American

Roberge, R. Whatever happened to Billy Brody?

Ross, A. Middleman

Shapiro, J. Night and day

Shepard, S. Costello

Terry, G. P. Grasping the bird's tail

Trevor, W. Good news

The **actors**. Davis, L.

ACTRESSES

See also Motion picture actors and actresses; Theater life

Black, H. The Aarne-Thompson Classification Revue

Blauner, P. Thank God for Charlie

Kronauer, B. The diva and her tricks

Novack, S. Conversions on the road to Damascus

O'Connor, S. Based on a true story

Read, C. Hungry enough

ACUPUNCTURE

McElroy, J. Mister X

Ada Liz. Rodoreda, M.

Adair, Danielle

Selma [excerpt]

Butler, B. 30 under 30; an anthology of innovative fiction by younger writers; Blake Butler & Lily Hoang, eds.

Adams, Ashlee

Bull of the Woods

Prairie Schooner v85 no2 p61-76 Summ 2011

Called Out

The Southern Review (Baton Rouge, La.) v46 no4 p546-62 Aut 2010

Adams, Brock

Audacious

The Sewanee Review v118 no3 p315-34 Summ 2010

Adams, Cleve F.

The key

The Black Lizard big book of Black Mask stories; edited and with a foreword by Otto Penzler; introduction by Keith Alan Deutsch.

Adcox, James Tadd

The Bed Frame

TriQuarterly no139 Wint/Spr 2011

A Dial Tone

TriQuarterly no139 Wint/Spr 2011

The Off Season

TriQuarterly no139 Wint/Spr 2011

The Weight of the Internet

TriQuarterly no139 Wint/Spr 2011

An **added** fraction. Diab, F.

Addicted to sweetness. Child, L.

Addison Howell and the clockroach. Priest, C.

Adichie, Chimamanda Ngozi

Birdsong

20 under 40; stories from the New Yorker; edited by Deborah Treisman.

The New Yorker v86 no28 p96-103 S 20 2010

Ceiling

The Best American short stories, 2011; selected from U.S. and Canadian magazines by Geraldine Brooks with Heidi Pitlor; with an introduction by Geraldine Brooks.

Granta no111 p65-80 Summ 2010

The headstrong historian

The Pen/O.Henry Prize stories, 2010; edited and with an introduction by Laura Furman; with essays on the stories they admire most by jurors Junot Diaz, Paula Fox, Yiyun Li.

Sola

Freedom; stories celebrating the Universal Declaration of Human Rights; Amnesty International.

Adlig Schwenkitten. Solzhenitsyn, A.

Admiralty. Anderson, P.

Admission. Senna, D.

Adnan, Yassin

Two stories

Beirut 39; new writing from the Arab world; edited by Samuel Shimon; with a preface by Hanan al-Shaykh

ADOLESCENCE

See also Boys; Girls; Youth

Baxter, C. Snow

Bingham, S. August ninth at Natural Bridge

Boggs, B. Homecoming

Chapman, J. Great Salt Lake

Eisenberg, D. What it was like, seeing Chris

Fleri, J. Gynecomastia

Fowler, C. Oh I do like to be beside the seaside

Fowler, K. J. The Pelican Bar

Franco, J. Emily

Gautier, A. The ease of living

Gautier, A. Held

Gifford, B. Bad girls

Gifford, B. Caca negra

Gifford, B. Close encounters of the right kind

Gifford, B. Portrait of the artist with four other guys

Gifford, B. Rain in the distance

Gifford, B. Roy's first car

Hamburger, A. The end of anti-Semitism

Hemmingson, M. Solid memories have the lifespan of tulips and sunflowers

Highsmith, P. In the plaza

Hodge, B. Just outside our windows, deep inside our walls

Hodge, B. An ounce of prevention is worth a pound of flesh

Hunter, L. Fifteen

Hunter, L. Peggy's brother

Hunter, L. Scales

Jones, S. G. So perfect

Jordan, N. Night in Tunisia

Kim, A. S. Beautiful white bodies

Marcus, H. Swimming

Millhauser, S. Clair de lune

Millhauser, S. Flying carpets

Millhauser, S. Tales of darkness and the unknown, vol. XIV: The white glove

Mullins, D. P. Arboretum

Neugeboren, J. You are my heart

Nutting, A. Teenager

Oates, J. C. Nowhere

Packer, A. Walk for Mankind

Percy, B. Refresh, refresh

Prill, D. Dating secrets of the dead

Ahmed, Saladin
Hooves and the hovel of Abdel Jameela
The Nebula Awards showcase; edited by Kevin J. Anderson.

AIDS (DISEASE)
Bear, E. The horrid glory of its wings
Beattie, A. Second question
Neugeboren, J. Comfort
Neugeboren, J. Here or there
Neugeboren, J. The Turetzky Trio

Aidt, Naja Marie
Women in Copenhagen
Copenhagen noir; edited by Bo Tao Michaëlis; translated by Mark Kline.

Aiken, Joan
The fluttering thing
Aiken, J. The monkey's wedding, and other stories
Girl in a whirl
Aiken, J. The monkey's wedding, and other stories
Hair
Aiken, J. The monkey's wedding, and other stories
Harp music
Aiken, J. The monkey's wedding, and other stories
The helper
Aiken, J. The monkey's wedding, and other stories
Honeymaroon
Aiken, J. The monkey's wedding, and other stories
The Magnesia Tree
Aiken, J. The monkey's wedding, and other stories
A mermaid too many
Aiken, J. The monkey's wedding, and other stories
Model wife
Aiken, J. The monkey's wedding, and other stories
The monkey's wedding
Aiken, J. The monkey's wedding, and other stories
Octopi in the sky
Aiken, J. The monkey's wedding, and other stories
The Paper Queen
Aiken, J. The monkey's wedding, and other stories
Reading in bed
Aiken, J. The monkey's wedding, and other stories
Red-hot favourite
Aiken, J. The monkey's wedding, and other stories
The sale of midsummer
Aiken, J. The monkey's wedding, and other stories
Second thoughts
Aiken, J. The monkey's wedding, and other stories
Spur of the moment
Aiken, J. The monkey's wedding, and other stories
Water of youth
Aiken, J. The monkey's wedding, and other stories

Wee Robin
Aiken, J. The monkey's wedding, and other stories
AIR CRASHES *See* Airplane accidents
AIR PILOTS
Hannah, B. Even Greenland
Hannah, B. Testimony of pilot
Levine, S. The flier
Stanger, V. The eye patch protocol
Wells, H. G. Little mother up the Mörderberg
AIR SHIPS *See* Airships
Air Space. Wingfield, A.
AIR TRAVEL
Emshwiller, C. Woman waiting
Nevins, F. M., Jr. Fair game
Vukcevich, R. In the flesh
AIRLINES
See also Airports
AIRMEN *See* Air pilots
AIRPLANE ACCIDENTS
Baumer, J. R. The forever sleep
Hannah, B. Even Greenland
Levine, S. Lax forb
Mofina, R. The last pursuit
Ruocco, J. Frog
AIRPLANES
Hand, E. The maiden flight of McCauley's Bellerophon
Ruocco, J. Flying monkeys
Wells, H. G. My first aeroplane
Accidents
See Airplane accidents
Pilots
See Air pilots
AIRPORTS
Shepard, S. Land of the living
AIRSHIPS
Pollexfen, M. Monsieur Fly-by-Night
Ronald, M. A serpent in the gears
Rosenbaum, B. Biographical notes to "A discourse on the nature of causality, with airplanes" by Benjamin Rosenbaum
Valentine, G. The Zeppelin Conductors' Society annual gentlemen's ball
Ajvaz, Michal
The wire book
Best European fiction 2011; edited by Aleksandr Hemon; preface by Colum McCann
Akalis, Scott
Terminal talk
Nature v475 no7357 p538 Jl 28 2011
Akitada's first case. Parker, I. J.
Akunin, Boris
Table talk, 1882
The greatest Russian stories of crime and suspense; edited by Otto Penzler.
Al. Emshwiller, C.
Al Ahdal, Wajdi
A crime in Mataeem Street
Beirut 39; new writing from the Arab world; edited by Samuel Shimon; with a preface by Hanan al-Shaykh
Al-Qatăryz. Marăr, M.
ALABAMA
Bierce, A. An occurance at Owl Creek Bridge
Bierce, A. An occurrence at Owl Creek Bridge
Hannah, B. Drummer down
McMillian, R. Escambia counties

ALABAMA—*Continued*
Birmingham
Lahens, Y. An American story
Alameddine, Rabih
The Half- Wall
　Ploughshares v37 no1 p10-23 Spr 2011
Alamo Plaza. Watson, B.
Alarcón, Daniel
The bridge
　The Pen/O.Henry Prize stories, 2010; edited
　and with an introduction by Laura Furman;
　with essays on the stories they admire most
　by jurors Junot Diaz, Paula Fox, Yiyun Li.
Second lives
　20 under 40; stories from the New Yorker;
　edited by Deborah Treisman.
(tr.) See Schweblin, Samanta
ALASKA
Kostival, B. Islanders
Matheson, R. C. Transfiguration
Nelson, K. The spirit bird
Simmons, D. Yukon River
Anchorage
Kurlansky, M. The soup
The **Albanian** florist. Gifford, B.
ALBANIANS
United States
Gifford, B. The Albanian florist
ALBANY (N.Y.) *See* New York (State)—Albany
Albert, Elisa
One good reason why not
　Promised lands; new Jewish American fiction
　on longing and belonging; edited by Derek
　Rubin.
ALCIBIADES, CA. 450-404 B.C.
About
Turtledove, H. The daimon
Alcoholic. Nutting, A.
ALCOHOLICS *See* Alcoholism; Drunkards
ALCOHOLISM
　See also Drunkards
Abbott, L. K. A great piece of elephant
Ballingrud, N. The way station
Barry, K. Doctor Sot
Baxter, C. The eleventh floor
Baxter, C. The old murderer
Boggs, B. Buckets of rain
Chuculate, E. D. Cheyenne Madonna
Chuculate, E. D. Dear Shorty
Chuculate, E. D. A famous Indian artist
Ferris, J. The pilot
Franklin, T. The ballad of Duane Juarez
Gorman, E. The long way back
Hannah, B. Rat-faced Auntie
McCabe, E. Music at Annahullion
Neugeboren, J. Overseas
O'Brien, E. Shovel kings
Parker, D. Big blonde
Ray, S. How we fall
Ray, S. The way home
Roberge, R. Love and hope and sex and dreams
Somerville, P. The machine of understanding
　other people
Trevor, W. A day
Williamson, E. M. Hope, among other vices and
　virtues
ALCORAN *See* Koran
Alcorian A-1949. Gates, D.

Alcott, Louisa May
My contraband
　The vintage book of American women writ-
　ers; edited and with an introduction by
　Elaine Showalter.
Alderman, Mitch
Family values
　Randisi, R. J. The Shamus winners: Ameri-
　ca's best private eye stories, volume II,
　1996-2009; collected and introduced by
　Robert J. Randisi; founder, Private Eye
　Writers of America
Aleas, Richard *See* Ardai, Charles, 1969-
Alenyikov, Michael
Barrel of laughs
　Alenyikov, M. Ivan and Misha; stories
It takes all kinds
　Alenyikov, M. Ivan and Misha; stories
Ivan and Misha
　Alenyikov, M. Ivan and Misha; stories
Whirling dervish
　Alenyikov, M. Ivan and Misha; stories
Who did what to whom?
　Alenyikov, M. Ivan and Misha; stories
Alex Rice Inc. Sneed, C.
Alexander, Gary
Charlie and the pirates
　The Best American mystery stories 2010; ed-
　ited and with an introduction by Lee Child;
　Otto Penzler, series editor
Alexie, Sherman
Green world
　Best of the West 2010; new stories from the
　wide side of the Missouri; edited by James
　Thomas and D. Seth Horton; foreword by
　Kent Meyers.
ALGERIA
Dib, M. The companion
Dib, M. The enchanted heir
Dib, M. A fine wedding
Dib, M. Forbidden lands
Dib, M. Little Cousin
Dib, M. The long wait
Dib, M. Naëma disappeared
Dib, M. The talisman
Dib, M. The traveler
Haydar Haydar. The dance of the savage prai-
　ries
Ali, Mohammed Naseehu
The long ride back home
　Freedom; stories celebrating the Universal
　Declaration of Human Rights; Amnesty In-
　ternational.
Alia. Levine, S.
ALIENATION (SOCIAL PSYCHOLOGY)
　See also Social isolation
Doctorow, E. L. All the time in the world
July, M. Something that needs nothing
Vonnegut, K. Girl pool
Alienation and love in the Hebrew alphabet.
　Tidhar, L.
ALIENS, ILLEGAL *See* Undocumented aliens
ALIENS, UNDOCUMENTED *See*
　Undocumented aliens
Aliens. Hemmingson, M.
ALKORAN *See* Koran
All around Atlantis. Eisenberg, D.
All Hallows' Eve. Gilley, T.

All I Know about Central Europeanism (with a bit
    of friendly help from Olomouc and Camus)
    [Part of special issue: Slovak Fiction]
    Vilikovský, P.
All I know about Gertrude Stein. Winterson, J.
All I want is my baby, woah woah, woah woah
    woah woah. Staun, S.
All in good time. O'Connor, S.
All love is a now. Bayley, E.
All moon-beasts. Cannon, P.
All over. Blatnik, A.
All the awful. Bill, F.
All the Bums in Rockaway. Vannatta, D.
All the day's sad stories: a novella. Hall, T. M.
All the myriad ways. Niven, L.
All the sex is west. Plummer, T. M.
All the time in the world. Doctorow, E. L.
All the time in the world. Dubus, A.
All the Way Down. Saknussemm, K.
All you can do is breathe. Warren, K.
Allan, John B.
    For works written by this author under oth-
    er names see Westlake, Donald E.
Allan, Nina
    Flying in the face of god
        The Year's best science fiction: twenty-eighth
        annual collection; edited by Gardner
        Dozois.
Allan, Stephen
    You're gonna get yours
        Blood, guts, & whiskey; edited by Todd Rob-
        inson; introduction by Max Allan Collins.
Alland, Sandra
    Things I don't remember
        Can'tLit; fearless fiction from Broken pencil
        magazine; edited by Richard Rosenbaum.
Allegiance. Kyle, A.
ALLEGORIES
        See also Fables; Fantasies; Good and
        evil; Parables; Symbolism
    Agee, J. A mother's tale
    Anderson, P. Goat song
    Chubak, S. The baboon whose buffoon was
        dead
    Davis, L. Once a very stupid man
    Finlay, C. C. Hail, conductor
    Gordimer, N. Look-alikes
    Gordimer, N. Tape measure
    Le Guin, U. H. The ones who walk away from
        Omelas
    Martin, G. R. R. In the lost lands
    Millhauser, S. People of the Book
    Sneed, C. Walled city
    Wells, H. G. The pearl of love
Allen, Dwight
    Among the missing
        Allen, D. The green suit; stories
    A bed of ice
        Allen, D. The green suit; stories
    Deferment
        Allen, D. The green suit; stories
    End of his tether
        Allen, D. The green suit; stories
    Fishing with Alex
        Allen, D. The green suit; stories
    Goat on a hill
        Allen, D. The green suit; stories
    The green suit
        Allen, D. The green suit; stories

    The Hazlett's dog
        Allen, D. The green suit; stories
    Invisible
        Allen, D. The green suit; stories
    Not Renata
        Allen, D. The green suit; stories
    Overtime
        Allen, D. The green suit; stories
    Succor
        Allen, D. The green suit; stories
Allen, Gilbert
    Trash
        The Southern Review (Baton Rouge, La.) v47
        no2 p177-86 Spr 2011
Allen, R. A.
    The Emerald Coast
        The Best American mystery stories 2010; ed-
        ited and with an introduction by Lee Child;
        Otto Penzler, series editor
    Monday Burning
        The Literary Review (Madison, N.J.) v53 no4
        p125-34 Summ 2010
ALLERGY
    Ruocco, J. Canary
    Vukcevich, R. The button
Allio, Kirstin
    Clothed, female figure
        The Pen/O.Henry Prize stories, 2010; edited
        and with an introduction by Laura Furman;
        with essays on the stories they admire most
        by jurors Junot Diaz, Paula Fox, Yiyun Li.
    Green
        New England Review v31 no3 p84-93 2010
Allog. Pearlman, E.
Allyn, Douglas
    An early Christmas
        The Best American mystery stories 2010; ed-
        ited and with an introduction by Lee Child;
        Otto Penzler, series editor
    Israfel
        On a raven's wing; new tales in honor of Ed-
        gar Allan Poe; edited by Stuart M.
        Kaminsky
    The Valhalla verdict
        By hook or by crook and 27 more of the best
        crime + mystery stories of the year; edited
        by Ed Gorman and Martin H. Greenberg.
Alma, Age Twelve: Assistant Babysitter & Future
    Failed Suicide. Milks, M. and Moore, L.
Almond, Steve
    The short goodbye
        Iowa Review v41 no1 p139 Spr 2011
    Testimony of a private
        Iowa Review v41 no1 p138 Spr 2011
    What retired engineer Roger Mudge thinks upon
        his son Patrick's announcement of his en-
        gagement
        Iowa Review v41 no1 p137 Spr 2011
Almost no memory. Davis, L.
Almost over: separate bedrooms. Davis, L.
Almost over: what's the word? Davis, L.
An **almost** perfect evening. Blatnik, A.
Alone. Reed, R.
Alone. Yiyun Li
Alpha. Greenfeld, K. T.
Alphabet. Lee, H. E.
Alpine, Texas (Highway 90). Shepard, S.

Alsup, Allison
Pioneers
River Styx no85 p78-9 2011
Alvarado, Beth
The Astonished Dead [Excerpt from The Adventures of Jillian O'Malley]
Western Humanities Review v65 no1 p82-8 Wint 2011
Alvin the typesetter. Davis, L.
Alwan, Mohammad Hassan
Haneef from Glasgow
Beirut 39; new writing from the Arab world; edited by Samuel Shimon; with a preface by Hanan al-Shaykh
Always. Fowler, K. J.
Always raining somewhere, said Jim Johnson. Wideman, J. E.
ALZHEIMER'S DISEASE
Fowler, K. J. The Marianas Islands
Amanda and the alien. Silverberg, R.
Amanuensis. Tuttle, S.
Amapola. Urrea, L. A.
Amaryllis. Vaughn, C.
AMATEUR THEATRICALS
Gordimer, N. The amateurs
The **amateurs**. Gordimer, N.
AMAZONS
Gifford, B. The age of fable
AMBASSADORS *See* Diplomatic life
AMBITION
See also Self-made men
Eugenides, J. Great experiment
Ambrose and the ancient spirits of east and west. Nix, G.
Ambrosio, Gabriella
Sticko
Freedom; stories celebrating the Universal Declaration of Human Rights; Amnesty International.
Amdahl, Gary
We Whistled While We Worked
The Massachusetts Review v51 no4 p746-73 Wint 2010
Amends. Trueblood, V.
AMERICA
See also Central America
American Boy. Pope, R.
AMERICAN CIVIL WAR, 1861-1865 *See* United States—Civil War, 1861-1865
The **American** dead. Lake, J.
American diary. Laurrent, E.
American history. Franco, J.
The **American** language. Gifford, B.
AMERICAN REVOLUTION, 1775-1783 *See* United States—Revolution, 1775-1783
AMERICAN SOLDIERS *See* Soldiers—United States
An **American** story. Lahens, Y.
AMERICANS
Argentina
Rubin, J. Toward Lithuania
Canada
Eisenberg, D. Transactions in a foreign currency
Central America
Eisenberg, D. Across the lake
Eisenberg, D. Holy Week
Eisenberg, D. Someone to talk to
Central Asia
Bissell, T. Expensive trips nowhere

Chile
Silverberg, R. How they pass the time in Pelpel
China
Dixon, S. China
Colombia
Fountain, B. Near-extinct birds of the central cordillera
Costa Rica
Murphy, B. Who do I have to kill to get a little respect up in here?
Nikitas, D. Trauma dyke
Czech Republic
Pearlman, E. ToyFolk
El Salvador
Shepard, L. Salvador
England
Eisenberg, D. In the station
Olsen, L. January
Pearlman, E. If love were all
Europe
Hardwick, E. A season's romance
France
Bingham, S. Found
Bingham, S. Sagesse
Bingham, S. Sweet peas
Davis, L. The bone
Davis, L. St. Martin
Ely, S. Mississippi rules
Gordimer, N. A meeting in space
Neugeboren, J. Comfort
Neugeboren, J. Make-a-wish
Neugeboren, J. The state of Israel
Neugeboren, J. Summer afternoon
Neugeboren, J. The Turetzky Trio
Wieland, L. Some churches
Germany
Cadigan, P. Picking up the pieces
Davis, L. Mr. Burdoff's visit to Germany
Dixon, S. Up and down the Drosselgasse
Stafford, J. The echo and the nemesis
Turtledove, H. The catcher in the Rhine
Greece
Horrocks, C. The lion gate
Honduras
Eisenberg, D. Under the 82nd Airborne
India
Mehta, R. Floating
Ireland
Hodge, B. When the bough doesn't break
Israel
Lovett, R. Leo's squid
Papernick, J. A kiss for Mrs. Fisch
Rapoport, N. Sovereignty
Silverberg, R. A thousand paces along the Via Dolorosa
Italy
Bunin, I. A. The gentleman from San Francisco
Eisenberg, D. Like it or not
Olsen, L. February
Woolson, C. F. Miss Grief
Japan
Packer, Z. Geese
Kosovo
Jordan, C. Rough justice
Lithuania
Doerr, A. The river nemunas
Majorca
Boylan, C. Villa Marta

AMERICANS—*Continued*
Malaysia
Ostlund, L. Bed death
Mexico
Boland, J. C. Tequila
Eisenberg, D. Tlaloc's paradise
Highsmith, P. In the plaza
Shepard, S. Land of the living
Simmons, D. Holy sisters
Simmons, D. Suitcase
Nigeria
Osondu, E. C. Our first American
Panama
Chambers, W. The black bottle
Russia
Laken, V. Family planning
Laken, V. Map of the city
Scotland
Rankin, I. Graduation day
South Africa
Gordimer, N. Open house
Spain
Leland, C. T. Memento mori
Vietnam
Chau, A. Relief
Hannah, B. Midnight and I'm not famous yet
Americca. Bender, A.
AMICK, STEVE
IN CASIMIR'S SHOES
Michigan Quarterly Review v50 no3 p411-
432 Summ 2011
AMISH
Horrocks, C. It looks like this
Amish in a Time of War. Groff, L.
Ammetis the sleeper. Lamrabet, R.
AMNESIA
Barry, K. See the tree, how big it's grown
Goodberg, D. Amnesia
Kurlansky, M. Red sea salt
Amnesia. Goodberg, D.
Amnesty. Gordimer, N.
Amnesty. Manilla, M.
Among the missing. Allen, D.
Among thieves. Anderson, P.
Amor vincit omnia. Parker, K. J.
The **amorous** corpse. Gautier, T.
Amorphous and mephitic. Cannon, P.
Amphetamine twitch. Bill, F.
AMPUTATION
Monzó, Q. Family life
Sedia, E. 1972: the lichenologist's visit
Amputee. Oates, J. C.
AMPUTEES
Beattie, A. The lawn party
Gordimer, N. The soft voice of the serpent
Hemmingson, M. What happens when my
wife's ex-boyfriend, back from Iraq, pays
us a visit
Kennedy, A. L. As God made us
Kilworth, G. Hats off to Mary
Laken, V. Spectators
Mankell, H. Sofia
Oates, J. C. Amputee
O'Connor, F. Good country people
Amqassim, Yahya
From the novel Raven's leg
Beirut 39; new writing from the Arab world;
edited by Samuel Shimon; with a preface
by Hanan al-Shaykh

AMSTERDAM (NETHERLANDS) *See* Nether-
lands—Amsterdam
Amsterdam at midnight. Parke, G.
AMULETS *See* Charms
AMUSEMENT PARKS
Boggs, B. Opportunity
Fowler, C. Oh I do like to be beside the seaside
Goodberg, D. The good book
Horn, D. Shtetl World
Loory, B. Husband and wife
Monk, D. Ducks in a row
Sands, B. The anals of piracy
Tremblay, P. We will never live in the castle
The **anachronist's** cookbook. Valente, C. M.
The **anals** of piracy. Sands, B.
ANARCHISM AND ANARCHISTS
Niven, L. Cloak of anarchy
Wells, H. G. The thumbmark
ANARCHISTS *See* Anarchism and anarchists
Anatomy. Curtis, C.
The **ancestors**. Balázs, B.
Ancestral voices. Dozois, G. R. and Swanwick,
M.
And all this unease. Lahens, Y.
And go like this. Crowley, J.
And ministers of grace. Williams, T.
And pray nobody sees you. Haywood, G. A.
And since I couldn't sleep. Blatnik, A.
And still you wonder why our first impulsr is to
kill you: an alphabetizes faux-manifesto
transcribes edited, and annotated (under du-
ress and protest). Braunbeck, G. A.
And the deep blue sea. Bear, E.
And the living is easy. Willis, D.
And the Stars Shone Brightly. Gray, V.
And then—the silence. Bradbury, R.
And they will come in the hour of our greatest
need. Hodge, B.
And you are? Levine, S.
Anders, Charlie
Yes man
Can'tLit; fearless fiction from Broken pencil
magazine; edited by Richard Rosenbaum.
Andersen, Hans Christian
1840: Venice: Tourist Destination [Excerpt from
a short story, What the Moon Saw]
Lapham's Quarterly v3 no4 p55 Fall 2010
The Nightingale [Retold by D. Wolkstein]
Parabola v35 no4 p38-43 Wint 2010
Anderson, Barth
Landlocked
Swenson, P. The Best of Talebones; edited by
Patrick Swenson.
Anderson, Kevin J.
Torn stitches, shattered glass
The monster's corner; stories through inhu-
man eyes; edited by Christopher Golden
Anderson, Poul
Admiralty
Anderson, P. Admiralty; edited by Rick
Katze.
The adventure of the misplaced hound
Anderson, P. Admiralty; edited by Rick
Katze.
Among thieves
Anderson, P. Admiralty; edited by Rick
Katze.

Anderson, Poul—*Continued*

The barrier moment
  Anderson, P. Admiralty; edited by Rick
    Katze.

The bitter bread
  Anderson, P. Admiralty; edited by Rick
    Katze.

Black bodies
  Anderson, P. Admiralty; edited by Rick
    Katze.

Delenda est
  Anderson, P. Admiralty; edited by Rick
    Katze.

Eutopia
  Anderson, P. Admiralty; edited by Rick
    Katze.

Flight to forever
  The end of the world; stories of the apoca-
    lypse; edited by Martin H. Greenberg.

Goat song
  Anderson, P. Admiralty; edited by Rick
    Katze.

Gypsy
  Anderson, P. Admiralty; edited by Rick
    Katze.

Holmgang
  Anderson, P. Admiralty; edited by Rick
    Katze.

Home
  Anderson, P. Admiralty; edited by Rick
    Katze.

Horse trader
  Anderson, P. Admiralty; edited by Rick
    Katze.

Inside straight
  Anderson, P. Admiralty; edited by Rick
    Katze.

Kyrie
  Anderson, P. Admiralty; edited by Rick
    Katze.

Lodestar
  Anderson, P. Admiralty; edited by Rick
    Katze.

Marius
  Anderson, P. Admiralty; edited by Rick
    Katze.

Murphy's Hall
  Anderson, P. Admiralty; edited by Rick
    Katze.

Operation changeling
  Anderson, P. Admiralty; edited by Rick
    Katze.

The problem of pain
  Anderson, P. Admiralty; edited by Rick
    Katze.

The pugilist
  Anderson, P. Admiralty; edited by Rick
    Katze.

Quixote and the windmill
  Anderson, P. Admiralty; edited by Rick
    Katze.

Sister planet
  Anderson, P. Admiralty; edited by Rick
    Katze.

The star beast
  Anderson, P. Admiralty; edited by Rick
    Katze.

Angel and Me. Klonaris, H.

The **angel** over the right shoulder, or, the beginning of a new year. Phelps, E. S.

Angela Perfidia. Benbow, M.

ANGELS
  Beagle, P. S. Uncle Chaim and Aunt Rifke and
    the angel
  Del Carlo, E. Nothing but fear
  Hodge, B. And they will come in the hour of
    our greatest need
  Loory, B. On the way down: a story for Ray
    Bradbury
  Matheson, R. C. Transfiguration
  Olsen, L. June
  Powers, T. The hour of Babel
  Rodoreda, M. It seemed like silk
  Silverberg, R. Basileus
  Woestijne, K. v. d. The saint of number

The **angel's** share. Hunt, M.

ANGER
  Bausch, R. Unjust
  Mehrotra, P. K. Fit of rage
  Phillips, H. The fights
  Somerville, P. People like me

ANGLICAN AND EPISCOPAL CLERGY
  Doctorow, E. L. Heist
  Gordimer, N. Not for publication

Animal. Emshwiller, C.

ANIMAL ABUSE *See* Animal welfare

Animal rescue. Lehane, D.

ANIMAL WELFARE
  See also Dogfighting
  Kronauer, B. Oh if you knew how the fishes do
  Kronauer, B. The woman in the pillows [ex-
    cerpt]

ANIMALS
  See also Extinct animals; Mythical ani-
    mals; Taxidermy names of individual ani-
    mals
  Bernheimer, K. A petting zoo tale
  Blatnik, A. One
  Reents, S. Creatures of the kingdom
        Training
  Chekhov, A. P. Kashtanka
        Treatment
  See Animal welfare

ANIMALS, MYTHICAL *See* Mythical animals

Animals. Doyle, R.

Aniruddha: the latest installment. Chaudhuri, A.

ANN ARBOR (MICH.) *See* Michigan—Ann Arbor

Annals of plagiary. McElroy, J.

ANNIE HALL (MOTION PICTURE)
  Yamauchi, W. Annie Hall, Annie Hall

Annie Hall, Annie Hall. Yamauchi, W.

ANNIVERSARIES, WEDDING *See* Wedding
  anniversaries

The **anniversary**. Mun, N.

The **anniversary** waltz. Estleman, L. D.

Annunication. Le Sueur, M.

Anointed. Baingana, D.

An **Anonymous** Island. Mun-Yol, Y.

ANOREXIA NERVOSA
  Engel, P. Green
  Mantel, H. The heart fails without warning
  Schappell, E. The joy of cooking

Another. Kennedy, A. L.

Another day, another dollar. Murphy, W.

Another story. Châteaureynaud, G. O.

Another young lust story. Sernotti, C.

Answer to prayer. Wells, H. G.
Ant colony. Nutting, A.
ANTARCTIC REGIONS
    See also Arctic regions
  Bailey, D. and Ballingrud, N. The crevasse
  Hemmingson, M. It's very cold down here
  Roden, B. The brink of eternity
  Roden, B. Endless night
  Turtledove, H. The scarlet band
The **Antelope** Birth.
Antes del sueño. Mamani, P.
Anthony, Meredith
  Fishtown odyssey
    Philadelphia noir; edited by Carlin Romano.
Anthony, Piers
  Possible to rue
    Before they were giants; edited by James L.
      Sutter; cover illustration by Kieran Yanner.
ANTHROPOLOGISTS
  Cisco, M. The Thing in the Jar
  Fowler, K. J. What I didn't see
  Latiolais, M. Gut
  Self, W. Understanding the Ur-Bororo
ANTIGRAVITY
    See also Gravitation
ANTIQUE DEALERS
    See also Art dealers
  Archer, J. I will survive
  Barrett, L. The noir boudoir
  Châteaureynaud, G. O. Delaunay the broker
  Hardwick, E. The final conflict
ANTIQUES
  Pearlman, E. Jan Term
  Villegas, H. The hair wreath
ANTISEMITISM
    See also Holocaust, Jewish (1933-1945)
  Kalechofsky, R. The enigmatic power of the let-
    ter "j"
  Neugeboren, J. The state of Israel
Antrim, Donald
  He knew
    The New Yorker v87 no12 p64-8, 69-71 My
    9 2011
ANTS
  Dick, P. K. Expendable
  Marār, M. The last covenant
  Stephenson, C. Leiningen versus the ants
  Wells, H. G. The empire of the ants
Ants. Novack, S.
Ants. Ruocco, J.
ANXIETY *See* Fear
Anywhere you send me. Bingham, S.
Anzaldúa, Gloria
  Ghost trap/Trampa de espanto
    Anzaldúa, G. The Gloria Anzaldúa reader;
      AnaLouise Keating, editor
  El paisano is a bird of omen
    Anzaldúa, G. The Gloria Anzaldúa reader;
      AnaLouise Keating, editor
  Reading LP
    Anzaldúa, G. The Gloria Anzaldúa reader;
      AnaLouise Keating, editor
The **aorta**. Idris, Y.
The **Apalachicola** night. Falk, M. R.
APARTHEID *See* South Africa—Race relations
APARTMENT HOUSES
  Assadi, M. An apartment to let!
  Ballard, J. G. Billennium
  Dixon, S. The neighbors

Eisenberg, D. A cautionary tale
Eisenberg, D. Twilight of the superheroes
'Izz al-Dīn, M. The path to madness
Jarrar, R. The story of my building (after Isaac
  Babel's "Story of my dovecote")
Monzó, Q. Centripetal force
Pera, B. Roman à clef
Powers, T. A journey of only two paces
Qiu Xiaolong. Housing assignment
Villegas, H. The hair wreath
An **apartment** to let!. Assadi, M.
APARTMENTS *See* Apartment houses
APES
    See also Gorillas
  Baker, L. The coming of age of Jane
Aphrodisiac. Jhabvala, R. P.
The **apocalypses**. Phillips, H.
Apolcalypse as foreplay. McQueen, G.
Apologies to Auden. Beattie, A.
Apostle of artillery. Snoek, P.
APOTHECARIES *See* Pharmacists
APPALACHIAN HIGHLANDERS
  Craddock, C. E. The "harnt" that walks
    Chilhowee
APPALACHIAN MOUNTAINS
  Willis, M. S. Speak well of the dead
  Willis, M. S. Triangulation
APPALACHIAN REGION
  Shepard, L. Halloween Town
  Willis, M. S. Evenings with Dotson
Appel, Anne Milano
  (tr.) *See* Pugno, Laura
  (tr.) *See* Voltolini, Dario
  (jt. auth) *See* Voltolini, Dario and Appel, Anne
    Milano
Appetite. McGoran, J.
Apple, Max
  Business talk
    Blue collar, white collar, no collar; stories of
      work; edited by Richard Ford.
The **apple**. Wells, H. G.
Apples. Butler, N.
The **applicant**. Bierce, A.
The **Apprentice**. Mozzi, G.
APPRENTICES
  Sherman, D. Wizard's apprentice
  Silverberg, R. The sorcerer's apprentice
Apricot jam. Solzhenitsyn, A.
Apricots. Bingham, S.
April. Olsen, L.
April. See Franco, J. April in three parts: part III,
  April
April 1863. Bell, M. S.
April in three parts: part 1, The rainbow goblins.
  Franco, J.
April in three parts: part II, Wasting. Franco, J.
April in three parts: part III, April. Franco, J.
AQUARIUMS
  Poulson, C. Fishy story
ARAB AMERICANS
  Jaber, R. From the novel America
  Kawtharani, H. Three stories
ARAB WOMEN
  Abu Lail, S. A letter to a betrayer
  Abu Lail, S. My neighbor is a whore!
  Abu Lail, S. A stranger at the bus stop!
  Assadi, M. An apartment to let!
  Assadi, M. Forbidden talk
  Assadi, M. The nightmare of a summer night

ARAB WOMEN—*Continued*

Assadi, M. Tea, biscuits and sugar

Bakriyya, R. Leave this world for me . . . for a woman . . . who seems to be the hope

Bakriyya, R. The story of perfume to you in the beginning of the year at the end of the story . . . . .

Diab, F. An added fraction

Diab, F. The power of silence

Diab, F. Thoughts of a sterile woman

Khalaylah, A. About spring, Marwah and the feast

Khalaylah, A. In the company of Jamal the trouble-maker

Khalaylah, A. The scabby woman's son

Khalaylah, A. Wafiyyah

Marjiyyah, R. A blessed whore: a story from life

Marjiyyah, R. The burning of a soul

Muwasi, E. Sin and eggs

Muwasi, E. The study hall monitor

Muwasi, E. Your love is soreness

Sirhan, A. Close to the bridge's edge

Sirhan, A. I will ask for a divorce

Sirhan, A. The wedding's night and the sacrifice

Uruq, S. The brightness of his eyes

Uruq, S. The path of deceit

Uruq, S. The student and the teacher

ARABIAN NIGHTS

Marār, M. The last covenant

Arabian nights. Gifford, B.

ARABIC LANGUAGE

Hassan, R. Y. Guardians of the air

ARABS

    See also Bedouins; Palestinian Arabs

Amqassim, Y. From the novel Raven's leg

Boukebba, A. From the novel Skin of shadow

Howard, R. E. The road of Azrael

Terrin, P. Clean-up; or, The adventures of Abdullah and me

United States

McElroy, J. No man's land

The **Arabs'** battle. Marār, M.

The **Arbitrarium**. Sansom, I.

Arboretum. Mullins, D. P.

Arcade games. Chau, A.

ARCHEOLOGISTS

Fowler, K. J. Private grave 9

ARCHEOLOGY

    See also Prehistoric man

Archer, Jeffrey

Better the devil you know

    Archer, J. And thereby hangs a tale

Blind date

    Archer, J. And thereby hangs a tale

Caste-off

    Archer, J. And thereby hangs a tale

Double-cross

    Archer, J. And thereby hangs a tale

A good eye

    Archer, J. And thereby hangs a tale

High heels

    Archer, J. And thereby hangs a tale

I will survive

    Archer, J. And thereby hangs a tale

The luck of Irish

    Archer, J. And thereby hangs a tale

Members only

    Archer, J. And thereby hangs a tale

No room at the inn

    Archer, J. And thereby hangs a tale

Politically correct

    Archer, J. And thereby hangs a tale

The queen's birthday telegram

    Archer, J. And thereby hangs a tale

Stuck on you

    Archer, J. And thereby hangs a tale

The undiplomatic diplomat

    Archer, J. And thereby hangs a tale

Where there's a will

    Archer, J. And thereby hangs a tale

Archer, Lynda

A Heart in Saskatoon

    Dalhousie Review v90 no2 p217-27 Summ 2010

Archer on horseback [excerpt]. Kronauer, B.

The **architect** of flowers. Lychack, W.

ARCHITECTS

    See also Building

Hampton, E. Mr. Gray

McElroy, J. Mister X

ARCHIVISTS

Archer, J. The undiplomatic diplomat

Grossman, V. S. The elk

ARCTIC REGIONS

    See also Alaska; Antarctic regions

London, J. The white silence

Ardai, Charles

Cold reading

    Christmas at the Mysterious Bookshop; 'tis the season to be deadly; stories of mistletoe and mayhem from 17 masters of suspense; edited by Otto Penzler.

Ardent. Cameron, D.

Are birds better at walking or flying? Zhang Kangkang

Are you comfortable? Schappell, E.

Aren't you dead yet? Schappell, E.

Argemi, Raul

The slender charm of Chinese women

    Barcelona noir; edited by Adriana V. Lopez & Cartmen Ospina; translated by Achy Obejas.

ARGENTINA

Buenos Aires

Rubin, J. Toward Lithuania

ARGENTINE REPUBLIC *See* Argentina

The **argonauts** of the air. Wells, H. G.

The **argument**. Dixon, S.

Ariadne Sees Dr. Frank. Wing, C.

ARISTOCRACY

    See also Courts and courtiers

England

McOmber, A. A man of history

France

Orczy, B. A question of passports

ARIZONA

Bierce, A. The stranger

Manilla, M. Still life with plums

Sheehan, A. Spin

Vukcevich, R. A funny smell

Phoenix

Urrea, L. A. Amapola

Tucson

Sheehan, A. Gentle future

St. Germain, J. Tortolita

The **Arkham** collector. Cannon, P.

Arkwright, John

The sundial

L. Ron Hubbard presents Writers of the Future volume XXVII; the year's thirteen best tales from the Writers of the Future international writers' program; illustrated by winners in the Illustrators of the Future international illustrators' program; with essays on writing & illustration by L. Ron Hubbard / Mike Resnick / Robert Cadtillo; edited by K. D. Wentworth

ARMADILLOS

Gray, A. The darkness

Armageddon-2419 A.D. Nowlan, P. F.

ARMAMENTS

Niven, L. The soft weapon

Snoek, P. Apostle of artillery

The **armor** of Sir Locust. Chapman, S.

ARMS AND ARMOR

See also Swords

Chapman, S. The armor of Sir Locust

Armstrong, Kelley

A haunted house of her own

The Year's best dark fantasy & horror; edited by Paula Guran

Rakshasi

The monster's corner; stories through inhuman eyes; edited by Christopher Golden

Zen and the art of vampirism

Vampires; the recent undead; edited by Paula Guran.

Armstrong, M. C.

The Seventy-Fourth Virgin

Gettysburg Review v24 no2 p265-76 Summ 2011

Armstrong, Scott

THE TEST

Dalhousie Review v91 no1 p67-75 Spr 2011

ARMY HOSPITALS *See* Hospitals and sanatoriums

Arnason, Eleanor

Mammoths of the great plains

The Year's best science fiction: twenty-eighth annual collection; edited by Gardner Dozois.

Arnegard, Iver

What Rises

The North American Review v296 no1 p32-3 Wint 2011

Arnheim & Sons. Epstein, J.

Arnold, Christopher Feliciano

Salt

The Kenyon Review v33 no1 p10-13 Wint 2011

An **Arranged** Honeymoon. Iromuanya, J.

An **arranged** marriage. Freudenberger, N.

An **arrest**. Bierce, A.

ARRESTS

Gilley, T. White

Greenland, S. Bad night in Hyannisport

Harrison, D. Mercy first, first mercy

Nagai, M. Confession

The **arrival**. Bayley, E.

Arsenijević, Vladimir

One minute: Dumbo's death

Best European fiction 2011; edited by Aleksandr Hemon; preface by Colum McCann

ARSON

Archer, J. High heels

Collinson, P. Arson plus

Downum, A. Blue valentine

Hannah, B. Lastward, deputy James

Hannah, B. Sick soldier at your door

Naipaul, V. S. The pyrotechnicist

Treadway, J. The nurse and the black lagoon

Tremblay, P. The Marlborough man meets the end

Woodrell, D. Returning the river

Arson plus. Collinson, P.

ART

Bakopoulos, N. Fresco, Byzantine

El-Mohtar, A. The singing fish

Lake, J. Taking the rats to Riga

Somerville, P. The universe in miniature in miniature

Williamson, M. Sacrament

Exhibitions

Nadjarian, N. Exhibition

ART COLLECTORS

Ely, S. Guatemala City

Silverberg, R. Not our brother

ART CRITICS

Tuten, F. The park in winter

Tuten, F. The park near Marienbad

ART DEALERS

See also Antique dealers

Baxter, C. Royal blue

ART EXHIBITIONS *See* Art—Exhibitions

ART FORGERIES *See* Forgery of works of art

ART GALLERIES AND MUSEUMS

Chuculate, E. D. Under the red star of Mars

Negarestani, R. The gallows-horse

Rozan, S. J. Seeing the moon

Art in heaven. Cardinale, J.

ART OBJECTS

See also Antiques

The **art** of negotiation. Ewan, C.

The **Art** of War. Shimoni, Y.

ART TEACHERS

Beattie, A. The lawn party

Boggs, B. Dear season

Watsmore, A. Bina

Arties aren't stupid. Tolbert, J.

ARTIFICIAL INSEMINATION

Penkov, M. A picture with Yuki

ARTIFICIAL INTELLIGENCE

Niven, L. The soft weapon

Niven, L. A teardrop falls

Petry, Y. The straggler

Reed, R. Alone

Skillingstead, J. Two

ARTIFICIAL SATELLITES

Bova, B. A long way back

ARTIST LIFE

Hardwick, E. The purchase

ARTISTS

See also Artist life; Illustrators; Painters; Women artists

Beagle, P. S. Uncle Chaim and Aunt Rifke and the angel

Beattie, A. Skeletons

Bingham, S. Benjamin

Black, A. The laziest form of revelation

Boland, J. C. Evocation of evil

Boland, J. C. The return of Jasper Kohl

Chuculate, E. D. Cheyenne Madonna

Chuculate, E. D. A famous Indian artist

Chuculate, E. D. Under the red star of Mars

ARTISTS—*Continued*

Franco, J. April in three parts: part II, Wasting
Gallari, A. Negative space
Goodman, A. La vita nuova
McOmber, A. Of wool
Mu Xin. Halo
Niedzviecki, H. The useless
Schappell, E. Aren't you dead yet?
Sneed, C. Portraits of a few of the people I've made cry
Tem, S. R. Miri
Tillman, L. The substitute
Tolbert, J. Arties aren't stupid
Tremblay, P. Figure 5
Vonnegut, K. $10,000 a year, easy
Vonnegut, K. The humbugs
Wieland, L. Out of the garden
Williamson, E. M. Creusa
Yant, C. The magician and the maid and other stories

ARTISTS' MODELS

Aiken, J. Model wife
Black, A. The laziest form of revelation
Novack, S. Cerulean skies

As always, unkind. Leland, C. T.
As dark as Christmas gets. Block, L.
As God made us. Kennedy, A. L.
As if. Emshwiller, C.
As if in time of war. Leland, C. T.
As If It Were the Last Time: Watching the Spring Tide Roll Into Alabama's Grand Bay. Finch, B.
As recorded on brass cylinders. Grant, J. L. and Mantchev, L.
As-Sayyed's space. Ibrāhim, .
As the Wall Came Tumbling Down: A Story. Timm, U.
As You've Planned It. Lång, L.-M.

ASEXUAL REPRODUCTION

Jones, G. A. La Cenerentola
Lindholm, M. Drum machine
Matheson, R. Counterfeit bills

Ash. Doyle, R.
Ash city stomp. Butner, R.
Ashes of the beacon. Bierce, A.
Ashfeldt, Lane

Snowmelt
Dancing with Mr. Darcy; stories inspired by Jane Austen and Chawton House Library; compiled by Sarah Waters.

ASIA

See also Southeast Asia

ASIA, SOUTHEASTERN *See* Southeast Asia
ASIA MINOR

Turtledove, H. Farmers' law

ASIANS

England

Wells, H. G. The Lord of the Dynamos

ASIMOV, ISAAC, 1920-1992

Parodies, imitations, etc.

Sands, B. Outside

Ask me another. Gruber, F.
The **asking** price. Hannah, S.
Aslam, Nadeem

Leila in the Wilderness
Granta no112 p7-53 Aut 2010
PUNNU'S JIHAD
Granta no116 p59-79 S 2011

Asleep in the Lord [Part of the Summer Fiction Issue] Eugenides, J.
Ass. Dixon, S.
Assadi, Mysoon

An apartment to let!
Loud sounds from the Holy Land; short fiction by Palestinian women; edited and translated by Jamal Assadi with assistance from Martha Moody.
Forbidden talk
Loud sounds from the Holy Land; short fiction by Palestinian women; edited and translated by Jamal Assadi with assistance from Martha Moody.
The nightmare of a summer night
Loud sounds from the Holy Land; short fiction by Palestinian women; edited and translated by Jamal Assadi with assistance from Martha Moody.
Tea, biscuits and sugar
Loud sounds from the Holy Land; short fiction by Palestinian women; edited and translated by Jamal Assadi with assistance from Martha Moody.

ASSASSINATION

Dozois, G. R. Counterfactual
Fowler, K. J. Standing room only
Jackson, A. A Tampa man
Orozco, D. Somoza's dream

ASSASSINS (ISMAILITES)

Shepard, J. The track of the Assassins

ASSAULT AND BATTERY

Bengtsson, J. T. One of the rough ones
Millhauser, S. The slap
Oates, J. C. The beating
O'Connor, F. Revelation
Sealy, I. A. Last in, first out
Stovall, T. Breakin' dishes
Vonnegut, K. Hundred-dollar kisses

ASSES AND MULES

Karay, R. H. The gray donkey
Sa'īd, M. A. Sheik Mabruk

Assimilation. Doctorow, E. L.
The **Asterisk** Company. Ríos, A. Á.

ASTEROIDS

Anderson, P. Holmgang
Buckell, T. S. Resistance
Dick, P. K. The infinites
Dick, P. K. Piper in the woods

ASTHMA

Daugherty, T. The inhalatorium
The **Astonished** Dead [Excerpt from The Adventures of Jillian O'Malley] Alvarado, B.

ASTROLOGERS

Smith, C. A. The last hieroglyph
Vukcevich, R. Tongues

ASTROLOGY

Matheson, R. Leo rising

ASTRONAUTS

See also Women astronauts
Farmer, P. J. The blasphemers
Mamatas, N. Your life, fifteen minutes from now
Niven, L. Neutron star
Ruocco, J. Dog

ASTRONOMERS

Wells, H. G. The star

ASTRONOMY
> *See also* Outer space; Stars names of individual planets

Cardinale, J. May I not seem to have lived

Asylum. Constantine, D.

At a loss for words. Ayau, K. J.

At central. Reed, K.

At night we play hearts. Mueller, D.

At night, when the demons come. Cluley, R.

At Old Man Eckert's. Bierce, A.

At Olivehill. Trevor, W.

At Phil & Joanna's 1: 60/40. Barnes, J.

At Phil & Joanna's 2: Marmalade. Barnes, J.

At Phil & Joanna's 3: Look, no hands. Barnes, J.

At Phil & Joanna's 4: One in five. Barnes, J.

At sea. Baker, L.

At the 24-hour. Nolan, W. F.

At the café. Dib, M.

At the conglomeroid cocktail party. Silverberg, R.

At the end of this story the door will open and under eight seconds will have passed. Martin, C.

At the post. Gold, H. L.

At the post office. Shibli, A.

At the rendezvous of victory. Gordimer, N.

At the riding school. Goodfellow, C.

At the zoo. Horrocks, C.

At Wanship. Wieland, L.

ATHEISM

Glover, E. M. Metaphysics

O'Connor, S. The professor of atheism: Department of refutation

O'Connor, S. The professor of atheism: Glue factory bowling

O'Connor, S. The professor of atheism: Magnum opus

O'Connor, S. The professor of atheism: Stealing peaches from Sam Snnow

ATHLETES
> *See also* Women athletes

Gallari, A. A beautiful lie

Gallari, A. Throwing stones

Haywood, G. A. The first rule is

Atkins, Elizabeth

The wrong side of Mr. Right

Price-Thompson, T. My blue suede shoes; four novellas; [edited by] Tracy Price-Thompson and Taressa Stovall.

Atkins, Marie

Seven brains, ten minutes

Z: zombie stories; edited by J. M. Lassen

Atkins, Peter

The Mystery

The Year's best dark fantasy & horror; edited by Paula Guran

Atkinson, Kate

The war on women

Freedom; stories celebrating the Universal Declaration of Human Rights; Amnesty International.

Atkinson, Lisa Michelle

Yule be sorry

Christmas at the Mysterious Bookshop; 'tis the season to be deadly; stories of mistletoe and mayhem from 17 masters of suspense; edited by Otto Penzler.

ATLANTIS

Smith, C. A. The death of Malygris

ATOMIC BOMB

Davis, C. Last year's grave undug

Prindle, J. Einstein's tears

Spinrad, N. The big flash

Stanger, V. The eye patch protocol

ATOMIC WARFARE *See* Nuclear warfare

ATONEMENT

Ryman, G. Pol Pot's beautiful daughter

ATONEMENT, DAY OF *See* Yom Kippur

Atop Beijing mountain of gold. Zhang Kangkang

Atria. Ausubel, R.

ATROCITIES
> *See also* Holocaust, Jewish (1933-1945); Massacres; Torture

Atta, Sefi

Green

Atta, S. News from home; stories

Hailstones on Zamfara

Atta, S. News from home; stories

Housekeeping

World Literature Today v84 no6 p24-7 N/D 2010

Last trip

Atta, S. News from home; stories

Lawless

Atta, S. News from home; stories

Madness in the family

Atta, S. News from home; stories

The miracle worker

Atta, S. News from home; stories

News from home

Atta, S. News from home; stories

Spoils

Atta, S. News from home; stories

A temporary position

Atta, S. News from home; stories

Twilight trek

Atta, S. News from home; stories

Yahoo yahoo

Atta, S. News from home; stories

An **attack** of hunger. Brennan, M.

Attack of the pod people. Novack, S.

An **attempt** at persuasion. Burbara, R.

ATTEMPTED MURDER *See* Murder stories

ATTEMPTED SUICIDE *See* Suicide

ATTITUDE (PSYCHOLOGY)
> *See also* Prejudices

Attitudes. Farmer, P. J.

Attlee and the long walk. Baker, K.

ATTORNEYS *See* Law and lawyers

Atwell, Mary Stewart

Maynard

The Best American mystery stories 2010; edited and with an introduction by Lee Child; Otto Penzler, series editor

AU PAIRS

Allio, K. Clothed, female figure

Doyle, R. The pram

Nolan, W. F. Child's care

The **Auble** gun. Hindmarch, W.

AUCTIONS

Black, H. Lot 558: Shadow of my nephew by Wells, Charlotte

Audacious. Adams, B.

AUDUBON, JOHN JAMES, 1785-1851
About
Turtledove, H. Audubon in Atlantis

Audubon in Atlantis. Turtledove, H.

August. Olsen, L.

August Eschenburg. Millhauser, S.
August ninth at Natural Bridge. Bingham, S.
Aunt Jules. O'Connor, S.
Aunt Résia and the spirits. Lahens, Y.
Aunt telephone. Pearlman, E.
Auntie Frosea. Ciocan, I.
AUNTS
    See also Nieces
  Bernheimer, K. A Garibaldi tale
  Chughtai, I. The quilt
  Engel, P. Paloma
  Fintushel, E. How the little rabbi grew
  Fisher, D. C. The bedquilt
  Gilb, D. Willows village
  Grover, L. L. The dance boots
  Hannah, B. Rat-faced Auntie
  Jensen, T. Looking for boll weevil
  Kyle, A. Company of strangers
  Lahens, Y. Aunt Résia and the spirits
  Lahens, Y. Petty corruption
  Large, J.-R. Rosanna
  Latiolais, M. The long table
  Levine, S. Alia
  Marãr, M. The home-coming guy!
  Mu Xin. Quiet afternoon tea
  Naipaul, V. S. My aunt Gold Teeth
  Simmons, D. Ticket
  Tóibín, C. The colour of shadows
  Trouillot, E. Which one?
  Yoshimoto, B. A special boy
Auspicious eggs. Morrow, J.
AUSTEN, JANE, 1775-1817
     About
  Owens, V. Jane Austen over the Styx
  Saunders, N. Tears fall on Orkney
    Parodies, imitations, etc.
  Bellamy, E. Miss Austen victorious
  Brendel, K. Somewhere
  Cowie, F. One character in search of her love
    story role
Austin, Mary Hunter
  The Walking Woman
    The vintage book of American women writ-
    ers; edited and with an introduction by
    Elaine Showalter.
AUSTIN (TEX.) *See* Texas—Austin
AUSTRALIA
  Dowling, T. Jarkman at the othergates
  Dowling, T. The library
  Lanagan, M. Machine maid
    Native peoples
    See Australian aborigines
Australia. Dorph, C. and Pasternak, S.
AUSTRALIAN ABORIGINES
  Wright, A. Be careful about playing with the
    path of least resistance
AUSTRALIANS
    United States
  Segal, L. G. Making good
AUSTRIA
    18th century
  Barnes, J. Harmony
Ausubel, Ramona
  Atria
    The New Yorker v87 no7 p62-9 Ap 4 2011
AUTHORITARIANISM *See* Totalitarianism

AUTHORS
    See also Art critics; Authorship; Drama-
    tists; Poets; Women authors names of indi-
    vidual authors, dramatists, poets, etc.
  Aguilar Camín, H. Comrade Vadillo
  Ajvaz, M. The wire book
  Barrett, L. Links
  Bradbury, R. Don't get technatal
  Bradbury, R. The wind
  Breen, J. L. William Allan Wilson
  Burnstein, M. A. I remember the future
  Châteaureynaud, G. O. Another story
  Clark, M. H. What's in a name?
  Clayton, L. Overlocked
  Connolly, L. C. Beneath between
  Crider, B. Pure pulp
  Davis, L. Cape Cod diary
  Davis, L. Sketches for a life of Wassily
  Delbanco, N. The writers' trade
  DeMille, N. Death benefits
  Dixon, S. An accurate acount
  Dixon, S. Can't win
  Dixon, S. Dawn
  Dixon, S. Dream
  Dixon, S. Meet the natives
  Dixon, S. Piers
  Dixon, S. Starting again
  Dixon, S. Storm
  Dixon, S. The talk show
  Dozois, G. R. Counterfactual
  Farmer, P. J. Father's in the basement
  Files, G. The jacaranda smile
  Fitzgerald, F. S. Pat Hobby and Orson Welles
  Galchen, R. The entire northern side was cov-
    ered with fire
  Galgut, D. The lover
  Gallari, A. Warwick Damon
  Garcia-Aguilera, C. Personal experience
  Goulart, R. Murder for dummies
  Gray, A. Thoughts while strolling
  Hannah, B. Drummer down
  Hannah, B. Two things, dimly, were going at
    each other
  Hardwick, E. Yes and no
  Haywood, G. A. Like something out of a comic
    book
  Kaminsky, S. M. Rattle, rattle, rattle
  Krauss, N. The young painters
  Lee, T. Black and white sky
  Lee, T. The persecution machine
  Levine, P. Development hell
  Lychack, W. The ghostwriter
  Mankell, H. Sofia
  Matheson, R. The house of the dead
  McElroy, J. Annals of plagiary
  Mehta, R. What we mean
  Mehta, R. Yours
  Monzó, Q. Literature
  Morris, E. Rejection letter
  Mu Xin. Notes from underground
  Munro, A. Material
  Nevins, F. M., Jr. The spark
  Noguchi, K. Foreign husband
  Perry, A. My object all sublime
  Rosen, J. The true world
  Ruocco, J. Hart
  Ruocco, J. Unicorns
  Ruocco, J. Wolves
  Ryman, G. The future of science fiction

AUTHORS—*Continued*

Schappell, E. Aren't you dead yet?

Schmitt, E.-E. The dreamer from Ostend

Self, W. Scale

Senna, D. There, there

Smith, C. A. Nemesis of the unfinished

Sneed, C. Interview with the second wife

Sneed, C. You're so different

Solzhenitsyn, A. Apricot jam

Stoltz, K. The elephant's tusks

Swirsky, R. 1943: a brief note pertaining to the absence of one olivaceous cormorant, stuffed

Tóibín, C. The pearl fishers

Uldes, E. Professional behavior

Villegas, H. His ghost

Villegas, H. Neighbours

Warsh, L. Endless embrace

Warsh, L. Mysterioso

Warsh, L. Secret

Wells, H. G. The wild asses of the devil

Wideman, J. E. Microstories

Wieland, L. The girl with radium eyes

Williamson, E. M. A wise man is known by his laughter

Woolson, C. F. Miss Grief

Zeman, A. Rue Morgue noir: the possible--probable--struggles Edgar Allan Poe might have faced while seeking success as a talented new writer in the world of today

AUTHORSHIP

See also Authors

Davis, L. The center of the story

Dixon, S. Next to nothing

Gifford, B. The secrets of the universe

Gribbons, D. A short story

Lovesey, P. The deadliest tale of all

Riippi, J. Something about my blood and yours

Sands, B. How to write a short story!

Yezierska, A. Wild winter love

AUTOBIOGRAPHICAL STORIES

Mehta, R. Quarantine

Noguchi, K. Foreign husband

Autobiography. Emshwiller, C.

Autobiography. Nagai, M.

The **automagic** horse. Hubbard, L. R.

AUTOMATA *See* Robots

The **automatic** garden. McOmber, A.

AUTOMOBILE ACCIDENTS *See* Traffic accidents

AUTOMOBILE DRIVERS

See also Chauffeurs; Hit-and-run drivers

Beattie, A. Shifting

Ehrenreich, B. Everything you see is real

AUTOMOBILES

Beattie, A. A vintage Thunderbird

Bingham, S. Red car

Franco, J. Jack-O'

Gifford, B. Roy's first car

Lansdale, J. R. The folding man

Roberge, R. Swiss engineering

Sands, B. A visitor's guide to lawn guyland

Self, W. Tough, tough toys for tough, tough boys

Sterling, P. One version of the story

Accidents

See Traffic accidents

Repairing

Naipaul, V. S. The mechanical genius

Service stations

Barrett, L. Texaco on Biscayne

Petry, A. L. The migraine workers

AUTOPSY

Solana, T. The offering

AVALANCHES

Shepard, J. Your fate hurtles down at you

AVANT GARDE STORIES *See* Experimental stories

AVARICE

Boland, J. C. Easy money

Hubbard, L. R. Greed

L'Amour, L. Off the mangrove coast

Phelan, T. Happine$$

Ava's apartment. Lethem, J.

AVIARIES

Narayan, S. The mechanical aviary of emperor Jalal-ud-din Muhammad Akbar

AVIATION *See* Aeronautics

Aviator on the prowl. Narayanan, K.

AVIATORS *See* Air pilots

Avigdor of the Apes. Stern, S.

AWARDS *See* Rewards (Prizes, etc.)

Away from home. Davis, L.

The **awkward** age. Liss, D.

Axis. Munro, A.

Ayau, Kurt Jose

At a loss for words

Ayau, K. J. The brick murder: a tragedy and other stories

Bob the negro

Ayau, K. J. The brick murder: a tragedy and other stories

The brick murder: a tragedy

Ayau, K. J. The brick murder: a tragedy and other stories

By the numbers

Ayau, K. J. The brick murder: a tragedy and other stories

Calling it off

Ayau, K. J. The brick murder: a tragedy and other stories

Culture clash

Ayau, K. J. The brick murder: a tragedy and other stories

Murray and the Holy Ghost

Ayau, K. J. The brick murder: a tragedy and other stories

Official friend

Ayau, K. J. The brick murder: a tragedy and other stories

Outsourcing

Ayau, K. J. The brick murder: a tragedy and other stories

Sand castle

Ayau, K. J. The brick murder: a tragedy and other stories

Spawning

Ayau, K. J. The brick murder: a tragedy and other stories

Ayres, Diane

Seeing nothing

Philadelphia noir; edited by Carlin Romano.

Ayres, Jedidiah

Mahogany and monogamy

Blood, guts, & whiskey; edited by Todd Robinson; introduction by Max Allan Collins.

Azathoth in analysis. Cannon, P.

Azathoth in Arkham. Cannon, P.

AZTECS
Bodard, A. D. Safe, child, safe
Kurlansky, M. Menudo

B

B. Wordsworth. Naipaul, V. S.
Babbitt, Natalie
The power of speech
Sympathy for the devil; edited by Tim Pratt.
Babcock, Dwight V.
Murder on the gayway
The Black Lizard big book of Black Mask stories; edited and with a foreword by Otto Penzler; introduction by Keith Alan Deutsch.
BABEL´, I. (ISAAC), 1894-1940
Jarrar, R. The story of my building (after Isaac Babel's "Story of my dovecote")
Babel´, Isaac *See* Babel´, I. (Isaac), 1894-1940
Babies. Gray, A.
The **baboon** whose buffoon was dead. Chubak, S.
BABOONS
Chubak, S. The baboon whose buffoon was dead
Freed, L. Sunshine
The **baby**. Dixon, S.
Baby. Emshwiller, C.
Baby brother. Hemmingson, M.
BABY SITTERS
Allen, D. Succor
Hemmingson, M. Baby brother
Oates, J. C. Babysitter
Villegas, H. The family
Willis, D. Frank
The **baby** spoon. Highsmith, P.
The **baby** store. Gorman, E.
A **baby** tramp. Bierce, A.
Baby, you were great. Wilhelm, K.
BABYLON (ANCIENT CITY)
Jones, W. The treachery of stone
Babysitter. Oates, J. C.
Bac Sierra, Benjamin
El Lobo [With an introduction by M. H. Kingston]
World Literature Today v84 no6 p17-19 N/D 2010
BACH, JOHANN SEBASTIAN, 1685-1750
About
Emshwiller, C. Destinations, premonitions and the nature of anxiety
BACHELORS *See* Single men
Bachman, Richard *See* King, Stephen, 1947-
Bacigalupi, Paolo
The gambler
The Nebula Awards showcase; edited by Kevin J. Anderson.
Pop squad
Brave new worlds; edited by John Joseph Adams.
Back in the woods. Shepard, S.
Back issues. Hardwick, E.
Back to Galicia [Part of a special issue: Roots and routes] White, E. R.
Backbone. Wallace, D. F.
Backup. Butcher, J.
The **Backward** Man. Terry, G. P.

BACTERIOLOGISTS
Wells, H. G. The stolen bacillus
Bad bargain. Nevins, F. M., Jr.
A **BAD** DAY FOR THE ZEBRAS. Meades, C.
Bad girls. Gifford, B.
A **Bad** Harvest. Hollander, D.
Bad move. Zeltserman, D.
Bad night at the Del Prado. Gifford, B.
Bad night in Hyannisport. Greenland, S.
Bad thoughts and the mechanism. Harland, R.
BADGERS
Boyle, P. Meles vulgaris
Badr, Liyānah
March of the dinosaurs
Freedom; stories celebrating the Universal Declaration of Human Rights; Amnesty International.
A **baffled** ambuscade. Bierce, A.
BAG LADIES *See* Homeless persons
BAGPIPE
Penkov, M. The night horizon
Bagworms. Nevins, F. M., Jr.
Bailat-Jones, Michelle
(tr.) *See* Ramuz, C. F.
Bailey, Dale and Ballingrud, Nathan
The crevasse
The Year's best dark fantasy & horror; edited by Paula Guran
Bailie, Tony
The druid's dance
Requiems for the departed; edited by Gerard Brennan & Mike Stone.
Baingana, Doreen
Anointed
Agni no72 p198-203 2010
Baker, Aimee
The persistence of memory
Best of the West 2009; new stories from the wide side of the Missouri; edited by James Thomas and D. Seth Horton; foreword by Rick Bass.
Baker, Deborah
DIY
Confrontation no109 p154-7 Spr 2011
Baker, Kage
Attlee and the long walk
Life on Mars: tales from the new frontier; an original science fiction anthology; edited by Jonathan Strahan
The books
The Year's best science fiction: twenty-eighth annual collection; edited by Gardner Dozois.
Two old men
Sympathy for the devil; edited by Tim Pratt.
The women of Nell Gwynne's
The Nebula Awards showcase; edited by Kevin J. Anderson.
Baker, Lori
At sea
Baker, L. Crash & tell; stories
The coming of age of Jane
Baker, L. Crash & tell; stories
Crash & tell
Baker, L. Crash & tell; stories
Experimental Maria
Baker, L. Crash & tell; stories
Ghost story
Baker, L. Crash & tell; stories

Baker, Lori—*Continued*
Still life
    Baker, L. Crash & tell; stories
Baker, Matt
The sunflower state
    Southern Humanities Review v45 no1 p87-99
    Wint 2011
Baker, Scott W.
Poison, inside the walls
    L. Ron Hubbard presents Writers of the Future volume XXVI; the year's twelve best tales from the Writers of the Future international writers' program; illustrated by winners in the Illustrators of the Future international illustrators' program; with essays on writing & illustration by L. Ron Hubbard/Dean Wesley Smith/ Stephen Youll; edited by K. D. Wentworth
BAKERIES AND BAKERS
Jemisin, N. K. 1929: the singular taffy puller
Naipaul, V. S. The baker's story
Ruocco, J. Flies
Ruocco, J. Marzipan lambs
The **baker's** story. Naipaul, V. S.
Bakopoulos, Natalie
Fresco, Byzantine
    The Pen/O.Henry Prize stories, 2010; edited and with an introduction by Laura Furman; with essays on the stories they admire most by jurors Junot Diaz, Paula Fox, Yiyun Li.
Bakriyya, Rajaa
Leave this world for me . . . for a woman . . . who seems to be the hope
    Loud sounds from the Holy Land; short fiction by Palestinian women; edited and translated by Jamal Assadi with assistance from Martha Moody.
The story of perfume to you in the beginning of the year at the end of the story . . . . . .
    Loud sounds from the Holy Land; short fiction by Palestinian women; edited and translated by Jamal Assadi with assistance from Martha Moody.
Bal, Hartosh Singh
Just another death
    Delhi noir; edited by Hirsh Sawhney
Balázs, Béla
The ancestors
    Balázs, B. The cloak of dreams; Chinese fairy tales; translated and introduced by Jack Zipes; illustrated by Mariette Lydis
The clay child
    Balázs, B. The cloak of dreams; Chinese fairy tales; translated and introduced by Jack Zipes; illustrated by Mariette Lydis
The cloak of dreams
    Balázs, B. The cloak of dreams; Chinese fairy tales; translated and introduced by Jack Zipes; illustrated by Mariette Lydis
The clumsy god
    Balázs, B. The cloak of dreams; Chinese fairy tales; translated and introduced by Jack Zipes; illustrated by Mariette Lydis
The flea
    Balázs, B. The cloak of dreams; Chinese fairy tales; translated and introduced by Jack Zipes; illustrated by Mariette Lydis

The friends
    Balázs, B. The cloak of dreams; Chinese fairy tales; translated and introduced by Jack Zipes; illustrated by Mariette Lydis
Li-Tai-Pe and springtime
    Balázs, B. The cloak of dreams; Chinese fairy tales; translated and introduced by Jack Zipes; illustrated by Mariette Lydis
Li-Tai-Pe and the thief
    Balázs, B. The cloak of dreams; Chinese fairy tales; translated and introduced by Jack Zipes; illustrated by Mariette Lydis
The moon fish
    Balázs, B. The cloak of dreams; Chinese fairy tales; translated and introduced by Jack Zipes; illustrated by Mariette Lydis
The old child
    Balázs, B. The cloak of dreams; Chinese fairy tales; translated and introduced by Jack Zipes; illustrated by Mariette Lydis
The opium smokers
    Balázs, B. The cloak of dreams; Chinese fairy tales; translated and introduced by Jack Zipes; illustrated by Mariette Lydis
The parasols
    Balázs, B. The cloak of dreams; Chinese fairy tales; translated and introduced by Jack Zipes; illustrated by Mariette Lydis
The revenge of the chestnut tree
    Balázs, B. The cloak of dreams; Chinese fairy tales; translated and introduced by Jack Zipes; illustrated by Mariette Lydis
The robbers of divine power
    Balázs, B. The cloak of dreams; Chinese fairy tales; translated and introduced by Jack Zipes; illustrated by Mariette Lydis
Tearful gaze
    Balázs, B. The cloak of dreams; Chinese fairy tales; translated and introduced by Jack Zipes; illustrated by Mariette Lydis
The victor
    Balázs, B. The cloak of dreams; Chinese fairy tales; translated and introduced by Jack Zipes; illustrated by Mariette Lydis
The **balcony** and the garden. Bayley, E.
Baljour and Meriwether in the adventure of the emperor's vengeance. Abraham, D.
Ball, David
(tr.) See Waberi, Abdourahman A.
Ball, K. C.
Coward's steel
    L. Ron Hubbard presents Writers of the Future volume XXVI; the year's twelve best tales from the Writers of the Future international writers' program; illustrated by winners in the Illustrators of the Future international illustrators' program; with essays on writing & illustration by L. Ron Hubbard/Dean Wesley Smith/ Stephen Youll; edited by K. D. Wentworth
Ball, Nicole
(tr.) See Waberi, Abdourahman A.
BALL GAMES
    See also Baseball; Basketball; Bowling; Football; Soccer; Tennis
The **ballad** of Duane Juarez. Franklin, T.
A **ballad** of Oyo. Mphahlele, E.

Ballard, J. G.
Billennium
Brave new worlds; edited by John Joseph Adams.
Ballard, W. T. (Willis Todhunter)
A little different
The Black Lizard big book of Black Mask stories; edited and with a foreword by Otto Penzler; introduction by Keith Alan Deutsch.
Ballard, Willis Todhunter See Ballard, W. T. (Willis Todhunter)
BALLET
See also Dancers
Ballingrud, Nathan
The way station
Naked city; tales of urban fantasy; edited by Ellen Datlow.
(jt. auth) See Bailey, Dale and Ballingrud, Nathan
BALLOONS
Langan, J. The unbearable proximity of Mr. Dunn's balloons
Loory, B. The little girl and the balloon
BALLS (PARTIES) See Parties
BALTIMORE (MD.) See Maryland—Baltimore
Bambara, Florentine
(tr.) See Devi, Ananda
BANANAS
Shapiro, J. Tiger beat
Band names. Lukasik-Foss, T.
BANDITS See Brigands and robbers
Bandleader's girlfriend. Nutting, A.
BANDS (MUSIC)
Adrian, C. The warm fuzzies
Calhoun, K. Nightblooming
Hannah, B. Testimony of pilot
Sterling, P. Coda
Bangalore. Fiore, L. C.
BANGKOK (THAILAND) See Thailand—Bangkok
BANGLADESH
Wiecek, M. The shipbreaker
BANK ROBBERS
Cole, W. Waiting for Rusty
Schirach, F. v. The Ethiopian
BANKERS
Archer, J. Politically correct
Baxter, C. The next building I plan to bomb
Boland, J. C. Marley's package
Hodge, B. An ounce of prevention is worth a pound of flesh
Ray, S. The miracles of Vincent Van Gogh
Roberts, W. O. The professionals
Solzhenitsyn, A. Fracture points
Tillman, L. Playing hurt
BANKRUPTCY
Cooper, D. Breakin' down
Delee, D. Bling, bling
DeMille, N. Death benefits
Kennedy, A. L. Confectioner's gold
Banks, L. A. See Banks, Leslie Esdaile
Banks, Leslie Esdaile
Wanted: dead or alive
Chicks kick butt; edited by Rachel Caine and Kerrie L. Hughes.

Banks, Russell
The gully
Blue collar, white collar, no collar; stories of work; edited by Richard Ford.
BANKS
See also Bankers
Sands, B. The heist
The **banks** of the Ohio. Bingham, S.
Banner Creek Summit. Cullen, N.
BANSHEES
Bruen, K. She wails through the fair
Banville, John
Summer voices
The Granta book of the Irish short story; [edited by] Anne Enright.
BAPTISTS
Willis, M. S. Scandalous Roy Critchfield
Bar Beach show. Osondu, E. C.
The **bar** on Tompkins Square Park. Tuten, F.
The **bar** sinister. Davis, R. H.
Barahona, Federico
(Never) fade away
Can'tLit; fearless fiction from Broken pencil magazine; edited by Richard Rosenbaum.
Barba, Andrés
The coming flood
Granta no113 p51-63 Wint 2010
Barba, David
Sweet croquette
Barcelona noir; edited by Adriana V. Lopez & Cartmen Ospina; translated by Achy Obejas.
Barbara Hutton Toujours. Terry, G. P.
The **barber** of Bariga. Mphahlele, E.
BARBERS
Mphahlele, E. The barber of Bariga
BARCELONA (SPAIN) See Spain—Barcelona
Barcelona, 1975. Tóibín, C.
Bardsley, Greg
Crazy Larry smells bacon
By hook or by crook and 27 more of the best crime + mystery stories of the year; edited by Ed Gorman and Martin H. Greenberg.
Barillas, Gabriel R.
The roads
San Diego noir; edited by Maryelizabeth Hart.
BARKENTINES See Sailing vessels
Barking man. Bell, M. S.
Barnes, Eric
Something Pretty, Something Beautiful
Prairie Schooner v84 no4 p80-96 Wint 2010
Barnes, John
Martian heart
Life on Mars: tales from the new frontier; an original science fiction anthology; edited by Jonathan Strahan
Barnes, Julian
At Phil & Joanna's 1: 60/40
Barnes, J. Pulse
At Phil & Joanna's 2: Marmalade
Barnes, J. Pulse
At Phil & Joanna's 3: Look, no hands
Barnes, J. Pulse
At Phil & Joanna's 4: One in five
Barnes, J. Pulse
Carcassonne
Barnes, J. Pulse
Complicity
Barnes, J. Pulse

Barnes, Julian—*Continued*
East wind
    Barnes, J. Pulse
Gardeners' world
    Barnes, J. Pulse
Harmony
    Barnes, J. Pulse
Homage to Hemingway
    The New Yorker v87 no19 p60-6 Jl 4 2011
The limner
    Barnes, J. Pulse
Marriage lines
    Barnes, J. Pulse
Pulse
    Barnes, J. Pulse
Sleeping with John Updike
    Barnes, J. Pulse
Trespass
    Barnes, J. Pulse
Barnes, Linda
Lucky penny
    The Shamus winners: America's best private
    eye stories, volume I: 1982-1995; collected
    and introduced by Robert J. Randisi; found-
    er, Private Eye Writers of America
Barnhill, Kelly
St. Brendan's shank
    The Thackery T. Lambshead cabinet of curi-
    osities; edited by Ann & Jeff VanderMeer.
The **Barnum** Museum. Millhauser, S.
BARONS *See* Aristocracy
BARQUENTINES *See* Sailing vessels
Barrel of laughs. Alenyikov, M.
Barrett, A. Igoni
Love Is Power, Or Something Like That
    Agni no72 p209-29 2010
Barrett, Lynne
Cave of the winds
    Barrett, L. Magpies
Gift wrap
    Barrett, L. Magpies
Gossip and toad
    Barrett, L. Magpies
Links
    Barrett, L. Magpies
The noir boudoir
    Barrett, L. Magpies
One hippopotamus
    Barrett, L. Magpies
Texaco on Biscayne
    Barrett, L. Magpies
When, he wondered
    Barrett, L. Magpies
Barrett, Neal, Jr.
Getting dark
    The Nebula Awards showcase; edited by Kev-
    in J. Anderson.
The **barrier** moment. Anderson, P.
BARRISTERS *See* Law and lawyers
Barrodale, Amie
William Wei
    The Paris Review v53 no197 p15-23 Summ
    2011
Barron, Laird
--30--
    The Best horror of the year: volume three;
    edited by Ellen Datlow.

Blackwood's baby
    Ghosts by gaslight; stories of steampunk and
    supernatural suspense; [edited by] Jack
    Dann [and] Nick Gevers
The siphon
    Blood and other cravings; edited by Ellen
    Datlow.
Barrow, Clyde *See* Clyde, 1909-1934
The **barrow** maid. Morgan, C.
Barry, Kevin
Doctor Sot
    Best European fiction 2011; edited by Alek-
    sandr Hemon; preface by Colum McCann
See the tree, how big it's grown
    The Granta book of the Irish short story; [ed-
    ited by] Anne Enright.
Barry, Quan
Ko-uta (Small Song)
    The Southern Review (Baton Rouge, La.) v47
    no3 p363-76 Summ 2011
BARS *See* Hotels, taverns, etc.
BARTENDERS
LaBrie, A. Princess
Lake, J. Tall spirits, blocking the night
Niven, L. The fourth profession
Riippi, J. Something about ipek (on a Valen-
    tine's Day)
The **barter**. Oates, J. C.
Barthelme, Donald
Me and Miss Mandible
    Blue collar, white collar, no collar; stories of
    work; edited by Richard Ford.
                    About
Williamson, E. M. The teaching of Don B.
Bartleby the scrivener. Melville, H.
Barzak, Christopher
Map of seventeen
    The beastly bride; tales of the animal people;
    edited by Ellen Datlow & Terri Windling;
    introduction by Terri Windling; selected
    decorations by Charles Vess.
    The Best science fiction and fantasy of the
    year: volume five; edited by Jonathan
    Strahan.
We do not come in peace
    Welcome to Bordertown; new stories and po-
    ems of the Borderlands; edited by Holly
    Black and Ellen Kushner; introduction by
    Terri Windling.
Barzini, Chiara
Three Stories
    Bomb no114 p Supp30 Wint 2010
BASEBALL
Dozois, G. R. The hanging curve
Gallari, A. A beautiful lie
Gallari, A. Throwing stones
Gilb, D. Uncle Rock
Kurlansky, M. Hot dog
Papernick, J. The last five-year plan
Based on a true story. O'Connor, S.
Basileus. Silverberg, R.
Baskervilles midgets. Oliver, R.
BASKETBALL
Bass, R. Coach
Ray, S. Three from Montana
Ray, S. When we rise

Bass, Rick
  Coach
    Best of the West 2011; new stories from the
      wild side of the Missouri; edited by James
      Thomas and D. Seth Horton; foreword by
      Ana Castillo.
  Fish story
    Best of the West 2010; new stories from the
      wide side of the Missouri; edited by James
      Thomas and D. Seth Horton; foreword by
      Kent Meyers.
  The hermit's story
Bassingthwaighte, Ian
  The Cardboard Dress
    TriQuarterly no139 Wint/Spr 2011
BASTARDY *See* Illegitimacy
The **bath**. Rodoreda, M.
BATHYSCAPHE
  Wells, H. G. In the abyss
  Wells, H. G. In the Avu observatory
Bats Out of Hell Division. Hannah, B.
BATTERED WIVES *See* Wife abuse
BATTLES
        See also names of individual battles
  Bierce, A. An affair of outposts
  Bierce, A. The coup de grâce
Bauer, Tricia
  Robin
    Western Humanities Review v64 no2 p155-9
      Summ 2010
Baumer, Jennifer Rachel
  The forever sleep
    Swenson, P. The Best of Talebones; edited by
      Patrick Swenson.
Bausch, Richard
  Unjust
    Blue collar, white collar, no collar; stories of
      work; edited by Richard Ford.
Baxt, George
  Schemes and variations
    Christmas at the Mysterious Bookshop; 'tis
      the season to be deadly; stories of mistletoe
      and mayhem from 17 masters of suspense;
      edited by Otto Penzler.
Baxter, Charles
  The cousins
    Pushcart Prize XXXV: best of the small
      presses 2011; edited by Bill Henderson
      with the Pushcart Prize editors.
    Baxter, C. Gryphon; new and selected stories
  The cures for love
    Baxter, C. Gryphon; new and selected stories
  The disappeared
    Baxter, C. Gryphon; new and selected stories
  The eleventh floor
    Baxter, C. Gryphon; new and selected stories
  Fenstad's mother
    Baxter, C. Gryphon; new and selected stories
  Ghosts
    Baxter, C. Gryphon; new and selected stories
  Gryphon
    Baxter, C. Gryphon; new and selected stories
  Harmony of the world
    Baxter, C. Gryphon; new and selected stories
  Horace and Margaret's fifty-second
    Baxter, C. Gryphon; new and selected stories
  Kiss away
    Baxter, C. Gryphon; new and selected stories

  Mr. Scary
    Baxter, C. Gryphon; new and selected stories
      Ploughshares v36 no2/3 p8-25 Fall 2010
  The next building I plan to bomb
    Baxter, C. Gryphon; new and selected stories
  The old murderer
    Baxter, C. Gryphon; new and selected stories
  Poor devil
    Baxter, C. Gryphon; new and selected stories
  Royal blue
    Baxter, C. Gryphon; new and selected stories
  Shelter
    Baxter, C. Gryphon; new and selected stories
  Snow
    Baxter, C. Gryphon; new and selected stories
  Surprised by joy
    Baxter, C. Gryphon; new and selected stories
  Westland
    Baxter, C. Gryphon; new and selected stories
  The winner
    Baxter, C. Gryphon; new and selected stories
  Winter journey
    Baxter, C. Gryphon; new and selected stories
  The would-be father
    Baxter, C. Gryphon; new and selected stories
Baxter, Stephen
  On Chryse Plain
    Life on Mars: tales from the new frontier; an
      original science fiction anthology; edited by
      Jonathan Strahan
  Return to Titan
    The Year's best science fiction: twenty-eighth
      annual collection; edited by Gardner
      Dozois.
  The unblinking eye
    Steampunk II: steampunk reloaded; edited by
      Ann & Jeff VanderMeer.
Bayer, Alexei
  An Excursion
    The Kenyon Review v33 no2 p87-104 Spr
      2011
Bayley, E.
  All love is a now
    Bayley, E. The life and memoirs of Dr. Pi
      and other stories; by Edgar Bayley; trans-
      lated by Emily Toder.
  The arrival
    Bayley, E. The life and memoirs of Dr. Pi
      and other stories; by Edgar Bayley; trans-
      lated by Emily Toder.
  The balcony and the garden
    Bayley, E. The life and memoirs of Dr. Pi
      and other stories; by Edgar Bayley; trans-
      lated by Emily Toder.
  The brunette and the miracle of the vial
    Bayley, E. The life and memoirs of Dr. Pi
      and other stories; by Edgar Bayley; trans-
      lated by Emily Toder.
  The bundle
    Bayley, E. The life and memoirs of Dr. Pi
      and other stories; by Edgar Bayley; trans-
      lated by Emily Toder.
  The charmer
    Bayley, E. The life and memoirs of Dr. Pi
      and other stories; by Edgar Bayley; trans-
      lated by Emily Toder.

Bayley, E.—*Continued*
The degroucher
  Bayley, E. The life and memoirs of Dr. Pi
    and other stories; by Edgar Bayley; trans-
    lated by Emily Toder.
Don Ascanio and his trumpet; or, Madariaga's
    cabin
  Bayley, E. The life and memoirs of Dr. Pi
    and other stories; by Edgar Bayley; trans-
    lated by Emily Toder.
Dr. Pi, Elena, and the glitch
  Bayley, E. The life and memoirs of Dr. Pi
    and other stories; by Edgar Bayley; trans-
    lated by Emily Toder.
Dulioto
  Bayley, E. The life and memoirs of Dr. Pi
    and other stories; by Edgar Bayley; trans-
    lated by Emily Toder.
Final act
  Bayley, E. The life and memoirs of Dr. Pi
    and other stories; by Edgar Bayley; trans-
    lated by Emily Toder.
Finished business
  Bayley, E. The life and memoirs of Dr. Pi
    and other stories; by Edgar Bayley; trans-
    lated by Emily Toder.
The four horsemen
  Bayley, E. The life and memoirs of Dr. Pi
    and other stories; by Edgar Bayley; trans-
    lated by Emily Toder.
The message
  Bayley, E. The life and memoirs of Dr. Pi
    and other stories; by Edgar Bayley; trans-
    lated by Emily Toder.
Miracle of poverty
  Bayley, E. The life and memoirs of Dr. Pi
    and other stories; by Edgar Bayley; trans-
    lated by Emily Toder.
The mix-up
  Bayley, E. The life and memoirs of Dr. Pi
    and other stories; by Edgar Bayley; trans-
    lated by Emily Toder.
Mr. Roux
  Bayley, E. The life and memoirs of Dr. Pi
    and other stories; by Edgar Bayley; trans-
    lated by Emily Toder.
The neighbor
  Bayley, E. The life and memoirs of Dr. Pi
    and other stories; by Edgar Bayley; trans-
    lated by Emily Toder.
The notebook with the black cover
  Bayley, E. The life and memoirs of Dr. Pi
    and other stories; by Edgar Bayley; trans-
    lated by Emily Toder.
Of poetry
  Bayley, E. The life and memoirs of Dr. Pi
    and other stories; by Edgar Bayley; trans-
    lated by Emily Toder.
An old lady travels by bus
  Bayley, E. The life and memoirs of Dr. Pi
    and other stories; by Edgar Bayley; trans-
    lated by Emily Toder.
The perfect angler
  Bayley, E. The life and memoirs of Dr. Pi
    and other stories; by Edgar Bayley; trans-
    lated by Emily Toder.

The political poet
  Bayley, E. The life and memoirs of Dr. Pi
    and other stories; by Edgar Bayley; trans-
    lated by Emily Toder.
The return
  Bayley, E. The life and memoirs of Dr. Pi
    and other stories; by Edgar Bayley; trans-
    lated by Emily Toder.
Sir Harrison and solitude
  Bayley, E. The life and memoirs of Dr. Pi
    and other stories; by Edgar Bayley; trans-
    lated by Emily Toder.
Staff recruitment
  Bayley, E. The life and memoirs of Dr. Pi
    and other stories; by Edgar Bayley; trans-
    lated by Emily Toder.
The tandem bike and the Archarm's envelope
  Bayley, E. The life and memoirs of Dr. Pi
    and other stories; by Edgar Bayley; trans-
    lated by Emily Toder.
Transparency
  Bayley, E. The life and memoirs of Dr. Pi
    and other stories; by Edgar Bayley; trans-
    lated by Emily Toder.
Typical scenes
  Bayley, E. The life and memoirs of Dr. Pi
    and other stories; by Edgar Bayley; trans-
    lated by Emily Toder.
Universal levitation
  Bayley, E. The life and memoirs of Dr. Pi
    and other stories; by Edgar Bayley; trans-
    lated by Emily Toder.
Valerio
  Bayley, E. The life and memoirs of Dr. Pi
    and other stories; by Edgar Bayley; trans-
    lated by Emily Toder.
The wait
  Bayley, E. The life and memoirs of Dr. Pi
    and other stories; by Edgar Bayley; trans-
    lated by Emily Toder.
The waltz
  Bayley, E. The life and memoirs of Dr. Pi
    and other stories; by Edgar Bayley; trans-
    lated by Emily Toder.
The waterfall and the linguist
  Bayley, E. The life and memoirs of Dr. Pi
    and other stories; by Edgar Bayley; trans-
    lated by Emily Toder.
The wedding
  Bayley, E. The life and memoirs of Dr. Pi
    and other stories; by Edgar Bayley; trans-
    lated by Emily Toder.
Bayley, Edgar
The Bundle
  The Massachusetts Review v51 no3 p600-1
    Aut 2010
The Neighbor
  The Massachusetts Review v51 no3 p601 Aut
    2010
Typical Scenes
  The Massachusetts Review v51 no3 p602-3
    Aut 2010
The Waterfall and the Linguist
  The Massachusetts Review v51 no3 p602 Aut
    2010
Bazzett, Leslie
Screen Test
  New England Review v32 no2 p90-107 Spr
    2011

Bazzle, Bradley
Gift Horse
  New England Review v31 no4 p54-68
  2010/2011
Be careful about playing with the path of least re-
  sistance. Wright, A.
Be swift, my darling. Moran, J.
Beach. Bolaño, R.
Beach Vacation. Sneed, C.
Beagle, Peter S.
The best worst monster
  Beagle, P. S. Sleight of hand
The bridge partner
  Beagle, P. S. Sleight of hand
The children of the shark god
  The beastly bride; tales of the animal people;
  edited by Ellen Datlow & Terri Windling;
  introduction by Terri Windling; selected
  decorations by Charles Vess.
  Beagle, P. S. Sleight of hand
Dirae
  Beagle, P. S. Sleight of hand
La lune t' attend
  Beagle, P. S. Sleight of hand
Music, when soft voices die
  Ghosts by gaslight; stories of steampunk and
  supernatural suspense; [edited by] Jack
  Dann [and] Nick Gevers
Oakland dragon blues
  Beagle, P. S. Sleight of hand
The rabbi's hobby
  Beagle, P. S. Sleight of hand
El regalo
  The way of the wizard; edited by John Joseph
  Adams.
The rock in the Park
  Beagle, P. S. Sleight of hand
Sleight of hand
  Beagle, P. S. Sleight of hand
Uncle Chaim and Aunt Rifke and the angel
  People of the book; a decade of Jewish sci-
  ence fiction & fantasy; edited by Rachel
  Swirsky & Sean Wallace.
Underbridge
  Naked city; tales of urban fantasy; edited by
  Ellen Datlow.
Up the down beanstalk: a wife remembers
  Beagle, P. S. Sleight of hand
Vanishing
  Beagle, P. S. Sleight of hand
What tune the enchantress plays
  Beagle, P. S. Sleight of hand
The woman who married the man in the moon
  Beagle, P. S. Sleight of hand
Beah, Ishmael
ABC antidote
  Freedom; stories celebrating the Universal
  Declaration of Human Rights; Amnesty In-
  ternational.
The **bean**. Levine, S.
Bean curd. Kurlansky, M.
Beano's deal. Roberge, R.
Bear, Astrid
(jt. auth) See Clark, Diane C. and Bear, Astrid
Bear, Elizabeth
And the deep blue sea
  Sympathy for the devil; edited by Tim Pratt.

The horrid glory of its wings
  The Year's best dark fantasy & horror; edited
  by Paula Guran
King pole, gallows pole, bottle tree
  Naked city; tales of urban fantasy; edited by
  Ellen Datlow.
Needles
  Blood and other cravings; edited by Ellen
  Datlow.
Bear, Greg
Destroyers
  Before they were giants; edited by James L.
  Sutter; cover illustration by Kieran Yanner.
The **bear** and the princess of light. Drakulic, S.
Bearing life. Monk, D.
BEARS
Black, H. Lot 558: Shadow of my nephew by
  Wells, Charlotte
Drakulic, S. The bear and the princess of light
Emshwiller, C. Hunting machine
Glass, J. The price of silver
Sinisalo, J. Bear's bride
Tuten, F. Self portrait with cheese
Bear's bride. Sinisalo, J.
Bears watching. Boland, J. C.
Beast. Hunt, S.
The **beating**. Oates, J. C.
Beatrixpark: An Illumination. Voltolini, D.
BEATRIXPARK: AN   ILLUMINATION.
  Voltolini, D. and Appel, A. M.
Beattie, Ann
Afloat
  Beattie, A. The New Yorker stories
Apologies to Auden
  Five Points v12 no3 p6-11 2009
The burning house
  Beattie, A. The New Yorker stories
The Cinderella waltz
  Beattie, A. The New Yorker stories
Colorado
  Beattie, A. The New Yorker stories
Coney Island
  Beattie, A. The New Yorker stories
The confidence decoy
  Beattie, A. The New Yorker stories
Coping stones
  Beattie, A. The New Yorker stories
Desire
  Beattie, A. The New Yorker stories
Distant music
  Beattie, A. The New Yorker stories
Downhill
  Beattie, A. The New Yorker stories
Dwarf house
  Beattie, A. The New Yorker stories
Fancy flights
  Beattie, A. The New Yorker stories
Find and replace
  Beattie, A. The New Yorker stories
Girl talk
  Beattie, A. The New Yorker stories
Gravity
  Beattie, A. The New Yorker stories
Greenwich time
  Beattie, A. The New Yorker stories
The Gypsy Chooses the Whatever Card
  The American Scholar v79 no4 p76-82 Aut
  2010

Beattie, Ann—*Continued*
Heaven on a summer night
    Beattie, A. The New Yorker stories
Home to Marie
    Beattie, A. The New Yorker stories
Horatio's trick
    Beattie, A. The New Yorker stories
In the white night
    Beattie, A. The New Yorker stories
Janus
    Beattie, A. The New Yorker stories
The lawn party
    Beattie, A. The New Yorker stories
Like glass
    Beattie, A. The New Yorker stories
Lofty
    Beattie, A. The New Yorker stories
Moving water
    Beattie, A. The New Yorker stories
One day
    Beattie, A. The New Yorker stories
A platonic relationship
    Beattie, A. The New Yorker stories
The rabbit hole as likely explanation
    Beattie, A. The New Yorker stories
Running dreams
    Beattie, A. The New Yorker stories
Second question
    Beattie, A. The New Yorker stories
Secrets and surprises
    Beattie, A. The New Yorker stories
Shifting
    Beattie, A. The New Yorker stories
Skeletons
    Beattie, A. The New Yorker stories
Snakes' shoes
    Beattie, A. The New Yorker stories
STARLIGHT
    The New Yorker v87 no28 p70-74 S 19 2011
Summer people
    Beattie, A. The New Yorker stories
Television
    Beattie, A. The New Yorker stories
That last odd day in L. A.
    Beattie, A. The New Yorker stories
Times
    Beattie, A. The New Yorker stories
Tuesday night
    Beattie, A. The New Yorker stories
Vermont
    Beattie, A. The New Yorker stories
A vintage Thunderbird
    Beattie, A. The New Yorker stories
Waiting
    Beattie, A. The New Yorker stories
Wanda's
    Beattie, A. The New Yorker stories
Weekend
    Beattie, A. The New Yorker stories
Where you'll find me
    Beattie, A. The New Yorker stories
Wolf dreams
    Beattie, A. The New Yorker stories
The women of this world
    Beattie, A. The New Yorker stories
The working girl
    Blue collar, white collar, no collar; stories of
    work; edited by Richard Ford.

Zalla
    Beattie, A. The New Yorker stories
The **beautiful** boy. Villegas, H.
The **beautiful** coalwoman. Châteaureynaud, G. O.
Beautiful even in death. Bill, F.
A **beautiful** lie. Gallari, A.
The **beautiful** suit. Wells, H. G.
Beautiful white bodies. Kim, A. S.
BEAUTY *See* Aesthetics
BEAUTY, PERSONAL *See* Personal beauty
BEAUTY CONTESTS
    Mphahlele, E. Grieg on a stolen piano
BEAUTY SHOPS
    Howell, M. We need to talk about Mr Collins
Beaverland. Burke, D.
Becalmed in hell. Niven, L.
Because the constable blundered. Nevins, F. M.,
    Jr.
Béchard, D. Y.
    The Boy and the Lioness
        Harvard Review (1992) no39 p86-119 2010
Beck, Randi
    A Decent Hand
        Michigan Quarterly Review v49 no3 p335-48
        Summ 2010
Beckett, Chris
    The peacock cloak
        The Year's best science fiction: twenty-eighth
        annual collection; edited by Gardner
        Dozois.
Becoming. Blatnik, A.
Becoming lucid. Sands, B.
Bed death. Ostlund, L.
The **Bed** Frame. Adcox, J. T.
A **bed** of ice. Allen, D.
BEDARD, BRIAN
    The Fallen
        The North American Review v296 no3 p38-41
        Summ 2011
Bedfellows. Turtledove, H.
Bedford, William
    The Factory Girl
        Dalhousie Review v90 no2 p283-90 Summ
        2010
Bedford-Jones, Henry
    Peace waits at Marokee
        The Big book of adventure stories; edited and
        with a introduction by Otto Penzler; fore-
        word by Douglas Preston.
BEDOUINS
    Errachidi, A. From the novel Bedouins on the
        edge
The **bedquilt**. Fisher, D. C.
Bedrock. Mas, A.
Bee & grim. May, R.
The **Beekeeper's** Wife. Geary, T. M.
Beer-bottle polka. Kornbluth, C. M.
Beer with a hamster chaser. Monk, D.
Beethoven one-sixteeth black. Gordimer, N.
BEETLES
    Monzó, Q. Gregor
Before I die. Rodoreda, M.
Before long. Laken, V.
BEGGARS
    Dozois, G. R. Disciples
Beginners. Boast, W.
The **beginning**. Rodoreda, M.

Begley, Louis
By Appointment Only
The American Scholar v79 no4 p83-8 Aut 2010
A **Beheading**. Hamid, M.
Behold the husband in his perfect agony. Hannah, B.
BEIJING (CHINA) *See* China—Beijing
Being mysterious strangers from distant shores. Emshwiller, C.
BEIRUT (LEBANON) *See* Lebanon—Beirut
The **belated** burial. Kiernan, C. R.
BELGIUM
Ostend
Kronauer, B. Desire for music and mountains [excerpt]
Believing it was George Harrison. Levine, S.
Bell, Celia Dovell
One Hundred Names for the Sea
Five Points v12 no3 p21-9 2009
Bell, Madison Smartt
April 1863
Five Points v13 no1 p61-7 2009
Barking man
Twenty dollars
Haiti noir; edited by Edwidge Danticat
Bell, Matt
Jumpman vs. the ape
Butler, B. 30 under 30; an anthology of innovative fiction by younger writers; Blake Butler & Lily Hoang, eds.
Xarles, Xavier, Xenos
The Literary Review (Madison, N.J.) v54 no1 p105-7 Fall 2010
Bell, Matthew
Dredge
The Best American mystery stories 2010; edited and with an introduction by Lee Child; Otto Penzler, series editor
Bell, Ted
The pirate of Palm Beach
Mystery Writers of America presents the rich and the dead; edited by Nelson DeMille.
BELL-RINGERS *See* Bells and bell ringers
Bellamy, Esther
Miss Austen victorious
Dancing with Mr. Darcy; stories inspired by Jane Austen and Chawton House Library; compiled by Sarah Waters.
BELLOW, SAUL, 1915-2005
About
Rosen, J. The true world
Bells. Hall, J. W.
BELLS AND BELL RINGERS
Hall, J. W. Bells
Belly Breathing. Thurber, B.
Belons. Kurlansky, M.
Beloved, you looked into space. Trueblood, V.
Beluthahatchie. Duncan, A.
Benali, Abdelkader
From the novel The trip to the slaughterhouse
Beirut 39; new writing from the Arab world; edited by Samuel Shimon; with a preface by Hanan al-Shaykh
Benbow, Margaret
Angela Perfidia
The Georgia Review v65 no1 p30-7 Spr 2011

Bender, Aimee
Americca
Fantastic women; 18 tales of the surreal and the sublime from Tin House; introduction by Joy Williams; edited by Rob Spillman.
The Fake Nazi
Ploughshares v36 no2/3 p26-39 Fall 2010
Skinless
Best of times, worst of times; contemporary American short stories from the new Gilded Age; edited by Wendy Martin and Cecelia Tichi.
Beneath between. Connolly, L. C.
Beneath us. McOmber, A.
BENEDICT, DIANNE
The Fox Pelt
The North American Review v296 no3 p21-23 Summ 2011
Benedicta, or A Guide to the Artist's Résumé. Hinnefeld, J.
Benford, Gregory
Centigrade 233
Future media; [edited by Rick Wilber]
To the storming gulf
The end of the world; stories of the apocalypse; edited by Martin H. Greenberg.
Bengal, Rebecca
Captioning for the blind
The best American nonrequired reading 2009; edited by Dave Eggers; introduction by Marjane Satrapi; managing editor, Jesse Nathan
Bengtsson, Jonas T.
One of the rough ones
Copenhagen noir; edited by Bo Tao Michaëlis; translated by Mark Kline.
Benjamin. Bingham, S.
Bennett, Andrea
The Falls
Dalhousie Review v90 no2 p229-38 Summ 2010
Bennett, Gertrude Barrows *See* Stevens, Francis, b. 1884
Benny. Gutstein, D.
Bentley, E. C. (Edmund Clerihew)
The sweet shot
Golf stories; edited by Charles McGrath.
Bentley, Edmund Clerihew *See* Bentley, E. C. (Edmund Clerihew), 1875-1956
Benvie, Robert
Into collapses
Can'tLit; fearless fiction from Broken pencil magazine; edited by Richard Rosenbaum.
Berckmans, J. M. H.
Just like Rasputin, we plod through mud and piss in search of Kellogg's Cornflakes
The Dedalus book of Flemish fantasy; edited by Eric Dickens and translated by Paul Vincent.
BEREAVEMENT
Barrett, N., Jr. Getting dark
Bergman, M. M. Housewifely arts
Bishop, M. Vinegar Peace (or, The Wrong-Way, Used-Adult Orphanage)
Ely, S. Dream fishing
Furman, L. A thousand words
Hamilton, H. The supremacy of grief
Heathcock, A. The daughter
Kennedy, A. L. What becomes

Bhattacharya, Nalinaksha
   Hissing cobras
      Delhi noir; edited by Hirsh Sawhney
Bi, Feiyu
   Wang Village and the World [With biographical
      note]
      Chinese Literature Today v1 no1 p8-12
         Summ 2010
Biancotti, Deborah
   Diamond shell
      The Year's best dark fantasy & horror; edited
         by Paula Guran
Biar Adass. Marār, M.
Bias. Muessig, C.
BIBLE
   Powers, T. The Bible repairman
   The **Bible** repairman. Powers, T.
   Bible stories for adults, no. 31: the covenant. Mor-
      row, J.
BIBLICAL STORIES
   Pollack, R. Burning beard: the dreams and vi-
      sions of Joseph ben Jacob, Lord Viceroy of
      Egypt
BICYCLES AND BICYCLING
   Le Clézio, J.-M. G. The mountain of the living
      god
   McElroy, J. Mister X
   McElroy, J. Silk, or the woman with the bike
   Wells, H. G. A perfect gentleman on wheels
Biddle, Cordelia Frances
   Reality
      Philadelphia noir; edited by Carlin Romano.
Bierce, Ambrose
   An adventure at Brownville
      Bierce, A. The devil's dictionary, tales, &
         memoirs; S. T. Joshi, editor
   The affair at Coulter's Notch
      Bierce, A. The devil's dictionary, tales, &
         memoirs; S. T. Joshi, editor
   An affair of outposts
      Bierce, A. The devil's dictionary, tales, &
         memoirs; S. T. Joshi, editor
   The applicant
      Bierce, A. The devil's dictionary, tales, &
         memoirs; S. T. Joshi, editor
   An arrest
      Bierce, A. The devil's dictionary, tales, &
         memoirs; S. T. Joshi, editor
   Ashes of the beacon
      Bierce, A. The devil's dictionary, tales, &
         memoirs; S. T. Joshi, editor
   At Old Man Eckert's
      Bierce, A. The devil's dictionary, tales, &
         memoirs; S. T. Joshi, editor
   A baby tramp
      Bierce, A. The devil's dictionary, tales, &
         memoirs; S. T. Joshi, editor
   A baffled ambuscade
      Bierce, A. The devil's dictionary, tales, &
         memoirs; S. T. Joshi, editor
   Beyond the wall
      Bierce, A. The devil's dictionary, tales, &
         memoirs; S. T. Joshi, editor
   The boarded window
      Bierce, A. The devil's dictionary, tales, &
         memoirs; S. T. Joshi, editor
   A bottomless grave
      Bierce, A. The devil's dictionary, tales, &
         memoirs; S. T. Joshi, editor

Charles Ashmore's trail
      Bierce, A. The devil's dictionary, tales, &
         memoirs; S. T. Joshi, editor
Chickamauga
      Bierce, A. The devil's dictionary, tales, &
         memoirs; S. T. Joshi, editor
A cold greeting
      Bierce, A. The devil's dictionary, tales, &
         memoirs; S. T. Joshi, editor
The coup de grâce
      Bierce, A. The devil's dictionary, tales, &
         memoirs; S. T. Joshi, editor
The damed thing
      Bierce, A. The devil's dictionary, tales, &
         memoirs; S. T. Joshi, editor
The death of Halpin Frayser
      Bierce, A. The devil's dictionary, tales, &
         memoirs; S. T. Joshi, editor
A diagnosis of death
      Bierce, A. The devil's dictionary, tales, &
         memoirs; S. T. Joshi, editor
The difficulty of crossing a field
      Bierce, A. The devil's dictionary, tales, &
         memoirs; S. T. Joshi, editor
The eyes of the panther
      Bierce, A. The devil's dictionary, tales, &
         memoirs; S. T. Joshi, editor
The famous Gilson bequest
      Bierce, A. The devil's dictionary, tales, &
         memoirs; S. T. Joshi, editor
For the Ahkoond
      Bierce, A. The devil's dictionary, tales, &
         memoirs; S. T. Joshi, editor
A fruitless assignment
      Bierce, A. The devil's dictionary, tales, &
         memoirs; S. T. Joshi, editor
George Thurston
      Bierce, A. The devil's dictionary, tales, &
         memoirs; S. T. Joshi, editor
Haïta the shepherd
      Bierce, A. The devil's dictionary, tales, &
         memoirs; S. T. Joshi, editor
The haunted valley
      Bierce, A. The devil's dictionary, tales, &
         memoirs; S. T. Joshi, editor
The hight-doings at "Deadman's"
      Bierce, A. The devil's dictionary, tales, &
         memoirs; S. T. Joshi, editor
A holy terror
      Bierce, A. The devil's dictionary, tales, &
         memoirs; S. T. Joshi, editor
A horseman in the sky
      Bierce, A. The devil's dictionary, tales, &
         memoirs; S. T. Joshi, editor
The inhabitant of Carcosa
      Bierce, A. The devil's dictionary, tales, &
         memoirs; S. T. Joshi, editor
The Isle of pines
      Bierce, A. The devil's dictionary, tales, &
         memoirs; S. T. Joshi, editor
John Bartine's watch
      Bierce, A. The devil's dictionary, tales, &
         memoirs; S. T. Joshi, editor
John Mortonson's funeral
      Bierce, A. The devil's dictionary, tales, &
         memoirs; S. T. Joshi, editor
A jug of sirup
      Bierce, A. The devil's dictionary, tales, &
         memoirs; S. T. Joshi, editor

Big people. Zucker, G.

The **big** switch: a Mike Hammer story. Spillane,
    M. and Collins, M. A.

BIGAMY

    Atta, S. Hailstones on Zamfara

    Atta, S. Madness in the family

    Naipaul, V. S. Bogart

Bigfoot. Loory, B.

BIGOTRY *See* Prejudices

Bill, Frank

    The accident

      Bill, F. Crimes in southern Indiana; stories

    All the awful

      Bill, F. Crimes in southern Indiana; stories

    Amphetamine twitch

      Bill, F. Crimes in southern Indiana; stories

    Beautiful even in death

      Bill, F. Crimes in southern Indiana; stories

    Cold, hard love

      Bill, F. Crimes in southern Indiana; stories

    A coon hunter's noir

      Bill, F. Crimes in southern Indiana; stories

    Crimes in southern Indiana

      Bill, F. Crimes in southern Indiana; stories

    Hill clan cross

      Bill, F. Crimes in southern Indiana; stories

    The Need

      Bill, F. Crimes in southern Indiana; stories

    Officer down (tweakers)

      Bill, F. Crimes in southern Indiana; stories

    The old mechanic

      Bill, F. Crimes in southern Indiana; stories

    Old testament wisdom

      Bill, F. Crimes in southern Indiana; stories

    The penance of Scoot McCutchen

      Bill, F. Crimes in southern Indiana; stories

    A rabbit in the lettuce patch

      Bill, F. Crimes in southern Indiana; stories

    Rough company

      Bill, F. Crimes in southern Indiana; stories

    These old bones

      Bill, F. Crimes in southern Indiana; stories

    Trespassing between heaven and hell

      Bill, F. Crimes in southern Indiana; stories

The **bill**. Krasznahorkai, L.

Bill Miller. Levine, S.

Billennium. Ballard, J. G.

BILOXI (MISS.) *See* Mississippi—Biloxi

Bilu, Dalya

    (tr.) *See* Shimoni, Youval

Bin Laden, Osama *See* Osama bin Laden

Bina. Watsmore, A.

Bingham, Sallie

    Anywhere you send me

      Bingham, S. Mending; new and selected stories

    Apricots

      Bingham, S. Mending; new and selected stories

    August ninth at Natural Bridge

      Bingham, S. Mending; new and selected stories

    The banks of the Ohio

      Bingham, S. Mending; new and selected stories

    Benjamin

      Bingham, S. Mending; new and selected stories

Found

    Bingham, S. Mending; new and selected stories

Heaven

    Bingham, S. Mending; new and selected stories

The hunt

    Bingham, S. Mending; new and selected stories

The ice party

    Bingham, S. Mending; new and selected stories

Mending

    Bingham, S. Mending; new and selected stories

Rachel's island

    Bingham, S. Mending; new and selected stories

Red car

    Bingham, S. Mending; new and selected stories

Sagesse

    Bingham, S. Mending; new and selected stories

Seagull

    Bingham, S. Mending; new and selected stories

Selling the farm

    Bingham, S. Mending; new and selected stories

Sweet peas

    Bingham, S. Mending; new and selected stories

The wedding

    Bingham, S. Mending; new and selected stories

Winter term

    Bingham, S. Mending; new and selected stories

BINGO

    Grove, L. L. Bingo night

Bingo and Bongo. Emshwiller, C.

Bingo night. Grove, L. L.

Binkley, Phyllis

    A convenient place to wait

      Binkley, P. Up from the marsh; stories and poems

    A day of quality

      Binkley, P. Up from the marsh; stories and poems

    Keepsakes

      Binkley, P. Up from the marsh; stories and poems

    The sisterhood

      Binkley, P. Up from the marsh; stories and poems

Binocular vision. Pearlman, E.

BINOCULARS

    Pearlman, E. Binocular vision

Binshatwan, Najwa

    The pools and the piano

      Beirut 39; new writing from the Arab world; edited by Samuel Shimon; with a preface by Hanan al-Shaykh

BIOGRAPHERS *See* Authors

Biographical notes to "A discourse on the nature of causality, with air-planes" by Benjamin Rosenbaum. Rosenbaum, B.

Biography of a porn star in three parts. Dwyer, J.

Biography of an uncircumcised man (including interview). Emshwiller, C.

BIOLOGISTS

Tiptree, J. The last flight of Doctor Ain

Birch memorial. Samarasan, P.

BIRD HUNTERS

Jewett, S. O. A white heron

The **Bird** Lady. Edwards, M.

Bird Shot. Mainieri, N.

BIRD WATCHERS

Nelson, K. The spirit bird

BIRDS

    See also Ostriches; Parrots; Pigeons

Alexie, S. Green world

Brennan, M. The twa corbies

Emshwiller, C. Looking down

Hemmingson, M. The birds

Lee, T. Black and white sky

Levine, S. Alia

Lychack, W. The old woman and her thief

Nutting, A. Magician

Okorafor, N. The go-slow

Royle, N. The obscure bird

Sterling, P. Empty nest

Tillman, L. That's how wrong my love is

The **birds**. Hemmingson, M.

The **birds**. Marãr, M.

Birdsall, Jill

Whisper Hill

    Southern Humanities Review v44 no4 p429-38 Fall 2010

Birdsong. Adichie, C. N.

Birdy num num. Self, W.

BIRMINGHAM (ALA.) *See* Alabama—Birmingham

BIRTH CONTROL

    See also Abortion

Morrow, J. Auspicious eggs

Birth days. Ryman, G.

BIRTHDAY PARTIES *See* Birthdays

BIRTHDAYS

Archer, J. The queen's birthday telegram

Beattie, A. Television

Bingham, S. August ninth at Natural Bridge

Black, A. I knew you'd be lovely

Butcher, J. It's my birthday, too

Hunter, L. Love song

Kurlansky, M. The icing on the cake

Manilla, M. Crystal City

McGarry, J. Family romance

Roncagliolo, S. The predator

Ruocco, J. Pests

A **bisel** this, a bisel that. Eidus, J.

BISEXUALITY

    See also Homosexuality

Tóibín, C. The pearl fishers

Bishop, Farnham and Brodeur, Arthur Gilchrist

The golden snare

    The Big book of adventure stories; edited and with a introduction by Otto Penzler; foreword by Douglas Preston.

Bishop, Michael

Vinegar Peace (or, The Wrong-Way, Used-Adult Orphanage)

    The Nebula Awards showcase; edited by Kevin J. Anderson.

BISHOPS

Wells, H. G. Answer to prayer

Bismarck rules. Tucher, A.

Bison Burgers. Henderson, L.

Bissell, Tom

A bridge under water

    The Best American short stories, 2011; selected from U.S. and Canadian magazines by Geraldine Brooks with Heidi Pitlor; with an introduction by Geraldine Brooks.

Expensive trips nowhere

    Best of times, worst of times; contemporary American short stories from the new Gilded Age; edited by Wendy Martin and Cecelia Tichi.

A **bit** of business. Trevor, W.

A **bit** on the side. Trevor, W.

Bitch. Oates, J. C.

Bites. Vasta, G.

The **bitter** bread. Anderson, P.

Bitter fruit. Nagai, M.

Bitter grounds. Gaiman, N.

Black, Alethea

Double-blind

    Black, A. I knew you'd be lovely; stories

The far side of the moon

    Black, A. I knew you'd be lovely; stories

Good in a crisis

    Black, A. I knew you'd be lovely; stories

I knew you'd be lovely

    Black, A. I knew you'd be lovely; stories

The laziest form of revelation

    Black, A. I knew you'd be lovely; stories

Mollusk makes

    Black, A. I knew you'd be lovely; stories

The only way out is through

    Black, A. I knew you'd be lovely; stories

Proof of love

    Black, A. I knew you'd be lovely; stories

Someday is today

    Black, A. I knew you'd be lovely; stories

The summer before

    Black, A. I knew you'd be lovely; stories

That of which we cannot speak

    Black, A. I knew you'd be lovely; stories

The thing itself

    Black, A. I knew you'd be lovely; stories

We've got a great future behind us

    Black, A. I knew you'd be lovely; stories

Black, Alex

Lisa with child

    L. Ron Hubbard presents Writers of the Future volume XXVI; the year's twelve best tales from the Writers of the Future international writers' program; illustrated by winners in the Illustrators of the Future international illustrators' program; with essays on writing & illustration by L. Ron Hubbard/Dean Wesley Smith/ Stephen Youll; edited by K. D. Wentworth

Black, Benjamin *See* Banville, John

Black, Holly

The Aarne-Thompson Classification Revue

    The Best science fiction and fantasy of the year: volume five; edited by Jonathan Strahan.

The coldest girl in Coldtown

    The Year's best dark fantasy & horror; edited by Paula Guran

    Vampires; the recent undead; edited by Paula Guran.

Black, Holly—*Continued*
  Lot 558: Shadow of my nephew by Wells,
      Charlotte
      The Thackery T. Lambshead cabinet of curi-
        osities; edited by Ann & Jeff VanderMeer.
  Noble rot
      Naked city; tales of urban fantasy; edited by
        Ellen Datlow.
  A reversal of fortune
      Sympathy for the devil; edited by Tim Pratt.
Black, Holly and Clare, Cassandra
  The Rowan gentleman
      Welcome to Bordertown; new stories and po-
        ems of the Borderlands; edited by Holly
        Black and Ellen Kushner; introduction by
        Terri Windling.
Black, Jenna
  Nine-tenths of the law
      Chicks kick butt; edited by Rachel Caine and
        Kerrie L. Hughes.
Black, Michael A.
  The golden bug
      On a raven's wing; new tales in honor of Ed-
        gar Allan Poe; edited by Stuart M.
        Kaminsky
Black, Scott
  Kaguya-hime: An Old Japanese Tale
      Western Humanities Review v65 no2 p110-
        135 Summ 2011
Black, Tony
  Hound of Culann
      Requiems for the departed; edited by Gerard
        Brennan & Mike Stone.
Black & white memories. Randisi, R. J.
The **black** abbot of puthuum. Smith, C. A.
Black and white sky. Lee, T.
The **black** angel's kiss. Swirsky, R.
Black bodies. Anderson, P.
The **black** book. Pamuk, O.
The **black** bottle. Chambers, W.
Black cargo. Woolrich, C.
Black dog. Lively, P.
Black flower. O'Brien, E.
BLACK HOLES (ASTRONOMY)
  Kosmatka, T. In-fall
  Lyman, J. The unreachable voices of ghosts
  Swanwick, M. Ginungagap
BLACK HUMOR *See* Humor; Satire
Black kids in lemon trees. Jones, S.
BLACK MAGIC *See* Witchcraft
BLACK MARKETS
  Guo Xiaolu. An Internet baby
Black oath. Shepard, S.
BLACK SERVANTS *See* African American ser-
    vants
The **black** side of memory. Salaets, L.
Black spider. Nevins, F. M., Jr.
The **black** square. Adrian, C.
Black step. Woodrell, D.
Black swan, white swan. Foster, E.
BLACK WOMEN *See* African American women
BLACKMAIL
        See also Extortion
  Bhattacharya, N. Hissing cobras
  Dick, P. K. Paycheck
  El Souwaim, M. From the novel The threshold
    of ashes
  Goodrich, J. Murder in the sixth
  Gorman, E. Favor and the princess

  Gorman, E. and Butler, T. Heritage
  James, D. Bottomed out
  Mariotte, J. J. Gold shield blues
  Penncavage, M. The cost of doing business
  Rozan, S. J. Iterations
  Trevor, W. The dressmaker's child
  Trevor, W. Men of Ireland
  Ursin, G. Sleipner's assignment
BLACKS
        See also African Americans
  Gordimer, N. Beethoven one-sixteeth black
  Gordimer, N. Parking Tax
          England
  Self, W. The Nonce prize
  Self, W. The rock of crack as big as the Ritz
BLACKSMITHS
  Van der Veer, K. L. Hammer song
Blackwood's baby. Barron, L.
Blades for France. Howard, R. E.
Blaine, Mark
  Four musicians
      South Carolina Review v43 no2 p24-31 Spr
        2011
BLAINESBEAUTIES.COM. Bradley, G.
Blake, Glenn
  Degüello
      Blake, G. Return fire; stories
  How far are we from the water?
      Blake, G. Return fire; stories
  The old and the lost
      Blake, G. Return fire; stories
  Return fire
      Blake, G. Return fire; stories
  Shooting stars
      Blake, G. Return fire; stories
  Thanksgiving
      Blake, G. Return fire; stories
  When the gods want to punish you
      Blake, G. Return fire; stories
Blakeslee, Vanessa
  Welcome, Lost Dogs
      The Southern Review (Baton Rouge, La.) v47
        no1 p21-35 Wint 2011
Blakinger, Kate
  Ice House
      Gettysburg Review v24 no1 p99-111 Spr 2011
Blanchard, John
  Cinema verite
      Best of the West 2010; new stories from the
        wide side of the Missouri; edited by James
        Thomas and D. Seth Horton; foreword by
        Kent Meyers.
The **blasphemers**. Farmer, P. J.
Blassingame, Wyatt
  Murder is bad luck
      The Black Lizard big book of Black Mask
        stories; edited and with a foreword by Otto
        Penzler; introduction by Keith Alan
        Deutsch.
Blatnik, Andrej
  All over
      Blatnik, A. You do understand; translated by
        Tamara M. Soban.
  An almost perfect evening
      Blatnik, A. You do understand; translated by
        Tamara M. Soban.
  And since I couldn't sleep
      Blatnik, A. You do understand; translated by
        Tamara M. Soban.

Blatnik, Andrej—*Continued*
   Words matter
     Blatnik, A. You do understand; translated by
      Tamara M. Soban.
Blauner, Peter
   Thank God for Charlie
     Mystery Writers of America presents the rich
      and the dead; edited by Nelson DeMille.
The **Bleach** Keeper. Hoppen, J.
Bleed. Oates, J. C.
Blessed Virgin Mary, Saint *See* Mary, Blessed
     Virgin, Saint
A **blessed** whore: a story from life. Marjiyyah, R.
BLIMPS *See* Airships
BLIND
   Alarcón, D. The bridge
   Archer, J. Blind date
   Barnes, J. Harmony
   Bengal, R. Captioning for the blind
   Gray, A. The picture window
   Laken, V. Before long
   Le Clézio, J.-M. G. People of the sky
   Niedzviecki, H. The colorist
   Osondu, E. C. Jimmy Carter's eyes
   Prentiss, N. In the porches of my ears
   Riippi, J. Something about Borges and the blind
     Chelsea
   Schmitt, E.-E. Getting better
   Simić, M. My girlfriend
   Terry, G. P. The promise
   Trevor, W. The piano tuner's wives
   Vukcevich, R. The wages of syntax
   Watson, B. Seeing eye
   Wells, H. G. The country of the blind
   Wells, H. G. The country of the blind (revised
     version)
Blind cat dance. Jablokov, A.
Blind date. Archer, J.
Blind date. Davis, L.
The **blind** owl [excerpt] Hidāyat, ;
Bling, bling. Delee, D.
Bliss. Gilley, T.
Bliss. Schirach, F. v.
BLIZZARDS *See* Storms
Bloch, Robert
   That hell-bound train
     Sympathy for the devil; edited by Tim Pratt.
Block, Francesca Lia
   Farewell, my zombie
     Zombies: the recent dead; edited by Paula
      Guran.
   Revenants anonymous
     Hungry for your love; an anthology of
      zombie romance; edited by Lori Perkins.
Block, Lawrence
   As dark as Christmas gets
     Christmas at the Mysterious Bookshop; 'tis
      the season to be deadly; stories of mistletoe
      and mayhem from 17 masters of suspense;
      edited by Otto Penzler.
   By the dawn's early light
     The Shamus winners: America's best private
      eye stories, volume I: 1982-1995; collected
      and introduced by Robert J. Randisi; found-
      er, Private Eye Writers of America

   The merciful angel of death
     The Shamus winners: America's best private
      eye stories, volume I: 1982-1995; collected
      and introduced by Robert J. Randisi; found-
      er, Private Eye Writers of America
Blocked. Ryman, G.
The **blog** at the end of the world. Tremblay, P.
BLOGS
   Galchen, R. The entire northern side was cov-
     ered with fire
   Tremblay, P. The blog at the end of the world
   Villegas, H. His ghost
Blond and blue. Estleman, L. D.
Blood. Doyle, R.
Blood. Rodoreda, M.
Blood. Ruocco, J.
Blood alone. Passarella, J.
Blood and dirt. Zimmerman, R.
Blood into Butterflies. Moses, J. A.
Blood not sap. Stevens, A. B.
The **blood** of Belshazzar. Howard, R. E.
The **blood** of leaves. Vo, T. H.
Blood sacrifices and the Catatonic Kid. Piccirilli,
   T.
Blood, sweat and biers. Reeves, R.
Blood washes off. Connelly, M.
Blood yesterday, blood tomorrow. Bowes, R.
The **bloody** Bokhara. Gault, W. C.
Bloody July. Estleman, L. D.
Bloom, Amy
   Love is not a pie
     I found this funny; my favorite pieces of hu-
      mor and some that may not be funny at all;
      edited by Judd Apatow.
Bloom, Steven
   A Work of Fiction
     Confrontation no109 p68-74 Spr 2011
Blue Bear. Chandler, E.
The **blue** birds come today. Furman, L.
The **blue** cart. Naipaul, V. S.
Blue clay blues. Jones, G. A.
The **blue** hill. Saint-Eloi, R.
The **blue** hotel. Crane, S.
The **Blue** laboratory. Meade, L. T.
Blue people. Gifford, B.
The **blue** room. Lahens, Y.
Blue roses. Hwang, F.
Blue valentine. Downum, A.
The **blue** wall. Furman, L.
Blue water djinn. Obreht, T.
BLUEBEARD (LEGENDARY CHARACTER)
   McDonald, S. Bluebeard by the sea
Bluebeard by the sea. McDonald, S.
BLUES (MUSIC)
   Downum, A. Blue valentine
   Duncan, A. Beluthahatchie
Blues for Irène. Victor, M.
Blumlein, Michael
   Fidelity: a primer
     People of the book; a decade of Jewish sci-
      ence fiction & fantasy; edited by Rachel
      Swirsky & Sean Wallace.
BLUNT, WILFRID SCAWEN, 1840-1922
              About
   Tóibín, C. Silence
The **boarded** window. Bierce, A.
BOARDERS *See* Boarding houses
BOARDING HOUSES
   Beagle, P. S. Music, when soft voices die

BOARDING HOUSES—*Continued*
  Clark, D. C. and Bear, A. The home front
  Fowler, K. J. Standing room only
  Freeman, M. E. W. The hall bedroom
  Hannah, B. Mother Rooney unscrolls the hurt
  Laken, V. Scavengers
  Le Sueur, M. Annunication
  Mehrotra, P. K. Fit of rage
  Naipaul, V. S. The perfect tenants
  O'Brien, E. Sinners
  Oliver, R. Baskervilles midgets
  Schmitt, E.-E. The dreamer from Ostend
BOARDING SCHOOLS *See* School life
Boast, Will
  Beginners
    The American Scholar v80 no4 p97-102 S
    2011
  Mr. Fern, Freestyle
    Five Points v14 no1 p133-48 2010
A **boat** that dislikes the riverbank. Salah al Azab,
  M.
BOATS AND BOATING
        See also Sailing vessels
  Boggs, B. Mattaponi Queen
  Dick, P. K. The builder
  Duffy, S. Lie, still, sleep becalmed
  Roche, T. S. Deepwater miracle
Bob the negro. Ayau, K. J.
Bobcat. Ruocco, J.
Boca Paila, Mexico. Shepard, S.
Bodard, Aliette de
  Eye of the destroyer
    Blood & devotion; tales of epic fantasy; ed-
      ited by W.H. Horner; illustrated by Nicole
      Cardiff
  Safe, child, safe
    Swenson, P. The Best of Talebones; edited by
      Patrick Swenson.
Bodsworth, Roxanne
  (jt. auth) See Kneebone, Eddie and Bodsworth,
    Roxanne
The **body**. Plummer, T. M.
Body and engine. Wieland, L.
Body snatcher. Tinsley, T. A.
BODYBUILDERS
  Gray, G. Mr. Universe
BODYGUARDS
  DeNiro, A. Comachrome
  Morrell, D. The controller
Bodyguards shoot second. Estleman, L. D.
Bog man. McAllister, J.
Bogart. Naipaul, V. S.
Boggs, Belle
  Buckets of rain
    Boggs, B. Mattaponi queen; stories
  Dear season
    Boggs, B. Mattaponi queen; stories
  Election day
    Boggs, B. Mattaponi queen; stories
  Good news for a hard time
    Boggs, B. Mattaponi queen; stories
  Homecoming
    Boggs, B. Mattaponi queen; stories
  Imperial Chrysanthemum
    Boggs, B. Mattaponi queen; stories
  It won't be long
    Boggs, B. Mattaponi queen; stories
  Jonas
    Boggs, B. Mattaponi queen; stories

Mattaponi Queen
  Boggs, B. Mattaponi queen; stories
Opportunity
  Boggs, B. Mattaponi queen; stories
Shelter
  Boggs, B. Mattaponi queen; stories
Youngest daughter
  Boggs, B. Mattaponi queen; stories
BOHR, NIELS HENRIK DAVID, 1885-1962
        About
  Sullivan, J. Niels Bohr and the sleeping Dane
Boland, John C.
  Bears watching
    Boland, J. C. 30 years in the pulps; stories of
      mystery & suspense
  Deep water
    Boland, J. C. 30 years in the pulps; stories of
      mystery & suspense
  Easy money
    Boland, J. C. 30 years in the pulps; stories of
      mystery & suspense
  Evidence seen
    Boland, J. C. 30 years in the pulps; stories of
      mystery & suspense
  Evocation of evil
    Boland, J. C. 30 years in the pulps; stories of
      mystery & suspense
  Last island south
    Boland, J. C. 30 years in the pulps; stories of
      mystery & suspense
  Mad hare
    Boland, J. C. 30 years in the pulps; stories of
      mystery & suspense
  Marley's ghost
    Boland, J. C. 30 years in the pulps; stories of
      mystery & suspense
  Marley's package
    Boland, J. C. 30 years in the pulps; stories of
      mystery & suspense
  Marley's woman
    Boland, J. C. 30 years in the pulps; stories of
      mystery & suspense
  Mountain fire
    Boland, J. C. 30 years in the pulps; stories of
      mystery & suspense
  No crime in the hills
    Boland, J. C. 30 years in the pulps; stories of
      mystery & suspense
  Out of her depth
    Boland, J. C. 30 years in the pulps; stories of
      mystery & suspense
  The passenger
    Boland, J. C. 30 years in the pulps; stories of
      mystery & suspense
  Past life
    Boland, J. C. 30 years in the pulps; stories of
      mystery & suspense
  The return of Jasper Kohl
    Boland, J. C. 30 years in the pulps; stories of
      mystery & suspense
  Reunion in Baineville
    Boland, J. C. 30 years in the pulps; stories of
      mystery & suspense
  Sargasso Sea
    Boland, J. C. 30 years in the pulps; stories of
      mystery & suspense
  Stand-in
    Boland, J. C. 30 years in the pulps; stories of
      mystery & suspense

Boland, John C.—*Continued*
The substitute
    Boland, J. C. 30 years in the pulps; stories of mystery & suspense
Swamp beast
    Boland, J. C. 30 years in the pulps; stories of mystery & suspense
Tequila
    Boland, J. C. 30 years in the pulps; stories of mystery & suspense
Two hundred big ones
    Boland, J. C. 30 years in the pulps; stories of mystery & suspense
Worth more dead
    Boland, J. C. 30 years in the pulps; stories of mystery & suspense
Bolaño, Roberto
Beach
    Granta no114 p23-8 Wint 2011
The Third Reich: Part 2
    The Paris Review v53 no197 p152-220 Summ 2011
The **bold** explorer in the place beyond. Nelson, D. E.
The **bolero** of Andi Rowe. Plummer, T. M.
BOLSHEVISM *See* Communism
Bomar. Vonnegut, K.
BOMBAY (INDIA) *See* India—Bombay
BOMBS
    See also Atomic bomb
Ibrāhīm, H. My young friend
Olsen, L. February
Olsen, L. January
Rodoreda, M. Orléans, three kilometers
Thomas, P. Short fuse
Bond, John
Trapped
    Florida heat wave; [edited and with an] introduction by Michael Lister.
The **bone**. Davis, L.
Bonehouse. Kehrli, K. R. M.
Bones. Jeter, K. W.
Bones. Ruocco, J.
The **bones** of hagerman. Wieland, M.
The **bone's** prayer. Kiernan, C. R.
Bonfiglio, Thomas
Puppies
    The Literary Review (Madison, N.J.) v54 no1 p70-6 Fall 2010
BONNER, NORA
Devil's Night
    The North American Review v296 no3 p7-12 Summ 2011
BONNIE, 1910-1934
                    About
Cook, K. L. Bonnie and Clyde in the backyard
Bonnie and Clyde in the backyard. Cook, K. L.
Bonnin, Gertrude Simmons *See* Zitkala-Ša, 1876-1938
Bonobo momma. Oates, J. C.
Boogiemen. Gautier, A.
The **book**. Loory, B.
BOOK BURNING
Binshatwan, N. The pools and the piano
BOOK OF A THOUSAND AND ONE NIGHTS
    See Arabian nights
The **book** of categories. Yu, C.
The **book** of Daniel. Vaughn, C.
BOOK RARITIES *See* Rare books

BOOK SHOPS *See* Booksellers and bookselling
BOOKS
        See also Books and reading; Manuscripts; Rare books
Loory, B. The book
Moore, A. Objects discovered in a novel under construction
Yu, C. The book of categories
BOOKS, RARE *See* Rare books
The **books**. Baker, K.
Books. Monzó, Q.
BOOKS AND READING
Anzaldúa, G. Reading LP
Baker, K. The books
Benford, G. Centigrade 233
Blatnik, A. Marks
Bradbury, R. Fahrenheit 451 [excerpt]
Châteaureynaud, G. O. A room on the abyss
Cook, T. H. The lesson of the season
Davis, L. Southward bound, reads Worstward ho
Doyle, R. The slave
Fultz, J. R. The thirteen texts of Arthyria
Gallari, A. Reading Rilke
Gonzalez Ledesma, F. The police inspector who loved books
Marías, J. A kind of nostalgia perhaps
McOmber, A. Gardens of the moon
McOmber, A. A man of history
Millhauser, S. People of the Book
Monzó, Q. Books
Powers, R. To the measures fall
Riippi, J. Something about my book
Ruocco, J. Small sharks
Schmitt, E.-E. The dreamer from Ostend
Schmitt, E.-E. Trashy reading
Spiers, H. Cleverclogs
Wells, H. G. How Pingwill was routed
Winslow, D. Poe, Jo, and I
Yant, C. The magician and the maid and other stories
The **bookseller**. Hardwick, E.
BOOKSELLERS AND BOOKSELLING
Ardai, C. Cold reading
Atkinson, L. M. Yule be sorry
Baxt, G. Schemes and variations
Connolly, L. C. Beneath between
Cook, T. H. The lesson of the season
Cowdrey, A. Twilight states
Goulart, R. Murder for dummies
Hardwick, E. The bookseller
Hoch, E. D. The theft of the rusty bookmark
Holmes, R. The long winter's nap
Klavan, A. The killer Christian
Kyle, A. Sex scenes from a chain bookstore
Marías, J. An epigram of fealty
McBain, E. I saw mommy killing Santa Claus
Perry, A. My object all sublime
Ressel, S. The legacy of between books
Rozan, S. J. The grift of the magi
Santlofer, J. The 74th tale
Boon, Louis Paul
Grim fairy tales
    The Dedalus book of Flemish fantasy; edited by Eric Dickens and translated by Paul Vincent.
The **booster** station. Ozturk, S.

Booth, Charles G.
One shot
> The Black Lizard big book of Black Mask stories; edited and with a foreword by Otto Penzler; introduction by Keith Alan Deutsch.

BOOTH, EDWIN, 1833-1893
About
Fowler, K. J. Booth's ghost
Booth, Reyna Feigher
Cat People
> *New England Review* v31 no3 p58-67 2010

Booth One. Levine, P.
Booth's ghost. Fowler, K. J.
BOOTS AND SHOES
Dick, P. K. The short happy life of the brown oxford
Qiu Xiaolong. Shoes of the cultural revolution
BORDEAUX (FRANCE) *See* France—Bordeaux
BORDER PATROL AGENTS
Holder, N. Beyond the pale
Plummer, T. M. The desert in green
Tremblay, P. Headstone in your pocket
Border radio. Roberge, R.
Bordered in black. Niven, L.
The **borderland** of Sol. Niven, L.
BOREDOM
Byer, J. Rats, homosex, saunas, and Simon
BORGES, JORGE LUIS, 1899-1986
About
Riippi, J. Something about Borges and the blind Chelsea
Boring friends. Davis, L.
Born, James O.
Revenge of the emerging market
> Florida heat wave; [edited and with an] introduction by Michael Lister.

Born, Kristina
The defining work of your career (excerpts from one hour of television)
> Butler, B. 30 under 30; an anthology of innovative fiction by younger writers; Blake Butler & Lily Hoang, eds.

Born on October Fourth. Suárez Cobián, A.
BORNEO
L'Amour, L. Off the mangrove coast
Borrowed crime. Woolrich, C.
Bosambo of Monrovia. Wallace, E.
BOSCH, HIERONYMUS, D. 1516
About
Olsen, L. September
Bosch, Lolita
In this world, and at the time Mercedes died
> Barcelona noir; edited by Adriana V. Lopez & Cartmen Ospina; translated by Achy Obejas.

Bose, Buddhadeva
Makhanlal's Sad Tale
> *The Literary Review (Madison, N.J.)* v54 no1 p108-24 Fall 2010

Boskovich, Desirina
Love is the spell that casts out fear
> The way of the wizard; edited by John Joseph Adams.

Bossier City, Louisiana (Highway 220). Shepard, S.
BOSTON (MASS.) *See* Massachusetts—Boston
BOTANISTS
Silverberg, R. How they pass the time in Pelpel

The **bottle** imp. Stevenson, R. L.
Bottomed out. James, D.
A **bottomless** grave. Bierce, A.
Boukebba, Abderrazak
From the novel Skin of shadow
> Beirut 39; new writing from the Arab world; edited by Samuel Shimon; with a preface by Hanan al-Shaykh.

Boundin. Kurlansky, M.
A **Boundless** Void. Takahashi, T.
Bounty. Minton, A.
Bounty hunter. Oates, J. C.
Bova, Ben
A long way back
> Before they were giants; edited by James L. Sutter; cover illustration by Kieran Yanner.

Bowen, Elizabeth
Summer night
> The Granta book of the Irish short story; [edited by] Anne Enright.

Bowes, Richard
Blood yesterday, blood tomorrow
> Blood and other cravings; edited by Ellen Datlow.
I needs must part, the policeman said
> The Nebula Awards showcase; edited by Kevin J. Anderson.
The margay's children
> The beastly bride; tales of the animal people; edited by Ellen Datlow & Terri Windling; introduction by Terri Windling; selected decorations by Charles Vess.
On the slide
> Naked city; tales of urban fantasy; edited by Ellen Datlow.

A **bowl** bigger than earth. Farmer, P. J.
BOWLING
Grover, L. L. Ojibwe boys
Nutting, A. She-man
BOXING
Gifford, B. The Sultan
Naipaul, V. S. The coward
Oates, J. C. Golden gloves
Roberge, R. Beano's deal
Roberge, R. A headache from Barstow to Salt Lake
Whitfield, R. Murder in the ring
The **Boy** and His Mother Are Stuck!. Lisicky, P.
The **boy** and the backpack. Land, J.
The **Boy** and the Lioness. Béchard, D. Y.
Boy in the cabinet. Shipp, J. C.
The **boy** next door. Mu Xin
Boy with Cane Pole. DeMarinis, R.
Boy with Finch. Majka, S.
Boyack, Neil
Country Junk
> *The Literary Review (Madison, N.J.)* v54 no1 p40-6 Fall 2010

Boyd, Manih
Trial day
> *Tribal College Journal of American Indian Higher Education* v23 no1 p50-1 Fall 2011

Boyd, Racquel
Pamatesēw
> *Tribal College Journal of American Indian Higher Education* v23 no1 p56-7 Fall 2011

Boylan, Clare
Villa Marta
The Granta book of the Irish short story; [edited by] Anne Enright.
Boyle, Patrick
Meles vulgaris
The Granta book of the Irish short story; [edited by] Anne Enright.
BOYLE, T. C.
In the Zone
The Kenyon Review v33 no4 p11-28 Fall 2011
What separates us from the animals
Harper's v321 p67-74 O 2010
Boyle, T. Coraghessan
Scorpion Ranch
Orion v29 no5 p33-48 S/O 2010
The silence
Best of the West 2011; new stories from the wild side of the Missouri; edited by James Thomas and D. Seth Horton; foreword by Ana Castillo.
Zapatos
Blue collar, white collar, no collar; stories of work; edited by Richard Ford.
BOYS
> *See also* Adolescence; Children; Youth

Allen, D. Among the missing
Atta, S. Yahoo yahoo
Ayau, K. J. Murray and the Holy Ghost
Baker, K. Two old men
Bardsley, G. Crazy Larry smells bacon
Baxter, C. Mr. Scary
Beagle, P. S. The rock in the Park
Beagle, P. S. Uncle Chaim and Aunt Rifke and the angel
Beattie, A. Zalla
Blake, G. Thanksgiving
Boggs, B. Homecoming
Bukiet, M. J. The Florida sunshine tree
Byer, J. Rats, homosex, saunas, and Simon
Chapman, J. Great Salt Lake
Chapman, T. Kiddieland
Châteaureynaud, G. O. The bronze schoolboy
Châteaureynaud, G. O. The gulf of the years
Châteaureynaud, G. O. A room on the abyss
Chuculate, E. D. Winter, 1979
Chuculate, E. D. Yoyo
Cook, K. L. Bonnie and Clyde in the backyard
Dozois, G. R. Chains of the sea
Dubus, A. Delivering
East, E. Second chance
Ford, J. Daddy long legs of the evening
Franco, J. April in three parts: part 1, The rainbow goblins
Franco, J. Camp
Franco, J. Chinatown in three parts
Franco, J. Halloween
Franco, J. I could kill someone
Franco, J. Jack-O'
Franco, J. Killing animals
Franco, J. Tar baby
Gautier, A. The ease of living
Gautier, A. Yearn
Gelasimov, A. The evil eye
Gifford, B. The age of fable
Gifford, B. The Albanian florist
Gifford, B. The American language
Gifford, B. Arabian nights

Gifford, B. Bad girls
Gifford, B. Blue people
Gifford, B. Caca negra
Gifford, B. The choice
Gifford, B. Chop suey joint
Gifford, B. Close encounters of the right kind
Gifford, B. Crime and punishment
Gifford, B. Einstein's son
Gifford, B. The exception
Gifford, B. Far from anywhere
Gifford, B. Force of evil
Gifford, B. The great failure
Gifford, B. In the land of the dead
Gifford, B. Innamorata
Gifford, B. Irredeemable
Gifford, B. Last plane out of Chungking
Gifford, B. The Liberian condition
Gifford, B. Lonely are the brave
Gifford, B. The man who swallowed the world
Gifford, B. Portrait of the artist with four other guys
Gifford, B. Rain in the distance
Gifford, B. Roy's first car
Gifford, B. Sad stories of the death of kings
Gifford, B. The secrets of the universe
Gifford, B. Six million and one
Gifford, B. The starving dogs of Little Croatia
Gifford, B. The sudden demise of Sharkface Bensky
Gifford, B. The Sultan
Gifford, B. The Swedish bakery
Gifford, B. War and peace
Gifford, B. The Weeper
Gilb, D. Uncle Rock
Gilley, T. Physical wisdom
Goodberg, D. Mercy blow
Goodman, A. La vita nuova
Gordimer, N. A meeting in space
Grodstein, L. Homewrecker
Hannah, B. A creature in the Bay of St. Louis
Hannah, B. Uncle high lonesome
Harland, R. Bad thoughts and the mechanism
Horrocks, C. At the zoo
Horrocks, C. Zero conditional
Hunter, L. Kid
Ibrāhim, H. The informer
Ibrāhim, H. My young friend
Jones, S. G. Father, son, holy rabbit
Jones, S. G. Monsters
Jones, S. G. The ones who got away
Jones, S. G. Till the morning comes
Khalaylah, A. In the company of Jamal the trouble-maker
Kim, S.-r. Into the light
King, S. The man in the black suit
Kitterman, B. Boys from poor families
Kitterman, B. A place in the opera
Kittredge, W. Stone boat
Kyle, A. Captain's club
Laken, V. Before long
Lanagan, M. Mulberry boys
Lansdale, J. R. The folding man
Le Clézio, J.-M. G. The mountain of the living god
Le Clézio, J.-M. G. The waterwheel
Lebbon, T. Naming of parts
Lethem, J. View from a headlock
Levine, S. Scoo boy
Lipsyte, S. The Dungeon Master

Bradbury, Ray—*Continued*
King of the gray spaces (R is for rocket)
  Bradbury, R. The collected stories of Ray
    Bradbury: volume I: 1938-1943; a critical
    edition; William F. Touponce, general edi-
    tor; Jonathan R. Eller, textual editor
The lake
  Bradbury, R. The collected stories of Ray
    Bradbury: volume I: 1938-1943; a critical
    edition; William F. Touponce, general edi-
    tor; Jonathan R. Eller, textual editor
Luana the living
  Bradbury, R. The collected stories of Ray
    Bradbury: volume I: 1938-1943; a critical
    edition; William F. Touponce, general edi-
    tor; Jonathan R. Eller, textual editor
The monster maker
  Bradbury, R. The collected stories of Ray
    Bradbury: volume I: 1938-1943; a critical
    edition; William F. Touponce, general edi-
    tor; Jonathan R. Eller, textual editor
Morgue ship
  Bradbury, R. The collected stories of Ray
    Bradbury: volume I: 1938-1943; a critical
    edition; William F. Touponce, general edi-
    tor; Jonathan R. Eller, textual editor
The parallel (A blade of grass)
  Bradbury, R. The collected stories of Ray
    Bradbury: volume I: 1938-1943; a critical
    edition; William F. Touponce, general edi-
    tor; Jonathan R. Eller, textual editor
The pedestrian
  Brave new worlds; edited by John Joseph Ad-
    ams.
The pendulum (first version)
  Bradbury, R. The collected stories of Ray
    Bradbury: volume I: 1938-1943; a critical
    edition; William F. Touponce, general edi-
    tor; Jonathan R. Eller, textual editor
The piper
  Bradbury, R. The collected stories of Ray
    Bradbury: volume I: 1938-1943; a critical
    edition; William F. Touponce, general edi-
    tor; Jonathan R. Eller, textual editor
The piper (first version)
  Bradbury, R. The collected stories of Ray
    Bradbury: volume I: 1938-1943; a critical
    edition; William F. Touponce, general edi-
    tor; Jonathan R. Eller, textual editor
Promotion to satellite
  Bradbury, R. The collected stories of Ray
    Bradbury: volume I: 1938-1943; a critical
    edition; William F. Touponce, general edi-
    tor; Jonathan R. Eller, textual editor
The scythe
  Bradbury, R. The collected stories of Ray
    Bradbury: volume I: 1938-1943; a critical
    edition; William F. Touponce, general edi-
    tor; Jonathan R. Eller, textual editor
The secret
  Bradbury, R. The collected stories of Ray
    Bradbury: volume I: 1938-1943; a critical
    edition; William F. Touponce, general edi-
    tor; Jonathan R. Eller, textual editor
The small assassin
  Bradbury, R. The collected stories of Ray
    Bradbury: volume I: 1938-1943; a critical
    edition; William F. Touponce, general edi-
    tor; Jonathan R. Eller, textual editor

Subterfuge
  Bradbury, R. The collected stories of Ray
    Bradbury: volume I: 1938-1943; a critical
    edition; William F. Touponce, general edi-
    tor; Jonathan R. Eller, textual editor
Tale of the mangledomvritch
  Bradbury, R. The collected stories of Ray
    Bradbury: volume I: 1938-1943; a critical
    edition; William F. Touponce, general edi-
    tor; Jonathan R. Eller, textual editor
Tomorrow and tomorrow
  Bradbury, R. The collected stories of Ray
    Bradbury: volume I: 1938-1943; a critical
    edition; William F. Touponce, general edi-
    tor; Jonathan R. Eller, textual editor
Undersea guardians
  Bradbury, R. The collected stories of Ray
    Bradbury: volume I: 1938-1943; a critical
    edition; William F. Touponce, general edi-
    tor; Jonathan R. Eller, textual editor
The wind
  Bradbury, R. The collected stories of Ray
    Bradbury: volume I: 1938-1943; a critical
    edition; William F. Touponce, general edi-
    tor; Jonathan R. Eller, textual editor
Bradbury, Ray and Hasse, Henry
Final victim
  Bradbury, R. The collected stories of Ray
    Bradbury: volume I: 1938-1943; a critical
    edition; William F. Touponce, general edi-
    tor; Jonathan R. Eller, textual editor
Gabriel's horn
  Bradbury, R. The collected stories of Ray
    Bradbury: volume I: 1938-1943; a critical
    edition; William F. Touponce, general edi-
    tor; Jonathan R. Eller, textual editor
Pendulum
  Bradbury, R. The collected stories of Ray
    Bradbury: volume I: 1938-1943; a critical
    edition; William F. Touponce, general edi-
    tor; Jonathan R. Eller, textual editor
BRADBURY, RAY, 1920-
          Parodies, imitations, etc.
Benford, G. Centigrade 233
Braddock, Paige
Jane's World [Graphic story]
  Women's Review of Books v27 no6 p18 N/D
    2010
Braddon, M. E.
Good Lady Ducayne
  The dreaming sex; early tales of scientific
    imagination by women; edited by Mike
    Ashley.
Braddon, Mary Elizabeth *See* Braddon, M. E.,
    1837-1915
Bradfield, Scott
The devil disinvests
  Sympathy for the devil; edited by Tim Pratt.
Bradley, George
BLAINESBEAUTIES.COM
  Southwest Review v96 no2 p208-30 2011
An East Egg update
  The Pen/O.Henry Prize stories, 2010; edited
    and with an introduction by Laura Furman;
    with essays on the stories they admire most
    by jurors Junot Diaz, Paula Fox, Yiyun Li.

Bradley, Marion Zimmer
The secret of the Blue Star
The way of the wizard; edited by John Joseph Adams.
BRAIN
Henderson, C. J. The wonderous boundless thought
Saare, J. I heart brains
Terry, G. P. A gray matter
BRAIN DAMAGE
Brackmann, L. Don't feed the bums
Roberge, R. Working backward from the worst moment of my life
Brain fever. Shepard, S.
Branches. Hemmingson, M.
Brand, Rebecca *See* Charnas, Suzy McKee
Brandon, Jay
A jury of his peers
The Best American mystery stories 2010; edited and with an introduction by Lee Child; Otto Penzler, series editor
Brau, Edgar
The Golem Project
The Antioch Review v68 no4 p668-87 Fall 2010
Braun, Remy
Why the World Is Not my Oyster
StoryQuarterly v44 p329-33 2010
Braunbeck, Gary A.
And still you wonder why our first impulsr is to kill you: an alphabetizes faux-manifesto transcribes edited, and annotated (under duress and protest)
The monster's corner; stories through inhuman eyes; edited by Christopher Golden
Glorietta
Zombies: the recent dead; edited by Paula Guran.
Bravado. Trevor, W.
Brave new world [excerpt] Huxley, A.
Bravo, Émile
Best American comic by a French artist
The best American nonrequired reading 2009; edited by Dave Eggers; introduction by Marjane Satrapi; managing editor, Jesse Nathan
Brawner's shadows. Cortijos, A.
BRAZIL
Wells, H. G. The empire of the ants
BRAZILIANS

United States
Hastings, W. Ten-year plan
BREAD
Marār, M. The loaf
Bread and water. Cisco, M.
Break it down. Davis, L.
Breakfast III. Meirose, J.
Breakin' dishes. Stovall, T.
Breakin' down. Cooper, D.
Breakthrough. Terry, G. P.
BREAST
Fleri, J. Gynecomastia
Harris, A. L. Still life with boobs
Nutting, A. Hellion
A **breath** of hot air. Kava, A. and Bremmer, P. A.
Breathe. Latiolais, M.
Breeding the demons. Kenyon, N.

Breen, Jon L.
William Allan Wilson
On a raven's wing; new tales in honor of Edgar Allan Poe; edited by Stuart M. Kaminsky
Breen, Susan
Triplet
The best American nonrequired reading 2009; edited by Dave Eggers; introduction by Marjane Satrapi; managing editor, Jesse Nathan
Bremmer, Patricia A.
(jt. auth) See Kava, Alex and Bremmer, Patricia A.
Brendel, Kelly
Somewhere
Dancing with Mr. Darcy; stories inspired by Jane Austen and Chawton House Library; compiled by Sarah Waters.
Brennan, Karen
Collected Stories
TriQuarterly v138 30177 bytes Summ/Fall 2010
Brennan, Maeve
An attack of hunger
The Granta book of the Irish short story; [edited by] Anne Enright.
Brennan, Marie
The twa corbies
Swenson, P. The Best of Talebones; edited by Patrick Swenson.
Brennan, Sarah Rees
The spy who never grew up
The Best science fiction and fantasy of the year: volume five; edited by Jonathan Strahan.
Brer Rabbit and the Tar-Baby. Harris, J. C.
Brett, Simon
Doctor theatre
Original sins; a Crime Writer's Association anthology; edited by Martin Edwards.
Breytenbach, Breyten
Four fictions [Excerpted from Catastrophes]
Harper's v322 no1930 p24-7 Mr 2011
Brezar, Aleksandar
(tr.) See Džamonja, Dario
Briceño, Carlos Martín
Insomnios
Archipiélago v19 no72 p31-32 Ap-Je 2011
The **brick** murder: a tragedy. Ayau, K. J.
The **bricks** of Gelecek. Kressel, M.
Bride of Azathoth. Cannon, P.
Brides. Kyle, A.
The **brides**. Phillips, H.
Bridesicle. McIntosh, W.
BRIDGE (GAME)
Beagle, P. S. The bridge partner
The **bridge**. Alarcón, D.
The **bridge**. Orozco, D.
The **Bridge** Named Desire. Džamonja, D.
The **bridge** partner. Beagle, P. S.
A **bridge** under water. Bissell, T.
The **bridgegroom**. Gordimer, N.
BRIDGES
Alarcón, D. The bridge
Gaiman, N. How to sell the Ponti Bridge
Sterling, P. The small bridge
Brief Lives. Zimmer, P.
The **briefcase**. Makkai, R.

Brieschke, Patricia
The prop master
  South Carolina Review v43 no2 p11-23 Spr
  2011
BRIGANDS AND ROBBERS
  See also Outlaws; Robbery
Balázs, B. The robbers of divine power
Briggs, Patricia
Fairy gifts
  Naked city; tales of urban fantasy; edited by
  Ellen Datlow.
Bright spots. Shepard, S.
The **brightness** of his eyes. Uruq, S.
BRIGHTON (ENGLAND) *See* England—Brighton
Brillig. Parks, R.
Brin, David
Just a hint
  Before they were giants; edited by James L.
  Sutter; cover illustration by Kieran Yanner.
Bringing down the moon. Miles, V.
The **brink** of eternity. Roden, B.
BRITISH
                     Africa
Gordimer, N. Livingstone's companions
                     Bulgaria
Penkov, M. The letter
                     Egypt
Mundy, T. The soul of a regiment
                     India
Kipling, R. The man who would be king
Wells, H. G. The flying man
                     Israel
Kadish, R. Come on Zion put your hands together
Wilson, J. The liars
                     Italy
Archer, J. No room at the inn
Drabble, M. A Pyrrhic victory
Trevor, W. After rain
Wells, H. G. Miss Winchelsea's heart
                     Jamaica
Wells, H. G. Mr. Ledbetter's vacation
                     Malaysia
Samarasan, P. Birch memorial
                     Morocco
Drabble, M. Hassan's tower
                     Nigeria
Mphahlele, E. Nigerian talking points
                     Palestine
Marār, M. The Arabs' battle
Marār, M. Ghanem's watermelon
Marār, M. Hard work
Marār, M. I want a rifle!
                     Russia
Meade, L. T. The Blue laboratory
                     Sierra Leone
Wells, H. G. Pollock and the Porroh man
                     South Africa
Buchan, J. The green wildebeest
Gordimer, N. Beethoven one-sixteeth black
Haggard, H. R. Hunter Quatermain's story
                     Spain
Marías, J. The resignation letter of Senor de
  Santiesteban
                     Tunisia
Jordan, N. Night in Tunisia
                     United States
Gordimer, N. Why haven't you written?

Griffiths, R. The obvious candidate
Kyle, A. Allegiance
BRITISH ARISTOCRACY *See* Aristocracy—England
BRITISH SOLDIERS *See* Soldiers—Great Britain
Brocklebank, Katherine
Bracelets
  The Black Lizard big book of Black Mask
  stories; edited and with a foreword by Otto
  Penzler; introduction by Keith Alan
  Deutsch.
Brockmeier, Kevin
These Hands
  The Georgia Review v65 no1 p38-64 Spr
  2011
Broderick, Damien
Under the moons of Venus
  The Best science fiction and fantasy of the
  year: volume five; edited by Jonathan
  Strahan.
  The Year's best science fiction: twenty-eighth
  annual collection; edited by Gardner
  Dozois.
Brodeur, Arthur Gilchrist
  (jt. auth) See Bishop, Farnham and Brodeur, Arthur Gilchrist
Broken glass. Eisenberg, D.
Broken words. Hughes, S. C.
BRONX (NEW YORK, N.Y.) *See* New York
  (N.Y.)—Bronx
The **bronze** schoolboy. Châteaureynaud, G. O.
Brooke, Keith
likeMe
  Nature v467 p494 S 23 2010
BROOKLYN (NEW YORK, N.Y.) *See* New
  York (N.Y.)—Brooklyn
Brooklyn Feast or Famine. Leahey, J.
Brooks, Gwendolyn
The rise of Maud Martha
  The vintage book of American women writers; edited and with an introduction by
  Elaine Showalter.
Brooks, Max
The Great Wall: a story from the zombie war
  Zombies: the recent dead; edited by Paula
  Guran.
BROTHELS *See* Prostitution
The **brother-in-law**. Davis, L.
Brotherly love. Price-Thompson, T.
BROTHERS
  See also Brothers and sisters; Stepbrothers; Twins
Abbott, L. K. A great piece of elephant
Alarcón, D. Second lives
Alenyikov, M. Barrel of laughs
Alenyikov, M. It takes all kinds
Alenyikov, M. Ivan and Misha
Alenyikov, M. Whirling dervish
Alenyikov, M. Who did what to whom?
Baxter, C. Snow
Beattie, A. Dwarf house
Beattie, A. One day
Beattie, A. Snakes' shoes
Bell, M. S. Barking man
Berry, W. Stand by me
Bierce, A. The mocking-bird
Burgis, B. Dark coffee, bright light and the paradoxes of omnipotence

Brown, Karen
   The Rubber Company Heiress
      Five Points v13 no3 p89-105 2010
   Swimming
      Five Points v13 no1 p87-95 2009
Brown, Raeford E.
   A Door Closes
      JAMA v305 no10 p977-8 Mr 9 2011
Brown, Randall
   About All Dolls
      Western Humanities Review v64 no2 p163
         Summ 2010
Brown, Rosellen
   The Shaggiest Dog
      Prairie Schooner v84 no3 p70-89 Fall 2010
   Wedding of the Week
      Five Points v12 no2 p48-52 2008
Brown, Stacy
   The magician's apprentice
      Hungry for your love; an anthology of
         zombie romance; edited by Lori Perkins.
Brown, Walter C.
   The parrot that wouldn't talk
      The Black Lizard big book of Black Mask
         stories; edited and with a foreword by Otto
         Penzler; introduction by Keith Alan
         Deutsch.
Browne, Laynie
   Mandrake, Hidden
      Chicago Review v55 no3/4 p162-3 Aut 2010
   Soporific
      Chicago Review v55 no3/4 p157-9 Aut 2010
   You Can Do This in a Sentence
      Chicago Review v55 no3/4 p160-1 Aut 2010
Brownies. Packer, Z.
Browning, Barbara
   Santutxo Etxeberria
      Bomb no112 p supp8-supp10 Summ 2010
Brownstein, Gabriel
   Occupations, Settlements, Territories
      Harvard Review (1992) no38 p157-75 2010
Brubaker, James
   Oh, Yoko
      Confrontation no109 p94-104 Spr 2011
Bruen, Ken
   She wails through the fair
      Requiems for the departed; edited by Gerard
         Brennan & Mike Stone.
Bruise for bruise. Davies, R.
The **brunette** and the miracle of the vial. Bayley,
   E.
A **Brush**. Berger, J.
Brushed in blackest silence. Hodge, B.
BRUTALITY *See* Cruelty; Violence
Bryant, Cullene
   Party time
      Dalhousie Review v90 no3 p397-402 Aut
         2010
Bryant, Edward
   Jody after the war
      The end of the world; stories of the apoca-
         lypse; edited by Martin H. Greenberg.
Bryant and May in the soup. Fowler, C.
BUBONIC PLAGUE *See* Plague
Buchan, John
   The green wildebeest
      The Big book of adventure stories; edited and
         with a introduction by Otto Penzler; fore-
         word by Douglas Preston.

Buck, James A. *See* Buck, Jim, 1929-
Buck, Jim
   The slave brand of Sleman Bin Ali
      The Big book of adventure stories; edited and
         with a introduction by Otto Penzler; fore-
         word by Douglas Preston.
Buckbee, Brian
   Wife Leaves Left
      The Southern Review (Baton Rouge, La.) v47
         no2 p215-20 Spr 2011
Buckell, Tobias
   The universe reef
      Nature v473 no7346 p248 My 12 2011
Buckell, Tobias S.
   The eve of the fall of Habesh
      Speculative Horizons; edited by Patrick St-
         Denis.
   Resistance
      Brave new worlds; edited by John Joseph Ad-
         ams.
   Trinkets
      Zombies: the recent dead; edited by Paula
         Guran.
Buckets of rain. Boggs, B.
Buday, Grant
   Retard
      Can'tLit; fearless fiction from Broken pencil
         magazine; edited by Richard Rosenbaum.
Buddha Jumps over the Wall. Ryu, S.
BUDDHISM
   Boyle, T. C. The silence
   Mu Xin. The moment childhood vanished
Budnitz, Judy
   Aboard
      Fantastic women; 18 tales of the surreal and
         the sublime from Tin House; introduction
         by Joy Williams; edited by Rob Spillman.
BUENOS AIRES (ARGENTINA) *See* Argenti-
   na—Buenos Aires
Buffalo Trace. Shepard, S.
Buford's last case. Nevins, F. M., Jr.
Bug Jack Barron [excerpt] Spinrad, N.
The **builder**. Dick, P. K.
BUILDING
   Dick, P. K. The builder
Built for pleasure. Emshwiller, C.
Bukiet, Melvin Jules
   The Florida sunshine tree
      Promised lands; new Jewish American fiction
         on longing and belonging; edited by Derek
         Rubin.
Bukowski, Charles
   A day
      Best of times, worst of times; contemporary
         American short stories from the new Gilded
         Age; edited by Wendy Martin and Cecelia
         Tichi.
Bulawayo, Noviolet
   Hitting Budapest
      Boston Review v35 no6 p43-7 N/D 2010
BULGARIA
   Penkov, M. East of the West
   Penkov, M. Makedonija
   Penkov, M. The night horizon
      Sofia
   Penkov, M. Cross thieves
   Penkov, M. A picture with Yuki

BULGARIANS
United States
Penkov, M. Buying Lenin
Penkov, M. Devshirmeh
Bulkin, Nadia
Everything dies, baby
    The Year's best dark fantasy & horror; edited
    by Paula Guran
Bull, Emma
Incunabulum
    Welcome to Bordertown; new stories and po-
    ems of the Borderlands; edited by Holly
    Black and Ellen Kushner; introduction by
    Terri Windling.
Bull of the Woods. Adams, A.
Bullet. Payne, M.
Bullfighting. Doyle, R.
BULLS
Doyle, R. Bullfighting
BULLYING
Benali, A. From the novel The trip to the
    slaughterhouse
Franco, J. I could kill someone
Gautier, A. Boogiemen
Gautier, A. Push
Hodge, B. An ounce of prevention is worth a
    pound of flesh
Kitterman, B. Someone like me
Kyle, A. Allegiance
Lindholm, M. Strays
Schweitzer, D. The dead kid
Bummer. Shapiro, J.
The **bundle**. Bayley, E.
The **Bundle**. Bayley, E.
Bunin, Ivan Alekseevich
The gentleman from San Francisco
    The greatest Russian stories of crime and sus-
    pense; edited by Otto Penzler.
Bunker, Eddie
Death of a rat
    Blood, guts, & whiskey; edited by Todd Rob-
    inson; introduction by Max Allan Collins.
Bunny. Lisicky, P.
Burbara, Rawya
An attempt at persuasion
    Loud sounds from the Holy Land; short fic-
    tion by Palestinian women; edited and
    translated by Jamal Assadi with assistance
    from Martha Moody.
The last stop: Street of the Prophets
    Loud sounds from the Holy Land; short fic-
    tion by Palestinian women; edited and
    translated by Jamal Assadi with assistance
    from Martha Moody.
A shelter, drizzle and a tempest
    Loud sounds from the Holy Land; short fic-
    tion by Palestinian women; edited and
    translated by Jamal Assadi with assistance
    from Martha Moody.
Until the green blossom opens . . .
    Loud sounds from the Holy Land; short fic-
    tion by Palestinian women; edited and
    translated by Jamal Assadi with assistance
    from Martha Moody.
Wipe your tears away, oh pine trees!
    Loud sounds from the Holy Land; short fic-
    tion by Palestinian women; edited and
    translated by Jamal Assadi with assistance
    from Martha Moody.

Burch, Beverly
Easy
    Southern Humanities Review v44 no3 p320-32
    Summ 2010
Burden. Wurzbacher, A.
BUREAUCRACY
    See also Civil service
Davis, C. Adrift on the policy level
Burgin, Richard
The justice society
    River Styx no85 p10-29 2011
Burgis, Ben
Dark coffee, bright light and the paradoxes of
    omnipotence
People of the book; a decade of Jewish sci-
    ence fiction & fantasy; edited by Rachel
    Swirsky & Sean Wallace.
BURGLARS *See* Thieves
Burglars. Dixon, S.
BURIAL *See* Funeral rites and ceremonies
BURIAL, PREMATURE *See* Premature burial
BURIED ALIVE *See* Premature burial
BURIED TREASURE
L'Amour, L. Off the mangrove coast
Prakash, U. The walls of Delhi
Smith, C. A. The master of the crabs
St. John, N. Further notes on my unfortunate
    condition
Wells, H. G. Mr. Brisher's treasure
Wells, H. G. The treasure in the forest
Burke, David
Beaverland
    Can'tLit; fearless fiction from Broken pencil
    magazine; edited by Richard Rosenbaum.
Burke, Thomas
The hollow man
    The book of the living dead; edited by John
    Richard Stephens.
BURKE, WILLIAM
About
Hodge, B. A good dead man is hard to find
BURN CARE UNITS
Roberge, R. Burn ward
Burn off by noon. Corncoran, T.
Burn ward. Roberge, R.
Burning beard: the dreams and visions of Joseph
    ben Jacob, Lord Viceroy of Egypt. Pollack,
    R.
Burning family members. Davis, L.
The **burning** house. Beattie, A.
The **burning** of a soul. Marjiyyah, R.
Burns, Tex, 1908-1988
    For works written by this author under oth-
    er names see L'Amour, Louis, 1908-
    1988
BURNS AND SCALDS
Osondu, E. C. Jimmy Carter's eyes
Roberge, R. Burn ward
Sterling, P. The pleasure of your company
Burnstein, Michael A.
I remember the future
    The Nebula Awards showcase; edited by Kev-
    in J. Anderson.
Burqa. Latiolais, M.
Burroughs, Edgar Rice
Tarzan the terrible
    The Big book of adventure stories; edited and
    with a introduction by Otto Penzler; fore-
    word by Douglas Preston.

BURROUGHS, EDGAR RICE, 1875-1950
   Parodies, imitations, etc.
   Farmer, P. J. Extracts from the memoirs of Lord
      Greystoke
Burton, Milton T.
   Cherry Coke
      Lone Star noir; edited by Bobby Byrd &
         Johnny Byrd.
BURYING GROUNDS *See* Cemeteries
BUS DRIVERS
   Mu Xin. Eighteen passengers on a bus
BUS TERMINALS
   Nair, M. Small fry
Busch, Frederick
   The World Began with Charlie Chan
      The Georgia Review v65 no1 p65-71 Spr
      2011
BUSES
   Boggs, B. Shelter
   Buday, G. Retard
   Dixon, S. The busses
   Mu Xin. Fellow passengers
   Riippi, J. Something about Ben Jensen
         Accidents
      See Traffic accidents
BUSH, GEORGE W.
         About
   Turtledove, H. Bedfellows
Bush, Peter
   (tr.) See Monzó, Quim
Bush meat. Renault, P.
BUSINESS
      See also Advertising; Merchants
   Bravo, É. Best American comic by a French art-
      ist
   Davis, C. Adrift on the policy level
   Kaczynski, T. Million year boom
   Millhauser, S. The next thing
   Ryman, G. Dead space for the unexpected
   Self, W. Grey area
Business philosophy. Lewycka, M.
Business talk. Apple, M.
BUSINESSMEN
   Apple, M. Business talk
   Archer, J. Better the devil you know
   Ayau, K. J. Bob the negro
   Baxter, C. The disappeared
   Binkley, P. A day of quality
   Boyle, T. C. Zapatos
   Cook, F. The gift
   Doctorow, C. Makers [excerpt]
   Goodberg, D. Double
   Kennedy, A. L. Wasps
   McElroy, J. The unknown kid
   Mulkerns, V. Memory and desire
   O'Brien, E. Inner cowboy
   Pearlman, E. ToyFolk
   Penncavage, M. The cost of doing business
   Ruocco, J. Hart
   Schirach, F. v. Summertime
   Vint, T. Beyond the window a park is dimming
   Vonnegut, K. Hundred-dollar kisses
   Vonnegut, K. With his hand on the throttle
BUSINESSWOMEN
   Holt, E. Fem care
The **busses**. Dixon, S.
Buster. Hicks, P.
Busy lines. Grace, P.
The **busy** road. Davis, L.

But soft what light... Emshwiller, C.
But there's a family resemblance. Tillman, L.
Butcher, Jim
   Backup
      Butcher, J. Side jobs; stories from the Dres-
         den files
   Curses
      Naked city; tales of urban fantasy; edited by
         Ellen Datlow.
   Day off
      Butcher, J. Side jobs; stories from the Dres-
         den files
   Heorot
      Butcher, J. Side jobs; stories from the Dres-
         den files
   It's my birthday, too
      Butcher, J. Side jobs; stories from the Dres-
         den files
   Last call
      Butcher, J. Side jobs; stories from the Dres-
         den files
   Love hurts
      Butcher, J. Side jobs; stories from the Dres-
         den files
   A restoration of faith
      Butcher, J. Side jobs; stories from the Dres-
         den files
   Something borrowed
      Butcher, J. Side jobs; stories from the Dres-
         den files
   Vignette
      Butcher, J. Side jobs; stories from the Dres-
         den files
   The warrior
      Butcher, J. Side jobs; stories from the Dres-
         den files
Butler, Ellis Parker
   Pigs is pigs
      21 essential American short stories; edited by
         Leslie M. Pockell
Butler, Nickolas
   Apples
      Ploughshares v37 no2/3 p15-28 Fall 2011
Butler, Robert Olen
   "This Is Earl Sandt"
      The Georgia Review v65 no1 p72-83 Spr
      2011
Butler, Terence
   (jt. auth) See Gorman, Edward and Butler, Ter-
      ence
BUTLERS
   Marías, J. What the butler said
Butner, Richard
   Ash city stomp
      Sympathy for the devil; edited by Tim Pratt.
Butt and Bhatti. Hanif, M.
Butte, Montana. Shepard, S.
Butterflies and Bugles. Ribeyro, J. R.
The **button**. Vukcevich, R.
Buying Lenin. Penkov, M.
BUZZARDS
   Russell, K. The dredgeman's revelation
By Appointment Only. Begley, L.
By hook or by crook. Drees, C.
By the dawn's early light. Block, L.
By the gleam of her teeth, she will light the path
      before her. Hall, T. M.
By the numbers. Ayau, K. J.
By the way. Sneed, C.

Byer, Josh
  Randal Isaac's suicide; y
    Can'tLit; fearless fiction from Broken pencil
      magazine; edited by Richard Rosenbaum.
  Rats, homosex, saunas, and Simon
    Can'tLit; fearless fiction from Broken pencil
      magazine; edited by Richard Rosenbaum.
Bynum, Sarah Shun-Lien
  The erlking
    20 under 40; stories from the New Yorker;
      edited by Deborah Treisman.
  The young wife's tale
    Fantastic women; 18 tales of the surreal and
      the sublime from Tin House; introduction
      by Joy Williams; edited by Rob Spillman.
Byrd, Bobby
  The dead man's wife
    Lone Star noir; edited by Bobby Byrd &
      Johnny Byrd.
Byrd, Robert James *See* Byrd, Bobby, 1942-
BYZANTINE EMPIRE
  Turtledove, H. Farmers' law

C

c. 1923: Hamburg: Danilo Kiš sends the flowers
  [Excerpt from Last respects] Kiš, D.
c. 1976: China: Yiyun Li observes a likeness [Ex-
  cerpt from Immortality] Li, Y.
CAB DRIVERS
  Silver, M. The passenger
The **caballero's** way. Henry, O.
The **cabinet** child. Tem, S. R.
Caca negra. Gifford, B.
Cacoethes scribendi. Sedgwick, C. M.
CACTUS
  Marār, M. Planting the cacti
Caddie crisis. Marquand, J. P.
Cadigan, Pat
  Picking up the pieces
    Naked city; tales of urban fantasy; edited by
      Ellen Datlow.
  Rock on
    Future media; [edited by Rick Wilber]
  The taste of night
    The Best science fiction and fantasy of the
      year: volume five; edited by Jonathan
      Strahan.
    The Year's best science fiction: twenty-eighth
      annual collection; edited by Gardner
      Dozois.
Caduceus. Latiolais, M.
Cady, Jack
  The parable of Satan's adversary
    Swenson, P. The Best of Talebones; edited by
      Patrick Swenson.
CAFÉS *See* Restaurants, lunchrooms, etc.
Cafeterias: A love story. Paul, D.
A **cageling** tale. Bernheimer, K.
Cain, Chelsea
  Less of a girl
    The monster's corner; stories through inhu-
      man eyes; edited by Christopher Golden
Caine, Rachel
  Dead man stalking: a Morganville Vampires sto-
    ry
    Vampires; the recent undead; edited by Paula
      Guran.

Shiny
    Chicks kick butt; edited by Rachel Caine and
      Kerrie L. Hughes.
CAIRO (EGYPT) *See* Egypt—Cairo
Caius. Pronzini, B. and Malzberg, B. N.
CAJUNS
  Chopin, K. The storm
Calcutta. Chew, R.
CALF *See* Calves
Calhoun, Kenneth
  Nightblooming
    The Pen/O.Henry Prize stories 2011; chosen
      and with an introduction by Laura Furman;
      with essays on the stories thety admire
      most by jurors A. M. Homes, Manuel Mu-
      ñoz, Christine Schutt
CALIFORNIA
  Barillas, G. R. The roads
  Bierce, A. The death of Halpin Frayser
  Bierce, A. The haunted valley
  Bierce, A. The lady from Redhorse
  Black, A. Someday is today
  Boland, J. C. No crime in the hills
  Gilb, D. Willows village
  Gilley, T. Physical wisdom
  Gilley, T. White
  Kitterman, B. Crazy people
  Orozco, D. Shakers
  Packer, A. Walk for Mankind
  Plummer, T. M. The bolero of Andi Rowe
  Powers, T. A journey of only two paces
  Roberge, R. Earthquake
  Senna, D. Admission
  Silverberg, R. Amanda and the alien
  Silverberg, R. The palace at midnight
  Yamauchi, W. Annie Hall, Annie Hall
  Yamauchi, W. A Christmas orange story
  Yamauchi, W. Dogs I owe to
  Yamauchi, W. McNisei
  Yamauchi, W. Pain and stuff
  Yamauchi, W. Rosebud
  Yiyun Li. Alone
                    Farm life
            See Farm life—California
                    Berkeley
  Packer, A. Things said or done
                    Hollywood
  Fitzgerald, F. S. Pat Hobby and Orson Welles
  Matheson, R. CU: Mannix
  Nolan, W. F. Vampire dollars
  Read, C. Hungry enough
  Shapiro, J. Night and day
                    Los Angeles
  Albert, E. One good reason why not
  Bacigalupi, P. The gambler
  Block, F. L. Farewell, my zombie
  Finney, E. J. Sequoia Gardens
  Gilb, D. Uncle Rock
  Mosley, W. Equal opportunity
  Nolan, W. F. At the 24-hour
  Nolan, W. F. The underdweller
  Plummer, T. M. All the sex is west
  Plummer, T. M. Forces
  Plummer, T. M. Happy hour
  Plummer, T. M. Olivia's roses
  Plummer, T. M. To visit the cemetery
  Plummer, T. M. Yard work
  Powers, T. The hour of Babel
  Powers, T. A soul in a bottle

CALIFORNIA—Los Angeles—*Continued*
Shapiro, J. Ennui
Silver, M. The passenger
Sizemore, S. Dancing with the star
Togneri, E. Paparazzo
Oakland
Beagle, P. S. Oakland dragon blues
San Diego
Brackmann, L. Don't feed the bums
Clark, D. C. and Bear, A. The home front
Ginsberg, D. The new girl
Haywood, G. A. Like something out of a comic book
Hughes, C. P. Moving black objects
Hunt, M. The angel's share
Kuhlken, K. Homes
Lawrence, M. C. Key witness
Lima, M. A scent of death
Mariotte, J. J. Gold shield blues
Parker, T. J. Vic Primeval
Urrea, L. A. The national city reparation society
Watson, B. Visitation
Winslow, D. After thirty
San Francisco
Bierce, A. The man out of the nose
Chau, A. Hunger
Dixon, S. What is all this?
Krinard, S. Mist
Mullins, D. P. Longing to love you
Mullins, D. P. True love versus the cigar-store Indian
Piccirilli, T. The return of inspiration
Call, Ryan
Somewhere ahead smoked the wreckage of my evening
Butler, B. 30 under 30; an anthology of innovative fiction by younger writers; Blake Butler & Lily Hoang, eds.
The **call** of blood. Row, J.
The **call** of Cthulhu. Lovecraft, H. P.
Call of the wild. Gifford, B.
Called Out. Adams, A.
Calling it off. Ayau, K. J.
Calvary. Lychack, W.
CALVES
Marãr, M. The day of the calf
CAMBODIA
Ryman, G. Blocked
Ryman, G. The last ten years in the life of hero Kai
Ryman, G. Pol Pot's beautiful daughter
Cambodia 1981. Morgan, S. S.
CAMBODIAN REFUGEES
Pearlman, E. Settlers
The **Cambrian**. Zebrowski, G.
Cameron, Dana
Ardent
Cape Cod noir; edited by David L. Ulin.
Femme sole
By hook or by crook and 27 more of the best crime + mystery stories of the year; edited by Ed Gorman and Martin H. Greenberg.
Cameron, Peter
The end of my life in New York
The Pen/O.Henry Prize stories, 2010; edited and with an introduction by Laura Furman; with essays on the stories they admire most by jurors Junot Diaz, Paula Fox, Yiyun Li.

CAMEROON
Smith, A. The go-between
Camín, Héctor Aguilar *See* Aguilar Camín, Héctor, 1946-
La **camisa** de Margarita. Palma, R.
Camp. Franco, J.
CAMP COUNSELORS
Rogers, I. Camp zombie
Camp Liberty. Fallon, S.
Camp zombie. Rogers, I.
The **campaign** trail. McElroy, J.
Campbell, Bonnie Jo
What There Was
The Southern Review (Baton Rouge, La.) v47 no2 p343-53 Spr 2011
Campbell, Felicia
4/18
Dead neon; tales of near-future Las Vegas; edited by Todd James Pierce and Jarret Keene.
Campbell, Ramsey
Respects
The Year's best dark fantasy & horror; edited by Paula Guran
CAMPBELL, RAMSEY, 1946-
Parodies, imitations, etc.
Cannon, P. The undercliffe sentences
Campbell-Such, Julia
The Napoleon difference
Can'tLit; fearless fiction from Broken pencil magazine; edited by Richard Rosenbaum.
CAMPING
See also Wilderness survival
Black, A. The only way out is through
MacLeod, I. The camping Wainwrights
Woodrell, D. Twin Forks
The **camping** Wainwrights. MacLeod, I.
CAMPS, SUMMER *See* Summer camps
CAMPUS LIFE *See* College life
CANADA
De Lint, C. Sisters
Hassan, R. Y. Guardians of the air
Villegas, H. Neighbours
Willis, D. The fiancée
Willis, D. Rely
Québec (Province)
Stefan, V. Doe a deer
Toronto
Armstrong, K. Zen and the art of vampirism
Willis, D. Traces
Yukon Territory
London, J. To build a fire
CANADIANS
England
Grotefeld, E. Eight years later
CANALS
Terrin, P. Clean-up; or, The adventures of Abdullah and me
Canary. Ruocco, J.
CANCER
Alland, S. Things I don't remember
Doyle, R. The photograph
Engel, P. Paloma
Fallon, S. Remission
Gilley, T. Invisible waves
Gorman, E. Flying solo
Hansen, P. Community property
Hemmingson, M. Last visit
Horrocks, C. Zolaria

CANCER—*Continued*
  Jones, S. G. Teeth
  King, S. Fair extension
  Kitterman, B. If I'd known you were going to stay this long
  Latiolais, M. Caduceus
  Ma, V. K. A child, a man
  McGarry, J. A full house
  Neugeboren, J. Make-a-wish
  Osondu, E. C. Pilgrimage
  Oyeyemi, H. The very shoe
  Pearlman, E. The little wife
  Pearlman, E. The noncombatant
  Pearlman, E. Self-reliance
  Perabo, S. Shelter
  Prentiss, N. In the porches of my ears
  Shapiro, J. Ennui
  Sterling, P. The last swim of the season
  Treadway, J. Please come back to me
  Trueblood, V. Choice in dreams
  Willis, M. S. Pie Knob
Candida, Marco
  Dream diary
    Best European fiction 2011; edited by Aleksandr Hemon; preface by Colum McCann
The **candle**. Bradbury, R.
CANDLES
  Bradbury, R. The candle
Candy. Falco, E.
Canfield, Dorothy *See* Fisher, Dorothy Canfield, 1879-1958
CANNIBALISM
  Barba, D. Sweet croquette
  Cain, C. Less of a girl
  Gray, A. Waste
  Jones, S. G. Father, son, holy rabbit
  Jones, S. G. The sons of Billy Clay
  Kurlansky, M. Margaret
  Nagai, M. Georgic
  Nolan, W. F. Zachry revisited
  Schirach, F. v. Love
  Terry, G. P. Spirit gobs
Cannon, Peter
  All moon-beasts
    Cannon, P. Forever Azathoth; parodies and pastiches
  Amorphous and mephitic
    Cannon, P. Forever Azathoth; parodies and pastiches
  The Arkham collector
    Cannon, P. Forever Azathoth; parodies and pastiches
  Azathoth in analysis
    Cannon, P. Forever Azathoth; parodies and pastiches
  Azathoth in Arkham
    Cannon, P. Forever Azathoth; parodies and pastiches
  Bride of Azathoth
    Cannon, P. Forever Azathoth; parodies and pastiches
  Cats, rats, and Bertie Wooster
    Cannon, P. Forever Azathoth; parodies and pastiches
  The house of Azathoth
    Cannon, P. Forever Azathoth; parodies and pastiches

  Old man
    Cannon, P. Forever Azathoth; parodies and pastiches
  The revenge of Azathoth
    Cannon, P. Forever Azathoth; parodies and pastiches
  The rummy affair of young Charlie
    Cannon, P. Forever Azathoth; parodies and pastiches
  Something foetid
    Cannon, P. Forever Azathoth; parodies and pastiches
  Son of Azathoth
    Cannon, P. Forever Azathoth; parodies and pastiches
  The sound and the fungi
    Cannon, P. Forever Azathoth; parodies and pastiches
  Tender is the night-gaunt
    Cannon, P. Forever Azathoth; parodies and pastiches
  The undercliffe sentences
    Cannon, P. Forever Azathoth; parodies and pastiches
Cannon, Taffy
  Instant karma
    San Diego noir; edited by Maryelizabeth Hart.
"**Cannot** easy normal die". Romano, C.
Canoe repair. McElroy, J.
CANOES AND CANOEING
  McElroy, J. Canoe repair
Can't win. Dixon, S.
Cantor, Rachel
  Love Drugstore
    The Kenyon Review v33 no3 p120-38 Summ 2011
CAPE COD (MASS.) *See* Massachusetts—Cape Cod
Cape Cod diary. Davis, L.
CAPE TOWN (SOUTH AFRICA) *See* South Africa—Cape Town
Capers. Pearlman, E.
CAPITAL PUNISHMENT
  Chekhov, A. P. The bet
  Gifford, B. Crime and punishment
  Matheson, R. The prisoner
  Tingle, T. Six dead cabbies
CAPITALISTS AND FINANCIERS
    See also Bankers; Millionaires; Wealth
CAPRI
  Wells, H. G. A dream of Armageddon
Captain's club. Kyle, A.
Captain's lament. Jones, S. G.
Captioning for the blind. Bengal, R.
Captive hearts. Keene, B.
Carcassonne. Barnes, J.
Card, Orson Scott
  Geriatric ward
    Brave new worlds; edited by John Joseph Adams.
  Jamaica
    The way of the wizard; edited by John Joseph Adams.
  Salvage
    The end of the world; stories of the apocalypse; edited by Martin H. Greenberg.
Card sharp. Khanna, R.
The **Cardboard** Dress. Bassingthwaighte, I.

Cardinale, Joseph
 Action at a distance
  Cardinale, J. The size of the universe
 Art in heaven
  Cardinale, J. The size of the universe
 The great disappointment
  Cardinale, J. The size of the universe
 May I not seem to have lived
  Cardinale, J. The size of the universe
 The singularity
  Cardinale, J. The size of the universe
Cardinale, Jospeh
 Proportions for the human figure
  Cardinale, J. The size of the universe
CARDS
 Khanna, R. Card sharp
 Monk, D. Christmas card
The **care** and feeding of your baby killer unicorn.
  Peterfreund, D.
Care of the circumcised penis. Doolittle, S.
The **care** of the self. Senna, D.
The **caretaker**. Faherty, T.
Carey, Elea
 One time
  Best of the West 2010; new stories from the
   wide side of the Missouri; edited by James
   Thomas and D. Seth Horton; foreword by
   Kent Meyers.
CARIBBEAN REGION
 Dent, L. Hell Cay
Caring, sharing. Self, W.
Carlson, Ron
 Escape from prison
  Best of the West 2011; new stories from the
   wild side of the Missouri; edited by James
   Thomas and D. Seth Horton; foreword by
   Ana Castillo.
 Esther Donnaly
  The Kenyon Review v33 no3 p3-12 Summ
   2011
 Victory at sea
  Best of the West 2010; new stories from the
   wide side of the Missouri; edited by James
   Thomas and D. Seth Horton; foreword by
   Kent Meyers.
CARNIVAL
 Rodoreda, M. Carnival
 Roncagliolo, S. The predator
Carnival. Rodoreda, M.
A **carnival** jangle. Dunbar-Nelson, A. M.
CARNIVALS (CIRCUS) *See* Amusement parks
Carolyn Came to Visit. Zimmerman, J.
Carpenter, Susan Streeter
 Elk medicine
  Best of the West 2009; new stories from the
   wide side of the Missouri; edited by James
   Thomas and D. Seth Horton; foreword by
   Rick Bass.
CARPENTERS
 Naipaul, V. S. The thing without a name
CARPETS
 Gault, W. C. The bloody Bokhara
CARRASQUEL, CHICO, 1928-2005
                About
 Gifford, B. Coda: the vanished gardens of Cor-
  doba
Carroll, Jonathan
 The Heidelberg cylinder
  Sympathy for the devil; edited by Tim Pratt.

Vedran
 The stories (in) between; edited by Greg
  Schauer, Jeanne B. Benzel, and W. H.
  Horner.
CARS (AUTOMOBILES) *See* Automobiles
El **Carterista**. Gifford, B.
The **Cartesian** Diver. Kinsella, J.
CARTHAGE (ANCIENT CITY)
 Anderson, P. Delenda est
Carver, Raymond
 Elephant
  I found this funny; my favorite pieces of hu-
   mor and some that may not be funny at all;
   edited by Judd Apatow.
La **Casa** de Serena. Denham, A.
The **case** of a boy's honour. Thomas, D.
The **case** of Colonel Crockett's violin. Linscott, G.
The **case** of Colonel Warburton's madness. Faye,
  L.
A **case** of criminal madness. Riccardi, T.
The **case** of Isadora Persano. Riccardi, T.
The **case** of the ghosts at Bly. Thomas, D.
The **case** of the matinee idol. Thomas, D.
The **case** of the missing lodger. Riccardi, T.
The **case** of the plangent colonel. Riccardi, T.
The **case** of the two Bohemes. Riccardi, T.
The **case** of the vermillion face. Riccardi, T.
Casey moan. Shepard, S.
Casing the promised land. Leland, C. T.
CASINOS
 Jensen, T. Looking for boll weevil
 Kiraly, A. Your recent acquisitions in the
  neonesque (microfables)
 Moss, P. Time machine
The **cask** of Castle Island. DuBois, B.
Cassirer, Nadine Gordimer *See* Gordimer, Na-
  dine, 1923-
CASTAWAYS
 Emshwiller, C. Venus rising
CASTE
                India
 Archer, J. Caste-off
Caste-off. Archer, J.
Castle, Shane
 DNA Smackdown
  The Humanist v70 no5 p38-9 S/O 2010
Castle in the desert: anno Dracula 1977. Newman,
  K.
CASTLES
 Turtledove, H. The catcher in the Rhine
Castro, Adam-Troy
 Cerile and the journeyer
  The way of the wizard; edited by John Joseph
   Adams.
 Of a sweet slow dance in the wake of temporary
  dogs
  Brave new worlds; edited by John Joseph Ad-
   ams.
Castronuovo, David
 (tr.) *See* Pirandello, Luigi
CASUALTIES (WORLD WAR, 1939-1945) *See*
  World War, 1939-1945—Casualties
The **cat**. Levine, S.
Cat. Ruocco, J.
The **Cat**. Selecky, S.
A **cat** horror story. Dozois, G. R.
Cat in a barn at night. Shepard, S.
The **cat-keeper** in Warsaw (Letter to the state
  prosecutor). Drakulic, S.

CELIBACY
See also Virginity
The **cello**. Schirach, F. v.
CEMETERIES
Loory, B. The graveyard
Lychack, W. Calvary
McOmber, A. Beneath us
Mu Xin. The Windsor cemetery diary
Plummer, T. M. To visit the cemetery
Rodoreda, M. It seemed like silk
Sikka, M. The railway aunty
Swirsky, R. The black angel's kiss
La **Cenerentola**. Jones, G. A.
CENSORSHIP
Emshwiller, C. If the word was to the wise
CENTAURS
Beagle, P. S. The rock in the Park
Turtledove, H. The horse of bronze
The **center** of the story. Davis, L.
Centers of Gravity. Hibbert, A.
Centigrade 233. Benford, G.
CENTRAL AMERICA
Eisenberg, D. Holy Week
CENTRAL INTELLIGENCE AGENCY (U.S.)
See United States. Central Intelligence
Agency
CENTRAL PARK (NEW YORK, N.Y.) See
New York (N.Y.)—Central Park
Centripetal force. Monzó, Q.
Cerat, Marie Lily
Maloulou
Haiti noir; edited by Edwidge Danticat
CEREBROVASCULAR DISEASE
Eisenberg, D. Revenge of the dinosaurs
CEREMONIES See Rites and ceremonies
Cerile and the journeyer. Castro, A.-T.
Certain death for a known person. Duffy, S.
Certain knowledge from Herodotus. Davis, L.
Cerulean skies. Novack, S.
CESTODA
Gordimer, N. Tape measure
Chabon, Michael
The god of dark laughter
Sympathy for the devil; edited by Tim Pratt.
Golems I have known, or, why my elder son's
middle name is Napoleon: a trickster's
memoir
People of the book; a decade of Jewish sci-
ence fiction & fantasy; edited by Rachel
Swirsky & Sean Wallace.
Ocean Avenue
I found this funny; my favorite pieces of hu-
mor and some that may not be funny at all;
edited by Judd Apatow.
Chacón, Daniel
The Color Red
Afro-Hispanic Review v29 no1 p195-206, 254
Spr 2010
Velocity of mass
Best of the West 2009; new stories from the
wide side of the Missouri; edited by James
Thomas and D. Seth Horton; foreword by
Rick Bass.
Chain. Vukcevich, R.
The **chain** of Aforgomon. Smith, C. A.
Chain of fools. Lake, J.
Chains of the sea. Dozois, G. R.
Challenger. Stashower, D.

Chambers, George
(I thought my father looked like FDR)
Blue collar, white collar, no collar; stories of
work; edited by Richard Ford.
Chambers, S. J.
2000: Dr. Lambshead's dark room
The Thackery T. Lambshead cabinet of curi-
osities; edited by Ann & Jeff VanderMeer.
Chambers, Whitman
The black bottle
The Black Lizard big book of Black Mask
stories; edited and with a foreword by Otto
Penzler; introduction by Keith Alan
Deutsch.
Chameleon. Claes, P.
Champion, D. L.
Death stops payment
The Black Lizard big book of Black Mask
stories; edited and with a foreword by Otto
Penzler; introduction by Keith Alan
Deutsch.
Champions of the World. Gorcheva-Newberry, K.
Chan, Jeffrey Paul
Russell Now and Then
Amerasia Journal v37 no1 p159-61 2011
Chance, Karen
In vino veritas
Chicks kick butt; edited by Rachel Caine and
Kerrie L. Hughes.
CHANCE
Jemison, N. K. Non-zero probabilities
Wells, H. G. A catastrophe
Chance. Pearlman, E.
Chance pattern. Nevins, F. M., Jr.
Chandler, Elizabeth
Blue Bear
The Kenyon Review v33 no1 p35-50 Wint
2011
Chandler, Raymond
Try the girl
The Black Lizard big book of Black Mask
stories; edited and with a foreword by Otto
Penzler; introduction by Keith Alan
Deutsch.
CHANDLER, RAYMOND, 1888-1959
Parodies, imitations, etc.
Nevins, F. M., Jr. Consultation in the dark
Chandler, Laurel See Holder, Nancy, 1953-
Chandra, Subhash
Death of the Two
Intersections no25 Ja 2011
The **changeling**. Silverberg, R.
CHANNEL ISLANDS
Archer, J. Members only
Chaon, Dan
I demand to know where you're taking me
I found this funny; my favorite pieces of hu-
mor and some that may not be funny at all;
edited by Judd Apatow.
Chapman, Jeffrey
Great Salt Lake
Best of the West 2009; new stories from the
wide side of the Missouri; edited by James
Thomas and D. Seth Horton; foreword by
Rick Bass.
Chapman, Stepan
The armor of Sir Locust
The Thackery T. Lambshead cabinet of curi-
osities; edited by Ann & Jeff VanderMeer.

CHILDBIRTH—*Continued*
Sa'id, M. A. The delivery
CHILDHOOD *See* Boys; Children; Girls
The **childhood** of the human hero. Emshwiller, C.
CHILDLESS MARRIAGE
Black, A. The thing itself
Diab, F. Thoughts of a sterile woman
Ely, S. The fishpond
Hall, T. M. All the day's sad stories: a novella
Kitterman, B. The window
Oates, J. C. Tetanus
Papernick, J. What is it then, between us?
Penkov, M. A picture with Yuki
Suong, N. M. Thirteen harbors
Tem, S. R. The cabinet child
Trevor, W. A day
CHILDLESSNESS
See also Childless marriage
Brendel, K. Somewhere
Foulds, A. The rules are the rules
Furman, L. The mother who stayed
Manilla, M. Childproof
Nolan, W. F. To be with Amy
Nutting, A. Dancing rat
Osondu, E. C. Miracle baby
Proulx, A. The sagebrush kid
Senna, D. You are free
Childproof. Manilla, M.
CHILDREN
See also Abandoned children; Adolescence; Boys; Foster children; Girls; Jewish children; Lost children; Mentally handicapped children; Missing children; Orphans; Physically handicapped children; War and children; Wild children
Baker, K. The books
Bierce, A. A baby tramp
Davis, L. We miss you: a study of get-well letters from a class of fourth graders
Dixon, S. Meet the natives
Eisenberg, D. Mermaids
Faolain, S. O. The trout
Farmer, P. J. Cats, dogs, and other creatures
Guène, F. Mimouna
Hunter, L. Marie Noe, talks to you about her kids
Kronauer, B. Stanzas for an observation
Kurlansky, M. The icing on the cake
Latiolais, M. The long table
Le Clézio, J.-M. G. The shepherds
Marãr, M. The day of the calf
Nolan, W. F. The underdweller
Phillips, H. The offspring
Scholes, K. Edward Bear and the very long walk
St. John, N. Further notes on my unfortunate condition
Story, K. Flame retarded
Trevor, W. Child's play
Adoption
See Adoption
CHILDREN, ABANDONED *See* Abandoned children
CHILDREN, ADOPTED *See* Adoption
CHILDREN, CRUELTY TO *See* Child abuse
CHILDREN, GIFTED *See* Gifted children
CHILDREN, JEWISH *See* Jewish children
CHILDREN, LOST *See* Lost children
CHILDREN, SICK *See* Sick children

The **children**. Trevor, W.
Children are the only ones who blush. Meno, J.
CHILDREN AS SLAVES *See* Slavery
The **children** of Cadmus. Kushner, E.
The **children** of gear. Thompson, N.
The **children** of the shark god. Beagle, P. S.
Child's care. Nolan, W. F.
Child's play. Trevor, W.
CHILE
Dorfman, A. Innocent passage
Kalechofsky, R. The enigmatic power of the letter "j"
Rural life
Silverberg, R. How they pass the time in Pelpel
CHILEANS
United States
Barrett, L. One hippopotamus
Chima, Cinda Williams
The trader and the slave
The way of the wizard; edited by John Joseph Adams.
Chimbwi. Hawkins, J.
CHIMPANZEES
Roberge, R. Beano's deal
Silverberg, R. The Pope of the chimps
Chin, Frank
Happy Chinatown Tours
Amerasia Journal v37 no1 p115-28 2011
Chin, Marilyn
Fox Girl [Part of special issue: Sex and Surveillance]
Feminist Studies v36 no3 p518-20 Fall 2010
Three buddhist tales
Pushcart Prize XXXV: best of the small presses 2011; edited by Bill Henderson with the Pushcart Prize editors.
CHINA
Balázs, B. The ancestors
Balázs, B. The clay child
Balázs, B. The cloak of dreams
Balázs, B. The clumsy god
Balázs, B. The flea
Balázs, B. The friends
Balázs, B. Li-Tai-Pe and springtime
Balázs, B. Li-Tai-Pe and the thief
Balázs, B. The moon fish
Balázs, B. The old child
Balázs, B. The opium smokers
Balázs, B. The parasols
Balázs, B. The revenge of the chestnut tree
Balázs, B. The robbers of divine power
Balázs, B. Tearful gaze
Balázs, B. The victor
De Bodard, A. The shipmaker
Kurlansky, M. Hot pot
Lake, J. The sky that wraps the world round, past the blue and into the black
Mu Xin. The moment childhood vanished
1949-
Mu Xin. Fong Fong no. 4
Mu Xin. Notes from underground
Mu Xin. Xia Mingzhu: a bright pearl
Zhang Kangkang. Are birds better at walking or flying?
Zhang Kangkang. Please take me with you
Zhang Kangkang. White poppies
Zhang Kangkang. Yanni's secret
College life
See College life—China

CHRISTMAS STORIES—*Continued*
Perry, A. My object all sublime
Vonnegut, K. While mortals sleep
A **Christmas** story. Naipaul, V. S.
The **Christmas** witch. Rickert, M.
Christopher Columbus. Shepard, S.
Christopher Raven. Goss, T.
Chrysalis. Bradbury, R.
Chu, John
THIRTY SECONDS FROM NOW
Boston Review v36 no5 p50-55 S 2011
Chubak, Sadeq
The baboon whose buffoon was dead
Tablet & pen; literary landscapes from the
modern Middle East, a words without bor-
ders anthology; edited by Reza Asian.
Chuculate, Eddie D.
Cheyenne Madonna
Chuculate, E. D. Cheyenne Madonna; [by]
Eddie Chuculate.
Dear Shorty
Chuculate, E. D. Cheyenne Madonna; [by]
Eddie Chuculate.
A famous Indian artist
Chuculate, E. D. Cheyenne Madonna; [by]
Eddie Chuculate.
Galveston Bay, 1826
Chuculate, E. D. Cheyenne Madonna; [by]
Eddie Chuculate.
Under the red star of Mars
Chuculate, E. D. Cheyenne Madonna; [by]
Eddie Chuculate.
Winter, 1979
Chuculate, E. D. Cheyenne Madonna; [by]
Eddie Chuculate.
Yoyo
Chuculate, E. D. Cheyenne Madonna; [by]
Eddie Chuculate.
Chughtai, Ismat
The quilt
Tablet & pen; literary landscapes from the
modern Middle East, a words without bor-
ders anthology; edited by Reza Asian.
The **church** in the wilderness. Child, L. M. F.
CHURCH SCHOOLS
See also School life
Gordimer, N. Not for publication
Prindle, J. Einstein's cross
CHURCHES
Ford, J. Relic
MacLeod, I. Topping off the spire
Wieland, L. Some churches
CHURCHILL, SIR WINSTON, 1874-1965
About
Loory, B. The tv and Winston Churchill
CIA *See* United States. Central Intelligence Agen-
cy
Ciechanowski, Walter
The dungeon out of time
The stories (in) between; edited by Greg
Schauer, Jeanne B. Benzel, and W. H.
Horner.
Cielito lindo. Engel, P.
Cigarette stop. Estleman, L. D.
CINCINNATI (OHIO) *See* Ohio—Cincinnati
CINDERELLA (LEGENDARY CHARACTER)
Dozois, G. R. Fairy tale
The **cinderella** game. Link, K.
The **Cinderella** waltz. Beattie, A.

Cinema verite. Blanchard, J.
Ciocan, Iulian
Auntie Frosea
Best European fiction 2011; edited by Alek-
sandr Hemon; preface by Colum McCann
Circling. Shepard, S.
The **circular** library of stones. Emshwiller, C.
CIRCUMCISION
Amqassim, Y. From the novel Raven's leg
Benali, A. From the novel The trip to the
slaughterhouse
Doolittle, S. Care of the circumcised penis
Papernick, J. Skin for skin
Circumstance. Spofford, H. E. P.
CIRCUMSTANTIAL EVIDENCE
Tolstoy, L., graf. God sees the truth, but waits
CIRCUS
Jewett, S. O. The circus at Denby
Porter, K. A. The circus
Tokarczuk, O. The ugliest woman in the world
Tuten, F. Self portrait with cheese
Tuten, F. Self portrait with circus
The **circus**. Porter, K. A.
The **circus** at Denby. Jewett, S. O.
Cisco, Michael
Bread and water
Blood and other cravings; edited by Ellen
Datlow.
The Thing in the Jar
The Thackery T. Lambshead cabinet of curi-
osities; edited by Ann & Jeff VanderMeer.
CITIES AND TOWNS
See also Extinct cities; Imaginary cities
Davis, L. City employment
Lampo, H. The city that never was
McElroy, J. Mister X
Millhauser, S. Phantoms
Rooney, K. and Gabbert, E. City walk IV, IX,
XII, XIV
Sa'id, M. A. The street
Sneed, C. Walled city
Tuttle, S. Amanuensis
CITIES AND TOWNS, RUINED, EXTINCT,
ETC. *See* Extinct cities
Citizen. Mehta, R.
A **citizen** speaks. Châteaureynaud, G. O.
CITIZENSHIP
Alarcón, D. Second lives
Mehta, R. Citizen
The **city**. Lahens, Y.
City employment. Davis, L.
A **city** of museums. Châteaureynaud, G. O.
City of the dog. Langan, J.
City people. Davis, L.
The **city** that never was. Lampo, H.
City walk IV, IX, XII, XIV. Rooney, K. and
Gabbert, E.
CIVIL SERVICE
Gogol, N. The overcoat
Civil Twilight. Hedges, T.
CIVIL WAR
United States
See United States—Civil War, 1861-1865
CIVILIZATION *See* Social problems
Civilization. Kaftan, V.
CIVILIZATION AND TECHNOLOGY *See*
Technology and civilization

Claes, Paul
  Chameleon
    The Dedalus book of Flemish fantasy; edited by Eric Dickens and translated by Paul Vincent.
Clair de lune. Millhauser, S.
Claire of the sea light. Danticat, E.
Clairval, Gio
  2003: the pea
    The Thackery T. Lambshead cabinet of curiosities; edited by Ann & Jeff VanderMeer.
CLAIRVOYANCE
  Holder, N. Beyond the pale
  Osondu, E. C. Jimmy Carter's eyes
  Updike, J. Farrell's caddie
  Wells, H. G. The crystal egg
The **Clan** of Ali Babas. Devi, A.
Clancy, Tom
  Tom Clancy's "Brain-Dead or Alive"
    The American Conservative v10 no2 p18-19 F 2011
CLANS
  See also Tribes
Clare, Cassandra
  (jt. auth) See Black, Holly and Clare, Cassandra
Clarity. Driscoll, D.
Clark, Curt
  For works written by this author under other names see Westlake, Donald E.
Clark, Dale
  The sound of the shot
    The Black Lizard big book of Black Mask stories; edited and with a foreword by Otto Penzler; introduction by Keith Alan Deutsch.
Clark, Diane C. and Bear, Astrid
  The home front
    San Diego noir; edited by Maryelizabeth Hart.
Clark, Mary Higgins
  The tell-tale purr
    On a raven's wing; new tales in honor of Edgar Allan Poe; edited by Stuart M. Kaminsky
    By hook or by crook and 27 more of the best crime + mystery stories of the year; edited by Ed Gorman and Martin H. Greenberg.
  What's in a name?
    Christmas at the Mysterious Bookshop; 'tis the season to be deadly; stories of mistletoe and mayhem from 17 masters of suspense; edited by Otto Penzler.
Clarke, Arthur C.
  "If I forget thee, oh Earth . . ."
    The end of the world; stories of the apocalypse; edited by Martin H. Greenberg.
Clarke, Brock
  Knock Knock
    Iowa Review v40 no2 p90-4 Fall 2010
Clarke, Susanna
  John Uskglass and the Cumbrian charcoal burner
    The way of the wizard; edited by John Joseph Adams.
Clarksville, Missouri (Little Dixie Highway). Shepard, S.
CLASS DISTINCTION
  Archer, J. Stuck on you
  Fitzgerald, F. S. Winter dreams
  Jen, G. In the American society

O'Brien, E. Green Georgette
Wells, H. G. The loyalty of Esau Common a fragment
Classic embrace. Shepard, S.
Classical scenes of farewell. Shepard, J.
The **classless** society. Hardwick, E.
The **classroom**. Knezevic, O.
Claus, Hugo
  Medieval
    The Dedalus book of Flemish fantasy; edited by Eric Dickens and translated by Paul Vincent.
Clausen, Jan
  The Gnat, the Hammer, and the Cruise Ship [Part of a special issue: Market]
    Women's Studies Quarterly v38 no3/4 p257-65 Fall/Wint 2010
CLAVICHORD
  Vukcevich, R. Over here
The **clay** child. Balázs, B.
Clayton, John J.
  The Name Changer
    Commentary v131 no3 p55-61 Mr 2011
Clayton, Lawrence
  Overlocked
    Blood, guts, & whiskey; edited by Todd Robinson; introduction by Max Allan Collins.
Clean-up; or, The adventures of Abdullah and me. Terrin, P.
CLEANING WOMEN
  See also Maids (Servants)
  Sa'id, M. A. The job
The **cleanup** man. Dixon, S.
Cleeves, Ann
  Neastly pleasures
    Original sins; a Crime Writer's Association anthology; edited by Martin Edwards.
Clemens, Samuel Langhorne See Twain, Mark, 1835-1910
Clements, David L.
  Last of the guerrilla gardeners
    Nature v469 no7330 p438 Ja 20 2011
CLEPTOMANIA See Kleptomania
Clerestory. Emshwiller, C.
CLERGY
  See also Rabbis; Women clergy
  Aiken, J. Second thoughts
  Ford, J. Relic
  Foulds, A. The rules are the rules
  Heathcock, A. Lazarus
  Hill, R. Where are all the naughty people?
  Kitterman, B. Wedding day
  Lake, J. The American dead
  Lansdale, J. R. The crawling sky
  Lansdale, J. R. The dark down there
  Lansdale, J. R. Deadman's road
  Lansdale, J. R. The gentleman's hotel
  McIlveen, J. Succumb
  Trevor, W. Of the cloth
  Vonnegut, K. Mr. Z
  Wells, H. G. Mr. Marshall's doppelganger
  Willis, M. S. The little harlots
  Willis, M. S. Scandalous Roy Critchfield
CLERGY, ANGLICAN AND EPISCOPAL See Anglican and Episcopal clergy
CLERGY, CATHOLIC See Catholic priests
CLERKS
  See also Civil service
Clever girl. Hanley, T.

A **Clever** Science. Fishbane, J.
Cleverclogs. Spiers, H.
Clézio, J.-M. G. le *See* Le Clézio, J.-M. G. (Jean-Marie Gustave), 1940-
CLICHES
Bradbury, R. It's not the heat, it's the hu—
Clifford, Sir Hugh Charles
The ghoul
The book of the living dead; edited by John Richard Stephens.
CLIFT, MONTGOMERY, 1920-1966
About
Warsh, L. A place in the sun
CLIMATE CHANGE
Goodberg, D. Weather channels
Shepard, J. The Netherlands lives with water
CLIPPER SHIPS *See* Sailing vessels
Clips [Part of special issue: Slovak Fiction] Juráňova, J.
Cloak of anarchy. Niven, L.
The **cloak** of dreams. Balázs, B.
CLOAKS
Balázs, B. The cloak of dreams
CLOCKS AND WATCHES
Bierce, A. John Bartine's watch
Prindle, J. Einstein's watch
CLONES *See* Asexual reproduction
CLONING
Levine, S. The cats
Close encounters of the right kind. Gifford, B.
Close to the bridge's edge. Sirhan, A.
Clothed, female figure. Allio, K.
CLOTHING AND DRESS
Jha, R. How I lost my clothes
McGarry, J. The wedding gowns
Wells, H. G. The beautiful suit
Cloudcroft. Dillman, D.
CLOUDS
Jones, S. Black kids in lemon trees
Smith, C. A. The primal city
Cloutier, Clarice
(tr.) See Hochel, Braňo
(tr.) See Johanides, Ján
(tr.) See Juráňova, Jana
(tr.) See Karvaš, Peter
(tr.) See Kompaníková, Monika
(tr.) See Kovalyk, Uršul´a
(tr.) See Rankov, Pavol
(tr.) See Šimko, Dušan
(tr.) See Vilikovský, Pavel
The **clown**. Konkka, A.
CLOWNS
Brotherton, M. Jack in the box
Chabon, M. The god of dark laughter
Konkka, A. The clown
Shipp, J. C. How to make a clown
CLUBS
See also Country clubs
Cluley, Ray
At night, when the demons come
The Best horror of the year: volume three; edited by Ellen Datlow.
The **clumsy** god. Balázs, B.
Clutter. Edwards, M.
CLYDE, 1909-1934
About
Cook, K. L. Bonnie and Clyde in the backyard
Coach. Bass, R.

COACHING (ATHLETICS)
Bass, R. Coach
Downey, G. First to score
Foulds, A. The rules are the rules
Franco, J. April in three parts: part III, April
The **Coal** Cellar. Spilman, R.
COAL MINERS *See* Coal mines and mining
COAL MINES AND MINING
Terry, G. P. Breakthrough
Warren, K. All you can do is breathe
COAL TOWNS *See* Coal mines and mining
The **coat**. Pearlman, E.
COBAIN, KURT, 1967-1994
About
Barahona, F. (Never) fade away
COCAINE
Sapper. Wheels within wheels
Taylor-Aragon, E. Epiphany
Cochrane, Mick
The Pound Game
Five Points v13 no3 p116-25 2010
COCKROACHES
Davis, L. Cockroaches in autumn
Cockroaches in autumn. Davis, L.
COCKTAIL PARTIES *See* Parties
Cocooning. Lazaroo, S.
Coda. Farmer, P. J.
Coda. Sterling, P.
Coda: the vanished gardens of Cordoba. Gifford, B.
Code of operation: snake farm. Gray, A.
Code Pink. Levine, P.
Coe, Tucker
For works written by this author under other names see Westlake, Donald E.
Coelho, Oliverio
After effects
Granta no113 p41-9 Wint 2010
Coelho, Paulo
In the prison of repose
Freedom; stories celebrating the Universal Declaration of Human Rights; Amnesty International.
Coexistence. Hlehel, A.
COFFEE
Blatnik, A. Cup of coffee
The **coffin-maker**. Pushkin, A. I.
COFFINS
Pushkin, A. I. The coffin-maker
Cohen, Joshua
Emission
The Paris Review v53 no196 p87-123 Spr 2011
Rip off the wings of dragonflies; virus; on location; still life with grapes; four art pieces; a Chinese folk tale, and the culture of pop art; anonymous anonymous
Butler, B. 30 under 30; an anthology of innovative fiction by younger writers; Blake Butler & Lily Hoang, eds.
Cohen, Phyllis
Designer justice
The Best American mystery stories 2010; edited and with an introduction by Lee Child; Otto Penzler, series editor
Cohen, Robert
Our Time with the Pirates
Ploughshares v36 no2/3 p40-54 Fall 2010
Cohiba. Puenzo, L.

COLD

Phillips, H. The long, cold goodbye

Cold comfort. Vukcevich, R.

A **cold** greeting. Bierce, A.

Cold, hard love. Bill, F.

Cold reading. Ardai, C.

The **coldest** girl in Coldtown. Black, H.

The **coldest** place. Niven, L.

Coldwell, Elizabeth

Everyone I love is dead

Hungry for your love; an anthology of zombie romance; edited by Lori Perkins.

Cole, William

Waiting for Rusty

The Black Lizard big book of Black Mask stories; edited and with a foreword by Otto Penzler; introduction by Keith Alan Deutsch.

Collaboration with fly. Davis, L.

Collected Stories. Brennan, K.

COLLECTIVE SETTLEMENTS

Love, Y. G. Lonely, lonely, lonely is the Lord of Hosts

Israel

Papernick, J. The miracle birth

COLLECTORS AND COLLECTING

Doctorow, C. Craphound

Evenson, B. 1995: kneel

Hoch, E. D. The Poe collector

McOmber, A. Egyptomania

COLLEGE LIFE

See also College students; School life; Students; Teachers

Gordimer, N. Look-alikes

Wells, H. G. A slip under the microscope

China

Qiu Xiaolong. Uniform

England

Trevor, W. Death of a professor

United States

Bingham, S. Winter term

Crucet, J. C. How to leave Hialeah

Dixon, S. The good fellow

Lupoff, R. A. Patterns

COLLEGE STUDENTS

See also College life

Adair, D. Selma [excerpt]

Atta, S. Lawless

Bailie, T. The druid's dance

Blatnik, A. Discourse

Burbara, R. An attempt at persuasion

Chowdhury, S. Hostel

Dillman, D. Cloudcroft

Evans, D. Harvest

Gallari, A. A beautiful lie

Greenland, S. Bad night in Hyannisport

Holmes, R. A nomad of the night

Irving, W. The adventure of the German student

Johnson, K. Names for water

Jones, K. The occidental tourist

Kyle, A. Economics

Kyle, A. Take care

Laken, V. Map of the city

Niedzviecki, H. Special topic: terrorism

Ross, A. The suicide room

Sabar, A. Sightlines

Schappell, E. Out of the blue and into the black

Shapiro, J. Ennui

Shapiro, J. Small

Sikka, M. The railway aunty

Stafford, J. The echo and the nemesis

Vincent, R. Hunt

Vonnegut, K. Guardian of the person

Wells, H. G. The thumbmark

Wieland, L. Body and engine

Willis, M. S. Speak well of the dead

Womack, C. The song of Roe Náld

Yi-Yang-ji. Koku

COLLEGE TEACHERS *See* Teachers

Collier, John

Thus i refute Beelzy

Sympathy for the devil; edited by Tim Pratt.

The **Colliers'** Venus (1893). Kiernan, C. R.

Collins, Max Allan

Dying in the post-war world

The Shamus winners: America's best private eye stories, volume I: 1982-1995; collected and introduced by Robert J. Randisi; founder, Private Eye Writers of America

(jt. auth) See Spillane, Mickey and Collins, Max Allan

Collinson, Peter

Arson plus

The Black Lizard big book of Black Mask stories; edited and with a foreword by Otto Penzler; introduction by Keith Alan Deutsch.

Collision. Jones, G. A.

Collision. Sabar, A.

COLOMBIA

Engel, P. Madre Patria

Fountain, B. Near-extinct birds of the central cordillera

Mason, E. B. The golden anaconda

COLONIALISM *See* Imperialism

The **colonization** of room 313. Farkas, A.

Colony. Dick, P. K.

COLOR

Niedzviecki, H. The colorist

The **color** of honor. Connell, R.

The **Color** Red. Chacón, D.

COLORADO

Carpenter, S. S. Elk medicine

Colorado. Beattie, A.

The **colorist.** Niedzviecki, H.

The **colour** of shadows. Tóibín, C.

Colston, Adam

Not in the flesh

L. Ron Hubbard presents Writers of the Future volume XXVI; the year's twelve best tales from the Writers of the Future international writers' program; illustrated by winners in the Illustrators of the Future international illustrators' program; with essays on writing & illustration by L. Ron Hubbard/Dean Wesley Smith/ Stephen Youll; edited by K. D. Wentworth

The **Columbus** School for Girls. Wieland, L.

COLUMNISTS *See* Journalists

COMA

Hemmingson, M. It's very cold down here

Meyer, P. What you do out here, when you're alone

Sterling, P. The good life

Comachrome. DeNiro, A.

Comanche. Shepard, S.

Combust. Milbrodt, T.

Come and get it. Gardner, E. S.

Come and Get Me. Marshall, A.
Come on Zion put your hands together. Kadish, R.
Come out, come out. Châteaureynaud, G. O.
Comeau, Joey
  Giraffes and everything
    Can'tLit; fearless fiction from Broken pencil
    magazine; edited by Richard Rosenbaum.
Comeback. Gorman, E.
COMEDIANS
  Pearlman, E. How to fall
COMETS
  O'Connor, S. All in good time
The comeuppance of Creegus Maxin. Frost, G.
Comfort. Neugeboren, J.
Comfort to the enemy. Leonard, E.
COMIC BOOKS, STRIPS, ETC.
  Bravo, É. Best American comic by a French art-
    ist
  Haywood, G. A. Like something out of a comic
    book
  Kaczynski, T. Million year boom
  Schrauwen, O. Best American hair analysis nar-
    rative
  St. John, N. Further notes on my unfortunate
    condition
Coming. Blatnik, A.
The coming. Emshwiller, C.
Coming close to Donna. Hannah, B.
The coming flood. Barba, A.
Coming for Green. Lake, J.
The coming of age of Jane. Baker, L.
COMING OF AGE STORIES See Adolescence;
  Youth
The coming of the white worm. Smith, C. A.
Commcomm. Saunders, G.
COMMENCEMENTS
  Rankin, I. Graduation day
COMMERCIAL TRAVELERS
  Gordimer, N. Through time and distance
  Kaczynski, T. Million year boom
  O'Connor, F. Good country people
  Welty, E. Death of a traveling salesman
A commonplace disaster. Lahens, Y.
COMMUNES See Collective settlements
COMMUNISM
    See also Totalitarianism
  Drakulic, S. The bear and the princess of light
  Drakulic, S. The cat-keeper in Warsaw (Letter
    to the state prosecutor)
  Drakulic, S. A communist with style
  Drakulic, S. From gulag to goulash: the intro-
    duction to Ms. Piggy's Hungarian cook-
    book
  Drakulic, S. A guided tour through the museum
    of communism
  Drakulic, S. An interview with the oldest dog in
    Bucharest
  Drakulic, S. The legend of the Berlin Wall–as
    presented by a mole
  Drakulic, S. The unusual case of the psychotic
    raven
  Penkov, M. Buying Lenin
        China
  Qiu Xiaolong. A Jing Dynasty goat
  Zhang Kangkang. Please take me with you
        Russia
  Grossman, V. S. A small life
  Grossman, V. S. A young woman and an old
    woman

Solzhenitsyn, A. Apricot jam
Solzhenitsyn, A. Ego
Solzhenitsyn, A. Fracture points
Solzhenitsyn, A. Times of crisis
A communist with style. Drakulic, S.
COMMUNISTS See Communism
Community. Dozois, G. R.
COMMUNITY LIFE
  Ibrāhīm, H. As-Sayyed's space
Community property. Hansen, P.
COMMUTERS
  Swierczynski, D. Lonergan's girl
Companion. Davis, L.
The companion. Dib, M.
COMPANIONS
  Beattie, A. Zalla
  Braddon, M. E. Good Lady Ducayne
  Marías, J. A kind of nostalgia perhaps
The Companionship of Stone. Thon, M. R.
Company. Davis, L.
Company of strangers. Kyle, A.
COMPASS
  Prindle, J. Einstein's compass
Complicity. Barnes, J.
COMPOSERS
  Black, A. We've got a great future behind us
  Goodberg, D. Rubber reality
  Gray, A. The movement
  Nevins, F. M., Jr. Funeral music
COMPUTER SIMULATION See Virtual reality
COMPUTERS
  Anderson, P. Goat song
  Buckell, T. S. Resistance
  Byer, J. Randal Isaac's suicide
  Dick, P. K. The Great C.
  Johnson, R. P. L. In apprehension, how like a
    god
  Kahaney, A. The temp
  Kehrli, K. R. M. Bonehouse
  Kessel, J. Iteration
  Morrow, J. Bible stories for adults, no. 31: the
    covenant
  Oliu, B. C\ping scopuli.com
  Padua, S. Lovelace & babbage
  Silverberg, R. Basileus
  Tolbert, J. One-click banishment
  Zeltserman, D. Julius Katz
Computers, VCR's & Football. Webber, C. R.
Comrade Vadillo. Aguilar Camín, H.
CON MEN See Swindlers and swindling
Con-science. Goodberg, D.
Conard, Robert C.
  (tr.) See Timm, Uwe
CONCENTRATION CAMPS
    See also Oranienberg (Germany: Concen-
    tration camp); Political prisoners;
    Ravensbrück (Germany: Concentration
    camp); World War, 1939-1945—Prisoners
    and prisons
  Oyeyemi, H. The very shoe
  Rodoreda, M. Night and fog
  Ryman, G. O Happy day !
CONCERTS
  Boggs, B. Opportunity
  Goodberg, D. Staging a scene
  Platana, J. Some of this is true
CONDEMNED PRISONERS
  King, D. Green Gables
Conditions for the revolution. Oloixarac, P.

Condon, Phil
Tanks
The Georgia Review v65 no1 p84-91 Spr 2011
The **cone**. Wells, H. G.
CONEY ISLAND (NEW YORK, N.Y.) *See* New York (N.Y.)—Coney Island
Coney Island. Beattie, A.
Confectioner's gold. Kennedy, A. L.
CONFEDERATE AGENTS *See* Spies
CONFEDERATE STATES OF AMERICA. ARMY
Bierce, A. One of the missing
Bierce, A. Parker Adderson, philosopher
CONFESSION
Bierce, A. A bottomless grave
Bierce, A. My favorite murder
Bierce, A. Oil of dog
Trevor, W. Solitude
CONFESSION (CATHOLIC)
Trevor, W. Justina's priest
Confession. Nagai, M.
Confession for Raymond Good Bird. Thon, M. R.
Confessions of a Teenage Cheerleading Ninja Wheelchairnapper. Mullane, E.
A **confidence** cap. Qiu Xiaolong
The **confidence** decoy. Beattie, A.
Confliction. Cooper, S.
CONFORMITY
Dozois, G. R. Community
Confucius and crab. Qiu Xiaolong
Confused aliens. Somerville, P.
The **congregation** of love. Leland, C. T.
CONGRESSES AND CONFERENCES
See also Meetings
Conklin, Lydia
Rockaway
New Letters v76 no4 p73-87 2010
Conley, Charles
Dragon Money
The North American Review v296 no1 p14-22 Wint 2011
CONNECTICUT
Matheson, R. The house of the dead
Connell, Richard
The color of honor
The Black Lizard big book of Black Mask stories; edited and with a foreword by Otto Penzler; introduction by Keith Alan Deutsch.
Connell, Richard Edward
The most dangerous game
The Big book of adventure stories; edited and with a introduction by Otto Penzler; foreword by Douglas Preston.
Connelly, Michael
Blood washes off
Mystery Writers of America presents the rich and the dead; edited by Nelson DeMille.
Connelly, Tina
Silverfin harbour
End of an Aeon; edited by Bridgett McKenna & Marti McKenna
Connolly, Lawrence C.
Beneath between
The stories (in) between; edited by Greg Schauer, Jeanne B. Benzel, and W. H. Horner.
Conquistador de la noche. Vaughn, C.

CONSCIENCE
See also Guilt
CONSPIRACIES
Barahona, F. (Never) fade away
Boland, J. C. Marley's package
D'Amico, D. A. Vector Victoria
Long, H. My grandfather was Adolf Hitler's roommate
Spinrad, N. Bug Jack Barron [excerpt]
Tremblay, P. The blog at the end of the world
Constantine, David
Asylum
Freedom; stories celebrating the Universal Declaration of Human Rights; Amnesty International.
CONSTANTINOPLE *See* Turkey—Istanbul
Constiner, Merle
Let the dead alone
The Black Lizard big book of Black Mask stories; edited and with a foreword by Otto Penzler; introduction by Keith Alan Deutsch.
Construction bid for poets [Love letter]. Petersen, K.
CONSTRUCTION INDUSTRY
Erdrich, L. Scales
Gilb, D. Willows village
Leland, C. T. As always, unkind
CONSULS *See* Diplomatic life
Consultation in the dark. Nevins, F. M., Jr.
CONSUMPTION (ECONOMICS)
Fowler, C. Oblivion by Calvin Klein
The **consumption**. Martin, C.
Contac. Dixon, S.
CONTENTMENT
See also Happiness
Contents May Have Shifted. Pearce, N.
Contents may have shifted #49 - #60. Houston, D.
CONTESTS
Evans, D. Someone ought to tell her there's nowhere to go
CONTRACEPTION *See* Birth control
CONTRACTORS
Ibrāhim, H Fathers and sons
The **controller**. Morrell, D.
A **convenient** place to wait. Binkley, P.
CONVENT LIFE
See also Nuns
Terry, G. P. The Holy Sisters of Shedir
CONVENTS *See* Convent life
CONVENTS AND NUNNERIES *See* Convent life
CONVERSATION
Barnes, J. At Phil & Joanna's 1: 60/40
Barnes, J. At Phil & Joanna's 2: Marmalade
Barnes, J. At Phil & Joanna's 3: Look, no hands
Barnes, J. At Phil & Joanna's 4: One in five
Conversation with Ord. Self, W.
The **conversion** of the Jews. Roth, P.
Conversions on the road to Damascus. Novack, S.
CONVICTS *See* Crime and criminals; Ex-convicts; Prisoners and prisons
CONVICTS, ESCAPED *See* Escaped convicts
Cook, Frank
The gift
Mystery Writers of America presents the rich and the dead; edited by Nelson DeMille.

Cook, K. L.
Bonnie and Clyde in the backyard
Best of the West 2011; new stories from the wild side of the Missouri; edited by James Thomas and D. Seth Horton; foreword by Ana Castillo.
Relative Peace
Prairie Schooner v85 no2 p123-43 Summ 2011
Cook, Thomas H.
The lesson of the season
Christmas at the Mysterious Bookshop; 'tis the season to be deadly; stories of mistletoe and mayhem from 17 masters of suspense; edited by Otto Penzler.
Nevermore
On a raven's wing; new tales in honor of Edgar Allan Poe; edited by Stuart M. Kaminsky
Cooke, Rose Terry
Odd Miss Todd
The vintage book of American women writers; edited and with an introduction by Elaine Showalter.
COOKERY
Davis, L. Kafka cooks dinner
Drakulic, S. From gulag to goulash: the introduction to Ms. Piggy's Hungarian cookbook
Kurlansky, M. Boundin
Kurlansky, M. Cholent
Wells, H. G. A misunderstood artist
COOKS
Barba, D. Sweet croquette
Gresh, L. H. Julia Brainchild
Makkai, R. The briefcase
Nadel, B. Two stars
A **coon** hunter's noir. Bill, F.
Cooper, Brenda
My father's singularity
The Year's best science fiction: twenty-eighth annual collection; edited by Gardner Dozois.
Cooper, Desiree
Breakin' down
Price-Thompson, T. My blue suede shoes; four novellas; [edited by] Tracy Price-Thompson and Taressa Stovall.
Cooper, Simon
Confliction
L. Ron Hubbard presents Writers of the Future volume XXVI; the year's twelve best tales from the Writers of the Future international writers' program; illustrated by winners in the Illustrators of the Future international illustrators' program; with essays on writing & illustration by L. Ron Hubbard/Dean Wesley Smith/ Stephen Youll; edited by K. D. Wentworth
Coovadia, Imraan
The Institute for Taxi Poetry
Agni no72 p179-88 2010
Coover, Robert
Going for a beer
The New Yorker v87 no4 p60-1 Mr 14 2011
Matinee
The New Yorker v87 no21 p66-71 Jl 25 2011
The **cop**. Somerville, P.
Coping stones. Beattie, A.

The **copper** bowl. Eliot, G. F.
Copping squid. Shea, M.
Corbett, David and Urrea, Luis Alberto
Who stole my monkey?
Lone Star noir; edited by Bobby Byrd & Johnny Byrd.
Cordingly, Beth
Marianne and Ellie
Dancing with Mr. Darcy; stories inspired by Jane Austen and Chawton House Library; compiled by Sarah Waters.
Corin, Lucy
The entire predicament
Fantastic women; 18 tales of the surreal and the sublime from Tin House; introduction by Joy Williams; edited by Rob Spillman.
Corncoran, Tom
Burn off by noon
Florida heat wave; [edited and with an] introduction by Michael Lister.
Cornea, Andrei
Oedipus and the Sphinx
World Literature Today v84 no5 p37 S/O 2010
Cornell, Jennifer C.
The swing of things
The Granta book of the Irish short story; [edited by] Anne Enright.
Corness, Patrick
(tr.) See Dovzhenko, Otar
CORPHQ (FIRM)
Kurlansky, M. Menudo
The **Corporate** Body [Part of a special issue: Thresholds] Nutt, D.
CORPORATIONS *See* Business
The **corpse** didn't kick. Ozaki, M. K.
Corpse smoker. Nutting, A.
CORPULENCE *See* Obesity
Corrie. Munro, A.
CORSAIRS *See* Pirates
Cortese, Katie
Thrill ride
River Styx no85 p74-5 2011
Cortez, Sarah
Montgomery Cleft
Lone Star noir; edited by Bobby Byrd & Johnny Byrd.
Cortijos, Antonia
Brawner's shadows
Barcelona noir; edited by Adriana V. Lopez & Cartmen Ospina; translated by Achy Obejas.
COSA NOSTRA *See* Mafia
COSSACKS
Lamb, H. The mighty manslayer
The **cost** of doing business. Penncavage, M.
Costa, Margaret Jull
(tr.) See Montes, Javier
Costello. Gavin, J.
Costello. Shepard, S.
COSTUME PARTIES *See* Parties
The **cottage** cheese diet. Gray, A.
The **cottages**. Davis, L.
Couch, Stephen
The dandelion clock
Swenson, P. The Best of Talebones; edited by Patrick Swenson.
Cougar. Lippman, L.

Counihan, Elizabeth
  Out of time
    Nature v467 p1000 O 21 2010
COUNTERESPIONAGE *See* Spies
Counterfactual. Dozois, G. R.
Counterfactual. Ebenbach, D. H.
Counterfeit bills. Matheson, R.
Counterplot. Nevins, F. M., Jr.
Counting backwards. Manilla, M.
Counting the shapes. Lee, Y. H.
COUNTRY CLUBS
  Archer, J. Members only
  Bell, T. The pirate of Palm Beach
Country Junk. Boyack, N.
COUNTRY LIFE
    See also Farm life; Mountain life; Planta-
    tion life; Ranch life; Small town life
  Berry, W. Stand by me
  Bingham, S. Apricots
  Davis, L. The house plans
  Lasdun, J. Oh, death
  O'Connor, F. Good country people
  Sa'id, M. A. The neighbors' story
COUNTRY MUSIC
  Black, A. We've got a great future behind us
A **Country** of Shoes. Welsch, G.
The **country** of the blind. Wells, H. G.
The **country** of the blind (revised version). Wells,
    H. G.
The **Country** Wife. Jia, P.
The **coup** de grâce. Bierce, A.
COURAGE
    See also Heroism
  Bierce, A. George Thurston
  Bierce, A. Killed at Resaca
  Bierce, A. A son of the gods
  Boyle, P. Meles vulgaris
The **court** is convening!. Marãr, M.
COURT LIFE *See* Courts and courtiers
COURTESANS
    See also Prostitutes
Courting the Lady Scythe. Parks, R.
COURTROOM SCENES *See* Trials
COURTS AND COURTIERS
    See also names of individual kings,
    queens, and rulers; also subdivision Kings
    and rulers under names of countries
  Smith, C. A. The witchcraft of Ulua
COURTSHIP
  Bryant, E. Jody after the war
  Ross, A. Middleman
  Wells, H. G. The jilting of Jane
  Wells, H. G. Miss Winchelsea's heart
COUSINS
  Atwell, M. S. Maynard
  Baker, L. Still life
  Baxter, C. The cousins
  Bill, F. Beautiful even in death
  Chau, A. They were dangerous
  Evans, D. Snakes
  Evans, D. Wherever you go, there you are
  Gifford, B. The man who swallowed the world
  Nagai, M. Love story
  Oates, J. C. Bounty hunter
  Oates, J. C. Honor code
  O'Brien, E. Old wounds
  O'Connor, S. Elodie
  Pearlman, E. Granski
  Penkov, M. East of the West

Sedgwick, C. M. Cacoethes scribendi
Sterling, P. A real deal
Trevor, W. The woman of the house
The **cousins**. Baxter, C.
Couture, Beth
  Fur: an autobiography [excerpt]
    Butler, B. 30 under 30; an anthology of inno-
    vative fiction by younger writers; Blake
    Butler & Lily Hoang, eds.
Couture, Kevin A.
  Mr money-maker
    Dalhousie Review v90 no3 p367-78 Aut 2010
COVERLETS
  Fisher, D. C. The bedquilt
The **Cow** Island Open. Williamson, E. M.
The **coward**. Naipaul, V. S.
Cowards die many times. Randisi, R. J.
Coward's steel. Ball, K. C.
Cowboy. Chinquee, K.
Cowboy. McGuane, T.
The **Cowboy**. Peterson, A.
COWBOYS
  Davis, L. The professor
  McGuane, T. Cowboy
Cowdrey, Albert
  Twilight states
    Vampires; the recent undead; edited by Paula
    Guran.
COWHANDS *See* Cowboys
Cowie, Felicity
  One character in search of her love story role
    Dancing with Mr. Darcy; stories inspired by
    Jane Austen and Chawton House Library;
    compiled by Sarah Waters.
COWS *See* Cattle
Cowshed. Walser, R.
Coxe, George Harmon
  Fall guy
    The Black Lizard big book of Black Mask
    stories; edited and with a foreword by Otto
    Penzler; introduction by Keith Alan
    Deutsch.
Coyne, Stephen
  How Love Feels
    The North American Review v296 no2 p25-29
    Spr 2011
Coyote and valorosa. Gearhart-Serna, T. L.
Coyote v. Acme. Frazier, I.
COYOTES
  Bengal, R. Captioning for the blind
  Gearhart-Serna, T. L. Coyote and valorosa
Coyotes. Idol, K.
C\ping scopuli.com. Oliu, B.
CRABS
  Qiu Xiaolong. Confucius and crab
  Smith, C. A. The master of the crabs
Cracker Barrel men's room (Highway 90 West).
  Shepard, S.
Cracks. Blatnik, A.
Craddock, Charles Egbert
  The "harnt" that walks Chilhowee
    The vintage book of American women writ-
    ers; edited and with an introduction by
    Elaine Showalter.
Craig, Kit, 1932-
    See also Reed, Kit, 1932-
Craig, Randolph *See* Page, Norvell W., 1904-
  1961

Crane, Stephen
  The blue hotel
    21 essential American short stories; edited by
      Leslie M. Pockell
Crank. Romo, I.
Craphound. Doctorow, C.
Crash & tell. Baker, L.
Crash site on a desert mountain outside Las Vegas. Mullins, D. P.
The **craving** woman. Marār, M.
Crawford, F. Marion (Francis Marion)
  For the blood is the life
    The book of the living dead; edited by John
      Richard Stephens.
Crawford, Francis Marion *See* Crawford, F.
  Marion (Francis Marion), 1854-1909
The **crawling** sky. Lansdale, J. R.
Crawlspace. Jones, S. G.
Crazy. Latiolais, M.
Crazy glue. Keret, E.
Crazy Larry smells bacon. Bardsley, G.
Crazy Legs. Kegel, C.
Crazy people. Kitterman, B.
CREATION (LITERARY, ARTISTIC, ETC.)
    See also Authorship
Creature. Emshwiller, C.
A **creature** in the Bay of St. Louis. Hannah, B.
Creatures of the kingdom. Reents, S.
CREDIBILITY *See* Truthfulness and falsehood
CREMATION
  Blatnik, A. Stains
  Ruocco, J. Marzipan lambs
Crème brûlée. Kurlansky, M.
Creswell, Robyn
  (tr.) See Kilito, Abdelfattah
Creusa. Williamson, E. M.
The **crevasse**. Bailey, D. and Ballingrud, N.
Crewed Up. Darcleight, D.
Cricket fighting. Qiu Xiaolong
CRICKETS
  Qiu Xiaolong. Cricket fighting
Crider, Bill
  Pure pulp
    By hook or by crook and 27 more of the best
      crime + mystery stories of the year; edited
      by Ed Gorman and Martin H. Greenberg.
CRIME AND CRIMINALS
    See also Arson; Bank robbers; Brigands
    and robbers; Child abuse; Escaped convicts;
    Extortion; Gangs; Gangsters; Hostages; Juvenile delinquency; Kidnapping; Kleptomania; Mafia; Murder stories; Rape; Swindlers
    and swindling; Thieves; Underworld; Vandalism; Vigilance committees; War criminals; Wife abuse
  Allen, R. A. The Emerald Coast
  Bierce, A. A bottomless grave
  Bierce, A. Oil of dog
  Black, T. Hound of Culann
  Boland, J. C. Mountain fire
  Boland, J. C. The substitute
  Brown, W. C. The parrot that wouldn't talk
  Cameron, D. Femme sole
  Cannon, P. Old man
  Doctorow, C. The things that make me weak
    and strange get engineered away
  Downey, G. First to score
  DuBois, B. The necessary brother
  Gifford, B. Caca negra

  Gifford, B. Crime and punishment
  Gorman, E. Flying solo
  Khair, T. The scam
  Lahens, Y. Petty corruption
  Lahens, Y. A shattered day
  Leidiger, L. Tell me
  Leonard, E. Showdown at checotah [variant title: How Carlos Webster changed his name
    to Carl and became a famous Oklahoma
    lawman]
  Levinson, R. S. Between sins
  Margolin, P. The house on Pine Terrace
  Martinovich, V. Taboo
  Matheson, R. Now die in it
  McDonald, C. These two guys . . .
  Nair, M. Small fry
  Phelan, T. Happine$$
  Riahi, K. From the novel The scalpel
  Ryman, G. VAO
  Schirach, F. v. Summertime
  Schirach, F. v. Tanata's tea bowl
  Somerville, P. The cop
  Trevor, W. A bit of business
  Unger, L. Wild Card
  Vonnegut, K. Girl pool
  Vukcevich, R. Tubs
  Warsh, L. Harry Cray
  Wells, H. G. Mr. Ledbetter's vacation
  Westlake, D. E. Give till it hurts
  Winchell, P. Ten carats of lead
Crime and punishment. Gifford, B.
The **crime** of Dr. Garine. Sokoloff, B.
A **Crime** of Opportunity. Finney, E. J.
Crimes in southern Indiana. Bill, F.
CRIMES OF PASSION
    See also Murder stories
CRIMINAL INVESTIGATION
  Nevins, F. M., Jr. Fair game
CRIMINALLY INSANE *See* Insane, Criminal
  and dangerous
CRIMINALS *See* Crime and criminals
Crimmins, Mark
  Slimer
    Confrontation no108 p165-71 Fall 2010
Crimson fruit. Kim, C.-s.
CRISIS ON EARTH-X. Puglsey, A.
CRO-MAGNON MAN *See* Prehistoric man
Croatan (from the encyclopedia orangutannicas).
  Sands, B.
CROATIAN AMERICANS
  Gifford, B. The starving dogs of Little Croatia
Crone, Moira
  Do Over
    StoryQuarterly v44 p200-12 2010
Crook, Jeff
  The last jar of mayo at the H&P
    End of an Aeon; edited by Bridgett McKenna
      & Marti McKenna
The **crooked** way. Estleman, L. D.
Cross, S. M.
  Through death to love
    Hungry for your love; an anthology of
      zombie romance; edited by Lori Perkins.
The **cross-eyed** bear. Dufresne, J.
Cross Keys. Henry, B.
Cross thieves. Penkov, M.
Cross-town. Hardwick, E.
The **Cross** Word [Part of the Culture Issue] Morris, M.

CROSSBONES. Farah, N.

Crosshill, Tom
Seeing double
L. Ron Hubbard presents Writers of the Future volume XXVI; the year's twelve best tales from the Writers of the Future international writers' program; illustrated by winners in the Illustrators of the Future international illustrators' program; with essays on writing & illustration by L. Ron Hubbard/Dean Wesley Smith/ Stephen Youll; edited by K. D. Wentworth

Crossing. Slouka, M.

Crossing over. Mphahlele, E.

Crossing the Alps. Drabble, M.

Crossing the dark river. Farmer, P. J.

Crossing the horizon. Blatnik, A.

Crossing the seven. Lake, J.

Crossings. Simner, J. L.

Crossroads. Sabar, A.

The **crowd**. Bradbury, R.

Crowley, John
And go like this
Naked city; tales of urban fantasy; edited by Ellen Datlow.

The **crown**. Loory, B.

A **crown** of sonnets dedicated to long-gone love. Hall, T. M.

Crownover, Drew
The Punks
Texas Bar Journal v74 no6 p478-80 Je 2011

CROWS
Kavukçu, C. The route of the crows
Shepard, L. The flock

Crucet, Jennine Capó
How to leave Hialeah
The Pen/O.Henry Prize stories 2011; chosen and with an introduction by Laura Furman; with essays on the stories thety admire most by jurors A. M. Homes, Manuel Muñoz, Christine Schutt
What Some Other Guys Can Call The Byron Story: Miami, 1996
The Virginia Quarterly Review v87 no3 p180-186 Summ 2011

The **cruel** theif of rosy infants. Piccirilli, T.

CRUELTY
See also Violence
Châteaureynaud, G. O. The peacocks
Ross, A. In the basement
Trevor, W. Folie à deux

CRUELTY TO CHILDREN *See* Child abuse

The **Cruise**. Ohlin, A.

Crumley, James
Luck
Lone Star noir; edited by Bobby Byrd & Johnny Byrd.

CRUSADES
See also Knights and knighthood
Howard, R. E. Hawks of Outremer
Howard, R. E. Red blades of black Cathay

Cruz, Angie
Wading
Callaloo v33 no3 p611-18 Summ 2010

Cry silence. Brown, F.

CRYOGENICS *See* Low temperatures

CRYONICS
McIntosh, W. Bridesicle
Niven, L. Rammer

Crystal City. Manilla, M.

A **crystal** clear dream. Flatmouth, M.

The **crystal** crypt. Dick, P. K.

The **crystal** egg. Wells, H. G.

CU: Mannix. Matheson, R.

La **cuadra**. Dib, M.

CUBANS
United States
Crucet, J. C. How to leave Hialeah
Rodriguez-Milanes, C. El Loco

The **cube**. Gray, A.

CUBS (BASEBALL TEAM) *See* Chicago Cubs (Baseball team)

A **cuckoo** tale. Bernheimer, K.

Cughtāi, 'Ismat *See* Chughtai, Ismat, 1915-1991

Cull. Padmanabhan, M.

Cullen, Nicole
Banner Creek Summit
Ploughshares v37 no1 p28-44 Spr 2011

CULTS
Chabon, M. The god of dark laughter
Doctorow, E. L. Walter John Harmon
Fowler, K. J. Always
Hodge, B. Hate the sinner, love the sin
Kiernan, C. R. The pearl diver
Lovecraft, H. P. The call of Cthulhu
Moles, D. Seven cities of gold
Silverberg, R. A thousand paces along the Via Dolorosa

Culture clash. Ayau, K. J.

CULTURE CONFLICT
See also East and West
Ayau, K. J. Culture clash
Hemmingson, M. The keepers
Lahiri, J. Gogol
Naipaul, V. S. My aunt Gold Teeth

Culver, Timothy J.
For works written by this author under other names see Westlake, Donald E.

Cummings, Ray
The girl in the golden atom
The Big book of adventure stories; edited and with a introduction by Otto Penzler; foreword by Douglas Preston.
T. McGuirk steals a diamond
The Black Lizard big book of Black Mask stories; edited and with a foreword by Otto Penzler; introduction by Keith Alan Deutsch.

Cunha, Carlos
The Frenchwoman's Letter
TriQuarterly no139 Wint/Spr 2011

Cup of coffee. Blatnik, A.

A **cup** of tea. Sa'id, M. A.

The **cure**. Mehta, R.

The **cures** for love. Baxter, C.

Curfew. O'Reilly, S.

Curie, Eve *See* Labouisse, Eve Curie, 1904-2007

Curie, Maria Sklodowska *See* Curie, Marie, 1867-1934

CURIE, MARIE, 1867-1934
About
Davis, L. Marie Curie, so honorable woman

The **curious** case of the moondawn daffodils murder. Nix, G.

A **curious** dream. Twain, M.

The **curious** experience of Thomas Dunbar. Stevens, F.

CURSES
Arkwright, J. The sundial
Hyde, D. The O'Kane and the corpse
Marías, J. Isaac's journey
Passarella, J. Blood alone
Curses. Butcher, J.
Curtis, Craig
Anatomy
  Confrontation no109 p172-9 Spr 2011
Vae Victis
  Harvard Review (1992) no40 p122-39 2011
Cusick, Gregg
Gutted
  The Saturday Evening Post v283 no3 p52-3
  My/Je 2011
The **custodian**. Eisenberg, D.
Custody Battle for Chelsea Tammy: At the Toys
  "R" Us, Aisle 6, in a Suburb of Atlanta,
  Georgia, December 24, 1983. Garriga, M.
CUSTODY OF CHILDREN
Kitterman, B. The man who raised rabbits
Tallent, E. Never come back
Custom sets. Wallace, J.
The **customer** is always right. Monso, I.
Cut. Kenyon, J.
Cut. Lindholm, M.
A **cut** above. Spagnoli, L.
Cyclops. Hemmingson, M.
The **cypress** dream. Haines, C.
CYPRESS GARDENS (FLA.) *See* Florida Cy-
  press Gardens
The **cypress** house. Koryta, M.
Czepiel, Kathy Leonard
Truth or Dare
  Calyx v26 no1 p12-25 Summ 2010
Czyzniejewski, Michael
The Daredevil Discovers His Doppelganger
  Indiana Review v32 no2 p3-9,151 Wint 2010

D

D in the underworld. Villegas, H.
Dacey's patent Automatic Nanny. Chiang, T.
Daddy. Hemmingson, M.
Daddy long legs of the evening. Ford, J.
Dahlia underground. Harris, C.
The **daimon**. Turtledove, H.
Daisne, Johan
Death on a motorbike
  The Dedalus book of Flemish fantasy; edited
  by Eric Dickens and translated by Paul
  Vincent.
Dalembert, Louis-Philippe
Dangerous crossroads
  Haiti noir; edited by Edwidge Danticat
DALLAS (TEX.) *See* Texas—Dallas
Daly, Carroll John
Knights of the Open Palm
  The Black Lizard big book of Black Mask
  stories; edited and with a foreword by Otto
  Penzler; introduction by Keith Alan
  Deutsch.
D'Ambrosio, Charles, Jr.
Drummond & son
  Blue collar, white collar, no collar; stories of
  work; edited by Richard Ford.
The **damed** thing. Bierce, A.

D'Amico, D. A.
Vector Victoria
  L. Ron Hubbard presents Writers of the Future volume XXVII; the year's thirteen best
  tales from the Writers of the Future international writers' program; illustrated by
  winners in the Illustrators of the Future in-
  ternational illustrators' program; with es-
  says on writing & illustration by L. Ron
  Hubbard / Mike Resnick / Robert Cadtillo;
  edited by K. D. Wentworth
Dammaj, Zayd Mutee'
A woman
  Tablet & pen; literary landscapes from the
  modern Middle East, a words without bor-
  ders anthology; edited by Reza Asian.
Damned spot. Latiolais, M.
The **danas**. Levine, S.
The **dance** boots. Grover, L. L.
Dance for me. Gautier, A.
The **dance** of the savage prairies. Haydar Haydar
DANCERS
Elrod, P. N. Vampires prefer blondes
Kozlowski, L. Nuclear wasted love song
Sneed, C. By the way
Swirsky, R. No longer you
Womack, C. The song of Roe Náld
Dancers in the time-flux. Silverberg, R.
DANCING
Trevor, W. The dancing-master's music
Vonnegut, K. Tango
Womack, C. Sappho's round dance
Lou **dancing**. Emmanuel, F.
The **dancing-master's** music. Trevor, W.
Dancing rat. Nutting, A.
The **dancing** rats. Sale, R.
Dancing with the star. Sizemore, S.
The **dandelion** clock. Couch, S.
Dandruff. Schneier, J.
DANES
  See also Vikings
Daneshvar, Simin *See* Danishvar, Simin, 1921-
Dangerous crossroads. Dalembert, L.-P.
DANIEL (BIBLICAL FIGURE)
Vaughn, C. The book of Daniel
Daniel who had never seen the sea. Le Clézio,
  J.-M. G.
Danishvar, Simin
The playhouse
  Tablet & pen; literary landscapes from the
  modern Middle East, a words without bor-
  ders anthology; edited by Reza Asian.
Danticat, Edwidge
Claire of the sea light
  Haiti noir; edited by Edwidge Danticat
Danticat, Edwige
Hot-air balloons
  Granta no115 p175-89 Spr 2011
Daphne, unrequited. Zeman, A.
Darcleight, Danner
Crewed Up
  The Kenyon Review v33 no1 p139-55 Wint
  2011
The **Daredevil** Discovers His Doppelganger.
  Czyzniejewski, M.
DARIUS I, KING OF PERSIA, 548-485 B.C.
  About
Vaughn, C. The book of Daniel
The **dark**. Fowler, K. J.

The **dark** age. Smith, C. A.
DARK AGES *See* Middle Ages
A **dark** and stormy night. Blatnik, A.
The **dark** between them. Ray, S.
Dark chocolate. Pickard, N.
Dark coffee, bright light and the paradoxes of om-
  nipotence. Burgis, B.
Dark, dark were the tunnels. Martin, G. R. R.
The **dark** down there. Lansdale, J. R.
The **dark** island. DuBois, B.
The **darkness**. Gray, A.
The **Darlingest**. Sills, J. B.
The **dart** of Rasasfa. Smith, C. A.
Darwin, Bernard
  The wooden putter
    Golf stories; edited by Charles McGrath.
DATING (SOCIAL CUSTOMS)
  Barnes, J. East wind
  Barnes, J. Trespass
  Bingham, S. The banks of the Ohio
  Black, A. Double-blind
  Blatnik, A. And since I couldn't sleep
  Block, F. L. Revenants anonymous
  Call, R. Somewhere ahead smoked the wreckage
    of my evening
  Coldwell, E. Everyone I love is dead
  Davis, L. Blind date
  Díaz, J. How to date a brown girl (black girl,
    white girl, or halfie)
  Dixon, S. Dawn
  Emshwiller, C. Hands
  Fievre, M. J. The rainbow's end
  Fredsti, D. First date
  Fried, G. Lindsey
  Graham, S. Eye of the beholder
  Gray, A. Dinner
  Kennedy, A. L. The effects of good government
    on the city
  Kurlansky, M. Hot dog
  Kyle, A. A lot like fun
  Latiolais, M. Thorns
  Loory, B. UFO: a love story
  Martinovich, V. Taboo
  McGarry, J. Dream date
  McIntosh, W. Bridesicle
  Novack, S. Fireflies
  Plummer, T. M. Olivia's roses
  Qiu Xiaolong. Iron rice bowl
  Riippi, J. Something about a finger
  Riippi, J. Something about perfecting a love
  Schappell, E. Monsters of the deep
  Trevor, W. An evening out
  Trueblood, V. Suitors
Dating secrets of the dead. Prill, D.
Daugherty, Tracy
  The inhalatorium
    Best of the West 2009; new stories from the
      wide side of the Missouri; edited by James
      Thomas and D. Seth Horton; foreword by
      Rick Bass.
The **daughter**. Heathcock, A.
DAUGHTERS *See* Fathers and daughters; Moth-
    ers and daughters
  Aiken, J. The helper
  Atta, S. Madness in the family
  Chau, A. In the season of milk
  Furman, L. A thousand words
  Kitterman, B. Mediators
  McGarry, J. A full house

McGarry, J. The sweetness of her name
Trouillot, E. Which one?
Trueblood, V. Phantom father
Trueblood, V. Suitors
Trueblood, V. Tom Thumb wedding
Wieland, L. Some churches
DAUGHTERS-IN-LAW
  Munro, A. Some women
The **daughters** of desire. Lake, J.
Davenport, T. F.
  The age of momentum
    Nature v468 no7324 p726 D 2 2010
Davidson, Hilary
  Son of so many tears
    Blood, guts, & whiskey; edited by Todd Rob-
      inson; introduction by Max Allan Collins.
Davidson, Sean
  High on the hog
    Nature v468 no7323 p594 N 25 2010
Davies, Robert
  Bruise for bruise
    The Year's best dark fantasy & horror; edited
      by Paula Guran
Davis, Chandler
  Adrift on the policy level
    Davis, C. It walks in beauty; selected prose of
      Chandler Davis; edited and with an intro-
      duction by Josh Lukin.
  It walks in beauty
    Davis, C. It walks in beauty; selected prose of
      Chandler Davis; edited and with an intro-
      duction by Josh Lukin.
  Last year's grave undug
    Davis, C. It walks in beauty; selected prose of
      Chandler Davis; edited and with an intro-
      duction by Josh Lukin.
  The names of Yanils
    Davis, C. It walks in beauty; selected prose of
      Chandler Davis; edited and with an intro-
      duction by Josh Lukin.
  The Statistomat pitch
    Davis, C. It walks in beauty; selected prose of
      Chandler Davis; edited and with an intro-
      duction by Josh Lukin.
Davis, Dorothy Salisbury
  Emily's time
    On a raven's wing; new tales in honor of Ed-
      gar Allan Poe; edited by Stuart M.
      Kaminsky
Davis, Frederick C.
  Flaming angel
    The Black Lizard big book of Black Mask
      stories; edited and with a foreword by Otto
      Penzler; introduction by Keith Alan
      Deutsch.
Davis, Lawrence-Minh Bùi
  Like Kissing Your Sister
    The Literary Review (Madison, N.J.) v53 no4
      p75-80 Summ 2010
Davis, Lydia
  20 sculptures in one hour
    Davis, L. The collected stories of Lydia Davis
  2001: Port Ewen, NY: Packaging [Excerpt from
    Letter to a Funeral Parlor]
    Lapham's Quarterly v4 no2 p50 Spr 2011
  Absentminded
    Davis, L. The collected stories of Lydia Davis
  Acknowledgment
    Davis, L. The collected stories of Lydia Davis

Davis, Lydia—*Continued*

The actors
  Davis, L. The collected stories of Lydia Davis
Affinity
  Davis, L. The collected stories of Lydia Davis
Agreement
  Davis, L. The collected stories of Lydia Davis
Almost no memory
  Davis, L. The collected stories of Lydia Davis
Almost over: separate bedrooms
  Davis, L. The collected stories of Lydia Davis
Almost over: what's the word?
  Davis, L. The collected stories of Lydia Davis
Alvin the typesetter
  Davis, L. The collected stories of Lydia Davis
Away from home
  Davis, L. The collected stories of Lydia Davis
Betrayal
  Davis, L. The collected stories of Lydia Davis
Blind date
  Davis, L. The collected stories of Lydia Davis
The bone
  Davis, L. The collected stories of Lydia Davis
Boring friends
  Davis, L. The collected stories of Lydia Davis
Break it down
  Davis, L. The collected stories of Lydia Davis
The brother-in-law
  Davis, L. The collected stories of Lydia Davis
Burning family members
  Davis, L. The collected stories of Lydia Davis
The busy road
  Davis, L. The collected stories of Lydia Davis
Cape Cod diary
  Davis, L. The collected stories of Lydia Davis
The caterpillar
  Davis, L. The collected stories of Lydia Davis
The cats in the prison recreation hall
  Davis, L. The collected stories of Lydia Davis
The cedar trees
  Davis, L. The collected stories of Lydia Davis
The center of the story
  Davis, L. The collected stories of Lydia Davis
Certain knowledge from Herodotus
  Davis, L. The collected stories of Lydia Davis
Child care
  Davis, L. The collected stories of Lydia Davis
City employment
  Davis, L. The collected stories of Lydia Davis
City people
  Davis, L. The collected stories of Lydia Davis
Cockroaches in autumn
  Davis, L. The collected stories of Lydia Davis
Collaboration with fly
  Davis, L. The collected stories of Lydia Davis
Companion
  Davis, L. The collected stories of Lydia Davis
Company
  Davis, L. The collected stories of Lydia Davis
The cottages
  Davis, L. The collected stories of Lydia Davis
A different man
  Davis, L. The collected stories of Lydia Davis
Disagreement
  Davis, L. The collected stories of Lydia Davis
Dog and me
  Davis, L. The collected stories of Lydia Davis
A double negative
  Davis, L. The collected stories of Lydia Davis

The dreadful mucamas
  Granta no115 p81-9 Spr 2011
Enlightened
  Davis, L. The collected stories of Lydia Davis
Ethics
  Davis, L. The collected stories of Lydia Davis
Example of the continuing past tense in a hotel
    room
  Davis, L. The collected stories of Lydia Davis
Examples of confusion
  Davis, L. The collected stories of Lydia Davis
Examples of remember
  Davis, L. The collected stories of Lydia Davis
Extracts from a life
  Davis, L. The collected stories of Lydia Davis
The family
  Davis, L. The collected stories of Lydia Davis
Fear
  Davis, L. The collected stories of Lydia Davis
The fears of Mrs. Orlando
  Davis, L. The collected stories of Lydia Davis
The fellowship
  Davis, L. The collected stories of Lydia Davis
A few things wrong with me
  Davis, L. The collected stories of Lydia Davis
Finances
  Davis, L. The collected stories of Lydia Davis
First grade: handwriting practice
  Davis, L. The collected stories of Lydia Davis
The fish
  Davis, L. The collected stories of Lydia Davis
The fish tank
  Davis, L. The collected stories of Lydia Davis
Five fictions from the middle of the night
  Fantastic women; 18 tales of the surreal and
    the sublime from Tin House; introduction
    by Joy Williams; edited by Rob Spillman.
Five signs of disturbance
  Davis, L. The collected stories of Lydia Davis
Five stories from Flaubert
  Harper's v321 p25-7 N 2010
The fly
  Davis, L. The collected stories of Lydia Davis
For sixty cents
  Davis, L. The collected stories of Lydia Davis
Forbidden subjects
  Davis, L. The collected stories of Lydia Davis
Foucault and pencil
  Davis, L. The collected stories of Lydia Davis
French lesson I: le meurtre
  Davis, L. The collected stories of Lydia Davis
A friend of mine
  Davis, L. The collected stories of Lydia Davis
From below, as a neighbor
  Davis, L. The collected stories of Lydia Davis
The furnace
  Davis, L. The collected stories of Lydia Davis
Getting better
  Davis, L. The collected stories of Lydia Davis
Getting to know your body
  Davis, L. The collected stories of Lydia Davis
Glenn Gould
  Davis, L. The collected stories of Lydia Davis
Go away
  Davis, L. The collected stories of Lydia Davis
The good taste contest
  Davis, L. The collected stories of Lydia Davis
Good times
  Davis, L. The collected stories of Lydia Davis

Davis, Lydia—*Continued*

Grammar questions
Davis, L. The collected stories of Lydia Davis
The great-grandmothers
Davis, L. The collected stories of Lydia Davis
Hand
Davis, L. The collected stories of Lydia Davis
Happiest moment
Davis, L. The collected stories of Lydia Davis
Happy memories
Davis, L. The collected stories of Lydia Davis
Head, heart
Davis, L. The collected stories of Lydia Davis
Helen and Vi: a study in health and vitality
Davis, L. The collected stories of Lydia Davis
Her damage
Davis, L. The collected stories of Lydia Davis
Her mother's mother
Davis, L. The collected stories of Lydia Davis
Honoring the subjunctive
Davis, L. The collected stories of Lydia Davis
The house behind
Davis, L. The collected stories of Lydia Davis
The house plans
Davis, L. The collected stories of Lydia Davis
The housemaid
Davis, L. The collected stories of Lydia Davis
How difficult
Davis, L. The collected stories of Lydia Davis
How he is often right
Davis, L. The collected stories of Lydia Davis
How it is done
Davis, L. The collected stories of Lydia Davis
How shall I mourn them?
Davis, L. The collected stories of Lydia Davis
How she could not drive
Davis, L. The collected stories of Lydia Davis
How W. H. Auden spends the night in a
    friend's house
Davis, L. The collected stories of Lydia Davis
Idea for a short documentary film
Davis, L. The collected stories of Lydia Davis
In a house besieged
Davis, L. The collected stories of Lydia Davis
In a northern country
Davis, L. The collected stories of Lydia Davis
In the everglades
Davis, L. The collected stories of Lydia Davis
In the garment district
Davis, L. The collected stories of Lydia Davis
Index entry
Davis, L. The collected stories of Lydia Davis
Information from the north concerning the ice:
Davis, L. The collected stories of Lydia Davis
Insomnia
Davis, L. The collected stories of Lydia Davis
Interesting
Davis, L. The collected stories of Lydia Davis
Jack in the country
Davis, L. The collected stories of Lydia Davis
Jane and the cane
Davis, L. The collected stories of Lydia Davis
Jury duty
Davis, L. The collected stories of Lydia Davis
Kafka cooks dinner
Davis, L. The collected stories of Lydia Davis
The letter
Davis, L. The collected stories of Lydia Davis

Letter to a funeral parlor
Davis, L. The collected stories of Lydia Davis
Liminal: the little man
Davis, L. The collected stories of Lydia Davis
Lonely
Davis, L. The collected stories of Lydia Davis
Lord Royston's tour
Davis, L. The collected stories of Lydia Davis
Losing memory
Davis, L. The collected stories of Lydia Davis
Lost things
Davis, L. The collected stories of Lydia Davis
Love
Davis, L. The collected stories of Lydia Davis
A man from her past
Davis, L. The collected stories of Lydia Davis
A man in our town
Davis, L. The collected stories of Lydia Davis
Marie Curie, so honorable woman
Davis, L. The collected stories of Lydia Davis
Meat, my husband
Davis, L. The collected stories of Lydia Davis
The meeting
Davis, L. The collected stories of Lydia Davis
The mice
Davis, L. The collected stories of Lydia Davis
Mildred and the oboe
Davis, L. The collected stories of Lydia Davis
Mir the Hessian
Davis, L. The collected stories of Lydia Davis
Money
Davis, L. The collected stories of Lydia Davis
The mother
Davis, L. The collected stories of Lydia Davis
Mothers
Davis, L. The collected stories of Lydia Davis
Mother's reaction to my travel plans
Davis, L. The collected stories of Lydia Davis
The mouse
Davis, L. The collected stories of Lydia Davis
A mown lawn
Davis, L. The collected stories of Lydia Davis
Mr. Burdoff's visit to Germany
Davis, L. The collected stories of Lydia Davis
Mr. Knockly
Davis, L. The collected stories of Lydia Davis
Mrs. D and her maids
Davis, L. The collected stories of Lydia Davis
Murder in Bohemia
Davis, L. The collected stories of Lydia Davis
My husband and I
Davis, L. The collected stories of Lydia Davis
My neighbors in a foreign place
Davis, L. The collected stories of Lydia Davis
My son
Davis, L. The collected stories of Lydia Davis
A natural disaster
Davis, L. The collected stories of Lydia Davis
New Year's resolution
Davis, L. The collected stories of Lydia Davis
Nietszche
Davis, L. The collected stories of Lydia Davis
Odd behavior
Davis, L. The collected stories of Lydia Davis
The old dictionary
Davis, L. The collected stories of Lydia Davis
Old Mother and the Grouch
Davis, L. The collected stories of Lydia Davis

Davis, Lydia—*Continued*

Once a very stupid man
  Davis, L. The collected stories of Lydia Davis
Oral history (with hiccups)
  Davis, L. The collected stories of Lydia Davis
Order
  Davis, L. The collected stories of Lydia Davis
The other
  Davis, L. The collected stories of Lydia Davis
Our kindness
  Davis, L. The collected stories of Lydia Davis
Our trip
  Davis, L. The collected stories of Lydia Davis
The outing
  Davis, L. The collected stories of Lydia Davis
Passing wind
  Davis, L. The collected stories of Lydia Davis
Pastor's Elaine's newsletter
  Davis, L. The collected stories of Lydia Davis
The patient
  Davis, L. The collected stories of Lydia Davis
A position at the university
  Davis, L. The collected stories of Lydia Davis
Priority
  Davis, L. The collected stories of Lydia Davis
Problem
  Davis, L. The collected stories of Lydia Davis
The professor
  Davis, L. The collected stories of Lydia Davis
The race of the patient motorcyclists
  Davis, L. The collected stories of Lydia Davis
The rape of the Tanuk women
  Davis, L. The collected stories of Lydia Davis
Reducing expenses
  Davis, L. The collected stories of Lydia Davis
Right and wrong
  Davis, L. The collected stories of Lydia Davis
Safe love
  Davis, L. The collected stories of Lydia Davis
Samuel Johnson is indignant
  Davis, L. The collected stories of Lydia Davis
A second chance
  Davis, L. The collected stories of Lydia Davis
Selfish
  Davis, L. The collected stories of Lydia Davis
The senses
  Davis, L. The collected stories of Lydia Davis
The silence of Mrs. Iln
  Davis, L. The collected stories of Lydia Davis
Sketches for a life of Wassilly
  Davis, L. The collected stories of Lydia Davis
Smoke
  Davis, L. The collected stories of Lydia Davis
The sock
  Davis, L. The collected stories of Lydia Davis
Southward bound, reads Worstward ho
  Davis, L. The collected stories of Lydia Davis
Special
  Davis, L. The collected stories of Lydia Davis
Special chair
  Davis, L. The collected stories of Lydia Davis
Spring spleen
  Davis, L. The collected stories of Lydia Davis
St. Martin
  Davis, L. The collected stories of Lydia Davis
Story
  Davis, L. The collected stories of Lydia Davis
A strange impulse
  Davis, L. The collected stories of Lydia Davis

The strangers
  Davis, L. The collected stories of Lydia Davis
Suddenly affraid
  Davis, L. The collected stories of Lydia Davis
Television
  Davis, L. The collected stories of Lydia Davis
Ten Stories from Flaubert
  The Paris Review v52 p121-7 Fall 2010
Therapy
  Davis, L. The collected stories of Lydia Davis
They take turns using a word they like
  Davis, L. The collected stories of Lydia Davis
The thirteenth woman
  Davis, L. The collected stories of Lydia Davis
This condition
  Davis, L. The collected stories of Lydia Davis
Thyroid diary
  Davis, L. The collected stories of Lydia Davis
To reiterate
  Davis, L. The collected stories of Lydia Davis
The transformation
  Davis, L. The collected stories of Lydia Davis
Traveling with mother
  Davis, L. The collected stories of Lydia Davis
Tropical storm
  Davis, L. The collected stories of Lydia Davis
Trying to learn
  Davis, L. The collected stories of Lydia Davis
Two sisters
  Davis, L. The collected stories of Lydia Davis
Two sisters (II)
  Davis, L. The collected stories of Lydia Davis
Two types
  Davis, L. The collected stories of Lydia Davis
Varieties of disturbance
  Davis, L. The collected stories of Lydia Davis
Visit to her husband
  Davis, L. The collected stories of Lydia Davis
The walk
  Davis, L. The collected stories of Lydia Davis
The way to perfection
  Davis, L. The collected stories of Lydia Davis
We miss you: a study of get-well letters from a
    class of fourth graders
  Davis, L. The collected stories of Lydia Davis
What an old woman will wear
  Davis, L. The collected stories of Lydia Davis
What I feel
  Davis, L. The collected stories of Lydia Davis
What she knew
  Davis, L. The collected stories of Lydia Davis
What was interesting
  Davis, L. The collected stories of Lydia Davis
What you learn about the baby
  Davis, L. The collected stories of Lydia Davis
The white tribe
  Davis, L. The collected stories of Lydia Davis
Wife one in country
  Davis, L. The collected stories of Lydia Davis
Workingmen
  Davis, L. The collected stories of Lydia Davis
Young and poor
  Davis, L. The collected stories of Lydia Davis
Davis, Norbert
Don't you cry for me
  The Black Lizard big book of Black Mask
    stories; edited and with a foreword by Otto
    Penzler; introduction by Keith Alan
    Deutsch.

Davis, Rebecca Harding
Marcia
    The vintage book of American women writers; edited and with an introduction by Elaine Showalter.
Davis, Richard Harding
The bar sinister
    21 essential American short stories; edited by Leslie M. Pockell
Davis, Wendi *See* Holder, Nancy, 1953-
Dawn. Dixon, S.
Dawson, Minnesota (Highway 212 East). Shepard, S.
Day, Cathy
The Jersey Devil
    The North American Review v295 no4 p7-12 Fall 2010
Day, R. W.
Magic's choice
    Blood & devotion; tales of epic fantasy; edited by W.H. Horner; illustrated by Nicole Cardiff
Day, Robert
Where I Am Now
    New Letters v76 no3 p73-100 2010
A **day**. Bukowski, C.
A **day**. Trevor, W.
Day at the beach. Emshwiller, C.
A **day** I loved you. Blatnik, A.
A **day** in the life of a smiling woman. Drabble, M.
A **day** like any other. Monzó, Q.
Day of awe. Pearlman, E.
DAY OF JUDGMENT *See* Judgment Day
A **day** of quality. Binkley, P.
The **day** of the calf. Marār, M.
Day off. Butcher, J.
A **day** that did not end hopelessly after all. Kronauer, B.
A **day** with interruption and an opponent. Kronauer, B.
Daykin, Rande
Errata
    Indiana Review v32 no2 p15-24,152 Wint 2010
Days. Eisenberg, D.
The **days** of flaming motorcycles. Valente, C. M.
Days of wonder. Ryman, G.
Dayward. Packer, Z.
De Bodard, Aliette
The shipmaker
    The Year's best science fiction: twenty-eighth annual collection; edited by Gardner Dozois.
De Coster, Saskia
Queen
    The Dedalus book of Flemish fantasy; edited by Eric Dickens and translated by Paul Vincent.
De Lint, Charles
Sisters
    Vampires; the recent undead; edited by Paula Guran.
A tangle of green men
    Welcome to Bordertown; new stories and poems of the Borderlands; edited by Holly Black and Ellen Kushner; introduction by Terri Windling.
Ten for the devil
    Sympathy for the devil; edited by Tim Pratt.

De Noux, O'Neil
The heart has reasons
    Randisi, R. J. The Shamus winners: America's best private eye stories, volume II, 1996-2009; collected and introduced by Robert J. Randisi; founder, Private Eye Writers of America
De Tocqueville, Alexis *See* Tocqueville, Alexis de
DEAD
    See also Funeral rites and ceremonies
Bierce, A. The inhabitant of Carcosa
Bulkin, N. Everything dies, baby
Carroll, J. The Heidelberg cylinder
Châteaureynaud, G. O. The styx
Clifford, Sir H. C. The ghoul
Gautier, T. The amorous corpse
Hearn, L. A dead love
Hodge, B. A good dead man is hard to find
Houser, N. First kisses from beyond the grave
Hyde, D. The O'Kane and the corpse
Knox, J. H. Wake not the dead
Lansdale, J. R. Deadman's road
Levine, S. Believing it was George Harrison
Link, K. The wrong grave
Loory, B. The rope and the sea
Lovecraft, H. P. Herbert West: reanimator
Lundberg, K. Savage city, cruel city
MacLeod, I. Re-crossing the Styx
Marr, M. Guns for the dead
Matheson, R. and Matheson, R. C. Where there's a will
Monk, D. When the train calls lonely
O'Connor, S. I think I'm happier
Park, P. Mysteries of the Old Quarter
Pushkin, A. I. The coffin-maker
Rich, M. Zothique mi amor
Saunders, G. Commcomm
Shepard, L. The skinny girl
Vukcevich, R. The next best thing
Wells, H. G. The plattner story
Dead drunk. Matera, L.
Dead girlfriend. Vukcevich, R.
The **dead** kid. Schweitzer, D.
A **dead** love. Hearn, L.
Dead man stalking: a Morganville Vampires story. Caine, R.
Dead man's land. Wellington, D.
Dead man's run. Reed, R.
The **dead** man's wife. Byrd, B.
Dead soldier. Estleman, L. D.
Dead space for the unexpected. Ryman, G.
Dead to the world. McMahon, G.
The **deadliest** tale of all. Lovesey, P.
Deadly force. Estleman, L. D.
Deadman's road. Lansdale, J. R.
DEAF
Balázs, B. The opium smokers
Barnes, J. The limner
Bierce, A. Chickamauga
Packer, Z. Dayward
    Means of communication
Wieland, L. Body and engine
DEAFNESS *See* Deaf
A **deal** in ostriches. Wells, H. G.
DEANS (CATHEDRAL AND COLLEGIATE)
    See Anglican and Episcopal clergy
DEAR LIFE. Munro, A.
Dear Nicole. Treadway, J.
Dear Ollie. Tillman, L.

The **death** of Malygris. Smith, C. A.
The **death** of Mycroft Holmes. Riccardi, T.
The **death** of Sherlock Holmes. Nolan, W. F.
Death of the Two. Chandra, S.
Death on a motorbike. Daisne, J.
Death stops payment. Champion, D. L.
Death Threat. Malone, M. A.
DEATHBED SCENES
  Ely, S. The poisoned arrow
  Hemmingson, M. Daddy
  Marley, L. Night shift
  Trevor, W. Faith
DEBATES AND DEBATING
  Franco, J. American history
The **debt**. Neugeboren, J.
Debt of honor. Rifbjerg, K.
The **debt** of the innocent. Swirsky, R.
DEBTOR AND CREDITOR
  Rifbjerg, K. Debt of honor
DEBTS
  Barillas, G. R. The roads
  Kuhlken, K. Homes
Debut. Emshwiller, C.
DECADENCE *See* Degeneration
December. Olsen, L.
December. Victoria, E.
A **Decent** Hand. Beck, R.
Decolta, Ramon
  Rainbow diamonds
    The Black Lizard big book of Black Mask
      stories; edited and with a foreword by Otto
      Penzler; introduction by Keith Alan
      Deutsch.
Dedman, Stephen
  Waste land
    Vampires; the recent undead; edited by Paula
      Guran.
Deep water. Boland, J. C.
Deepwater miracle. Roche, T. S.
DEER
  Lychack, W. Hawkins
  Rickert, M. Memoir of a deer woman
  Stefan, V. Doe a deer
DEFECTORS
  Knezevic, O. The classroom
The **defenders**. Dick, P. K.
The **defenseless** dead. Niven, L.
Deferment. Allen, D.
Defiled imagination. Swirsky, R.
The **defining** work of your career (excerpts from
  one hour of television). Born, K.
DEFORMITIES
    See also Monsters
  Châteaureynaud, G. O. Icarus saved from the
    skies
  Emshwiller, C. Chicken Icarus
  Minh, C. A father and his children
  Nguyen, Q. L. The goat horn bell
  O'Connor, S. Man in the moon
  Phan, N. T. A dream
DEGENERACY *See* Degeneration
DEGENERATION
  Sheckley, R. The store of the worlds
DeGhett, Stephanie Coyne
  Old Dime's Last Show
    Southern Humanities Review v45 no2 p164-91
      Spr 2011
The **degroucher**. Bayley, E.
Degüello. Blake, G.

Dehan, Richard
  Lady Clanbevan's baby
    The dreaming sex; early tales of scientific
      imagination by women; edited by Mike
      Ashley.
Deja vu. Sterling, P.
Dejong, Lewis
  Lita Noble, Or, The Saddest Books Are the
    Stolen Ones
    The North American Review v296 no2 p31-35
      Spr 2011
Del Carlo, Eric
  Nothing but fear
    Swenson, P. The Best of Talebones; edited by
      Patrick Swenson.
Del Rey, Lester
  Kindness
    The end of the world; stories of the apoca-
      lypse; edited by Martin H. Greenberg.
The **Delaford** Ladies' Detective Agency. Hopkin-
  son, E.
Delany, Samuel R.
  Through the Valley of the Nest of Spiders
    Boston Review v35 no4 p35-7 Jl/Ag 2010
Delaunay the broker. Châteaureynaud, G. O.
Delbanco, Nicholas
  The writers' trade
    Blue collar, white collar, no collar; stories of
      work; edited by Richard Ford.
Delee, David
  Bling, bling
    Mystery Writers of America presents the rich
      and the dead; edited by Nelson DeMille.
Delenda est. Anderson, P.
DELHI (INDIA) *See* India—Delhi
A **delicate** architecture. Valente, C. M.
DeLillo, Don
  Hammer and Sickle
    Harper's v321 no1927 p63-6, 68-74 D 2010
Delivering. Dubus, A.
The **delivery**. Sa'id, M. A.
Deliverywoman. Nutting, A.
Delury, Jane
  Nothing of consequence
    The Pen/O.Henry Prize stories 2011; chosen
      and with an introduction by Laura Furman;
      with essays on the stories thety admire
      most by jurors A. M. Homes, Manuel Mu-
      ñoz, Christine Schutt
DeMarinis, Rick
  Boy with Cane Pole
    The Antioch Review v68 no3 p436-41 Summ
      2010
Dembo, Margot Bettauer
  (tr.) See Hermann, Judith
DEMENTIA
  Chacón, D. Velocity of mass
  Cook, F. The gift
  Mariotte, J. J. Janey in Amber
  Schappell, E. Are you comfortable?
DeMille, Nelson
  Death benefits
    Mystery Writers of America presents the rich
      and the dead; edited by Nelson DeMille.

Deming, Richard
The man who chose the devil
The Black Lizard big book of Black Mask stories; edited and with a foreword by Otto Penzler; introduction by Keith Alan Deutsch.
Demon in the woods. Shepard, S.
DEMONIAC POSSESSION
See also Exorcism
Black, J. Nine-tenths of the law
Nolan, W. F. Child's care
DEMONOLOGY
See also Demoniac possession; Satanism; Witchcraft
Armstrong, K. Rakshasi
Kenyon, N. Breeding the demons
Lovecraft, H. P. The call of Cthulhu
Nix, G. Ambrose and the ancient spirits of east and west
DEMONSTRATIONS
Hatoum, M. Torn
Sa'id, M. A. The delivery
Sa'id, M. A. The procession
'Demption road. Porter, J.
Denham, Alice
La Casa de Serena
Confrontation no108 p222-7 Fall 2010
Deniers. Lipsyte, S.
DeNiro, Alan
Comachrome
Swenson, P. The Best of Talebones; edited by Patrick Swenson.
DENMARK
Holm, B. Q. The great actor
Lundberg, K. Savage city, cruel city
Ozturk, S. The booster station
Stoltz, K. The elephant's tusks
Copenhagen
Aidt, N. M. Women in Copenhagen
Bengtsson, J. T. One of the rough ones
Dorph, C. and Pasternak, S. Australia
Helle Helle. A fine boy
Holm, G. When it's tough out there
Kaaberbol, L. and Friis, A. When the time came
Rifbjerg, K. Debt of honor
Staalesen, G. Last train from central station
Staun, S. All I want is my baby, woah woah, woah woah woah woah
Ursin, G. Sleipner's assignment
Dennis, Chris
Here is what you do
Granta no114 p235-56 Wint 2011
Dent, Catherine Zobal
Rise
Harvard Review (1992) no39 p16-24 2010
Dent, Lester
Hell Cay
The Big book of adventure stories; edited and with a introduction by Otto Penzler; foreword by Douglas Preston.
Luck
The Black Lizard big book of Black Mask stories; edited and with a foreword by Otto Penzler; introduction by Keith Alan Deutsch.
DENTISTS
Dixon, S. Who he?
Kennedy, A. L. Story of my life
Kyle, A. Take care

Laken, V. Before long
MacLaverty, B. Language, truth and lockjaw
Ruocco, J. Lighting bug
Ruocco, J. Ugly ducks
Department lounge. Pinede, N.
Departure. Rodoreda, M.
The **deposition**. Wolff, T.
Depression. Wilbur, E.
Deprivation. Treadway, J.
Depths. Sabar, A.
Desai, Mira
(tr.) See Chavda, Pravinsinh
Desaliento. Engel, P.
Descendancy. Shepard, S.
Descent. Nolan, W. F.
The **desert**: a field guide. Guidubaldi, D.
The **desert** in green. Plummer, T. M.
DESERTED HOUSES
Bierce, A. A vine on a house
Terry, G. P. This is not a pipe
Wells, H. G. The thing in no. 7
DESERTION AND NONSUPPORT
Beattie, A. Wanda's
DESERTS
Boyle, T. C. The silence
Emshwiller, C. After shock
Guerrero, L. A memory
Guidubaldi, D. The desert: a field guide
Hunter, L. Out there
Kressel, M. The bricks of Gelecek
Silverberg, R. Smithers and the ghosts of the Thar
Design faults in the Volvo 760 Turbo: a manual. Self, W.
Designer justice. Cohen, P.
Desire. Beattie, A.
Desire. Uphoff, M.
Desire for music and mountains [excerpt]. Kronauer, B.
DESPAIR
Thon, M. R. Confession for Raymond Good Bird
The **destination**. Dib, M.
Destinations, premonitions and the nature of anxiety. Emshwiller, C.
DESTINY See Fate and fatalism
Destroyers. Bear, G.
Destruction Bay. Tanaka, S.
DESTRUCTION OF EARTH See Earth, Destruction of
DESTRUCTION OF THE JEWS See Holocaust, Jewish (1933-1945)
Details. Miéville, C.
DETECTIVE AND MYSTERY STORIES See Mystery and detective stories
DETECTIVES
Aniskin, Fyodor. See stories by Lipatov, V.
Bakshi, Inspector Raghav. See stories by Bhattacharya, N.
Bosch, Harry. See stories by Connelly, M.
Brown, Father. See stories by Chesterton, G. K.
Calhoun, Rory. See stories by Healy, J. F.
Carlyle, Carlotta. See stories by Barnes, L.
Carter, Lloyd. See stories by Powell, T.
Casey, Jack "Flashgun". See stories by Coxe, G. H.
Caye, Lucien. See stories by De Noux, O.
Crockett, Ben. See stories by Long, J.
Cuddy, John Francis. See stories by Healy, J. F.

DETECTIVES—*Continued*

Dalton, Smokey. See stories by Nelscott, K.
Devlin, Inspector Benedict. See stories by McGilloway, B.
Drummond, Hugh "Bulldog". See stories by Sapper
Dupin, C. Auguste. See stories by Poe, E. A.
Elliott, Scott. See stories by Faherty, T.
Fandorin, Erast Petrovich. See stories by Akunin, B.
Frost, Jerry. See stories by McCoy, H.
Gar, Jo. See stories by Decolta, R.
Gunner, Aaron. See stories by Haywood, G. A.
Haggerty, Leo. See stories by Schutz, B. M.
Hammer, Mike. See stories by Spillane, M.
Hammer, Mike. See stories by Spillane, M. and Collins, M. A.
Heller, Nate. See stories by Collins, M. A.
Holmes, Sherlock. See stories by Faye, L.
Holmes, Sherlock. See stories by Linscott, G.
Holmes, Sherlock. See stories by Nikitin, P.
Holmes, Sherlock. See stories by Nolan, W. F.
Holmes, Sherlock. See stories by Riccardi, T.
Holmes, Sherlock. See stories by Thomas, D.
Jenkins, Ed. See stories by Gardner, E. S.
Kane, Karl. See stories by Millar, S.
Katz, Julius. See stories by Zeltserman, D.
Lee, Jack. See stories by Rozan, S. J.
Lennon, Bill. See stories by Ballard, W. T.
Lewis, Truxton. See stories by Randisi, R. J.
MacBride, Steve. See stories by Nebel, F.
Masterson, Bat. See stories by Randisi, R. J.
McCone, Sharon. See stories by Muller, M.
McGavock, Luther. See stories by Constiner, M.
McGuirk, T. See stories by Cummings, R.
Mensing, Loren. See stories by Nevins, F. M., Jr.
Millhone, Kinsey. See stories by Grafton, S.
Moon, Manny. See stories by Deming, R.
Nudger, Alo. See stories by Lutz, J.
O'Farrell, Val. See stories by Randisi, R. J.
O'Hanna, Mike. See stories by Clark, D.
Paris, Charles. See stories by Brett, S.
Plunkett, Lee. See stories by Nethercott, M.
Po, Henry. See stories by Randisi, R. J.
Rutledge, Ian. See stories by Todd, C.
Sail, Oscar. See stories by Dent, L.
Scudder, Matt. See stories by Block, L.
Shayne, Mike. See stories by Halliday, B.
Shugak, Kate. See stories by Stabenow, D.
Simms, Bubba. See stories by Alderman, M.
Skeat, T. See stories by Kornbluth, C. M.
Smith, Cellini. See stories by Reeves, R.
Spades, Sam. See stories by Hammett, D.
Street, Delilah. See stories by Douglas, C. N.
Sugawara, Akitada. See stories by Parker, I. J.
Sullivan, Billy. See stories by DuBois, B.
Tex of the Border Patrol. See stories by Brocklebank, K.
Tracy, Jerry. See stories by Tinsley, T. A.
Walker, Amos. See stories by Estleman, L. D.

DETECTIVES, PRIVATE

Ahmad, O. Yesterday man
Block, F. L. Farewell, my zombie
Block, L. As dark as Christmas gets
Boland, J. C. Out of her depth
Cave, H. B. Smoke in your eyes
Chandler, R. Try the girl
Daisne, J. Death on a motorbike

Davis, N. Don't you cry for me
DuBois, B. The road's end
Farmer, P. J. Skinburn
Gorman, E. Favor and the princess
Hart, R. G. My partner the zombie
Hopkinson, E. The Delaford Ladies' Detective Agency
Johnson, R. P. L. In apprehension, how like a god
Lutz, J. Lily & men
Nevins, F. M., Jr. Consultation in the dark
Nevins, F. M., Jr. Doomchild
Nix, G. The curious case of the moondawn daffodils murder
Nolan, W. F. Vampire dollars
Pickard, N. Dust devil
Pronzini, B. Cat's-paw
Reed, R. Dead man's run
Sandlin, L. Phelan's first case
Shipp, J. C. The sun never rises in the big city
Stinson, H. H. Three apes from the east
Turtledove, H. The scarlet band
Waggoner, T. Disarmed and dangerous
Wiecek, M. A death in Ueno
Detours on the way to nothing. Swirsky, R.
DETROIT (MICH.) *See* Michigan—Detroit
Development hell. Levine, P.

Devi, Ananda

The Clan of Ali Babas
The Massachusetts Review v51 no4 p645-51 Wint 2010

DEVIL

Aiken, J. Octopi in the sky
Aiken, J. Reading in bed
Archer, J. Better the devil you know
Babbitt, N. The power of speech
Black, H. A reversal of fortune
Bloch, R. That hell-bound train
Bradfield, S. The devil disinvests
Butner, R. Ash city stomp
Cady, J. The parable of Satan's adversary
De Lint, C. Ten for the devil
Dikeman, K. Nine sundays in a row
Downum, A. Blue valentine
Ford, J. On the road to New Egypt
Glover, E. M. Metaphysics
Green, S. R. Jesus and Satan go jogging in the desert
Hawthorne, N. Young Goodman Brown
Hodge, B. Guardian
King, S. Fair extension
King, S. The man in the black suit
Lake, J. The goat cutter
Richerson, C. . . . With [ord crossed out] by good intentions
Schwartz, D. J. Mike's place
Smith, C. A. Schizoid creator
Stross, C. Snowball's chance
Twain, M. Sold to Satan
Wells, H. G. The devotee of art
Wells, H. G. The temptation of Harringay
Wells, H. G. The wild asses of the devil
Westerfeld, S. Non-disclosure agreement
Wildt, J. Like riding a bike
Zettel, S. The redemption of Silky Bill
The **devil** disinvests. Bradfield, S.
The **devil** in iron. Howard, R. E.
DEVIL WORSHIP *See* Satanism
The **devil** you don't. Ackley-McPhail, D.

The **Devil's** Circle. Nadzam, B.
Devil's music (Montana, Highway 2). Shepard, S.
Devil's Night. BONNER, N.
Devil's pocket. Gilman, K.
Devilsbridge [excerpt]. Kronauer, B.
Devlin, Anne
  Naming the names
    The Granta book of the Irish short story; [edited by] Anne Enright.
The **devotee** of art. Wells, H. G.
Devshirmeh. Penkov, M.
DeWitt, Helen
  Re: Awesomeness, or The Internet as Consolation
    The Review of Contemporary Fiction v31 no1 p146-152,170 Spr 2011
Dia. Engel, P.
Diab, Fatmah
  An added fraction
    Loud sounds from the Holy Land; short fiction by Palestinian women; edited and translated by Jamal Assadi with assistance from Martha Moody.
  The power of silence
    Loud sounds from the Holy Land; short fiction by Palestinian women; edited and translated by Jamal Assadi with assistance from Martha Moody.
  Thoughts of a sterile woman
    Loud sounds from the Holy Land; short fiction by Palestinian women; edited and translated by Jamal Assadi with assistance from Martha Moody.
DIABETES
  Gautier, A. Some other kind of happiness
  Rodoreda, M. The mirror
A **diagnosis** of death. Bierce, A.
A **Dial** Tone. Adcox, J. T.
DIALOGUE *See* Conversation
The **diamond** as big as the Ritz. Fitzgerald, F. S.
The **diamond** maker. Wells, H. G.
The **diamond** mine. Gordimer, N.
Diamond shell. Biancotti, D.
DIAMONDS
  Archer, J. Double-cross
  Archer, J. Stuck on you
  Fitzgerald, F. S. The diamond as big as the Ritz
  Wells, H. G. A deal in ostriches
  Wells, H. G. The diamond maker
Diamonds mean death. Walsh, T.
DIARIES (STORIES ABOUT)
  Candida, M. Dream diary
  Furman, L. The mother who stayed
DIARIES (STORIES IN DIARY FORM)
    See also Letters (Stories in letter form)
  Baker, L. The coming of age of Jane
  Barthelme, D. Me and Miss Mandible
  Coelho, P. In the prison of repose
  Freeman, M. E. W. The hall bedroom
  Gilman, C. P. The yellow wall-paper
  Gilman, C. P. The yellow wallpaper
  Gomel, E. Going east
  Gray, A. Diary of the blockage
  Laurrent, E. American diary
  Loring, F. G. The tomb of Sarah
  McOmber, A. Beneath us
  Naipaul, V. S. The nightwatchman's occurance book
  Shteyngart, G. Lenny hearts Eunice

Simpson, H. Diary of an interesting year
Somerville, P. Pangea
Tremblay, P. The strange case of Nicholas Thomas: an excerpt from a history of the Longesian Library
Diarmaid and Grainne. McKinty, A.
Diary of an interesting year. Simpson, H.
Diary of the blockage. Gray, A.
Díaz, Jaquira
  Section 8
    The Southern Review (Baton Rouge, La.) v47 no1 p145-55 Wint 2011
Díaz, Junot
  Edison, New Jersey
    Blue collar, white collar, no collar; stories of work; edited by Richard Ford.
  How to date a brown girl (black girl, white girl, or halfie)
    Best of times, worst of times; contemporary American short stories from the new Gilded Age; edited by Wendy Martin and Cecelia Tichi.
Diaz, Natalie
  How to love a woman with no legs
    Best of the West 2010; new stories from the wide side of the Missouri; edited by James Thomas and D. Seth Horton; foreword by Kent Meyers.
Dib, Mohammed
  At the café
    Dib, M. At the café & The talisman; translated by C. Dickson; afterword by Mildred Mortimer.
  The companion
    Dib, M. At the café & The talisman; translated by C. Dickson; afterword by Mildred Mortimer.
  La cuadra
    Dib, M. At the café & The talisman; translated by C. Dickson; afterword by Mildred Mortimer.
  The destination
    Dib, M. At the café & The talisman; translated by C. Dickson; afterword by Mildred Mortimer.
  The enchanted heir
    Dib, M. At the café & The talisman; translated by C. Dickson; afterword by Mildred Mortimer.
  The end
    Dib, M. At the café & The talisman; translated by C. Dickson; afterword by Mildred Mortimer.
  A fine wedding
    Dib, M. At the café & The talisman; translated by C. Dickson; afterword by Mildred Mortimer.
  Forbidden lands
    Dib, M. At the café & The talisman; translated by C. Dickson; afterword by Mildred Mortimer.
  He who bestows all worldly goods
    Dib, M. At the café & The talisman; translated by C. Dickson; afterword by Mildred Mortimer.
  Little Cousin
    Dib, M. At the café & The talisman; translated by C. Dickson; afterword by Mildred Mortimer.

Dib, Mohammed—*Continued*

The long wait

Dib, M. At the café & The talisman; translated by C. Dickson; afterword by Mildred Mortimer.

Naëma disappeared

Dib, M. At the café & The talisman; translated by C. Dickson; afterword by Mildred Mortimer.

The stone inscription

Dib, M. At the café & The talisman; translated by C. Dickson; afterword by Mildred Mortimer.

The talisman

Dib, M. At the café & The talisman; translated by C. Dickson; afterword by Mildred Mortimer.

Though birdsong fills the air

Dib, M. At the café & The talisman; translated by C. Dickson; afterword by Mildred Mortimer.

The traveler

Dib, M. At the café & The talisman; translated by C. Dickson; afterword by Mildred Mortimer.

Dick, Philip K.

Beyond lies the wub

Dick, P. K. The collected stories of Philip K. Dick, volume one: The King of the Elves (1947-1952)

The builder

Dick, P. K. The collected stories of Philip K. Dick, volume one: The King of the Elves (1947-1952)

Colony

Dick, P. K. The collected stories of Philip K. Dick, volume one: The King of the Elves (1947-1952)

The crystal crypt

Dick, P. K. The collected stories of Philip K. Dick, volume one: The King of the Elves (1947-1952)

The defenders

Dick, P. K. The collected stories of Philip K. Dick, volume one: The King of the Elves (1947-1952)

Expendable

Dick, P. K. The collected stories of Philip K. Dick, volume one: The King of the Elves (1947-1952)

The Great C.

Dick, P. K. The collected stories of Philip K. Dick, volume one: The King of the Elves (1947-1952)

The gun

Dick, P. K. The collected stories of Philip K. Dick, volume one: The King of the Elves (1947-1952)

The indefatigable frog

Dick, P. K. The collected stories of Philip K. Dick, volume one: The King of the Elves (1947-1952)

The infinites

Dick, P. K. The collected stories of Philip K. Dick, volume one: The King of the Elves (1947-1952)

The King of the Elves

Dick, P. K. The collected stories of Philip K. Dick, volume one: The King of the Elves (1947-1952)

The little movement

Dick, P. K. The collected stories of Philip K. Dick, volume one: The King of the Elves (1947-1952)

Meddler

Dick, P. K. The collected stories of Philip K. Dick, volume one: The King of the Elves (1947-1952)

Menace react

Dick, P. K. The collected stories of Philip K. Dick, volume one: The King of the Elves (1947-1952)

The monority report

Brave new worlds; edited by John Joseph Adams.

Mr. Spaceship

Dick, P. K. The collected stories of Philip K. Dick, volume one: The King of the Elves (1947-1952)

Nanny

Dick, P. K. The collected stories of Philip K. Dick, volume one: The King of the Elves (1947-1952)

Out in the garden

Dick, P. K. The collected stories of Philip K. Dick, volume one: The King of the Elves (1947-1952)

Paycheck

Dick, P. K. The collected stories of Philip K. Dick, volume one: The King of the Elves (1947-1952)

Piper in the woods

Dick, P. K. The collected stories of Philip K. Dick, volume one: The King of the Elves (1947-1952)

The preserving machine

Dick, P. K. The collected stories of Philip K. Dick, volume one: The King of the Elves (1947-1952)

Prize ship

Dick, P. K. The collected stories of Philip K. Dick, volume one: The King of the Elves (1947-1952)

Roog

Dick, P. K. The collected stories of Philip K. Dick, volume one: The King of the Elves (1947-1952)

The short happy life of the brown oxford

Dick, P. K. The collected stories of Philip K. Dick, volume one: The King of the Elves (1947-1952)

The skull

Dick, P. K. The collected stories of Philip K. Dick, volume one: The King of the Elves (1947-1952)

Stability

Dick, P. K. The collected stories of Philip K. Dick, volume one: The King of the Elves (1947-1952)

The variable man

Dick, P. K. The collected stories of Philip K. Dick, volume one: The King of the Elves (1947-1952)

Dickinson, Helen

(tr.) See Diome, Fatou

DIVORCED PERSONS

Barnes, J. East wind
Baxter, C. Poor devil
Beattie, A. The Cinderella waltz
Beattie, A. Horatio's trick
Beattie, A. A platonic relationship
Beattie, A. Tuesday night
Beattie, A. Wolf dreams
Black, A. That of which we cannot speak
Black, A. We've got a great future behind us
Blake, G. How far are we from the water?
Blatnik, A. Other paths
Boggs, B. It won't be long
Boggs, B. Mattaponi Queen
Buday, G. Retard
Chau, A. Arcade games
Davis, L. The letter
Davis, L. The sock
Dixon, S. What is all this?
Drabble, M. The caves of God
Drabble, M. Homework
Eisenberg, D. Like it or not
Gilley, T. All Hallows' Eve
Gordimer, N. A find
Grodstein, L. Homewrecker
Hampton, E. Mr. Gray
Heathcock, A. Lazarus
Hemmingson, M. Pictures of houses with water
    damage
Hunt, A. Sliabh Ban
'Izz al-Dīn, M. The path to madness
Kim, C.-s. Crimson fruit
Latiolais, M. Burqa
Latiolais, M. The legal case
Leidiger, L. Tell me
Leland, C. T. As if in time of war
Manilla, M. Childproof
Manilla, M. The wife you wanted
McDonald, S. Seven sexy cowboy robots
Nelson, A. Iff
Novack, S. Rilke
Parks, R. The finer points of destruction
Penkov, M. Devshirmeh
Ray, S. The dark between them
Rosenbaum, T. The Yehuda triangle
Self, W. The five-swing wlak
Self, W. Scale
Shapiro, J. Death and disaster
Sneed, C. By the way
Sneed, C. Twelve + Twelve
Trevor, W. On the streets
Trueblood, V. Trespass
Wieland, L. At Wanship
Wieland, M. The bones of hagerman
Willis, M. S. On the road with C. T. Savage
Yiyun Li. Alone
Zeman, A. Daphne, unrequited

DIVORCÉES *See* Divorced persons
DIVORCÉS *See* Divorced persons

Dixon, Stephen

An accurate acount
    Dixon, S. What is all this?; uncollected stories

The argument
    Dixon, S. What is all this?; uncollected stories

Ass
    Dixon, S. What is all this?; uncollected stories

The baby
    Dixon, S. What is all this?; uncollected stories

Biff
    Dixon, S. What is all this?; uncollected stories

Burglars
    Dixon, S. What is all this?; uncollected stories

The busses
    Dixon, S. What is all this?; uncollected stories

Can't win
    Dixon, S. What is all this?; uncollected stories

China
    Dixon, S. What is all this?; uncollected stories

The chocolate sampler
    Dixon, S. What is all this?; uncollected stories

The cleanup man
    Dixon, S. What is all this?; uncollected stories

Contac
    Dixon, S. What is all this?; uncollected stories

Dawn
    Dixon, S. What is all this?; uncollected stories

Dream
    Dixon, S. What is all this?; uncollected stories

End of a friend
    Dixon, S. What is all this?; uncollected stories

Ends
    Dixon, S. What is all this?; uncollected stories

Evening
    Dixon, S. What is all this?; uncollected stories

Fired
    Dixon, S. What is all this?; uncollected stories

For a quiet English Sunday
    Dixon, S. What is all this?; uncollected stories

Getting lost
    Dixon, S. What is all this?; uncollected stories

The good fellow
    Dixon, S. What is all this?; uncollected stories

Green pea eater
    Dixon, S. What is all this?; uncollected stories

A home away from home
    Dixon, S. What is all this?; uncollected stories

In memoriam
    Dixon, S. What is all this?; uncollected stories

Interest
    Dixon, S. What is all this?; uncollected stories

Jackie
    Dixon, S. What is all this?; uncollected stories

Dixon, Stephen—*Continued*

The killer
  Dixon, S. What is all this?; uncollected stories
Knock knock
  Dixon, S. What is all this?; uncollected stories
The leader
  Dixon, S. What is all this?; uncollected stories
Leaves
  Dixon, S. What is all this?; uncollected stories
Long made short
  Dixon, S. What is all this?; uncollected stories
Meet the natives
  Dixon, S. What is all this?; uncollected stories
Mr. Greene
  Dixon, S. What is all this?; uncollected stories
The neighbors
  Dixon, S. What is all this?; uncollected stories
Next to nothing
  Dixon, S. What is all this?; uncollected stories
Night
  Dixon, S. What is all this?; uncollected stories
No knocks
  Dixon, S. What is all this?; uncollected stories
Nothing new
  Dixon, S. What is all this?; uncollected stories
One thing
  Dixon, S. What is all this?; uncollected stories
An outing
  Dixon, S. What is all this?; uncollected stories
Overtime
  Dixon, S. What is all this?; uncollected stories
P
  Dixon, S. What is all this?; uncollected stories
Pale cheeks of a butcher's boy
  Dixon, S. What is all this?; uncollected stories
The phone
  Dixon, S. What is all this?; uncollected stories
Piers
  Dixon, S. What is all this?; uncollected stories
Produce
  Dixon, S. What is all this?; uncollected stories
Question
  Dixon, S. What is all this?; uncollected stories
Reinsertion
  Dixon, S. What is all this?; uncollected stories

Sex
  Dixon, S. What is all this?; uncollected stories
She
  Dixon, S. What is all this?; uncollected stories
Shoelaces
  Dixon, S. What is all this?; uncollected stories
Starting again
  Dixon, S. What is all this?; uncollected stories
Stories
  Dixon, S. What is all this?; uncollected stories
Storm
  Dixon, S. What is all this?; uncollected stories
The talk show
  Dixon, S. What is all this?; uncollected stories
Up and down the Drosselgasse
  Dixon, S. What is all this?; uncollected stories
Walt
  Dixon, S. What is all this?; uncollected stories
What is all this?
  Dixon, S. What is all this?; uncollected stories
Who he?
  Dixon, S. What is all this?; uncollected stories
The wild bird reserve
  Dixon, S. What is all this?; uncollected stories
Yo-yo
  Dixon, S. What is all this?; uncollected stories
The young man who read brilliant books
  Dixon, S. What is all this?; uncollected stories

DIY. Baker, D.
DNA Smackdown. Castle, S.
Do it quickly, she said,. Blatnik, A.
Do not concern yourself with things Lee Nading has left out. Roberge, R.
Do Over. Crone, M.
Do You Know Meier? Walser, R.
Do you suppose it's the east winds? Fatima, A.
Dobozy, Tamas
The restoration of the villa where Tibor Kalman once lived
  The Pen/O.Henry Prize stories 2011; chosen and with an introduction by Laura Furman; with essays on the stories thety admire most by jurors A. M. Homes, Manuel Muñoz, Christine Schutt
The **doctor**. Goodberg, D.
Doctor Nine. Maberry, J.
Doctor Sot. Barry, K.
Doctor theatre. Brett, S.
Doctorow, Cory
Chicken little
  The Year's best science fiction: twenty-eighth annual collection; edited by Gardner Dozois.

Doctorow, Cory—*Continued*
  Craphound
    Before they were giants; edited by James L.
      Sutter; cover illustration by Kieran Yanner.
  The Jammie Dodgers and the adventure of the
      Leicester Square screening
    The Best science fiction and fantasy of the
      year: volume five; edited by Jonathan
      Strahan.
  Makers [excerpt]
    Future media; [edited by Rick Wilber]
  Martian chronicles
    Life on Mars: tales from the new frontier; an
      original science fiction anthology; edited by
      Jonathan Strahan
  Shannon's law
    Welcome to Bordertown; new stories and po-
      ems of the Borderlands; edited by Holly
      Black and Ellen Kushner; introduction by
      Terri Windling.
  The things that make me weak and strange get
      engineered away
    Brave new worlds; edited by John Joseph Ad-
      ams.
Doctorow, E. L.
  All the time in the world
    Doctorow, E. L. All the time in the world;
      new and selected stories
  Assimilation
    Doctorow, E. L. All the time in the world;
      new and selected stories
    The New Yorker v86 no37 p116-18, 119-25 N
      22 2010
  Edgemont Drive
    Doctorow, E. L. All the time in the world;
      new and selected stories
  Heist
    Doctorow, E. L. All the time in the world;
      new and selected stories
  A house on the plains
    Doctorow, E. L. All the time in the world;
      new and selected stories
  The hunter
    Doctorow, E. L. All the time in the world;
      new and selected stories
  Jolene: a life
    Doctorow, E. L. All the time in the world;
      new and selected stories
  Liner notes: the songs of Billy Bathgate
    Doctorow, E. L. All the time in the world;
      new and selected stories
  Wakefield
    Doctorow, E. L. All the time in the world;
      new and selected stories
  Walter John Harmon
    Doctorow, E. L. All the time in the world;
      new and selected stories
  Willi
    Doctorow, E. L. All the time in the world;
      new and selected stories
  The writer in the family
    Doctorow, E. L. All the time in the world;
      new and selected stories
DOCTORS *See* Physicians; Women physicians
DOCUMENTS *See* Manuscripts

Dodson, Zach
  I write to you of this
    Butler, B. 30 under 30; an anthology of inno-
      vative fiction by younger writers; Blake
      Butler & Lily Hoang, eds.
Doe a deer. Stefan, V.
Doenges, Judy
  Melinda
    The Pen/O.Henry Prize stories 2011; chosen
      and with an introduction by Laura Furman;
      with essays on the stories thety admire
      most by jurors A. M. Homes, Manuel Mu-
      ñoz, Christine Schutt
  Best of the West 2011; new stories from the
      wild side of the Missouri; edited by James
      Thomas and D. Seth Horton; foreword by
      Ana Castillo.
Doerr, Anthony
  The river nemunas
    Pushcart Prize XXXV: best of the small
      presses 2011; edited by Bill Henderson
      with the Pushcart Prize editors.
The **dog**. Doyle, R.
The **dog**. Grossman, V. S.
Dog. Ruocco, J.
Dog and me. Davis, L.
Dog bites. Nuila, R.
The **Dog** Dies. Reece, B.
Dog is dead. Emshwiller, C.
The **dog** prince. Prineas, S.
A **dog** story. Schappell, E.
DOGFIGHTING
  Bill, F. Crimes in southern Indiana
  Waite, U. Don't look away
DOGS
  Adrian, C. The black square
  Beattie, A. Distant music
  Bengal, R. Captioning for the blind
  Berry, J. Twenty-eight scenes for neglected
      guests
  Bill, F. A coon hunter's noir
  Black, T. Hound of Culann
  Bradbury, R. The emissary
  Bradley, G. An East Egg update
  Chekhov, A. P. Kashtanka
  Chesterton, G. K. The oracle of the dog
  Cooper, B. My father's singularity
  Davis, R. H. The bar sinister
  Dick, P. K. Roog
  Doyle, R. Animals
  Doyle, R. The dog
  Drakulic, S. An interview with the oldest dog in
      Bucharest
  Emshwiller, C. Pelt
  Farmer, P. J. Cats, dogs, and other creatures
  Ginsberg, D. The new girl
  Gold, H. L. A matter of form
  Grossman, V. S. The dog
  Harte, B. A yellow dog
  Havazelet, E. Gurov in Manhattan
  Henry, O. Memoirs of a yellow dog
  Highsmith, P. There I was, struck with Bubsy
  Horrocks, C. Steal small
  Hunter, L. The fence
  Jones, G. A. One of Sandy's dreams
  Jones, S. G. Monsters
  Kennedy, A. L. Whole family with young chil-
      dren devastated
  Kipling, R. Garm - a hostage

Dowling, Terry—*Continued*

He tried to catch the light
  Dowling, T. Amberjack; tales of fear and wonder

Jarkman at the othergates
  Dowling, T. Amberjack; tales of fear and wonder

The lagan fishers
  Dowling, T. Amberjack; tales of fear and wonder

The library
  Dowling, T. Amberjack; tales of fear and wonder

The magikkers
  Dowling, T. Amberjack; tales of fear and wonder

The shaddowwes box
  Ghosts by gaslight; stories of steampunk and supernatural suspense; [edited by] Jack Dann [and] Nick Gevers

Some roses for the bonestell man
  Dowling, T. Amberjack; tales of fear and wonder

The suits at Auderlene
  Dowling, T. Amberjack; tales of fear and wonder

Toother
  Dowling, T. Amberjack; tales of fear and wonder

Truth window: a tale of the bedlam rose
  Dowling, T. Amberjack; tales of fear and wonder

The view in Nancy's window
  Dowling, T. Amberjack; tales of fear and wonder

Down in the black gang. Farmer, P. J.

Down the quiet street. Mphahlele, E.

Down Time. Sonde, S.

Downey, Garbhan

First to score
  Requiems for the departed; edited by Gerard Brennan & Mike Stone.

Downey, Ryan

The world, the words, this man
  Butler, B. 30 under 30; an anthology of innovative fiction by younger writers; Blake Butler & Lily Hoang, eds.

Downhill. Beattie, A.

Downs, Michael

The Greatest Show
  New Letters v76 no3 p9-30 2010

History Class
  The Kenyon Review v33 no1 p73-85 Wint 2011

DOWN'S SYNDROME

Pearlman, E. Inbound

Downstream. Scott, J.

Downum, Amanda

Blue valentine
  End of an Aeon; edited by Bridgett McKenna & Marti McKenna

DOWRY *See* Marriage customs

DOYLE, SIR ARTHUR CONAN, 1859-1930
Parodies, imitations, etc.

Anderson, P. The adventure of the misplaced hound

Faye, L. The case of Colonel Warburton's madness

Linscott, G. The case of Colonel Crockett's violin

Nikitin, P. The strangler

Nolan, W. F. The death of Sherlock Holmes

Riccardi, T. An affair in Ravello

Riccardi, T. A case of criminal madness

Riccardi, T. The case of Isadora Persano

Riccardi, T. The case of the missing lodger

Riccardi, T. The case of the plangent colonel

Riccardi, T. The case of the two Bohemes

Riccardi, T. The case of the vermillion face

Riccardi, T. The death of Mycroft Holmes

Riccardi, T. The mountain of fear

Riccardi, T. Porlock's demise

Riccardi, T. A singular event in Tranquebar

Thomas, D. The case of a boy's honour

Thomas, D. The case of the ghosts at Bly

Thomas, D. The case of the matinee idol

Thomas, D. Sherlock Holmes the actor

Turtledove, H. The scarlet band

Doyle, Brian

King of the Losers
  New Letters v76 no4 p40-9 2010

Doyle, Conan *See* Doyle, Sir Arthur Conan, 1859-1930

Doyle, Roddy

Animals
  Doyle, R. Bullfighting and other stories

Ash
  Doyle, R. Bullfighting and other stories

Blood
  Doyle, R. Bullfighting and other stories

Bullfighting
  Doyle, R. Bullfighting and other stories

The dog
  Doyle, R. Bullfighting and other stories

Funerals
  Doyle, R. Bullfighting and other stories

The joke
  Doyle, R. Bullfighting and other stories

The photograph
  Doyle, R. Bullfighting and other stories

The plate
  Doyle, R. Bullfighting and other stories

The pram
  The Granta book of the Irish short story; [edited by] Anne Enright.

Recuperation
  Doyle, R. Bullfighting and other stories

The slave
  Doyle, R. Bullfighting and other stories

Sleep
  Doyle, R. Bullfighting and other stories

Teaching
  Doyle, R. Bullfighting and other stories

Dozois, Gardner R.

A cat horror story.
  Dozois, G. R. When the great days come; [by] Gardner Dozois

Chains of the sea
  Dozois, G. R. When the great days come; [by] Gardner Dozois

Community
  Dozois, G. R. When the great days come; [by] Gardner Dozois

Counterfactual
  Dozois, G. R. When the great days come; [by] Gardner Dozois

Dozois, Gardner R.—*Continued*

Dinner party
    Dozois, G. R. When the great days come; [by] Gardner Dozois
Disciples
    Dozois, G. R. When the great days come; [by] Gardner Dozois
A dream at noonday
    Dozois, G. R. When the great days come; [by] Gardner Dozois
Fairy tale
    Dozois, G. R. When the great days come; [by] Gardner Dozois
The hanging curve
    Dozois, G. R. When the great days come; [by] Gardner Dozois
A kingdom by the sea
    Dozois, G. R. When the great days come; [by] Gardner Dozois
A knight of ghosts and shadows
    Dozois, G. R. When the great days come; [by] Gardner Dozois
Morning child
    Dozois, G. R. When the great days come; [by] Gardner Dozois
The peacemaker
    Dozois, G. R. When the great days come; [by] Gardner Dozois
Recidivist
    Dozois, G. R. When the great days come; [by] Gardner Dozois
Solace
    Dozois, G. R. When the great days come; [by] Gardner Dozois
A special kind of morning
    Dozois, G. R. When the great days come; [by] Gardner Dozois
When the great days come
    Dozois, G. R. When the great days come; [by] Gardner Dozois

Dozois, Gardner R. and Swanwick, Michael

Ancestral voices
    Dozois, G. R. When the great days come; [by] Gardner Dozois

Dr. Johnson's daughter. Villegas, H.

Dr. Lash remembers. Ford, J.

Dr. Pi, Elena, and the glitch. Bayley, E.

Dr. Time. Snyder, M. V.

Drabble, Margaret

The caves of God
    Drabble, M. A day in the life of a smiling woman; complete short stories; edited by José Francisco Fernández
Crossing the Alps
    Drabble, M. A day in the life of a smiling woman; complete short stories; edited by José Francisco Fernández
A day in the life of a smiling woman
    Drabble, M. A day in the life of a smiling woman; complete short stories; edited by José Francisco Fernández
The dower house at Kellynch: a Somerset romance
    Drabble, M. A day in the life of a smiling woman; complete short stories; edited by José Francisco Fernández

Faithful lovers
    Drabble, M. A day in the life of a smiling woman; complete short stories; edited by José Francisco Fernández
The gifts of war
    Drabble, M. A day in the life of a smiling woman; complete short stories; edited by José Francisco Fernández
Hassan's tower
    Drabble, M. A day in the life of a smiling woman; complete short stories; edited by José Francisco Fernández
Homework
    Drabble, M. A day in the life of a smiling woman; complete short stories; edited by José Francisco Fernández
Les liaisons dangereuses
    Drabble, M. A day in the life of a smiling woman; complete short stories; edited by José Francisco Fernández
The merry widow
    Drabble, M. A day in the life of a smiling woman; complete short stories; edited by José Francisco Fernández
A Pyrrhic victory
    Drabble, M. A day in the life of a smiling woman; complete short stories; edited by José Francisco Fernández
Stepping westward: a topographical tale
    Drabble, M. A day in the life of a smiling woman; complete short stories; edited by José Francisco Fernández
A success story
    Drabble, M. A day in the life of a smiling woman; complete short stories; edited by José Francisco Fernández
A voyage to Cythera
    Drabble, M. A day in the life of a smiling woman; complete short stories; edited by José Francisco Fernández

Draculalucard. Emshwiller, C.

Dragged fighting from his tomb. Hannah, B.

Dragon Money. Conley, C.

DRAGONS

Beagle, P. S. Oakland dragon blues
Lanagan, M. The miracle aquilina
Yolen, J. and Stemple, A. The tsar's dragon

Drakulic, Slavenka

The bear and the princess of light
    Drakulić, S. A guided tour through the museum of communism; fables from a mouse, a parrot, a bear, a cat, a mole, a pig, a dog, and a raven
The cat-keeper in Warsaw (Letter to the state prosecutor)
    Drakulić, S. A guided tour through the museum of communism; fables from a mouse, a parrot, a bear, a cat, a mole, a pig, a dog, and a raven
A communist with style
    Drakulić, S. A guided tour through the museum of communism; fables from a mouse, a parrot, a bear, a cat, a mole, a pig, a dog, and a raven

Drakulic, Slavenka—*Continued*

From gulag to goulash: the introduction to Ms. Piggy's Hungarian cookbook

Drakulić, S. A guided tour through the museum of communism; fables from a mouse, a parrot, a bear, a cat, a mole, a pig, a dog, and a raven

A guided tour through the museum of communism

Drakulić, S. A guided tour through the museum of communism; fables from a mouse, a parrot, a bear, a cat, a mole, a pig, a dog, and a raven

An interview with the oldest dog in Bucharest

Drakulić, S. A guided tour through the museum of communism; fables from a mouse, a parrot, a bear, a cat, a mole, a pig, a dog, and a raven

The legend of the Berlin Wall–as presented by a mole

Drakulić, S. A guided tour through the museum of communism; fables from a mouse, a parrot, a bear, a cat, a mole, a pig, a dog, and a raven

The unusual case of the psychotic raven

Drakulić, S. A guided tour through the museum of communism; fables from a mouse, a parrot, a bear, a cat, a mole, a pig, a dog, and a raven

DRAMA CRITICS

Wells, H. G. The sad story of a dramatic critic

DRAMATISTS

Bingham, S. Seagull

Senna, D. Admission

DRAWING

Hodge, B. Just outside our windows, deep inside our walls

The **dreadful** mucamas. Davis, L.

Dream. Dixon, S.

The **Dream**. Heynen, J.

A **dream**. Phan, N. T.

A **dream** at noonday. Dozois, G. R.

Dream date. McGarry, J.

Dream diary. Candida, M.

Dream fishing. Ely, S.

Dream girl. Kishore, S.

A **dream** of Armageddon. Wells, H. G.

Dream spot. Woodrell, D.

The **dreamer** from Ostend. Schmitt, E.-E.

Dreaming of the dead. Gordimer, N.

DREAMS

Baumer, J. R. The forever sleep

Bierce, A. The death of Halpin Frayser

Bowes, R. I needs must part, the policeman said

Brennan, M. An attack of hunger

Candida, M. Dream diary

Dixon, S. Dream

Dixon, S. Mr. Greene

Emshwiller, C. Nightmare call

Gifford, B. In the land of the dead

Gifford, B. Last plane out of Chungking

Gordimer, N. Dreaming of the dead

Goss, T. Christopher Raven

Harland, R. Bad thoughts and the mechanism

Hossein, R. S. The sultana's dream

Hunter, L. Loofah

Matheson, R. He wanted to live

Nagai, M. Drowning land

Sa'id, M. A. Devouring: a very short story

Sands, B. Abridged version

Sands, B. Becoming lucid

Silverberg, R. Gate of horn, gate of ivory

Sturgeon, T. The professor's teddy bear

Thurber, J. The secret life of Walter Mitty

Trueblood, V. Choice in dreams

Twain, M. A curious dream

Villegas, H. In the grass

Wells, H. G. The devotee of art

Wells, H. G. A dream of Armageddon

Dredge. Bell, M.

The **dredgeman's** revelation. Russell, K.

Drees, Charlie

By hook or by crook

By hook or by crook and 27 more of the best crime + mystery stories of the year; edited by Ed Gorman and Martin H. Greenberg.

DREHER, PETER, 1932-

About

Tillman, L. Impressions of an artist, with Haiku

DREIDEL (GAME)

Prindle, J. Einstein's dreidel

DRESDEN (GERMANY) *See* Germany—Dresden

Dress Up. McDowell, D.

Dresser, Davis *See* Halliday, Brett, 1904-1977

DRESSMAKERS

Rodoreda, M. Threaded needle

The **dressmaker's** child. Trevor, W.

Driscoll, David

Clarity

TriQuarterly v138 48679 bytes Summ/Fall 2010

Driscoll, Jack

That Story

The Georgia Review v64 no4 p690-702 Wint 2010

Wanting Only to Be Heard

The Georgia Review v65 no1 p92-103 Spr 2011

Drive. Gwyn, A.

Drive-through hosue. Slavin, J.

DRIVING

Burke, D. Beaverland

Gwyn, A. Drive

Driving lessons. Mullins, D. P.

Drop dead twice. Searls, H.

Drought. Spafford, R.

DROUGHTS

Ely, S. Lovers of hurricanes

Phillips, H. The droughts

The **droughts**. Phillips, H.

The **Drowned** Man at Sanderlings. Freeman, C.

DROWNING

Banville, J. Summer voices

Bingham, S. The banks of the Ohio

Bradbury, R. The lake

Chuculate, E. D. Winter, 1979

Cook, T. H. Nevermore

Gorman, E. The baby store

Guo Xiaolu. An Internet baby

Oates, J. C. The Spill

Obreht, T. Blue water djinn

Ray, S. Rodin's hand of god

Rodoreda, M. Friday, June 8

Solomon, A. Secret pool

Willis, M. S. On the road with C. T. Savage

Drowning land. Nagai, M.

DRUG ABUSE
> *See also* Drugs; Marijuana

Eisenberg, D. Presents
Hannah, B. Coming close to Donna
Robinson, K. S. In Pierson's orchestra

DRUG ADDICTION
Eisenberg, D. Rosie gets a soul
Gautier, A. Pan is dead
Gorman, E. Such a good girl
Hannah, B. Two things, dimly, were going at each other
Schappell, E. Out of the blue and into the black
Self, W. Scale
Thon, M. R. Home
Thon, M. R. Xmas, Jamaica Plain

DRUG ADDICTS
Arsenijević, V. One minute: Dumbo's death
Bill, F. Amphetamine twitch
Galchen, R. Wild berry blue
Gautier, A. Some other kind of happiness
Hemmingson, M. Fishpole Pete
Jha, R. How I lost my clothes
Romo, I. Crank
Self, W. Birdy num num
Simms, C. Tick-tock
Tremblay, P. Headstone in your pocket

DRUG INDUSTRY *See* Drug trade

DRUG TRADE
LaSalle, P. Lunch across the bridge
Roberge, R. Whatever happened to Billy Brody?

DRUG TRAFFIC
Atta, S. Last trip
Boggs, B. Homecoming
Child, L. Addicted to sweetness
DuBois, B. The cask of Castle Island
Margolin, P. The house on Pine Terrace
Moore, T. A. Red milk
Self, W. The Nonce prize
Self, W. The rock of crack as big as the Ritz

DRUGGISTS *See* Pharmacists

DRUGS
> *See also* Drug addiction; Drug traffic

Barillas, G. R. The roads
Bell, M. S. Twenty dollars
Bill, F. Crimes in southern Indiana
Bill, F. Hill clan cross
Bill, F. Officer down (tweakers)
Clayton, L. Overlocked
Doenges, J. Melinda
Egan, J. Out of body
Fenn, J. Twilight at the change house
Finney, E. J. Sequoia Gardens
Ford, J. The summer palace
Franco, J. Jack-O'
Lahens, Y. Who is that man?
Lippman, L. Cougar
MacLean, A. MacHinery and the cauliflowers
McMillian, R. Escambia counties
Murphy, B. Who do I have to kill to get a little respect up in here?
Nesbit, E. The five senses
Saunders, G. Escape from Spiderhead
Silverberg, R. A thousand paces along the Via Dolorosa
Smith, C. A. Double cosmos
Solomon, A. Secret pool
Thompson, N. The children of gear
Urrea, L. A. Amapola
Wells, H. G. The new accelerator

Woodrell, D. Twin Forks

DRUGSTORES *See* Pharmacists

DRUIDS AND DRUIDISM
Bailie, T. The druid's dance
The **druid's** dance. Bailie, T.
Drum machine. Lindholm, M.
Drummer down. Hannah, B.

DRUMMERS
Hannah, B. Testimony of pilot
Drummond & son. D'Ambrosio, C., Jr.

DRUNKARDS
> *See also* Alcoholism

Baxter, C. Winter journey
Hannah, B. Ride, fly, penetrate, loiter
Wells, H. G. Mr. Marshall's doppelganger

DRUNKENNESS
Abasiyanik, S. F. Such a story
Black, H. The coldest girl in Coldtown
Blatnik, A. Was I?
Chuculate, E. D. Winter, 1979
Comeau, J. Giraffes and everything
Dib, M. He who bestows all worldly goods
Dixon, S. Up and down the Drosselgasse
Franco, J. April in three parts: part 1, The rainbow goblins
Franco, J. Halloween
Franco, J. Tar baby
Greenland, S. Bad night in Hyannisport
Horrocks, C. Going to Estonia
Hunter, L. Love song
Novack, S. A good woman's love
Nutting, A. Alcoholic
Pushkin, A. I. The coffin-maker
Simmons, D. In the garden
Smith, C. A. Strange shadows
Staun, S. All I want is my baby, woah woah, woah woah woah woah
Thon, M. R. Father, lover, deadman, dreamer
Treadway, J. Shirley wants her nickel back

DRUZES
Rakha, Y. Suicide 20, or the Hakimi Maqama

DUAL PERSONALITY
> *See also* Multiple personality; Personality disorders

The **dualist**. Hughes, V. A.
Duarte. Shepard, S.
Dubé, Peter
Echo
> Life as we show it; writing on film; co-edited by Masha Tupitsyn & Brian Pera; introduction by Masha Tupitsyn

DUBLIN (IRELAND) *See* Ireland—Dublin

DuBois, Brendan
The cask of Castle Island
> On a raven's wing; new tales in honor of Edgar Allan Poe; edited by Stuart M. Kaminsky
The dark island
> By hook or by crook and 27 more of the best crime + mystery stories of the year; edited by Ed Gorman and Martin H. Greenberg.
The necessary brother
> The Shamus winners: America's best private eye stories, volume I: 1982-1995; collected and introduced by Robert J. Randisi; founder, Private Eye Writers of America

DuBois, Brendan—*Continued*
The road's end
Randisi, R. J. The Shamus winners: America's best private eye stories, volume II, 1996-2009; collected and introduced by Robert J. Randisi; founder, Private Eye Writers of America

duBois, Jennifer
Wolf
The Kenyon Review v33 no3 p90-103 Summ 2011

Dubus, Andre
All the time in the world
I found this funny; my favorite pieces of humor and some that may not be funny at all; edited by Judd Apatow.
Delivering
Blue collar, white collar, no collar; stories of work; edited by Richard Ford.

The **duck**. Loory, B.
Duck. Vukcevich, R.
Ducker, Matthew
The Wilderness
Five Points v13 no1 p143-55 2009
DUCKS
Dick, P. K. Out in the garden
Loory, B. The duck
Ducks in a row. Monk, D.
Duckweed. Wier, G.
Ducornet, Rikki
The Dickmare
Fantastic women; 18 tales of the surreal and the sublime from Tin House; introduction by Joy Williams; edited by Rob Spillman.

Due, Tananarive
The lake
The monster's corner; stories through inhuman eyes; edited by Christopher Golden
Duffy, Steve
Certain death for a known person
The Year's best dark fantasy & horror; edited by Paula Guran
Lie, still, sleep becalmed
Zombies: the recent dead; edited by Paula Guran.
X for Demetrious
Blood and other cravings; edited by Ellen Datlow.
Dufresne, John
The cross-eyed bear
The Best American mystery stories 2010; edited and with an introduction by Lee Child; Otto Penzler, series editor
Iffy
Florida heat wave; [edited and with an] introduction by Michael Lister.
Duke of Earl. Shepard, S.
The **duke** of Riverside. Kushner, E.
Dukes and Duchesses of Park Ridge. Stansel, I.
Dulac, Brian
A Final Brooklyn
The Massachusetts Review v52 no1 p101-4 Spr 2011
Dulioto. Bayley, E.
Dunbar-Nelson, Alice Moore
A carnival jangle
The vintage book of American women writers; edited and with an introduction by Elaine Showalter.

Duncan, Andy
Beluthahatchie
Sympathy for the devil; edited by Tim Pratt
Zora and the zombie
Zombies: the recent dead; edited by Paula Guran.
Duncan, Hal
The death of a love
Speculative Horizons; edited by Patrick St-Denis.
DUNES *See* Sand dunes
The **Dungeon** Master. Lipsyte, S.
The **dungeon** out of time. Ciechanowski, W.
Dunmore, Helen
Where I keep my faith
Freedom; stories celebrating the Universal Declaration of Human Rights; Amnesty International.
Durango, Mexico. Shepard, S.
During the war. Monzó, Q.
Dusi. Monk, D.
Dust. Sprenger, S.
Dust catchers. Packer, N. H.
Dust devil. Pickard, N.
DUTCH
United States
Salter, J. Foreign shores
Dwarf house. Beattie, A.
DWARFS
Beattie, A. Dwarf house
Campbell-Such, J. The Napoleon difference
Hart, R. G. My partner the zombie
Oliver, R. Baskervilles midgets
Shapiro, J. Small
Verbeke, A. Love, hope and dwarfs
Wagner, W. N. The secret of calling rabbits
Wells, H. G. Our little neighbour
Dwell time. Packer, A.
Dwyer, Jaclyn
Biography of a porn star in three parts
Butler, B. 30 under 30; an anthology of innovative fiction by younger writers; Blake Butler & Lily Hoang, eds.
The **dybbuk** in love. Taaffe, S.
Dybek, Stuart
Here comes the sun
Iowa Review v41 no1 p82-3 Spr 2011
Sauerkraut soup
Blue collar, white collar, no collar; stories of work; edited by Richard Ford.
Dying in the post-war world. Collins, M. A.
Dying Is All I Think About. Nutting, A.
Džamonja, Dario
The Bridge Named Desire
The Massachusetts Review v51 no3 p541-4 Aut 2010

E

EAR
Vukcevich, R. My eyes, your ears
Earley, Tony
Mr. Tall
Pushcart Prize XXXV: best of the small presses 2011; edited by Bill Henderson with the Pushcart Prize editors.
An **early** Christmas. Allyn, D.
The **early** crossing. Jones, G. A.

Ears. Levine, S.
EARTH
  Helfers, J. Afterword
  Niven, L. Inconstant moon
EARTH, DESTRUCTION OF
  Clarke, A. C. "If I forget thee, oh Earth . . ."
  Farmer, P. J. Toward the beloved city
  Silverberg, R. When we went to see the end of
    the world
The **earth** slept: a vision. Knapp, A.
Earthquake. Roberge, R.
EARTHQUAKES
      See also Disasters
  Gilley, T. Physical wisdom
  Orozco, D. Shakers
  Roberge, R. Earthquake
  Silverberg, R. Waiting for the earthquake
  Sylvain, P. Odette
  Zoboi, I. A. The harem
The **ease** of living. Gautier, A.
East, Elyssa
  Second chance
    Cape Cod noir; edited by David L. Ulin.
EAST AND WEST
  Mu Xin. Halo
An **East** Egg update. Bradley, G.
EAST INDIANS
              England
  Chaudhuri, A. Aniruddha: the latest installment
  Naipaul, V. S. Tell me who to kill
              South Africa
  Gordimer, N. A chip of glass ruby
              Trinidad and Tobago
  Naipaul, V. S. The mechanical genius
              United States
  Lahiri, J. Gogol
  Mehta, R. A better life
  Mehta, R. Citizen
  Naipaul, V. S. One out of many
East of the West. Penkov, M.
EAST SIDE, LOWER (NEW YORK, N.Y.) *See*
      New York (N.Y.)—Lower East Side
East wind. Barnes, J.
The **Eastern** succession. Jones, G. A.
Easy. Burch, B.
Easy love. Somerville, P.
Easy money. Boland, J. C.
Eat, drink and be wary. Bradbury, R.
Eating and drinking salesman. Qiu Xiaolong
Eating potato salad on the lawn of the damned.
    Starkey, L.
Eaton, Edith Maude *See* Sui Sin Far, 1865-1914
EAVESDROPPING
  O'Brien, E. Sinners
Ebenbach, David Harris
  Counterfactual
    Agni no73 p82-4 2011
  The Guy We Didn't Invite to the Orgy
    Iowa Review v40 no2 p149-51 Fall 2010
ECCENTRICS AND ECCENTRICITIES
      See also Recluses
  Baxter, C. Gryphon
  Blanchard, J. Cinema verite
  Cooke, R. T. Odd Miss Todd
  Davis, L. Alvin the typesetter
  Hannah, B. Scandale d'estime
  Naipaul, V. S. Man-man
  Reed, K. Weston walks
  Roden, B. The brink of eternity

  Schmitt, E.-E. The dreamer from Ostend
Echidna Dreaming [Retold by R. Bodsworth]
    Kneebone, E. and Bodsworth, R.
Echo. Dubé, P.
The **echo** and the nemesis. Stafford, J.
The **echo** of neighborly bones. Woodrell, D.
Eck, Matthew
  Fucking the Mermaid
    The Massachusetts Review v51 no4 p730-7
    Wint 2010
Eclipse. Emshwiller, C.
Economics. Kyle, A.
Ecorcheville. Châteaureynaud, G. O.
Ed Luby's key club. Vonnegut, K.
Edelman, Scott
  The human race
    Z: zombie stories; edited by J. M. Lassen
  The last supper
    Zombies: the recent dead; edited by Paula
    Guran.
EDEN
  O'Connor, S. The professor of atheism: Paradise
  Wells, H. G. The apple
Edge, T. D.
  Repairs
    End of an Aeon; edited by Bridgett McKenna
    & Marti McKenna
Edgemont Drive. Doctorow, E. L.
EDINBURGH (SCOTLAND) *See* Scotland—Ed-
    inburgh
Edinburgh. Kennedy, A. L.
Edison, New Jersey. Díaz, J.
EDITORS
      See also Journalists
  Eugenides, J. Great experiment
  Pearlman, E. Fidelity
  Senna, D. There, there
EDUCATION
      See also Books and reading; Teachers
  Beah, I. ABC antidote
  Williams, T. A short history of Dunkelblau's
    Meistergarten
An **education** for the ages. Goodberg, D.
EDUCATORS *See* Teachers
Edward Bear and the very long walk. Scholes, K.
Edwards, Martin
  Clutter
    Original sins; a Crime Writer's Association
    anthology; edited by Martin Edwards.
Edwards, Melodie
  The Bird Lady
    Prairie Schooner v85 no2 p83-6 Summ 2011
Edwards, Sarah L.
  If we shadows have offended
    End of an Aeon; edited by Bridgett McKenna
    & Marti McKenna
The **effects** of good government on the city. Ken-
    nedy, A. L.
Egan, Jennifer
  Out of body
    The Best American short stories, 2011; select-
    ed from U.S. and Canadian magazines by
    Geraldine Brooks with Heidi Pitlor; with an
    introduction by Geraldine Brooks.
Eggers, Dave
  Your mother and I
    I found this funny; my favorite pieces of hu-
    mor and some that may not be funny at all;
    edited by Judd Apatow.

Eggers, Dave—*Continued*

Best of times, worst of times; contemporary American short stories from the new Gilded Age; edited by Wendy Martin and Cecelia Tichi.

Ego. Solzhenitsyn, A.

EGYPT

Ḥaqqī, Y. The first lesson

Howard, R. E. Hawks over Egypt

Maḥfūẓ, N. The seventh heaven

Mamatas, N. Summon, bind, banish

To 640

Smith, P. A. The perils of twilight

Cairo

Idris, Y. The aorta

Rakha, Y. Suicide 20, or the Hakimi Maqama

Egyptomania. McOmber, A.

Ehrenreich, Ben

Everything you see is real

Best of the West 2010; new stories from the wide side of the Missouri; edited by James Thomas and D. Seth Horton; foreword by Kent Meyers.

Eidus, Janice

A bisel this, a bisel that

Promised lands; new Jewish American fiction on longing and belonging; edited by Derek Rubin.

Eight Mile & Dequindre. Estleman, L. D.

Eight Mile and Dequindre. Estleman, L. D.

Eight years later. Grotefeld, E.

Eighteen passengers on a bus. Mu Xin

The **eighth** voyage of Sinbad. Millhauser, S.

EINSTEIN, ALBERT, 1879-1955

About

Prindle, J. Einstein's compass

Prindle, J. Einstein's cross

Prindle, J. Einstein's dreidel

Prindle, J. Einstein's proof

Prindle, J. Einstein's socks

Prindle, J. Einstein's tears

Prindle, J. Einstein's violin

Ryman, G. No bad thing

Einstein's compass. Prindle, J.

Einstein's cross. Prindle, J.

Einstein's dreidel. Prindle, J.

Einstein's proof. Prindle, J.

Einstein's socks. Prindle, J.

Einstein's son. Gifford, B.

Einstein's tears. Prindle, J.

Einstein's violin. Prindle, J.

Einstein's watch. Prindle, J.

Eiríksdóttir, Kristín

Holes in people

Best European fiction 2011; edited by Aleksandr Hemon; preface by Colum McCann

Eisenberg, Deborah

Across the lake

Eisenberg, D. The collected stories of Deborah Eisenberg

All around Atlantis

Eisenberg, D. The collected stories of Deborah Eisenberg

Broken glass

Eisenberg, D. The collected stories of Deborah Eisenberg

A cautionary tale

Eisenberg, D. The collected stories of Deborah Eisenberg

The custodian

Eisenberg, D. The collected stories of Deborah Eisenberg

Days

Eisenberg, D. The collected stories of Deborah Eisenberg

The flaw in the design

Eisenberg, D. The collected stories of Deborah Eisenberg

Blue collar, white collar, no collar; stories of work; edited by Richard Ford.

Flotsam

Eisenberg, D. The collected stories of Deborah Eisenberg

The girl who left her sock on the floor

Eisenberg, D. The collected stories of Deborah Eisenberg

Holy Week

Eisenberg, D. The collected stories of Deborah Eisenberg

In the station

Eisenberg, D. The collected stories of Deborah Eisenberg

A lesson in traveling light

Eisenberg, D. The collected stories of Deborah Eisenberg

Like it or not

Eisenberg, D. The collected stories of Deborah Eisenberg

Mermaids

Eisenberg, D. The collected stories of Deborah Eisenberg

Presents

Eisenberg, D. The collected stories of Deborah Eisenberg

Rafe's coat

Eisenberg, D. The collected stories of Deborah Eisenberg

Recalculating

The New York Review of Books v58 no12 p54, 56-60 Jl 14 2011

Revenge of the dinosaurs

Eisenberg, D. The collected stories of Deborah Eisenberg

The robbery

Eisenberg, D. The collected stories of Deborah Eisenberg

Rosie gets a soul

Eisenberg, D. The collected stories of Deborah Eisenberg

Some other, better Otto

Eisenberg, D. The collected stories of Deborah Eisenberg

Someone to talk to

Eisenberg, D. The collected stories of Deborah Eisenberg

Tlaloc's paradise

Eisenberg, D. The collected stories of Deborah Eisenberg

Transactions in a foreign currency

Eisenberg, D. The collected stories of Deborah Eisenberg

Twilight of the superheroes

Eisenberg, D. The collected stories of Deborah Eisenberg

Under the 82nd Airborne

Eisenberg, D. The collected stories of Deborah Eisenberg

The **emissary**. Bradbury, R.
Emissary. Emshwiller, C.
Emission. Cohen, J.
Emmanuel, François
  Lou dancing
    Best European fiction 2011; edited by Aleksandr Hemon; preface by Colum McCann
Emmerich, Karen
  (tr.) See Michalopoulou, Amanda
Emmons, Jeanne
  Vinyl
    River Styx no85 p80-1 2011
EMPATHY
  Dick, P. K. Beyond lies the wub
  Sebold, G. Inspection day
  Somerville, P. The machine of understanding other people
The **emperor** of Mars. Steele, A. M.
The **empire** of the ants. Wells, H. G.
EMPIRE STATE BUILDING (NEW YORK, N.Y.)
  Sabar, A. Elevation
EMPLOYEES, DISMISSAL OF *See* Dismissal of employees
The **empty** family. Tóibín, C.
Empty nest. Sterling, P.
The **Empty** Room. Lethem, J.
An **empty** room. Mu Xin
Emshwiller, Carol
  Abominable
    Emshwiller, C. The Collected Stories of Carol Emshwiller
  The abominable child's tale
    The beastly bride; tales of the animal people; edited by Ellen Datlow & Terri Windling; introduction by Terri Windling; selected decorations by Charles Vess.
  Acceptance speech
    Emshwiller, C. The Collected Stories of Carol Emshwiller
  After shock
    Emshwiller, C. The Collected Stories of Carol Emshwiller
  Al
    Emshwiller, C. The Collected Stories of Carol Emshwiller
  Animal
    Emshwiller, C. The Collected Stories of Carol Emshwiller
  As if
    Emshwiller, C. The Collected Stories of Carol Emshwiller
  Autobiography
    Emshwiller, C. The Collected Stories of Carol Emshwiller
  Baby
    Emshwiller, C. The Collected Stories of Carol Emshwiller
  Being mysterious strangers from distant shores
    Emshwiller, C. The Collected Stories of Carol Emshwiller
  Bingo and Bongo
    Emshwiller, C. The Collected Stories of Carol Emshwiller
  Biography of an uncircumcised man (including interview)
    Emshwiller, C. The Collected Stories of Carol Emshwiller

Built for pleasure
    Emshwiller, C. The Collected Stories of Carol Emshwiller
But soft what light...
    Emshwiller, C. The Collected Stories of Carol Emshwiller
Chicken Icarus
    Emshwiller, C. The Collected Stories of Carol Emshwiller
The childhood of the human hero
    Emshwiller, C. The Collected Stories of Carol Emshwiller
The circular library of stones
    Emshwiller, C. The Collected Stories of Carol Emshwiller
Clerestory
    Emshwiller, C. The Collected Stories of Carol Emshwiller
The coming
    Emshwiller, C. The Collected Stories of Carol Emshwiller
Creature
    Emshwiller, C. The Collected Stories of Carol Emshwiller
Day at the beach
    Emshwiller, C. The Collected Stories of Carol Emshwiller
Debut
    Emshwiller, C. The Collected Stories of Carol Emshwiller
Destinations, premonitions and the nature of anxiety
    Emshwiller, C. The Collected Stories of Carol Emshwiller
Dog is dead
    Emshwiller, C. The Collected Stories of Carol Emshwiller
Draculalucard
    Emshwiller, C. The Collected Stories of Carol Emshwiller
Eclipse
    Emshwiller, C. The Collected Stories of Carol Emshwiller
Emissary
    Emshwiller, C. The Collected Stories of Carol Emshwiller
Eohippus
    Emshwiller, C. The Collected Stories of Carol Emshwiller
Escape is no accident
    Emshwiller, C. The Collected Stories of Carol Emshwiller
Expecting sunshine and getting it
    Emshwiller, C. The Collected Stories of Carol Emshwiller
Fledged
    Emshwiller, C. The Collected Stories of Carol Emshwiller
Foster mother
    Emshwiller, C. The Collected Stories of Carol Emshwiller
The futility of fixed positions
    Emshwiller, C. The Collected Stories of Carol Emshwiller
Grandma
    Emshwiller, C. The Collected Stories of Carol Emshwiller

Emshwiller, Carol—*Continued*

  To the association

    Emshwiller, C. The Collected Stories of Carol Emshwiller

  Two-step for six legs

    Emshwiller, C. The Collected Stories of Carol Emshwiller

  Venus rising

    Emshwiller, C. The Collected Stories of Carol Emshwiller

  Verging on the pertinent

    Emshwiller, C. The Collected Stories of Carol Emshwiller

  The victim

    Emshwiller, C. The Collected Stories of Carol Emshwiller

  Vilcabamba

    Emshwiller, C. The Collected Stories of Carol Emshwiller

  What every woman knows

    Emshwiller, C. The Collected Stories of Carol Emshwiller

  White dove

    Emshwiller, C. The Collected Stories of Carol Emshwiller

  Woman waiting

    Emshwiller, C. The Collected Stories of Carol Emshwiller

  Yes, Virginia

    Emshwiller, C. The Collected Stories of Carol Emshwiller

  You'll feel better...

    Emshwiller, C. The Collected Stories of Carol Emshwiller

  Yukon

    Emshwiller, C. The Collected Stories of Carol Emshwiller

The **enchanted** heir. Dib, M.

The **end**. Dib, M.

The **End**. Wallace, D.

End of a friend. Dixon, S.

The **end** of anti-Semitism. Hamburger, A.

The **end** of England. Lisicky, P.

End of his tether. Allen, D.

The **end** of it all. Loory, B.

The **end** of my life in New York. Cameron, P.

End of novel. Blatnik, A.

The **End** of Old History. Gaddis, S. M.

END OF THE WORLD

    See also Earth, Destruction of

Anderson, P. Murphy's Hall

Atkins, M. Seven brains, ten minutes

Baker, K. The books

Bear, E. And the deep blue sea

Bierce, A. For the Ahkoond

Dozois, G. R. Chains of the sea

Dozois, G. R. When the great days come

Hautala, R. The hum

Lee, T. Black and white sky

Mosher, C. J. A girl and her cat

Phillips, H. The apocalypses

Silverberg, R. Waiting for the earthquake

Swirsky, R. The lady who plucked red flowers beneath the queen's window

Wells, H. G. The story of the Last Trump

The **end** zone. Gilley, T.

Endangered Species. Hanson, E.

Endangered species. Ruocco, J.

Endgame. Grossman, L.

Endless embrace. Warsh, L.

Endless night. Roden, B.

ENDOWMENTS

Bierce, A. The applicant

Pearlman, E. Rules

Ends. Dixon, S.

Endurance. Tomasula, S.

The **enemies**. Tamir, Z.

The **enemy**. Naipaul, V. S.

Engaged. Rodoreda, M.

ENGAGEMENTS *See* Betrothals

Engel, Patricia

  Cielito lindo

    Engel, P. Vida

  Desaliento

    Engel, P. Vida

  Dia

    Engel, P. Vida

  Green

    Engel, P. Vida

  Lucho

    Engel, P. Vida

  Madre Patria

    Engel, P. Vida

  Paloma

    Engel, P. Vida

  Refuge

    Engel, P. Vida

  Vida

    Engel, P. Vida

The **engines** of Sodom. Papernick, J.

ENGLAND

    See also Lake District (England)

Archer, J. Double-cross

Lee, T. Black and white sky

Mantel, H. The heart fails without warning

Self, W. Chest

Trevor, W. A perfect relationship

    19th century

Baker, K. The women of Nell Gwynne's

Wells, H. G. A perfect gentleman on wheels

    Aristocracy

    See Aristocracy—England

    College life

    See College life—England

    Politics

    See Politics—England

    Prisoners and prisons

    See Prisoners and prisons—England

    Rural life

Wells, H. G. Mr. Marshall's doppelganger

Wodehouse, P. G. The mixer

    World War, 1939-1945

    See World War, 1939-1945—England

    Brighton

Fowler, C. Oh I do like to be beside the seaside

    Channel Islands

    See Channel Islands

    Lake District

    See Lake District (England)

    Lancashire

Kennedy, A. L. The effects of good government on the city

    Liverpool

Atkins, P. The Mystery

    London

Abraham, D. Baljour and Meriwether in the adventure of the emperor's vengeance

Archer, J. Politically correct

ENGLAND—London—*Continued*
  Baker, K. The women of Nell Gwynne's
  Beagle, P. S. Music, when soft voices die
  Bell, M. S. Barking man
  Chaudhuri, A. Aniruddha: the latest installment
  Cleeves, A. Neastly pleasures
  Dehan, R. Lady Clanbevan's baby
  Doctorow, C. The Jammie Dodgers and the adventure of the Leicester Square screening
  Edelman, S. The human race
  Fowler, C. Bryant and May in the soup
  Green, S. R. Street wizard
  MacLeod, I. Elementals
  Marías, J. An epigram of fealty
  McOmber, A. Beneath us
  Naipaul, V. S. Tell me who to kill
  Nevins, F. M., Jr. The other man in the pinstripe
  Nix, G. The curious case of the moondawn daffodils murder
  Pearlman, E. If love were all
  Rohmer, S. The hand of the Mandarin Quong
  Sabatini, R. Intelligence
  Self, W. Birdy num num
  Self, W. Conversation with Ord
  Self, W. Design faults in the Volvo 760 Turbo: a manual
  Self, W. The Nonce prize
  Self, W. The North London book of the dead
  Self, W. The rock of crack as big as the Ritz
  Self, W. Ward 9
  Trevor, W. A bit on the side
            Manchester
  Edwards, M. Clutter
  Valente, C. M. The anachronist's cookbook
            Oxford
  Davis, L. The walk
            Somerset
  Archer, J. The queen's birthday telegram
            Suffolk
  Self, W. Flytopia
            Yorkshire
  Powers, R. To the measures fall
Englander, Nathan
  Free fruit for young widows
    The Best American short stories, 2011; selected from U.S. and Canadian magazines by Geraldine Brooks with Heidi Pitlor; with an introduction by Geraldine Brooks.
ENGLISH LANGUAGE
  Levine, S. How do breasts feels?
The **English** mutiny. MacLeod, I.
ENGLISH PEOPLE *See* British
The **enigma** of her voice. Franc, I.
The **enigmatic** power of the letter "j". Kalechofsky, R.
Enigwe, Chika
  Saving Agu's Wife
    Agni no72 p230-6 2010
Enlightened. Davis, L.
ENNUI *See* Boredom
Ennui. Shapiro, J.
Entanglement. Lingen, M.
ENTERTAINERS
        See also Actors; Actresses; Clowns
  Baker, K. The books
  Kennedy, A. L. Another
  Manilla, M. Crystal City
  Millhauser, S. The knife thrower

Nutting, A. Dancing rat
  Spinrad, N. The big flash
ENTERTAINING *See* Parties
The **entire** northern side was covered with fire. Galchen, R.
The **entire** predicament. Corin, L.
ENTOMOLOGISTS
  Wells, H. G. The moth
Entropia / Entropy. Kerbaker, A.
The **envies**. Phillips, H.
ENVY *See* Jealousy
Eohippus. Emshwiller, C.
EPIDEMICS
        See also Plague
  Tremblay, P. The blog at the end of the world
An **epigram** of fealty. Marías, J.
EPILEPTICS
  Gray, A. There will be sense
Epiphany. Taylor-Aragon, E.
Episcatory. Terry, G. P.
EPISCOPAL CLERGY *See* Anglican and Episcopal clergy
Epitaph for an age. Kalechofsky, R.
The **epizootic**. Vonnegut, K.
Epstein, Joseph
  Arnheim & Sons
    Commentary v132 no1 p63-8 Jl/Ag 2011
  Wild About Harry
    Commentary v131 no1 p34-40 Ja 2011
Equal opportunity. Mosley, W.
The **equine** theft. Randisi, R. J.
ER (...) Ellipses. Obarrio, J.
Erby, Sharon
  Pushing
    Feminist Studies v36 no2 p313-29 Summ 2010
Erdrich, Louise
  The reptile garden
    Best of the West 2009; new stories from the wide side of the Missouri; edited by James Thomas and D. Seth Horton; foreword by Rick Bass.
  Scales
    Best of times, worst of times; contemporary American short stories from the new Gilded Age; edited by Wendy Martin and Cecelia Tichi.
  The years of my birth
    The New Yorker v86 no43 p64-8 Ja 10 2011
The **Ereshkigal** working. Howard, J. L.
The **erlking**. Bynum, S. S.-L.
EROTICISM *See* Sex
Errachidi, Abdelaziz
  From the novel Bedouins on the edge
    Beirut 39; new writing from the Arab world; edited by Samuel Shimon; with a preface by Hanan al-Shaykh
Errata. Daykin, R.
Erratum: insert "r" in "transgressors". Hall, T. M.
ERRORS
  Phillips, H. The mistakes
Escambia counties. McMillian, R.
Escape. Willis, D.
Escape from prison. Carlson, R.
Escape from Spiderhead. Saunders, G.
Escape is no accident. Emshwiller, C.
ESCAPED CONVICTS
  Boland, J. C. Mountain fire
  Erdrich, L. Scales

ESCAPED CONVICTS—*Continued*

Mofina, R. The last pursuit

Nolan, W. F. The Pelican's brother

Wallace, E. Bosambo of Monrovia

ESCAPES

Dick, P. K. Paycheck

Piccirilli, T. Blood sacrifices and the Catatonic Kid

The **escapist**. Shipp, J. C.

Esdaile, Leslie *See* Banks, Leslie Esdaile

ESKIMOS *See* Inuit

Eslami, Elizabeth

Yana Land

The Literary Review (Madison, N.J.) v54 no3 p126-31 Spr 2011

Esmeralda and the flipping hammer (Highway 152, continued). Shepard, S.

ESP *See* Extrasensory perception

ESP. Tang, J.

ESPIONAGE *See* Spies

ESPN. Simon, N.

Esposito, Bliss

Kirby and the portal to Hell

Dead neon; tales of near-future Las Vegas; edited by Todd James Pierce and Jarret Keene.

Espresso. Kurlansky, M.

Il **est** ne. Vaughn, C.

ESTATES *See* Houses

Esther Donnaly. Carlson, R.

ESTHETICS *See* Aesthetics

Estleman, Loren D.

The anniversary waltz

Estleman, L. D. Amos Walker; the complete story collection

Blond and blue

Estleman, L. D. Amos Walker; the complete story collection

Bloody July

Estleman, L. D. Amos Walker; the complete story collection

Bodyguards shoot second

Estleman, L. D. Amos Walker; the complete story collection

Cigarette stop

Estleman, L. D. Amos Walker; the complete story collection

The crooked way

The Shamus winners: America's best private eye stories, volume I: 1982-1995; collected and introduced by Robert J. Randisi; founder, Private Eye Writers of America

Estleman, L. D. Amos Walker; the complete story collection

Dead soldier

Estleman, L. D. Amos Walker; the complete story collection

Deadly force

Estleman, L. D. Amos Walker; the complete story collection

Dogs

Estleman, L. D. Amos Walker; the complete story collection

Eight Mile & Dequindre

Estleman, L. D. Amos Walker; the complete story collection

Eight Mile and Dequindre

The Shamus winners: America's best private eye stories, volume I: 1982-1995; collected and introduced by Robert J. Randisi; founder, Private Eye Writers of America

Fast burn

Estleman, L. D. Amos Walker; the complete story collection

Greektown

Estleman, L. D. Amos Walker; the complete story collection

I'm in the book

Estleman, L. D. Amos Walker; the complete story collection

Kill the cat

Estleman, L. D. Amos Walker; the complete story collection

Lady on ice

Randisi, R. J. The Shamus winners: America's best private eye stories, volume II, 1996-2009; collected and introduced by Robert J. Randisi; founder, Private Eye Writers of America

Estleman, L. D. Amos Walker; the complete story collection

Major crimes

Estleman, L. D. Amos Walker; the complete story collection

The man who loved noir

Estleman, L. D. Amos Walker; the complete story collection

Necessary evil

Estleman, L. D. Amos Walker; the complete story collection

Needle

Estleman, L. D. Amos Walker; the complete story collection

People who kill

Estleman, L. D. Amos Walker; the complete story collection

Pickups and shotguns

Estleman, L. D. Amos Walker; the complete story collection

The prettiest dead girl in Detroit

Estleman, L. D. Amos Walker; the complete story collection

Redneck

Estleman, L. D. Amos Walker; the complete story collection

Robber's roost

Estleman, L. D. Amos Walker; the complete story collection

Rumble strip

Estleman, L. D. Amos Walker; the complete story collection

Safe house

Estleman, L. D. Amos Walker; the complete story collection

Slipstream

Estleman, L. D. Amos Walker; the complete story collection

Snow angels

Estleman, L. D. Amos Walker; the complete story collection

Sometimes a hyena

Estleman, L. D. Amos Walker; the complete story collection

Estleman, Loren D.—*Continued*
  Square one
    Estleman, L. D. Amos Walker; the complete
      story collection
  Sunday
    Estleman, L. D. Amos Walker; 'the complete
      story collection
  Trust me
    Estleman, L. D. Amos Walker; the complete
      story collection
  The Woodward Plan
    Estleman, L. D. Amos Walker; the complete
      story collection
Estranged. Phillips, C. L.
ETHICS
        See also Honesty; Sin; Truthfulness and
    falsehood
Ethics. Davis, L.
The **Ethiopian**. Schirach, F. v.
ETHIOPIANS
                    Germany
  Schirach, F. v. The Ethiopian
Eugenides, Jeffrey
  Asleep in the Lord [Part of the Summer Fiction
    Issue]
    The New Yorker v87 no17 p86-90, 92-3, 95-9
      Je 13-20 2011
  Great experiment
    Blue collar, white collar, no collar; stories of
      work; edited by Richard Ford.
EUROPE
  McOmber, A. This new and poisonous air
EUTHANASIA
  Bierce, A. The coup de grâce
  Gorman, E. Turn away
Eutopia. Anderson, P.
An **evanescent** book. Ureta, T.
Evans, Danielle
  Harvest
    Evans, D. Before you suffocate your own fool
      self
  Jellyfish
    Evans, D. Before you suffocate your own fool
      self
  The king of a vast empire
    Evans, D. Before you suffocate your own fool
      self
  Robert E. Lee dead
    Evans, D. Before you suffocate your own fool
      self
  Snakes
    Evans, D. Before you suffocate your own fool
      self
  Someone ought to tell her there's nowhere to go
    Evans, D. Before you suffocate your own fool
      self
  Virgins
    Evans, D. Before you suffocate your own fool
      self
  Wherever you go, there you are
    Evans, D. Before you suffocate your own fool
      self
Evans, David Allan
  Invisible trophies
    South Dakota Magazine v26 no5 p88-90 Ja/F
      2011

Evans, Mary Anna
  Low-budget monster flick
    Florida heat wave; [edited and with an] intro-
      duction by Michael Lister.
The **eve** of the fall of Habesh. Buckell, T. S.
Even Greenland. Hannah, B.
Evening. Dixon, S.
Evening of the Yarp. Hannah, B.
An **evening** out. Trevor, W.
Evenings at home. Hardwick, E.
Evenings with Dotson. Willis, M. S.
Evenson, Brian
  1995: kneel
    The Thackery T. Lambshead cabinet of curi-
      osities; edited by Ann & Jeff VanderMeer.
  Windeye
    The Pen/O.Henry Prize stories 2011; chosen
      and with an introduction by Laura Furman;
      with essays on the stories thety admire
      most by jurors A. M. Homes, Manuel Mu-
      ñoz, Christine Schutt
Evensong. Nevins, F. M., Jr.
Event horizon. Hecht, J.
Events with odd and even endings. Kronauer, B.
Every girl dreams of falling in love. Li, S.
Everyone I love is dead. Coldwell, E.
Everything dies, baby. Bulkin, N.
Everything forbidden. Chau, A.
Everything in this country must. McCann, C.
Everything you see is real. Ehrenreich, B.
Everywhere. Ryman, G.
EVIDENCE, CIRCUMSTANTIAL *See* Circum-
    stantial evidence
Evidence of love in a case of abandonment.
    Rickert, M.
Evidence of love in a case of abandonment: one
    daughter's personal account. Rickert, M.
Evidence seen. Boland, J. C.
EVIL *See* Good and evil
The **evil** eye. Gelasimov, A.
Evison, Jonathan
  The Revised Fundamentals of Caregiving
    TriQuarterly v138 55715 bytes Summ/Fall
      2010
Evocation of evil. Boland, J. C.
EVOLUTION
  Dick, P. K. The infinites
The **Evolution** Rapist. McConnell, S.
Ewan, Chris
  The art of negotiation
    Original sins; a Crime Writer's Association
      anthology; edited by Martin Edwards.
EX-CONVICTS
  Aiken, J. The Paper Queen
  Allen, R. A. The Emerald Coast
  Baxter, C. The old murderer
  Bengtsson, J. T. One of the rough ones
  Boland, J. C. Swamp beast
  Dib, M. At the café
  Drees, C. By hook or by crook
  Gorman, E. Loose ends
  Hastings, W. Ten-year plan
  Jeter, K. W. Bones
  McHugh, M. The naturalist
  Mosley, W. Equal opportunity
  Oates, J. C. Nowhere
  Sandlin, L. Phelan's first case
  Trueblood, V. Amends
  Tucher, A. Bismarck rules

EXPERIMENTAL STORIES—*Continued*
Pulver, J. S. Just another desert night with blood
Sanders, T. Obit
Seabrook, T. When Robin Hood fell with an arrow through his heart
Somerville, P. The abacus
Stein, G. Miss Furr and Miss Skeene
Tamir, Z. The enemies
Tidhar, L. Alienation and love in the Hebrew alphabet
Tillman, L. Love sentence
Van den Broeck, W. Successor to the throne
Verhelst, P. Swarm 10
Vukcevich, R. Grocery list
Young, M. The age of the tire boat
EXPERIMENTS, SCIENTIFIC *See* Scientific experiments
Experts. Blatnik, A.
EXPLORERS
Bailey, D. and Ballingrud, N. The crevasse
Reynolds, A. The old man and the Martian sea
EXPLOSIONS
Wiecek, M. The shipbreaker
EXTERMINATION *See* Pests—Control
EXTERMINATION, JEWISH *See* Holocaust, Jewish (1933-1945)
The **exterminator**. Roberge, R.
The **exterminator's** want ad. Sterling, B.
EXTINCT ANIMALS
Wells, H. G. Aepyornis Island
EXTINCT CITIES
Bierce, A. The inhabitant of Carcosa
Le Clézio, J.-M. G. The waterwheel
EXTORTION
Trevor, W. Against the odds
Extracts from a life. Davis, L.
Extracts from the memoirs of Lord Greystoke. Farmer, P. J.
EXTRASENSORY PERCEPTION
        See also Clairvoyance; Telepathy
Cadigan, P. The taste of night
Sylvain, P. Odette
EYE
        See also Vision
The **eye**. Furman, L.
Eye of the beholder. Graham, S.
Eye of the destroyer. Bodard, A. d.
The **eye** patch protocol. Stanger, V.
Eye to Eye. Heynen, J.
Eyes and Ears. O, T. C.
The **eyes** of the panther. Bierce, A.
EYEWITNESSES *See* Witnesses

F

FABLES
        See also Allegories
Bierce, A. Haïta the shepherd
Drakulic, S. The bear and the princess of light
Drakulic, S. The cat-keeper in Warsaw (Letter to the state prosecutor)
Drakulic, S. A communist with style
Drakulic, S. From gulag to goulash: the introduction to Ms. Piggy's Hungarian cookbook
Drakulic, S. A guided tour through the museum of communism

Drakulic, S. An interview with the oldest dog in Bucharest
Drakulic, S. The legend of the Berlin Wall–as presented by a mole
Drakulic, S. The unusual case of the psychotic raven
Knapp, A. The earth slept: a vision
Lychack, W. A stand of fables
McElroy, J. The last disarmament but one
Proulx, A. The sagebrush kid
Tuten, F. Self portrait with cheese
Fabra, Jordi Sierra I.
A high-end neighborhood
        Barcelona noir; edited by Adriana V. Lopez & Cartmen Ospina; translated by Achy Obejas.
The **Fabric** of Nostalgia. Zarankin, J.
Face. Shepard, S.
Face from Atlantis. Gordimer, N.
FACE MASKS *See* Masks (for the face)
Face to face. Harwood, J.
FACTORIES
        See also Labor and laboring classes
Bukowski, C. A day
Dybek, S. Sauerkraut soup
Katelnikoff, J. Small game hunter
Levine, S. Sausage
Pascoe, J. Paper
Phelps, E. S. The tenth of January
Solzhenitsyn, A. Fracture points
The **Factory** Girl. Bedford, W.
The **facts** of M. Valdemar's case. Poe, E. A.
FACULTY (EDUCATION) *See* Teachers
Faherty, Terence
The caretaker
        By hook or by crook and 27 more of the best crime + mystery stories of the year; edited by Ed Gorman and Martin H. Greenberg.
The second coming
        Randisi, R. J. The Shamus winners: America's best private eye stories, volume II, 1996-2009; collected and introduced by Robert J. Randisi; founder, Private Eye Writers of America
Fähner. Schirach, F. v.
Fahrenheit 451 [excerpt] Bradbury, R.
FAILURE
Hannah, B. Getting ready
Hannah, B. Rat-faced Auntie
Phillips, H. The failures
Yates, R. A glutton for punishment
The **failures**. Phillips, H.
Fair extension. King, S.
Fair game. Nevins, F. M., Jr.
Fair Ladies. Goss, T.
Fair trade. Ryan, S.
FAIRIES
Briggs, P. Fairy gifts
Henderson, S. Wild copper
Jones, G. A. In the forest of the queen
Mingin, W. From sunset to the white sea
Monk, D. Moonlighting
Moorcock, M. Shamalung (the diminutions)
Rickert, M. Was she wicked? was she good?
Sherman, D. How the pooka came to New York City
Spenst, K. Hands held at religious angles
Wells, H. G. Mr. Skelmersdale in Fairyland

FAIRS

Aiken, J. Water of youth
Fisher, D. C. The bedquilt
Galchen, R. Wild berry blue
Hall, T. M. Last night of the county fair
Fairy gifts. Briggs, P.
Fairy tale. Dozois, G. R.
Fairy tale. Hemmerchts, K.
Fairy Tale. Kleeman, A.
FAIRY TALES *See* Fantasies

FAITH

Anderson, P. The problem of pain
Black, A. Proof of love
Burgis, B. Dark coffee, bright light and the paradoxes of omnipotence
Doctorow, E. L. Heist
Dunmore, H. Where I keep my faith
Kitterman, B. Wedding day
Loory, B. The magic pig
Lychack, W. The ghostwriter
Nagai, M. How we touch the ground, how we touch
Novack, S. Morty, el morto
Shapiro, J. Tiger beat
Faith. Trevor, W.
Faith-based initiative. Shea, K.

FAITH CURE

Barnhill, K. St. Brendan's shank
FAITH HEALERS *See* Faith cure
Faith is three parts formaldehyde, one part ethyl alcohol. Hall, T. M.
Faith, South Dakota (Interstate 25). Shepard, S.
Faithful lovers. Drabble, M.

FAITHFULNESS

Engel, P. Cielito lindo
Henry, O. The caballero's way
The **Fake** Nazi. Bender, A.

Falco, Ed
Candy
Five Points v12 no3 p98-113 2009

Falco, Federico
In Utah there are mountains too
Granta no113 p195-215 Wint 2010

Falk, Mark Raymond
The Apalachicola night
Florida heat wave; [edited and with an] introduction by Michael Lister.

Falksen, G. D.
The strange case of Mr. Salad Monday
Steampunk II: steampunk reloaded; edited by Ann & Jeff VanderMeer.

Fall, Tyler
Taxidermy
Gettysburg Review v23 no3 p469-76 Aut 2010

Fall guy. Coxe, G. H.
Fall, Orpheum. McOmber, A.

Fallaras, Cristina
The story of a scar
Barcelona noir; edited by Adriana V. Lopez & Cartmen Ospina; translated by Achy Obejas.

The **Fallen**. BEDARD, B.
Fallen boys. Morris, M.
Falling with wings. Monk, D.

Fallon, Siobhan
Camp Liberty
Fallon, S. You know when the men are gone

Gold star
Fallon, S. You know when the men are gone
Inside the break
Fallon, S. You know when the men are gone
The last stand
Fallon, S. You know when the men are gone
Leave
Fallon, S. You know when the men are gone
Lost and Found
Good Housekeeping v252 no3 p167-8, 171-2, 174-7 Mr 2011
Remission
Fallon, S. You know when the men are gone
You know when the men are gone
Fallon, S. You know when the men are gone
You survived the war, now survive the homecoming
Fallon, S. You know when the men are gone

The **Falls**. Bennett, A.

FALSE ACCUSATION

Todd, C. Yesterday
Tolstoy, L., graf. God sees the truth, but waits
Vonnegut, K. Ed Luby's key club
False Gods. Cherry, K.
False Steps. Meruane, L.

FAME

Cook, K. L. Bonnie and Clyde in the backyard
Mamatas, N. Your life, fifteen minutes from now
Familiar birds. Fowler, K. J.
A **familiar** face of death. Goodberg, D.
A **familiar** place. Mullins, D. P.

FAMILY

Amqassim, Y. From the novel Raven's leg
Engel, P. Madre Patria
Ibrāhīm, H. Family re-union
Kawtharani, H. Three stories
Kronauer, B. The handkerchief [excerpt]
Levine, S. The danas
Marār, M. And we used to squeeze the olives for oil
Saʿīd, M. A. Sheik Mabruk
The **family**. Davis, L.
The **family**. Villegas, H.
Family affair a Smokey Dalton story. Nelscott, K.
Family business. Maberry, J.

FAMILY CHRONICLES

See also Family life
Furman, L. The blue birds come today
A **family** elopement. Wells, H. G.
Family gifting. Yamauchi, W.
Family happiness. McGarry, J.

FAMILY LIFE

See also Aunts; Brothers; Brothers and sisters; Family chronicles; Fathers; Fathers and sons; Fathers-in-law; Grandchildren; Granddaughters; Grandfathers; Grandmothers; Grandparents; Grandsons; Marriage; Marriage problems; Mothers and daughters; Mothers and sons; Mothers-in-law; Nephews; Nieces; Parent and child; Sisters; Stepbrothers; Stepfathers; Stepmothers; Stepsons; Twins; Uncles
Adrian, C. The warm fuzzies
Aiken, J. The monkey's wedding
Atta, S. Yahoo yahoo
Baker, L. Still life
Barrett, L. Gift wrap
Beattie, A. Times

FAMILY LIFE—*Continued*

Beattie, A. Where you'll find me
Benali, A. From the novel The trip to the slaughterhouse
Bender, A. Americca
Bierce, A. A bottomless grave
Bingham, S. Found
Bloom, A. Love is not a pie
Blumlein, M. Fidelity: a primer
Boggs, B. Shelter
Brooks, G. The rise of Maud Martha
Bukowski, C. A day
Carlson, R. Escape from prison
Doctorow, E. L. The writer in the family
Doyle, R. Animals
Doyle, R. Recuperation
DuBois, B. The necessary brother
Eisenberg, D. The custodian
Evans, D. Wherever you go, there you are
Farmer, P. J. Down in the black gang
Gilley, T. Vanishing world
Goodberg, D. The good book
Grover, L. L. Refugees living and dying in the west end of Duluth
Hall, T. M. By the gleam of her teeth, she will light the path before her
Hemmingson, M. Branches
Hoang, M. T. The story of a family
Jarrar, R. The story of my building (after Isaac Babel's "Story of my dovecote")
Jen, G. In the American society
Kearney, G. L-o-v-e
Kronauer, B. Events with odd and even endings
Kurlansky, M. Bean curd
Lavin, M. Lilacs
Leland, C. T. A mother's love
Levine, S. Uppsala
Manilla, M. Hand. Me. Down.
McGarry, J. Family happiness
McGarry, J. The offering
McGarry, J. The sweetness of her name
Meyer, P. What you do out here, when you're alone
Millhauser, S. Getting closer
Millhauser, S. A protest against the sun
Monzó, Q. Family life
Moore, L. Four calling birds, three french hens
Mu Xin. Xia Mingzhu: a bright pearl
Naipaul, V. S. The enemy
Niedzviecki, H. Sometime next sunrise
O'Connor, F. The mad Lomasneys
O'Connor, S. All in good time
O'Connor, S. Disappearance and
Osondu, E. C. Stars in my mother's eyes, stripes on my back
Phelan, T. Happine$$
Phelps, E. S. The angel over the right shoulder, or, the beginning of a new year
Phillips, H. The far-flung families
Ruocco, J. Lighting bug
Shapiro, J. 1966
Shapiro, J. In its place
Shapiro, J. Tiger beat
Shields, S. The watershed
Skurnick, L. Spectacle Pond
Somerville, P. The universe in miniature in miniature
Tillman, L. But there's a family resemblance
Tóibín, C. The new Spain

Tremblay, P. It's against the law to feed the ducks
Tremblay, P. The teacher
Trevor, W. Lost ground
Villegas, H. Twenty-first-century design
Vukcevich, R. Love story
Watson, B. Alamo Plaza
Wieland, L. Vision
Willis, M. S. Fellowship of kindred minds
Womack, C. Uncle Jimmy's personal emissary
Yamauchi, W. Family gifting
Yellin, T. Reuben
Family life. Monzó, Q.
The **Family** Man. Karnes, J. W.
A **Family** Matter. MITRA, K.
Family planning. Laken, V.
Family re-union. Ibrāhim, .

FAMILY REUNIONS

Beattie, A. The lawn party
Bingham, S. The hunt
Eisenberg, D. Revenge of the dinosaurs
Hardwick, E. Evenings at home
Family romance. McGarry, J.

FAMILY SAGAS *See* Family chronicles
Family tree. Kirtley, D. B.
Family values. Alderman, M.

FAMINES

Tremblay, P. Growing things
Famous for Crabs. Oates, N.
The **famous** Gilson bequest. Bierce, A.
A **famous** Indian artist. Chuculate, E. D.

FANATICISM

Dozois, G. R. Community
FANATICS *See* Fanaticism
Fancy flights. Beattie, A.
Fans. Hannah, B.

FANTASIES

See also Allegories; End of the world; Experimental stories; Future; Improbable stories; Science fiction; Utopias
Abercrombie, J. The fool jobs
Abraham, D. Baljour and Meriwether in the adventure of the emperor's vengeance
Ackert, D. and Rosenbaum, B. The king of the djinn
Ahmed, S. Hooves and the hovel of Abdel Jameela
Aiken, J. The fluttering thing
Aiken, J. Honeymaroon
Aiken, J. The Magnesia Tree
Anderson, P. Operation changeling
Anthony, P. Possible to rue
Anzaldúa, G. Reading LP
Arkwright, J. The sundial
Baker, K. Two old men
Balázs, B. The ancestors
Balázs, B. The clay child
Balázs, B. The cloak of dreams
Balázs, B. The clumsy god
Balázs, B. The flea
Balázs, B. The friends
Balázs, B. Li-Tai-Pe and springtime
Balázs, B. Li-Tai-Pe and the thief
Balázs, B. The moon fish
Balázs, B. The old child
Balázs, B. The opium smokers
Balázs, B. The parasols
Balázs, B. The revenge of the chestnut tree
Balázs, B. The robbers of divine power

FANTASIES—*Continued*

Ryman, G. The last ten years in the life of hero Kai

Ryman, G. Pol Pot's beautiful daughter

Salvatore, R. A. A sparkle for Homer

Schoen, L. M. The wrestler and the spear fisher

Scholes, K. Edward Bear and the very long walk

Sedia, E. 1972: the lichenologist's visit

Sedia, E. Cherrystone and shards of ice

Shea, M. Copping squid

Shehadeh, R. The unbecoming of Virgil Smythe

Shepard, J. In cretaceous seas

Shepard, L. Halloween Town

Sherman, D. How the pooka came to New York City

Sherman, D. Wizard's apprentice

Shetterly, W. The sages of elsewhere

Shipp, J. C. Boy in the cabinet

Shipp, J. C. The escapist

Shipp, J. C. Fungus of the heart

Shipp, J. C. Ula Morales

Silverberg, R. Basileus

Silverberg, R. The regulars

Silverberg, R. The sorcerer's apprentice

Silverberg, R. Thesme and the Ghayrog

Simner, J. L. Crossings

Sinisalo, J. Bear's bride

Smith, C. A. The black abbot of puthuum

Smith, C. A. The coming of the white worm

Smith, C. A. The death of Ilalotha

Smith, C. A. The death of Malygris

Smith, C. A. The garden of Adompha

Smith, C. A. The last hieroglyph

Smith, C. A. Necromancy in Naat

Smith, C. A. The primal city

Smith, C. A. The seven geases

Smith, C. A. Symposium of the Gorgon

Smith, C. A. The treader of the dust

Smith, C. A. Xeethra

Smith, P. A. The perils of twilight

Snyder, M. The monkey bride

St. John, N. Further notes on my unfortunate condition

Stashower, D. Challenger

Stein, J. C. The ghost of Leadville

Stockton, F. The lady or the tiger?

Sullivan, J. Niels Bohr and the sleeping Dane

Swirsky, R. Detours on the way to nothing

Swirsky, R. Heartstrung

Swirsky, R. The lady who plucked red flowers beneath the queen's window

Tem, S. R. The cabinet child

Terry, G. P. The tale of the glass man

Terry, G. P. The Ustek Cloudy

Thomas, P. Short fuse

Tidhar, L. The projected girl

Tobler, E. C. Island lake

Tolbert, J. One-click banishment

Tom, L. Living rooms

Tregillis, I. Still life (a sexagesimal fairy tale)

Turtledove, H. The genetics lecture

Turtledove, H. The horse of bronze

Turtledove, H. Uncle Alf

Twain, M. Sold to Satan

Valente, C. M. A delicate architecture

Valente, C. M. A voice like a hole

Valentine, G. The Zeppelin Conductors' Society annual gentlemen's ball

Van der Veer, K. L. Hammer song

Vaughan, E. A. A rose by any other name would still be red

Vaughn, C. God's creatures

Vincent, R. Hunt

Vukcevich, R. Glinky

Wagner, W. N. The secret of calling rabbits

Wells, H. G. The wild asses of the devil

Williams, T. A short history of Dunkelblau's Meistergarten

Woestijne, K. v. d. The saint of number

Womack, C. Sappho's round dance

Yant, C. The magician and the maid and other stories

Yolen, J. and Stemple, A. The tsar's dragon

Youmans, M. The salamander fire

Yu, C. The book of categories

Zeman, A. Rue Morgue noir: the possible--probable--struggles Edgar Allan Poe might have faced while seeking success as a talented new writer in the world of today

FANTASTIC FICTION *See* Fantasies; Science fiction

Fantasy for six electrodes and one adrenaline drip (a play in the form of a feelie script). Haldeman, J.

Faolain, Sean O.

The trout

The Granta book of the Irish short story; [edited by] Anne Enright.

The **far-flung** families. Phillips, H.

Far from anywhere. Gifford, B.

Far from here. Vila-Matas, E.

The **far** side of the bell-shaped curve. Silverberg, R.

The **far** side of the moon. Black, A.

Far Woods. Willey, B.

Farah, Nuruddin

CROSSBONES

Granta no116 p35-50 S 2011

Young Thing

The New Yorker v86 no40 p80-7 D 13 2010

Farewell, my zombie. Block, F. L.

FAREWELLS

Rodoreda, M. Departure

Farid, Tarek Hussein *See* Heim, Aribert Ferdinand, 1914-1992

Farkas, Andrew

The colonization of room 313

Butler, B. 30 under 30; an anthology of innovative fiction by younger writers; Blake Butler & Lily Hoang, eds.

Farland, David

Feeding the feral children

The way of the wizard; edited by John Joseph Adams.

FARM LIFE

See also Peasant life

Couch, S. The dandelion clock

Heathcock, A. The staying freight

Jewett, S. O. A white heron

McOmber, A. Gardens of the moon

Null, M. N. Something you can't live without

Oates, J. C. High lonesome

Sterling, P. The good life

California

Yamamoto, H. Seventeen syllables

Ireland

Trevor, W. The children

FARM LIFE—Ireland—*Continued*

Trevor, W. The hill bachelors

Kansas

Baker, A. The persistence of memory

Minnesota

Grove, L. L. Shonnud's girl

Nebraska

King, S. 1922

South Africa

Gordimer, N. Six feet of the country

Mphahlele, E. The master of Doornvlei

Southern States

O'Connor, F. Revelation

FARM TENANCY *See* Tenant farming

Farmer, Philip José

After King Kong fell

The Big book of adventure stories; edited and with a introduction by Otto Penzler; foreword by Douglas Preston.

Attitudes

Farmer, P. J. Up the bright river; the worlds of Philip José Farmer; edited by Gary K. Wolfe.

The blasphemers

Farmer, P. J. Up the bright river; the worlds of Philip José Farmer; edited by Gary K. Wolfe.

A bowl bigger than earth

Farmer, P. J. Up the bright river; the worlds of Philip José Farmer; edited by Gary K. Wolfe.

Cats, dogs, and other creatures

Swenson, P. The Best of Talebones; edited by Patrick Swenson.

Coda

Farmer, P. J. Up the bright river; the worlds of Philip José Farmer; edited by Gary K. Wolfe.

Crossing the dark river

Farmer, P. J. Up the bright river; the worlds of Philip José Farmer; edited by Gary K. Wolfe.

Down in the black gang

Farmer, P. J. Up the bright river; the worlds of Philip José Farmer; edited by Gary K. Wolfe.

Extracts from the memoirs of Lord Greystoke

Farmer, P. J. Up the bright river; the worlds of Philip José Farmer; edited by Gary K. Wolfe.

Father's in the basement

Farmer, P. J. Up the bright river; the worlds of Philip José Farmer; edited by Gary K. Wolfe.

How deep the grooves

Farmer, P. J. Up the bright river; the worlds of Philip José Farmer; edited by Gary K. Wolfe.

Skinburn

Farmer, P. J. Up the bright river; the worlds of Philip José Farmer; edited by Gary K. Wolfe.

St. Francis kisses his ass goodbye

Farmer, P. J. Up the bright river; the worlds of Philip José Farmer; edited by Gary K. Wolfe.

The Sumerian oath

Farmer, P. J. Up the bright river; the worlds of Philip José Farmer; edited by Gary K. Wolfe.

Toward the beloved city

Farmer, P. J. Up the bright river; the worlds of Philip José Farmer; edited by Gary K. Wolfe.

The two-edged gift

Farmer, P. J. Up the bright river; the worlds of Philip José Farmer; edited by Gary K. Wolfe.

Up the bright river

Farmer, P. J. Up the bright river; the worlds of Philip José Farmer; edited by Gary K. Wolfe.

Voice of the sonar in my vermiform appendix

Farmer, P. J. Up the bright river; the worlds of Philip José Farmer; edited by Gary K. Wolfe.

FARMERS *See* Farm life

Farmers' law. Turtledove, H.

Farnsworth, Vanessa

A JOKE TOLD BY PILOTS

Dalhousie Review v91 no1 p61-66 Spr 2011

Napoleon's Eyes

Dalhousie Review v90 no2 p241-50 Summ 2010

Farrell, Frank B.

A History of Foolishness

The North American Review v295 no4 p15-23 Fall 2010

Farrell's caddie. Updike, J.

FASCISM

See also Communism; Dictators; National socialism; Totalitarianism

FASHION MODELS

Mitchell, K. Jayne

Nutting, A. Model's assistant

Fast burn. Estleman, L. D.

FASTING

Le Clézio, J.-M. G. Hazaran

Fat man. Lake, J.

FATE AND FATALISM

Goodberg, D. Timing of a mad man

The **fate** of Lisa Sperling. Rodoreda, M.

A **father** and his children. Minh, C.

Father and son. Qiu Xiaolong

Father, lover, deadman, dreamer. Thon, M. R.

Father, son, holy rabbit. Jones, S. G.

Father Woytzski leads a Jewish youth group to the Holocaust memorial in Oswiecim, Poland. Kalechofsky, R.

FATHERS

See also Fathers and daughters; Fathers and sons; Fathers-in-law; Stepfathers

Bingham, S. The ice party

Blatnik, A. Stains

Boggs, B. It won't be long

Chau, A. Quiet as they come

Davis, L. Grammar questions

Eiríksdóttir, K. Holes in people

Ely, S. Dream fishing

Ely, S. The poisoned arrow

Fowler, K. J. King Rat

Hemmingson, M. Branches

Kuhlken, K. Homes

Leland, C. T. As if in time of war

Levine, S. The man who was always a father

FATHERS AND SONS—*Continued*

Dixon, S. A home away from home
Dixon, S. Reinsertion
Dixon, S. Who he?
Doolittle, S. Care of the circumcised penis
Dozois, G. R. Morning child
Ely, S. 84 Avenue Foch
Ely, S. The oldest man in Mississippi
Ely, S. Rocks
Emshwiller, C. Destinations, premonitions and the nature of anxiety
Englander, N. Free fruit for young widows
Farmer, P. J. How deep the grooves
Fowler, C. Bryant and May in the soup
Gallari, A. Go piss on Jane
Gallari, A. Good friend
Gautier, A. Pan is dead
Gifford, B. The theory of the leisure class
Gilley, T. Bliss
Gordimer, N. Letter from his father
Goss, T. Fair Ladies
Grodstein, L. Homewrecker
Hannah, B. Fans
Hannah, B. Hey, have you got a cig, the time, the news, my face?
Ḥaqqī, Y. The first lesson
Heathcock, A. Smoke
Heathcock, A. The staying freight
Hemmingson, M. Pictures of houses with water damage
Hodge, B. When the silence gets too loud
Hussein, A. The refugees
Ibrāhīm, H. Fathers and sons
Jones, S. G. Crawlspace
Jones, S. G. Father, son, holy rabbit
Kennedy, A. L. Wasps
King, S. 1922
Kitterman, B. If I'd known you were going to stay this long
Kyle, A. Captain's club
Kyle, A. A lot like fun
Laken, V. Separate kingdoms
Lanagan, M. The miracle aquilina
Lebbon, T. Naming of parts
Leland, C. T. Peach Queen
Leland, C. T. Swim
Leonard, E. Showdown at checotah [variant title: How Carlos Webster changed his name to Carl and became a famous Oklahoma lawman]
Liss, D. The awkward age
London, J. A thousand deaths
Loory, B. The well
Lychack, W. Calvary
Lychack, W. Thin end of the wedge
MacLeod, I. The camping Wainwrights
Marār, M. The orange tree
Matheson, R. The hunt
McCann, C. Everything in this country must
McElroy, J. Canoe repair
McElroy, J. Night soul
McElroy, J. Particle of difference
Meyer, P. What you do out here, when you're alone
Monzó, Q. Helvetian freedoms
Moody, D. Big man
Mullins, D. P. Crash site on a desert mountain outside Las Vegas
Neugeboren, J. A missing year: letter to my son

Neugeboren, J. Overseas
Niedzviecki, H. Sometime next sunrise
Nuila, R. Dog bites
Oates, J. C. The barter
Oates, J. C. Lost daddy
O'Reilly, S. Curfew
Osondu, E. C. Bar Beach show
Parks, R. The man who carved skulls
Pearlman, E. Day of awe
Percy, B. Refresh, refresh
Powers, J. Preacher's kid
Qiu Xiaolong. Father and son
Ray, S. The dark between them
Ray, S. In the half-light
Ray, S. Three from Montana
Reents, S. Creatures of the kingdom
Riippi, J. Something about birthdays
Roberge, R. Working backward from the worst moment of my life
Rubin, J. Toward Lithuania
Schwarzschild, E. Midhusband
Scibona, S. The kid
Shapiro, J. Predation
Shepard, S. Livingston, Montana
Shipp, J. C. Kingdom come
Slouka, M. Crossing
Slouka, M. The hare's mask
Smith, M. M. The things he said
Sterling, P. Deja vu
Sullivan, J. Niels Bohr and the sleeping Dane
Tuten, F. The ship at anchor
Ulin, D. L. La jetée
Van den Broeck, W. Successor to the throne
Vila-Matas, E. Far from here
Watson, B. Visitation
Wells, H. G. The magic shop
Wieland, M. The bones of hagerman
Williamson, E. M. Mr. Murphy's wedding
Willis, D. And the living is easy
Woodrell, D. Woe to live on
Woolrich, C. Borrowed crime

Fathers and sons. Ibrāhīm, :

FATHERS-IN-LAW

Bill, F. The accident
Bill, F. Cold, hard love

Father's in the basement. Farmer, P. J.

Fatima, Altaf

Do you suppose it's the east winds?
   Tablet & pen; literary landscapes from the modern Middle East, a words without borders anthology; edited by Reza Asian.

Faulds, Jessica

Sickness
   Can'tLit; fearless fiction from Broken pencil magazine; edited by Richard Rosenbaum.

FAULKNER, GRANT

The Names of All Things
   Southwest Review v96 no3 p445-461 Je 2011

Faulkner, William

A rose for Emily
   21 essential American short stories; edited by Leslie M. Pockell

FAULKNER, WILLIAM, 1897-1962
                    Parodies, imitations, etc.

Cannon, P. The sound and the fungi

Faust, Minister Y.

The electrical neurheographiton
   The Thackery T. Lambshead cabinet of curiosities; edited by Ann & Jeff VanderMeer.

FILICIDE
Chapman, T. Kiddieland
Davidson, H. Son of so many tears
Kloess, C. The hardest button
Rodoreda, M. Friday, June 8
Villegas, H. The other side
The **film-makers** of Mars. Ryman, G.
Filmer. Wells, H. G.
Filmflam. Nevins, F. M., Jr.
Final act. Bayley, E.
A **Final** Brooklyn. Dulac, B.
The **final** conflict. Hardwick, E.
Final dispositions. Moore, L. M.
Final enemy. Hubbard, L. R.
The **final** nail. Randisi, R. J.
The **final** nail: a Val O'Farrel story. Randisi, R. J.
Final resting place. Muller, M.
Final statement. Blatnik, A.
Final victim. Bradbury, R. and Hasse, H.
FINANCE
See also Banks
Finances. Davis, L.
Finch, Bill
As If It Were the Last Time: Watching the Spring Tide Roll Into Alabama's Grand Bay
Nature Conservancy v60 no3 p80 Aut 2010
Fincke, Gary
Weepers
South Carolina Review v43 no2 p59-68 Spr 2011
A **find**. Gordimer, N.
Find and replace. Beattie, A.
Finding Love, Sex and Gender [Part of a special issue: XYZ Transformations of Urban Space: Transgendered and Transsexual Experiences of the City] Pacquing, M.
Finding Picasso. Haskins, M.
Finding there. Hunter, L.
A **fine** boy. Helle Helle
A **FINE** MEMORY WHILE IN DETOX. MURPHY, D.
A **fine** wedding. Dib, M.
The **finer** points of destruction. Parks, R.
The **finger**. Victor, G.
FINGERS
Riippi, J. Something about a finger
Victor, G. The finger
Finis. Lindholm, M.
Finished business. Bayley, E.
FINLAND
Horrocks, C. Going to Estonia
Olsen, L. June
Finlay, Charles Coleman
Hail, conductor
Swenson, P. The Best of Talebones; edited by Patrick Swenson.
Life so dear or peace so sweet
The way of the wizard; edited by John Joseph Adams.
Pervert
Brave new worlds; edited by John Joseph Adams.
Finney, Ernest J.
A Crime of Opportunity
The Sewanee Review v118 no3 p335-50 Summ 2010

Sequoia Gardens
Best of the West 2009; new stories from the wide side of the Missouri; edited by James Thomas and D. Seth Horton; foreword by Rick Bass.
Fintushel, Eliot
How the little rabbi grew
People of the book; a decade of Jewish science fiction & fantasy; edited by Rachel Swirsky & Sean Wallace.
Fiore, L. C.
Bangalore
Michigan Quarterly Review v49 no3 p365-81 Summ 2010
Fire. Greene, L. P.
Fire water. Hannah, B.
FIREARMS
Franco, J. I could kill someone
Gifford, B. Six million and one
Hemmingson, M. Give me the gun, he says
Hindmarch, W. The Auble gun
Kitterman, B. Boys from poor families
Lee, Y. H. Flower, mercy, needle, chain
Marār, M. I want a rifle!
Nevins, F. M., Jr. Dogsbody
Sheinin, L. The hunting knife
The **firebrand** symphony. Hodge, B.
Fired. Dixon, S.
Fired. Vukcevich, R.
FIREFIGHTERS
Harris, C. Dahlia underground
Sterling, P. First response
Trueblood, V. Trespass
Fireflies. Novack, S.
FIRES
See also Arson; Disasters
Blake, G. When the gods want to punish you
Boland, J. C. No crime in the hills
Boland, J. C. The substitute
Child, L. Addicted to sweetness
Gifford, B. Irredeemable
Greene, L. P. Fire
Hannah, B. Fire water
Hannah, B. Rangoon Green
London, J. To build a fire
Nolan, W. F. Descent
Novack, S. Save my soul
Phelps, E. S. The tenth of January
FIREWORKS
Naipaul, V. S. The pyrotechnicist
First, body. Thon, M. R.
First breath. Leboeuf, N. J.
First date. Fredsti, D.
First, Do No Harm. Kirchheimer, G. D.
First grade: handwriting practice. Davis, L.
The **first** husband. Oates, J. C.
First kisses from beyond the grave. Houser, N.
The **first** lesson. Ḥaqqī, Y.
First love never dies. Kozlowski, J.
First, marriage. Wieland, L.
First principle. Kress, N.
First response. Sterling, P.
The **first** rule is. Haywood, G. A.
First sight. Mullins, D. P.
First to score. Downey, G.
The **First** Wife. Sneed, C.

Firth, Matthew
Some kind of betrayal
Can'tLit; fearless fiction from Broken pencil magazine; edited by Richard Rosenbaum.
Fischer, Bruno
Middleman for murder
The Black Lizard big book of Black Mask stories; edited and with a foreword by Otto Penzler; introduction by Keith Alan Deutsch.
Fischer, Jason
The house of nameless
L. Ron Hubbard presents Writers of the Future volume XXVI; the year's twelve best tales from the Writers of the Future international writers' program; illustrated by winners in the Illustrators of the Future international illustrators' program; with essays on writing & illustration by L. Ron Hubbard/Dean Wesley Smith/ Stephen Youll; edited by K. D. Wentworth
The **fish**. Davis, L.
Fish. Gray, A.
The **fish** in the teapot. Loory, B.
Fish story. Bass, R.
The **fish** tank. Davis, L.
Fishbane, Joel
A Clever Science
New England Review v32 no2 p68-84 Spr 2011
Fisher, Dorothy Canfield
The bedquilt
The vintage book of American women writers; edited and with an introduction by Elaine Showalter.
Fisher, Steve
Wait for me
The Black Lizard big book of Black Mask stories; edited and with a foreword by Otto Penzler; introduction by Keith Alan Deutsch.
The **fisherman**. Thorne, T.
Fisherman's blues. McGilloway, B.
FISHERMEN
See also Fishing
Balázs, B. The moon fish
Gray, A. Fish
Hannah, B. Getting ready
Fishermen. Obioma, C. J.
FISHES
See also Aquariums
Loory, B. The fish in the teapot
Poulson, C. Fishy story
FISHING
See also Fishermen
Allen, D. Fishing with Alex
Ayau, K. J. Spawning
Ely, S. Dream fishing
Grace, P. Busy lines
Hannah, B. Fire water
Hannah, B. High-water railers
Fishing the edge of the world. Monk, D.
Fishing with Alex. Allen, D.
Fishpole Pete. Hemmingson, M.
The **fishpond**. Ely, S.
Fishtown odyssey. Anthony, M.
Fishy story. Poulson, C.
Fit of rage. Mehrotra, P. K.

FITCH, BRIAN
Better Than Dead
The North American Review v296 no3 p32-37 Summ 2011
Fitts, Tim
No *Rabio*
Gettysburg Review v24 no1 p33-47 Spr 2011
Fitzgerald, F. Scott (Francis Scott)
The diamond as big as the Ritz
21 essential American short stories; edited by Leslie M. Pockell
Pat Hobby and Orson Welles
I found this funny; my favorite pieces of humor and some that may not be funny at all; edited by Judd Apatow.
Winter dreams
Golf stories; edited by Charles McGrath.
FITZGERALD, F. SCOTT (FRANCIS SCOTT), 1896-1940
Parodies, imitations, etc.
Bradley, G. An East Egg update
Cannon, P. Tender is the night-gaunt
Fitzgerald, Francis Scott *See* Fitzgerald, F. Scott (Francis Scott), 1896-1940
Fitzgerald, Samar Farah
Where Do You Go?
New England Review v32 no1 p77-88 2011
Five fictions from the middle of the night. Davis, L.
A **five-minute** conversation. Novack, S.
Five Movie Endings (I Would Banish from This World if I Were Ruler Supreme of Hollywood). Ramirez, S.
The **Five** Points of Performance. Mohar, C.
The **five** senses. Nesbit, E.
Five Shorts. Nissen, T.
Five shorts. Shepard, S.
Five signs of disturbance. Davis, L.
Five spot. Shepard, S.
Five stories from Flaubert. Davis, L.
The **five-swing** wlak. Self, W.
The **five** wounds. Quade, K. V.
A **flag** on the island. Naipaul, V. S.
Flame retarded. Story, K.
FLAMENCO DANCERS *See* Dancers
Flaming angel. Davis, F. C.
Flann, Kathy
Half a brother
Michigan Quarterly Review v50 no2 p210-224 Spr 2011
Somebody for Everybody
The North American Review v296 no3 p13-19 Summ 2011
Flash crowd. Niven, L.
Flashmen. Dowling, T.
Flatlander. Niven, L.
Flatmouth, Mary
A crystal clear dream
Tribal College Journal of American Indian Higher Education v23 no1 p58-9 Fall 2011
The **flaw** in the design. Eisenberg, D.
The **flea**. Balázs, B.
Fledged. Emshwiller, C.
Fleischman, Cyrille
The Neighbor on Rue de Jarente
World Literature Today v84 no5 p40-1 S/O 2010

Fleischmann, Raymond
  Shannon the Cannon
    River Styx no83 p62-78 2010
Fleming, Ian
  Goldfinger [excerpt]
    Golf stories; edited by Charles McGrath.
Fleri, Janine
  Gynecomastia
    Can'tLit; fearless fiction from Broken pencil
      magazine; edited by Richard Rosenbaum.
The **Flesh**. Handler, J. C.
Flick, Sherrie
  The Lake
    Ploughshares v36 no4 p36 Wint 2010/2011
The **flier**. Levine, S.
FLIERS *See* Air pilots
Flies. Ruocco, J.
FLIGHT
  Hand, E. The maiden flight of McCauley's Bel-
    lerophon
  Loory, B. The well
  McOmber, A. A memory of his rising
  O'Connor, S. The professor of atheism: Here
    comes another lesson
  Russo, P. Swoop
Flight. McGuane, T.
The **flight** of the horse. Niven, L.
Flight to forever. Anderson, P.
Flint. Ruckley, B.
Floating. Mehta, R.
The **flock**. Shepard, L.
FLOODS
    See also Disasters
  Cardinale, J. The great disappointment
  Dick, P. K. The builder
  Phillips, H. The floods
  Shepard, S. Saving Fats
The **floods**. Phillips, H.
Florianne. Woodrell, D.
FLORIDA
  Allen, R. A. The Emerald Coast
  Ayau, K. J. Sand castle
  Barrett, L. Cave of the winds
  Bingham, S. Red car
  Boland, J. C. Deep water
  Boland, J. C. Out of her depth
  Boland, J. C. Past life
  Bond, J. Trapped
  Born, J. O. Revenge of the emerging market
  Bukiet, M. J. The Florida sunshine tree
  Corncoran, T. Burn off by noon
  Due, T. The lake
  Dufresne, J. Iffy
  Engel, P. Desaliento
  Evans, D. Snakes
  Evans, M. A. Low-budget monster flick
  Falk, M. R. The Apalachicola night
  Gautier, A. The ease of living
  Haines, C. The cypress dream
  Hannah, B. A creature in the Bay of St. Louis
  Hannah, B. Two gone over
  Kava, A. and Bremmer, P. A. A breath of hot
    air
  King, J. Quiet
  Koryta, M. The cypress house
  Lister, M. Ultima forsan
  McMillian, R. Escambia counties
  Pascoe, J. Paper
  Russell, K. The dredgeman's revelation

  Unger, L. Wild Card
                      Key West
  Boland, J. C. Last island south
  DuBois, B. The road's end
  Isleib, R. The itinerary
                        Miami
  Barrett, L. Texaco on Biscayne
  Engel, P. Dia
  Lutz, J. Lily & men
                     Miami Beach
  Garcia-Aguilera, C. Personal experience
                      Palm Beach
  Bell, T. The pirate of Palm Beach
                        Tampa
  Gifford, B. The exception
  Jackson, A. A Tampa man
FLORIDA CYPRESS GARDENS
  Haines, C. The cypress dream
The **Florida** sunshine tree. Bukiet, M. J.
FLORISTS
  Gifford, B. The Albanian florist
Flotsam. Eisenberg, D.
Flower, mercy, needle, chain. Lee, Y. H.
The **flowering** of the strange orchild. Wells, H. G.
FLOWERS
        See also Orchids
  De Coster, S. Queen
  Latiolais, M. Thorns
  Lychack, W. The architect of flowers
  Rodoreda, M. Paralysis
Floyd, Charles Arthur *See* Floyd, Pretty Boy,
    1904-1934
FLOYD, PRETTY BOY, 1904-1934
                       About
  Leonard, E. Louly and Pretty Boy
FLUTISTS
  Vukcevich, R. Gas
  Williamson, E. M. Creusa
The **fluttering** thing. Aiken, J.
The **fly**. Davis, L.
FLYING *See* Flight
Flying Backwards. Rogers, H.
Flying carpets. Millhauser, S.
Flying cars. Goodberg, D.
Flying fish "prometheus" (a fantasy of the future).
    Bergsoe, V.
Flying in the face of god. Allan, N.
The **flying** man. Wells, H. G.
Flying monkeys. Ruocco, J.
Flying pigs. Goodberg, D.
Flying solo. Gorman, E.
Flytopia. Self, W.
Foer, Jonathan Safran
  Here we aren't, so quickly
    20 under 40; stories from the New Yorker;
      edited by Deborah Treisman.
FOETUS *See* Fetus
FOG
  Fowler, C. Bryant and May in the soup
The **folding** man. Lansdale, J. R.
Folie à deux. Trevor, W.
Folktales of North America. Mitchell, E.
Following Slowly. Rea, A. E.
Fong Fong no. 4. Mu Xin
FOOD
  Dybek, S. Sauerkraut soup
  Kurlansky, M. Hot dog
  Kurlansky, M. Muffins
  Latiolais, M. Gut

Found. Bingham, S.
FOUNDATIONS (ENDOWMENTS) *See* Endowments
FOUNDLINGS *See* Abandoned children
Fountain, Ben
   Near-extinct birds of the central cordillera
      Best of times, worst of times; contemporary American short stories from the new Gilded Age; edited by Wendy Martin and Cecelia Tichi.
Four calling birds, three french hens. Moore, L.
Four fictions [Excerpted from Catastrophes] Breytenbach, B.
The **four** horsemen. Bayley, E.
Four indians in the mirror. Grove, L. L.
Four musicians. Blaine, M.
Four stories. Brown, G.
Four women from Ravensbrück. Kalechofsky, R.
Fourteen small stories. Adolphsen, P.
FOURTH DIMENSION
   Bradbury, R. Tale of the mangledomvritch
   Smith, C. A. Double cosmos
   Smith, C. A. Strange shadows
FOURTH OF JULY
   Chau, A. Hunger
The **fourth** profession. Niven, L.
Fowler, Christopher
   Bryant and May in the soup
      Original sins; a Crime Writer's Association anthology; edited by Martin Edwards.
   Oblivion by Calvin Klein
      Naked city; tales of urban fantasy; edited by Ellen Datlow.
   Oh I do like to be beside the seaside
      The Best horror of the year: volume three; edited by Ellen Datlow.
Fowler, Karen Joy
   Always
      Fowler, K. J. What I didn't see and other stories
   Booth's ghost
      Fowler, K. J. What I didn't see and other stories
   The dark
      Fowler, K. J. What I didn't see and other stories
   Familiar birds
      Fowler, K. J. What I didn't see and other stories
   Halfway people
      Fowler, K. J. What I didn't see and other stories
   King Rat
      Fowler, K. J. What I didn't see and other stories
   The last worders
      Fowler, K. J. What I didn't see and other stories
   The Marianas Islands
      Fowler, K. J. What I didn't see and other stories
   The Pelican Bar
      Fowler, K. J. What I didn't see and other stories
   Private grave 9
      Fowler, K. J. What I didn't see and other stories

   Standing room only
      Fowler, K. J. What I didn't see and other stories
   What I didn't see
      Fowler, K. J. What I didn't see and other stories
Fox Girl [Part of special issue: Sex and Surveillance] Chin, M.
The **Fox** Pelt. BENEDICT, D.
Fracture points. Solzhenitsyn, A.
A **Fragile** Life. Kinder, R. M.
Fragments of a hologram rose. Gibson, W.
Franc, Isabel
   The enigma of her voice
      Barcelona noir; edited by Adriana V. Lopez & Cartmen Ospina; translated by Achy Obejas.
FRANCE
   Charnas, S. M. Lowland sea
   Kurlansky, M. Orangina
               15th century
   Shepard, J. Classical scenes of farewell
               16th century
   Howard, R. E. Blades for France
   Howard, R. E. Sword woman
               18th century
   Orczy, B. A question of passports
               Aristocracy
      See Aristocracy—France
               Army
      Foreign Legion
   Surdez, G. Suicide patrol
   Wren, P. C. A gentleman of color
               Rural life
   Davis, L. French lesson I: le meurtre
               Bordeaux
   Wieland, L. La fenêtre
               Normandy
   Bingham, S. Sagesse
               Paris
   Bingham, S. Sweet peas
   Goodrich, J. Murder in the sixth
   Kurlansky, M. Belons
   McElroy, J. The man with the bagful of boomerangs in the Bois de Boulogne
   Rodoreda, M. Orléans, three kilometers
   Schmitt, E.-E. Getting better
   Trevor, W. Folie à deux
   Villegas, H. The other door
   Wieland, L. Out of the garden
Franchini, Antonio
   It Is Proper for Men to Remember
      Chicago Review v56 no1 p71-5 Spr 2011
FRANCINI, THOMAS, 1571-1651
               About
   McOmber, A. The automatic garden
Francis, David
   Once Removed
      Harvard Review (1992) no38 p28-48 2010
Francis, H. E.
   About Love
      Southwest Review v95 no4 p614-30 2010
Franco, James
   American history
      Franco, J. Palo Alto; stories
   April in three parts: part 1, The rainbow goblins
      Franco, J. Palo Alto; stories
   April in three parts: part II, Wasting
      Franco, J. Palo Alto; stories

Franco, James—_Continued_
April in three parts: part III, April
Franco, J. Palo Alto; stories
Camp
Franco, J. Palo Alto; stories
Chinatown in three parts
Franco, J. Palo Alto; stories
Emily
Franco, J. Palo Alto; stories
Halloween
Franco, J. Palo Alto; stories
I could kill someone
Franco, J. Palo Alto; stories
Jack-O'
Franco, J. Palo Alto; stories
Killing animals
Franco, J. Palo Alto; stories
Lockheed
Franco, J. Palo Alto; stories
Tar baby
Franco, J. Palo Alto; stories
Frank, Brian P.
Test of faith
Nature v472 no7343 p384 Ap 21 2011
Frank. Willis, D.
FRANKENSTEIN (FICTITIOUS CHARAC-TER)
Anderson, K. J. Torn stitches, shattered glass
Frankenstein. Shelley, M. W.
Franklin, Tom
The ballad of Duane Juarez
Best of times, worst of times; contemporary American short stories from the new Gilded Age; edited by Wendy Martin and Cecelia Tichi.
Fraser, Bruce
The Partner
The Advocate (Vancouver, B.C.) v68 pt4 p563-8 Jl 2010
Squires & Morley
The Advocate (Vancouver, B.C.) v69 pt3 p372-7 My 2011
FRATRICIDE
Wells, H. G. Walcote
Zimmerman, R. Blood and dirt
FRAUD
See also Tax evasion
Bill, F. Rough company
Born, J. O. Revenge of the emerging market
Catalona, K. The Sadowsky manifesto
Frazier, Ian
Coyote v. Acme
I found this funny; my favorite pieces of humor and some that may not be funny at all; edited by Judd Apatow.
FREAK SHOWS
Jewett, S. O. The circus at Denby
Fredsti, Dana
First date
Hungry for your love; an anthology of zombie romance; edited by Lori Perkins.
Free fruit for young widows. Englander, N.
Free Lunch at the Poseidon. Gnidzeijko-Smith, E.
Free you are. Senna, D.

Freed, Lynn
Sunshine
The Pen/O.Henry Prize stories 2011; chosen and with an introduction by Laura Furman; with essays on the stories thety admire most by jurors A. M. Homes, Manuel Muñoz, Christine Schutt
FREEDOM _See_ Liberty
Freeman, Castle, Jr.
The Drowned Man at Sanderlings
New England Review v32 no1 p65-73 2011
The Secret Sits in the Middle
Southwest Review v96 no3 p355-366 Je 2011
Freeman, Mary Eleanor Wilkins
The hall bedroom
The dreaming sex; early tales of scientific imagination by women; edited by Mike Ashley.
A New England nun
The vintage book of American women writers; edited and with an introduction by Elaine Showalter.
Noblesse
The vintage book of American women writers; edited and with an introduction by Elaine Showalter.
Old Woman Magoun
The vintage book of American women writers; edited and with an introduction by Elaine Showalter.
Freestanding. Sabar, A.
FREEZING OF HUMAN BODIES _See_ Cryonics
FREIGHTERS _See_ Ships
French, Paul _See_ Asimov, Isaac, 1920-1992
FRENCH
United States
Laurrent, E. American diary
FRENCH CAMEROONS _See_ Cameroon
FRENCH LANGUAGE
Davis, L. French lesson I: le meurtre
French lesson I: le meurtre. Davis, L.
The **Frenchwoman's** Letter. Cunha, C.
Fresco, Byzantine. Bakopoulos, N.
Fresno. King, G.
Freudenberger, Nell
An arranged marriage
20 under 40; stories from the New Yorker; edited by Deborah Treisman.
Friday, June 8. Rodoreda, M.
Friday's footprint. Gordimer, N.
Fried, Golda
Lindsey
Can'tLit; fearless fiction from Broken pencil magazine; edited by Richard Rosenbaum.
Summer
Can'tLit; fearless fiction from Broken pencil magazine; edited by Richard Rosenbaum.
Fried, John
Nueve
The North American Review v295 no2 p14-21 Spr 2010
Fried, Seth
Frost mountain picnic massacre
Pushcart Prize XXXV: best of the small presses 2011; edited by Bill Henderson with the Pushcart Prize editors.
The Year's best dark fantasy & horror; edited by Paula Guran

From the novel Skin of shadow. Boukebba, A.

From the novel The last hanging poem. Hussein al Abri

From the novel The scalpel. Riahi, K.

From the novel The threshold of ashes. El Souwaim, M.

from Whosoever Fears the Sea. Forster, D.

FRONT NATIONAL (FRANCE)

Neugeboren, J. Summer afternoon

FRONTIER AND PIONEER LIFE
Ohio

Bierce, A. The boarded window
Wyoming

Proulx, A. Them old cowboy songs

Frost, Gregory

The comeuppance of Creegus Maxin

The beastly bride; tales of the animal people; edited by Ellen Datlow & Terri Windling; introduction by Terri Windling; selected decorations by Charles Vess.

Swift decline

The stories (in) between; edited by Greg Schauer, Jeanne B. Benzel, and W. H. Horner.

Frost mountain picnic massacre. Fried, S.

Frozen in time. Goodberg, D.

Frozen mouth [(1966), chapters one and two] Kim, H.-y.

Frucht, Abby

Tamarinds

New Letters v77 no1 p17-35 2010/2011

Fruelund, Simon

Hair

World Literature Today v84 no5 p42-3 S/O 2010

FRUIT

Marãr, M. The wall of cacti

FRUIT PICKERS See Migrant labor

A **fruitless** assignment. Bierce, A.

Frumkin, Rebekah

Monster

The best American nonrequired reading 2009; edited by Dave Eggers; introduction by Marjane Satrapi; managing editor, Jesse Nathan

Ft. Robinson, Nebraska (Highway 20). Shepard, S.

Fucking the Mermaid. Eck, M.

FUGITIVES

See also Escaped convicts; Manhunts; Outlaws

Blatnik, A. I can't decide

Goodrich, J. Murder in the sixth

Matheson, R. The hunt

Sa'īd, M. A. Hayat: a short story

Fugue. Nagai, M.

Fukuoka and the Way to Be Free. White, M. J.

A **full** house. McGarry, J.

Full house. Yu, M. R.

Fuller, Alice W.

A wife manufactured to order

The dreaming sex; early tales of scientific imagination by women; edited by Mike Ashley.

Fultz, John R.

The thirteen texts of Arthyria

The way of the wizard; edited by John Joseph Adams.

Los **fundadores.** Martínez-Salguero, J.

The **funeral.** Sa'īd, M. A.

The **funeral.** Wilhelm, K.

Funeral music. Nevins, F. M., Jr.

FUNERAL RITES AND CEREMONIES

Bierce, A. John Mortonson's funeral

Doyle, R. Funerals

Furman, L. A thousand words

Glass, J. C. Robbie

Gordimer, N. Six feet of the country

Gray, A. The movement

Hirshberg, G. Shomer

Ibrãhim, H As-Sayyed's space

Kiernan, C. R. The belated burial

Kyle, A. Brides

Leland, C. T. Fellatio

Manilla, M. The wife you wanted

Morrow, J. The iron shroud

Mphahlele, E. Down the quiet street

Mphahlele, E. In Corner B

Neugeboren, J. Summer afternoon

Niedzviecki, H. Undead

Sa'īd, M. A. The funeral

Willis, M. S. Fellowship of kindred minds

Willis, M. S. Speak well of the dead

Funerals. Doyle, R.

Fungus of the heart. Shipp, J. C.

A **funny** smell. Vukcevich, R.

Fur: an autobiography [excerpt] Couture, B.

FUR TRADE

See also Trading posts

Furlough. Heathcock, A.

Furman, Laura

The blue birds come today

Furman, L. The mother who stayed; stories

The blue wall

Furman, L. The mother who stayed; stories

The eye

Furman, L. The mother who stayed; stories

Here it was, November

Furman, L. The mother who stayed; stories

The hospital room

Furman, L. The mother who stayed; stories

The mother who stayed

Furman, L. The mother who stayed; stories

Plum Creek

Furman, L. The mother who stayed; stories

The thief

Furman, L. The mother who stayed; stories

A thousand words

Furman, L. The mother who stayed; stories

The **furnace.** Davis, L.

Further notes on my unfortunate condition. St. John, N.

Fusilli, Jim

Digby, attorney at law

By hook or by crook and 27 more of the best crime + mystery stories of the year; edited by Ed Gorman and Martin H. Greenberg.

The **futility** of fixed positions. Emshwiller, C.

FUTURE

See also Science fiction

Anderson, P. Goat song

Anderson, P. The pugilist

Bacigalupi, P. The gambler

Bacigalupi, P. Pop squad

Ballard, J. G. Billennium

Bear, E. And the deep blue sea

Beckett, C. The peacock cloak

Benford, G. Centigrade 233

FUTURE—*Continued*

Bergsoe, V. Flying fish "prometheus" (a fantasy of the future)
Bierce, A. For the Ahkoond
Bradbury, R. Fahrenheit 451 [excerpt]
Bradbury, R. King of the gray spaces (R is for rocket)
Bradbury, R. The pedestrian
Bradbury, R. The pendulum (first version)
Bradbury, R. and Hasse, H. Pendulum
Brin, D. Just a hint
Bryant, E. Jody after the war
Cadigan, P. Rock on
Card, O. S. Salvage
Clarke, A. C. "If I forget thee, oh Earth . . ."
Cluley, R. At night, when the demons come
Davis, C. Adrift on the policy level
De Bodard, A. The shipmaker
Del Rey, L. Kindness
Dick, P. K. The defenders
Dick, P. K. Mr. Spaceship
Doctorow, C. Craphound
Doctorow, C. The Jammie Dodgers and the adventure of the Leicester Square screening
Doctorow, C. The things that make me weak and strange get engineered away
Dowling, T. The library
Dowling, T. Truth window: a tale of the bedlam rose
Dozois, G. R. Dinner party
Dozois, G. R. A knight of ghosts and shadows
Dozois, G. R. Morning child
Dozois, G. R. The peacemaker
Dozois, G. R. Recidivist
Dozois, G. R. Solace
Dozois, G. R. A special kind of morning
Ellison, H. "Repent, harlequin!" said the ticktockman
Emshwiller, C. Baby
Emshwiller, C. Day at the beach
Farmer, P. J. How deep the grooves
Finlay, C. C. Pervert
Gaiman, N. and Talbot, B. From homogenous to honey
Genge, S. Sins of the father
Goodberg, D. A letter from vesta
Goodberg, D. A letter to vesta
Goodberg, D. The new world
Goodberg, D. The preservation society
Goodberg, D. Staging a scene
Goodberg, D. World at war
Gorman, E. The baby store
Haines, J. P. Ten with a flag
Haldeman, J. Sleeping dogs
Harris, C. W. The miracle of the lily
Hawkins, J. Chimbwi
Henderson, C. J. The wonderous boundless thought
Huxley, A. Brave new world [excerpt]
Irvine, A. Peter Shilling
Jablokov, A. Blind cat dance
Jones, G. A. Blue clay blues
Jones, G. A. Identifying the object
Kiernan, C. R. The pearl diver
Kress, N. By fools like me
Lake, J. The American dead
Lake, J. The sky that wraps the world round, past the blue and into the black
Langan, S. Independence day

Lindsley, H. Just do it
MacLeod, I. Re-crossing the Styx
MacLeod, I. Taking good care of myself
Miéville, C. Highway 61 revisited
Monk, D. Stringing tomorrow
Morris, E. Rejection letter
Morrow, J. Auspicious eggs
Niven, L. Cloak of anarchy
Niven, L. The defenseless dead
Niven, L. Flash crowd
Niven, L. Flatlander
Niven, L. The flight of the horse
Niven, L. The hole man
Payne, M. Bullet
Popkes, S. Jackie's boy
Popov, A. Plumbers
Rajaniemi, H. Elegy for a young elk
Reed, K. At central
Reed, R. Dead man's run
Reynolds, A. Sleepover
Rickert, M. Evidence of love in a case of abandonment
Rickert, M. Evidence of love in a case of abandonment: one daughter's personal account
Robinson, K. S. In Pierson's orchestra
Ryman, G. Birth days
Ryman, G. Days of wonder
Ryman, G. Dead space for the unexpected
Ryman, G. Everywhere
Ryman, G. The future of science fiction
Ryman, G. Home
Ryman, G. Talk is cheap
Ryman, G. VAO
Ryman, G. You
Sanders, T. Obit
Saunders, G. Escape from Spiderhead
Self, W. Caring, sharing
Sheckley, R. The store of the worlds
Shehadeh, R. The unbecoming of Virgil Smythe
Shepard, J. The Netherlands lives with water
Shipp, J. C. Kingdom come
Silverberg, R. At the conglomeroid cocktail party
Silverberg, R. Caught in the organ draft
Silverberg, R. Dancers in the time-flux
Silverberg, R. Gate of horn, gate of ivory
Silverberg, R. Gianni
Silverberg, R. Homefaring
Silverberg, R. The palace at midnight
Silverberg, R. When we went to see the end of the world
Sisson, A. Patriot girls
Smith, C. A. The dark age
Smith, C. A. The great god Awto
Spinrad, N. Bug Jack Barron [excerpt]
Sterling, B. The exterminator's want ad
Swanwick, M. The feast of Saint Janis
Swanwick, M. Libertarian Russia
Swirsky, R. Again and again and again
Swirsky, R. The debt of the innocent
Swirsky, R. The lady who plucked red flowers beneath the queen's window
Tidhar, L. The night train
Tolbert, J. Arties aren't stupid
Torgersen, B. R. Exanastasis
Valentine, G. Is this your day to join revolution?
Vaughn, C. Amaryllis
Vonnegut, K. Harrison Bergeron

FUTURE—*Continued*
Wells, H. G. The star
Wells, H. G. A story of the days to come
Wells, H. G. A tale of the twentieth century for advanced thinkers
Williamson, M. Sacrament
Wyndham, J. The wheel
Zelazny, R. Lucifer
FUTURE LIFE
Simpson, H. Diary of an interesting year
The **future** of science fiction. Ryman, G.
Futures. Ross, A.
Fytton Armstrong, Terence Ian *See* Gawsworth, John, 1912-1970

G

Gabbert, Elisa
(jt. auth) See Rooney, Kathleen and Gabbert, Elisa
Gabel, Aja
The seven stages of camping with the poet
South Carolina Review v43 no2 p90-4 Spr 2011
Gabel-Hartman, Laura
The Tea Guy
Southern Humanities Review v44 no4 p442-9 Fall 2010
Gabriel's horn. Bradbury, R. and Hasse, H.
Gaddis, Sarah M.
The End of Old History
Agni no72 p59-68 2010
Gaiman, Neil
Bitter grounds
Zombies: the recent dead; edited by Paula Guran.
How to sell the Ponti Bridge
The way of the wizard; edited by John Joseph Adams.
The price
Sympathy for the devil; edited by Tim Pratt.
The problem of Susan
People of the book; a decade of Jewish science fiction & fantasy; edited by Rachel Swirsky & Sean Wallace.
"The truth is a cave in the Black Mountains. . . ."
The Best science fiction and fantasy of the year: volume five; edited by Jonathan Strahan.
We can get them for you wholesale
Sympathy for the devil; edited by Tim Pratt.
The end of the world; stories of the apocalypse; edited by Martin H. Greenberg.
Gaiman, Neil and Talbot, Bryan
From homogenous to honey
Brave new worlds; edited by John Joseph Adams.
Gaitskill, Mary
The other place
The New Yorker v87 no1 p112-19 F 14-21 2011
Galatea in Situ. Feinsilber, M.
Galchen, Rivka
The entire northern side was covered with fire
20 under 40; stories from the New Yorker; edited by Deborah Treisman.

Wild berry blue
The best American nonrequired reading 2009; edited by Dave Eggers; introduction by Marjane Satrapi; managing editor, Jesse Nathan
GALES *See* Storms
Galgut, Damon
The lover
The Pen/O.Henry Prize stories, 2010; edited and with an introduction by Laura Furman; with essays on the stories they admire most by jurors Junot Diaz, Paula Fox, Yiyun Li.
Gallari, Adam
A beautiful lie
Gallari, A. We are never as beautiful as we are now; stories
Chasing Adonis
Gallari, A. We are never as beautiful as we are now; stories
Go piss on Jane
Gallari, A. We are never as beautiful as we are now; stories
Good friend
Gallari, A. We are never as beautiful as we are now; stories
Negative space
Gallari, A. We are never as beautiful as we are now; stories
No cause for concern
Gallari, A. We are never as beautiful as we are now; stories
Reading Rilke
Gallari, A. We are never as beautiful as we are now; stories
Throwing stones
Gallari, A. We are never as beautiful as we are now; stories
Warwick Damon
Gallari, A. We are never as beautiful as we are now; stories
The **gallows-horse.** Negarestani, R.
Galveston Bay, 1826. Chuculate, E. D.
Gálvez Ronceros, Antonio
Jutito
Callaloo v34 no2 p252-3 Spr 2011
Monologue for Jutito
Callaloo v34 no2 p254-5 Spr 2011
The **gambler.** Bacigalupi, P.
GAMBLERS *See* Gambling
GAMBLING
See also Lotteries; Wagers
Anderson, P. Inside straight
Barillas, G. R. The roads
Burton, M. T. Cherry Coke
Chekhov, A. P. The bet
Crane, S. The blue hotel
DuBois, B. The necessary brother
Gorman, E. The long way back
Khanna, R. Card sharp
Kilworth, G. Hats off to Mary
Mankiewicz, D. M. Odds on death
Pushkin, A. The queen of spades
Shapiro, J. Bummer
Tremblay, P. Nineteen snapshots of Dennisport
Twain, M. The celebrated jumping frog of Calaveras County
Willis, D. Escape
A **game** of golf. Goodberg, D.

GAMES

See also Bingo; Video games

Boland, J. C. Mad hare
Cardinale, J. The singularity
Carlson, R. Escape from prison
Ciechanowski, W. The dungeon out of time
Evenson, B. Windeye
Kronauer, B. Stanzas for an observation
Lipsyte, S. The Dungeon Master

The **Games** Room. Gordimer, N.

GANEŚA (HINDU DEITY)

Ford, J. Ganesha

Ganesha. Ford, J.

Gangrene. Kilpatrick, S.

GANGS

See also Juvenile delinquency

Tafoya, D. Above the Imperial

GANGSTERS

See also Mafia

Boland, J. C. Marley's ghost
Chance, K. In vino veritas
Hemingway, E. The killers
Howard, C. The way they limp
Lake, J. The sky that wraps the world round, past the blue and into the black
Leonard, E. Louly and Pretty Boy
Vukcevich, R. Suddenly speaking

Gappah, Petina

An incident at lunchtime

Freedom; stories celebrating the Universal Declaration of Human Rights; Amnesty International.

The **garbage** man. Goodberg, D.

Garcia, Nancy

(tr.) See Palma, Ricardo

Garcia-Aguilera, Carolina

Personal experience

Florida heat wave; [edited and with an] introduction by Michael Lister.

A **garden** in Hell. Parks, R.

The **garden** of Adompha. Smith, C. A.

GARDEN PARTIES *See* Parties

The **Gardener**. Myerson, J.

Gardener. Nutting, A.

Gardeners' world. Barnes, J.

GARDENING *See* Gardens

Gardening in the dark. Shepard, S.

GARDENS

Barnes, J. Gardeners' world
Gray, A. The picture window
McOmber, A. The automatic garden
Parks, R. A garden in Hell

Gardens of the moon. McOmber, A.

Gardiner, John Rolfe

Virgin Summer

The American Scholar v80 no3 p82-91 Summ 2011

Gardner, Erle Stanley

Come and get it

The Black Lizard big book of Black Mask stories; edited and with a foreword by Otto Penzler; introduction by Keith Alan Deutsch.

GARIBALDI, GIUSEPPE, 1807-1882

About

Barnes, J. Carcassonne

A **Garibaldi** tale. Bernheimer, K.

Garm - a hostage. Kipling, R.

Garner, Alan

Gray Wolf, Prince Jack, and the Firebird

Freedom; stories celebrating the Universal Declaration of Human Rights; Amnesty International.

Garriga, Michael

Custody Battle for Chelsea Tammy: At the Toys "R" Us, Aisle 6, in a Suburb of Atlanta, Georgia, December 24, 1983

The Southern Review (Baton Rouge, La.) v47 no2 p335-8 Spr 2011

Gartner, Zsuzsi

We Come in Peace

The Walrus v8 no4 p44-9, 51-2 My 2011

Gas. Lachaîne, A.

Gas. Vukcevich, R.

Gash, Jonathan

The life business

Requiems for the departed; edited by Gerard Brennan & Mike Stone.

GASOLINE STATIONS *See* Automobiles—Service stations

Gate of horn, gate of ivory. Silverberg, R.

Gates, David

Alcorian A-1949

The Paris Review v53 no197 p61-77 Summ 2011

Gates of empire. Howard, R. E.

Gault, William Campbell

The bloody Bokhara

The Black Lizard big book of Black Mask stories; edited and with a foreword by Otto Penzler; introduction by Keith Alan Deutsch.

Gautam under a tree. Sawhney, H.

Gautier, Amina

Afternoon tea

Gautier, A. At-risk; stories

Boogiemen

Gautier, A. At-risk; stories

Dance for me

Gautier, A. At-risk; stories

Directory Assistance

Southwest Review v96 no2 p249-62 2011

The ease of living

Gautier, A. At-risk; stories

Girl of wisdom

Gautier, A. At-risk; stories

Held

Gautier, A. At-risk; stories

Pan is dead

Gautier, A. At-risk; stories

Push

Gautier, A. At-risk; stories

Some other kind of happiness

Gautier, A. At-risk; stories

Yearn

Gautier, A. At-risk; stories

Gautier, Théophile

The amorous corpse

The book of the living dead; edited by John Richard Stephens.

Gauvin, Edward

(tr.) See Châteaureynaud, Georges-Olivier

Gavin, Jim

Costello

The New Yorker v86 no39 p70-81 D 6 2010

GAWSWORTH, JOHN, 1912-1970
About
Marías, J. An epigram of fealty
Gay, William
I Hate to See That Evening Sun Go Down
The Georgia Review v65 no1 p104-22 Spr 2011
GAY MEN *See* Homosexuality
GAY WOMEN *See* Lesbianism
GAYE, MARVIN
About
Tillman, L. Later
GAYNOR, GLORIA
About
Archer, J. I will survive
GAZA STRIP
Jarrar, R. The story of my building (after Isaac Babel's "Story of my dovecote")
Kanafāni, G. Letter from Gaza
Marār, M. It means ... : a pimp
Marār, M. The wall of cacti
Gearhart-Serna, Terra L.
Coyote and valorosa
The beastly bride; tales of the animal people; edited by Ellen Datlow & Terri Windling; introduction by Terri Windling; selected decorations by Charles Vess.
Geary, Tracy Miller
The Beekeeper's Wife
Good Housekeeping v251 no4 p219-20, 222-7 O 2010
Geddarien. Lemberg, R.
Geeraerts, Jef
Indian summer
The Dedalus book of Flemish fantasy; edited by Eric Dickens and translated by Paul Vincent.
Geeraerts, Jozef Adriaan *See* Geeraerts, Jef, 1930-
GEESE
Teodorovici, L. D. Goose chase
Geese. Packer, Z.
Gelasimov, Andrei
The evil eye
Best European fiction 2011; edited by Aleksandr Hemon; preface by Colum McCann
GEMS *See* Diamonds
Gen Papa-Georgio. Sands, B.
GENERALS
Balázs, B. The victor
Gordimer, N. At the rendezvous of victory
Terry, G. P. The general's tears
The **general's** tears. Terry, G. P.
The **generation** gap. Gordimer, N.
Genetic Drift. Naimon, D.
GENETIC ENGINEERING
Tolbert, J. Arties aren't stupid
GENETIC EXPERIMENTATION *See* Genetics
GENETIC RESEARCH *See* Genetics
GENETICS
Lindholm, M. Cut
Ryman, G. Days of wonder
Turtledove, H. The genetics lecture
The **genetics** lecture. Turtledove, H.
GENEVA (SWITZERLAND) *See* Switzerland—Geneva

Genge, Sara
Sins of the father
The Best science fiction and fantasy of the year: volume five; edited by Jonathan Strahan.
GENGHIS KHAN, 1162-1227
About
Howard, R. E. Red blades of black Cathay
GENIUS
See also Gifted children
Genka Paltsevson of Dmitri. Lipatov, V.
GENOCIDE
Padmanabhan, M. Cull
Gentle future. Sheehan, A.
Gentle Heart [With commentary] Martin, R.
The **gentleman** from San Francisco. Bunin, I. A.
A **gentleman** of color. Wren, P. C.
A **gentleman** of the old school. Yarbro, C. Q.
The **gentleman's** hotel. Lansdale, J. R.
The **Geography** of Stars. Nelson, K.
GEOLOGISTS
Gordimer, N. Town and country lovers
George, Nina
The Light in the West
World Literature Today v85 no3 p18-21 My/Je 2011
George and Priti. Naranbhai, A. O.
George and the pink house. Naipaul, V. S.
George Thurston. Bierce, A.
Georgic. Nagai, M.
Geriatric ward. Card, O. S.
GERMAN WEST AFRICA *See* Cameroon
GERMANS
Murphy, Y. The good word
England
Trevor, W. The telephone game
United States
Gordimer, N. Face from Atlantis
Leonard, E. Comfort to the enemy
GERMANY
Archer, J. A good eye
Popov, A. Plumbers
Sprenger, S. Dust
19th century
Mu Xin. Weimar in early spring
1918-1945
Anderson, K. J. Torn stitches, shattered glass
World War, 1939-1945
See World War, 1939-1945—Germany
Berlin
Cadigan, P. Picking up the pieces
Prindle, J. Einstein's dreidel
Prindle, J. Einstein's watch
Dresden
Hodge, B. And they will come in the hour of our greatest need
Hamburg
Kronauer, B. Devilsbridge [excerpt]
Munich
Prindle, J. Einstein's compass
Prindle, J. Einstein's cross
The **Gernsback** continuum. Gibson, W.
GERONTOLOGISTS *See* Physicians
GESTAPO *See* National socialism
Get out of Butte altogether. Shepard, S.
Get ready. Manilla, M.
Get some young. Hannah, B.
Getting along just fine. Nolan, W. F.
Getting better. Davis, L.

Getting better. Schmitt, E.-E.
Getting closer. Millhauser, S.
Getting dark. Barrett, N., Jr.
Getting lost. Dixon, S.
Getting ready. Hannah, B.
Getting to know your body. Davis, L.
Getting together. Matheson, R.
Ghanem's watermelon. Marãr, M.
GHETTOS *See* Jews—Segregation
The **ghost** of Leadville. Stein, J. C.
Ghost ship. Gifford, B.
GHOST STORIES
> *See also* Horror stories; Supernatural
> phenomena

Aiken, J. Wee Robin
Anzaldúa, G. Ghost trap/Trampa de espanto
Atkins, P. The Mystery
Beagle, P. S. Music, when soft voices die
Beagle, P. S. Vanishing
Bierce, A. An arrest
Bierce, A. At Old Man Eckert's
Bierce, A. A baffled ambuscade
Bierce, A. A cold greeting
Bierce, A. The famous Gilson bequest
Bierce, A. A fruitless assignment
Bierce, A. The Isle of pines
Bierce, A. A jug of sirup
Bierce, A. The middle toe of the right foot
Bierce, A. The moonlit road
Bierce, A. The other lodgers
Bierce, A. Present at a hanging
Bierce, A. A resumed identity
Bierce, A. The spook house
Bierce, A. The stranger
Bierce, A. The suitable surroundings [y]
Bierce, A. The thing at Nolan
Bierce, A. Three and one are one
Bierce, A. Two military executions
Bierce, A. A wireless message
Burke, T. The hollow man
Craddock, C. E. The "harnt" that walks
    Chilhowee
Doyle, R. The pram
Ford, J. The summer palace
Goss, T. Christopher Raven
Harwood, J. Face to face
Hearn, L. The name on the stone
Hendee, B. The winds of Brennan Marcher
Hirshberg, G. The muldoon
Hirshberg, G. Shomer
Hoffman, N. K. Snow on snow
Irvine, A. Semaphore
Jacobs, W. W. The monkey's paw
Lanagan, M. The proving of Smollett Standforth
Landon, P. Thurnley Abbey
Langan, J. The third always beside you
Levine, S. Believing it was George Harrison
Marías, J. A kind of nostalgia perhaps
Marías, J. The resignation letter of Senor de
    Santiesteban
Mariotte, J. J. Janey in Amber
Millhauser, S. Phantoms
Millhauser, S. We others
Monk, D. Last tour of duty
Morrow, J. The iron shroud
Nolan, W. F. Horror at Winchester House
Nutting, A. Knife thrower
Phillips, H. The hauntings
Powers, T. A journey of only two paces

Powers, T. Parallel lines
Powers, T. A soul in a bottle
Rickert, M. Holiday
Rickert, M. Journey into the kingdom
Rickert, M. War is beautiful
Sands, B. Terror in the haunted house
Shepard, L. Rose Street attractors
Shipp, J. C. The haunted house
Silverberg, R. Smithers and the ghosts of the
    Thar
Taaffe, S. The dybbuk in love
Terry, G. P. The importance of cheese
Terry, G. P. On Orly's border
Twain, M. A curious dream
Villegas, H. The beautiful boy
Villegas, H. His ghost
Villegas, H. Salvage
Villegas, H. Twenty-first-century design
Villegas, H. While he sleeps
Villegas, H. Winter
Vukcevich, R. Over here
Wells, H. G. The inexperienced ghost
Wells, H. G. The moth
Wharton, E. The pomegranate seed
Williams, S. The Jade Woman of the Luminous
    Star
Willis, M. S. Big boss is back
Youmans, M. The grave reflection
Ghost story. Baker, L.
GHOST TOWNS *See* Extinct cities
Ghost trap/Trampa de espanto. Anzaldúa, G.
Ghost walk. Holladay, C.
Ghosted. Lovesey, P.
GHOSTS *See* Ghost stories
Ghosts. Baxter, C.
The **ghostwriter.** Lychack, W.
The **ghoul.** Clifford, Sir H. C.
GHOULS AND OGRES
Liss, D. The awkward age
Parks, R. The twa corbies, revisited
Wellington, D. Dead man's land
Giacomo's Rug. Gill, E.
Gianni. Silverberg, R.
GIANTS
Beagle, P. S. Up the down beanstalk: a wife re-
members
Gibson, William
The age of fable
The Gernsback continuum
Fragments of a hologram rose
Before they were giants; edited by James L.
Sutter; cover illustration by Kieran Yanner.
The Gernsback continuum
Steampunk II: steampunk reloaded; edited by
Ann & Jeff VanderMeer.
Gifford, Barry
The age of fable
Gifford, B. Sad stories of the death of kings
The Albanian florist
Gifford, B. Sad stories of the death of kings
The American language
Gifford, B. Sad stories of the death of kings
Arabian nights
Gifford, B. Sad stories of the death of kings
Bad girls
Gifford, B. Sad stories of the death of kings
Bad night at the Del Prado
Gifford, B. Sad stories of the death of kings
Blue people
Gifford, B. Sad stories of the death of kings

Gifford, Barry—*Continued*

Caca negra
    Gifford, B. Sad stories of the death of kings
Call of the wild
    Gifford, B. Sad stories of the death of kings
El Carterista
    Gifford, B. Sad stories of the death of kings
The choice
    Gifford, B. Sad stories of the death of kings
Chop suey joint
    Gifford, B. Sad stories of the death of kings
Close encounters of the right kind
    Gifford, B. Sad stories of the death of kings
Coda: the vanished gardens of Cordoba
    Gifford, B. Sad stories of the death of kings
Crime and punishment
    Gifford, B. Sad stories of the death of kings
Einstein's son
    Gifford, B. Sad stories of the death of kings
The exception
    Gifford, B. Sad stories of the death of kings
Far from anywhere
    Gifford, B. Sad stories of the death of kings
Force of evil
    Gifford, B. Sad stories of the death of kings
Ghost ship
    Gifford, B. Sad stories of the death of kings
The great failure
    Gifford, B. Sad stories of the death of kings
In the land of the dead
    Gifford, B. Sad stories of the death of kings
Innamorata
    Gifford, B. Sad stories of the death of kings
Irredeemable
    Gifford, B. Sad stories of the death of kings
Last plane out of Chungking
    Gifford, B. Sad stories of the death of kings
The Liberian condition
    Gifford, B. Sad stories of the death of kings
Lonely are the brave
    Gifford, B. Sad stories of the death of kings
The man who swallowed the world
    Gifford, B. Sad stories of the death of kings
Portrait of the artist with four other guys
    Gifford, B. Sad stories of the death of kings
Rain in the distance
    Gifford, B. Sad stories of the death of kings
Roy's first car
    Gifford, B. Sad stories of the death of kings
Sad stories of the death of kings
    Gifford, B. Sad stories of the death of kings
The secrets of the universe
    Gifford, B. Sad stories of the death of kings
Significance
    Gifford, B. Sad stories of the death of kings
Six million and one
    Gifford, B. Sad stories of the death of kings
The starving dogs of Little Croatia
    Gifford, B. Sad stories of the death of kings
The sudden demise of Sharkface Bensky
    Gifford, B. Sad stories of the death of kings
The Sultan
    Gifford, B. Sad stories of the death of kings
The Swedish bakery
    Gifford, B. Sad stories of the death of kings
The theory of the leisure class
    Gifford, B. Sad stories of the death of kings
War and peace
    Gifford, B. Sad stories of the death of kings

The Weeper
    Gifford, B. Sad stories of the death of kings
The **gift**. Cook, F.
Gift Horse. Bazzle, B.
The **gift** of the magi. Henry, O.
Gift wrap. Barrett, L.
GIFTED CHILDREN
    Gordimer, N. Not for publication
GIFTS
    Henry, O. The gift of the magi
    McGarry, J. Gold leaf
    Wieland, L. Resolution Trust
The **gifts** of Avalae. McHugh, I.
The **gifts** of war. Drabble, M.
Gigantomachy. Gutiérrez, P.
GIGOLOS
    Popov, A. Plumbers
Gilb, Dagoberto
    Uncle Rock
        Best of the West 2011; new stories from the
            wild side of the Missouri; edited by James
            Thomas and D. Seth Horton; foreword by
            Ana Castillo.
    Willows village
        Best of the West 2009; new stories from the
            wide side of the Missouri; edited by James
            Thomas and D. Seth Horton; foreword by
            Rick Bass.
Gilbert's mother. Trevor, W.
Gilbey, John
    The last laboratory
        Nature v469 no7328 p126 Ja 6 2011
Gilbow, S. L.
    Red card
        Brave new worlds; edited by John Joseph Ad-
            ams.
Gilchrist, Ellen
    Tell Me the Truth About Love
        Good Housekeeping v252 no5 p205-8, 210,
            212-13 My 2011
Gildner, Gary
    If I Could Be with You
        Confrontation no108 p133-46 Fall 2010
    Stories Under the Stars
        The North American Review v295 no2 p34-5
            Spr 2010
Gilgul. Hayim Yerushalmi, Y.
Gillett, Regan Runnels
    The Karmic Cabbie
        Texas Bar Journal v74 no6 p494-6 Je 2011
Gilley, Ted
    All Hallows' Eve
        Gilley, T. Bliss and other short stories
    Bliss
        Gilley, T. Bliss and other short stories
    The end zone
        Gilley, T. Bliss and other short stories
    House of prayer
        Gilley, T. Bliss and other short stories
    Invisible waves
        Gilley, T. Bliss and other short stories
    Mountains of the moon
        Gilley, T. Bliss and other short stories
    Physical wisdom
        Gilley, T. Bliss and other short stories
    Vanishing world
        Gilley, T. Bliss and other short stories
    White
        Gilley, T. Bliss and other short stories

GIRLS—*Continued*

Miéville, C. Highway 61 revisited
Millet, L. Snow white, rose red
Monk, D. That Saturday
Monk, D. X_day
Mosher, C. J. A girl and her cat
Munro, A. Some women
Narayan, S. Pishaach
Niedzviecki, H. Prenatal
Nolan, W. F. Child's care
Nutting, A. Dancing rat
Nutting, A. Teenager
Oates, J. C. Bonobo momma
Oates, J. C. ID
Oates, J. C. Nowhere
Oates, J. C. The story of the stabbing
Oates, J. C. Strip poker
O'Brien, E. Green Georgette
O'Brien, E. Plunder
Osondu, E. C. Jimmy Carter's eyes
Packer, A. Walk for Mankind
Packer, Z. Brownies
Papernick, J. Skin for skin
Pearlman, E. Girl in blue with brown bag
Phan, N. T. A dream
Priest, C. Addison Howell and the clockroach
Randall, P. The Oxfam dress
Reynolds, A. The old man and the Martian sea
Rickert, M. The Christmas witch
Rickert, M. Evidence of love in a case of abandonment
Rickert, M. Evidence of love in a case of abandonment: one daughter's personal account
Rickert, M. Traitor
Rickert, M. Was she wicked? was she good?
Riippi, J. Something about the Zombies
Ruocco, J. Seabird
Schappell, E. Monsters of the deep
Seamans, S. Survival instincts
Sheehan, A. Spin
Shipp, J. C. Ula Morales
Smith, C. Catgirl
Smith, M. M. What happens when you wake up in the night
Somerville, P. The wildlife biologist
Stashower, D. Challenger
Swirsky, R. Heartstrung
Terry, G. P. Now you see it ..
Tidhar, L. Alienation and love in the Hebrew alphabet
Tremblay, P. The teacher
Trevor, W. An afternoon
Trevor, W. The children
Trevor, W. The dancing-master's music
Trevor, W. Good news
Trevor, W. Rose wept
Uphoff, M. Desire
Vaughn, C. The girl with the pre-Raphaelite hair
Vukcevich, R. Jumping
Vukcevich, R. Over here
Watsmore, A. Bina
Wieland, L. Quickening
Wolff, T. The deposition
Young, J. Written in light

Girls. Henderson, K.
Give me the gun, he says. Hemmingson, M.
Give me your heart. Oates, J. C.
Give till it hurts. Westlake, D. E.
Give us some dirt. Tillman, L.

GLADNESS *See* Happiness

Glaser, Rachel B.
Infections
Butler, B. 30 under 30; an anthology of innovative fiction by younger writers; Blake Butler & Lily Hoang, eds.

A **Glasgow** Rose. Smith, R. M.

Glaspell, Susan
A jury of her peers
The vintage book of American women writers; edited and with an introduction by Elaine Showalter.

Glass, James C.
Robbie
Swenson, P. The Best of Talebones; edited by Patrick Swenson.

Glass, Julia
The price of silver
Best of the West 2010; new stories from the wide side of the Missouri; edited by James Thomas and D. Seth Horton; foreword by Kent Meyers.
Five Points v12 no2 p137-66 2008

GLASS
Terry, G. P. The tale of the glass man

GLASS BLOWING AND WORKING
Youmans, M. The salamander fire

Glenn Gould. Davis, L.

Glinky. Vukcevich, R.

Glitter Gulch. Mullins, D. P.

GLOBAL WARMING
Valentine, G. So deep that the bottom could not be seen

Glonze. Regier, G. T.

Glorietta. Braunbeck, G. A.

Glover, Elizabeth M.
Metaphysics
Sympathy for the devil; edited by Tim Pratt.

GLOVES
Millhauser, S. Tales of darkness and the unknown, vol. XIV: The white glove

A **glutton** for punishment. Yates, R.

The **Gnat,** the Hammer, and the Cruise Ship [Part of a special issue: Market] Clausen, J.

Gnidzeijko-Smith, Erin
Free Lunch at the Poseidon
TriQuarterly no139 Wint/Spr 2011

GNOMES *See* Fairies

Go away. Davis, L.
The **go-between**. Smith, A.
Go piss on Jane. Gallari, A.
The **go-slow**. Okorafor, N.
Go to the Ant, Thou Sluggard. Heynen, J.
The **goat** cutter. Lake, J.
The **goat** horn bell. Nguyen, Q. L.
Goat on a hill. Allen, D.
Goat song. Anderson, P.

GOATS
Babbitt, N. The power of speech
Naipaul, V. S. The raffle

GOD
Dowling, T. He tried to catch the light
Niedzviecki, H. Doing God's work
O'Connor, S. The professor of atheism: Stealing peaches from Sam Snnow
Smith, C. A. Schizoid creator
Vukcevich, R. A funny smell
Wells, H. G. The story of the Last Trump
Wells, H. G. A vision of judgment

GOD—*Continued*
Woestijne, K. v. d. The saint of number
The **god** of dark laughter. Chabon, M.
God of exile. McGarry, T.
God of fire. Laken, V.
God sees the truth, but waits. Tolstoy, L., graf
The **Goddess** of Outen. Terry, G. P.
GODDESSES
Emshwiller, C. If not forever, when?
Terry, G. P. The Goddess of Outen
GODMOTHERS
Treadway, J. Oregon
GODS
Balázs, B. The old child
Emshwiller, C. Looking down
Krinard, S. Mist
Milks, M. My father and I were bent
groundward
Torgersen, B. R. Exanastasis
Uncle River. Love of the true God
Wells, H. G. Jimmy Goggles the god
God's creatures. Vaughn, C.
The **Gods** Wear Funny Hats. Rinaldi, N.
GODZILLA (FICTITIOUS CHARACTER)
Shepard, J. Gojira, king of the monsters
Goedjen, Tara
Orphans of Holy Week
New England Review v31 no4 p158-71
2010/2011
**GOETHE, JOHANN WOLFGANG VON, 1749-
1832**
About
Mu Xin. Weimar in early spring
Gogol, Nikolai
1842: St. Petersburg: Nikolai Gogol on a labor
of love [Excerpt from The Overcoat]
Lapham's Quarterly v4 no2 p165-8 Spr 2011
The overcoat
The greatest Russian stories of crime and sus-
pense; edited by Otto Penzler.
The portrait
The greatest Russian stories of crime and sus-
pense; edited by Otto Penzler.
Gogol. Lahiri, J.
Going back west. Osondu, E. C.
Going deep. Kelly, J. P.
Going east. Gomel, E.
Going for a beer. Coover, R.
Going to Estonia. Horrocks, C.
Gojira, king of the monsters. Shepard, J.
Gold, H. L.
At the post
Gold, H. L. Perfect murders; introduction to
the Bison Books edition by E. J. Gold.
I know suicide
Gold, H. L. Perfect murders; introduction to
the Bison Books edition by E. J. Gold.
Love in the dark
Gold, H. L. Perfect murders; introduction to
the Bison Books edition by E. J. Gold.
A matter of form
Gold, H. L. Perfect murders; introduction to
the Bison Books edition by E. J. Gold.
The old die rich
Gold, H. L. Perfect murders; introduction to
the Bison Books edition by E. J. Gold.
Perfect murder
Gold, H. L. Perfect murders; introduction to
the Bison Books edition by E. J. Gold.

Problem in murder
Gold, H. L. Perfect murders; introduction to
the Bison Books edition by E. J. Gold.
Gold, Horace Leonard *See* Gold, H. L., 1914-
1996
GOLD
Gaiman, N. "The truth is a cave in the Black
Mountains. . . ."
Gold leaf. McGarry, J.
Gold Mine. Watkins, C. V.
GOLD MINES AND MINING
Bierce, A. A holy terror
Gold shield blues. Mariotte, J. J.
Gold star. Fallon, S.
Goldberg, Matthew
Perfect Practice Makes Perfect
StoryQuarterly v44 p75-92 2010
Goldbloom, Goldie
The Telephone of the Dead
Prairie Schooner v84 no3 p43-57 Fall 2010
The **golden** anaconda. Mason, E. B.
The **golden** bug. Black, M. A.
Golden gloves. Oates, J. C.
The **golden** snare. Bishop, F. and Brodeur, A. G.
Goldenstern, Joyce
The Girl Who Left the Village
Western Humanities Review v65 no2 p33-34
Summ 2011
Hungry Mother
Western Humanities Review v65 no2 p31-32
Summ 2011
More
Western Humanities Review v65 no2 p30
Summ 2011
Goldfinger [excerpt] Fleming, I.
Goldstein, Imré
(tr.) *See* Nádas, Péter
Goldstein, Rebecca
The afterlife of skeptics
Promised lands; new Jewish American fiction
on longing and belonging; edited by Derek
Rubin.
GOLEM
Chabon, M. Golems I have known, or, why my
elder son's middle name is Napoleon: a
trickster's memoir
Morrow, J. The iron shroud
Sullivan, J. Niels Bohr and the sleeping Dane
The **Golem** Project. Brau, E.
Golems I have known, or, why my elder son's
middle name is Napoleon: a trickster's
memoir. Chabon, M.
GOLF
Archer, J. Members only
Bentley, E. C. The sweet shot
Darwin, B. The wooden putter
Fitzgerald, F. S. Winter dreams
Fleming, I. Goldfinger [excerpt]
Goodberg, D. A game of golf
Hall, H. The last round
Jenkins, D. Tees and teens
Kaplan, J. The mower
Laken, V. Spectators
Lardner, R. Triumph at Crestwood
Lardner, R. Mr. Frisbie
Leacock, S. B. The golfomaniac
Marquand, J. P. Caddie crisis
McGrath, C. Sneaking on
Rankin, I. Graduation day

Goodberg, David—*Continued*
  An opportunity of a lifetime
    Goodberg, D. Selected shorts and other methods of time travel
  The others
    Goodberg, D. Selected shorts and other methods of time travel
  The perfectionist
    Goodberg, D. Selected shorts and other methods of time travel
  Precautions
    Goodberg, D. Selected shorts and other methods of time travel
  The preservation society
    Goodberg, D. Selected shorts and other methods of time travel
  Research methods
    Goodberg, D. Selected shorts and other methods of time travel
  Rubber reality
    Goodberg, D. Selected shorts and other methods of time travel
  Selected shorts
    Goodberg, D. Selected shorts and other methods of time travel
  Staging a scene
    Goodberg, D. Selected shorts and other methods of time travel
  Synecdoche
    Goodberg, D. Selected shorts and other methods of time travel
  Timing of a mad man
    Goodberg, D. Selected shorts and other methods of time travel
  Weather channels
    Goodberg, D. Selected shorts and other methods of time travel
  World at war
    Goodberg, D. Selected shorts and other methods of time travel
GOODBYES *See* Farewells
Goodfellow, Cody
  At the riding school
    The Best horror of the year: volume three; edited by Ellen Datlow.
The **goodly** race. Randisi, R. J.
Goodman, Allegra
  La vita nuova
    The Best American short stories, 2011; selected from U.S. and Canadian magazines by Geraldine Brooks with Heidi Pitlor; with an introduction by Geraldine Brooks.
Goodnight moons. Klages, E.
Goodrich, Joseph
  Murder in the sixth
    Mystery Writers of America presents the rich and the dead; edited by Nelson DeMille.
Goolsby, Jesse
  Resurrecting a Body Half
    The Literary Review (Madison, N.J.) v54 no2 p130-7 Wint 2011
Goose chase. Teodorovici, L. D.
Gorcheva-Newberry, Kristina
  Champions of the World
    The Southern Review (Baton Rouge, La.) v47 no3 p487-507 Summ 2011
Gordimer, Nadine
  The amateurs
    Gordimer, N. Life times; stories, 1952-2007

Amnesty
  Freedom; stories celebrating the Universal Declaration of Human Rights; Amnesty International.
At the rendezvous of victory
  Gordimer, N. Life times; stories, 1952-2007
Beethoven one-sixteeth black
  Gordimer, N. Life times; stories, 1952-2007
The bridgegroom
  Gordimer, N. Life times; stories, 1952-2007
A chip of glass ruby
  Gordimer, N. Life times; stories, 1952-2007
The diamond mine
  Gordimer, N. Life times; stories, 1952-2007
Dreaming of the dead
  Gordimer, N. Life times; stories, 1952-2007
Face from Atlantis
  Gordimer, N. Life times; stories, 1952-2007
A find
  Gordimer, N. Life times; stories, 1952-2007
For dear life
  Gordimer, N. Life times; stories, 1952-2007
Friday's footprint
  Gordimer, N. Life times; stories, 1952-2007
The Games Room
  The American Scholar v80 no2 p96-105 Spr 2011
The generation gap
  Gordimer, N. Life times; stories, 1952-2007
Letter from his father
  Gordimer, N. Life times; stories, 1952-2007
A lion on the freeway
  Gordimer, N. Life times; stories, 1952-2007
Livingstone's companions
  Gordimer, N. Life times; stories, 1952-2007
Look-alikes
  Gordimer, N. Life times; stories, 1952-2007
Loot
  Gordimer, N. Life times; stories, 1952-2007
A meeting in space
  Gordimer, N. Life times; stories, 1952-2007
The moment before the gun went off
  Gordimer, N. Life times; stories, 1952-2007
Not for publication
  Gordimer, N. Life times; stories, 1952-2007
Once upon a time
  Gordimer, N. Life times; stories, 1952-2007
Open house
  Gordimer, N. Life times; stories, 1952-2007
Oral history
  Gordimer, N. Life times; stories, 1952-2007
Parking Tax
  Gordimer, N. Life times; stories, 1952-2007
Rain-queen
  Gordimer, N. Life times; stories, 1952-2007
Second coming
  Gordimer, N. Life times; stories, 1952-2007
Six feet of the country
  Gordimer, N. Life times; stories, 1952-2007
The smell of death and flowers
  Gordimer, N. Life times; stories, 1952-2007
The soft voice of the serpent
  Gordimer, N. Life times; stories, 1952-2007
A soldier's embrace
  Gordimer, N. Life times; stories, 1952-2007
Some Monday for sure
  Gordimer, N. Life times; stories, 1952-2007
Something out there
  Gordimer, N. Life times; stories, 1952-2007

Gordimer, Nadine—*Continued*

Tape measure

Gordimer, N. Life times; stories, 1952-2007

Through time and distance

Gordimer, N. Life times; stories, 1952-2007

Town and country lovers

Gordimer, N. Life times; stories, 1952-2007

The ultimate safari

Gordimer, N. Life times; stories, 1952-2007

Which new era would that be?

Gordimer, N. Life times; stories, 1952-2007

Why haven't you written?

Gordimer, N. Life times; stories, 1952-2007

Gordon, Mary

Trio

Salmagundi no168/169 p211-32 Fall 2010/Wint 2011

Gordon, Peter

Maxine

Southwest Review v95 no4 p572-7 2010

Gordon, Sarah

Parade

Can'tLit; fearless fiction from Broken pencil magazine; edited by Richard Rosenbaum.

The worst of us

Can'tLit; fearless fiction from Broken pencil magazine; edited by Richard Rosenbaum.

GORILLAS

Farmer, P. J. After King Kong fell

Fowler, K. J. What I didn't see

Gorky, Maksim

A strange murderer

The greatest Russian stories of crime and suspense; edited by Otto Penzler.

Gorky, Maxim *See* Gorky, Maksim, 1868-1936

Gorman, Edward

Aftermath

Gorman, E. Noir 13; [by] Ed Gorman

The baby store

Gorman, E. Noir 13; [by] Ed Gorman

Comeback

Gorman, E. Noir 13; [by] Ed Gorman

Favor and the princess

Gorman, E. Noir 13; [by] Ed Gorman

Flying solo

Gorman, E. Noir 13; [by] Ed Gorman

Killing Kate

Gorman, E. Noir 13; [by] Ed Gorman

A little something to believe in

Gorman, E. Noir 13; [by] Ed Gorman

The long way back

Gorman, E. Noir 13; [by] Ed Gorman

Loose ends

Gorman, E. Noir 13; [by] Ed Gorman

Such a good girl

Gorman, E. Noir 13; [by] Ed Gorman

That day at Eagle's Point

Gorman, E. Noir 13; [by] Ed Gorman

Turn away

The Shamus winners: America's best private eye stories, volume I: 1982-1995; collected and introduced by Robert J. Randisi; founder, Private Eye Writers of America

Gorman, Edward and Butler, Terence

Heritage

Gorman, E. Noir 13; [by] Ed Gorman

Gorman, Edward and Morrish, Robert

Rafferty's comeback

Gorman, E. Noir 13; [by] Ed Gorman

The **gospel** according to Octavio Ruiz. Kitterman, B.

Goss, Theodora

Christopher Raven

Ghosts by gaslight; stories of steampunk and supernatural suspense; [edited by] Jack Dann [and] Nick Gevers

Fair Ladies

The Best science fiction and fantasy of the year: volume five; edited by Jonathan Strahan.

The wings of Meister Wilhelm

People of the book; a decade of Jewish science fiction & fantasy; edited by Rachel Swirsky & Sean Wallace.

GOSSIP

Barrett, L. Gossip and toad

Gossip and toad. Barrett, L.

GOTHIC ROMANCES

See also Horror stories

Goto, Hiromi

The hikikomori

The beastly bride; tales of the animal people; edited by Ellen Datlow & Terri Windling; introduction by Terri Windling; selected decorations by Charles Vess.

Gottlieb, Daphne

Somewhere, over

Life as we show it; writing on film; co-edited by Masha Tupitsyn & Brian Pera; introduction by Masha Tupitsyn

Gough, Thomas

House of Spiders

New England Review v32 no1 p128-38 2011

Goulart, Ron

Murder for dummies

Christmas at the Mysterious Bookshop; 'tis the season to be deadly; stories of mistletoe and mayhem from 17 masters of suspense; edited by Otto Penzler.

GOULD, GLENN, 1932-1982

About

Davis, L. Glenn Gould

GOVERNESSES

See also Housekeepers

Atta, S. News from home

Chiang, T. Dacey's patent Automatic Nanny

Meade, L. T. The Blue laboratory

Pearlman, E. Vallies

Vaughn, C. Threads

GOYA, FRANCISCO, 1746-1828

About

Hodge, B. Brushed in blackest silence

Goya y Lucientes, Francisco José de *See* Goya, Francisco, 1746-1828

Goyen, William

Precious Door

TriQuarterly no139 Wint/Spr 2011

Goytisolo, Juan

Mr. President . . .

Freedom; stories celebrating the Universal Declaration of Human Rights; Amnesty International.

Grace, Patricia

Busy lines

Freedom; stories celebrating the Universal Declaration of Human Rights; Amnesty International.

Grace. Hoang, M. T.

Gracias. Shepard, S.
GRADUATION *See* Commencements
Graduation day. Rankin, I.
Grafting. Nagai, M.
Grafton, Sue
  A little missionary work
    The Shamus winners: America's best private
      eye stories, volume I: 1982-1995; collected
      and introduced by Robert J. Randisi; found-
      er, Private Eye Writers of America
Graham, Heather
  Wicked be
    The monster's corner; stories through inhu-
      man eyes; edited by Christopher Golden
Graham, Stacey
  Eye of the beholder
    Hungry for your love; an anthology of
      zombie romance; edited by Lori Perkins.
Graillis's legacy. Trevor, W.
Grammar questions. Davis, L.
Grand Central. LaSalle, P.
**GRAND CENTRAL TERMINAL (NEW
  YORK, N.Y.)**
  Sabar, A. Navigation
The **grand** lady of my soul. Taraqqi, G.
GRANDCHILDREN
      See also Granddaughters; Grandsons
  Phelan, T. Happine$$
GRANDDAUGHTERS
  Emshwiller, C. Peri
  Plummer, T. M. Olivia's roses
  Rodoreda, M. The bath
  Vukcevich, R. Over here
GRANDFATHERS
  Bill, F. All the awful
  Bill, F. The old mechanic
  Bill, F. Old testament wisdom
  Dixon, S. The chocolate sampler
  Doerr, A. The river nemunas
  Edwards, M. Clutter
  Ely, S. Rocks
  Farmer, P. J. After King Kong fell
  Gautier, A. The ease of living
  Gifford, B. The age of fable
  Gifford, B. Force of evil
  Gilley, T. Invisible waves
  Hirshberg, G. The muldoon
  Horrocks, C. At the zoo
  Lemberg, R. Geddarien
  Monzó, Q. Helvetian freedoms
  Papernick, J. The engines of Sodom
  Pearlman, E. Day of awe
  Penkov, M. Buying Lenin
  Qiu Xiaolong. Confucius and crab
  Qiu Xiaolong. Shoes of the cultural revolution
  Riippi, J. Something about a nail
  Riippi, J. Something about swimming with sea
    turtles
  Riippi, J. Something (entirely true) about your
    grandfather
  Roberge, R. Border radio
  Salah al Azab, M. A boat that dislikes the river-
    bank
  Schappell, E. Are you comfortable?
  Sneed, C. Portraits of a few of the people I've
    made cry
  St. John, N. Further notes on my unfortunate
    condition
  Terry, G. P. Meeting the Dog Girls

  Vukcevich, R. In the flesh
  Vukcevich, R. Over here
  Woodrell, D. The horse in our history
  Zhang Kangkang. Atop Beijing mountain of
    gold
Grandma. Emshwiller, C.
GRANDMOTHERS
  Alland, S. Things I don't remember
  Arnason, E. Mammoths of the great plains
  Ayau, K. J. Bob the negro
  Baxter, C. Mr. Scary
  Blatnik, A. Sunday dinners
  Blatnik, A. Videotapes
  Boggs, B. Homecoming
  Clark, M. H. The tell-tale purr
  Clark, M. H. What's in a name?
  Davis, L. The strangers
  Diaz, N. How to love a woman with no legs
  Eisenberg, D. Revenge of the dinosaurs
  Emshwiller, C. Grandma
  Evans, D. Snakes
  Fowler, K. J. The Marianas Islands
  Freeman, M. E. W. Old Woman Magoun
  Gautier, A. Some other kind of happiness
  Gautier, A. Yearn
  Gresh, L. H. Julia Brainchild
  Latiolais, M. The moon
  Levine, S. Parthenogenetic grandmother
  Mehta, R. Citizen
  Mehta, R. Ten thousand years
  Pinede, N. Department lounge
  Riippi, J. Something about the rest
  Spiers, H. Cleverclogs
  Tuten, F. Self portrait with Sicily
  Yamauchi, W. Family gifting
Grandmother's footsteps. Jones, G. A.
GRANDPARENTS
  Ayau, K. J. Spawning
  Chuculate, E. D. Yoyo
  Somerville, P. The peach
  Tallent, E. Never come back
  Teodorovici, L. D. Goose chase
  Verbeke, A. Love, hope and dwarfs
  Willis, M. S. Triangulation
GRANDSONS
  Kitterman, B. The man who raised rabbits
Granski. Pearlman, E.
Grant, Colin
  Lino
    Granta no111 p189-201 Summ 2010
Grant, James L. and Mantchev, Lisa
  As recorded on brass cylinders; adagio for two
    dancers
    Steampunk II: steampunk reloaded; edited by
      Ann & Jeff VanderMeer.
Grant, John *See* Gash, Jonathan, 1933-
GRAPHIC SHORT STORIES
  Bethman, D. Squeeze me
  Gaiman, N. and Talbot, B. From homogenous to
    honey
  Padua, S. Lovelace & babbage
  Ressel, S. The legacy of between books
  Ryan, S. Fair trade
Grasping the bird's tail. Terry, G. P.
The **grave** reflection. Youmans, M.
GRAVE ROBBERS
  Bierce, A. One summer night
  Hodge, B. A good dead man is hard to find

GRAVEDIGGERS
Hodge, B. Our turn too will one day come
Gravegoods. Jones, G. A.
Gravel. Munro, A.
Graves, Clo *See* Dehan, Richard, 1863-1932
Gravetending. Hall, T. M.
The **graveyard**. Loory, B.
GRAVEYARDS *See* Cemeteries
GRAVITATION
Niven, L. Neutron star
GRAVITY *See* Gravitation
Gravity. Beattie, A.
GRAVITY'S GOD. O'KANE, J.
Gray, Amelia
Babies
Gray, A. Museum of the weird
Code of operation: snake farm
Gray, A. Museum of the weird
The cottage cheese diet
Gray, A. Museum of the weird
The cube
Gray, A. Museum of the weird
The darkness
Gray, A. Museum of the weird
Death of a beast
Gray, A. Museum of the weird
Diary of the blockage
Gray, A. Museum of the weird
Dinner
Gray, A. Museum of the weird
Fish
Gray, A. Museum of the weird
A javelina story
Gray, A. Museum of the weird
Love, mortar
Gray, A. Museum of the weird
The movement
Gray, A. Museum of the weird
The picture window
Gray, A. Museum of the weird
The pit
Gray, A. Museum of the weird
The suitcase
Gray, A. Museum of the weird
There will be sense
Gray, A. Museum of the weird
This quiet complex
Gray, A. Museum of the weird
Thoughts while strolling
Gray, A. Museum of the weird
The tortoise and the hare
Gray, A. Museum of the weird
Trip advisory: the boyhood home of former
president Ronald Reagan
Gray, A. Museum of the weird
Unsolved mystery
Gray, A. Museum of the weird
The vanished
Gray, A. Museum of the weird
Vultures
Gray, A. Museum of the weird
Waste
Gray, A. Museum of the weird
Gray, Glenn
Mr. Universe
Blood, guts, & whiskey; edited by Todd Rob-
inson; introduction by Max Allan Collins.
Gray, Russell *See* Fischer, Bruno, 1908-1992

Gray, Victoria
And the Stars Shone Brightly
Critical Quarterly v52 no3 p87-92 O 2010
The Little Soldier
Critical Quarterly v53 no2 p80-92 Jl 2011
The **gray** donkey. Karay, R. H.
A **gray** matter. Terry, G. P.
Gray matters. Dietrich, B. D.
Gray Wolf, Prince Jack, and the Firebird. Garner,
A.
Grazing the long acre. Jones, G. A.
The **great** actor. Holm, B. Q.
GREAT AUNTS *See* Aunts
Great breakthroughs in darkness. Laidlaw, M.
GREAT BRITAIN
See also England; Northern Ireland;
Scotland; Wales
GREAT BRITAIN. ARMY
MacLeod, I. The English mutiny
The **Great** C. Dick, P. K.
The **great** cardhouse. Highsmith, P.
The **great** disappointment. Cardinale, J.
The **great** divide. Ray, S.
Great experiment. Eugenides, J.
The **great** failure. Gifford, B.
The **great** god Awto. Smith, C. A.
The **great-grandmothers**. Davis, L.
A **great** piece of elephant. Abbott, L. K.
Great Salt Lake. Chapman, J.
The **Great** Wall: a story from the zombie war.
Brooks, M.
The **Greatest** Gift. Stern, P. V. D.
The **greatest** science-fiction story ever written.
Stone, E. J.
The **Greatest** Show. Downs, M.
Greatshadow. Maxey, J.
Grebowicz, Margret
Philosophy Seminar: The Carnivore
Agni no73 p159 2011
GREECE
Bakopoulos, N. Fresco, Byzantine
Peloponnesian War, 431-404 B.C.
Turtledove, H. The daimon
GREED *See* Avarice
Greed. Hubbard, L: R.
A **greek** story. Tillman, L.
Greektown. Estleman, L. D.
Green, Simon R.
Jesus and Satan go jogging in the desert
The monster's corner; stories through inhu-
man eyes; edited by Christopher Golden
Street wizard
The way of the wizard; edited by John Joseph
Adams.
Green. Allio, K.
Green. Atta, S.
Green. Engel, P.
Green. Sabar, A.
Green. Schirach, F. v.
The **Green** Dress. Hedden, K.
Green future. Walker, D.
Green Gables. King, D.
Green Georgette. O'Brien, E.
Green grass blues. Lake, J.
Green legs and glam. Randisi, R. J.
Green pea eater. Dixon, S.
The **green** suit. Allen, D.
The **green** wildebeest. Buchan, J.
Green world. Alexie, S.

Greene, L. Patrick
Fire
    The Big book of adventure stories; edited and
        with a introduction by Otto Penzler; fore-
        word by Douglas Preston.
Greenfeld, Karl Taro
Alpha
    Commentary v131 no2 p46-53 F 2011
The Jews of the North
    Commentary v132 no1 p46-54 Jl/Ag 2011
Greenie and yellow. Naipaul, V. S.
Greenland, Seth
Bad night in Hyannisport
    Cape Cod noir; edited by David L. Ulin.
Greenlaw, Duncan
DISTINCTION
    Dalhousie Review v91 no1 p77-89 Spr 2011
Greenman, Ben
Letterhead
    TriQuarterly no139 29964 bytes Wint/Spr
        2011
Viva Regina
    Cape Cod noir; edited by David L. Ulin.
Greenspon, Jaq
Mirrors and infinity
    Dead neon; tales of near-future Las Vegas;
        edited by Todd James Pierce and Jarret
        Keene.
Greenwich time. Beattie, A.
GREENWICH VILLAGE (NEW YORK, N.Y.)
    See New York (N.Y.)—Greenwich Village
Gregor. Monzó, Q.
GREGORY, LADY, 1852-1932
                About
Tóibín, C. Silence
Gregory, Isabella Augusta Persse, Lady *See*
    Gregory, Lady, 1852-1932
Gresh, Lois H.
Julia Brainchild
    Hungry for your love; an anthology of
        zombie romance; edited by Lori Perkins.
Grey area. Self, W.
Gribbons, Devin
A short story
    Butler, B. 30 under 30; an anthology of inno-
        vative fiction by younger writers; Blake
        Butler & Lily Hoang, eds.
GRIEF *See* Bereavement
Grieg on a stolen piano. Mphahlele, E.
Griffith, Nicola
Mirrors and burnstone
    Before they were giants; edited by James L.
        Sutter; cover illustration by Kieran Yanner.
Griffiths, Richard
The obvious candidate
    Freedom; stories celebrating the Universal
        Declaration of Human Rights; Amnesty In-
        ternational.
The **grift** of the magi. Rozan, S. J.
Grim fairy tales. Boon, L. P.
Grimes, Stacy
Zig Zag Lane
    Five Points v12 no2 p90-109 2008
Grimshaw on the Ice. Schultz, K.
The **grisly** folk. Wells, H. G.
Griswald. Lychack, W.
GROCERS
Dixon, S. Produce
Jones, E. P. The store

Kennedy, A. L. Edinburgh
Grocery list. Vukcevich, R.
Grodstein, Lauren
Homewrecker
    Promised lands; new Jewish American fiction
        on longing and belonging; edited by Derek
        Rubin.
Groff, Lauren
Above and below [Part of the Summer Fiction
        Issue]
    The New Yorker v87 no17 p106-19 Je 13-20
        2011
Amish in a Time of War
    Five Points v12 no1 p32-50 2008
Rue
    The monster's corner; stories through inhu-
        man eyes; edited by Christopher Golden
Grogan, Greg
Old Friends
    Georgia Bar Journal v16 no7 p34-6, 38-43 Je
        2011
Grooming. Manilla, M.
Grossman, Edith
    (tr.) See Roncagliolo, Santiago
Grossman, Lev
Endgame
    The way of the wizard; edited by John Joseph
        Adams.
Sir Ranulph Wykeham-Rackham, GBE, a.k.a.
        Roboticus the All-Knowing
    The Thackery T. Lambshead cabinet of curi-
        osities; edited by Ann & Jeff VanderMeer.
Grossman, Vasiliĭ Semenovich
The dog
    Grossman, V. S. The road; stories, journalism,
        and essays; [by] Vasily Grossman; translat-
        ed from the Russian by Robert and Eliza-
        beth Chandler with Olga Mukovnikova;
        commentary and notes by Robert Chandler
        with Yury Bit-Yunan; afterword by Fyodor
        Guber
The elk
    Grossman, V. S. The road; stories, journalism,
        and essays; [by] Vasily Grossman; translat-
        ed from the Russian by Robert and Eliza-
        beth Chandler with Olga Mukovnikova;
        commentary and notes by Robert Chandler
        with Yury Bit-Yunan; afterword by Fyodor
        Guber
In Kislavodsk
    Grossman, V. S. The road; stories, journalism,
        and essays; [by] Vasily Grossman; translat-
        ed from the Russian by Robert and Eliza-
        beth Chandler with Olga Mukovnikova;
        commentary and notes by Robert Chandler
        with Yury Bit-Yunan; afterword by Fyodor
        Guber
In the town of Berdichev
    Grossman, V. S. The road; stories, journalism,
        and essays; [by] Vasily Grossman; translat-
        ed from the Russian by Robert and Eliza-
        beth Chandler with Olga Mukovnikova;
        commentary and notes by Robert Chandler
        with Yury Bit-Yunan; afterword by Fyodor
        Guber

Grossman, Vasiliĭ Semenovich—*Continued*
Living space
Grossman, V. S. The road; stories, journalism, and essays; [by] Vasily Grossman; translated from the Russian by Robert and Elizabeth Chandler with Olga Mukovnikova; commentary and notes by Robert Chandler with Yury Bit-Yunan; afterword by Fyodor Guber
Mama
Grossman, V. S. The road; stories, journalism, and essays; [by] Vasily Grossman; translated from the Russian by Robert and Elizabeth Chandler with Olga Mukovnikova; commentary and notes by Robert Chandler with Yury Bit-Yunan; afterword by Fyodor Guber
The road
Grossman, V. S. The road; stories, journalism, and essays; [by] Vasily Grossman; translated from the Russian by Robert and Elizabeth Chandler with Olga Mukovnikova; commentary and notes by Robert Chandler with Yury Bit-Yunan; afterword by Fyodor Guber
A small life
Grossman, V. S. The road; stories, journalism, and essays; [by] Vasily Grossman; translated from the Russian by Robert and Elizabeth Chandler with Olga Mukovnikova; commentary and notes by Robert Chandler with Yury Bit-Yunan; afterword by Fyodor Guber
A young woman and an old woman
Grossman, V. S. The road; stories, journalism, and essays; [by] Vasily Grossman; translated from the Russian by Robert and Elizabeth Chandler with Olga Mukovnikova; commentary and notes by Robert Chandler with Yury Bit-Yunan; afterword by Fyodor Guber
Grotefeld, Elaine
Eight years later
Dancing with Mr. Darcy; stories inspired by Jane Austen and Chawton House Library; compiled by Sarah Waters.
Grounding the Tutu Girl. Sween, G. S.
Groundscratchers. Welsch, G.
Grove, Linda Legarde
Bingo night
Grover, L. L. The dance boots
Four indians in the mirror
Grover, L. L. The dance boots
Shonnud's girl
Grover, L. L. The dance boots
Three seasons
Grover, L. L. The dance boots
Grover, Linda Legarde
The dance boots
Grover, L. L. The dance boots
Maggie and Louis, 1914
Grover, L. L. The dance boots
Ojibwe boys
Grover, L. L. The dance boots
Refugees living and dying in the west end of Duluth
Grover, L. L. The dance boots
Growing things. Tremblay, P.
Grozny. Torres, D.

Gruber, Frank
Ask me another
The Black Lizard big book of Black Mask stories; edited and with a foreword by Otto Penzler; introduction by Keith Alan Deutsch.
Gryphon. Baxter, C.
Grytten, Frode
Hotel by a railroad
Best European fiction 2011; edited by Aleksandr Hemon; preface by Colum McCann
GUADALAJARA (MEXICO) *See* Mexico—Guadalajara
GUADALCANAL CAMPAIGN *See* World War, 1939-1945—Solomon Islands
Gualta. Marías, J.
Guardian. Hodge, B.
GUARDIAN AND WARD
See also Adoption
Saki. Sredni Vashtar
Guardian of the person. Vonnegut, K.
Guardians of the air. Hassan, R. Y.
The **guardicci** masterpiece. Châteaureynaud, G. O.
Guatemala City. Ely, S.
GUATEMALANS
United States
Manilla, M. Amnesty
Guène, Faïza
Mimouna
Beirut 39; new writing from the Arab world; edited by Samuel Shimon; with a preface by Hanan al-Shaykh
Guerrero, Lucrecia
A memory
Best of the West 2009; new stories from the wide side of the Missouri; edited by James Thomas and D. Seth Horton; foreword by Rick Bass.
Sisters
The Antioch Review v69 no2 p314-16 Spr 2011
GUERRILLAS
Gordimer, N. Oral history
GUESTS
Marār, M. The sleeping person is dead!
Osondu, E. C. Nigerians in America
Schulze, I. Oranges and angel
A **guided** tour through the museum of communism. Drakulic, S.
Guided walks. Good, A.
Guidubaldi, Dina
The desert: a field guide
Best of the West 2010; new stories from the wide side of the Missouri; edited by James Thomas and D. Seth Horton; foreword by Kent Meyers.
GUILT
See also Sin
Bierce, A. The man out of the nose
Gappah, P. An incident at lunchtime
Gorman, E. The baby store
Heathcock, A. Furlough
Horrocks, C. Steal small
Leegant, J. Remittances
Mofina, R. The last pursuit
O'Nan, S. Monsters
Orozco, D. Hunger tales
Ridgway, K. Shame
Thon, M. R. Father, lover, deadman, dreamer

GUILT—*Continued*

Thon, M. R. Heavenly creatures: for wandering children and their delinquent mother

Tóibín, C. The colour of shadows

Tóibín, C. The new Spain

Treadway, J. Dear Nicole

Trevor, W. The dressmaker's child

Zhang Kangkang. Please take me with you

The **guilt** edge. Randisi, R. J.

GUINEA FOWL

Rodoreda, M. Guinea fowls

Guinea fowls. Rodoreda, M.

Guinea pig. Johnson, C.

GUINEA PIGS

Butler, E. P. Pigs is pigs

GULF OF ADEN

Horrocks, C. In the Gulf of Aden, past the Cape of Guardafui

The **gulf** of the years. Châteaureynaud, G. O.

The **gully**. Banks, R.

The **gun**. Dick, P. K.

GUNS *See* Firearms

Guns for the dead. Marr, M.

Guo Xiaolu

An Internet baby

Freedom; stories celebrating the Universal Declaration of Human Rights; Amnesty International.

Gurov in Manhattan. Havazelet, E.

Gut. Latiolais, M.

Guterson, David

Paradise

The American Scholar v80 no4 p88-96 S 2011

Gutiérrez, Pablo

Gigantomachy

Granta no113 p115-22 Wint 2010

Gutstein, Daniel

Benny

Iowa Review v40 no2 p88-9 Fall 2010

Gutted. Cusick, G.

The **Guy** We Didn't Invite to the Orgy. Ebenbach, D. H.

The **guy** with the eyes. Robinson, S.

Gwyn, Aaron

Drive

Best of the West 2011; new stories from the wild side of the Missouri; edited by James Thomas and D. Seth Horton; foreword by Ana Castillo.

Gwyn, Richard

(tr.) *See* Neuman, Andrés

Gynecomastia. Fleri, J.

GYPSIES

Teodorovici, L. D. Goose chase

Gypsy. Anderson, P.

The **Gypsy** Chooses the Whatever Card. Beattie, A.

H

Habila, Helon

The Iron Gate

Agni no72 p237-9 2010

Hadley, Tessa

Honor

The New Yorker v86 no47 p66-72 F 7 2011

Post Production

Ploughshares v37 no1 p50-61 Spr 2011

The Trojan prince

The New Yorker v86 no36 p76-83 N 15 2010

Hadley. Loory, B.

Haggard, H. Rider (Henry Rider)

Hunter Quatermain's story

The Big book of adventure stories; edited and with a introduction by Otto Penzler; foreword by Douglas Preston.

Haggard, Henry Rider *See* Haggard, H. Rider (Henry Rider), 1856-1925

Haggerty, John

The Language of Fireflies

Confrontation no109 p57-67 Spr 2011

HAIFA (ISRAEL) *See* Israel—Haifa

Haigh, Jennifer

Favorite Son

The Virginia Quarterly Review v86 no4 p154-9 Fall 2010

Something Sweet

Harvard Review (1992) no40 p78-95 2011

Thrift

Five Points v14 no1 p18-37 2010

Hail, conductor. Finlay, C. C.

Hailstones on Zamfara. Atta, S.

Haines, Carolyn

The cypress dream

Florida heat wave; [edited and with an] introduction by Michael Lister.

Haines, Joseph Paul

Ten with a flag

Brave new worlds; edited by John Joseph Adams.

HAIR

Aiken, J. Hair

Couture, B. Fur: an autobiography [excerpt]

Gray, A. Dinner

Nutting, A. Corpse smoker

Schrauwen, O. Best American hair analysis narrative

Somerville, P. Hair university

Hair. Aiken, J.

Hair. Fruelund, S.

The **hair**. Heuler, K.

Hair university. Somerville, P.

The **hair** wreath. Villegas, H.

Haircut. Matheson, R.

HAIRDRESSERS *See* Beauty shops

Haïta the shepherd. Bierce, A.

HAITI

Bell, M. S. Twenty dollars

Cerat, M. L. Maloulou

Dalembert, L.-P. Dangerous crossroads

Duncan, A. Zora and the zombie

Lahens, Y. And all this unease

Lahens, Y. Aunt Résia and the spirits

Lahens, Y. A commonplace disaster

Lahens, Y. Death in July

Lahens, Y. Madness had come with the rain

Lahens, Y. Moon bathing

Lahens, Y. The neighborhood, the ravine, and the old Peugeot

Lahens, Y. Petty corruption

Lahens, Y. A shattered day

Lahens, Y. Soursop, orange, and lemongrass

Lahens, Y. The survivors

Lahens, Y. Three natural deaths

HAITI—*Continued*
Lahens, Y. Wash your memory with lots of water
Lahens, Y. The weight of the night
Mars, K. Paradise Inn
Pinede, N. Department lounge
Saint-Eloi, R. The blue hill
Sylvain, P. Odette
Theodore-Pharel, M. K. Mercy at the gate
Ulysse, K. D. The last department
Zoboi, I. A. The harem
Port-au-Prince
Lahens, Y. The city
Lahens, Y. Who is that man?
Large, J.-R. Rosanna
Victor, G. The finger
Victor, M. Blues for Irène
HAITIAN REFUGEES
Bingham, S. Anywhere you send me
HAITIANS
United States
Buckell, T. S. Trinkets
Lahens, Y. An American story
Trouillot, E. Which one?
Ulysse, K. D. The last department
Halam, Ann
See also Jones, Gwyneth A., 1952-
Haldeman, Joe
Fantasy for six electrodes and one adrenaline drip (a play in the form of a feelie script)
Future media; [edited by Rick Wilber]
Out of phase
Before they were giants; edited by James L. Sutter; cover illustration by Kieran Yanner.
Sleeping dogs
The Year's best science fiction: twenty-eighth annual collection; edited by Gardner Dozois.
A !tangled web
The Nebula Awards showcase; edited by Kevin J. Anderson.
Hale, Daniel J.
The precipice
Mystery Writers of America presents the rich and the dead; edited by Nelson DeMille.
Half a brother. Flann, K.
HALF-CASTES *See* Mixed bloods
Half-Life. Slouka, M.
The **Half-** Wall. Alameddine, R.
Halfway people. Fowler, K. J.
Hall, Holworthy
The last round
Golf stories; edited by Charles McGrath.
Hall, James W.
Bells
On a raven's wing; new tales in honor of Edgar Allan Poe; edited by Stuart M. Kaminsky
Overexposure
Florida heat wave; [edited and with an] introduction by Michael Lister.
Hall, Tina May
All the day's sad stories: a novella
Hall, T. M. The physics of imaginary objects
By the gleam of her teeth, she will light the path before her
Hall, T. M. The physics of imaginary objects
A crown of sonnets dedicated to long-gone love
Hall, T. M. The physics of imaginary objects

Erratum: insert "r" in "transgressors"
Hall, T. M. The physics of imaginary objects
Faith is three parts formaldehyde, one part ethyl alcohol
Hall, T. M. The physics of imaginary objects
For dear Pearl, who drowned
Hall, T. M. The physics of imaginary objects
Gravetending
Hall, T. M. The physics of imaginary objects
How to remember a bird
Hall, T. M. The physics of imaginary objects
In your endeavors, you may feel my ghostly presence
Hall, T. M. The physics of imaginary objects
Kick
Hall, T. M. The physics of imaginary objects
Last night of the county fair
Hall, T. M. The physics of imaginary objects
Skinny girls' constitution and bylaws
Hall, T. M. The physics of imaginary objects
There is a factory in Sierra Vista where Jesus is resurrected every hour in hot plastic and the stench of chicken
Hall, T. M. The physics of imaginary objects
This is a love story, too
Hall, T. M. The physics of imaginary objects
Visitations
Hall, T. M. The physics of imaginary objects
The woman who fell in love with a meteorologist and stopped the rain
Hall, T. M. The physics of imaginary objects
The **hall** bedroom. Freeman, M. E. W.
Halliday, Brett
A taste for cognac
The Black Lizard big book of Black Mask stories; edited and with a foreword by Otto Penzler; introduction by Keith Alan Deutsch.
HALLOWEEN
Frost, G. The comeuppance of Creegus Maxin
Holladay, C. Ghost walk
Lansdale, J. R. The folding man
Moore, S. One thin dime
O'Nan, S. Monsters
Story, K. Flame retarded
Halloween. Franco, J.
Halloween Town. Shepard, L.
HALLUCINATIONS AND ILLUSIONS
See also Personality disorders
Bierce, A. An occurance at Owl Creek Bridge
Bierce, A. An occurrence at Owl Creek Bridge
Bierce, A. The realm of the unreal
Dozois, G. R. A kingdom by the sea
Ely, S. Dream fishing
Gibson, W. The Gernsback continuum
Lively, P. Black dog
Millhauser, S. Eisenheim the illusionist
Shepard, L. Salvador
Vukcevich, R. Some other time
Wells, H. G. The door in the wall
Wells, H. G. The moth
Wells, H. G. The remarkable case of Davidson's eyes
Halo. Mu Xin
Halvorsen, Cheryl
Smart Cows
Nebraska Life v15 no5 p43 S 2011

Hamburger, Aaron
  The end of anti-Semitism
    Promised lands; new Jewish American fiction
      on longing and belonging; edited by Derek
      Rubin.
Hamby, Barbara
  Lani Dances the Zombie Hula in LA
    Five Points v13 no3 p16-26 2010
Hamid, Mohsin
  A Beheading
    Granta no112 p191-5 Aut 2010
Hamilton, Clive *See* Lewis, C. S. (Clive Staples),
    1898-1963
Hamilton, Hugo
  The supremacy of grief
    The Granta book of the Irish short story; [ed-
      ited by] Anne Enright.
Hamilton, Jane
  The Scarf Dancers
    TriQuarterly v138 46009 bytes Summ/Fall
      2010
Hammer and Sickle. DeLillo, D.
Hammer song. Van der Veer, K. L.
The **Hammerpond** Park burglary. Wells, H. G.
Hammett, Dashiell
  The maltese falcon
    The Black Lizard big book of Black Mask
      stories; edited and with a foreword by Otto
      Penzler; introduction by Keith Alan
      Deutsch.
Hammett, Samuel Dashiell *See* Hammett,
    Dashiell, 1894-1961
Hampton, Evelyn
  Mr. Gray
    Butler, B. 30 under 30; an anthology of inno-
      vative fiction by younger writers; Blake
      Butler & Lily Hoang, eds.
Hand, Elizabeth
  The maiden flight of McCauley's Bellerophon
    The Best science fiction and fantasy of the
      year: volume five; edited by Jonathan
      Strahan.
HAND
  Maupassant, G. d. The hand
  Rohmer, S. The hand of the Mandarin Quong
Hand. Davis, L.
The **hand**. Maupassant, G. d.
Hand. Me. Down. Manilla, M.
The **hand** of the Mandarin Quong. Rohmer, S.
HAND-TO-HAND FIGHTING
  Crane, S. The blue hotel
The **Handbag** Incident. Donoghue, W.
Handey, Jack
  My first day in Hell
    I found this funny; my favorite pieces of hu-
      mor and some that may not be funny at all;
      edited by Judd Apatow.
The **handkerchief** [excerpt]. Kronauer, B.
Handler, Joan Cusack
  The Flesh
    Southern Humanities Review v44 no3 p335-9
      Summ 2010
Hands. Emshwiller, C.
Hands held at religious angles. Spenst, K.
HANDYMEN *See* Hired men
HANDYWOMEN *See* Hired women
Haneef from Glasgow. Alwan, M. H.
The **hanging** curve. Dozois, G. R.
Hanging fire. Pearlman, E.

HANGINGS
  Bierce, A. An occurance at Owl Creek Bridge
  Bierce, A. An occurrence at Owl Creek Bridge
  Loory, B. The sea monster
  Rodoreda, M. Guinea fowls
Hangman. Williamson, E. M.
Hanif, Mohammed
  Butt and Bhatti
    Granta no112 p119-31 Aut 2010
Hanley, Tessa
  Clever girl
    The New Yorker v87 no16 p66-72 Je 6 2011
Hannah, Barry
  Bats Out of Hell Division
    Hannah, B. Long, last, happy; new and select-
      ed stories
  Behold the husband in his perfect agony
    Hannah, B. Long, last, happy; new and select-
      ed stories
  Coming close to Donna
    Hannah, B. Long, last, happy; new and select-
      ed stories
  A creature in the Bay of St. Louis
    Hannah, B. Long, last, happy; new and select-
      ed stories
  Dragged fighting from his tomb
    Hannah, B. Long, last, happy; new and select-
      ed stories
  Drummer down
    Hannah, B. Long, last, happy; new and select-
      ed stories
  Even Greenland
    Hannah, B. Long, last, happy; new and select-
      ed stories
  Evening of the Yarp; a report by Roonswent
    Dover
    Hannah, B. Long, last, happy; new and select-
      ed stories
  Fans
    Hannah, B. Long, last, happy; new and select-
      ed stories
  Fire water
    Hannah, B. Long, last, happy; new and select-
      ed stories
  Get some young
    Hannah, B. Long, last, happy; new and select-
      ed stories
  Getting ready
    Hannah, B. Long, last, happy; new and select-
      ed stories
  Hey, have you got a cig, the time, the news, my
    face?
    Hannah, B. Long, last, happy; new and select-
      ed stories
  High-water railers
    Hannah, B. Long, last, happy; new and select-
      ed stories
  Knowing he was not my kind yet I followed
    Hannah, B. Long, last, happy; new and select-
      ed stories
  Lastward, deputy James
    Hannah, B. Long, last, happy; new and select-
      ed stories
  Love too long
    Hannah, B. Long, last, happy; new and select-
      ed stories
  Midnight and I'm not famous yet
    Hannah, B. Long, last, happy; new and select-
      ed stories

Hannah, Barry—*Continued*
Mother mouth
Hannah, B. Long, last, happy; new and select-
ed stories
Mother Rooney unscrolls the hurt
Hannah, B. Long, last, happy; new and select-
ed stories
Rangoon Green
Hannah, B. Long, last, happy; new and select-
ed stories
Harper's v321 p67-74 N 2010
Rat-faced Auntie
Hannah, B. Long, last, happy; new and select-
ed stories
Ride, fly, penetrate, loiter
Hannah, B. Long, last, happy; new and select-
ed stories
Scandale d'estime
Hannah, B. Long, last, happy; new and select-
ed stories
Sick soldier at your door
Hannah, B. Long, last, happy; new and select-
ed stories
Testimony of pilot
Hannah, B. Long, last, happy; new and select-
ed stories
Trek
Hannah, B. Long, last, happy; new and select-
ed stories
Two gone over
Hannah, B. Long, last, happy; new and select-
ed stories
Two things, dimly, were going at each other
Hannah, B. Long, last, happy; new and select-
ed stories
Uncle high lonesome
Hannah, B. Long, last, happy; new and select-
ed stories
Water liars
Hannah, B. Long, last, happy; new and select-
ed stories
Hannah, Sophie
The asking price
Original sins; a Crime Writer's Association
anthology; edited by Martin Edwards.
Hannibal, Edward
Misery Island
Commonweal v138 no13 p18-24 Jl 15 2011
Hanoosh, Yasmeen
(tr.) See Abbas, Luay Hamza
Hansen, Pearce
Community property
Blood, guts, & whiskey; edited by Todd Rob-
inson; introduction by Max Allan Collins.
Hanson, Erik
Endangered Species
The North American Review v295 no3 p21-3
Summ 2010
Happiest moment. Davis, L.
Happine$$. Phelan, T.
HAPPINESS
Bierce, A. Haïta the shepherd
Bloch, R. That hell-bound train
Mueenuddin, D. A spoiled man
Happiness. Rodoreda, M.
Happy Chinatown Tours. Chin, F.
O **Happy** day !. Ryman, G.
A **Happy** Family. Trevor, W.
Happy hour. Plummer, T. M.

Happy man. Shepard, S.
Happy memories. Davis, L.
Happy with crocodiles. Shepard, J.
Ḥaqqi, Yaḥyá
The first lesson
Tablet & pen; literary landscapes from the
modern Middle East, a words without bor-
ders anthology; edited by Reza Asian.
HARASSMENT, SEXUAL *See* Sexual harass-
ment
Harassment [Part of special issue: Sex and Sur-
veillance] Parkison, A.
Hard currency. Willis, D.
Hard work. Marãr, M.
The **hardest** button. Kloess, C.
Harding, Rebecca Blaine *See* Davis, Rebecca
Harding, 1831-1910
Hardwick, Elizabeth
Back issues
Hardwick, E. The New York stories of Eliza-
beth Hardwick; selected and with an intro-
duction by Darryl Pinckney
The bookseller
Hardwick, E. The New York stories of Eliza-
beth Hardwick; selected and with an intro-
duction by Darryl Pinckney
The classless society
Hardwick, E. The New York stories of Eliza-
beth Hardwick; selected and with an intro-
duction by Darryl Pinckney
Cross-town
Hardwick, E. The New York stories of Eliza-
beth Hardwick; selected and with an intro-
duction by Darryl Pinckney
Evenings at home
Hardwick, E. The New York stories of Eliza-
beth Hardwick; selected and with an intro-
duction by Darryl Pinckney
The final conflict
Hardwick, E. The New York stories of Eliza-
beth Hardwick; selected and with an intro-
duction by Darryl Pinckney
The oak and the axe
Hardwick, E. The New York stories of Eliza-
beth Hardwick; selected and with an intro-
duction by Darryl Pinckney
On the eve
Hardwick, E. The New York stories of Eliza-
beth Hardwick; selected and with an intro-
duction by Darryl Pinckney
The purchase
Hardwick, E. The New York stories of Eliza-
beth Hardwick; selected and with an intro-
duction by Darryl Pinckney
A season's romance
Hardwick, E. The New York stories of Eliza-
beth Hardwick; selected and with an intro-
duction by Darryl Pinckney
Shot: a New York story
Hardwick, E. The New York stories of Eliza-
beth Hardwick; selected and with an intro-
duction by Darryl Pinckney
Yes and no
Hardwick, E. The New York stories of Eliza-
beth Hardwick; selected and with an intro-
duction by Darryl Pinckney

Hare, Augustus
The vampire of Croglin Grange
The book of the living dead; edited by John Richard Stephens.
HARE, WILLIAM
About
Hodge, B. A good dead man is hard to find
The **harem**. Zoboi, I. A.
The **hare's** mask. Slouka, M.
Harland, Richard
Bad thoughts and the mechanism
Ghosts by gaslight; stories of steampunk and supernatural suspense; [edited by] Jack Dann [and] Nick Gevers
The fear
The Best horror of the year: volume three; edited by Ellen Datlow.
HARLEM (NEW YORK, N.Y.) *See* New York (N.Y.)—Harlem
Harman, Mark
(jt. auth) See Kafka, Franz and Harman, Mark
Harmony. Barnes, J.
Harmony of the world. Baxter, C.
The **"harnt"** that walks Chilhowee. Craddock, C. E.
Harold the spider man. Tremblay, P.
Harp music. Aiken, J.
Harper, Jordan
Red hair and black leather
Blood, guts, & whiskey; edited by Todd Robinson; introduction by Max Allan Collins.
HARPS
Aiken, J. Harp music
Harris, Anne L.
Still life with boobs
Swenson, P. The Best of Talebones; edited by Patrick Swenson.
Harris, Charlaine
Dahlia underground
Vampires; the recent undead; edited by Paula Guran.
Harris, Clare Winger
The miracle of the lily
The dreaming sex; early tales of scientific imagination by women; edited by Mike Ashley.
Harris, Elizabeth
(tr.) See Mozzi, Giulio
Harris, George Washington
The Snake-Bit Irishman [1867]
Southern Quarterly v48 no2 p114-17 Wint 2011
Tripetown: Twenty Minutes For Breakfastt [1867]
Southern Quarterly v48 no2 p117-19 Wint 2011
Harris, Joel Chandler
Brer Rabbit and the Tar-Baby
21 essential American short stories; edited by Leslie M. Pockell
Harris, John Wyndham Parkes Lucas Beynon
See Wyndham, John, 1903-1969
Harris, Lynn
Mummy dust tea
Before; short stories about pregnancy from our top writers; edited by Emily Franklin and Heather Swain

Harrison, David
Mercy first, first mercy
Blood, guts, & whiskey; edited by Todd Robinson; introduction by Max Allan Collins.
Harrison Bergeron. Vonnegut, K.
Harry Cray. Warsh, L.
Harry Sprague meets the masters. Wind, H. W.
Hart, R. G.
My partner the zombie
Hungry for your love; an anthology of zombie romance; edited by Lori Perkins.
Hart. Ruocco, J.
Harte, Bret
A yellow dog
Harvest. Evans, D.
The **Harvest**. Heynen, J.
Harvey, Brennan
The truth, from a lie of convenience
L. Ron Hubbard presents Writers of the Future volume XXVII; the year's thirteen best tales from the Writers of the Future international writers' program; illustrated by winners in the Illustrators of the Future international illustrators' program; with essays on writing & illustration by L. Ron Hubbard / Mike Resnick / Robert Cadtillo; edited by K. D. Wentworth
Harvey, Henry
UNION ROAD
Dalhousie Review v91 no1 p45-51 Spr 2011
Harvey, Jack *See* Rankin, Ian, 1960-
Harvey, Miles
The Master of Patina
Agni no73 p39-58 2011
Harvey, Ryan
An acolyte of black spires
L. Ron Hubbard presents Writers of the Future volume XXVII; the year's thirteen best tales from the Writers of the Future international writers' program; illustrated by winners in the Illustrators of the Future international illustrators' program; with essays on writing & illustration by L. Ron Hubbard / Mike Resnick / Robert Cadtillo; edited by K. D. Wentworth
Harwood, John
Face to face
Ghosts by gaslight; stories of steampunk and supernatural suspense; [edited by] Jack Dann [and] Nick Gevers
Hasbún, Rodrigo
The place of losses
Granta no113 p65-79 Wint 2010
HASHISH
Beattie, A. Fancy flights
Hasidic noir. Abraham, P.
HASIDISM
Abraham, P. Hasidic noir
Haskell, Arkansas (Highway 70). Shepard, S.
Haskins, Michael
Finding Picasso
The Saturday Evening Post v283 no1 p24-7, 56-8 Ja/F 2011
Hassan, Ihab
Hawk
Agni no73 p69-81 2011
Ma'lesh
The Antioch Review v69 no3 p534-544 Summ 2011

Hassan, Rosa Yassin
  Guardians of the air
    Beirut 39; new writing from the Arab world;
      edited by Samuel Shimon; with a preface
      by Hanan al-Shaykh
Hassan's tower. Drabble, M.
Hasse, Henry
  (jt. auth) See Bradbury, Ray and Hasse, Henry
Hastings, William
  Ten-year plan
    Cape Cod noir; edited by David L. Ulin.
The **hat**. Loory, B.
Hat. Naipaul, V. S.
HATE
  See also Misogyny
Hate the sinner, love the sin. Hodge, B.
Hatoum, Milton
  Torn
    Freedom; stories celebrating the Universal
      Declaration of Human Rights; Amnesty In-
      ternational.
HATS
  Loory, B. The hat
Hats off to Mary. Kilworth, G.
The **haunted** house. Shipp, J. C.
A **haunted** house of her own. Armstrong, K.
HAUNTED HOUSES *See* Ghost stories
The **haunted** valley. Bierce, A.
The **hauntings**. Phillips, H.
Hautala, Rick
  The hum
    The end of the world; stories of the apoca-
      lypse; edited by Martin H. Greenberg.
Havazelet, Ehud
  Gurov in Manhattan
    The Best American short stories, 2011; select-
      ed from U.S. and Canadian magazines by
      Geraldine Brooks with Heidi Pitlor; with an
      introduction by Geraldine Brooks.
HAWAII
  Sale, R. The dancing rats
  Stevenson, R. L. The bottle imp
HAWAIIAN ISLANDS *See* Hawaii
Hawk, Tiffany
  Into the Frying Pan
    StoryQuarterly v44 p334-46 2010
Hawk. Hassan, I.
Hawkins, Jim
  Chimbwi
    The Year's best science fiction: twenty-eighth
      annual collection; edited by Gardner
      Dozois.
Hawkins. Lychack, W.
Hawks of Outremer. Howard, R. E.
Hawks over Egypt. Howard, R. E.
Hawthorne, Nathaniel
  Young Goodman Brown
    Sympathy for the devil; edited by Tim Pratt.
HAWTHORNE, NATHANIEL, 1804-1864
  About
  Youmans, M. The grave reflection
Hayat: a short story. Sa'id, M. A.
Haydar Haydar
  The dance of the savage prairies
    Tablet & pen; literary landscapes from the
      modern Middle East, a words without bor-
      ders anthology; edited by Reza Asian.

Hayes, Martin
  Me am Petri
    Nature v466 p1148 Ag 26 2010
Hayim Yerushalmi, Yosef
  Gilgul
    The New Yorker v87 no24 p76-83 Ag 15
      2011
Haynsworth, Leslie
  The Other Girls
    Confrontation no108 p35-45 Fall 2010
Haywood, Gar Anthony
  And pray nobody sees you
    Randisi, R. J. The Shamus winners: Ameri-
      ca's best private eye stories, volume II,
      1996-2009; collected and introduced by
      Robert J. Randisi; founder, Private Eye
      Writers of America
  The first rule is
    The Best American mystery stories 2010; ed-
      ited and with an introduction by Lee Child;
      Otto Penzler, series editor
  Like something out of a comic book
    San Diego noir; edited by Maryelizabeth Hart.
Hazaran. Le Clézio, J.-M. G.
Hazell, Jacqui
  The school trip
    Dancing with Mr. Darcy; stories inspired by
      Jane Austen and Chawton House Library;
      compiled by Sarah Waters.
The **Hazlett's** dog. Allen, D.
Hazzan, Dave
  Some dead guys
    Can'tLit; fearless fiction from Broken pencil
      magazine; edited by Richard Rosenbaum.
He, Qifang
  Streets
    Chinese Literature Today v1 no1 p78-81
      Summ 2010
  The Weeping Yangtze
    Chinese Literature Today v1 no1 p73-7
      Summ 2010
He and the cat. Mphahlele, E.
He knew. Antrim, D.
He Remembered His Life. Kotker, Z.
He tried to catch the light. Dowling, T.
He wanted to live. Matheson, R.
He who bestows all worldly goods. Dib, M.
He will not see me stopping here. O'Connor, S.
The **head-gardener's** story. Chekhov, A. P.
Head, heart. Davis, L.
Head in the world. Shepard, S.
The **head** reflects. Shepard, S.
A **headache** from Barstow to Salt Lake. Roberge,
  R.
HEADMASTERS *See* School superintendents and
  principals; Teachers
HEADMISTRESSES *See* School superintendents
  and principals; Teachers
Heads You Lose. Meltzer, D.
Headstone in your pocket. Tremblay, P.
The **headstrong** historian. Adichie, C. N.
Healey, Emma
  Last winter here
    Can'tLit; fearless fiction from Broken pencil
      magazine; edited by Richard Rosenbaum.
Health Nuts. Hodges, J. O.
HEALTH RESORTS
    See also Summer resorts

Healy, J. F. (Jeremiah F.)
Aftermath
　　Randisi, R. J. The Shamus winners: America's best private eye stories, volume II, 1996-2009; collected and introduced by Robert J. Randisi; founder, Private Eye Writers of America
The holiday fairy
　　Christmas at the Mysterious Bookshop; 'tis the season to be deadly; stories of mistletoe and mayhem from 17 masters of suspense; edited by Otto Penzler.
In my ancestor's image: a Rory Calhoun short story
　　On a raven's wing; new tales in honor of Edgar Allan Poe; edited by Stuart M. Kaminsky
Healy, Jeremiah F. *See* Healy, J. F. (Jeremiah F.), 1948-
Hearn, Lafcadio
A dead love
　　The book of the living dead; edited by John Richard Stephens.
The name on the stone
　　The book of the living dead; edited by John Richard Stephens.
HEART
　　　　　　Disease
Oates, J. C. The barter
　　　　　　Diseases
Chopin, K. The story of an hour
Shepard, S. Wisconsin wilderness
Welty, E. Death of a traveling salesman
The **heart**. Naipaul, V. S.
The **heart** fails without warning. Mantel, H.
The **heart** has reasons. De Noux, O.
A **Heart** in Saskatoon. Archer, L.
Heartstrung. Swirsky, R.
Heat engine. Swirsky, R.
Heath, Aloise Buckley
It Says Here . . . [Reprint]
　　National Review v62 no24 p20-1 D 31 2010
Heathcock, Alan
The daughter
　　Heathcock, A. Volt; stories
Fort Apache
　　Heathcock, A. Volt; stories
Furlough
　　Heathcock, A. Volt; stories
Lazarus
　　Heathcock, A. Volt; stories
Peacekeeper
　　Heathcock, A. Volt; stories
Smoke
　　Heathcock, A. Volt; stories
The staying freight
　　Heathcock, A. Volt; stories
Volt
　　Heathcock, A. Volt; stories
HEAVEN
Bingham, S. Heaven
Maḥfūẓ, N. The seventh heaven
O'Connor, S. The professor of atheism: Department of refutation
Ruocco, J. Bones
Heaven. Bingham, S.
Heaven Is Full of Windows. Stern, S.
Heaven on a summer night. Beattie, A.

Heavenly creatures: for wandering children and their delinquent mother. Thon, M. R.
Hecht, Jeff
Event horizon
　　Nature v475 no7356 p418 Jl 21 2011
Hedayat, Sadegh *See* Hidāyat, Ṣādiq, 1903-1951
Hedden, Kim
The Green Dress
　　Confrontation no108 p172-82 Fall 2010
The **hedgehog**. Schirach, F. v.
Hedges, Timothy
Civil Twilight
　　Gettysburg Review v24 no2 p173-87 Summ 2011
The **Heidelberg** cylinder. Carroll, J.
HEIM, ARIBERT FERDINAND, 1914-1992
　　　　　　About
Gifford, B. Far from anywhere
HEINE, HEINRICH, 1797-1856
　　　　　　About
Mu Xin. Weimar in early spring
HEIRESSES *See* Inheritance and succession; Wealth
HEIRS *See* Inheritance and succession; Wealth
Heist. Doctorow, E. L.
The **heist**. Sands, B.
Held. Gautier, A.
Helen and Vi: a study in health and vitality. Davis, L.
The **Helens**. Phillips, H.
Helfers, John
Afterword
　　The end of the world; stories of the apocalypse; edited by Martin H. Greenberg.
HELL
Cady, J. The parable of Satan's adversary
Carroll, J. The Heidelberg cylinder
Duncan, A. Beluthahatchie
Esposito, B. Kirby and the portal to Hell
Handey, J. My first day in Hell
Nutting, A. Hellion
O'Connor, S. The professor of atheism: Glue factory bowling
Parks, R. A garden in Hell
Stevenson, R. L. The bottle imp
Westerfeld, S. Non-disclosure agreement
Youmans, M. The salamander fire
Hell Cay. Dent, L.
Helle Helle
A fine boy
　　Copenhagen noir; edited by Bo Tao Michaëlis; translated by Mark Kline.
Hellenes, McKinley M.
The Jesus
　　Can'tLit; fearless fiction from Broken pencil magazine; edited by Richard Rosenbaum.
Hellion. Nutting, A.
Hello, nations!. Marār, M.
The **helper**. Aiken, J.
Helvetian freedoms. Monzó, Q.
Hemingway, Ernest
The killers
　　I found this funny; my favorite pieces of humor and some that may not be funny at all; edited by Judd Apatow.
　　21 essential American short stories; edited by Leslie M. Pockell

HEMINGWAY, ERNEST, 1899-1961
About
Oates, J. C. Papa at Ketchum, 1961
Hemmerchts, Kristien
Fairy tale
The Dedalus book of Flemish fantasy; edited
by Eric Dickens and translated by Paul
Vincent.
Hemmingson, Michael
Adventure
Hemmingson, M. Pictures of houses with wa-
ter damage; stories
Aliens
Hemmingson, M. Pictures of houses with wa-
ter damage; stories
Baby brother
Hemmingson, M. Pictures of houses with wa-
ter damage; stories
The birds
Hemmingson, M. Pictures of houses with wa-
ter damage; stories
Branches
Hemmingson, M. Pictures of houses with wa-
ter damage; stories
Cyclops
Hemmingson, M. Pictures of houses with wa-
ter damage; stories
Daddy
Hemmingson, M. Pictures of houses with wa-
ter damage; stories
Fishpole Pete
Hemmingson, M. Pictures of houses with wa-
ter damage; stories
Forbidden scenes of affection
Hemmingson, M. Pictures of houses with wa-
ter damage; stories
Give me the gun, he says
Hemmingson, M. Pictures of houses with wa-
ter damage; stories
It's very cold down here
Hemmingson, M. Pictures of houses with wa-
ter damage; stories
The keepers
Hemmingson, M. Pictures of houses with wa-
ter damage; stories
Last visit
Hemmingson, M. Pictures of houses with wa-
ter damage; stories
Looking for Wanda beyond the Salton Sea
Hemmingson, M. Pictures of houses with wa-
ter damage; stories
Pictures of houses with water damage
Hemmingson, M. Pictures of houses with wa-
ter damage; stories
Solid memories have the life-span of tulips and
sunflowers
Hemmingson, M. Pictures of houses with wa-
ter damage; stories
What happened?
Hemmingson, M. Pictures of houses with wa-
ter damage; stories
What happens when my wife's ex-boyfriend,
back from Iraq, pays us a visit
Hemmingson, M. Pictures of houses with wa-
ter damage; stories
Why don't you use your parking space?
Hemmingson, M. Pictures of houses with wa-
ter damage; stories

You can call and ask a question
Hemmingson, M. Pictures of houses with wa-
ter damage; stories
You will not believe what happens to me, but
does it matter? it only matters that I know
what happens
Hemmingson, M. Pictures of houses with wa-
ter damage; stories
Hempel, Amy
In the cemetery where Al Jolson is buried
Best of times, worst of times; contemporary
American short stories from the new Gilded
Age; edited by Wendy Martin and Cecelia
Tichi.
Hendee, Barb
The winds of Brennan Marcher
Swenson, P. The Best of Talebones; edited by
Patrick Swenson.
Henderson, C. J.
The wonderous boundless thought
The stories (in) between; edited by Greg
Schauer, Jeanne B. Benzel, and W. H.
Horner.
Henderson, Kim
Girls
River Styx no85 p82-3 2011
Henderson, Samantha
Wild copper
Steampunk II: steampunk reloaded; edited by
Ann & Jeff VanderMeer.
Hendrickson, Janet
(tr.) See Madrid, Fabrizio Mejía
(tr.) See Pron, Patricio
HENRY VIII, KING OF ENGLAND, 1491-1547
About
Vaughn, C. A princess of Spain
Henry, Brian
Cross Keys
The Antioch Review v69 no3 p440-448 Summ
2011
Henry, O.
The caballero's way
The Big book of adventure stories; edited and
with a introduction by Otto Penzler; fore-
word by Douglas Preston.
The gift of the magi
21 essential American short stories; edited by
Leslie M. Pockell
Memoirs of a yellow dog
Heorot. Butcher, J.
Her dagger before me. Powell, T.
Her damage. Davis, L.
Her dog. Wolff, T.
Her firstborn. Packer, A.
Her Last Affair. Hiller, C.
Her mother's mother. Davis, L.
Her name was Jane. Ho, J.
HERACLES (LEGENDARY CHARACTER)
See Hercules (Legendary character)
Herbert, Stephanie
Kindness and Other Inalienable Rights
Texas Bar Journal v74 no6 p486-8 Je 2011
Herbert West: reanimator. Lovecraft, H. P.
HERCULES (LEGENDARY CHARACTER)
Piccirilli, T. Caucasus
Herdbound. Shepard, S.
Here after life. Monk, D.
Here comes the sun. Dybek, S.
Here is what you do. Dennis, C.

Here it was, November. Furman, L.

Here or there. Neugeboren, J.

Here we aren't, so quickly. Foer, J. S.

Heritage. Gorman, E. and Butler, T.

Hermann, Judith

Misha

The Literary Review (Madison, N.J.) v54 no2 p41-61 Wint 2011

HERMAPHRODITISM

Roberge, R. Working backward from the worst moment of my life

HERMITS

See also Recluses

Ahmed, S. Hooves and the hovel of Abdel Jameela

The **hermit's** story. Bass, R.

Hernández, Sònia

The survivor

Granta no113 p147-56 Wint 2010

HEROES

See also Heroism

Banks, R. The gully

Howard, R. E. The devil in iron

McCulley, J. Zorro deals with treason

Page, N. W. The wings of Kali

Scholes, K. Edward Bear and the very long walk

Shepard, J. In cretaceous seas

Vukcevich, R. Superpowers

HEROIN

Atta, S. Last trip

Simms, C. Tick-tock

HEROISM

See also Courage; Heroes

Emshwiller, C. The childhood of the human hero

Mankell, H. Sofia

Ryman, G. The last ten years in the life of hero Kai

Heron, E. *See* Prichard, Kate O'Brien Ryall

Heron, H. *See* Prichard, Hesketh Vernon, 1876-1922

HERONS

Jewett, S. O. A white heron

HERRIOT, JAMES

Parodies, imitations, etc.

Cannon, P. All moon-beasts

Cannon, P. Amorphous and mephitic

Hertmans, Stefan

Lock-up no. 14

The Dedalus book of Flemish fantasy; edited by Eric Dickens and translated by Paul Vincent.

Heuler, Karen

The hair

Michigan Quarterly Review v50 no2 p263-274 Spr 2011

Hey, have you got a cig, the time, the news, my face? Hannah, B.

Hey You!. Jankovic, M.

Heynen, Jim

The Dream

The Georgia Review v65 no1 p130 Spr 2011

Electricity

The Georgia Review v65 no1 p126-8 Spr 2011

Eye to Eye

The Georgia Review v65 no1 p123 Spr 2011

Go to the Ant, Thou Sluggard

The Georgia Review v65 no1 p134-5 Spr 2011

The Harvest

The Georgia Review v65 no1 p131-2 Spr 2011

House Visitation

The Georgia Review v65 no1 p129-30 Spr 2011

One Dead Chicken

The Georgia Review v65 no1 p128-9 Spr 2011

The Parrot

The Georgia Review v65 no1 p136-7 Spr 2011

The Robin's Nest

The Georgia Review v65 no1 p133-4 Spr 2011

Scar Tissue

The Georgia Review v65 no1 p125-6 Spr 2011

That Could Have Been You

The Georgia Review v65 no1 p132-3 Spr 2011

What If

The Georgia Review v65 no1 p130-1 Spr 2011

Yellow Girl

The Georgia Review v65 no1 p124-5 Spr 2011

Hibbert, Andra

Centers of Gravity

Five Points v14 no1 p38-61 2010

Hicks, Jim

(tr.) See Devi, Ananda

(tr.) See Marchis, Vittorio

Hicks, Patrick

Buster

Dalhousie Review v90 no2 p293-301 Summ 2010

Hidāyat, Ṣādiq

The blind owl [excerpt]

Tablet & pen; literary landscapes from the modern Middle East, a words without borders anthology; edited by Reza Asian.

A **high-end** neighborhood. Fabra, J. S. I.

High heels. Archer, J.

High lonesome. Oates, J. C.

High Noon moon (Highway 152, continued). Shepard, S.

High on the hog. Davidson, S.

HIGH SCHOOLS *See* School life

High-water railers. Hannah, B.

Highsmith, Patricia

The baby spoon

Highsmith, P. Patricia Highsmith: selected novels and short stories; edited with an introduction by Joan Schenkar.

The great cardhouse

Highsmith, P. Patricia Highsmith: selected novels and short stories; edited with an introduction by Joan Schenkar.

In the plaza

Highsmith, P. Patricia Highsmith: selected novels and short stories; edited with an introduction by Joan Schenkar.

Highsmith, Patricia—*Continued*

A mighty nice man
Highsmith, P. Patricia Highsmith: selected novels and short stories; edited with an introduction by Joan Schenkar.

Not one of us
Highsmith, P. Patricia Highsmith: selected novels and short stories; edited with an introduction by Joan Schenkar.

Oona, the jolly cave woman
Highsmith, P. Patricia Highsmith: selected novels and short stories; edited with an introduction by Joan Schenkar.

Quiet night
Highsmith, P. Patricia Highsmith: selected novels and short stories; edited with an introduction by Joan Schenkar.

The still point of the turning world
Highsmith, P. Patricia Highsmith: selected novels and short stories; edited with an introduction by Joan Schenkar.

The terrors of basket-weaving
Highsmith, P. Patricia Highsmith: selected novels and short stories; edited with an introduction by Joan Schenkar.

There I was, struck with Bubsy

The trouble with Mrs. Blynn, the trouble with the world
Highsmith, P. Patricia Highsmith: selected novels and short stories; edited with an introduction by Joan Schenkar.

Two disagreeable pigeons
Highsmith, P. Patricia Highsmith: selected novels and short stories; edited with an introduction by Joan Schenkar.

Where the door is always open and the welcome mat is out
Highsmith, P. Patricia Highsmith: selected novels and short stories; edited with an introduction by Joan Schenkar.

Woodrow, Wilson's necktie
Highsmith, P. Patricia Highsmith: selected novels and short stories; edited with an introduction by Joan Schenkar.

The **hight-doings** at "Deadman's". Bierce, A.

Highway 61 revisited. Miéville, C.

Highway, high beams. Blatnik, A.

The **hikikomori**. Goto, H.

HIKING
Barnes, J. Trespass

Hill, Lawrence
Meet you at the door
The Walrus v8 no1 p60-5, 67 Ja/F 2011

Hill, Lindsay Stuart
Water Running on the Moon
Five Points v12 no1 p114-19 2008

Hill, Miranda
Petitions to Saint Chronic
Dalhousie Review v90 no3 p335-44 Aut 2010

Hill, Reginald
Where are all the naughty people?
Original sins; a Crime Writer's Association anthology; edited by Martin Edwards.

The **hill** bachelors. Trevor, W.

Hill clan cross. Bill, F.

Hiller, Catherine
Her Last Affair
The Antioch Review v68 no3 p537-44 Summ 2010

Hindmarch, Will
The Auble gun
The Thackery T. Lambshead cabinet of curiosities; edited by Ann & Jeff VanderMeer.

HINDUS
Fatima, A. Do you suppose it's the east winds?
Naipaul, V. S. A Christmas story
Naipaul, V. S. My aunt Gold Teeth
                    England
                See also East Indians—England

Hinnefeld, Joyce
Benedicta, or A Guide to the Artist's Résumé
The Literary Review (Madison, N.J.) v54 no2 p86-95 Wint 2011

HIPPIES
Pearlman, E. Mates
Willis, D. The separation

Hired by a Witch. VanBuren, K.

HIRED KILLERS
Alexander, G. Charlie and the pirates
Ewan, C. The art of negotiation
Gaiman, N. We can get them for you wholesale
Kenyon, J. Cut
Land, J. Killing time
Lansdale, J. R. Six-finger Jack
Nevins, F. M., Jr. Evensong
Vaughan, E. A. A rose by any other name would still be red

HIRED MEN
Faherty, T. The caretaker
Lindholm, M. Finis
Trevor, W. The woman of the house

HIRED WOMEN
Mphahlele, E. Mrs. Plum
Salter, J. Foreign shores

Hirshberg, Glen
The muldoon
People of the book; a decade of Jewish science fiction & fantasy; edited by Rachel Swirsky & Sean Wallace.

Shomer
The Best horror of the year: volume three; edited by Ellen Datlow.

His Actual Mark. Murray, S.

His chosen calling. Naipaul, V. S.

His ghost. Villegas, H.

HISPANIC AMERICANS
Anzaldúa, G. El paisano is a bird of omen
Doctorow, E. L. Assimilation
Engel, P. Desaliento
Engel, P. Lucho
Engel, P. Paloma
Engel, P. Vida

Hissing cobras. Bhattacharya, N.

HISTORIANS
Davis, L. Cape Cod diary

History Class. Downs, M.

History of a disturbance. Millhauser, S.

A **History** of Foolishness. Farrell, F. B.

A **history** of terraforming. Reed, R.

The **history** within us. Kressel, M.

HIT AND RUN DRIVERS
Bill, F. Trespassing between heaven and hell
Franco, J. April in three parts: part 1, The rainbow goblins
Franco, J. Halloween
Hodge, B. De fortuna
Thon, M. R. Father, lover, deadman, dreamer

HITCHHIKERS
 Blatnik, A. Highway, high beams
 Ford, J. On the road to New Egypt
 Gilley, T. Vanishing world
 Hannah, B. Evening of the Yarp
 Olsen, L. February
 Self, W. Tough, tough toys for tough, tough
  boys
 Woodrell, D. Dream spot
HITLER, ADOLF, 1889-1945
          About
 Dixon, S. The leader
 Long, H. My grandfather was Adolf Hitler's
  roommate
 Turtledove, H. Uncle Alf
Hitting Budapest. Bulawayo, N.
Hitting Trees with Sticks. Rogers, J.
Hlehel, Ala
 Coexistence
  Beirut 39; new writing from the Arab world;
   edited by Samuel Shimon; with a preface
   by Hanan al-Shaykh
Ho, Joses
 Her name was Jane
  Nature v476 no7360 p366 Ag 18 2011
Hoang, Minh Tuong
 Grace
  Family of fallen leaves; stories of Agent Or-
   ange by Vietnamese writers; edited by
   Charles Waugh and Huy Lien.
 The story of a family
  Family of fallen leaves; stories of Agent Or-
   ange by Vietnamese writers; edited by
   Charles Waugh and Huy Lien.
Hoarding. Latiolais, M.
HOAXES
 Reed, K. At central
 Smith, C. A. Morthylla
 Trevor, W. Death of a professor
 Wells, H. G. A deal in ostriches
The **hob** carpet. MacLeod, I.
Hobb, Robin
 Cat's meat
  Lindholm, M. and Hobb, R. The inheritance
   and other stories; [by] Megan Lindholm
   [and] Robin Hobb
 Homecoming
  Lindholm, M. and Hobb, R. The inheritance
   and other stories; [by] Megan Lindholm
   [and] Robin Hobb
 The inheritance
  Lindholm, M. and Hobb, R. The inheritance
   and other stories; [by] Megan Lindholm
   [and] Robin Hobb
Hoch, Edward D.
 The Poe collector
  On a raven's wing; new tales in honor of Ed-
   gar Allan Poe; edited by Stuart M.
   Kaminsky
 The theft of the rusty bookmark
  Christmas at the Mysterious Bookshop; 'tis
   the season to be deadly; stories of mistletoe
   and mayhem from 17 masters of suspense;
   edited by Otto Penzler.
Hochel, Braňo
 My Best Story [Part of special issue: Slovak
  Fiction]
  The Review of Contemporary Fiction v30 no2
   p24-8 Summ 2010

HOCHSTEIN, ROLAINE
 The Two of Us
  Southwest Review v96 no3 p337-347 Je 2011
Hodge, Brian
 And they will come in the hour of our greatest
  need
  Hodge, B. Picking the bones
 Brushed in blackest silence
  Hodge, B. Picking the bones
 The firebrand symphony
  Hodge, B. Picking the bones
 De fortuna
  Hodge, B. Picking the bones
 A good dead man is hard to find
  Hodge, B. Picking the bones
 Guardian
  Hodge, B. Picking the bones
 Hate the sinner, love the sin
  Hodge, B. Picking the bones
 If I should wake before I die
  Hodge, B. Picking the bones
 Just outside our windows, deep inside our walls
  The Best horror of the year: volume three;
   edited by Ellen Datlow.
 An ounce of prevention is worth a pound of
  flesh
  Hodge, B. Picking the bones
 Our turn too will one day come
  Hodge, B. Picking the bones
 The passion of the beast
  Hodge, B. Picking the bones
 Pull
  Hodge, B. Picking the bones
 Re: your application of 5/5
  Hodge, B. Picking the bones
 When the bough doesn't break
  Hodge, B. Picking the bones
 When the silence gets too loud
  Hodge, B. Picking the bones
 Where the black stars fall
  Hodge, B. Picking the bones
 With acknowledgements to Sun Tzu
  Hodge, B. Picking the bones
Hodges, John Oliver
 Health Nuts
  StoryQuarterly v44 p60-74 2010
Hoffman, Alice
 Owl and Mouse
  Five Points v12 no3 p54-61 2009
 Treasure
  Ploughshares v37 no2/3 p49-60 Fall 2011
Hoffman, Nina Kiriki
 Snow on snow
  Swenson, P. The Best of Talebones; edited by
   Patrick Swenson.
 The third dead boy
  Z: zombie stories; edited by J. M. Lassen
Holden, Mark
 The New Baby
  Indiana Review v32 no2 p101-106,152 Wint
   2010
Holder, Nancy
 Beyond the pale
  Chicks kick butt; edited by Rachel Caine and
   Kerrie L. Hughes.
HOLDUPS *See* Robbery
A **Hole** in the Head. Oates, J. C.
The **hole** man. Niven, L.
Holes in people. Eiríksdóttir, K.

Holiday. Niedzviecki, H.
Holiday. Rickert, M.
The **holiday** fairy. Healy, J. F.
HOLIDAYS
>   *See also* Christmas stories; Fourth of
>   July; New Year; Thanksgiving Day; Vacations; Yom Kippur
Holladay, Cary
>   Ghost walk
>   Philadelphia noir; edited by Carlin Romano.
>   "Horseman, pass by!"
>   *The Sewanee Review* v119 no1 p1-17 Wint 2011
HOLLAND *See* Netherlands
Hollander, David
>   A Bad Harvest
>   *Agni* no73 p150-8 2011
Hollerbochen comes back. Bradbury, R.
Hollerbochen's dilemma. Bradbury, R.
Holliday, Doc *See* Holliday, John Henry, 1851-1887
HOLLIDAY, JOHN HENRY, 1851-1887
>   **About**
>   Stein, J. C. The ghost of Leadville
The **hollow** man. Burke, T.
HOLLYWOOD (CALIF.) *See* California—Hollywood
Holm, Benn Q.
>   The great actor
>   Copenhagen noir; edited by Bo Tao
>   Michaëlis; translated by Mark Kline.
Holm, Gretelise
>   When it's tough out there
>   Copenhagen noir; edited by Bo Tao
>   Michaëlis; translated by Mark Kline.
Holmes, Rupert
>   The long winter's nap
>   Christmas at the Mysterious Bookshop; 'tis
>   the season to be deadly; stories of mistletoe
>   and mayhem from 17 masters of suspense;
>   edited by Otto Penzler.
>   A nomad of the night
>   On a raven's wing; new tales in honor of Edgar Allan Poe; edited by Stuart M.
>   Kaminsky
Holmgang. Anderson, P.
HOLOCAUST, JEWISH (1933-1945)
>   Goldstein, R. The afterlife of skeptics
>   Kalechofsky, R. Epitaph for an age
>   Kalechofsky, R. Father Woytzski leads a Jewish
>   youth group to the Holocaust memorial in
>   Oswiecim, Poland
>   Kalechofsky, R. Four women from Ravensbrück
>   Kalechofsky, R. My poor prisoner
>   Sullivan, J. Niels Bohr and the sleeping Dane
HOLOCAUST SURVIVORS
>   Eisenberg, D. All around Atlantis
>   Englander, N. Free fruit for young widows
>   Gifford, B. Six million and one
>   Niedzviecki, H. Displacement
>   Pearlman, E. Vaquita
>   Raphael, L. Money
>   Rosenbaum, T. The Yehuda triangle
>   Segal, L. G. Making good
>   Thon, M. R. Tu B'Shvat: for the drowned and
>   the saved

Holt, Elliott
>   Fem care
>   Pushcart Prize XXXV: best of the small
>   presses 2011; edited by Bill Henderson
>   with the Pushcart Prize editors.
Holy sisters. Simmons, D.
The **Holy** Sisters of Shedir. Terry, G. P.
A **holy** site. Ibrãhim, H.
A **holy** terror. Bierce, A.
Holy Terror. Takahashi, T.
HOLY WEEK
>   Quade, K. V. The five wounds
Holy Week. Eisenberg, D.
Holyoke. Shepard, S.
Holzer, Heide
>   (tr.) *See* George, Nina
Homage to Hemingway. Barnes, J.
HOME
>   Gottlieb, D. Somewhere, over
>   Kronauer, B. A sort of achievement like nature's
>   Marãr, M. Biar Adass
Home. Anderson, P.
Home. Martin, W.
Home. Ryman, G.
Home. Thon, M. R.
Home [Part of the Summer Fiction Issue]
>   Saunders, G.
A **home** away from home. Dixon, S.
Home Brew. King, O.
The **home-coming** guy!. Marãr, M.
Home from xpand. Blatnik, A.
The **home** front. Clark, D. C. and Bear, A.
The **Home** Jar. Zafris, N.
Home schooling. Pearlman, E.
Home Schooling. Quarry, J.
Home to Marie. Beattie, A.
Homecoming. Boggs, B.
Homecoming. Fosse, J.
Homecoming. Hobb, R.
Homecoming. O'Berry, T. S.
HOMECOMINGS
>   Fosse, J. Homecoming
>   Gordimer, N. Amnesty
>   Lahens, Y. The city
>   O'Connor, S. White fire
>   Sterling, P. Within an inch of the burnished
>   knob
>   Tóibín, C. The empty family
>   Tóibín, C. The new Spain
>   Wieland, L. At Wanship
>   Zhang Kangkang. Please take me with you
Homefaring. Silverberg, R.
HOMELESS PERSONS
>   Ballingrud, N. The way station
>   Baxter, C. Shelter
>   Brackmann, L. Don't feed the bums
>   Châteaureynaud, G. O. A city of museums
>   Doctorow, E. L. Edgemont Drive
>   Esposito, B. Kirby and the portal to Hell
>   Glaser, R. B. Infections
>   Gordimer, N. Look-alikes
>   Lethem, J. Ava's apartment
>   Matera, L. Dead drunk
>   Means, D. The junction
>   Nair, M. Small fry
>   Porter, J. 'Demption road
>   Row, J. Sheep may safely graze
>   Thon, M. R. Home

Horn, Dara
Shtetl World
Promised lands; new Jewish American fiction on longing and belonging; edited by Derek Rubin.
Horn hunter. MacLeod, M.
Horowitz, James *See* Salter, James
The **horrid** glory of its wings. Bear, E.
Horrocks, Caitlin
At the zoo
Horrocks, C. This is not your city; stories
Embodied
Horrocks, C. This is not your city; stories
Going to Estonia
Horrocks, C. This is not your city; stories
In the Gulf of Aden, past the Cape of Guardafui
Horrocks, C. This is not your city; stories
It looks like this
Horrocks, C. This is not your city; stories
The lion gate
Horrocks, C. This is not your city; stories
The sleep
The Best American short stories, 2011; selected from U.S. and Canadian magazines by Geraldine Brooks with Heidi Pitlor; with an introduction by Geraldine Brooks.
Steal small
Pushcart Prize XXXV: best of the small presses 2011; edited by Bill Henderson with the Pushcart Prize editors.
Horrocks, C. This is not your city; stories
This is not your city
Horrocks, C. This is not your city; stories
World Champion Cow of the Insane
Horrocks, C. This is not your city; stories
Zero conditional
Horrocks, C. This is not your city; stories
Zolaria
Horrocks, C. This is not your city; stories
Horror at Winchester House. Nolan, W. F.
HORROR STORIES
See also Ghost stories; Murder stories; Supernatural phenomena; Vampires; Werewolves
Bailey, D. and Ballingrud, N. The crevasse
Barron, L. --30--
Barron, L. Blackwood's baby
Bierce, A. An adventure at Brownville
Bierce, A. The boarded window
Bierce, A. The death of Halpin Frayser
Bierce, A. A diagnosis of death
Bierce, A. The secret of Macarger's Gulch
Bierce, A. A watcher by the dead
Bradbury, R. The emissary
Bradbury, R. The small assassin
Bradbury, R. The wind
Braddon, M. E. Good Lady Ducayne
Cain, C. Less of a girl
Campbell, R. Respects
Cannon, P. The Arkham collector
Cannon, P. Cats, rats, and Bertie Wooster
Cannon, P. The rummy affair of young Charlie
Cannon, P. Something foetid
Cannon, P. Tender is the night-gaunt
Cannon, P. The undercliffe sentences
Carroll, J. The Heidelberg cylinder
Charnas, S. M. Lowland sea
Ciechanowski, W. The dungeon out of time
Claus, H. Medieval

Clifford, Sir H. C. The ghoul
Cluley, R. At night, when the demons come
Connell, R. E. The most dangerous game
Crook, J. The last jar of mayo at the H&P
Dinan, K. Nub Hut
Dowling, T. The fooly
Dowling, T. The suits at Auderlene
Due, T. The lake
Eliot, G. F. The copper bowl
Farmer, P. J. Father's in the basement
Ford, J. Daddy long legs of the evening
Fowler, C. Oh I do like to be beside the seaside
Gaiman, N. The price
Gautier, T. The amorous corpse
Goodfellow, C. At the riding school
Harland, R. The fear
Highsmith, P. Woodrow, Wilson's necktie
Hirshberg, G. The muldoon
Hodge, B. A good dead man is hard to find
Hodge, B. Guardian
Hodge, B. Hate the sinner, love the sin
Hodge, B. Just outside our windows, deep inside our walls
Hodge, B. Our turn too will one day come
Hodge, B. The passion of the beast
Hodge, B. Pull
Hodge, B. When the bough doesn't break
Hodge, B. When the silence gets too loud
Holmes, R. A nomad of the night
Houarner, G. The other box
Irving, W. The adventure of the German student
Jackson, S. The lottery
Jones, G. A. Grandmother's footsteps
Jones, S. G. Captain's lament
Jones, S. G. Crawlspace
Jones, S. G. The meat tree
Jones, S. G. Monsters
Jones, S. G. Raphael
Jones, S. G. So perfect
Jones, S. G. Till the morning comes
Kaminsky, S. M. Rattle, rattle, rattle
Knox, J. H. Wake not the dead
Koja, K. Toujours
Konrath, J. A. The screaming
Kowal, M. R. Death comes but twice
Laidlaw, M. Leng
Lanagan, M. Mulberry boys
Langan, J. City of the dog
Lansdale, J. R. The crawling sky
Lansdale, J. R. The dark down there
Lansdale, J. R. The gentleman's hotel
Lansdale, J. R. Torn away
Link, K. The hortlak
Loring, F. G. The tomb of Sarah
Lovecraft, H. P. The call of Cthulhu
Lovecraft, H. P. Herbert West: reanimator
Mantooth, J. The water tower
Matheson, R. Haircut
Matheson, R. The last blah in the etc
Matheson, R. Life size
Matheson, R. Pride
Matheson, R. and Matheson, R. C. Where there's a will
Matheson, R. C. Transfiguration
Maupassant, G. d. The hand
McMahon, G. Strange scenes from an unfinished film
Miéville, C. Details
Monette, S. White Charles

HORROR STORIES—*Continued*
Morris, M. Fallen boys
Newman, K. Castle in the desert: anno Dracula 1977
Niven, L. Bordered in black
Niven, L. Night on Mispec Moor
Nolan, W. F. The man who stalked Hyde
Nolan, W. F. Zachry revisited
Oates, J. C. Babysitter
Oliver, R. Mr. Pigsny
Partridge, N. Lesser demons
Piccirilli, T. Caucasus
Piccirilli, T. The cruel theif of rosy infants
Prentiss, N. In the porches of my ears
Pulver, J. S. Just another desert night with blood
Raes, H. The smell of fresh linen
Rath, T. A trick iof the dark
Reed, K. The zombie prince
Roden, B. The brink of eternity
Rohmer, S. The hand of the Mandarin Quong
Royle, N. The obscure bird
Ruyslinck, W. The slugs
Sands, B. A performance
Shawl, N. To the moment
Shea, M. Copping squid
Shelley, M. W. Frankenstein
Silverberg, R. Not our brother
Smith, C. A. Mother of toads
Smith, C. A. The seed from the sepulcher
Smith, C. A. The tomb-spawn
Smith, C. A. The treader of the dust
Smith, C. A. The witchcraft of Ulua
Smith, M. M. What happens when you wake up in the night
Spofford, H. E. P. The moonstone mass
Strand, J. Specimen 313
Straub, P. Variations on a theme from Seinfeld
Sturgeon, T. The professor's teddy bear
Valente, C. M. Proverbs of hell
Warren, K. All you can do is breathe
Wells, H. G. The flowering of the strange orchild
Wells, H. G. Pollock and the Porroh man
Wells, H. G. The valley of spiders
Horse. Shepard, S.
The **horse** in our history. Woodrell, D.
The **horse** of bronze. Turtledove, H.
HORSE RACING
    See also Jockeys
Blassingame, W. Murder is bad luck
Horse trader. Anderson, P.
A **horseman** in the sky. Bierce, A.
"**Horseman,** pass by!". Holladay, C.
HORSES
Boland, J. C. The substitute
Goodfellow, C. At the riding school
Grove, L. L. Shonnud's girl
Hubbard, L. R. The automagic horse
Hunt, A. Sliabh Ban
McCann, C. Everything in this country must
Niven, L. The flight of the horse
Ryman, G. Days of wonder
Sheehan, A. Spin
Tuten, F. The bar on Tompkins Square Park
Wieland, M. The bones of hagerman
Woodrell, D. The horse in our history
Horses racing men. Shepard, S.
The **hortlak**. Link, K.
Hospice on ice. Wilson, M. J.

HOSPICES
Platana, J. Some of this is true
The **hospital** room. Furman, L.
HOSPITALS
Cook, T. H. Nevermore
Marãr, M. The court is convening!
HOSPITALS AND SANATORIUMS
    See also Burn care units
Alcott, L. M. My contraband
Bowes, R. I needs must part, the policeman said
Furman, L. The hospital room
Gray, A. The tortoise and the hare
Laken, V. God of fire
Leidiger, L. Tell me
Marra, A. Chechnya
Oates, J. C. Bitch
Pearlman, E. Tess
Rickert, M. You have never been here
Schmitt, E.-E. Getting better
Thon, M. R. First, body
Zeltserman, D. Bad move
Hossein, Roquia Sakhawat
The sultana's dream
    The dreaming sex; early tales of scientific imagination by women; edited by Mike Ashley.
HOSTAGES
Brandon, J. A jury of his peers
Gray, A. A javelina story
Horrocks, C. In the Gulf of Aden, past the Cape of Guardafui
Keene, B. Captive hearts
Olsen, L. February
Hostel. Chowdhury, S.
Hot-air balloons. Danticat, E.
Hot dog. Kurlansky, M.
Hot, fast, and sad. Nutting, A.
Hot on the Hunt. Samalin, Z.
Hot pot. Kurlansky, M.
Hotel by a railroad. Grytten, F.
The **hotel** life. Montes, J.
HOTELS, TAVERNS, ETC.
    See also Motels
Adnan, Y. Two stories
Archer, J. No room at the inn
Bierce, A. The other lodgers
Blatnik, A. I write these words
Blatnik, A. Qed
Blatnik, A. Words matter
Boland, J. C. Worth more dead
Burke, D. Beaverland
Cameron, D. Femme sole
Crane, S. The blue hotel
Dixon, S. Ass
Gallari, A. Go piss on Jane
Gallari, A. Good friend
Gallari, A. No cause for concern
Gold, H. L. I know suicide
Gordimer, N. Friday's footprint
Gordimer, N. Livingstone's companions
Gray, A. The darkness
Grove, L. L. Four indians in the mirror
Hannah, B. Fans
Hardwick, E. The final conflict
Harper, J. Red hair and black leather
Lake, J. Tall spirits, blocking the night
Levine, S. The girl
Lutz, J. Poe, Poe, Poe
Mars, K. Paradise Inn

How to make a clown. Shipp, J. C.

How to remember a bird. Hall, T. M.

How to sell the Ponti Bridge. Gaiman, N.

How to write a short story!. Sands, B.

How W. H. Auden spends the night in a friend's house. Davis, L.

How we fall. Ray, S.

How we touch the ground, how we touch. Nagai, M.

Howard, Clark
The way they limp
By hook or by crook and 27 more of the best crime + mystery stories of the year; edited by Ed Gorman and Martin H. Greenberg.

Howard, Jonathan L.
The Ereshkigal working
The way of the wizard; edited by John Joseph Adams.

Howard, Robert Ervin
Blades for France
Howard, R. E. Sword woman and other historical adventures; [by] Robert E. Howard; fully illustrated by John Watkiss.
The blood of Belshazzar
Howard, R. E. Sword woman and other historical adventures; [by] Robert E. Howard; fully illustrated by John Watkiss.
The devil in iron
The Big book of adventure stories; edited and with a introduction by Otto Penzler; foreword by Douglas Preston.
Gates of empire
Howard, R. E. Sword woman and other historical adventures; [by] Robert E. Howard; fully illustrated by John Watkiss.
Hawks of Outremer
Howard, R. E. Sword woman and other historical adventures; [by] Robert E. Howard; fully illustrated by John Watkiss.
Hawks over Egypt
Howard, R. E. Sword woman and other historical adventures; [by] Robert E. Howard; fully illustrated by John Watkiss.
The lion of Tiberias
Howard, R. E. Sword woman and other historical adventures; [by] Robert E. Howard; fully illustrated by John Watkiss.
Lord of Samarcand
Howard, R. E. Sword woman and other historical adventures; [by] Robert E. Howard; fully illustrated by John Watkiss.
Red blades of black Cathay
Howard, R. E. Sword woman and other historical adventures; [by] Robert E. Howard; fully illustrated by John Watkiss.
The road of Azrael
Howard, R. E. Sword woman and other historical adventures; [by] Robert E. Howard; fully illustrated by John Watkiss.
The road of the eagles
Howard, R. E. Sword woman and other historical adventures; [by] Robert E. Howard; fully illustrated by John Watkiss.
The shadow of the vulture
Howard, R. E. Sword woman and other historical adventures; [by] Robert E. Howard; fully illustrated by John Watkiss.

The sowers of the thunder
Howard, R. E. Sword woman and other historical adventures; [by] Robert E. Howard; fully illustrated by John Watkiss.
Spears of Clontarf
Howard, R. E. Sword woman and other historical adventures; [by] Robert E. Howard; fully illustrated by John Watkiss.
Sword woman
Howard, R. E. Sword woman and other historical adventures; [by] Robert E. Howard; fully illustrated by John Watkiss.

HOWARD, ROBERT ERVIN, 1906-1936
Parodies, imitations, etc.
Lake, J. The leopard's paw

Howell, Mary
We need to talk about Mr Collins
Dancing with Mr. Darcy; stories inspired by Jane Austen and Chawton House Library; compiled by Sarah Waters.

HOWLEY, KERRY
Pretty Citadel
The Paris Review no198 p15-21 Fall 2011

Hrbek, Greg
Tomorrow People
Prairie Schooner v85 no1 p13-37 Spr 2011

Hrgovic, Maja
Zlatka
Granta no115 p229-42 Spr 2011

Hu, Zongfeng
(tr.) See Jia, Pingwa

Hubbard, L. Ron (La Fayette Ron)
The automagic horse
Hubbard, L. R. Greed
Final enemy
Hubbard, L. R. Greed
Greed
Hubbard, L. R. Greed

Hubbard, La Fayette Ron *See* Hubbard, L. Ron (La Fayette Ron), 1911-1986

Huff, Tanya
No matter where you go
Vampires; the recent undead; edited by Paula Guran.

Hughes, Cameron Pierce
Moving black objects
San Diego noir; edited by Maryelizabeth Hart.

Hughes, Mary-Beth
Double happiness
Pushcart Prize XXXV: best of the small presses 2011; edited by Bill Henderson with the Pushcart Prize editors.

Hughes, Suzy Ceulan
Broken words
Dancing with Mr. Darcy; stories inspired by Jane Austen and Chawton House Library; compiled by Sarah Waters.

Hughes, Van Aaron
The dualist
L. Ron Hubbard presents Writers of the Future volume XXVII; the year's thirteen best tales from the Writers of the Future international writers' program; illustrated by winners in the Illustrators of the Future international illustrators' program; with essays on writing & illustration by L. Ron Hubbard / Mike Resnick / Robert Cadtillo; edited by K. D. Wentworth

Hulme, Juliet *See* Perry, Anne, 1938-

The **hum**. Hautala, R.
HUMAN ANATOMY
 See also Nose; Teeth
The **human** race. Edelman, S.
HUMAN SACRIFICE
 Dozois, G. R. The peacemaker
 Wells, H. G. The Lord of the Dynamos
Human subjects. Vukcevich, R.
The **humbugs**. Vonnegut, K.
HUMOR
 See also Parodies; Practical jokes; Satire
 Bierce, A. Jupiter Doke, Brigadier General
 Bierce, A. Mrs. Dennison's head
 Bierce, A. My favorite murder
 Bierce, A. Oil of dog
 Bradbury, R. It's not the heat, it's the hu—
 Dozois, G. R. The hanging curve
 Frazier, I. Coyote v. Acme
 Gray, A. Death of a beast
 Handey, J. My first day in Hell
 Harris, A. L. Still life with boobs
 Horn, D. Shtetl World
 Kitterman, B. A place in the opera
 Knight, D. F. To serve man
 Matheson, R. Getting together
 Meno, J. Children are the only ones who blush
 Naipaul, V. S. The mechanical genius
 Riippi, J. Something about marriage, pt 2
 Simms, P. For immediate release
 Sneed, C. Walled city
 Thurber, J. The secret life of Walter Mitty
 Twain, M. The celebrated jumping frog of
  Calaveras County
 Twain, M. A curious dream
 Wells, H. G. The Hammerpond Park burglary
 Wells, H. G. How Pingwill was routed
 Westlake, D. E. Give till it hurts
 Wodehouse, P. G. The salvation of George
  Mackintosh
HUMOROUS STORIES *See* Humor
Humphries, Clair
 The Jane Austen hen weekend
  Dancing with Mr. Darcy; stories inspired by
  Jane Austen and Chawton House Library;
  compiled by Sarah Waters.
HUNCHBACKS
 Qiu Xiaolong. Old hunchback Fang
Hundred-dollar kisses. Vonnegut, K.
HUNGARIANS
    United States
 Eisenberg, D. In the station
HUNGARY
 Pearlman, E. On Junius Bridge
HUNGER
 See also Starvation
 Gordimer, N. The ultimate safari
 Marār, M. The loaf
 Nagai, M. Fugue
 Nagai, M. Georgic
 Sa'ıd, M. A. The procession
Hunger. Chau, A.
A **hunger** and thirst for justice. Monzó, Q.
Hunger tales. Orozco, D.
Hungry enough. Read, C.
Hungry Mother. Goldenstern, J.
Hunk. Novack, S.

Hunt, Arlene
 Sliabh Ban
  Requiems for the departed; edited by Gerard
  Brennan & Mike Stone.
Hunt, Erica
 My life with cars
  Bomb no116 p VII-XI Summ 2011
Hunt, Gabriel
 Nor idolatry blind the eye
  The Big book of adventure stories; edited and
  with a introduction by Otto Penzler; fore-
  word by Douglas Preston.
Hunt, Morgan
 The angel's share
  San Diego noir; edited by Maryelizabeth Hart.
Hunt, Samantha
 Beast
  Fantastic women; 18 tales of the surreal and
  the sublime from Tin House; introduction
  by Joy Williams; edited by Rob Spillman.
 The Yellow
  The New Yorker v86 no38 p66-70 N 29 2010
The **hunt**. Bingham, S.
The **Hunt**. Donoghue, E.
The **Hunt**. Lee, L.
The **hunt**. Matheson, R.
Hunt. Vincent, R.
Hunter, Evan, 1926-2005
 For works written by this author under oth-
 er names see McBain, Ed, 1926-2005
Hunter, Lindsay
 The fence
  Hunter, L. Daddy's; 24 fictions
 Fifteen
  Hunter, L. Daddy's; 24 fictions
 Finding there
  Hunter, L. Daddy's; 24 fictions
 Food luck
  Hunter, L. Daddy's; 24 fictions
 It all go by
  Hunter, L. Daddy's; 24 fictions
 Kid
  Hunter, L. Daddy's; 24 fictions
 Let
  Hunter, L. Daddy's; 24 fictions
 Loofah
  Hunter, L. Daddy's; 24 fictions
 Love song
  Hunter, L. Daddy's; 24 fictions
 Marie Noe, talks to you about her kids
  Hunter, L. Daddy's; 24 fictions
 My brother
  Hunter, L. Daddy's; 24 fictions
 Note
  Hunter, L. Daddy's; 24 fictions
 Out there
  Hunter, L. Daddy's; 24 fictions
 Peggy's brother
  Hunter, L. Daddy's; 24 fictions
 Scales
  Hunter, L. Daddy's; 24 fictions
 Sex armageddon
  Hunter, L. Daddy's; 24 fictions
 That baby
  Hunter, L. Daddy's; 24 fictions
 This one
  Hunter, L. Daddy's; 24 fictions
 Tuesday
  Hunter, L. Daddy's; 24 fictions

I

I Could Kill Someone [Excerpt from I could kill someone] Franco, J.

I demand to know where you're taking me. Chaon, D.

I Hate to See That Evening Sun Go Down. Gay, W.

I heart brains. Saare, J.

I knew you'd be lovely. Black, A.

I know suicide. Gold, H. L.

I Looked For You, I Called Your Name. Van Den Berg, L.

I love you. Emshwiller, C.

I needs must part, the policeman said. Bowes, R.

I reach, I climb, I reach again [Part of special issue: Honoring Student Voices] Kittle, P.

I remember the future. Burnstein, M. A.

I, rocket. Bradbury, R.

I run every day. Orozco, D.

I saw mommy killing Santa Claus. McBain, E.

I think. Blatnik, A.

I think I'm happier. O'Connor, S.

(I thought my father looked like FDR). Chambers, G.

I thought there was a Hawk. Shepard, S.

I want a rifle!. Marãr, M.

I Want You to Know That I Know That He Loved You. Weil, J.

I will ask for a divorce. Sirhan, A.

I will lend you my wife. Osondu, E. C.

I will survive. Archer, J.

I write these words. Blatnik, A.

I write to you of this. Dodson, Z.

Ibarz, Mercè
Nela and the virgins
Best European fiction 2011; edited by Aleksandr Hemon; preface by Colum McCann

Ibrãhim, Hannã
As-Sayyed's space
Ibrãhim, H. and Sa'id, M. A. Father and son; selected short fiction; by Hanna Ibrahim Elias and Mohammad Ali Saeid; translated by Jamal Assadi
Family re-union
Ibrãhim, H. and Sa'id, M. A. Father and son; selected short fiction; by Hanna Ibrahim Elias and Mohammad Ali Saeid; translated by Jamal Assadi
Fathers and sons
Ibrãhim, H. and Sa'id, M. A. Father and son; selected short fiction; by Hanna Ibrahim Elias and Mohammad Ali Saeid; translated by Jamal Assadi
A holy site
Ibrãhim, H. and Sa'id, M. A. Father and son; selected short fiction; by Hanna Ibrahim Elias and Mohammad Ali Saeid; translated by Jamal Assadi
The informer
Ibrãhim, H. and Sa'id, M. A. Father and son; selected short fiction; by Hanna Ibrahim Elias and Mohammad Ali Saeid; translated by Jamal Assadi
Intruders?!
Ibrãhim, H. and Sa'id, M. A. Father and son; selected short fiction; by Hanna Ibrahim Elias and Mohammad Ali Saeid; translated by Jamal Assadi

My young friend
Ibrãhim, H. and Sa'id, M. A. Father and son; selected short fiction; by Hanna Ibrahim Elias and Mohammad Ali Saeid; translated by Jamal Assadi

Icarus saved from the skies. Châteaureynaud, G. O.

ICE
McDonald, S. Seven sexy cowboy robots
Nutting, A. Ice melter
Ice. Tuck, L.
ICE AGE *See* Prehistoric times
ICE CREAM, ICES, ETC.
Rodoreda, M. Ice cream
Ice cream. Rodoreda, M.
Ice House. Blakinger, K.
Ice, Mating. Khan, U. A.
Ice melter. Nutting, A.
The **ice** party. Bingham, S.
ICE SKATING
Williamson, E. M. Skaters
Iceland. Pugno, L.
The **icing** on the cake. Kurlansky, M.
Icon. Terry, G. P.
ID. Oates, J. C.
IDAHO
Reents, S. Creatures of the kingdom
Simmons, D. Roll
Simmons, D. Ticket
Vestal, S. Opposition in all things
Wieland, M. The bones of hagerman
Idea for a short documentary film. Davis, L.
Identifying the object. Jones, G. A.
IDENTITY *See* Personality
IDENTITY (PSYCHOLOGY)
Foster, E. Sinner, baker, fabulist, priest; red mask, gentleman, beast
Marías, J. Gualta
IDENTITY THEFT
Evans, D. The king of a vast empire
Spagnoli, L. A cut above
Idol, Kim
Coyotes
Dead neon; tales of near-future Las Vegas; edited by Todd James Pierce and Jarret Keene.
Idol's eye. Emshwiller, C.
Idris, Yusif
The aorta
Tablet & pen; literary landscapes from the modern Middle East, a words without borders anthology; edited by Reza Asian.
If I Could Be with You. Gildner, G.
"If I forget thee, oh Earth . . .". Clarke, A. C.
If I should wake before I die. Hodge, B.
If I were Lee's girlfriend, I wouldn't want to drown children in the duck pond. Kneeland, A.
If I'd known you were going to stay this long. Kitterman, B.
If love were all. Pearlman, E.
If not forever, when? Emshwiller, C.
If the word was to the wise. Emshwiller, C.
If we shadows have offended. Edwards, S. L.
Iff. Nelson, A.
Iffy. Dufresne, J.
Ifowodo, Ogaga
The Treasonable Parrot
Agni no72 p151-61 2010

Ikstena, Nora
Elza Kuga's old-age dementia
Best European fiction 2011; edited by Aleksandr Hemon; preface by Colum McCann
ILLEGAL ALIENS *See* Undocumented aliens
ILLEGITIMACY
See also Unmarried mothers
Naipaul, V. S. The blue cart
ILLINOIS
Laken, V. Remedies
Chicago
Butcher, J. Backup
Butcher, J. Curses
Butcher, J. Day off
Butcher, J. Heorot
Butcher, J. Last call
Butcher, J. Love hurts
Butcher, J. A restoration of faith
Butcher, J. Something borrowed
Butcher, J. The warrior
Dybek, S. Sauerkraut soup
Eugenides, J. Great experiment
Gifford, B. The American language
Gifford, B. Arabian nights
Gifford, B. Bad girls
Gifford, B. The choice
Gifford, B. Chop suey joint
Gifford, B. Close encounters of the right kind
Gifford, B. Einstein's son
Gifford, B. Ghost ship
Gifford, B. In the land of the dead
Gifford, B. The man who swallowed the world
Gifford, B. Rain in the distance
Gifford, B. The starving dogs of Little Croatia
Gifford, B. The sudden demise of Sharkface Bensky
Gifford, B. The theory of the leisure class
Gifford, B. The Weeper
Makkai, R. Peter Torrelli, falling apart
Somerville, P. The machine of understanding other people
ILLNESS
See also Invalids; Mental illness; Terminal illness
Beattie, A. The rabbit hole as likely explanation
Bill, F. The penance of Scoot McCutchen
Davis, L. Thyroid diary
Doyle, R. The plate
Drabble, M. Crossing the Alps
Gray, A. Diary of the blockage
Havazelet, E. Gurov in Manhattan
Levine, S. The kidney problem
McCormack, D. Scarlatina!
ILLUSIONS *See* Hallucinations and illusions
ILLUSTRATORS
Aiken, J. Red-hot favourite
I'm a dork. Lawson, P.
I'm in the book. Estleman, L. D.
I'm only going to tell you this once. Schappell, E.
IMAGINARY ANIMALS *See* Mythical animals
IMAGINARY CITIES
Smith, C. A. The seven geases
Wells, H. G. The country of the blind
Wells, H. G. The country of the blind (revised version)
Wells, H. G. In the abyss
Wells, H. G. In the Avu observatory
IMAGINARY KINGDOMS
Howard, R. E. The devil in iron

Howard, R. E. The road of the eagles
IMAGINARY PLAYMATES
Bernheimer, K. A doll's tale
IMAGINARY WARS AND BATTLES
Bodard, A. d. Eye of the destroyer
Day, R. W. Magic's choice
Houarner, G. D. In the light of dying fires
Howard, R. E. The road of the eagles
Niven, L. Not long before the end
Wells, H. G. A dream of Armageddon
Wells, H. G. The land ironclads
IMMIGRANTS
Alenyikov, M. Barrel of laughs
Alenyikov, M. It takes all kinds
Alenyikov, M. Ivan and Misha
Alenyikov, M. Whirling dervish
Alenyikov, M. Who did what to whom?
Allio, K. Clothed, female figure
Argemi, R. The slender charm of Chinese women
Atta, S. Green
Doctorow, E. L. Assimilation
Gilley, T. All Hallows' Eve
Goldstein, R. The afterlife of skeptics
Horrocks, C. This is not your city
Lychack, W. Love is a temper
Mirvis, T. Potatoes
O'Brien, E. Shovel kings
Osondu, E. C. I will lend you my wife
Pung, A. The shed
Schirach, F. v. Bliss
Sherman, D. How the pooka came to New York City
Stern, S. Avigdor of the Apes
Vapnyar, L. Things that are not yours
Yiyun Li. The science of flight
IMMORTALITY
Arkwright, J. The sundial
Armstrong, K. Rakshasi
Bacigalupi, P. Pop squad
Fowler, K. J. Always
Jones, G. A. Total internal reflection
Lansdale, J. R. Torn away
MacLeod, I. Re-crossing the Styx
Niven, L. Cautionary tales
Ryman, G. No bad thing
Shelley, M. W. The mortal immortal
Spinrad, N. Bug Jack Barron [excerpt]
Swirsky, R. 1943: a brief note pertaining to the absence of one olivaceous cormorant, stuffed
Impaired. Sterling, P.
Imperfections. Quatro, J.
Imperial Chrysanthemum. Boggs, B.
IMPERIALISM
Ridgway, K. Shame
IMPERSONATIONS
See also Impostors; Mistaken identity; Transvestism
Archer, J. I will survive
Claes, P. Chameleon
Land, J. Killing time
Nevins, F. M., Jr. Superscam
Swanwick, M. The feast of Saint Janis
Terry, G. P. Grasping the bird's tail
Vukcevich, R. My shoes
The **importance** of cheese. Terry, G. P.

INTERVIEWING—*Continued*

Lafferty, M. 1963: the argument against Louis Pasteur

Ross, A. Futures

INTERVIEWS (STORIES IN INTERVIEW FORM)

Riippi, J. An exchange

Into collapses. Benvie, R.

Into the Frying Pan. Hawk, T.

Into the gorge. Rash, R.

Into the light. Kim, S.-r.

An **intriguing** teacher, from Charlotte Temple [excerpt] Rowson, S. H.

Intruders?!. Ibrāhim, .

INUIT

Valentine, G. So deep that the bottom could not be seen

INVALIDS

Bradbury, R. The emissary

Hendee, B. The winds of Brennan Marcher

Marār, M. And we used to squeeze the olives for oil

Munro, A. Some women

Wells, H. G. Through a window

The **invasion** from outer space. Millhauser, S.

INVENTIONS

Aiken, J. The helper

Dick, P. K. The short happy life of the brown oxford

Faust, M. Y. The electrical neurheographiton

Jemisin, N. K. 1929: the singular taffy puller

Miéville, C. Pulvadmonitor: the dust's warning

Millhauser, S. The wizard of West Orange

Wells, H. G. A tale of the twentieth century for advanced thinkers

Williams, T. A short history of Dunkelblau's Meistergarten

INVENTORS

Chiang, T. Dacey's patent Automatic Nanny

Doctorow, C. Makers [excerpt]

Hindmarch, W. The Auble gun

Matheson, R. Professor Fritz and the runaway house

INVESTMENTS

Kurlansky, M. Muffins

INVISIBILITY

La Spina, G. The ultimate ingredient

Terry, G. P. Now you see it ..

Invisible. Allen, D.

Invisible river. Trueblood, V.

Invisible trophies. Evans, D. A.

Invisible waves. Gilley, T.

Involution. Latiolais, M.

Iona Moon. Thon, M. R.

IOWA

Gorman, E. The long way back

Thompson, J. Pie of the month

IPHIGENIA (LEGENDARY CHARACTER)

Olsen, L. March

Swirsky, R. A memory of wind

IRA *See* Irish Republican Army

IRAN

Danishvar, S. The playhouse

Golshiri, H. My China doll

Hidāyat, . The blind owl [excerpt]

Jamalzadeh, M. A. Persian is sugar

Taraqqi, G. The grand lady of my soul

Vaughn, C. The book of Daniel

IRAQ WAR, 2003-

Fallon, S. Camp Liberty

Percy, B. Refresh, refresh

Vukcevich, R. Over here

IRAQIS

United States

Somerville, P. Easy love

IRELAND

See also Northern Ireland; Ulster (Ireland and Northern Ireland)

Barry, K. Doctor Sot

Barry, K. See the tree, how big it's grown

Bruen, K. She wails through the fair

Donovan, G. Visit

Downey, G. First to score

Doyle, R. Funerals

Doyle, R. Teaching

Gash, J. The life business

Hodge, B. When the bough doesn't break

Hunt, A. Sliabh Ban

Keegan, C. Foster

McAllister, J. Bog man

McCormack, U. The sea is not full

Moore, T. A. Red milk

Mulkerns, V. Memory and desire

Ní Dhuibhne, E. Trespasses

O'Brien, E. Black flower

O'Brien, E. Inner cowboy

O'Connor, F. The mad Lomasneys

Thompson, N. The children of gear

Tóibín, C. The colour of shadows

Tóibín, C. The empty family

Tóibín, C. A priest in the family

Tóibín, C. Two women

Trevor, W. At Olivehill

Trevor, W. Big bucks

Trevor, W. A bit of business

Trevor, W. The dressmaker's child

Trevor, W. Justina's priest

Trevor, W. Low Sunday, 1950

Trevor, W. Men of Ireland

Trevor, W. The potato dealer

Trevor, W. Sacred statues

Trevor, W. Timothy's birthday

Trevor, W. The Virgin's gift

Farm life

See Farm life—Ireland

Rural life

Keegan, C. Men and women

McCabe, E. Music at Annahullion

McGahern, J. The key

Ni Dhuibhne, E. Midwife to the fairies

O'Reilly, S. Curfew

Trevor, W. Of the cloth

Trevor, W. Sitting with the dead

Trevor, W. The woman of the house

Dublin

Doyle, R. Blood

Doyle, R. Recuperation

Doyle, R. The slave

Jakubowski, M. A price to pay

O'Brien, E. Send my roots rain

Ridgway, K. Shame

Tóibín, C. One minus one

Trevor, W. Bravado

Trevor, W. Faith

Irish, William, 1903-1968
> *For works written by this author under other names see* Woolrich, Cornell, 1903-1968

IRISH
England
O'Brien, E. Shovel kings
O'Connor, J. Mothers were all the same
Trevor, W. The mourning
Germany
Mathews, A. Train tracks
Spain
Doyle, R. Bullfighting
United States
Neville, S. The last dance
Sherman, D. How the pooka came to New York City
Tóibín, C. The empty family
Tóibín, C. One minus one

IRISH AMERICANS
Jones, K. The occidental tourist
Leland, C. T. A mother's love
McGarry, J. Dream date

IRISH REPUBLICAN ARMY
Devlin, A. Naming the names
O'Brien, E. Black flower

Iromuanya, Julie
An Arranged Honeymoon
> *The Kenyon Review* v32 no4 p93-103 Fall 2010

The **Iron** Gate. Habila, H.
Iron rice bowl. Qiu Xiaolong
The **iron** shroud. Morrow, J.

IRON-WORKS
Kitterman, B. Union wages

IRONY
Bierce, A. An affair of outposts
Bierce, A. The applicant
Bierce, A. A son of the gods
Chekhov, A. P. The bet
Henry, O. The gift of the magi
Irvine, A. Peter Shilling
Wells, H. G. A family elopement
Wells, H. G. The Rajah's treasure

Irredeemable. Gifford, B.
Irreverence. Lisicky, P.

Irvine, Alex
Peter Shilling
> Brave new worlds; edited by John Joseph Adams.
Semaphore
> People of the book; a decade of Jewish science fiction & fantasy; edited by Rachel Swirsky & Sean Wallace.

Irving, Washington
The adventure of the German student
> The book of the living dead; edited by John Richard Stephens.
Rip Van Winkle
> 21 essential American short stories; edited by Leslie M. Pockell

Is that you, Bert? Bradbury, R.
Is this your day to join revolution? Valentine, G.

Isaacs, Haim
Zouhira
> *The Massachusetts Review* v51 no3 p563-77 Aut 2010

Isaac's journey. Marías, J.

ISLAM
> *See also* Muslims
Saeed, M. Warriors of the sky

ISLAMIC LAW
Atkinson, K. The war on women

Island lake. Tobler, E. C.
Islanders. Kostival, B.

ISLANDS
> *See also* names of individual islands and groups of islands
Aiken, J. Honeymaroon
Archer, J. The undiplomatic diplomat
Barnes, J. Marriage lines
Châteaureynaud, G. O. Another story
Châteaureynaud, G. O. The excursion
Connelly, T. Silverfin harbour
Dent, L. Hell Cay
MacLeod, I. On the sighting of other islands
Simmons, D. In the garden
Terry, G. P. The Goddess of Outen
Tobler, E. C. Island lake
Wells, H. G. Aepyornis Island

ISLANDS OF THE PACIFIC
> *See also* Solomon Islands
Worts, G. F. The python pit

The **Isle** of pines. Bierce, A.

Isleib, Roberta
The itinerary
> Mystery Writers of America presents the rich and the dead; edited by Nelson DeMille.

The **Isles** of the Blessed. Drabble, M.

ISRAEL
> *See also* Jerusalem
Englander, N. Free fruit for young widows
Kadish, R. Come on Zion put your hands together
Kirshenbaum, B. The lunatic
Leegant, J. Remittances
Lovett, R. Leo's squid
Neugeboren, J. The state of Israel
Papernick, J. The miracle birth
Rapoport, N. Sovereignty
Haifa
Tidhar, L. The projected girl
Tel Aviv
Burgis, B. Dark coffee, bright light and the paradoxes of omnipotence

ISRAELI-ARAB RELATIONS
Ibrāhim, H Family re-union
Ibrāhim, H. Fathers and sons
Ibrāhim, H. A holy site
Ibrāhim, H. The informer
Ibrāhim, H Intruders?!
Ibrāhim, H My young friend
Marār, M. Al-Qatāryz
Marār, M. Biar Adass
Marār, M. The craving woman
Marār, M. From the bag of others!
Marār, M. Hello, nations!
Marār, M. Planting the cacti
Marār, M. Teneem
Marār, M. The wall of cacti
Sa'īd, M. A. Ahmad and Mordekhai
Sa'īd, M. A. The delivery

ISRAELITES *See* Jews
Israfel. Allyn, D.
ISTANBUL (TURKEY) *See* Turkey—Istanbul
It all go by. Hunter, L.

It Can Be Hard to Educate Elected Officials. Trimble, R.

It Is Proper for Men to Remember. Franchini, A.

It looks like this. Horrocks, C.

It means ... : a pimp. Marār, M.

It Says Here . . . [Reprint] Heath, A. B.

It seemed like silk. Rodoreda, M.

It takes a universe. Terry, G. P.

It takes all kinds. Alenyikov, M.

It Takes Two Hands to Clap. Rashid, F.

It walks in beauty. Davis, C.

It will end in tears. Michiels, I.

It won't be long. Boggs, B.

ITALIAN AMERICANS

Tuten, F. Self portrait with Sicily

ITALIANS

Zaire

Gordimer, N. Rain-queen

ITALY

See also Capri; Sicily

Cheever, J. The world of apples

Elba

Drabble, M. A Pyrrhic victory

Rome

Eisenberg, D. Like it or not

Venice

Wieland, L. Pound in Venice

Iteration. Kessel, J.

Iterations. Rozan, S. J.

The **itinerary.** Isleib, R.

It's against the law to feed the ducks. Tremblay, P.

It's All Good. Nunez, S.

It's my birthday, too. Butcher, J.

It's not the heat, it's the hu—. Bradbury, R.

It's very cold down here. Hemmingson, M.

Ivan and Misha. Alenyikov, M.

'Izz al-Dīn, Manṣūrah

The path to madness

Beirut 39; new writing from the Arab world; edited by Samuel Shimon; with a preface by Hanan al-Shaykh

J

Jaber, Rabee

From the novel America

Beirut 39; new writing from the Arab world; edited by Samuel Shimon; with a preface by Hanan al-Shaykh

Jablokov, Alexander

Blind cat dance

The Year's best science fiction: twenty-eighth annual collection; edited by Gardner Dozois.

The **jacaranda** smile. Files, G.

Jack in the box. Brotherton, M.

Jack in the country. Davis, L.

Jack-O'. Franco, J.

Jackie. Dixon, S.

Jackie's boy. Popkes, S.

Jackson, Alice

A Tampa man

Florida heat wave; [edited and with an] introduction by Michael Lister.

Jackson, Helen Hunt

The prince's little sweetheart

The vintage book of American women writers; edited and with an introduction by Elaine Showalter.

Jackson, Shirley

The lottery

Brave new worlds; edited by John Joseph Adams.

The vintage book of American women writers; edited and with an introduction by Elaine Showalter.

21 essential American short stories; edited by Leslie M. Pockell

Jacobs, Mark

Loss Leader

Southern Humanities Review v44 no3 p306-15 Summ 2010

Jacobs, W. W. (William Wymark)

The monkey's paw

The book of the living dead; edited by John Richard Stephens.

Jacobs, William Wymark *See* Jacobs, W. W. (William Wymark), 1863-1943

Jacobsen, Rob

SCENT ADDICT

Dalhousie Review v91 no1 p99-106 Spr 2011

Jacoff, Samuel

Sickness

Gettysburg Review v24 no3 p425-435 S 2011

The **Jade** Woman of the Luminous Star. Williams, S.

Jakubowski, Maxim

A price to pay

Requiems for the departed; edited by Gerard Brennan & Mike Stone.

Jamaica. Card, O. S.

Jamalzadeh, Mohammad Ali

Persian is sugar

Tablet & pen; literary landscapes from the modern Middle East, a words without borders anthology; edited by Reza Asian.

James, Cyan

Justin

Harvard Review (1992) no38 p207-23 2010

James, Dean

Bottomed out

Lone Star noir; edited by Bobby Byrd & Johnny Byrd.

JAMES, HENRY, 1843-1916

About

Tóibín, C. Silence

The **Jammie** Dodgers and the adventure of the Leicester Square screening. Doctorow, C.

Jan Term. Pearlman, E.

Jančar, Drago

The prophecy

Best European fiction 2011; edited by Aleksandr Hemon; preface by Colum McCann

Jane and the cane. Davis, L.

The **Jane** Austen hen weekend. Humphries, C.

Jane Austen over the Styx. Owens, V.

Jane's World [Graphic story] Braddock, P.

Janey in Amber. Mariotte, J. J.

JANITORS

Dixon, S. The cleanup man

Gifford, B. Arabian nights

Prakash, U. The walls of Delhi

Ross, A. The rest of it

Janjaweed wife. Osondu, E. C.
Jankovic, Marko
  Hey You!
  Nature v467 p628 S 30 2010
Jansen, Patty
  This peaceful state of war
    L. Ron Hubbard presents Writers of the Future volume XXVII; the year's thirteen best tales from the Writers of the Future international writers' program; illustrated by winners in the Illustrators of the Future international illustrators' program; with essays on writing & illustration by L. Ron Hubbard / Mike Resnick / Robert Cadtillo; edited by K. D. Wentworth
January. Olsen, L.
Janus. Beattie, A.
JAPAN
  Goto, H. The hikikomori
  Parks, R. The feather cloak
  Parks, R. Lord Goji's wedding
  Parks, R. Mooning viewing at Shijo Bridge
    1867-1945
  Kim, S.-r. Into the light
    1945-
  Chong, C.-w. The Korean women I love
  Kim, C.-s. Crimson fruit
  Kim, H.-y. Frozen mouth [(1966), chapters one and two]
  Kim, T.-s. In the shadow of Mount Fuji
  Noguchi, K. Foreign husband
  Yu, M. R. Full house
    Marriage customs
    See Marriage customs—Japan
JAPANESE
    United States
  Yamamoto, H. Seventeen syllables
JAPANESE AMERICANS
  Yamauchi, W. Annie Hall, Annie Hall
  Yamauchi, W. A Christmas orange story
  Yamauchi, W. Dogs I owe to
  Yamauchi, W. Family gifting
  Yamauchi, W. McNisei
  Yamauchi, W. Onna
  Yamauchi, W. Pain and stuff
  Yamauchi, W. Rosebud
  Yamauchi, W. Shigin
    Evacuation and relocation, 1942-1945
  Manilla, M. Crystal City
JAPANESE LANGUAGE
    Study and teaching
  Pearlman, E. Relic and type
Jared Bruckheiny. Sands, B.
Jarkman at the othergates. Dowling, T.
Jarrar, Randa
  The story of my building (after Isaac Babel's "Story of my dovecote")
    Beirut 39; new writing from the Arab world; edited by Samuel Shimon; with a preface by Hanan al-Shaykh
JARRY, ALFRED, 1873-1907
    About
  Farmer, P. J. Coda
A **javelina** story. Gray, A.
Jayne. Mitchell, K.
Jayne Mansfield. Singleton, G.

Jazzār, Ḥamdī
  From the novel Secret pleasures
    Beirut 39; new writing from the Arab world; edited by Samuel Shimon; with a preface by Hanan al-Shaykh
JEALOUSY
  Baxter, C. Kiss away
  Black, A. I knew you'd be lovely
  Emshwiller, C. Mrs. Jones
  Fallon, S. Leave
  Gorman, E. Comeback
  Hannah, B. Water liars
  Haywood, G. A. The first rule is
  Highsmith, P. Oona, the jolly cave woman
  Oates, J. C. The first husband
  Pascoe, J. Paper
  Penkov, M. Makedonija
  Phillips, H. The envies
  Self, W. Conversation with Ord
  Sneed, C. You're so different
  Somerville, P. Vaara in the woods
Jellyfish. Evans, D.
Jemisin, N. K.
  1929: the singular taffy puller
    The Thackery T. Lambshead cabinet of curiosities; edited by Ann & Jeff VanderMeer.
Jemison, N. K.
  Non-zero probabilities
    The Nebula Awards showcase; edited by Kevin J. Anderson.
Jen, Gish
  In the American society
    Best of times, worst of times; contemporary American short stories from the new Gilded Age; edited by Wendy Martin and Cecelia Tichi.
Jenkins, Dan
  Tees and teens
    Golf stories; edited by Charles McGrath.
Jennifer's lover. Silverberg, R.
Jenny. Vonnegut, K.
Jensen, Mrs. Oliver *See* Stafford, Jean, 1915-1979
Jensen, Toni
  Looking for boll weevil
    Best of the West 2011; new stories from the wild side of the Missouri; edited by James Thomas and D. Seth Horton; foreword by Ana Castillo.
The **Jersey** Devil. Day, C.
JERUSALEM
  Howard, R. E. The sowers of the thunder
  MacLeod, I. Second journey of the magus
  Pearlman, E. Allog
  Rapoport, N. Sovereignty
  Wilson, J. The liars
JESTERS *See* Fools and jesters
JESUITS
  Child, L. M. F. The church in the wilderness
The **Jesus**. Hellenes, M. M.
Jesus and Satan go jogging in the desert. Green, S. R.
JESUS CHRIST
    About
  Ford, J. On the road to New Egypt
  Gordimer, N. Second coming
  Green, S. R. Jesus and Satan go jogging in the desert
  Hellenes, M. M. The Jesus

JESUS CHRIST—About—*Continued*
MacLeod, I. Second journey of the magus

Crucifixion
Green, S. R. Jesus and Satan go jogging in the desert
La **jetée**. Ulin, D. L.
Jeter, K. W.
   Bones
      Dead neon; tales of near-future Las Vegas; edited by Todd James Pierce and Jarret Keene.
JEWEL ROBBERIES *See* Robbery
JEWELERS
   Buckell, T. S. Trinkets
JEWELRY
      See also Diamonds; Pearls; Rings
   Pung, A. The shed
Jewett, Sarah Orne
   The circus at Denby
      The vintage book of American women writers; edited and with an introduction by Elaine Showalter.
   A white heron
      The vintage book of American women writers; edited and with an introduction by Elaine Showalter.
JEWISH CHILDREN
   Fintushel, E. How the little rabbi grew
   Yellin, T. Reuben
JEWISH HOLOCAUST (1933-1945) *See* Holocaust, Jewish (1933-1945)
JEWISH REFUGEES
      See also Holocaust survivors
   Pearlman, E. If love were all
   Pearlman, E. Purim night
JEWISH WOMEN
   Albert, E. One good reason why not
   Kalechofsky, R. Four women from Ravensbrück
   Rapoport, N. Sovereignty
   Tremblay, P. Rhymes with Jew
   Vapnyar, L. Things that are not yours
JEWS
      See also Antisemitism; Hasidism; Jewish women; Judaism
   Allen, D. Not Renata
   Beagle, P. S. The rabbi's hobby
   Bernheimer, K. A cuckoo tale
   Blumlein, M. Fidelity: a primer
   Burgis, B. Dark coffee, bright light and the paradoxes of omnipotence
   Chabon, M. Golems I have known, or, why my elder son's middle name is Napoleon: a trickster's memoir
   Cook, T. H. Nevermore
   Eidus, J. A bisel this, a bisel that
   Gomel, E. Going east
   Goss, T. The wings of Meister Wilhelm
   Hirshberg, G. The muldoon
   Hirshberg, G. Shomer
   Hutchinson, D. The fortunate isles
   Irvine, A. Semaphore
   Kadish, R. Come on Zion put your hands together
   Kalechofsky, R. Father Woytzski leads a Jewish youth group to the Holocaust memorial in Oswiecim, Poland
   Kirshenbaum, B. The lunatic
   Kressel, M. The history within us

Kurlansky, M. Cholent
Kurlansky, M. Muffins
Leegant, J. Remittances
Love, Y. G. Lonely, lonely, lonely is the Lord of Hosts
Lovett, R. Leo's squid
Neugeboren, J. Summer afternoon
Niedzviecki, H. Displacement
Papernick, J. The engines of Sodom
Papernick, J. A kiss for Mrs. Fisch
Papernick, J. The last five-year plan
Papernick, J. The miracle birth
Pearlman, E. Day of awe
Raphael, L. Money
Rosen, J. The true world
Rosenbaum, T. The Yehuda triangle
Roth, P. The conversion of the Jews
Rubin, J. Toward Lithuania
Sparber, M. Eliyahu-ha-Navi
Thon, M. R. Tu B'Shvat: for the drowned and the saved
Wilson, J. The liars
Persecutions
      See also Holocaust, Jewish (1933-1945)
Religion
      See Judaism
Segregation
Anderson, K. J. Torn stitches, shattered glass
Lemberg, R. Geddarien
Brooklyn (New York, N.Y.)
Neugeboren, J. You are my heart
Chicago (Ill.)
Gifford, B. Ghost ship
Denmark
Sullivan, J. Niels Bohr and the sleeping Dane
Haiti
Kurlansky, M. The leopard of Ti Morne
Massachusetts
Pearlman, E. Relic and type
New York (N.Y.)
Beagle, P. S. Uncle Chaim and Aunt Rifke and the angel
Dozois, G. R. Disciples
Stern, S. Avigdor of the Apes
Yezierska, A. Wild winter love
New York (State)
Papernick, J. Skin for skin
Russia
Yolen, J. and Stemple, A. The tsar's dragon
South America
Pearlman, E. Vaquita
United States
Bukiet, M. J. The Florida sunshine tree
Galchen, R. Wild berry blue
Goldstein, R. The afterlife of skeptics
Hamburger, A. The end of anti-Semitism
Horn, D. Shtetl World
Mirvis, T. Potatoes
Papernick, J. There is no other
Pearlman, E. Chance
Pearlman, E. Settlers
Schwarzschild, E. Midhusband
Wilson, A. The Porchies
The **Jews** of the North. Greenfeld, K. T.
Jha, Radhika
   How I lost my clothes
      Delhi noir; edited by Hirsh Sawhney

Jhabvala, Ruth Prawer
Aphrodisiac
The New Yorker v87 no20 p80-7 Jl 11-18 2011
Jia, Pingwa
The Country Wife
New Letters v77 no1 p89-142 2010/2011
JILTING
Goodman, A. La vita nuova
The **jilting** of Jane. Wells, H. G.
Jimmy Carter's eyes. Osondu, E. C.
Jimmy Goggles the god. Wells, H. G.
A **Jing** Dynasty goat. Qiu Xiaolong
JINN
Ackert, D. and Rosenbaum, B. The king of the djinn
Caine, R. Shiny
The **job**. Sa'id, M. A.
Job history. Proulx, A.
The **jockey**. McCullers, C.
JOCKEYS
McCullers, C. The jockey
Jody after the war. Bryant, E.
Johanides, Ján
Berlin in the Afternoon, at a Quarter to Winter [Part of special issue: Slovak Fiction]
The Review of Contemporary Fiction v30 no2 p36-43 Summ 2010
JOHANNESBURG (SOUTH AFRICA) *See* South Africa—Johannesburg
John Bartine's watch. Bierce, A.
John, for Christmas. Rutherford, E.
John Mortonson's funeral. Bierce, A.
John Uskglass and the Cumbrian charcoal burner. Clarke, S.
Johns, Rebecca
Perpetua in Glory
Ploughshares v36 no4 p44-57 Wint 2010/2011
Johnson, Adam
THE THIRD MATE
Granta no116 p95-117 S 2011
Johnson, Alaya Dawn
A prince of thirteen days
Welcome to Bordertown; new stories and poems of the Borderlands; edited by Holly Black and Ellen Kushner; introduction by Terri Windling.
Johnson, Charles
Guinea pig
Boston Review v36 no1 p45-9 Ja/F 2011
Johnson, Dana
Palm Springs, 1985
Iowa Review v40 no3 p146-56 Wint 2010/2011
What American is
Callaloo v33 no4 p929-34 Fall 2010
Johnson, Kij
Names for water
The Best science fiction and fantasy of the year: volume five; edited by Jonathan Strahan.
Spar
The Nebula Awards showcase; edited by Kevin J. Anderson.

Johnson, R. P. L.
In apprehension, how like a god
L. Ron Hubbard presents Writers of the Future volume XXVII; the year's thirteen best tales from the Writers of the Future international writers' program; illustrated by winners in the Illustrators of the Future international illustrators' program; with essays on writing & illustration by L. Ron Hubbard / Mike Resnick / Robert Cadtillo; edited by K. D. Wentworth
Johnston, Bret Anthony
Soldier of fortune
The Best American short stories, 2011; selected from U.S. and Canadian magazines by Geraldine Brooks with Heidi Pitlor; with an introduction by Geraldine Brooks.
Johnston, Tim
Two years
Best of the West 2011; new stories from the wild side of the Missouri; edited by James Thomas and D. Seth Horton; foreword by Ana Castillo.
The **joke**. Doyle, R.
A **JOKE** TOLD BY PILOTS. Farnsworth, V.
JOKES, PRACTICAL *See* Practical jokes
Jolene: a life. Doctorow, E. L.
Jonas. Boggs, B.
Jonathan Seabreeze Upward. Sands, B.
Jones, Edward P.
The store
Blue collar, white collar, no collar; stories of work; edited by Richard Ford.
Jones, Gareth D.
World Wire Web
Nature v468 no7322 p470 N 18 2010
Jones, Gwyneth A.
Blue clay blues
Jones, G. A. The universe of things; short fiction; by Gwyneth Jones.
La Cenerentola
Jones, G. A. The universe of things; short fiction; by Gwyneth Jones.
Collision
Jones, G. A. The universe of things; short fiction; by Gwyneth Jones.
The early crossing
Jones, G. A. The universe of things; short fiction; by Gwyneth Jones.
The Eastern succession
Jones, G. A. The universe of things; short fiction; by Gwyneth Jones.
Grandmother's footsteps
Jones, G. A. The universe of things; short fiction; by Gwyneth Jones.
Gravegoods
Jones, G. A. The universe of things; short fiction; by Gwyneth Jones.
Grazing the long acre
Jones, G. A. The universe of things; short fiction; by Gwyneth Jones.
Identifying the object
Jones, G. A. The universe of things; short fiction; by Gwyneth Jones.
In the forest of the queen
Jones, G. A. The universe of things; short fiction; by Gwyneth Jones.

Jones, Gwyneth A.—*Continued*

One of Sandy's dreams
  Jones, G. A. The universe of things; short fiction; by Gwyneth Jones.

Red Sonja and Lessingham in Dreamland
  Jones, G. A. The universe of things; short fiction; by Gwyneth Jones.

The thief, the princess, and the Cartesian circle
  Jones, G. A. The universe of things; short fiction; by Gwyneth Jones.

Total internal reflection
  Jones, G. A. The universe of things; short fiction; by Gwyneth Jones.

The universe of things
  Jones, G. A. The universe of things; short fiction; by Gwyneth Jones.

Jones, Henry Bedford- *See* Bedford-Jones, Henry, 1887-1949

Jones, Jeff P.

Maybe We're the Angels
  Five Points v14 no1 p122-32 2010

Jones, Kaylie

The occidental tourist
  Cape Cod noir; edited by David L. Ulin.

Jones, Shane

Black kids in lemon trees
  Butler, B. 30 under 30; an anthology of innovative fiction by younger writers; Blake Butler & Lily Hoang, eds.

Jones, Solomon

Scarred
  Philadelphia noir; edited by Carlin Romano.

Jones, Stephen Graham

Captain's lament
  Jones, S. G. The ones that got away

Crawlspace
  Jones, S. G. The ones that got away

Father, son, holy rabbit
  Jones, S. G. The ones that got away

Lonegan's luck
  Jones, S. G. The ones that got away

The meat tree
  Jones, S. G. The ones that got away

Monsters
  Jones, S. G. The ones that got away

The ones who got away
  The Year's best dark fantasy & horror; edited by Paula Guran
  Jones, S. G. The ones that got away

Raphael
  Jones, S. G. The ones that got away

So perfect
  Jones, S. G. The ones that got away

The sons of Billy Clay
  Jones, S. G. The ones that got away

Teeth
  Jones, S. G. The ones that got away

Till the morning comes
  Jones, S. G. The ones that got away
  The Best horror of the year: volume three; edited by Ellen Datlow.

Wolf Island
  Jones, S. G. The ones that got away

Jones, William

The treachery of stone
  Blood & devotion; tales of epic fantasy; edited by W.H. Horner; illustrated by Nicole Cardiff

JOPLIN, JANIS, 1943-1970

About

Swanwick, M. The feast of Saint Janis

Jordan, Ceri

Rough justice
  Randisi, R. J. The Shamus winners: America's best private eye stories, volume II, 1996-2009; collected and introduced by Robert J. Randisi; founder, Private Eye Writers of America

Jordan, Neil

Night in Tunisia
  The Granta book of the Irish short story; [edited by] Anne Enright.

Jordan's waterhammer. Mastroianni, J.

JOSEPH (BIBLICAL FIGURE)

About

Pollack, R. Burning beard: the dreams and visions of Joseph ben Jacob, Lord Viceroy of Egypt

Josephine has her day. Thurber, J.

Joshi, Ruchir

Parking
  Delhi noir; edited by Hirsh Sawhney

Journal of an inmate. Lake, J.

JOURNALISTS

See also Women journalists

Adichie, C. N. Sola
Bacigalupi, P. The gambler
Bal, H. S. Just another death
Barrett, L. Gossip and toad
Baxter, C. The winner
Doctorow, C. Makers [excerpt]
Dowling, T. The suits at Auderlene
Dozois, G. R. Counterfactual
Gold, H. L. Problem in murder
Gordimer, N. Livingstone's companions
Gordimer, N. Open house
Haines, C. The cypress dream
Khair, T. The scam
Minh, C. A father and his children
Niven, L. Flash crowd
Olsen, L. November
Pearlman, E. Fidelity
Roberge, R. Beano's deal
Rozan, S. J. Iterations
Sands, B. Gen Papa-Georgio
Sands, B. Jonathan Seabreeze Upward
Senna, D. You are free
Taylor, A. Little Russia
Turtledove, H. News from the front
Vaughn, C. Threads
Vonnegut, K. While mortals sleep
Zeman, A. Daphne, unrequited

JOURNALS *See* Diaries (Stories about); Diaries (Stories in diary form)

Journey Home. Hadley, T.

Journey into the kingdom. Rickert, M.

A **journey** of only two paces. Powers, T.

JOURNEYS *See* Overland journeys; Voyages and travels

JOY AND SORROW

See also Happiness

Joy in our cause. Emshwiller, C.

The **joy** of cooking. Schappell, E.

Joyriders. Schutz, G.

Juana Has a Friend. Samudio, Á. C. and O'Leary, G.

JUDAISM
>*See also* Hasidism; Jews; Synagogues; Yom Kippur

Papernick, J. The Madonna of Temple Beth Elohim

Papernick, J. There is no other

Willis, M. S. Elvissa and the rabbi

JUDGES
>Levinson, R. S. Between sins

JUDGMENT DAY
>Owens, V. Jane Austen over the Styx

Wells, H. G. A vision of judgment

A **jug** of sirup. Bierce, A.

Julia Brainchild. Gresh, L. H.

Julius Katz. Zeltserman, D.

July, Miranda
>Majesty
>>I found this funny; my favorite pieces of humor and some that may not be funny at all; edited by Judd Apatow.

>Oranges
>>Fantastic women; 18 tales of the surreal and the sublime from Tin House; introduction by Joy Williams; edited by Rob Spillman.

>Something that needs nothing
>>Best of times, worst of times; contemporary American short stories from the new Gilded Age; edited by Wendy Martin and Cecelia Tichi.

July. Olsen, L.

JULY FOURTH *See* Fourth of July

Jump. Packer, A.

Jumping. Vukcevich, R.

Jumpman vs. the ape. Bell, M.

The **junction.** Means, D.

June. Olsen, L.

June bugs. Shepard, S.

JUNGLES
>Buck, J. The slave brand of Sleman Bin Ali

Burroughs, E. R. Tarzan the terrible

Fowler, K. J. What I didn't see

Gonzalez, V. In a jungle

Jupiter Doke, Brigadier General. Bierce, A.

Juráňová, Jana
>Clips [Part of special issue: Slovak Fiction]
>*The Review of Contemporary Fiction* v30 no2 p44-8 Summ 2010

JURY DUTY *See* Trials

Jury duty. Davis, L.

A **jury** of her peers. Glaspell, S.

A **jury** of his peers. Brandon, J.

Just a hint. Brin, D.

Just another death. Bal, H. S.

Just another desert night with blood. Pulver, J. S.

Just another vampire story. Shipp, J. C.

Just do it. Lindsley, H.

Just like Rasputin, we plod through mud and piss in search of Kellogg's Cornflakes. Berckmans, J. M. H.

Just outside our windows, deep inside our walls. Hodge, B.

Just things. Kalinauskaitė, D.

Justice, Jean Ross
>Mysteries
>*The Antioch Review* v68 no4 p656-67 Fall 2010

JUSTICE
>McCormack, U. The sea is not full

Mosley, W. The trial

O'Connor, S. The professor of atheism: Glue factory bowling

Stockton, F. The lady or the tiger?

The **justice** society. Burgin, R.

Justin. James, C.

Justina's priest. Trevor, W.

Jutito. Gálvez Ronceros, A.

JUVENILE DELINQUENCY
>Cather, W. Paul's case: a study in temperament

Jones, S. G. The ones who got away

K

K is for Kosovo (or, Massimo's career). Ryman, G.

Kaaberbol, Lene and Friis, Agnete
>When the time came
>>Copenhagen noir; edited by Bo Tao Michaëlis; translated by Mark Kline.

Kaczynski, Tom
>Million year boom
>>The best American nonrequired reading 2009; edited by Dave Eggers; introduction by Marjane Satrapi; managing editor, Jesse Nathan

Kadish, Rachel
>Come on Zion put your hands together
>>Promised lands; new Jewish American fiction on longing and belonging; edited by Derek Rubin.

Kafka, Franz
>1920: Prague: Senior management
>*Lapham's Quarterly* v4 no2 p90 Spr 2011

>1920: Prague: Urban Renewal [Excerpt from story, The City Coat of Arms]
>*Lapham's Quarterly* v3 no4 p159 Fall 2010

Kafka, Franz and Harman, Mark
>Kafka's 'A Message from the Emperor': A New Translation
>*The New York Review of Books* v58 no14 p41 S 29 2011

KAFKA, FRANZ, 1883-1924
>**About**
>Davis, L. Kafka cooks dinner

Gordimer, N. Letter from his father

KAFKA, HERMANN
>**About**
>Gordimer, N. Letter from his father

Kafka cooks dinner. Davis, L.

Kafka's 'A Message from the Emperor': A New Translation. Kafka, F. and Harman, M.

Kaftan, Vylar
>Civilization
>>Brave new worlds; edited by John Joseph Adams.

>The orange-tree sacrifice
>>The way of the wizard; edited by John Joseph Adams.

Kaguya-hime: An Old Japanese Tale. Black, S.

Kahaney, Amelia
>The temp
>>The best American nonrequired reading 2009; edited by Dave Eggers; introduction by Marjane Satrapi; managing editor, Jesse Nathan

Kalechofsky, Roberta
The enigmatic power of the letter "j"
  Kalechofsky, R. Four women from Ravensbrück: five stories from the Shoa
Epitaph for an age
  Kalechofsky, R. Four women from Ravensbrück: five stories from the Shoa
Father Woyztski leads a Jewish youth group to the Holocaust memorial in Oswiecim, Poland
  Kalechofsky, R. Four women from Ravensbrück: five stories from the Shoa
Four women from Ravensbrück
  Kalechofsky, R. Four women from Ravensbrück: five stories from the Shoa
My poor prisoner
  Kalechofsky, R. Four women from Ravensbrück: five stories from the Shoa
Kalenda, Judi
Planet Canada
  Calyx v26 no2 p49-59 Wint 2011
KALI (HINDU DIETY)
Parks, R. The finer points of destruction
Kalinauskaitė, Danutė
Just things
  Best European fiction 2011; edited by Aleksandr Hemon; preface by Colum McCann
Kaminsky, Stuart M.
Rattle, rattle, rattle
  On a raven's wing; new tales in honor of Edgar Allan Poe; edited by Stuart M. Kaminsky
Kamlani, Beena
Palisades
  World Literature Today v84 no6 p49 N/D 2010
Kamoche, Ken N.
Secondhand Wife
  World Literature Today v85 no5 p17-22 S 2011
KAMPUCHEA *See* Cambodia
Kanafāni, Ghassān
Letter from Gaza
  Tablet & pen; literary landscapes from the modern Middle East, a words without borders anthology; edited by Reza Asian.
Kanakia, Rahul
Ted Agonistes
  Nature v476 no7358 p120 Ag 4 2011
KANSAS
Doctorow, E. L. Walter John Harmon
  Farm life
  See Farm life—Kansas
Kaplan, Hester
Natural Wonder
  Ploughshares v37 no1 p71-89 Spr 2011
Kaplan, James
The mower
  Golf stories; edited by Charles McGrath.
Karay, Refik Halit
The gray donkey
  Tablet & pen; literary landscapes from the modern Middle East, a words without borders anthology; edited by Reza Asian.
Karl Marx. Last, B.
The **Karmic** Cabbie. Gillett, R. R.
Karnes, Julie Woods
The Family Man
  Confrontation no109 p75-93 Spr 2011

Karvaš, Peter
Xerox of a Document about One Half of (the Art of) Life [Part of special issue: Slovak Fiction]
  The Review of Contemporary Fiction v30 no2 p61-6 Summ 2010
KASHMIR VALLEY (INDIA) *See* India—Vale of Kashmir
Kashtanka. Chekhov, A. P.
Katelnikoff, Joel
Small game hunter
  Can'tLit; fearless fiction from Broken pencil magazine; edited by Richard Rosenbaum.
Kava, Alex and Bremmer, Patricia A.
A breath of hot air
  Florida heat wave; [edited and with an] introduction by Michael Lister.
Kava, Sharon M. *See* Kava, Alex
Kavanagh, Dan *See* Barnes, Julian, 1946-
Kavanagh, Paul *See* Block, Lawrence, 1938-
Kavukçu, Cemil
The route of the crows
  Tablet & pen; literary landscapes from the modern Middle East, a words without borders anthology; edited by Reza Asian.
Kawtharani, Hala
Three stories
  Beirut 39; new writing from the Arab world; edited by Samuel Shimon; with a preface by Hanan al-Shaykh
Kearney, Greg
L-o-v-e
  Can'tLit; fearless fiction from Broken pencil magazine; edited by Richard Rosenbaum.
Panties
  Can'tLit; fearless fiction from Broken pencil magazine; edited by Richard Rosenbaum.
Keegan, Claire
Foster
  The Best American short stories, 2011; selected from U.S. and Canadian magazines by Geraldine Brooks with Heidi Pitlor; with an introduction by Geraldine Brooks.
Men and women
  The Granta book of the Irish short story; [edited by] Anne Enright.
KEELER, HARRY STEPHEN, 1890-1967
  Parodies, imitations, etc.
Nevins, F. M., Jr. The skull of the stuttering gunfighter
Keene, Brian
Captive hearts
  Hungry for your love; an anthology of zombie romance; edited by Lori Perkins.
Selected scenes from the end of the world: three stories from the universe of The rising
  Zombies: the recent dead; edited by Paula Guran.
Keene, Day
Sauce for the gander
  The Black Lizard big book of Black Mask stories; edited and with a foreword by Otto Penzler; introduction by Keith Alan Deutsch.
The **keepers**. Hemmingson, M.
Keeping Corky. Tem, M.
Keepsakes. Binkley, P.

Kegel, Carolyn
Crazy Legs
  Confrontation no109 p119-32 Spr 2011
Kehrli, Keffy R. M.
Bonehouse
  L. Ron Hubbard presents Writers of the Fu-
  ture volume XXVII; the year's thirteen best
  tales from the Writers of the Future inter-
  national writers' program; illustrated by
  winners in the Illustrators of the Future in-
  ternational illustrators' program; with es-
  says on writing & illustration by L. Ron
  Hubbard / Mike Resnick / Robert Cadtillo;
  edited by K. D. Wentworth
Keith, Esme
My lips are sealed
  Can'tLit; fearless fiction from Broken pencil
  magazine; edited by Richard Rosenbaum.
Kelly, James Patrick
Feel the zaz
  Future media; [edited by Rick Wilber]
Going deep
  The Nebula Awards showcase; edited by Kev-
  in J. Anderson.
Plus or minus
  The Best science fiction and fantasy of the
  year: volume five; edited by Jonathan
  Strahan.
Kemal, Yaşar *See* Yaşar Kemal, 1922-
Kennedy, A. L.
Another
  Kennedy, A. L. What becomes; stories
As God made us
  Kennedy, A. L. What becomes; stories
Confectioner's gold
  Kennedy, A. L. What becomes; stories
Edinburgh
  Kennedy, A. L. What becomes; stories
The effects of good government on the city
  Freedom; stories celebrating the Universal
  Declaration of Human Rights; Amnesty In-
  ternational.
Marriage
  Kennedy, A. L. What becomes; stories
Saturday teatime
  Kennedy, A. L. What becomes; stories
Story of my life
  Kennedy, A. L. What becomes; stories
Sympathy
  Kennedy, A. L. What becomes; stories
Vanish
  Kennedy, A. L. What becomes; stories
Wasps
  Kennedy, A. L. What becomes; stories
What becomes
  Kennedy, A. L. What becomes; stories
Whole family with young children devastated
  Kennedy, A. L. What becomes; stories
Kennedy, Jake
Parking her car in Michigan Theatre
  Can'tLit; fearless fiction from Broken pencil
  magazine; edited by Richard Rosenbaum.
Kennedy, Thomas E.
(jt. auth) See Lång, Line-Maria
KENTUCKY
Allen, D. Deferment
Allen, D. Fishing with Alex
Allen, D. The Hazlett's dog
Berry, W. Stand by me

Davis, C. Last year's grave undug
Hardwick, E. Evenings at home
KENYA
                        Nairobi
Minot, S. Pole, pole
Kenyon, John
Cut
  Blood, guts, & whiskey; edited by Todd Rob-
  inson; introduction by Max Allan Collins.
Kenyon, Kay
The acid test
  Swenson, P. The Best of Talebones; edited by
  Patrick Swenson.
Kenyon, Nate
Breeding the demons
  The monster's corner; stories through inhu-
  man eyes; edited by Christopher Golden
Keret, Etgar
Crazy glue
  Can'tLit; fearless fiction from Broken pencil
  magazine; edited by Richard Rosenbaum.
One kiss on the mouth in Mombasa
  Can'tLit; fearless fiction from Broken pencil
  magazine; edited by Richard Rosenbaum.
Keret, Etgar and Shlesinger, Miriam
What animal are you?
  Harper's v322 no1933 p29-30 Je 2011
Kessel, John
Faustfeathers
  Sympathy for the devil; edited by Tim Pratt.
Iteration
  The Best science fiction and fantasy of the
  year: volume five; edited by Jonathan
  Strahan.
The **key**. Adams, C. F.
The **key**. McGahern, J.
A **key** to the Castleblakeney Key. Kiernan, C. R.
KEY WEST (FLA.) *See* Florida—Key West
Key witness. Lawrence, M. C.
Khair, Tabish
The scam; y
  Delhi noir; edited by Hirsh Sawhney
Khalaylah, Asmahan
About spring, Marwah and the feast
  Loud sounds from the Holy Land; short fic-
  tion by Palestinian women; edited and
  translated by Jamal Assadi with assistance
  from Martha Moody.
In the company of Jamal the trouble-maker
  Loud sounds from the Holy Land; short fic-
  tion by Palestinian women; edited and
  translated by Jamal Assadi with assistance
  from Martha Moody.
The scabby woman's son
  Loud sounds from the Holy Land; short fiction by Palestinian women; edited and
  translated by Jamal Assadi with assistance
  from Martha Moody.
Wafiyyah
  Loud sounds from the Holy Land; short fiction by Palestinian women; edited and
  translated by Jamal Assadi with assistance
  from Martha Moody.
Khan, Uzma Aslam
Ice, Mating
  Granta no112 p89-111 Aut 2010

Khanna, Rajan
Card sharp
The way of the wizard; edited by John Joseph
Adams.
Khunta. Sussman, S.
KIBBUTZIM *See* Collective settlements—Israel
Kick. Hall, T. M.
Kicking the habit. Saus, S.
Kickshaws. Williamson, E. M.
Kid. Hunter, L.
The **kid**. Scibona, S.
Kiddie land; ambrosia; rumors; the paragraphs.
Kraft, R. J.
Kiddieland. Chapman, T.
KIDNAPPING
See also Hostages
Ayau, K. J. By the numbers
Boland, J. C. Reunion in Baineville
Fallon, S. Camp Liberty
Fountain, B. Near-extinct birds of the central
cordillera
Groff, L. Rue
Hale, D. J. The precipice
Jones, S. G. The ones who got away
Large, J.-R. Rosanna
Osondu, E. C. An incident at Pat's Bar
Powers, J. Preacher's kid
Powers, T. The Bible repairman
Shipp, J. C. Fungus of the heart
Villegas, H. D in the underworld
The **kidney** problem. Levine, S.
Kiernan, Caitlín R.
The belated burial
Vampires; the recent undead; edited by Paula
Guran.
The bone's prayer
The Year's best dark fantasy & horror; edited
by Paula Guran
The Colliers' Venus (1893)
Naked city; tales of urban fantasy; edited by
Ellen Datlow.
A key to the Castleblakeney Key
The Thackery T. Lambshead cabinet of curi-
osities; edited by Ann & Jeff VanderMeer.
The pearl diver
Brave new worlds; edited by John Joseph Ad-
ams.
The steam dancer
Steampunk II: steampunk reloaded; edited by
Ann & Jeff VanderMeer.
Kilito, Abdelfattah
Revolt in the *Msid*
Chicago Review v55 no3/4 p168-75 Aut 2010
The Wife of R.
Chicago Review v55 no3/4 p164-7 Aut 2010
Kill the cat. Estleman, L. D.
Killed at Resaca. Bierce, A.
The **killer**. Dixon, S.
The **killer** Christian. Klavan, A.
The **killers**. Hemingway, E.
Killing animals. Franco, J.
Killing Kate. Gorman, E.
The **killing** man. Spillane, M.
Killing time. Land, J.
Kilpatrick, Kilt
Last times at Ridgemont High
Hungry for your love; an anthology of
zombie romance; edited by Lori Perkins.

Kilpatrick, Nancy
Vampire anonymous
Vampires; the recent undead; edited by Paula
Guran.
Kilpatrick, Sean
Gangrene
Butler, B. 30 under 30; an anthology of inno-
vative fiction by younger writers; Blake
Butler & Lily Hoang, eds.
Kilworth, Garry
Hats off to Mary
Requiems for the departed; edited by Gerard
Brennan & Mike Stone.
Kim, Alice Sola
Beautiful white bodies
Zombies: the recent dead; edited by Paula
Guran.
Kim, Ch'ang-saeng
Crimson fruit
Into the light; an anthology of literature by
Koreans in Japan; edited by Melissa L.
Wender.
Kim, Eson
Most at Rest
The Massachusetts Review v51 no4 p678-91
Wint 2010
Kim, Hak-yong
Frozen mouth [(1966), chapters one and two]
Into the light; an anthology of literature by
Koreans in Japan; edited by Melissa L.
Wender.
Kim, Sa-ryang
Into the light
Into the light; an anthology of literature by
Koreans in Japan; edited by Melissa L.
Wender.
Kim, Saryang *See* Kim, Sa-ryang, 1914-1950
Kim, Tal-su
In the shadow of Mount Fuji
Into the light; an anthology of literature by
Koreans in Japan; edited by Melissa L.
Wender.
The **kind** of neighbor you used to have. Meek, J.
A **kind** of nostalgia perhaps. Marías, J.
Kinder, R. M.
A Fragile Life
Confrontation no108 p212-21 Fall 2010
Kindness. Del Rey, L.
Kindness and Other Inalienable Rights. Herbert, S.
King, Dana
Green Gables
Blood, guts, & whiskey; edited by Todd Rob-
inson; introduction by Max Allan Collins.
King, Gillian
Fresno
River Styx no84 p28-9 2011
King, Grace Elizabeth
The little convent girl
The vintage book of American women writ-
ers; edited and with an introduction by
Elaine Showalter.
King, Jonathon
Quiet
Florida heat wave; [edited and with an] intro-
duction by Michael Lister.
King, Owen
Home Brew
Prairie Schooner v85 no2 p5-16 Summ 2011

King, Stephen
1922
King, S. Full dark, no stars
Big driver
King, S. Full dark, no stars
Fair extension
King, S. Full dark, no stars
A good marriage
King, S. Full dark, no stars
The man in the black suit
Sympathy for the devil; edited by Tim Pratt.
KING KONG (MOTION PICTURE: 1933)
Farmer, P. J. After King Kong fell
The **king** of a vast empire. Evans, D.
The **King** of Norway. Oz, A.
The **king** of the djinn. Ackert, D. and Rosenbaum, B.
The **King** of the Elves. Dick, P. K.
King of the gray spaces (R is for rocket). Bradbury, R.
King of the Losers. Doyle, B.
King pole, gallows pole, bottle tree. Bear, E.
King Rat. Fowler, K. J.
A **kingdom** by the sea. Dozois, G. R.
Kingdom come. Shipp, J. C.
Kingman, Arizona (Andy Devine Boulevard). Shepard, S.
KINGS AND RULERS
See also Courts and courtiers names of kings and rulers
Bynum, S. S.-L. The young wife's tale
Châteaureynaud, G. O. The pavilion and the linden
Kipling, R. The man who would be king
Loory, B. The crown
Prineas, S. The dog prince
Sa'īd, M. A. The statue
Smith, C. A. The death of Malygris
Smith, C. A. The garden of Adompha
Smith, C. A. The seven geases
Wells, H. G. The Rajah's treasure
Kinsella, John
The Cartesian Diver
The Literary Review (Madison, N.J.) v54 no2 p81-3 Wint 2011
Kipling, Rudyard
Garm - a hostage
The man who would be king
The Big book of adventure stories; edited and with a introduction by Otto Penzler; foreword by Douglas Preston.
Kiraly, Andrew
Your recent acquisitions in the neonesque (microfables)
Dead neon; tales of near-future Las Vegas; edited by Todd James Pierce and Jarret Keene.
Kirby and the portal to Hell. Esposito, B.
Kirchheimer, Gloria DeVidas
First, Do No Harm
The Antioch Review v68 no4 p732-46 Fall 2010
Kirshenbaum, Binnie
The lunatic
Promised lands; new Jewish American fiction on longing and belonging; edited by Derek Rubin.

Kirtley, David Barr
Family tree
The way of the wizard; edited by John Joseph Adams.
The skull-faced boy
Z: zombie stories; edited by J. M. Lassen
Kiš, Danilo
c. 1923: Hamburg: Danilo Kiš sends the flowers [Excerpt from Last respects]
Lapham's Quarterly v4 no1 p134-7 Wint 2011
Kishore, Swapna
Dream girl
Nature v470 no7334 p430 F 17 2011
Kiss away. Baxter, C.
A **kiss** for Mrs. Fisch. Papernick, J.
KISSING
Blatnik, A. Say that
Keret, E. One kiss on the mouth in Mombasa
Novack, S. Morty, el morto
Kitchen. Shepard, S.
Kitterman, Barry
Boys from poor families
Kitterman, B. From the San Joaquin; stories
Crazy people
Kitterman, B. From the San Joaquin; stories
The gospel according to Octavio Ruiz
Kitterman, B. From the San Joaquin; stories
If I'd known you were going to stay this long
Kitterman, B. From the San Joaquin; stories
In dog years
Kitterman, B. From the San Joaquin; stories
The man who raised rabbits
Kitterman, B. From the San Joaquin; stories
Mediators
Kitterman, B. From the San Joaquin; stories
A place in the opera
Kitterman, B. From the San Joaquin; stories
Rivers of wood
Kitterman, B. From the San Joaquin; stories
Someone like me
Kitterman, B. From the San Joaquin; stories
Union wages
Kitterman, B. From the San Joaquin; stories
Wedding day
Kitterman, B. From the San Joaquin; stories
The window
Kitterman, B. From the San Joaquin; stories
Kittle, Penny
I reach, I climb, I reach again [Part of special issue: Honoring Student Voices]
Voices from the Middle v18 no3 p55-6 Mr 2011
Kittredge, William
Stone boat
Best of the West 2010; new stories from the wide side of the Missouri; edited by James Thomas and D. Seth Horton; foreword by Kent Meyers.
Kitty and the mosh pit of the damned. Vaughn, C.
Kitty's zombie New Year. Vaughn, C.
KKK See Ku Klux Klan
Klages, Ellen
Goodnight moons
Life on Mars: tales from the new frontier; an original science fiction anthology; edited by Jonathan Strahan

Klause, Annette Curtis
Elf blood
    Welcome to Bordertown; new stories and poems of the Borderlands; edited by Holly Black and Ellen Kushner; introduction by Terri Windling.
Klavan, Andrew
The killer Christian
    Christmas at the Mysterious Bookshop; 'tis the season to be deadly; stories of mistletoe and mayhem from 17 masters of suspense; edited by Otto Penzler.
Kleeman, Alexandra
Fairy Tale
    The Paris Review v52 no195 p15-22 Wint 2010
KLEIN, T. E. D., 1947-
        Parodies, imitations, etc.
Cannon, P. The Arkham collector
Klein, Ted *See* Klein, T. E. D., 1947-
Klempt, lever puller. Madigan, C.
KLEPTOMANIA
Bell, T. The pirate of Palm Beach
Kloess, Christina
The hardest button
    Butler, B. 30 under 30; an anthology of innovative fiction by younger writers; Blake Butler & Lily Hoang, eds.
Klonaris, Helen
Angel and Me
    Calyx v26 no3 p56-57 Summ 2011
Knapp, Adeline
The earth slept: a vision
    The dreaming sex; early tales of scientific imagination by women; edited by Mike Ashley.
Kneebone, Eddie and Bodsworth, Roxanne
Echidna Dreaming [Retold by R. Bodsworth]
    Parabola v36 no2 p60-65 Summ 2011
Kneeland, Andrea
If I were Lee's girlfriend, I wouldn't want to drown children in the duck pond
    Butler, B. 30 under 30; an anthology of innovative fiction by younger writers; Blake Butler & Lily Hoang, eds.
Knezevic, Olja
The classroom
    Freedom; stories celebrating the Universal Declaration of Human Rights; Amnesty International.
Knickerbocker, Alyssa
Same as it was when you left
    Best of the West 2011; new stories from the wild side of the Missouri; edited by James Thomas and D. Seth Horton; foreword by Ana Castillo.
The **knife.** Loory, B.
Knife, Barn, My Harvey. Houtrides, R.
The **knife** thrower. Millhauser, S.
Knife thrower. Nutting, A.
KNIFE THROWING
Loory, B. The knife
Knight, Damon Francis
To serve man
    The Big book of adventure stories; edited and with a introduction by Otto Penzler; foreword by Douglas Preston.
A **knight** of ghosts and shadows. Dozois, G. R.
KNIGHTHOOD *See* Knights and knighthood

KNIGHTS AND KNIGHTHOOD
    See also Middle Ages
Brennan, M. The twa corbies
Châteaureynaud, G. O. The beautiful coalwoman
McOmber, A. A man of history
The **Knights** of Liberty. Randisi, R. J.
Knights of the Open Palm. Daly, C. J.
Knock Knock. Clarke, B.
Knock knock. Dixon, S.
Knowing he was not my kind yet I followed. Hannah, B.
KNOWLEDGE AND LEARNING
Blatnik, A. Learning
Knowles, Brent
Digital rights
    L. Ron Hubbard presents Writers of the Future volume XXVI; the year's twelve best tales from the Writers of the Future international writers' program; illustrated by winners in the Illustrators of the Future international illustrators' program; with essays on writing & illustration by L. Ron Hubbard/Dean Wesley Smith/ Stephen Youll; edited by K. D. Wentworth
Knox, John H.
Wake not the dead
    The book of the living dead; edited by John Richard Stephens.
Knoxville, Tennessee (Highway 40). Shepard, S.
Ko-uta (Small Song). Barry, Q.
Koizumi, Yakumo *See* Hearn, Lafcadio, 1850-1904
Koja, Kathe
Toujours
    Blood and other cravings; edited by Ellen Datlow.
Koku. Yi-Yang-ji
Kole, Diana
Listened
    The Kenyon Review v33 no1 p14-17 Wint 2011
Kolpan, Gerald
The ratcatcher
    Philadelphia noir; edited by Carlin Romano.
Kompaníková, Monika
Slávko [Part of special issue: Slovak Fiction]
    The Review of Contemporary Fiction v30 no2 p67-73 Summ 2010
Konkka, Anita
The clown
    Best European fiction 2011; edited by Aleksandr Hemon; preface by Colum McCann
Konrath, J. A.
The screaming
    Vampires; the recent undead; edited by Paula Guran.
Konrath, Joe *See* Konrath, J. A., 1970-
KORAN
Boukebba, A. From the novel Skin of shadow
        Study and teaching
Jazzār, ₁ From the novel Secret pleasures
KOREA
            Seoul
Yi-Yang-ji. Koku
KOREAN AMERICANS
Beagle, P. S. El regalo
Row, J. The call of blood

Kronauer, Brigitte—*Continued*

Desire for music and mountains [excerpt]
Kronauer, B. Constructs of desire; selections from Brigitte Kronauer; translated and edited by Jutta Ittner

Devilsbridge [excerpt]
Kronauer, B. Constructs of desire; selections from Brigitte Kronauer; translated and edited by Jutta Ittner

The diva and her tricks
Kronauer, B. Constructs of desire; selections from Brigitte Kronauer; translated and edited by Jutta Ittner

Events with odd and even endings
Kronauer, B. Constructs of desire; selections from Brigitte Kronauer; translated and edited by Jutta Ittner

The handkerchief [excerpt]
Kronauer, B. Constructs of desire; selections from Brigitte Kronauer; translated and edited by Jutta Ittner

Martens and rabbits
Kronauer, B. Constructs of desire; selections from Brigitte Kronauer; translated and edited by Jutta Ittner

Mrs. Mühlenbeck in her house [excerpt]
Kronauer, B. Constructs of desire; selections from Brigitte Kronauer; translated and edited by Jutta Ittner

Oh if you knew how the fishes do
Kronauer, B. Constructs of desire; selections from Brigitte Kronauer; translated and edited by Jutta Ittner

Rita Münster [excerpt]
Kronauer, B. Constructs of desire; selections from Brigitte Kronauer; translated and edited by Jutta Ittner

A sort of achievement like nature's
Kronauer, B. Constructs of desire; selections from Brigitte Kronauer; translated and edited by Jutta Ittner

Stanzas for an observation
Kronauer, B. Constructs of desire; selections from Brigitte Kronauer; translated and edited by Jutta Ittner

A successful effort for Miss Block
Kronauer, B. Constructs of desire; selections from Brigitte Kronauer; translated and edited by Jutta Ittner

The woman in the pillows [excerpt]
Kronauer, B. Constructs of desire; selections from Brigitte Kronauer; translated and edited by Jutta Ittner

KU KLUX KLAN

Connell, R. The color of honor

Daly, C. J. Knights of the Open Palm

Kubla Khan. Tran, V.

Kuhlken, Ken

Homes
San Diego noir; edited by Maryelizabeth Hart.

Kuitenbrouwer, Kathryn

LAIKAS I
Granta no116 p203-222 S 2011

Kumar, Amitava

Milk Is Good for You
World Literature Today v84 no6 p32 N/D 2010

Postmortem
World Literature Today v84 no6 p33 N/D 2010

The **kumquats** affair. Nevins, F. M., Jr.

Kunzru, Hari

Memories of the decadence
Pushcart Prize XXXV: best of the small presses 2011; edited by Bill Henderson with the Pushcart Prize editors.

Kurlansky, Mark

Bean curd
Kurlansky, M. Edible stories; a novel in 16 parts

Belons
Kurlansky, M. Edible stories; a novel in 16 parts

Boundin
Kurlansky, M. Edible stories; a novel in 16 parts

Cholent
Kurlansky, M. Edible stories; a novel in 16 parts

Crème brûlée
Kurlansky, M. Edible stories; a novel in 16 parts

Espresso
Kurlansky, M. Edible stories; a novel in 16 parts

Hot dog
Kurlansky, M. Edible stories; a novel in 16 parts

Hot pot
Kurlansky, M. Edible stories; a novel in 16 parts

The icing on the cake
Kurlansky, M. Edible stories; a novel in 16 parts

The leopard of Ti Morne
Haiti noir; edited by Edwidge Danticat

Margaret
Kurlansky, M. Edible stories; a novel in 16 parts

Menudo
Kurlansky, M. Edible stories; a novel in 16 parts

Muffins
Kurlansky, M. Edible stories; a novel in 16 parts

Orangina
Kurlansky, M. Edible stories; a novel in 16 parts

Osetra
Kurlansky, M. Edible stories; a novel in 16 parts

Red sea salt
Kurlansky, M. Edible stories; a novel in 16 parts

The soup
Kurlansky, M. Edible stories; a novel in 16 parts

Kushner, Anna

(tr.) See Gutiérrez, Pablo

Kushner, Ellen

The children of Cadmus
The beastly bride; tales of the animal people; edited by Ellen Datlow & Terri Windling; introduction by Terri Windling; selected decorations by Charles Vess.

Kushner, Ellen—*Continued*
The duke of Riverside
Naked city; tales of urban fantasy; edited by
Ellen Datlow.
The man with the knives
The Best science fiction and fantasy of the
year: volume five; edited by Jonathan
Strahan.
Kushner, Ellen and Windling, Terri
Welcome to Bordertown
Welcome to Bordertown; new stories and po-
ems of the Borderlands; edited by Holly
Black and Ellen Kushner; introduction by
Terri Windling.
Kutsch. Walser, R.
Kuzmanovic, Tomislav
(tr.) See Hrgovic, Maja
Kyle, Aryn
Allegiance
Kyle, A. Boys and girls like you and me; sto-
ries
Boys and girls like you and me
Kyle, A. Boys and girls like you and me; sto-
ries
Brides
Kyle, A. Boys and girls like you and me; sto-
ries
Captain's club
Kyle, A. Boys and girls like you and me; sto-
ries
Company of strangers
Kyle, A. Boys and girls like you and me; sto-
ries
Economics
Kyle, A. Boys and girls like you and me; sto-
ries
Femme
Kyle, A. Boys and girls like you and me; sto-
ries
A lot like fun
Kyle, A. Boys and girls like you and me; sto-
ries
Nine
Kyle, A. Boys and girls like you and me; sto-
ries
Sex scenes from a chain bookstore
Kyle, A. Boys and girls like you and me; sto-
ries
Take care
Kyle, A. Boys and girls like you and me; sto-
ries
Kyrie. Anderson, P.

L

L-o-v-e. Kearney, G.
La Spina, Greye
The ultimate ingredient
The dreaming sex; early tales of scientific
imagination by women; edited by Mike
Ashley.
LABELLE, PATTI
About
Boggs, B. Opportunity
Labinger, Andrea G.
(tr.) See Brau, Edgar

LABOR AND LABORING CLASSES
See also Apprentices; Labor unions; Mi-
grant labor
Marãr, M. Hard work
O'Brien, E. Shovel kings
Rodoreda, M. Love
Trevor, W. The mourning
LABOR UNIONS
See also Labor and laboring classes
Dixon, S. Produce
Kitterman, B. Union wages
LABOUISSE, EVE CURIE, 1904-2007
About
Wieland, L. The girl with radium eyes
LaBrie, Aimee
Princess
Philadelphia noir; edited by Carlin Romano.
LABYRINTHS
Heathcock, A. The daughter
O'Connor, S. Ziggurat
Lachaîne, Alexis
Gas
Dalhousie Review v90 no2 p253-62 Summ
2010
Ladies and gentlemen. Ross, A.
Lady Clanbevan's baby. Dehan, R.
The **lady** from Redhorse. Bierce, A.
Lady on ice. Estleman, L. D.
The **lady** or the tiger? Stockton, F.
The **lady** who plucked red flowers beneath the
queen's window. Swirsky, R.
Lafferty, Mur
1963: the argument against Louis Pasteur
The Thackery T. Lambshead cabinet of curi-
osities; edited by Ann & Jeff VanderMeer.
The **lagan** fishers. Dowling, T.
LAGOS (NIGERIA) *See* Nigeria—Lagos
Lahens, Yanick
An American story
Lahens, Y. Aunt Resia and the spirits and
other stories; translated by Betty Wilson;
afterword by Marie-Agnes Sourieau
And all this unease
Lahens, Y. Aunt Resia and the spirits and
other stories; translated by Betty Wilson;
afterword by Marie-Agnes Sourieau
Aunt Résia and the spirits
Lahens, Y. Aunt Resia and the spirits and
other stories; translated by Betty Wilson;
afterword by Marie-Agnes Sourieau
The blue room
Lahens, Y. Aunt Resia and the spirits and
other stories; translated by Betty Wilson;
afterword by Marie-Agnes Sourieau
The city
Lahens, Y. Aunt Resia and the spirits and
other stories; translated by Betty Wilson;
afterword by Marie-Agnes Sourieau
A commonplace disaster
Lahens, Y. Aunt Resia and the spirits and
other stories; translated by Betty Wilson;
afterword by Marie-Agnes Sourieau
Death in July
Lahens, Y. Aunt Resia and the spirits and
other stories; translated by Betty Wilson;
afterword by Marie-Agnes Sourieau

Lahens, Yanick—*Continued*
  Madness had come with the rain
    Lahens, Y. Aunt Resia and the spirits and
      other stories; translated by Betty Wilson;
      afterword by Marie-Agnes Sourieau
  Moon bathing
    Lahens, Y. Aunt Resia and the spirits and
      other stories; translated by Betty Wilson;
      afterword by Marie-Agnes Sourieau
  The neighborhood, the ravine, and the old
      Peugeot
    Lahens, Y. Aunt Resia and the spirits and
      other stories; translated by Betty Wilson;
      afterword by Marie-Agnes Sourieau
  Petty corruption
    Lahens, Y. Aunt Resia and the spirits and
      other stories; translated by Betty Wilson;
      afterword by Marie-Agnes Sourieau
  A shattered day
    Lahens, Y. Aunt Resia and the spirits and
      other stories; translated by Betty Wilson;
      afterword by Marie-Agnes Sourieau
  Soursop, orange, and lemongrass
    Lahens, Y. Aunt Resia and the spirits and
      other stories; translated by Betty Wilson;
      afterword by Marie-Agnes Sourieau
  The survivors
    Lahens, Y. Aunt Resia and the spirits and
      other stories; translated by Betty Wilson;
      afterword by Marie-Agnes Sourieau
  Three natural deaths
    Lahens, Y. Aunt Resia and the spirits and
      other stories; translated by Betty Wilson;
      afterword by Marie-Agnes Sourieau
  Wash your memory with lots of water
    Lahens, Y. Aunt Resia and the spirits and
      other stories; translated by Betty Wilson;
      afterword by Marie-Agnes Sourieau
  The weight of the night
    Lahens, Y. Aunt Resia and the spirits and
      other stories; translated by Betty Wilson;
      afterword by Marie-Agnes Sourieau
  Who is that man?
    Haiti noir; edited by Edwidge Danticat
Lahiri, Jhumpa
  Gogol
    Best of times, worst of times; contemporary
      American short stories from the new Gilded
      Age; edited by Wendy Martin and Cecelia
      Tichi.
  Interpreter of maladies
    Blue collar, white collar, no collar; stories of
      work; edited by Richard Ford.
  A temporary matter
    The vintage book of American women writ-
      ers; edited and with an introduction by
      Elaine Showalter.
Laidlaw, Marc
  Great breakthroughs in darkness
    Steampunk II: steampunk reloaded; edited by
      Ann & Jeff VanderMeer.
  Leng
    The Year's best dark fantasy & horror; edited
      by Paula Guran
LAIKAS I. Kuitenbrouwer, K.
Lake, Jay
  Achilles, sulking in his Buick
    Lake, J. The sky that wraps; collected short
      fiction

The American dead
  Lake, J. The sky that wraps; collected short
    fiction
Chain of fools
  Lake, J. The sky that wraps; collected short
    fiction
Coming for Green
  Lake, J. The sky that wraps; collected short
    fiction
Crossing the seven
  Lake, J. The sky that wraps; collected short
    fiction
The daughters of desire
  Blood & devotion; tales of epic fantasy; ed-
    ited by W.H. Horner; illustrated by Nicole
    Cardiff
A different way into the life
  Lake, J. The sky that wraps; collected short
    fiction
Dogs in the moonlight
  Lake, J. The sky that wraps; collected short
    fiction
Fat man
  Lake, J. The sky that wraps; collected short
    fiction
The goat cutter
  Sympathy for the devil; edited by Tim Pratt.
Green grass blues
  Lake, J. The sky that wraps; collected short
    fiction
Journal of an inmate
  Lake, J. The sky that wraps; collected short
    fiction
Lehr, Rex
  Lake, J. The sky that wraps; collected short
    fiction
The leopard's paw
  Lake, J. The sky that wraps; collected short
    fiction
Little Pig, Berry Brown and the hard moon
  Lake, J. The sky that wraps; collected short
    fiction
The man with one bright eye
  Lake, J. The sky that wraps; collected short
    fiction
Number of the bus
  Lake, J. The sky that wraps; collected short
    fiction
On the human plan
  Lake, J. The sky that wraps; collected short
    fiction
People of leaf and branch
  Lake, J. The sky that wraps; collected short
    fiction
Promises
  Lake, J. The sky that wraps; collected short
    fiction
Skinhorse goes to Mars
  Lake, J. The sky that wraps; collected short
    fiction
The sky that wraps the world round, past the
    blue and into the black
  Lake, J. The sky that wraps; collected short
    fiction
Taking the rats to Riga
  The Thackery T. Lambshead cabinet of curi-
    osities; edited by Ann & Jeff VanderMeer.

Lake, Jay—*Continued*

Tall spirits, blocking the night

Swenson, P. The Best of Talebones; edited by Patrick Swenson.

To raise a mutiny betwixt yourselves

Lake, J. The sky that wraps; collected short fiction

To this their late escape

Lake, J. The sky that wraps; collected short fiction

A very old man with no wings at all

Lake, J. The sky that wraps; collected short fiction

A water matter

Lake, J. The sky that wraps; collected short fiction

Witness to the fall

Lake, J. The sky that wraps; collected short fiction

Lake, Jay and Scholes, Ken

The starship mechanic

The Year's best science fiction: twenty-eighth annual collection; edited by Gardner Dozois.

Lake, Robert

Rock of ages

Dalhousie Review v90 no3 p385-94 Aut 2010

The **lake**. Bradbury, R.

The **lake**. Due, T.

The **Lake**. Flick, S.

LAKE DISTRICT (ENGLAND)

Drabble, M. Stepping westward: a topographical tale

Laken, Valerie

Before long

Laken, V. Separate kingdoms; stories

Family planning

Laken, V. Separate kingdoms; stories

God of fire

Laken, V. Separate kingdoms; stories

Map of the city

Laken, V. Separate kingdoms; stories

Remedies

Laken, V. Separate kingdoms; stories

Scavengers

Laken, V. Separate kingdoms; stories

Separate kingdoms

Laken, V. Separate kingdoms; stories

Spectators

Laken, V. Separate kingdoms; stories

LAKES

Due, T. The lake

Lakewood, New Jersey. Neugeboren, J.

Lamb, Harold

The mighty manslayer

The Big book of adventure stories; edited and with a introduction by Otto Penzler; foreword by Douglas Preston.

Lambert, Shaena

The War Between the Men and the Women

Ploughshares v37 no1 p94-105 Spr 2011

Lamborghini mommy. Kozak, H. J.

LaMere, Brandon

The reunion

Tribal College Journal of American Indian Higher Education v23 no1 p52-3 Fall 2011

L'Amour, Louis

Off the mangrove coast

The Big book of adventure stories; edited and with a introduction by Otto Penzler; foreword by Douglas Preston.

Lampe, Michael *See* MacLeod, Michael, 1953-

Lampo, Hubert

The city that never was

The Dedalus book of Flemish fantasy; edited by Eric Dickens and translated by Paul Vincent.

Lamrabet, Rachida

Ammetis the sleeper

The Dedalus book of Flemish fantasy; edited by Eric Dickens and translated by Paul Vincent.

Lanagan, Margo

Machine maid

Steampunk II: steampunk reloaded; edited by Ann & Jeff VanderMeer.

The miracle aquilina

The Best science fiction and fantasy of the year: volume five; edited by Jonathan Strahan.

Mulberry boys

Blood and other cravings; edited by Ellen Datlow.

The proving of Smollett Standforth

Ghosts by gaslight; stories of steampunk and supernatural suspense; [edited by] Jack Dann [and] Nick Gevers

Sea-hearts

The Year's best dark fantasy & horror; edited by Paula Guran

LANCASHIRE (ENGLAND) *See* England—Lancashire

Lancelotta, Victoria

Practice

The Southern Review (Baton Rouge, La.) v46 no4 p611-20 Aut 2010

Land, Jon

The boy and the backpack

The Saturday Evening Post v282 no6 p24-6, 70-2, 74 N/D 2010

Killing time

The Best American mystery stories 2010; edited and with an introduction by Lee Child; Otto Penzler, series editor

The leap year rule

The Saturday Evening Post v283 no4 p52-5, 60, 62, 64 Jl/Ag 2011

The **land** ironclads. Wells, H. G.

The **land** of Beulah. Senna, D.

Land of the living. Shepard, S.

LAND REFORM *See* Land tenure

LAND TENURE

Sa'id, M. A. The neighbors' story

Landers, Scott

The Age of Heroes

New England Review v32 no2 p38-51 Spr 2011

Landis, Geoffrey A.

The sultan of the clouds

The Best science fiction and fantasy of the year: volume five; edited by Jonathan Strahan.

The Year's best science fiction: twenty-eighth annual collection; edited by Gardner Dozois.

LANDLADIES *See* Landlord and tenant
Landlocked. Anderson, B.
The **landlord**. Tower, W.
LANDLORD AND TENANT
    See also Tenant farming
  Chowdhury, S. Hostel
  Gray, A. This quiet complex
  Marār, M. From the bag of others!
  McCracken, E. Property
  Naipaul, V. S. The perfect tenants
  Tower, W. The landlord
LANDLORDS *See* Landlord and tenant
Landon, Perceval
  Thurnley Abbey
    The book of the living dead; edited by John
      Richard Stephens.
LANDSCAPE GARDENING
    See also Trees
Lanesskog, Geir
  Sailing the sky sea
    L. Ron Hubbard presents Writers of the Fu-
      ture volume XXVII; the year's thirteen best
      tales from the Writers of the Future inter-
      national writers' program; illustrated by
      winners in the Illustrators of the Future in-
      ternational illustrators' program; with es-
      says on writing & illustration by L. Ron
      Hubbard / Mike Resnick / Robert Cadtillo;
      edited by K. D. Wentworth.
Lang, Kyle
  The Little Things
    StoryQuarterly v44 p277-91 2010
Lång, Line-Maria
  As You've Planned It
    The Southern Review (Baton Rouge, La.) v47
      no1 p11-13 Wint 2011
  Doll
    The Literary Review (Madison, N.J.) v54 no1
      p95-7 Fall 2010
Langan, John
  City of the dog
    The Best horror of the year: volume three;
      edited by Ellen Datlow.
  The revel
    The Best horror of the year: volume three;
      edited by Ellen Datlow.
  The third always beside you
    Blood and other cravings; edited by Ellen
      Datlow.
  The unbearable proximity of Mr. Dunn's bal-
    loons
    Ghosts by gaslight; stories of steampunk and
      supernatural suspense; [edited by] Jack
      Dann [and] Nick Gevers
  The wide, carnivorous sky
    The Year's best dark fantasy & horror; edited
      by Paula Guran
    Vampires; the recent undead; edited by Paula
      Guran.
Langan, Sarah
  Independence day
    Brave new worlds; edited by John Joseph Ad-
      ams.
LANGUAGE AND LANGUAGES
    See also English language; French lan-
      guage
  Kurlansky, M. The soup
  Le Guin, U. K. She unnames them
  McElroy, J. Night soul

  Millhauser, S. History of a disturbance
  Vukcevich, R. Suddenly speaking
  Vukcevich, R. The wages of syntax
The **Language** of Fireflies. Haggerty, J.
Language, truth and lockjaw. MacLaverty, B.
Lani Dances the Zombie Hula in LA. Hamby, B.
Lanigan, Susan
  Roundabouts
    Nature v473 no7345 p118 My 5 2011
  Stay special
    Nature v466 p1014 Ag 19 2010
Lansdale, Joe R.
  The crawling sky
    Lansdale, J. R. Deadman's road
  The dark down there
    Lansdale, J. R. Deadman's road
  Deadman's road
    Lansdale, J. R. Deadman's road
    Zombies: the recent dead; edited by Paula
      Guran.
  The folding man
    The Best horror of the year: volume three;
      edited by Ellen Datlow.
  The gentleman's hotel
    Lansdale, J. R. Deadman's road
  Six-finger Jack
    Lone Star noir; edited by Bobby Byrd &
      Johnny Byrd.
  Torn away
    The Year's best dark fantasy & horror; edited
      by Paula Guran
LAOTIANS
United States

  Bacigalupi, P. The gambler
LAPLAND
  Geeraerts, J. Indian summer
LARCENY *See* Theft
Lardner, Rex
  Triumph at Crestwood
    Golf stories; edited by Charles McGrath.
Lardner, Ring
  Mr. Frisbie
    Golf stories; edited by Charles McGrath.
Large, Josaphat-Robert
  Rosanna
    Haiti noir; edited by Edwidge Danticat
Larp of Mars. Roberson, C.
LAS VEGAS (NEV.) *See* Nevada—Las Vegas
LaSalle, Peter
  Grand Central
    The Antioch Review v69 no1 p102-14 Wint
      2011
  Lunch across the bridge
    Best of the West 2011; new stories from the
      wild side of the Missouri; edited by James
      Thomas and D. Seth Horton; foreword by
      Ana Castillo.
Lasdun, James
  Oh, death
    The Pen/O.Henry Prize stories, 2010; edited
      and with an introduction by Laura Furman;
      with essays on the stories they admire most
      by jurors Junot Diaz, Paula Fox, Yiyun Li.
Last, Bob
  Karl Marx
    Critical Quarterly v53 no1 p88-92 Ap 2011
The **last** blah in the etc. Matheson, R.
Last call. Butcher, J.
The **last** covenant. Marār, M.

The **last** dance. Neville, S.
The **last** department. Ulysse, K. D.
The **last** disarmament but one. McElroy, J.
The **last** five-year plan. Papernick, J.
The **last** flight of Doctor Ain. Tiptree, J.
Last frontier. Leland, C. T.
The **last** hieroglyph. Smith, C. A.
Last in, first out. Sealy, I. A.
Last island south. Boland, J. C.
The **last** jar of mayo at the H&P. Crook, J.
The **last** laboratory. Gilbey, J.
Last night of the county fair. Hall, T. M.
Last of the guerrilla gardeners. Clements, D. L.
The **last** passenger. Nevins, F. M., Jr.
Last plane out of Chungking. Gifford, B.
The **last** pursuit. Mofina, R.
Last Rites. Waters, D.
The **last** round. Hall, H.
Last seen. Lee, M. J.
The **last** stand. Fallon, S.
The **last** stop: Street of the Prophets. Burbara, R.
The **last** supper. Edelman, S.
The **last** swim of the season. Sterling, P.
The **last** ten years in the life of hero Kai. Ryman,
   G.
The **last** thing we need. Watkins, C. V.
Last times at Ridgemont High. Kilpatrick, K.
Last tour of duty. Monk, D.
Last train from central station. Staalesen, G.
Last trip. Atta, S.
Last visit. Hemmingson, M.
Last winter here. Healey, E.
The **last** worders. Fowler, K. J.
Last year's grave undug. Davis, C.
Lastward, deputy James. Hannah, B.
The **Late** Interiors. MacKenzie, I.
Later. Smith, M. M.
Later. Tillman, L.
Later That Night. Pierce, G.
LATIN AMERICA
   Boyle, T. C. Zapatos
LATINOS (U.S.) *See* Hispanic Americans
Latiolais, Michelle
   Boys
      Latiolais, M. Widow; stories
   Breathe
      Latiolais, M. Widow; stories
   Burqa
      Latiolais, M. Widow; stories
   Caduceus
      Latiolais, M. Widow; stories
   Crazy
      Latiolais, M. Widow; stories
   Damned spot
      Latiolais, M. Widow; stories
   Gut
      Latiolais, M. Widow; stories
   Hoarding
      Latiolais, M. Widow; stories
   Involution
      Latiolais, M. Widow; stories
   The legal case
      Latiolais, M. Widow; stories
   The long table
      Latiolais, M. Widow; stories
   The moon
      Latiolais, M. Widow; stories
   Pink
      Latiolais, M. Widow; stories

   Place
      Latiolais, M. Widow; stories
   Tattoo
      Latiolais, M. Widow; stories
   Thorns
      Latiolais, M. Widow; stories
   Widow
      Latiolais, M. Widow; stories
LATVIA
   Sokoloff, B. The crime of Dr. Garine
Laurrent, Eric
   American diary
      Best European fiction 2011; edited by Alek-
      sandr Hemon; preface by Colum McCann
LaValle, Victor
   Poor me
      Callaloo v33 no4 p968-73 Fall 2010
Lavin, Mary
   Lilacs
      The Granta book of the Irish short story; [ed-
      ited by] Anne Enright.
Law, Janice
   The Secrets of a Client Are Inviolate
      Texas Bar Journal v74 no6 p490-3 Je 2011
LAW AND LAWYERS
               See also Judges; Trials; Women lawyers
   Allyn, D. An early Christmas
   Beattie, A. The confidence decoy
   Beattie, A. Television
   Black, A. The thing itself
   Boland, J. C. Out of her depth
   Brandon, J. A jury of his peers
   Cohen, P. Designer justice
   Doctorow, E. L. Wakefield
   Dorfman, A. Innocent passage
   Drees, C. By hook or by crook
   Fusilli, J. Digby, attorney at law
   Gordimer, N. A soldier's embrace
   Latiolais, M. The legal case
   Melville, H. Bartleby the scrivener
   Mphahlele, E. He and the cat
   Phelan, T. Time will tell
   Roberge, R. Do not concern yourself with things
      Lee Nading has left out
   Ross, A. When in Rome
   Schirach, F. v. Bliss
   Schirach, F. v. The cello
   Schirach, F. v. The Ethiopian
   Schirach, F. v. Fähner
   Schirach, F. v. Green
   Schirach, F. v. The hedgehog
   Schirach, F. v. Love
   Schirach, F. v. Self-defense
   Schirach, F. v. Summertime
   Schirach, F. v. Tanata's tea bowl
   Schirach, F. v. The thorn
   Vila-Matas, E. Far from here
   Wolff, T. The deposition
   Zeltserman, D. Bad move
The **law** of escape. Martín, A.
Lawless. Atta, S.
The **lawn** party. Beattie, A.
Lawrence, Bill
   The Intelligentcia
      StoryQuarterly v44 p156-67 2010
Lawrence, Martha C.
   Key witness
      San Diego noir; edited by Maryelizabeth Hart.

Laws, Karen
Paolo's Turn
The Georgia Review v65 no2 p311-324
Summ 2011
Lawson, April Ayers
Virgin
The Paris Review v52 p13-35 Fall 2010
Lawson, Patricia
I'm a dork
Dalhousie Review v90 no3 p379-84 Aut 2010
LAWSUITS *See* Law and lawyers
LAWYERS *See* Law and lawyers
Lax forb. Levine, S.
Layla's belly. Yared, H.
Lazaroo, Simone
Cocooning
Amerasia Journal v36 no2 p153-64 2010
Lazarus. Heathcock, A.
The **laziest** form of revelation. Black, A.
Le Clézio, J.-M. G. (Jean-Marie Gustave)
Daniel who had never seen the sea
Le Clézio, J.-M. G. Mondo and other stories
= Mondo et autres histoires; translated
[from the French] by Alison Anderson.
Hazaran
Le Clézio, J.-M. G. Mondo and other stories
= Mondo et autres histoires; translated
[from the French] by Alison Anderson.
Lullaby
Le Clézio, J.-M. G. Mondo and other stories
= Mondo et autres histoires; translated
[from the French] by Alison Anderson.
The mountain of the living god
Le Clézio, J.-M. G. Mondo and other stories
= Mondo et autres histoires; translated
[from the French] by Alison Anderson.
People of the sky
Le Clézio, J.-M. G. Mondo and other stories
= Mondo et autres histoires; translated
[from the French] by Alison Anderson.
The shepherds
Le Clézio, J.-M. G. Mondo and other stories
= Mondo et autres histoires; translated
[from the French] by Alison Anderson.
The waterwheel
Le Clézio, J.-M. G. Mondo and other stories
= Mondo et autres histoires; translated
[from the French] by Alison Anderson.
Le Clézio, Jean-Marie Gustave *See* Le Clézio,
J.-M. G. (Jean-Marie Gustave), 1940-
Le Guin, Ursula H.
The ones who walk away from Omelas
Brave new worlds; edited by John Joseph Ad-
ams.
Le Guin, Ursula K.
She unnames them
The vintage book of American women writ-
ers; edited and with an introduction by
Elaine Showalter.
The word of unbinding
The way of the wizard; edited by John Joseph
Adams.
Le Sueur, Meridel
Annunication
The vintage book of American women writ-
ers; edited and with an introduction by
Elaine Showalter.

Leacock, Stephen Butler
The golfomaniac
Golf stories; edited by Charles McGrath.
The **leader.** Dixon, S.
Leahey, Jason
Brooklyn Feast or Famine
The Antioch Review v69 no3 p545-570 Summ
2011
Leahy, Krista Hoeppner
Too fatal a poison
The way of the wizard; edited by John Joseph
Adams.
The **Leak.** Eliasson, G. and Kravec, A.
Leap day. Nevins, F. M., Jr.
The **leap** year rule. Land, J.
Lear, Peter *See* Lovesey, Peter
Learning. Blatnik, A.
LEARNING AND SCHOLARSHIP *See* Scholars
Leave. Fallon, S.
LEAVE-TAKINGS *See* Farewells
Leave this world for me . . . for a woman . . .
who seems to be the hope. Bakriyya, R.
Leaves. Dixon, S.
LEBANESE

Germany
Schirach, F. v. The hedgehog
LEBANON

Beirut
Kawtharani, H. Three stories
Lebbon, Tim
Naming of parts
Zombies: the recent dead; edited by Paula
Guran.
Leboeuf, Nicole J.
First breath
Blood and other cravings; edited by Ellen
Datlow.
LECTURES AND LECTURING
See also Speeches, addresses, etc.
Smith, C. A. The great god Awto
Turtledove, H. The genetics lecture
Lee, Geoffrey
Niramiai
Gettysburg Review v24 no1 p5-13 Spr 2011
Lee, Helen Elaine
Alphabet
Prairie Schooner v85 no1 p59-64 Spr 2011
Lee, Lisa
The Hunt
The North American Review v295 no3 p25-31
Summ 2010
Lee, Michael J.
Last seen
Butler, B. 30 under 30; an anthology of inno-
vative fiction by younger writers; Blake
Butler & Lily Hoang, eds.
Lee, Nicole
Toyol
World Literature Today v84 no5 p34-6 S/O
2010
Lee, Tanith
Black and white sky
The Best horror of the year: volume three;
edited by Ellen Datlow.
The persecution machine
Steampunk II: steampunk reloaded; edited by
Ann & Jeff VanderMeer.

Lee, Tanith—*Continued*

The puma's daughter

The beastly bride; tales of the animal people; edited by Ellen Datlow & Terri Windling; introduction by Terri Windling; selected decorations by Charles Vess.

La vampiresse

Vampires; the recent undead; edited by Paula Guran.

Lee, Tien-Yi

Miranda Visits the Holiday Inn

Gettysburg Review v23 no3 p341-55 Aut 2010

Lee, Yoon Ha

Counting the shapes

The way of the wizard; edited by John Joseph Adams.

Flower, mercy, needle, chain

The Year's best science fiction: twenty-eighth annual collection; edited by Gardner Dozois.

Leebron, Fred G.

The exchange student

Cape Cod noir; edited by David L. Ulin.

Leegant, Joan

Remittances

Promised lands; new Jewish American fiction on longing and belonging; edited by Derek Rubin.

Leeward to the sky. Monk, D.

LEGACIES *See* Inheritance and succession

The **legacy** of between books. Ressel, S.

The **legal** case. Latiolais, M.

LEGAL PROFESSION *See* Law and lawyers

LEGAL STORIES *See* Law and lawyers

The **legend** of the Berlin Wall–as presented by a mole. Drakulic, S.

LEGENDS AND FOLK TALES

Aiken, J. The sale of midsummer

Wells, H. G. The flying man

Ireland

Hyde, D. The O'Kane and the corpse

United States

Harris, J. C. Brer Rabbit and the Tar-Baby

Irving, W. Rip Van Winkle

LeGuin, Ursula *See* Le Guin, Ursula K., 1929-

Lehane, Dennis

Animal rescue

The Best American mystery stories 2010; edited and with an introduction by Lee Child; Otto Penzler, series editor

By hook or by crook and 27 more of the best crime + mystery stories of the year; edited by Ed Gorman and Martin H. Greenberg.

Lehr, Rex. Lake, J.

Leiber, Fritz

The seven black priests

The Big book of adventure; edited and with a introduction by Otto Penzler; foreword by Douglas Preston.

Leidiger, Lynda

Tell me

The Best American mystery stories 2010; edited and with an introduction by Lee Child; Otto Penzler, series editor

Leila in the Wilderness. Aslam, N.

Leiningen versus the ants. Stephenson, C.

Leka, Arian

Brothers of the blade

Best European fiction 2011; edited by Aleksandr Hemon; preface by Colum McCann

Leland, Christopher T.

As always, unkind

Leland, C. T. Love/imperfect; stories

As if in time of war

Leland, C. T. Love/imperfect; stories

Casing the promised land

Leland, C. T. Love/imperfect; stories

The congregation of love

Leland, C. T. Love/imperfect; stories

Fellatio

Leland, C. T. Love/imperfect; stories

How the Coe boys got their names

Leland, C. T. Love/imperfect; stories

In conclusion

Leland, C. T. Love/imperfect; stories

Last frontier

Leland, C. T. Love/imperfect; stories

Memento mori

Leland, C. T. Love/imperfect; stories

A mother's love

Leland, C. T. Love/imperfect; stories

Peach Queen

Leland, C. T. Love/imperfect; stories

Reprise

Leland, C. T. Love/imperfect; stories

Swim

Leland, C. T. Love/imperfect; stories

Traveler

Leland, C. T. Love/imperfect; stories

What do you do with your nights?

Leland, C. T. Love/imperfect; stories

What it came to

Leland, C. T. Love/imperfect; stories

The woman who loved Claude Rains

Leland, C. T. Love/imperfect; stories

Wonderful town

Leland, C. T. Love/imperfect; stories

Lemberg, Rose

Geddarien

People of the book; a decade of Jewish science fiction & fantasy; edited by Rachel Swirsky & Sean Wallace.

Lemmings. Ruocco, J.

Leng. Laidlaw, M.

LENINGRAD (SOVIET UNION) *See* Russia— St. Petersburg

Lenny hearts Eunice. Shteyngart, G.

Leo rising. Matheson, R.

Leonard, Elmore

Comfort to the enemy

Leonard, E. Comfort to the enemy and other Carl Webster stories

Louly and Pretty Boy

Leonard, E. Comfort to the enemy and other Carl Webster stories

Showdown at checotah [variant title: How Carlos Webster changed his name to Carl and became a famous Oklahoma lawman]

Leonard, E. Comfort to the enemy and other Carl Webster stories

Leong, Sandra

We Don't Deserve This

Ploughshares v36 no2/3 p55-74 Fall 2010

The **leopard** of Ti Morne. Kurlansky, M.

Levine, Peter

Booth One

The Southern Review (Baton Rouge, La.) v47 no3 p409-18 Summ 2011

Code Pink

Commentary v130 no4 p39-47 N 2010

Levine, Stacey

Alia

Levine, S. The girl with brown fur; tales & stories

And you are?

Levine, S. The girl with brown fur; tales & stories

The bean

Levine, S. The girl with brown fur; tales & stories

Believing it was George Harrison

Levine, S. The girl with brown fur; tales & stories

Bill Miller

Levine, S. The girl with brown fur; tales & stories

The cat

Levine, S. The girl with brown fur; tales & stories

The cats

Levine, S. The girl with brown fur; tales & stories

The danas

Levine, S. The girl with brown fur; tales & stories

Ears

Levine, S. The girl with brown fur; tales & stories

The fields

Levine, S. The girl with brown fur; tales & stories

The flier

Levine, S. The girl with brown fur; tales & stories

The girl

Levine, S. The girl with brown fur; tales & stories

How do breasts feels?

Levine, S. The girl with brown fur; tales & stories

The kidney problem

Levine, S. The girl with brown fur; tales & stories

Lax forb

Levine, S. The girl with brown fur; tales & stories

The man who was always a father

Levine, S. The girl with brown fur; tales & stories

Milk boy

Levine, S. The girl with brown fur; tales & stories

Parthenogenetic grandmother

Levine, S. The girl with brown fur; tales & stories

Pat Smash

Levine, S. The girl with brown fur; tales & stories

Sausage

Levine, S. The girl with brown fur; tales & stories

Scoo boy

Levine, S. The girl with brown fur; tales & stories

Tippy flowery

Levine, S. The girl with brown fur; tales & stories

The tree

Levine, S. The girl with brown fur; tales & stories

Uppsala

Levine, S. The girl with brown fur; tales & stories

The water

Levine, S. The girl with brown fur; tales & stories

The wedding

Levine, S. The girl with brown fur; tales & stories

The wolf

Levine, S. The girl with brown fur; tales & stories

The world of Barry

Levine, S. The girl with brown fur; tales & stories

Levinson, Robert S.

Between sins

By hook or by crook and 27 more of the best crime + mystery stories of the year; edited by Ed Gorman and Martin H. Greenberg.

LEWIS, C. S. (CLIVE STAPLES), 1898-1963

Parodies, imitations, etc.

Gaiman, N. The problem of Susan

Lewis, Clive Staples *See* Lewis, C. S. (Clive Staples), 1898-1963

Lewis, Trudy

Old Wives' Mail: a short story [Part of a special issue: Stirrings: Journeys through emotion]

DisClosure no16 p37-54 2007

Lewycka, Marina

Business philosophy

Freedom; stories celebrating the Universal Declaration of Human Rights; Amnesty International.

Lezhava, Zurab

Sex for fridge

Best European fiction 2011; edited by Aleksandr Hemon; preface by Colum McCann

Li, Shelly

Every girl dreams of falling in love

Nature v477 no7365 p504 S 22 2011

A good time

Nature v472 no7344 p508 Ap 28 2011

(jt. auth) See Liu, Ken and Li, Shelly

Li, Yiyun

c. 1976: China: Yiyun Li observes a likeness [Excerpt from Immortality]

Lapham's Quarterly v4 no1 p58-61 Wint 2011

Li-Tai-Pe and springtime. Balázs, B.

Li-Tai-Pe and the thief. Balázs, B.

Les **liaisons** dangereuses. Drabble, M.

LIARS

Hannah, B. High-water railers

Hannah, B. Water liars

Kurlansky, M. Boundin

Monzó, Q. A day like any other

Nelson, A. Or else

The **liars**. Wilson, J.

Lib. Emshwiller, C.

LIBERIA
  Wallace, E. Bosambo of Monrovia
The **Liberian** condition. Gifford, B.
Libertarian Russia. Swanwick, M.
LIBERTY
  Anderson, P. The pugilist
  Chubak, S. The baboon whose buffoon was
    dead
The **Librarian**. Trevor, D.
LIBRARIANS
  Ashfeldt, L. Snowmelt
  Baker, L. Ghost story
  Oates, J. C. Amputee
  O'Brien, E. Send my roots rain
  Ruocco, J. Wolves
  Solzhenitsyn, A. Nastenka
  Tremblay, P. The strange case of Nicholas
    Thomas: an excerpt from a history of the
    Longesian Library
  Trevor, W. Graillis's legacy
LIBRARIES
  Bingham, S. Winter term
  Emshwiller, C. The circular library of stones
  Emshwiller, C. If the word was to the wise
  Franco, J. April in three parts: part II, Wasting
  Hardwick, E. Back issues
  Vukcevich, R. The library of pi
The **library**. Dowling, T.
The **library** of pi. Vukcevich, R.
LIBYA
  Binshatwan, N. The pools and the piano
Lie, still, sleep becalmed. Duffy, S.
LIFE (PHILOSOPHY OF LIFE)
  Meyer, C. The sweet taste of slavery
The **life** and death of Marcelino Iturriaga. Marías,
  J.
The **life** business. Gash, J.
LIFE INSURANCE
  Vonnegut, K. The epizootic
Life is so short. Monzó, Q.
Life is the teacher. Vaughn, C.
LIFE ON OTHER PLANETS
      See also Interplanetary visitors
  Anderson, P. Horse trader
  Anderson, P. Kyrie
  Anderson, P. Lodestar
  Anderson, P. Sister planet
  Baker, S. W. Poison, inside the walls
  Baxter, S. Return to Titan
  Dick, P. K. Beyond lies the wub
  Dick, P. K. Colony
  Emshwiller, C. Puritan planet
  Emshwiller, C. Two-step for six legs
  Farmer, P. J. The blasphemers
  Farmer, P. J. A bowl bigger than earth
  Goodberg, D. The others
  Hubbard, L. R. Final enemy
  Hughes, V. A. The dualist
  Johnson, K. Spar
  Jones, G. A. Gravegoods
  Lake, J. The sky that wraps the world round,
    past the blue and into the black
  Niven, L. Bordered in black
  Niven, L. Cautionary tales
  Niven, L. Flatlander
  Niven, L. The soft weapon
  Novik, N. Seven years from home
  Silverberg, R. The trouble with Sempoanga
  Silverberg, R. Waiting for the earthquake

  Smith, C. A. The dart of Rasasfa
  Somerville, P. Confused aliens
  Young, J. Written in light
A **life** on paper. Châteaureynaud, G. O.
Life size. Matheson, R.
Life so dear or peace so sweet. Finlay, C. C.
Light. Link, K.
The **Light** in the West. George, N.
Light Opera. Martin, L.
Lighting bug. Ruocco, J.
Lightning Man. Shepard, S.
Like a demon. Lychack, W.
Like glass. Beattie, A.
Like it or not. Eisenberg, D.
Like Kissing Your Sister. Davis, L.-M. B.
Like riding a bike. Wildt, J.
Like something out of a comic book. Haywood,
  G. A.
likeMe. Brooke, K.
Lilacs. Lavin, M.
Lily & men. Lutz, J.
Lima, Maria
  A scent of death
    San Diego noir; edited by Maryelizabeth Hart.
LIMA (PERU) *See* Peru—Lima
Liminal: the little man. Davis, L.
Limits. Niven, L.
The **limner**. Barnes, J.
LIN-GREENBERG, KAREN
  What Was There Long Ago
    The North American Review v296 no3 p25-31
    Summ 2011
Lin-Greenberg, Karin
  A Good Brother
    The Antioch Review v68 no3 p473-88 Summ
    2010
LINDBERGH, CHARLES, 1902-1974
              About
  Dozois, G. R. Counterfactual
Lindholm, Megan
  Cut
    Lindholm, M. and Hobb, R. The inheritance
      and other stories; [by] Megan Lindholm
      [and] Robin Hobb
  Drum machine
    Lindholm, M. and Hobb, R. The inheritance
      and other stories; [by] Megan Lindholm
      [and] Robin Hobb
  The fifth squashed cat
    Lindholm, M. and Hobb, R. The inheritance
      and other stories; [by] Megan Lindholm
      [and] Robin Hobb
  Finis
    Lindholm, M. and Hobb, R. The inheritance
      and other stories; [by] Megan Lindholm
      [and] Robin Hobb
  Silver lady and the fortyish man
    Lindholm, M. and Hobb, R. The inheritance
      and other stories; [by] Megan Lindholm
      [and] Robin Hobb
  Strays
    Lindholm, M. and Hobb, R. The inheritance
      and other stories; [by] Megan Lindholm
      [and] Robin Hobb
  A touch of lavender
    Lindholm, M. and Hobb, R. The inheritance
      and other stories; [by] Megan Lindholm
      [and] Robin Hobb
Lindsey. Fried, G.

Liu, Aimee
The Repairman
Good Housekeeping v251 no3 p177-82 S 2010
Liu, Ken and Li, Shelly
To the stars
Nature v470 no7332 p134 F 3 2011
Liu, Xiaofeng
(tr.) See Jia, Pingwa
Lively, Penelope
Black dog
LIVERPOOL (ENGLAND) *See* England—Liverpool
The **lives** of the prophets. Monzó, Q.
The **living** and the dead. Mphahlele, E.
Living at the center. Emshwiller, C.
Living Light. Miller, I.
Living rooms. Tom, L.
Living space. Grossman, V. S.
Livingston, Montana. Shepard, S.
LIVINGSTONE, DAVID, 1813-1873
About
Gordimer, N. Livingstone's companions
Livingstone's companions. Gordimer, N.
Llamada anónima. Llovera Baranda, J. L.
Llanos. Shepard, S.
Llovera Baranda, José Luis
Llamada anónima
Archipiélago v19 no70 p40 O-D 2010
The **loaf**. Marãr, M.
LOANS
Carver, R. Elephant
El **Lobo** [With an introduction by M. H. Kingston]
Bac Sierra, B.
Lock-up no. 14. Hertmans, S.
Lockheed. Franco, J.
LOCKS AND KEYS
Hertmans, S. Lock-up no. 14
LaBrie, A. Princess
El **Loco**. Rodriguez-Milanes, C.
LOCUSTS
Baker, A. The persistence of memory
Gordimer, N. The soft voice of the serpent
Lodestar. Anderson, P.
Lofty. Beattie, A.
LOGGERS
Somerville, P. Vaara in the woods
London, Jack
A thousand deaths
The book of the living dead; edited by John Richard Stephens.
To build a fire
21 essential American short stories; edited by Leslie M. Pockell
The white silence
The Big book of adventure stories; edited and with a introduction by Otto Penzler; foreword by Douglas Preston.
LONDON (ENGLAND) *See* England—London
Lonegan's luck. Jones, S. G.
LONELINESS
Blatnik, A. Other paths
Brennan, M. An attack of hunger
Chau, A. The pussycats
Couture, B. Fur: an autobiography [excerpt]
Davis, L. Five signs of disturbance
Doyle, R. Recuperation
Emshwiller, C. Foster mother
Grossman, V. S. Mama

Hemmingson, M. Why don't you use your parking space?
Highsmith, P. Where the door is always open and the welcome mat is out
July, M. Majesty
Kennedy, A. L. Sympathy
Kennedy, A. L. Vanish
Kyle, A. Boys and girls like you and me
Kyle, A. Company of strangers
Latiolais, M. Hoarding
Leland, C. T. The congregation of love
Levine, S. The cats
Oates, J. C. Sourland
Orozco, D. Hunger tales
Pearlman, E. How to fall
Rodoreda, M. Ada Liz
Roncagliolo, S. The predator
Tremblay, P. The people who live near me
Trevor, W. An evening out
Trevor, W. Graillis's legacy
Willis, D. Escape
Lonely. Davis, L.
Lonely are the brave. Gifford, B.
Lonely, lonely, lonely is the Lord of Hosts. Love, Y. G.
Lonergan's girl. Swierczynski, D.
Long, Henry
My grandfather was Adolf Hitler's roommate
The stories (in) between; edited by Greg Schauer, Jeanne B. Benzel, and W. H. Horner.
Long, Julius
Merely murder
The Black Lizard big book of Black Mask stories; edited and with a foreword by Otto Penzler; introduction by Keith Alan Deutsch.
The **long,** cold goodbye. Phillips, H.
LONG ISLAND (N.Y.)
Bradley, G. An East Egg update
Millhauser, S. The slap
Long made short. Dixon, S.
The **long** ride back home. Ali, M. N.
The **long** table. Latiolais, M.
Long time waiting. Vaughn, C.
The **long** wait. Dib, M.
A **long** way back. Bova, B.
The **long** way back. Gorman, E.
The **long** winter's nap. Holmes, R.
LONGEVITY
See also Aging
Longing to love you. Mullins, D. P.
Loofah. Hunter, L.
Look-alikes. Gordimer, N.
Look down, this is where it must have happened. Niedzviecki, H.
Looking after family. Vaughn, C.
Looking down. Emshwiller, C.
Looking for boll weevil. Jensen, T.
Looking for Service. Oates, N.
Looking for Wanda beyond the Salton Sea. Hemmingson, M.
Loomis, Mercy
White night, black horse
Hungry for your love; an anthology of zombie romance; edited by Lori Perkins.
The **Loop** Trail. Rechner, M.

Loory, Ben

The afterlife is what you leave behind
  Loory, B. Stories for nighttime and some for
    the day
Bigfoot
  Loory, B. Stories for nighttime and some for
    the day
The book
  Loory, B. Stories for nighttime and some for
    the day
The crown
  Loory, B. Stories for nighttime and some for
    the day
Death and the fruits of the tree
  Loory, B. Stories for nighttime and some for
    the day
The duck
  Loory, B. Stories for nighttime and some for
    the day
The end of it all
  Loory, B. Stories for nighttime and some for
    the day
The fish in the teapot
  Loory, B. Stories for nighttime and some for
    the day
The girl in the storm
  Loory, B. Stories for nighttime and some for
    the day
The graveyard
  Loory, B. Stories for nighttime and some for
    the day
Hadley
  Loory, B. Stories for nighttime and some for
    the day
The hat
  Loory, B. Stories for nighttime and some for
    the day
The house on the cliff and the sea
  Loory, B. Stories for nighttime and some for
    the day
The hunter's head
  Loory, B. Stories for nighttime and some for
    the day
Husband and wife
  Loory, B. Stories for nighttime and some for
    the day
The knife
  Loory, B. Stories for nighttime and some for
    the day
The little girl and the balloon
  Loory, B. Stories for nighttime and some for
    the day
The magic pig
  Loory, B. Stories for nighttime and some for
    the day
The man and the moose
  Loory, B. Stories for nighttime and some for
    the day
The man who went to China
  Loory, B. Stories for nighttime and some for
    the day
  The Antioch Review v69 no2 p310-13 Spr
    2011
The Martian
  Loory, B. Stories for nighttime and some for
    the day
The octopus
  Loory, B. Stories for nighttime and some for
    the day

On the way down: a story for Ray Bradbury
  Loory, B. Stories for nighttime and some for
    the day
The path
  Loory, B. Stories for nighttime and some for
    the day
Photographs
  Loory, B. Stories for nighttime and some for
    the day
The poet
  Loory, B. Stories for nighttime and some for
    the day
The rope and the sea
  Loory, B. Stories for nighttime and some for
    the day
The sea monster
  Loory, B. Stories for nighttime and some for
    the day
The shadow
  Loory, B. Stories for nighttime and some for
    the day
The shield
  Loory, B. Stories for nighttime and some for
    the day
The snake in the throat
  Loory, B. Stories for nighttime and some for
    the day
The swimming pool
  Loory, B. Stories for nighttime and some for
    the day
The tree
  Loory, B. Stories for nighttime and some for
    the day
The tunnel
  Loory, B. Stories for nighttime and some for
    the day
The tv and Winston Churchill
  Loory, B. Stories for nighttime and some for
    the day
UFO: a love story
  Loory, B. Stories for nighttime and some for
    the day
The walk that replaced understanding
  Loory, B. Stories for nighttime and some for
    the day
The well
  Loory, B. Stories for nighttime and some for
    the day
The woman and the basement
  Loory, B. Stories for nighttime and some for
    the day

Loose ends. Gorman, E.

Loot. Gordimer, N.

Lopez, Barry

The Mappist
  The Georgia Review v65 no1 p175-85 Spr
    2011

Lord Dunsany's teapot. Novik, N.

Lord Goji's wedding. Parks, R.

Lord of Samarcand. Howard, R. E.

The **Lord** of the Dynamos. Wells, H. G.

Lord Rendall's song. Marías, J.

Lord Royston's tour. Davis, L.

Loring, F. G.

The tomb of Sarah
  The book of the living dead; edited by John
    Richard Stephens.

LOS ALAMOS (N.M.) *See* New Mexico—Los
  Alamos

LOVE AFFAIRS—*Continued*

Novack, S. Conversions on the road to Damascus

Oates, J. C. Amputee

O'Brien, E. Manhattan medley

Pearlman, E. Unravished bride

Rodoreda, M. In a whisper

Rodoreda, M. The mirror

Ross, A. Ladies and gentlemen

Samarasan, P. Birch memorial

Sawhney, H. Gautam under a tree

Self, W. Design faults in the Volvo 760 Turbo: a manual

Silverberg, R. Snake and ocean, ocean and snake

Sneed, C. Portraits of a few of the people I've made cry

Somerville, P. Easy love

Tem, S. R. Miri

Theodore-Pharel, M. K. Mercy at the gate

Thon, M. R. First, body

Thon, M. R. Necessary angels

Tóibín, C. Silence

Trevor, W. After rain

Trevor, W. A bit on the side

Trevor, W. Child's play

Trevor, W. A day

Trevor, W. A friendship

Trevor, W. Marrying Damian

Trevor, W. Old flame

Trevor, W. The room

Trueblood, V. She had coarsened

Trueblood, V. Trespass

Wannous, D. Two stories

Warsh, L. Endless embrace

Warsh, L. Harry Cray

Warsh, L. Mysterioso

Yared, H. Layla's belly

Love and hope and sex and dreams. Roberge, R.

Love Drugstore. Cantor, R.

Love forest. Trung, T. D.

Love, hope and dwarfs. Verbeke, A.

Love hurts. Butcher, J.

Love in the dark. Gold, H. L.

Love is a temper. Lychack, W.

Love is not a pie. Bloom, A.

Love Is Power, Or Something Like That. Barrett, A. I.

Love is the spell that casts out fear. Boskovich, D.

Love leans in from the left. Vukcevich, R.

Love, love, love, alone. Naipaul, V. S.

Love me again. Emshwiller, C.

Love me for my yellow hair alone. Wheat, C.

Love, mortar. Gray, A.

Love of the true God. Uncle River

Love sentence. Tillman, L.

Love song. Hunter, L.

LOVE STORIES

See also Courtship; Love affairs; Lovers

Anderson, P. The bitter bread

Archer, J. Caste-off

Barnes, J. Carcassonne

Baxter, C. Winter journey

Beattie, A. Skeletons

Bierce, A. Beyond the wall

Bierce, A. The lady from Redhorse

Blatnik, A. The moment of decision

Brown, S. The magician's apprentice

Cross, S. M. Through death to love

Davies, R. Bruise for bruise

Davis, L. Story

Diab, F. An added fraction

Dillman, D. Cloudcroft

Dubus, A. All the time in the world

Emshwiller, C. But soft what light..

Emshwiller, C. Love me again

Emshwiller, C. Omens

Fitzgerald, F. S. Winter dreams

Friedman. C. S. Soul mate

Galchen, R. Wild berry blue

Gorman, E. That day at Eagle's Point

Grotefeld, E. Eight years later

Hardwick, E. The final conflict

Hardwick, E. A season's romance

Hemmingson, M. It's very cold down here

Jazzār, ; From the novel Secret pleasures

Johnson, A. D. A prince of thirteen days

Kadish, R. Come on Zion put your hands together

Love, Y. G. Lonely, lonely, lonely is the Lord of Hosts

Ma, V. K. Thay phung

Marār, M. The internal pages

Mu Xin. An empty room

Nagai, M. Love story

Neugeboren, J. You are my heart

Nolan, W. F. What love is this?

O'Brien, E. Send my roots rain

O'Connor, S. He will not see me stopping here

Penkov, M. East of the West

Pitts, J. A. Three chords and the truth

Prill, D. Dating secrets of the dead

Ray, S. The miracles of Vincent Van Gogh

Rickert, M. You have never been here

Riippi, J. Something about L—

Sabar, A. Collision

Sabar, A. Crossroads

Sabar, A. Depths

Sabar, A. Elevation

Sabar, A. Freestanding

Sabar, A. Green

Sabar, A. Navigation

Sabar, A. Renovations

Sabar, A. Sightlines

Sedgwick, C. M. Cacoethes scribendi

Silverberg, R. Needle in a timestack

Tanpinar, A. H. A mind at peace

Tillman, L. Love sentence

Trevor, W. Big bucks

Trevor, W. A perfect relationship

Trung, T. D. Love forest

Tuten, F. Self portrait with circus

Urrea, L. A. Amapola

Vestal, S. Opposition in all things

Vo, T. H. The blood of leaves

Vonnegut, K. Jenny

Vukcevich, R. Gas

Vukcevich, R. Human subjects

Wells, H. G. In the modern vein: an unsympathetic love story

Love story. Nagai, M.

Love story. Vukcevich, R.

LOVE, SWEET LOVE. Roscoe, P.

Love too long. Hannah, B.

Lovecraft, H. P. (Howard Phillips)

The call of Cthulhu

21 essential American short stories; edited by Leslie M. Pockell

Lovecraft, H. P. (Howard Phillips)—*Continued*
　Herbert West: reanimator
　　The book of the living dead; edited by John
　　Richard Stephens.
LOVECRAFT, H. P. (HOWARD PHILLIPS),
　　1890-1937
　　　　Parodies, imitations, etc.
　Cannon, P. Azathoth in analysis
　Cannon, P. Azathoth in Arkham
　Cannon, P. Bride of Azathoth
　Cannon, P. The house of Azathoth
　Cannon, P. Old man
　Cannon, P. The revenge of Azathoth
　Cannon, P. Son of Azathoth
　Smith, C. A. The seven geases
Lovecraft, Howard Phillips *See* Lovecraft, H. P.
　　(Howard Phillips), 1890-1937
Lovelace & babbage. Padua, S.
The **lover**. Galgut, D.
LOVERS
　Adichie, C. N. Birdsong
　Aiken, J. Spur of the moment
　Barrett, L. One hippopotamus
　Barzak, C. Map of seventeen
　Beattie, A. Vermont
　Bezmozgis, D. The train of their departure
　Black, A. I knew you'd be lovely
　Black, A. The laziest form of revelation
　Blatnik, A. On paper
　Caine, R. Shiny
　Chabon, M. Ocean Avenue
　Châteaureynaud, G. O. Icarus saved from the
　　skies
　Chuculate, E. D. Under the red star of Mars
　Dixon, S. Biff
　Dixon, S. Leaves
　Dixon, S. Piers
　Dixon, S. Sex
　Dixon, S. She
　Dixon, S. Starting again
　Drabble, M. Crossing the Alps
　Ely, S. Wasps
　Emmanuel, F. Lou dancing
　Engel, P. Cielito lindo
　Foer, J. S. Here we aren't, so quickly
　Franc, I. The enigma of her voice
　Gallari, A. A beautiful lie
　Gallari, A. Chasing Adonis
　Gallari, A. Reading Rilke
　Glass, J. The price of silver
　Greenman, B. Viva Regina
　Guidubaldi, D. The desert: a field guide
　Guo Xiaolu. An Internet baby
　Hall, T. M. A crown of sonnets dedicated to
　　long-gone love
　Hardwick, E. Yes and no
　Hemmingson, M. Give me the gun, he says
　Horrocks, C. The lion gate
　Hunter, L. Loofah
　Hunter, L. Sex armageddon
　Hunter, L. Unpreparing
　Kurlansky, M. Menudo
　Kyle, A. Sex scenes from a chain bookstore
　Langan, J. City of the dog
　Latiolais, M. Boys
　Leland, C. T. In conclusion
　Levinson, R. S. Between sins
　Loomis, M. White night, black horse
　Marcus, H. Swimming

　Marjiyyah, R. The burning of a soul
　McQueen, G. Apolcalypse as foreplay
　Mullins, D. P. Longing to love you
　Neugeboren, J. The debt
　Neugeboren, J. The Turetzky Trio
　Novack, S. Fireflies
　Nutting, A. Bandleader's girlfriend
　Oates, J. C. Death certificate
　Pearlman, E. The ministry of restraint
　Pearlman, E. Purim night
　Pearlman, E. ToyFolk
　Poulson, C. Fishy story
　Roman, I. Zombified
　Ruocco, J. Blood
　Ruocco, J. Lemmings
　Ruocco, J. Pests
　Saare, J. I heart brains
　Senna, D. There, there
　Shapiro, J. Maternity
　Simmons, D. Suitcase
　Simmons, D. Yukon River
　Sneed, C. By the way
　Sneed, C. Quality of life
　Sneed, C. Twelve + Twelve
　Spagnoli, L. A cut above
　Stevens, A. B. Blood not sap
　Swirsky, R. No longer you
　Tillman, L. Dear Ollie
　Tillman, L. The recipe
　Tillman, L. The substitute
　Tóibín, C. Two women
　Tuten, F. Self portrait with beach
　Tuten, F. Voyagers
　Uruq, S. The brightness of his eyes
　Vukcevich, R. The wages of syntax
　Williamson, E. M. Hangman
　Williamson, E. M. Hope, among other vices and
　　virtues
　Winslow, D. After thirty
　Zoboi, I. A. The harem
Lovers of hurricanes. Ely, S.
Lovesey, Peter
　The deadliest tale of all
　　On a raven's wing; new tales in honor of Ed-
　　gar Allan Poe; edited by Stuart M.
　　Kaminsky
　Ghosted
　　Original sins; a Crime Writer's Association
　　anthology; edited by Martin Edwards.
Lovett, Rivka
　Leo's squid
　　Promised lands; new Jewish American fiction
　　on longing and belonging; edited by Derek
　　Rubin.
Low-budget monster flick. Evans, M. A.
Low-hanging fruit. Shepard, J.
Low Sunday, 1950. Trevor, W.
LOW TEMPERATURES
　Nutting, A. Deliverywoman
　Reynolds, A. Sleepover
LOWER EAST SIDE (NEW YORK, N.Y.) *See*
　　New York (N.Y.)—Lower East Side
Lowland sea. Charnas, S. M.
The **loyalty** of Esau Common a fragment. Wells,
　　H. G.
LSD (DRUG)
　Erdrich, L. The reptile garden
Luana the living. Bradbury, R.
Lucho. Engel, P.

Lucientes, Francisco José de Goya y *See* Goya, Francisco, 1746-1828
Lucifer. Zelazny, R.
Luck. Crumley, J.
Luck. Dent, L.
Luck. Trueblood, V.
The **luck** of Irish. Archer, J.
Luck of the dead. Nevins, F. M., Jr.
Lucky penny. Barnes, L.
Lucy Hardin's missing period. Marche, S.
Lukasik-Foss, Tor
   Band names
      Can'tLit; fearless fiction from Broken pencil magazine; edited by Richard Rosenbaum.
Lull. Link, K.
Lullaby. Le Clézio, J.-M. G.
LUMBER INDUSTRY
      See also Loggers
   Kitterman, B. Rivers of wood
LUMBERJACKS *See* Loggers
LUMBERMEN *See* Loggers
Lunacies. Tillman, L.
The **lunatic**. Kirshenbaum, B.
The **lunatics**. Robinson, K. S.
Lunch across the bridge. LaSalle, P.
Lundberg, Kristian
   Savage city, cruel city
      Copenhagen noir; edited by Bo Tao Michaëlis; translated by Mark Kline.
La **lune** t' attend. Beagle, P. S.
Luo, Xuanmin
   Peels for Salt
      Amerasia Journal v37 no1 p191-3 2011
Lupoff, Richard A.
   Patterns
      By hook or by crook and 27 more of the best crime + mystery stories of the year; edited by Ed Gorman and Martin H. Greenberg.
Lutz, John
   Lily & men
      Florida heat wave; [edited and with an] introduction by Michael Lister.
   Poe, Poe, Poe
      On a raven's wing; new tales in honor of Edgar Allan Poe; edited by Stuart M. Kaminsky
   Second story sunlight
      Randisi, R. J. The Shamus winners: America's best private eye stories, volume II, 1996-2009; collected and introduced by Robert J. Randisi; founder, Private Eye Writers of America
   What you don't know can hurt you
      The Shamus winners: America's best private eye stories, volume I: 1982-1995; collected and introduced by Robert J. Randisi; founder, Private Eye Writers of America
Lychack, William
   The architect of flowers
      Lychack, W. The architect of flowers
   Calvary
      Lychack, W. The architect of flowers
   Chickens
      Lychack, W. The architect of flowers
   The ghostwriter
      Lychack, W. The architect of flowers
   Griswald
      Lychack, W. The architect of flowers

Hawkins
   Lychack, W. The architect of flowers
Like a demon
   Lychack, W. The architect of flowers
Love is a temper
   Lychack, W. The architect of flowers
The old woman and her thief
   Lychack, W. The architect of flowers
A stand of fables
   Lychack, W. The architect of flowers
Stolpestad
   Lychack, W. The architect of flowers
Thin end of the wedge
   Lychack, W. The architect of flowers
To the farm
   Lychack, W. The architect of flowers
Lyeskov, Nikolai
   The sentry
      The greatest Russian stories of crime and suspense; edited by Otto Penzler.
Lyman, Jeffrey
   The unreachable voices of ghosts
      L. Ron Hubbard presents Writers of the Future volume XXVII; the year's thirteen best tales from the Writers of the Future international writers' program; illustrated by winners in the Illustrators of the Future international illustrators' program; with essays on writing & illustration by L. Ron Hubbard / Mike Resnick / Robert Cadtillo; edited by K. D. Wentworth
LYSERGIC ACID DIETHYLAMIDE *See* LSD (Drug)

M

M&M World. Walbert, K.
Ma, Van Khang
   A child, a man
      Family of fallen leaves; stories of Agent Orange by Vietnamese writers; edited by Charles Waugh and Huy Lien.
   Thay phung
      Family of fallen leaves; stories of Agent Orange by Vietnamese writers; edited by Charles Waugh and Huy Lien.
Mabanckou, Alain
   We Will Win the World Cup 2010
      The Massachusetts Review v51 no4 p641-4 Wint 2010
Maberry, Jonathan
   Doctor Nine
      The stories (in) between; edited by Greg Schauer, Jeanne B. Benzel, and W. H. Horner.
   Family business
      Z: zombie stories; edited by J. M. Lassen
   Saint John
      The monster's corner; stories through inhuman eyes; edited by Christopher Golden
Mac Adam, Alfred
   (tr.) See Falco, Federico
   (tr.) See Yushimito, Carlos
MACABRE STORIES *See* Horror stories

MacDonald, John D. (John Dann)
Murder in one syllable
  The Black Lizard big book of Black Mask stories; edited and with a foreword by Otto Penzler; introduction by Keith Alan Deutsch.
The **MacGuffin**. Terry, G. P.
The **machine**. Rickert, M.
Machine maid. Lanagan, M.
The **machine** of understanding other people. Somerville, P.
MACHINERY AND CIVILIZATION See Technology and civilization
MACHINERY AND MACHINISTS
Wells, H. G. The Lord of the Dynamos
MacHinery and the cauliflowers. MacLean, A.
MacKenzie, Ian
The Late Interiors
  Gettysburg Review v24 no3 p349-383 S 2011
MacLaverty, Bernard
Language, truth and lockjaw
  The Granta book of the Irish short story; [edited by] Anne Enright.
MacLean, Alistair
MacHinery and the cauliflowers
  The Big book of adventure stories; edited and with a introduction by Otto Penzler; foreword by Douglas Preston.
Macleod, Catherine
Seepage
  Swenson, P. The Best of Talebones; edited by Patrick Swenson.
MacLeod, Ian
The camping Wainwrights
  MacLeod, I. Journeys; stories; by Ian R. Macleod
Elementals
  MacLeod, I. Journeys; stories; by Ian R. Macleod
The English mutiny
  MacLeod, I. Journeys; stories; by Ian R. Macleod
The hob carpet
  MacLeod, I. Journeys; stories; by Ian R. Macleod
The master Miller's tale
  MacLeod, I. Journeys; stories; by Ian R. Macleod
On the sighting of other islands
  MacLeod, I. Journeys; stories; by Ian R. Macleod
Re-crossing the Styx
  The Year's best science fiction: twenty-eighth annual collection; edited by Gardner Dozois.
Second journey of the magus
  MacLeod, I. Journeys; stories; by Ian R. Macleod
Taking good care of myself
  MacLeod, I. Journeys; stories; by Ian R. Macleod
Topping off the spire
  MacLeod, I. Journeys; stories; by Ian R. Macleod

MacLeod, Michael
Horn hunter
  Best of the West 2011; new stories from the wild side of the Missouri; edited by James Thomas and D. Seth Horton; foreword by Ana Castillo.
Mad hare. Boland, J. C.
The **mad** Lomasneys. O'Connor, F.
MADAGASCAR
Delury, J. Nothing of consequence
Madame Cassandra. O'Brien, E.
Madame Poirer's Dog. Winter, K.
Madame Realism's conscience. Tillman, L.
Maddy Dune's first and only spelling bee. O'Sullivan, P.
Madigan, Conor
Klempt, lever puller
  Butler, B. 30 under 30; an anthology of innovative fiction by younger writers; Blake Butler & Lily Hoang, eds.
MADNESS See Insanity; Mental illness
Madness had come with the rain. Lahens, Y.
Madness in the family. Atta, S.
The **Madonna** of Temple Beth Elohim. Papernick, J.
Madre Patria. Engel, P.
Madrid, Fabrizio Mejía
Rancor
  The Virginia Quarterly Review v87 no2 p164-173 Spr 2011
MAFIA
  See also Gangsters
Ayres, D. Seeing nothing
Blauner, P. Thank God for Charlie
Lansdale, J. R. Six-finger Jack
Rankin, I. Graduation day
Maggie and Louis, 1914. Grover, L. L.
Maggio, Christopher
Exclamatory Statements
  River Styx no83 p80-1 2010
MAGI
MacLeod, I. Second journey of the magus
MAGIC
  See also Supernatural phenomena; Talismans; Witchcraft
Anderson, P. Operation changeling
Ball, K. C. Coward's steel
Beagle, P. S. El regalo
Black, H. and Clare, C. The Rowan gentleman
Brennan, M. The twa corbies
Buckell, T. S. The eve of the fall of Habesh
Card, O. S. Jamaica
De Lint, C. A tangle of green men
Doctorow, C. Shannon's law
Dowling, T. The magikkers
Krinard, S. Mist
Lake, J. A different way into the life
Lake, J. Green grass blues
Lake, J. Number of the bus
Lake, J. Witness to the fall
Leahy, K. H. Too fatal a poison
Lima, M. A scent of death
Mamatas, N. Summon, bind, banish
Maxey, J. Greatshadow
McHugh, I. The gifts of Avalae
Monk, D. Christmas card
O'Sullivan, P. Maddy Dune's first and only spelling bee
Pratt, T. A. Mommy issues of the dead

MAGIC—*Continued*

Riley, R. Undying love

Shetterly, W. The sages of elsewhere

Smith, C. A. The coming of the white worm

Smith, C. A. The master of the crabs

Smith, P. A. The perils of twilight

Stevenson, R. L. The bottle imp

Valentine, G. So deep that the bottom could not be seen

Van der Veer, K. L. Hammer song

Wells, H. G. The magic shop

The **magic** goes away. Niven, L.

Magic makeup. Vukcevich, R.

The **magic** pig. Loory, B.

The **magic** shop. Wells, H. G.

Magician. Nutting, A.

The **magician** and the maid and other stories. Yant, C.

MAGICIANS

Beagle, P. S. Sleight of hand

Beagle, P. S. The woman who married the man in the moon

Berman, S. Thimbleriggery and fledgling

Bradley, M. Z. The secret of the Blue Star

Brown, S. The magician's apprentice

Butcher, J. Backup

Butcher, J. Curses

Butcher, J. Day off

Butcher, J. Heorot

Butcher, J. It's my birthday, too

Butcher, J. Last call

Butcher, J. Love hurts

Butcher, J. A restoration of faith

Butcher, J. Something borrowed

Butcher, J. Vignette

Butcher, J. The warrior

Chima, C. W. The trader and the slave

Clarke, S. John Uskglass and the Cumbrian charcoal burner

Farland, D. Feeding the feral children

Ford, J. The sorcerer Minus

Green, S. R. Street wizard

Grossman, L. Endgame

Howard, J. L. The Ereshkigal working

Kennedy, A. L. Vanish

Khanna, R. Card sharp

Kirtley, D. B. Family tree

Lee, Y. H. Counting the shapes

Lindholm, M. Silver lady and the fortyish man

Martin, G. R. R. In the lost lands

Millhauser, S. Eisenheim the illusionist

O'Connor, S. Sawed-in-half girl

Sherman, D. Wizard's apprentice

Silverberg, R. The sorcerer's apprentice

Tidhar, L. The projected girl

Tom, L. Living rooms

Wagner, W. N. The secret of calling rabbits

Willis, D. Escape

Yant, C. The magician and the maid and other stories

The **magician's** apprentice. Brown, S.

Magic's choice. Day, R. W.

The **magikkers**. Dowling, T.

Magliocco, Peter

Monsieur Dombo in glitter town

Dead neon; tales of near-future Las Vegas; edited by Todd James Pierce and Jarret Keene.

The **Magnesia** Tree. Aiken, J.

Mahfouz, Naguib *See* Maḥfūẓ, Najīb, 1911-2006

Maḥfūẓ, Najīb

The seventh heaven

Tablet & pen; literary landscapes from the modern Middle East, a words without borders anthology; edited by Reza Asian.

Mahogany and monogamy. Ayres, J.

The **maiden** flight of McCauley's Bellerophon. Hand, E.

MAIDS (SERVANTS)

See also Cleaning women

Davis, L. The housemaid

Davis, L. Mrs. D and her maids

Ely, S. The fishpond

Hardwick, E. Shot: a New York story

Trevor, W. The dancing-master's music

MAINE

McCracken, E. Property

Nolan, W. F. A woods encounter

Nolan, W. F. Zachry revisited

Robinson, L. Officer Friendly

Spofford, H. E. P. Circumstance

Strout, E. Pharmacy

Mainieri, Nicholas

Bird Shot

The Southern Review (Baton Rouge, La.) v47 no2 p302-7 Spr 2011

Maizell, Sylvia

(tr.) *See* Makanin, Vladimir

Majesty. July, M.

Majesty (Highway 101 South). Shepard, S.

Majka, Sara

Boy with Finch

Gettysburg Review v24 no2 p213-27 Summ 2011

Major crimes. Estleman, L. D.

MAJORCA (SPAIN)

Archer, J. The luck of Irish

Boylan, C. Villa Marta

Makamane, Ret'sepile

Monrovia Scripture

Agni no73 p167-76 2011

Makanin, Vladimir

The Old-Timers

The Kenyon Review v33 no3 p44-61 Summ 2011

Make-a-wish. Neugeboren, J.

Makedonija. Penkov, M.

Makers [excerpt] Doctorow, C.

Makhanlal's Sad Tale. Bose, B.

Making good. Segal, L. G.

Makkai, Rebecca

The briefcase

The best American nonrequired reading 2009; edited by Dave Eggers; introduction by Marjane Satrapi; managing editor, Jesse Nathan

Peter Torrelli, falling apart

The Best American short stories, 2011; selected from U.S. and Canadian magazines by Geraldine Brooks with Heidi Pitlor; with an introduction by Geraldine Brooks.

Maksik, Alexander

A Tobogganist

Harvard Review (1992) no40 p40-67 2011

MALARIA

El Souwaim, M. From the novel The threshold of ashes

MALAYA
    See also Malaysia
MALAYSIA
    Clifford, Sir H. C. The ghoul
    Samarasan, P. Birch memorial
Ma'lesh. Hassan, I.
Malloy, Stacey Leigh
    How She Set Him Up
    Georgia Bar Journal v16 no7 p44-51 Je 2011
Malone, Megan Anderegg
    Death Threat
    The Kenyon Review v33 no1 p6-9 Wint 2011
Malone, Michael
    Christmas spirit
        Christmas at the Mysterious Bookshop; 'tis
        the season to be deadly; stories of mistletoe
        and mayhem from 17 masters of suspense;
        edited by Otto Penzler.
Maloulou. Cerat, M. L.
The **maltese** falcon. Hammett, D.
Malzberg, Barry N.
    (jt. auth) See Pronzini, Bill and Malzberg, Barry
    N.
Mama. Grossman, V. S.
Mamani, Porfirio
    Antes del sueño
    Archipiélago v19 no71 p35-36 Ja-Mr 2011
Mamatas, Nick
    Summon, bind, banish
        Sympathy for the devil; edited by Tim Pratt.
    Your life, fifteen minutes from now
        Swenson, P. The Best of Talebones; edited by
        Patrick Swenson.
MAMMOTHS
    Arnason, E. Mammoths of the great plains
Mammoths of the great plains. Arnason, E.
MAN
    Del Rey, L. Kindness
    Emshwiller, C. Baby
    Emshwiller, C. Strangers
MAN, PREHISTORIC *See* Prehistoric man; Pre-
    historic times
The **man** and the moose. Loory, B.
The **man** and the snake. Bierce, A.
A **man** from her past. Davis, L.
The **Man** I Love. McDonnell, M.
A **man** in our town. Davis, L.
The **man** in the black suit. King, S.
Man in the moon. O'Connor, S.
Man-man. Naipaul, V. S.
Man must live. Mphahlele, E.
A **man** of history. McOmber, A.
Man of steel, woman of Kleenex. Niven, L.
Man on the Run. Ford, K.
The **man** out of the nose. Bierce, A.
The **man** overboard. Bierce, A.
Man O'War. Shepard, S.
The **man** who carved skulls. Parks, R.
The **man** who chose the devil. Deming, R.
The **man** who could work miracles. Wells, H. G.
The **man** who didn't throw himself under a train
    speaks. Blatnik, A.
The **man** who floated in time. Silverberg, R.
The **man** who loved noir. Estleman, L. D.
The **man** who raised rabbits. Kitterman, B.
The **man** who stalked Hyde. Nolan, W. F.
The **man** who swallowed the world. Gifford, B.
The **man** who was always a father. Levine, S.
The **man** who went to China. Loory, B.

The **man** who would be king. Kipling, R.
Man with a club. Matheson, R.
The **man** with a nose. Wells, H. G.
The **man** with one bright eye. Lake, J.
The **man** with the bagful of boomerangs in the
    Bois de Boulogne. McElroy, J.
The **man** with the knives. Kushner, E.
A **man** with two lives. Bierce, A.
The **man** without no kiddleys. Vonnegut, K.
Mance Lipscomb. Trueblood, V.
MANCHESTER (ENGLAND) *See* England—
    Manchester
Mandan, North Dakota (Highway 94). Shepard, S.
Mandrake, Hidden. Browne, L.
MANHATTAN (NEW YORK, N.Y.) *See* New
    York (N.Y.)—Manhattan
Manhattan medley. O'Brien, E.
MANHUNTS
    See also Adventure
    Anderson, P. Eutopia
    Sheckley, R. The prize of peril
    Wells, H. G. Through a window
Manickavel, Kuzhali
    The underground bird sanctuary
    Michigan Quarterly Review v50 no1 p60-5
    Wint 2011
Manilla, Marie
    Amnesty
        Manilla, M. Still life with plums; a collection
        of short stories
    Childproof
        Manilla, M. Still life with plums; a collection
        of short stories
    Counting backwards
        Manilla, M. Still life with plums; a collection
        of short stories
    Crystal City
        Manilla, M. Still life with plums; a collection
        of short stories
    Distillation
        Manilla, M. Still life with plums; a collection
        of short stories
    Get ready
        Manilla, M. Still life with plums; a collection
        of short stories
    Grooming
        Manilla, M. Still life with plums; a collection
        of short stories
    Hand. Me. Down.
        Manilla, M. Still life with plums; a collection
        of short stories
    Still life with plums
        Manilla, M. Still life with plums; a collection
        of short stories
    The wife you wanted
        Manilla, M. Still life with plums; a collection
        of short stories
Mankell, Henning
    Sofia
        Freedom; stories celebrating the Universal
        Declaration of Human Rights; Amnesty In-
        ternational.
Mankiewicz, Don M.
    Odds on death
        The Black Lizard big book of Black Mask
        stories; edited and with a foreword by Otto
        Penzler; introduction by Keith Alan
        Deutsch.

Mann, Ben
Unfamiliar territory
L. Ron Hubbard presents Writers of the Future volume XXVII; the year's thirteen best tales from the Writers of the Future international writers' program; illustrated by winners in the Illustrators of the Future international illustrators' program; with essays on writing & illustration by L. Ron Hubbard / Mike Resnick / Robert Cadtillo; edited by K. D. Wentworth
Manning, Kevin
South
The Virginia Quarterly Review v87 no3 p80-85 Summ 2011
MANORS *See* Houses
Mansbach, Adam
Variations on a fifty-pound bale
Cape Cod noir; edited by David L. Ulin.
MANSIONS *See* Houses
Mantchev, Lisa
(jt. auth) See Grant, James L. and Mantchev, Lisa
Mantel, Hilary
The heart fails without warning
Best European fiction 2011; edited by Aleksandr Hemon; preface by Colum McCann
Mantooth, John
The water tower
The Year's best dark fantasy & horror; edited by Paula Guran
MANUSCRIPTS
Ajvaz, M. The wire book
Ardai, C. Cold reading
Baxt, G. Schemes and variations
Catalona, K. The Sadowsky manifesto
Châteaureynaud, G. O. Delaunay the broker
Emshwiller, C. Modillion
Harwood, J. Face to face
Smith, C. A. The chain of Aforgomon
Yu, C. The book of categories
A **map** back to the world and into your heart. Chau, A.
Map of seventeen. Barzak, C.
Map of the city. Laken, V.
The **Mappist**. Lopez, B.
Marans. Roberts, B.
Marār, Muṣṭafá
Al-Qatāryz
Mārar, M. "The internal pages" and other stories; [by] Mustafa Murrar; edited and translated by Janal Assadi; with assistance from Martha Moody
And we used to squeeze the olives for oil
Mārar, M. "The internal pages" and other stories; [by] Mustafa Murrar; edited and translated by Janal Assadi; with assistance from Martha Moody
The Arabs' battle
Mārar, M. "The internal pages" and other stories; [by] Mustafa Murrar; edited and translated by Janal Assadi; with assistance from Martha Moody
Biar Adass
Mārar, M. "The internal pages" and other stories; [by] Mustafa Murrar; edited and translated by Janal Assadi; with assistance from Martha Moody

The birds
Mārar, M. "The internal pages" and other stories; [by] Mustafa Murrar; edited and translated by Janal Assadi; with assistance from Martha Moody
The court is convening!
Mārar, M. "The internal pages" and other stories; [by] Mustafa Murrar; edited and translated by Janal Assadi; with assistance from Martha Moody
The craving woman
Mārar, M. "The internal pages" and other stories; [by] Mustafa Murrar; edited and translated by Janal Assadi; with assistance from Martha Moody
The day of the calf
Mārar, M. "The internal pages" and other stories; [by] Mustafa Murrar; edited and translated by Janal Assadi; with assistance from Martha Moody
From the bag of others!
Mārar, M. "The internal pages" and other stories; [by] Mustafa Murrar; edited and translated by Janal Assadi; with assistance from Martha Moody
Ghanem's watermelon
Mārar, M. "The internal pages" and other stories; [by] Mustafa Murrar; edited and translated by Janal Assadi; with assistance from Martha Moody
Hard work
Mārar, M. "The internal pages" and other stories; [by] Mustafa Murrar; edited and translated by Janal Assadi; with assistance from Martha Moody
Hello, nations!
Mārar, M. "The internal pages" and other stories; [by] Mustafa Murrar; edited and translated by Janal Assadi; with assistance from Martha Moody
The home-coming guy!
Mārar, M. "The internal pages" and other stories; [by] Mustafa Murrar; edited and translated by Janal Assadi; with assistance from Martha Moody
I want a rifle!
Mārar, M. "The internal pages" and other stories; [by] Mustafa Murrar; edited and translated by Janal Assadi; with assistance from Martha Moody
The internal pages
Mārar, M. "The internal pages" and other stories; [by] Mustafa Murrar; edited and translated by Janal Assadi; with assistance from Martha Moody
It means ... : a pimp
Mārar, M. "The internal pages" and other stories; [by] Mustafa Murrar; edited and translated by Janal Assadi; with assistance from Martha Moody
The last covenant
Mārar, M. "The internal pages" and other stories; [by] Mustafa Murrar; edited and translated by Janal Assadi; with assistance from Martha Moody

Marjiyyah, Rania
  A blessed whore: a story from life
    Loud sounds from the Holy Land; short fiction by Palestinian women; edited and translated by Jamal Assadi with assistance from Martha Moody.
  The burning of a soul
    Loud sounds from the Holy Land; short fiction by Palestinian women; edited and translated by Jamal Assadi with assistance from Martha Moody.
Marks. Blatnik, A.
The **Marlborough** man meets the end. Tremblay, P.
Marley, Louise
  Night shift
    Swenson, P. The Best of Talebones; edited by Patrick Swenson.
Marley's ghost. Boland, J. C.
Marley's package. Boland, J. C.
Marley's woman. Boland, J. C.
Marquand, John P. (John Phillips)
  Caddie crisis
    Golf stories; edited by Charles McGrath.
Marr, Melissa
  Guns for the dead
    Naked city; tales of urban fantasy; edited by Ellen Datlow.
Marra, Anthony
  Chechnya
    Pushcart Prize XXXV: best of the small presses 2011; edited by Bill Henderson with the Pushcart Prize editors.
MARRIAGE
    See also Childless marriage; Divorce; Family life; Husband and wife; Interfaith marriage; Marriage problems; Weddings
Apple, M. Business talk
Atta, S. The miracle worker
Barnes, J. Marriage lines
Barnes, J. Pulse
Beattie, A. The burning house
Beattie, A. In the white night
Beattie, A. Running dreams
Beattie, A. Times
Beattie, A. The working girl
Blatnik, A. Thirty years
Brennan, M. An attack of hunger
Campbell-Such, J. The Napoleon difference
Doctorow, E. L. Assimilation
Doyle, R. The slave
Doyle, R. Sleep
Drabble, M. The dower house at Kellynch: a Somerset romance
Earley, T. Mr. Tall
Jackson, H. H. The prince's little sweetheart
Keret, E. Crazy glue
Leland, C. T. Fellatio
Levine, S. The kidney problem
Nagai, M. Love story
Osondu, E. C. I will lend you my wife
Packer, A. Dwell time
Pearlman, E. Elder Jinks
Phillips, H. The brides
Qiu Xiaolong. Lottery
Qiu Xiaolong. Uniform
Ray, S. How we fall
Ray, S. Mrs. Secrest
Ray, S. The way home

Riippi, J. Something about marriage, pt 2
Riippi, J. Something about marriage, pt 3
Riippi, J. Something about rings
Roberge, R. Love and hope and sex and dreams
Ross, A. In the basement
Row, J. Sheep may safely graze
Sa'id, M. A. Hayat: a short story
Schappell, E. A dog story
Senna, D. Replacement theory
Senna, D. What's the matter with Helga and Dave?
Shapiro, J. The old bean
Shapiro, J. Tiger beat
Simmons, D. Letters
Sirhan, A. The wedding's night and the sacrifice
Snyder, M. The monkey bride
Sterling, P. Impaired
Tem, S. R. Miri
Theodore-Pharel, M. K. Mercy at the gate
Tillman, L. Playing hurt
Tokarczuk, O. The ugliest woman in the world
Trevor, W. The piano tuner's wives
Trevor, W. The potato dealer
Trueblood, V. Phantom father
Trueblood, V. Suitors
Tuck, L. Ice
Vaughn, V. Some new blood
Wells, H. G. The devotee of art
Wieland, L. First, marriage
Williamson, E. M. Mr. Murphy's wedding
Willis, M. S. Pie Knob
MARRIAGE, CHILDLESS *See* Childless marriage
MARRIAGE, INTERFAITH *See* Interfaith marriage
Marriage. Kennedy, A. L.
MARRIAGE COUNSELING *See* Marriage problems
MARRIAGE CUSTOMS
        China
Qiu Xiaolong. Housing assignment
        Japan
Hemmingson, M. The keepers
Marriage lines. Barnes, J.
MARRIAGE PROBLEMS
    See also Divorce; Family life; Interfaith marriage; Love affairs
Adichie, C. N. Ceiling
Aiken, J. Model wife
Allen, D. Among the missing
Allen, D. End of his tether
Atta, S. Hailstones on Zamfara
Barrett, L. When, he wondered
Beattie, A. Downhill
Beattie, A. Fancy flights
Beattie, A. Home to Marie
Beattie, A. The lawn party
Beattie, A. Secrets and surprises
Beattie, A. Shifting
Beattie, A. Summer people
Beattie, A. Vermont
Beattie, A. Waiting
Beattie, A. Wanda's
Bhattacharya, N. Hissing cobras
Bierce, A. An affair of outposts
Bill, F. Officer down (tweakers)
Bill, F. A rabbit in the lettuce patch
Bingham, S. Rachel's island
Bingham, S. Red car

MARRIAGE PROBLEMS—*Continued*

Bissell, T. Expensive trips nowhere
Blatnik, A. Say that
Blumlein, M. Fidelity: a primer
Boland, J. C. The passenger
Bowen, E. Summer night
Brendel, K. Somewhere
Chaon, D. I demand to know where you're taking me
Chau, A. A map back to the world and into your heart
Chopin, K. The storm
Chowdhury, S. Hostel
Chughtai, I. The quilt
Davis, L. Visit to her husband
Dixon, S. Nothing new
Dixon, S. The phone
Dixon, S. Walt
Doctorow, E. L. Jolene: a life
Doctorow, E. L. Wakefield
Doyle, R. Ash
Doyle, R. The dog
Doyle, R. The joke
Dubus, A. Delivering
Eisenberg, D. The flaw in the design
Ely, S. Guatemala City
Fallon, S. You survived the war, now survive the homecoming
Ford, R. Under the radar
Furman, L. The mother who stayed
Fusilli, J. Digby, attorney at law
Galchen, R. The entire northern side was covered with fire
Gilley, T. Vanishing world
Gold, H. L. Love in the dark
Gordimer, N. Friday's footprint
Gordimer, N. The generation gap
Gordimer, N. Why haven't you written?
Grytten, F. Hotel by a railroad
Hannah, B. Get some young
Hannah, B. Love too long
Hardwick, E. The oak and the axe
Heathcock, A. The staying freight
Hemmingson, M. Adventure
Hemmingson, M. Cyclops
Hemmingson, M. Forbidden scenes of affection
Hemmingson, M. Looking for Wanda beyond the Salton Sea
Hunt, S. Beast
Hurston, Z. N. Sweat
Keegan, C. Men and women
Kennedy, A. L. Wasps
Kennedy, A. L. What becomes
Kitterman, B. The gospel according to Octavio Ruiz
Kitterman, B. In dog years
Kitterman, B. Mediators
Kostival, B. Islanders
Kurlansky, M. Crème brûlée
Kyle, A. Sex scenes from a chain bookstore
Kyle, A. Take care
Lahiri, J. Interpreter of maladies
Lahiri, J. A temporary matter
Langan, J. The third always beside you
Latiolais, M. Crazy
Le Guin, U. K. She unnames them
Leland, C. T. The woman who loved Claude Rains
Matheson, R. CU: Mannix

McKinty, A. Diarmaid and Grainne
Mullins, D. P. First sight
Munro, A. Material
Naipaul, V. S. Love, love, love, alone
Naipaul, V. S. Until the soldiers came
Neugeboren, J. Overseas
Novack, S. Cerulean skies
Novack, S. Save my soul
Novack, S. The thin border between here and disaster
Nutting, A. Gardener
Oates, J. C. Babysitter
Oates, J. C. Tetanus
O'Brien, E. Madame Cassandra
O'Connor, S. Aunt Jules
Osondu, E. C. The men they married
Papernick, J. What is it then, between us?
Parker, D. Big blonde
Phillips, H. The fights
Popov, A. Plumbers
Roberge, R. Do not concern yourself with things Lee Nading has left out
Rodoreda, M. Before I die
Rodoreda, M. The beginning
Rodoreda, M. Blood
Rodoreda, M. The salamander
Salter, J. My lord you
Schirach, F. v. Fähner
Schmitt, E.-E. Perfect crime
Schwarzschild, E. Midhusband
Shepard, S. Land of the living
Shipp, J. C. Just another vampire story
Silverberg, R. Jennifer's lover
Silverberg, R. Needle in a timestack
Stovall, T. Breakin' dishes
Treadway, J. Dear Nicole
Treadway, J. Shirley wants her nickel back
Trevor, W. A friendship
Trevor, W. Old flame
Trevor, W. The room
Trevor, W. Rose wept
Trueblood, V. Choice in dreams
Trueblood, V. Mance Lipscomb
Turner, A. Fool in search of a country song
Vint, T. Beyond the window a park is dimming
Vonnegut, K. With his hand on the throttle
Waite, U. Don't look away
Warsh, L. Mysterioso
Watkins, M. Two midnights in a jug
Watson, B. Visitation
Wells, H. G. A family elopement
Wells, H. G. How Gabriel became Thompson
Wells, H. G. Le mari terrible
Wells, H. G. The purple pileus
Wieland, L. Vision
Willis, D. Caught
Willis, D. The separation
Willis, D. Traces
Wilson, L. Precious things
Yamamoto, H. Seventeen syllables
Yezbek, S. From the novel The scent of cinnamon
Yezierska, A. Wild winter love
Zeltserman, D. Bad move

MARRIAGE PROPOSALS

Atkins, E. The wrong side of Mr. Right
Baker, L. Crash & tell
Saunders, N. Tears fall on Orkney
Solender, E. A. Second thoughts

Marrying Damian. Trevor, W.

Mars, Kettly
Paradise Inn
Haiti noir; edited by Edwidge Danticat

MARS (PLANET)
Baker, K. Attlee and the long walk
Barnes, J. Martian heart
Baxter, S. On Chryse Plain
Bradbury, R. The piper
Bradbury, R. The piper (first version)
Doctorow, C. Martian chronicles
Klages, E. Goodnight moons
Kress, N. First principle
McDonald, I. Digging
Niven, L. The hole man
Reed, R. A history of terraforming
Reynolds, A. The old man and the Martian sea
Roberson, C. Larp of Mars
Robinson, K. S. Discovering life
Steele, A. M. The emperor of Mars
Swirsky, R. The taste of promises

Marshall, Alexandra
Come and Get Me
Five Points v12 no3 p114-18 2009

Marshall, Brenda A.
In Which a Coffin is a Bed but an Ox is not a Coffin
Michigan Quarterly Review v49 no3 p309, 308, 310-24 Summ 2010

Marsten, Richard, 1926-2005
For works written by this author under other names see McBain, Ed, 1926-2005

Martel, Yann
The moon above his head
Freedom; stories celebrating the Universal Declaration of Human Rights; Amnesty International.

MARTENS
Kronauer, B. Martens and rabbits

Martens and rabbits. Kronauer, B.

MARTHA'S VINEYARD (MASS.)
Mansbach, A. Variations on a fifty-pound bale

MARTIAL ARTS
Benali, A. From the novel The trip to the slaughterhouse

The **Martian**. Loory, B.

Martian chronicles. Doctorow, C.

Martian heart. Barnes, J.

MARTIANS
See also Interplanetary visitors; Mars (Planet)
Dick, P. K. The crystal crypt
Loory, B. The end of it all
Loory, B. The Martian
Okorafor, N. Wahala

Martín, Andreu
The law of escape
Barcelona noir; edited by Adriana V. Lopez & Cartmen Ospina; translated by Achy Obejas.

Martin, Chelsea
At the end of this story the door will open and under eight seconds will have passed
Martin, C. The really funny thing about apathy
The consumption
Martin, C. The really funny thing about apathy

McDonald's is impossible
Martin, C. The really funny thing about apathy
Moments before the future begins to approach
Martin, C. The really funny thing about apathy

Martin, George R. R.
Dark, dark were the tunnels
The end of the world; stories of the apocalypse; edited by Martin H. Greenberg.
In the lost lands
The way of the wizard; edited by John Joseph Adams.

Martin, Hugh
Three months before we ship to Iraq
River Styx no85 p86 2011

Martin, Lee
Light Opera
The Georgia Review v65 no1 p186-208 Spr 2011

Martin, Rafe
Gentle Heart [With commentary]
Parabola v35 no3 p75-9 Fall 2010

Martin, Tomas L.
Activation
Nature v467 p362 S 16 2010

Martin, Wolfe
Home
Five Points v13 no1 p130-42 2009

Martínez-Salguero, Jaime
Los fundadores
Archipiélago v19 no72 p12-14 Ap-Je 2011

Martinovich, Victor
Taboo
Best European fiction 2011; edited by Aleksandr Hemon; preface by Colum McCann

MARTYRS
Ibrāhīm, H. A holy site

MARX BROTHERS
About
Kessel, J. Faustfeathers

MARY, BLESSED VIRGIN, SAINT
About
Jones, G. A. Grazing the long acre
Plummer, T. M. What would Mary do: a Christmas story

Mary, Mary, shut the door. Schutz, B. M.

MARY TYLER MOORE SHOW (TELEVISION PROGRAM)
Davis, L. Glenn Gould

MARYLAND
Baltimore
Mullen, C. Poetic justice

Marzipan lambs. Ruocco, J.

Mas, Alexandre
Bedrock
The Antioch Review v68 no4 p704-17 Fall 2010

MASKS (FOR THE FACE)
Foster, E. Sinner, baker, fabulist, priest; red mask, gentleman, beast
Grossman, L. Sir Ranulph Wykeham-Rackham, GBE, a.k.a. Roboticus the All-Knowing
Rodoreda, M. Carnival

MASKS (SCULPTURE)
Silverberg, R. Not our brother

MASOCHISM
Holm, G. When it's tough out there

Mason, Bobbie Ann
Shiloh
Best of times, worst of times; contemporary American short stories from the new Gilded Age; edited by Wendy Martin and Cecelia Tichi.
Mason, Daniel
The miraculous discovery of Psammetichus I
Harper's v322 no1930 p62-5 Mr 2011
Mason, Elmer Brown
The golden anaconda
The Big book of adventure stories; edited and with a introduction by Otto Penzler; foreword by Douglas Preston.
MASSACHUSETTS
See also Martha's Vineyard (Mass.); Nantucket Island (Mass.)
Boland, J. C. Evidence seen
Cameron, D. Ardent
Greenman, B. Viva Regina
Horn, D. Shtetl World
Jewett, S. O. The circus at Denby
Jones, K. The occidental tourist
King, S. Big driver
Lahiri, J. Gogol
Love, Y. G. Lonely, lonely, lonely is the Lord of Hosts
Phelps, E. S. The tenth of January
Rickert, M. The Christmas witch
Vonnegut, K. Guardian of the person
Wieland, L. Quickening
Boston
DuBois, B. The dark island
Dufresne, J. The cross-eyed bear
Hardwick, E. The final conflict
Lehane, D. Animal rescue
Pearlman, E. Girl in blue with brown bag
Pearlman, E. Settlers
Thon, M. R. Home
Thon, M. R. Xmas, Jamaica Plain
18th century
Cameron, D. Femme sole
Cape Cod
Baker, L. At sea
Berry, J. Twenty-eight scenes for neglected guests
East, E. Second chance
Greenland, S. Bad night in Hyannisport
Hastings, W. Ten-year plan
Skurnick, L. Spectacle Pond
Tremblay, P. Nineteen snapshots of Dennisport
Ulin, D. L. La jetée
Vonnegut, K. Money talks
Zeltserman, D. When death shines bright
Provincetown
Leebron, F. G. The exchange student
MASSACRES
Child, L. M. F. The church in the wilderness
Fried, S. Frost mountain picnic massacre
Gordimer, N. Oral history
Nagai, M. Song
MASSEURS
Qiu Xiaolong. Foot masseur
The **master** magician. Worts, G. F.
The **master** Miller's tale. MacLeod, I.
The **master** of Doornvlei. Mphahlele, E.
The **Master** of Patina. Harvey, M.
The **master** of the crabs. Smith, C. A.

Masters, Hilary
Wonder Bread
Ploughshares v36 no4 p74-7 Wint 2010/2011
Mastroianni, Joe
Jordan's waterhammer
Brave new worlds; edited by John Joseph Adams.
MASTURBATION
Hunter, L. Loofah
Matar, Hisham
Naima
The New Yorker v86 no45 p62-71 Ja 24 2011
Matas, Enrique Vila- *See* Vila-Matas, Enrique, 1948-
Matera, Lia
Dead drunk
Randisi, R. J. The Shamus winners: America's best private eye stories, volume II, 1996-2009; collected and introduced by Robert J. Randisi; founder, Private Eye Writers of America
Material. Munro, A.
The **maternal** instinct. Naipaul, V. S.
Maternity. Shapiro, J.
Mates. Pearlman, E.
MATHEMATICS
Lee, Y. H. Counting the shapes
Matheson, Richard
1984 1/2
Matheson, R. Matheson uncollected: volume one
Counterfeit bills
Matheson, R. Matheson uncollected: volume one
CU: Mannix
Matheson, R. Matheson uncollected: volume two
An element never forgets
Matheson, R. Matheson uncollected: volume two
Getting together
Matheson, R. Matheson uncollected: volume two
Haircut
Matheson, R. Matheson uncollected: volume two
He wanted to live
Matheson, R. Matheson uncollected: volume one
The house of the dead
Matheson, R. Matheson uncollected: volume two
The hunt
Matheson, R. Matheson uncollected: volume two
The last blah in the etc
Matheson, R. Matheson uncollected: volume one
Leo rising
Matheson, R. Matheson uncollected: volume two
Life size
Matheson, R. Matheson uncollected: volume one
Man with a club
Matheson, R. Matheson uncollected: volume one

Matheson, Richard—*Continued*
Mountains of the mind
    Matheson, R. Matheson uncollected: volume
    two
Now die in it
    Matheson, R. Matheson uncollected: volume
    two
Person to person
    Matheson, R. Matheson uncollected: volume
    two
Portrait
    Matheson, R. Matheson uncollected: volume
    two
Pride
    Matheson, R. Matheson uncollected: volume
    one
The prisoner
    Matheson, R. Matheson uncollected: volume
    one
Professor Fritz and the runaway house
    Matheson, R. Matheson uncollected: volume
    one
Purge among peanuts
    Matheson, R. Matheson uncollected: volume
    one
Red is the color of desire
    Matheson, R. Matheson uncollected: volume
    two

Matheson, Richard and Matheson, Richard Christian
Where there's a will
    Matheson, R. Matheson uncollected: volume
    two

Matheson, Richard Christian
Transfiguration
    The Best horror of the year: volume three;
    edited by Ellen Datlow.
(jt. auth) See Matheson, Richard and Matheson,
    Richard Christian

Mathews, Aidan
Train tracks
    The Granta book of the Irish short story; [ed-
    ited by] Anne Enright.
Matilda, or, A Man of Maxims. VanDonkelaar, C.
Matinee. Coover, R.
MATRIARCHS *See* Mothers
MATRIARCHY
    Emshwiller, C. Debut
MATRICIDE *See* Parricide
Mattaponi Queen. Boggs, B.
A **matter** of form. Gold, H. L.
Matthews, A. J. *See* Hautala, Rick
Maupassant, Guy de
The hand
    The book of the living dead; edited by John
    Richard Stephens.
Mautam. Yost, D.
Max. Ockert, J.
Maxey, James
Greatshadow
    Blood & devotion; tales of epic fantasy; ed-
    ited by W.H. Horner; illustrated by Nicole
    Cardiff
Maxine. Gordon, P.
Maxwell, Mary Elizabeth *See* Braddon, M. E.,
    1837-1915

May, Rachel
Bee & grim
    Michigan Quarterly Review v50 no1 p50-9
    Wint 2011
May. Olsen, L.
May I not seem to have lived. Cardinale, J.
May nobody save anything!. Marär, M.
Maybe another long march across China 80,000
    strong. Emshwiller, C.
Maybe We're the Angels. Jones, J. P.
Maynard. Atwell, M. S.
Mayo, Jim, 1908-1988
    *For works written by this author under oth-
    er names see* L'Amour, Louis, 1908-
    1988
MAYORS
    Aiken, J. The Paper Queen
McAdam, Jeanine
Inhuman resources
    Hungry for your love; an anthology of
    zombie romance; edited by Lori Perkins.
McAllister, John
Bog man
    Requiems for the departed; edited by Gerard
    Brennan & Mike Stone.
McBain, Ed
I saw mommy killing Santa Claus
    Christmas at the Mysterious Bookshop; 'tis
    the season to be deadly; stories of mistletoe
    and mayhem from 17 masters of suspense;
    edited by Otto Penzler.
McCabe, Eugene
Music at Annahullion
    The Granta book of the Irish short story; [ed-
    ited by] Anne Enright.
McCann, Colum
Everything in this country must
    The Granta book of the Irish short story; [ed-
    ited by] Anne Enright.
McCann, Jessica
Night Window
    River Styx no83 p84-5 2010
McCarthy, T. C.
Private Exploration
    Nature v474 no7349 p120 Je 2 2011
McChrystal, Stanley
Sad Lieutenant [Excerpt from story]
    Harper's v321 p22-3 S 2010
McConnell, Sean
The Evolution Rapist
    The Literary Review (Madison, N.J.) v54 no2
    p21-35 Wint 2011
McCormack, Derek
Scarlatina!
    Can'tLit; fearless fiction from Broken pencil
    magazine; edited by Richard Rosenbaum.
McCormack, Una
The sea is not full
    Requiems for the departed; edited by Gerard
    Brennan & Mike Stone.
McCoy, Horace
Dirty work
    The Black Lizard big book of Black Mask
    stories; edited and with a foreword by Otto
    Penzler; introduction by Keith Alan
    Deutsch.

McCoy, Maureen
Your Children and Mine
The Antioch Review v68 no3 p408-35 Summ
2010

McCracken, Elizabeth
Property
The Best American short stories, 2011; select-
ed from U.S. and Canadian magazines by
Geraldine Brooks with Heidi Pitlor; with an
introduction by Geraldine Brooks.
Granta no111 p169-88 Summ 2010

McCray, Cheyenne
Double dead
Chicks kick butt; edited by Rachel Caine and
Kerrie L. Hughes.

McCrumb, Sharyn
Rattler and the Mothman
The monster's corner; stories through inhu-
man eyes; edited by Christopher Golden

McCullers, Carson
The jockey
I found this funny; my favorite pieces of humor and some that may not be funny at all;
edited by Judd Apatow.

McCulley, Johnston
Zorro deals with treason
The Big book of adventure stories; edited and
with a introduction by Otto Penzler; foreword by Douglas Preston.

McDonald, Craig
These two guys . . .
Blood, guts, & whiskey; edited by Todd Rob-
inson; introduction by Max Allan Collins.

McDonald, Ian
Digging
Life on Mars: tales from the new frontier; an
original science fiction anthology; edited by
Jonathan Strahan

McDonald, Sandra
Bluebeard by the sea
Swenson, P. The Best of Talebones; edited by
Patrick Swenson.
Seven sexy cowboy robots
The Best science fiction and fantasy of the
year: volume five; edited by Jonathan
Strahan.

McDonald's is impossible. Martin, C.

McDonnell, Madeline
The Man I Love
Harvard Review (1992) no40 p142-63 2011

McDowell, Drew
Dress Up
Dalhousie Review v90 no2 p269-79 Summ
2010

McElrea, Karen
Nine ball tourney, lotza prizes
Can'tLit; fearless fiction from Broken pencil
magazine; edited by Richard Rosenbaum.

McElroy, Joseph
Annals of plagiary
McElroy, J. Night soul and other stories
The campaign trail
McElroy, J. Night soul and other stories
Canoe repair
McElroy, J. Night soul and other stories
Character
McElroy, J. Night soul and other stories
The last disarmament but one
McElroy, J. Night soul and other stories

The man with the bagful of boomerangs in the
Bois de Boulogne
McElroy, J. Night soul and other stories
Mister X
McElroy, J. Night soul and other stories
Night soul
McElroy, J. Night soul and other stories
No man's land
McElroy, J. Night soul and other stories
Particle of difference
McElroy, J. Night soul and other stories
Silk, or the woman with the bike
McElroy, J. Night soul and other stories
The unknown kid
McElroy, J. Night soul and other stories

McFadden, Dennis
Chickens' Revenge
Confrontation no108 p228-40 Fall 2010

McGahern, John
The key
The Granta book of the Irish short story; [ed-
ited by] Anne Enright.

McGarry, Jean
Dream date
McGarry, J. Ocean state; stories
Family happiness
McGarry, J. Ocean state; stories
Family romance
McGarry, J. Ocean state; stories
A full house
McGarry, J. Ocean state; stories
Gold leaf
McGarry, J. Ocean state; stories
The night before
McGarry, J. Ocean state; stories
Ocean state
McGarry, J. Ocean state; stories
The offering
McGarry, J. Ocean state; stories
The sweetness of her name
McGarry, J. Ocean state; stories
Transference
McGarry, J. Ocean state; stories
The tree of life
McGarry, J. Ocean state; stories
The wedding gowns
McGarry, J. Ocean state; stories
Welcome wherever he went
McGarry, J. Ocean state; stories

McGarry, Terry
God of exile
Swenson, P. The Best of Talebones; edited by
Patrick Swenson.

McGilloway, Brian
Fisherman's blues
Requiems for the departed; edited by Gerard
Brennan & Mike Stone.

McGoran, Jonathan
Appetite
The stories (in) between; edited by Greg
Schauer, Jeanne B. Benzel, and W. H.
Horner.

McGrath, Charles
Sneaking on
Golf stories; edited by Charles McGrath.

MCGRAW, ERIN
Punchline
The Kenyon Review v33 no4 p35-48 Fall
2011

McGuane, Thomas
Cowboy
Blue collar, white collar, no collar; stories of work; edited by Richard Ford.

The Good Samaritan
The New Yorker v87 no10 p66-73 Ap 25 2011
McGuill, Robert
The Outskirts of Nowhere
Southwest Review v96 no1 p33-45 2011
McHugh, Ian
The gifts of Avalae
Blood & devotion; tales of epic fantasy; edited by W.H. Horner; illustrated by Nicole Cardiff
McHugh, Maura
Vic
The Year's best dark fantasy & horror; edited by Paula Guran
McHugh, Maureen
The naturalist
The Best science fiction and fantasy of the year: volume five; edited by Jonathan Strahan.
McIntosh, Will
Bridesicle
The Nebula Awards showcase; edited by Kevin J. Anderson.
McKinty, Adrian
Diarmaid and Grainne
Requiems for the departed; edited by Gerard Brennan & Mike Stone.
McLaverty, Michael
The road to the shore
The Granta book of the Irish short story; [edited by] Anne Enright.
McLean, Anne
(tr.) See Coelho, Oliverio
McLennan, Jeanna
The Southwest Rapist
Can'tLit; fearless fiction from Broken pencil magazine; edited by Richard Rosenbaum.
McLeod, Charles
The State Bird of Minnesota
Michigan Quarterly Review v49 no3 p325-34 Summ 2010
McIlveen, John
Succumb
The monster's corner; stories through inhuman eyes; edited by Christopher Golden
McLoughlin, Margo
(tr.) See The antelope birth
McMahon, Gary
Dead to the world
Zombies: the recent dead; edited by Paula Guran.
Strange scenes from an unfinished film
The Year's best dark fantasy & horror; edited by Paula Guran
McMahon, Pat *See* Hoch, Edward D., 1930-2008
McManus, John
The Ninety-Fifth Percentile
Harvard Review (1992) no39 p36-54 2010
McMillian, Raven
Escambia counties
Florida heat wave; [edited and with an] introduction by Michael Lister.
McNeile, Herman Cyril *See* Sapper, 1888-1937

McNisei. Yamauchi, W.
McOmber, Adam
The automatic garden
McOmber, A. This new & poisonous air; stories
Beneath us
McOmber, A. This new & poisonous air; stories
Egyptomania
McOmber, A. This new & poisonous air; stories
Fall, Orpheum
McOmber, A. This new & poisonous air; stories
Gardens of the moon
McOmber, A. This new & poisonous air; stories
A man of history
McOmber, A. This new & poisonous air; stories
A memory of his rising
McOmber, A. This new & poisonous air; stories
Of wool
McOmber, A. This new & poisonous air; stories
There are no bodies such as this
McOmber, A. This new & poisonous air; stories
This new and poisonous air
McOmber, A. This new & poisonous air; stories
McPhail, Mike
Beyond imagine
The stories (in) between; edited by Greg Schauer, Jeanne B. Benzel, and W. H. Horner.
McPherson, James Alan
A solo song: for Doc
Blue collar, white collar, no collar; stories of work; edited by Richard Ford.
McQueen, Gina
Apolcalypse as foreplay
Hungry for your love; an anthology of zombie romance; edited by Lori Perkins.
McReynolds, Erin
VIVA!
The North American Review v296 no1 p25-9 Wint 2011
Me am Petri. Hayes, M.
Me and Miss Mandible. Barthelme, D.
Meade, Elizabeth Thomasina *See* Meade, L. T., 1854-1914
Meade, L. T.
The Blue laboratory
The dreaming sex; early tales of scientific imagination by women; edited by Mike Ashley.
Meades, Christopher
A BAD DAY FOR THE ZEBRAS
Dalhousie Review v91 no1 p53-59 Spr 2011
Meadowdene Estates. Villegas, H.
Mean green. Shepard, S.

Means, David
The junction
The Pen/O.Henry Prize stories 2011; chosen and with an introduction by Laura Furman; with essays on the stories thety admire most by jurors A. M. Homes, Manuel Muñoz, Christine Schutt
El Morro
The New Yorker v87 no25 p62-68 Ag 29 2011
The tree line, Kansas, 1934
The New Yorker v86 no33 p74-7 O 25 2010
MEAT INDUSTRY
Levine, S. Sausage
Meat, my husband. Davis, L.
The **meat** tree. Jones, S. G.
The **mechanical** aviary of emperor Jalal-ud-din Muhammad Akbar. Narayan, S.
The **mechanical** genius. Naipaul, V. S.
MECHANICS (PERSONS)
Boggs, B. It won't be long
Jones, G. A. The universe of things
Leland, C. T. The woman who loved Claude Rains
Meddler. Dick, P. K.
Medea. Petrushevskaya, L. and others
Mediators. Kitterman, B.
Medic!. Perin, A.
MEDICAL LIFE *See* Physicians
MEDICAL RESEARCH *See* Medicine—Research
MEDICAL STUDENTS *See* Students
MEDICINE
See also Surgery
Research
Baker, L. Experimental Maria
Sedia, E. 1972: the lichenologist's visit
MEDICINE, EXPERIMENTAL *See* Medicine—Research
MEDICINE, PRACTICE OF *See* Physicians
MEDICINES, PATENT, PROPRIETARY, ETC.
Wells, H. G. The truth about Pyecraft
Medieval. Claus, H.
MEDIEVAL LIFE *See* Middle Ages
MEDIUMS *See* Spiritualism
MEDUSA (LEGENDARY CHARACTER)
Pinborough, S. The screaming room
Roscoe, T. Snake-head
Medusa's Daughter. Rothenberg, P.
Meek, James
The kind of neighbor you used to have
Freedom; stories celebrating the Universal Declaration of Human Rights; Amnesty International.
Meet the natives. Dixon, S.
Meet you at the door. Hill, L.
The **meeting**. Davis, L.
A **meeting** in space. Gordimer, N.
Meeting the Dog Girls. Terry, G. P.
MEETINGS
Davis, L. The meeting
Sterling, P. The small bridge
Mehrotra, Palash Krishna
Fit of rage
Delhi noir; edited by Hirsh Sawhney
Mehta, Rahul
A better life
Mehta, R. Quarantine; stories

The better person
Mehta, R. Quarantine; stories
Citizen
Mehta, R. Quarantine; stories
The cure
Mehta, R. Quarantine; stories
Floating
Mehta, R. Quarantine; stories
Quarantine
Mehta, R. Quarantine; stories
Ten thousand years
Mehta, R. Quarantine; stories
What we mean
Mehta, R. Quarantine; stories
Yours
Mehta, R. Quarantine; stories
Meikle, William
Twitterspace
Nature v477 no7364 p364 S 15 2011
Meirose, Jim
Breakfast III
Dalhousie Review v90 no3 p355-60 Aut 2010
Meles vulgaris. Boyle, P.
Melinda. Doenges, J.
Melko, Paul
Ten sigmas
Swenson, P. The Best of Talebones; edited by Patrick Swenson.
Melnick, M. A.
Obediently Yours
The Literary Review (Madison, N.J.) v53 no4 p15-24 Summ 2010
Melnyczuk, Askold
We Are Family
The Antioch Review v69 no1 p115-39 Wint 2011
Melting point. Blatnik, A.
Meltzer, Daniel
Heads You Lose
Confrontation no108 p183-94 Fall 2010
Melville, Herman
Bartleby the scrivener
21 essential American short stories; edited by Leslie M. Pockell
Members only. Archer, J.
Memed, my hawk. Yaşar Kemal
Memento mori. Leland, C. T.
Memoir of a deer woman. Rickert, M.
Memoirs of a yellow dog. Henry, O.
Memories of the decadence. Kunzru, H.
MEMORY
See also Amnesia
Bear, E. King pole, gallows pole, bottle tree
Blake, G. The old and the lost
Bowes, R. I needs must part, the policeman said
Davis, L. Almost no memory
Davis, L. Happy memories
Dozois, G. R. A dream at noonday
Haldeman, J. Sleeping dogs
Jones, G. A. Collision
Kennedy, A. L. Saturday teatime
Kurlansky, M. Red sea salt
Lahens, Y. And all this unease
Lychack, W. Griswald
McElroy, J. Annals of plagiary
O'Brien, E. My two mother
O'Brien, E. Send my roots rain
Rodoreda, M. The mirror
Salaets, L. The black side of memory

MEMORY—*Continued*
Slouka, M. The hare's mask
Sneed, C. By the way
Sneed, C. Interview with the second wife
Sterling, P. Deja vu
Tidhar, L. The river came; fragmented recall
Tidhar, L. The spontaneous knotting of an agitated string
Treadway, J. Oregon
Treadway, J. Testomony
Trevor, W. Folie à deux
Tuten, F. Self portrait with Sicily
Vukcevich, R. Strong suits
Willis, D. Remember, relive
A **memory**. Guerrero, L.
Memory and desire. Mulkerns, V.
A **memory** of his rising. McOmber, A.
A **memory** of wind. Swirsky, R.
MEMPHIS (TENN.) *See* Tennessee—Memphis
Memphis. Novack, S.
MEN
    See also Single men
Blatnik, A. All over
Doyle, R. Bullfighting
Emshwiller, C. Abominable
Hodge, B. When the silence gets too loud
Kronauer, B. Archer on horseback [excerpt]
Levine, S. Pat Smash
Levine, S. The tree
Manilla, M. Grooming
Qiu Xiaolong. Chinese chess
Ray, S. The miracles of Vincent Van Gogh
Roberge, R. Burn ward
Sands, B. A visitor's guide to lawn guyland
Tran, V. Kubla Khan
Men and women. Keegan, C.
Men of Ireland. Trevor, W.
The **men** they married. Osondu, E. C.
Men with Wings. Stone, L. F.
Mena, María Cristina
The vine-leaf
    The vintage book of American women writers; edited and with an introduction by Elaine Showalter.
Menace react. Dick, P. K.
Menders. Monk, D.
Mending. Bingham, S.
Menéndez, Ana
The shunting trains trace iron labyrinths
    Boston Review v36 no3 p42-5 My/Je 2011
You Are the Heirs of All My Terrors
    World Literature Today v84 no5 p28-9 S/O 2010
Mengestu, Dinaw
An honest exit
    20 under 40; stories from the New Yorker; edited by Deborah Treisman.
    The New Yorker v86 no20 p72-8, 80-1 Jl 12-19 2010
Meno, Joe
Children are the only ones who blush
    Pushcart Prize XXXV: best of the small presses 2011; edited by Bill Henderson with the Pushcart Prize editors.
Homo Sapiens
    TriQuarterly v138 32439 bytes Summ/Fall 2010
MENSERVANTS
Naipaul, V. S. One out of many

MENSTRUATION
Emshwiller, C. I love you
Hunter, L. Us
MENTAL DEPRESSION
Allen, D. Fishing with Alex
Davis, L. Therapy
Tremblay, P. Rhymes with Jew
MENTAL DISORDERS *See* Mental illness
Mental health and its alternative. Emshwiller, C.
MENTAL HOSPITALS *See* Mentally ill—Care and treatment
MENTAL ILLNESS
    See also Hallucinations and illusions; Nervous breakdown; Paranoia; Personality disorders; Schizophrenia
Atta, S. Madness in the family
Beattie, A. Downhill
Bell, M. Dredge
Bierce, A. The man out of the nose
Châteaureynaud, G. O. The pest
Eisenberg, D. Some other, better Otto
Emshwiller, C. The circular library of stones
Emshwiller, C. Draculalucard
Gifford, B. Call of the wild
Gifford, B. The man who swallowed the world
Gilman, C. P. The yellow wall-paper
Gilman, C. P. The yellow wallpaper
Horrocks, C. Embodied
Jeter, K. W. Bones
Lively, P. Black dog
Matheson, R. Person to person
Oates, J. C. Uranus
Olsen, L. May
Whittall, Z. Check mate
MENTAL TELEPATHY *See* Telepathy
MENTALLY HANDICAPPED
    See also Mentally handicapped children
Atta, S. Last trip
Buday, G. Retard
D'Ambrosio, C., Jr. Drummond & son
Oates, J. C. The Spill
O'Brien, E. Inner cowboy
Tem, M. Keeping Corky
Terry, G. P. Slowdown in Paxville
Van Pelt, J. The yard god
Wells, H. G. Our little neighbour
MENTALLY HANDICAPPED CHILDREN
Pearlman, E. Tess
MENTALLY ILL
    See also Insane, Criminal and dangerous
Bingham, S. The wedding
Harrison, D. Mercy first, first mercy
Roberge, R. Do not concern yourself with things Lee Nading has left out
Trueblood, V. Luck
Williams, S. The Jade Woman of the Luminous Star
Care and treatment
Coelho, P. In the prison of repose
Constantine, D. Asylum
Erdrich, L. The reptile garden
Gilley, T. Bliss
Nix, G. The curious case of the moondawn daffodils murder
Piccirilli, T. Blood sacrifices and the Catatonic Kid
Rodriguez-Milanes, C. El Loco
Self, W. Ward 9
Somerville, P. Pangea

Menudo. Kurlansky, M.
MERCENARIES *See* Soldiers of fortune
Mercenary takes a stab at self-improvement.
  Shepard, S.
MERCHANT MARINE *See* Seamen
MERCHANTS
  Englander, N. Free fruit for young widows
  Gifford, B. Far from anywhere
  Marãr, M. Teneem
  Marr, M. Guns for the dead
  Somerville, P. Easy love
  Wells, H. G. A catastrophe
  Woodrell, D. Florianne
The merciful angel of death. Block, L.
MERCURY (PLANET)
  Niven, L. The coldest place
Mercy at the gate. Theodore-Pharel, M. K.
Mercy blow. Goodberg, D.
MERCY DEATH *See* Euthanasia
Mercy first, first mercy. Harrison, D.
Merely murder. Long, J.
MERLIN (LEGENDARY CHARACTER)
  Resnick, M. Winter solstice
A mermaid too many. Aiken, J.
MERMAIDS
  Aiken, J. A mermaid too many
  Anderson, B. Landlocked
  Bradbury, R. Undersea guardians
  Genge, S. Sins of the father
  Parks, R. A pinch of salt
  Terry, G. P. Episcatory
Mermaids. Eisenberg, D.
MERMEN
  Terry, G. P. Episcatory
The merry widow. Drabble, M.
Meruane, Lina
  False Steps
    The Literary Review (Madison, N.J.) v53 no4
    p144-50 Summ 2010
Mesmer, Sharon
  from Metaxu
    Hanging Loose no98 p73-80 2011
The message. Bayley, E.
METAMORPHOSIS
  Allan, N. Flying in the face of god
  Bierce, A. The eyes of the panther
  Bradbury, R. Chrysalis
  Davis, L. The transformation
  Monzó, Q. Gregor
  Moody, D. Big man
  Rickert, M. Memoir of a deer woman
  Silverberg, R. At the conglomeroid cocktail par-
    ty
  Silverberg, R. Dancers in the time-flux
Metamorphosis. Updike, J.
Metaphysics. Glover, E. M.
METEORITES
  Dowling, T. The suits at Auderlene
  Goodberg, D. Con-science
METEOROLOGISTS
  Hall, T. M. The woman who fell in love with
    a meteorologist and stopped the rain
Methapyrilene hydrochloride sometimes helps.
  Emshwiller, C.
METROPOLITAN MUSEUM OF ART (NEW
    YORK, N.Y.)
  Gallari, A. Negative space
  Sabar, A. Renovations

MEXICAN-AMERICAN BORDER REGION
  Tremblay, P. Headstone in your pocket
MEXICAN AMERICANS
    See also Mexicans—United States
  Kitterman, B. The gospel according to Octavio
    Ruiz
  Plummer, T. M. The bolero of Andi Rowe
  Plummer, T. M. To visit the cemetery
  Plummer, T. M. What would Mary do: a Christ-
    mas story
MEXICANS
              United States
  Breen, S. Triplet
  Finney, E. J. Sequoia Gardens
  Urrea, L. A. Amapola
MEXICO
  Aguilar Camín, H. Comrade Vadillo
  Boland, J. C. Out of her depth
  Eisenberg, D. Tlaloc's paradise
  Marías, J. A kind of nostalgia perhaps
              Rural life
  Silverberg, R. Not our brother
              Guadalajara
  Monzó, Q. Family life
              Mexico City
  Mena, M. C. The vine-leaf
              Nuevo Laredo
  LaSalle, P. Lunch across the bridge
MEXICO. ARMY *See* Mexico. Ejército
MEXICO. EJÉRCITO
  Brandon, J. A jury of his peers
MEXICO CITY (MEXICO) *See* Mexico—Mexi-
    co City
Meyer, Christoph
  The sweet taste of slavery
    Can'tLit; fearless fiction from Broken pencil
    magazine; edited by Richard Rosenbaum.
Meyer, Philipp
  What you do out here, when you're alone
    20 under 40; stories from the New Yorker;
    edited by Deborah Treisman.
    Best of the West 2011; new stories from the
    wild side of the Missouri; edited by James
    Thomas and D. Seth Horton; foreword by
    Ana Castillo.
Mí Encanta Panama. Kostuck, R.
MIAMI (FLA.) *See* Florida—Miami
MIAMI BEACH (FLA.) *See* Florida—Miami
    Beach
MICE
  Aiken, J. Honeymaroon
  Davis, L. The mice
  Davis, L. The mouse
  Drakulic, S. A guided tour through the museum
    of communism
  Millhauser, S. Cat 'n' mouse
The mice. Davis, L.
Mice. Ruocco, J.
Michalopoulou, Amanda
  A Mother Knows Best
    World Literature Today v84 no5 p47-9 S/O
    2010
Michiels, Ivo
  It will end in tears
    The Dedalus book of Flemish fantasy; edited
    by Eric Dickens and translated by Paul
    Vincent.
MICHIGAN
  Allyn, D. An early Christmas

Millhauser, Steven—*Continued*

Eisenheim the illusionist
    Millhauser, S. We others; new and selected
        stories

Flying carpets
    Millhauser, S. We others; new and selected
        stories

Getting closer
    Millhauser, S. We others; new and selected
        stories
    The New Yorker v86 no42 p58-61 Ja 3 2011

History of a disturbance
    Millhauser, S. We others; new and selected
        stories

The invasion from outer space
    Millhauser, S. We others; new and selected
        stories

The knife thrower
    Millhauser, S. We others; new and selected
        stories

The next thing
    Millhauser, S. We others; new and selected
        stories

People of the Book
    Millhauser, S. We others; new and selected
        stories

Phantoms
    The Best American short stories, 2011; select-
        ed from U.S. and Canadian magazines by
        Geraldine Brooks with Heidi Pitlor; with an
        introduction by Geraldine Brooks.

A protest against the sun
    Millhauser, S. We others; new and selected
        stories

The slap
    Millhauser, S. We others; new and selected
        stories

Snowmen
    Millhauser, S. We others; new and selected
        stories

Tales of darkness and the unknown, vol. XIV:
        The white glove
    Millhauser, S. We others; new and selected
        stories

A visit
    Millhauser, S. We others; new and selected
        stories

We others
    Millhauser, S. We others; new and selected
        stories

The wizard of West Orange
    Millhauser, S. We others; new and selected
        stories

A **million** dollars. Sneed, C.

Million year boom. Kaczynski, T.

MILLIONAIRES
    See also Wealth
    Papernick, J. The last five-year plan

Mills, Richard
    Of All His Good Life
        Raritan v30 no2 p57-84 Fall 2010

Mimouna. Guène, F.

MIND AND BODY
    Kronauer, B. A day that did not end hopelessly
        after all

A **mind** at peace. Tanpinar, A. H.

MIND READING *See* Telepathy

Miner, Valerie
    Moving In
        Southwest Review v95 no3 p449-55 2010

MINERS *See* Coal mines and mining; Gold mines
        and mining; Mines and mining

Miners and Trappers. MOUSTAKIS, M.

Mines. Straight, S.

MINES AND MINING
        See also Coal mines and mining; Gold
        mines and mining
    Lansdale, J. R. The dark down there
    Mastroianni, J. Jordan's waterhammer
    Morris, M. Fallen boys
    Robinson, K. S. The lunatics

Minevski, Blaže
    Academician Sisoye's inaugural speech
        Best European fiction 2011; edited by Alek-
        sandr Hemon; preface by Colum McCann

Mingin, William
    From sunset to the white sea
        Swenson, P. The Best of Talebones; edited by
        Patrick Swenson.

Minh, Chuyen
    A father and his children
        Family of fallen leaves; stories of Agent Or-
        ange by Vietnamese writers; edited by
        Charles Waugh and Huy Lien.

MINIATURE OBJECTS
    Loory, B. The man who went to China

Minichillo, John
    Moe Tucker
        The Literary Review (Madison, N.J.) v54 no3
        p113-18 Spr 2011

MINISTERS *See* Clergy

The **ministry** of restraint. Pearlman, E.

MINNESOTA
    Grove, L. L. Bingo night
    Grove, L. L. Three seasons
    Oates, J. C. Sourland
                Farm life
            See Farm life—Minnesota
                Duluth
    Grover, L. L. Ojibwe boys
    Grover, L. L. Refugees living and dying in the
        west end of Duluth

Minnesota. Ferriss, L.

Minnows. Robinson, E.

The **minor** character. Self, W.

MINOR PLANETS *See* Asteroids

Minot, Susan
    Pole, pole
        The Pen/O.Henry Prize stories 2011; chosen
        and with an introduction by Laura Furman;
        with essays on the stories thety admire
        most by jurors A. M. Homes, Manuel Mu-
        ñoz, Christine Schutt

MINOTAUR (GREEK MYTHOLOGY)
    Fischer, J. The house of nameless

Minotaur. Shepard, J.

Minton, Amy
    Bounty
        Indiana Review v32 no2 p31-43,153 Wint
        2010

Mir the Hessian. Davis, L.

The **miracle** aquilina. Lanagan, M.

Miracle baby. Osondu, E. C.

The **miracle** birth. Papernick, J.

Miracle of poverty. Bayley, E.

The **miracle** of the lily. Harris, C. W.

The **miracle** worker. Atta, S.
MIRACLES
  Atta, S. The miracle worker
  Dozois, G. R. The hanging curve
  Papernick, J. The Madonna of Temple Beth Elo-
    him
  Wells, H. G. The man who could work miracles
The **miracles** of Vincent Van Gogh. Ray, S.
The **miraculous** discovery of Psammetichus I. Ma-
    son, D.
Miranda Visits the Holiday Inn. Lee, T.-Y.
Miri. Tem, S. R.
The **mirror**. Rodoreda, M.
Mirror images. Swirsky, R.
MIRRORS
  Dubé, P. Echo
Mirrors and burnstone. Griffith, N.
Mirrors and infinity. Greenspon, J.
Mirvis, Tova
  Potatoes
    Promised lands; new Jewish American fiction
      on longing and belonging; edited by Derek
      Rubin.
MISCARRIAGE
  Baxter, C. Royal blue
  Hall, J. W. Bells
  Hemmingson, M. Solid memories have the life-
    span of tulips and sunflowers
  Hodge, B. If I should wake before I die
  Latiolais, M. Burqa
  Schappell, E. A dog story
MISCEGENATION
  Gordimer, N. Town and country lovers
Misery Island. Hannibal, E.
Misha. Hermann, J.
MISOGYNY
  Highsmith, P. Oona, the jolly cave woman
Miss Austen victorious. Bellamy, E.
Miss Furr and Miss Skeene. Stein, G.
Miss Grief. Woolson, C. F.
Miss Winchelsea's heart. Wells, H. G.
MISSING CHILDREN
    See also Lost children
  Gilley, T. Mountains of the moon
  Houarner, G. The other box
  Jones, S. G. The meat tree
  Le Clézio, J.-M. G. Daniel who had never seen
    the sea
  Lee, M. J. Last seen
  Pinborough, S. The nowhere man
  Roden, B. Sweet sorrow
  Shipp, J. C. Kingdom come
  Smith, C. Catgirl
The **missing** mass. Niven, L.
Missing Out. Aboulela, L.
MISSING PERSONS
    See also Missing children
  Adichie, C. N. Sola
  Aidt, N. M. Women in Copenhagen
  Biancotti, D. Diamond shell
  Bierce, A. Charles Ashmore's trail
  Bierce, A. The difficulty of crossing a field
  Bierce, A. An unfinished race
  Bill, F. A rabbit in the lettuce patch
  Butcher, J. Heorot
  Clark, D. C. and Bear, A. The home front
  Dib, M. Naëma disappeared
  Doolittle, S. Care of the circumcised penis
  Eiríksdóttir, K. Holes in people

  Fowler, K. J. King Rat
  Fowler, K. J. What I didn't see
  Freeman, M. E. W. The hall bedroom
  Gray, A. The vanished
  Isleib, R. The itinerary
  Jakubowski, M. A price to pay
  Johnston, T. Two years
  McOmber, A. Fall, Orpheum
  Millhauser, S. The disaooearance of Elaine
    Coleman
  Mingin, W. From sunset to the white sea
  Nelson, A. Iff
  Packer, A. Dwell time
  Schirach, F. v. Green
  Shapiro, J. Small
  Staalesen, G. Last train from central station
  Sterling, P. An account in her name
  Wells, H. G. The plattner story
  Willis, D. Vanishing
  Woodrell, D. Florianne
A **missing** year: letter to my son. Neugeboren, J.
Mission San Juan Capistrano. Shepard, S.
MISSIONARIES
  Dozois, G. R. Disciples
  Jansen, P. This peaceful state of war
  Shepard, S. Little people
  Waters, D. Mormons in heat
Missis Flinders. Slesinger, T.
MISSISSIPPI
  Ely, S. The oldest man in Mississippi
  Hannah, B. Fire water
  Hannah, B. High-water railers
  Hannah, B. Lastward, deputy James
  Hannah, B. Rangoon Green
  Hannah, B. Scandale d'estime
  Hannah, B. Sick soldier at your door
                    Biloxi
  Watson, B. Alamo Plaza
Mississippi rules. Ely, S.
MISSOURI
  Bierce, A. The thing at Nolan
  Watkins, M. Two midnights in a jug
Mist. Krinard, S.
MISTAKEN IDENTITY
    See also Impersonations
  Kyle, A. Take care
  Matheson, R. The prisoner
  O'Connor, S. Based on a true story
The **mistakes**. Phillips, H.
Mister X. McElroy, J.
MISTRESSES
  Kyle, A. Boys and girls like you and me
  Mu Xin. Xia Mingzhu: a bright pearl
  Villegas, H. An unexpected thing
  Yezbek, S. From the novel The scent of cinna-
    mon
Mistry, Rohinton
  The scream
    Freedom; stories celebrating the Universal
      Declaration of Human Rights; Amnesty In-
      ternational.
Misunderstanding. Blatnik, A.
A **misunderstood** artist. Wells, H. G.
Mitchell, David
  Character development
    Freedom; stories celebrating the Universal
      Declaration of Human Rights; Amnesty In-
      ternational.

Mitchell, Emily
Folktales of North America
TriQuarterly v138 36566 bytes Summ/Fall 2010
On Friendship
New England Review v31 no3 p50-7 2010
Mitchell, Kirsty
Jayne
Dancing with Mr. Darcy; stories inspired by Jane Austen and Chawton House Library; compiled by Sarah Waters.
MITRA, KEYA
A Family Matter
The Kenyon Review v33 no4 p118-131 Fall 2011
The **mix-up**. Bayley, E.
MIXED BLOODS
See also Mulattoes
Senna, D. Admission
The **mixer**. Wodehouse, P. G.
The **mocking-bird**. Bierce, A.
Model wife. Aiken, J.
MODELS, ARTISTS' *See* Artists' models
MODELS, FASHION *See* Fashion models
Model's assistant. Nutting, A.
Modesitt, L. E., Jr.
The stranger
Speculative Horizons; edited by Patrick St-Denis.
Modica, Matthew
Hunting Season
The Antioch Review v68 no4 p718-31 Fall 2010
Modillion. Emshwiller, C.
Moe Tucker. Minichillo, J.
Moffett, Kevin
The perfect age
Iowa Review v41 no1 p13-28 Spr 2011
Mofina, Rick
The last pursuit
Original sins; a Crime Writer's Association anthology; edited by Martin Edwards.
Mogelson, Luke
Visitors
The Hudson Review v63 no3 p399-423 Aut 2010
MOHAMMEDANISM *See* Islam
MOHAMMEDANS *See* Muslims
Mohar, Christopher
The Five Points of Performance
Southwest Review v95 no4 p578-92 2010
Mojado. Shepard, S.
Moles, David
Seven cities of gold
The Year's best science fiction: twenty-eighth annual collection; edited by Gardner Dozois.
MOLES (ANIMALS)
Drakulic, S. The legend of the Berlin Wall–as presented by a mole
Mollet, Daniel
Checking fields
South Dakota Magazine v26 no5 p84-7 Ja/F 2011
Mollusk makes. Black, A.
Molten. Packer, A.
The **moment** before the gun went off. Gordimer, N.
The **moment** childhood vanished. Mu Xin

The **moment** of decision. Blatnik, A.
Moments before the future begins to approach. Martin, C.
Mommy issues of the dead. Pratt, T. A.
MONASTERIES *See* Monasticism and religious orders
MONASTICISM AND RELIGIOUS ORDERS
See also Convent life; Jesuits; Monks
Timmermans, F. The white vase
Monday Burning. Allen, R. A.
Monette, Sarah
White Charles
The Year's best dark fantasy & horror; edited by Paula Guran
MONEY
Brackmann, L. Don't feed the bums
Mehta, R. The cure
Sneed, C. Quality of life
Vonnegut, K. Money talks
Zhang Kangkang. White poppies
Money. Davis, L.
Money. Raphael, L.
Money talks. Vonnegut, K.
MONEYLENDERS
See also Loans
MONGOLISM (DISEASE) *See* Down's syndrome
MONGOLS
See also Tatars
Howard, R. E. The sowers of the thunder
Monk, Devon
Bearing life
Monk, D. A cup of normal
Beer with a hamster chaser
Monk, D. A cup of normal
Christmas card
Monk, D. A cup of normal
Ducks in a row
Monk, D. A cup of normal
Dusi
Monk, D. A cup of normal
Falling with wings
Monk, D. A cup of normal
Fishing the edge of the world
Monk, D. A cup of normal
Here after life
Monk, D. A cup of normal
Last tour of duty
Monk, D. A cup of normal
Leeward to the sky
Monk, D. A cup of normal
Menders
Monk, D. A cup of normal
Moonlighting
Monk, D. A cup of normal
Oldblade
Monk, D. A cup of normal
Probe
Monk, D. A cup of normal
Singing down the sun
Monk, D. A cup of normal
Skein of sunlight
Monk, D. A cup of normal
Stitchery
Monk, D. A cup of normal
Stringing tomorrow
Monk, D. A cup of normal

Monk, Devon—*Continued*
  Sugar 'n' spice
    Swenson, P. The Best of Talebones; edited by
      Patrick Swenson.
  That Saturday
    Monk, D. A cup of normal
  When the train calls lonely
    Monk, D. A cup of normal
  The wishing time
    Monk, D. A cup of normal
  X_day
    Monk, D. A cup of normal
Monkey Boy and the monsters. Shipp, J. C.
The **monkey** bride. Snyder, M.
MONKEYS
      See also Baboons
  Snyder, M. The monkey bride
The **monkey's** paw. Jacobs, W. W.
The **monkey's** wedding. Aiken, J.
MONKS
      See also Monasticism and religious or-
      ders
  Barnhill, K. St. Brendan's shank
  Farmer, P. J. St. Francis kisses his ass goodbye
  Parks, R. Lord Goji's wedding
  Ryman, G. The last ten years in the life of hero
    Kai
  Smith, C. A. The black abbot of puthuum
  Terry, G. P. Icon
  Timmermans, F. The white vase
  Trevor, W. The Virgin's gift
Monologue for Jutito. Gálvez Ronceros, A.
The **monority** report. Dick, P. K.
MONROE, MARILYN, 1926-1962
                About
  Wheat, C. Love me for my yellow hair alone
Monrovia Scripture. Makamane, R.
Monsieur Dombo in glitter town. Magliocco, P.
Monsieur Fly-by-Night. Pollexfen, M.
Monso, Imma
  The customer is always right
    Barcelona noir; edited by Adriana V. Lopez
      & Cartmen Ospina; translated by Achy
      Obejas.
Monster. Frumkin, R.
The **Monster** in the Mountain. Yang, M.
The **monster** maker. Bradbury, R.
Monster mash. Douglas, C. N.
MONSTERS
  Beagle, P. S. The best worst monster
  Braunbeck, G. A. And still you wonder why our
    first impulsr is to kill you: an alphabetizes
    faux-manifesto transcribes edited, and anno-
    tated (under duress and protest)
  Cain, C. Less of a girl
  Emshwiller, C. Mrs. Jones
  Lansdale, J. R. The crawling sky
  Lansdale, J. R. The folding man
  Lovecraft, H. P. The call of Cthulhu
  McCrumb, S. Rattler and the Mothman
  Monk, D. Dusi
  Moody, D. Big man
  Nix, G. The curious case of the moondawn daf-
    fodils murder
  O'Connor, S. Ziggurat
  Phillips, H. The monsters
  Shipp, J. C. Monkey Boy and the monsters
  Sturgeon, T. The professor's teddy bear
  Watts, P. The things

Monsters. Jones, S. G.
Monsters. O'Nan, S.
The **monsters**. Phillips, H.
Monsters. Saintcrow, L.
Monsters in the night. Smith, C. A.
Monsters of the deep. Schappell, E.
MONTANA
  Bass, R. Coach
  Briggs, P. Fairy gifts
  Kitterman, B. Union wages
  McGuane, T. Cowboy
  Ray, S. The great divide
  Ray, S. In the half-light
  Ray, S. The miracles of Vincent Van Gogh
  Ray, S. When we rise
  Thon, M. R. Father, lover, deadman, dreamer
Montes, Javier
  The hotel life
    Granta no113 p99-114 Wint 2010
Montgomery Cleft. Cortez, S.
Monumental City. Muir, S.
MONUMENTS
  Wells, H. G. The pearl of love
Monzó, Quim
  Books
    Monzó, Q. Guadalajara; stories; translated
      from the Catalan by Peter Bush.
    Bomb no116 p XXII-XXIII Summ 2011
  Centripetal force
    Monzó, Q. Guadalajara; stories; translated
      from the Catalan by Peter Bush.
  A day like any other
    Monzó, Q. Guadalajara; stories; translated
      from the Catalan by Peter Bush.
  During the war
    Monzó, Q. Guadalajara; stories; translated
      from the Catalan by Peter Bush.
  Family life
    Monzó, Q. Guadalajara; stories; translated
      from the Catalan by Peter Bush.
  Gregor
    Monzó, Q. Guadalajara; stories; translated
      from the Catalan by Peter Bush.
  Helvetian freedoms
    Monzó, Q. Guadalajara; stories; translated
      from the Catalan by Peter Bush.
    The Massachusetts Review v52 no1 p31-4 Spr
      2011
  A hunger and thirst for justice
    Monzó, Q. Guadalajara; stories; translated
      from the Catalan by Peter Bush.
  Life is so short
    Monzó, Q. Guadalajara; stories; translated
      from the Catalan by Peter Bush.
  Literature
    Monzó, Q. Guadalajara; stories; translated
      from the Catalan by Peter Bush.
  The lives of the prophets
    Monzó, Q. Guadalajara; stories; translated
      from the Catalan by Peter Bush.
  Outside the gates of Troy
    Monzó, Q. Guadalajara; stories; translated
      from the Catalan by Peter Bush.
  The power of words
    Monzó, Q. Guadalajara; stories; translated
      from the Catalan by Peter Bush.
  Strategies
    Monzó, Q. Guadalajara; stories; translated
      from the Catalan by Peter Bush.

Moody, David
  Big man
    The monster's corner; stories through inhu-
    man eyes; edited by Christopher Golden
MOON
  Harvey, B. The truth, from a lie of convenience
  Payne, M. Bullet
  Robinson, K. S. The lunatics
  Tillman, L. Lunacies
The **moon**. Latiolais, M.
The **moon** above his head. Martel, Y.
Moon bathing. Lahens, Y.
The **moon** fish. Balázs, B.
Moon songs. Emshwiller, C.
Mooning viewing at Shijo Bridge. Parks, R.
Moonlight sonata. Woollcott, A.
Moonlighting. Monk, D.
The **moonlit** road. Bierce, A.
The **moonstone** mass. Spofford, H. E. P.
The **Moor**. Stroud, B.
Moorcock, Michael
  Shamalung (the diminutions)
    The Thackery T. Lambshead cabinet of curi-
    osities; edited by Ann & Jeff VanderMeer.
Moore, Alan
  Objects discovered in a novel under construction
    The Thackery T. Lambshead cabinet of curi-
    osities; edited by Ann & Jeff VanderMeer.
Moore, Edwaard Kelsey
  Signs and Deliverance
    African American Review v43 no2/3 p493-8
    Summ/Fall 2009
Moore, Leeyanne
  (jt. auth) See Milks, Megan and Moore,
    Leeyanne
Moore, Linda McCullough
  Final dispositions
    Pushcart Prize XXXV: best of the small
    presses 2011; edited by Bill Henderson
    with the Pushcart Prize editors.
Moore, Lorrie
  Four calling birds, three french hens
    I found this funny; my favorite pieces of hu-
    mor and some that may not be funny at all;
    edited by Judd Apatow.
Moore, Phyllis
  Rembrandt's Bones
    The Georgia Review v65 no1 p209-24 Spr
    2011
Moore, Stewart
  One thin dime
    The beastly bride; tales of the animal people;
    edited by Ellen Datlow & Terri Windling;
    introduction by Terri Windling; selected
    decorations by Charles Vess.
Moore, T. A.
  Red milk
    Requiems for the departed; edited by Gerard
    Brennan & Mike Stone.
MOOSE
  Loory, B. The man and the moose
Moral hazard. Sublett, J.
MORALITY
  Ayau, K. J. Outsourcing
Moran, John
  Be swift, my darling
    Nature v473 no7348 p550 My 27 2011
More. Goldenstern, J.
More sex. Tillman, L.

Morgan, C. E.
  Twins
    20 under 40; stories from the New Yorker;
    edited by Deborah Treisman.
Morgan, Christine
  The barrow maid
    Z: zombie stories; edited by J. M. Lassen
Morgan, Staci Stokes
  Cambodia 1981
    StoryQuarterly v44 p195-9 2010
Morgue ship. Bradbury, R.
MORMONISM *See* Mormons and Mormonism
MORMONS AND MORMONISM
  Card, O. S. Salvage
  Vestal, S. Opposition in all things
  Waters, D. Mormons in heat
Mormons in heat. Waters, D.
Morning child. Dozois, G. R.
Morning Cloud, Evening Rain. Ping, W.
Morning meditation. Vukcevich, R.
MOROCCANS
  Benali, A. From the novel The trip to the
    slaughterhouse
MOROCCO
                    Tangier
  Terry, G. P. Barbara Hutton Toujours
Morrell, David
  The controller
    Mystery Writers of America presents the rich
    and the dead; edited by Nelson DeMille.
Morris, Edward
  Rejection letter
    End of an Aeon; edited by Bridgett McKenna
    & Marti McKenna
Morris, J. M. *See* Morris, Mark, 1963-
Morris, Mark
  Fallen boys
    The Best horror of the year: volume three;
    edited by Ellen Datlow.
Morris, Mary
  The Cross Word [Part of the Culture Issue]
    Atlantic Monthly (1993) v307 no4 p72-6, 78-
    83 My 2011
Morrish, Robert
  (jt. auth) See Gorman, Edward and Morrish,
    Robert
El **Morro**. Means, D.
Morrow, James
  Auspicious eggs
    Brave new worlds; edited by John Joseph Ad-
    ams.
  Bible stories for adults, no. 31: the covenant
    Sympathy for the devil; edited by Tim Pratt.
  The iron shroud
    Ghosts by gaslight; stories of steampunk and
    supernatural suspense; [edited by] Jack
    Dann [and] Nick Gevers
Morse, Canaan
  (tr.) See He, Qifang
The **mortal** immortal. Shelley, M. W.
MORTALITY
  Niven, L. Limits
Morthylla. Smith, C. A.
Morty, el morto. Novack, S.
MOSCOW (RUSSIA) *See* Russia—Moscow
Moses, Jennifer Anne
  Blood into Butterflies
    Confrontation no108 p16-33 Fall 2010

Mosher, C. J.
A girl and her cat
Dead neon; tales of near-future Las Vegas; edited by Todd James Pierce and Jarret Keene.
Mosley, Walter
Equal opportunity
Best of times, worst of times; contemporary American short stories from the new Gilded Age; edited by Wendy Martin and Cecelia Tichi.
The trial
Freedom; stories celebrating the Universal Declaration of Human Rights; Amnesty International.
Mosquitoes. Shepard, S.
Moss, P.
Time machine
Dead neon; tales of near-future Las Vegas; edited by Todd James Pierce and Jarret Keene.
Most at Rest. Kim, E.
The **most** dangerous game. Connell, R. E.
MOTELS
Seamans, S. Survival instincts
Shepard, S. Indianapolis (Highway 74)
Williamson, E. M. Wamsutter in Dali vision
The **moth**. Wells, H. G.
The **mother**. Davis, L.
The **mother**. Somerville, P.
A **Mother** Knows Best. Michalopoulou, A.
Mother mouth. Hannah, B.
Mother of toads. Smith, C. A.
Mother Rooney unscrolls the hurt. Hannah, B.
The **mother** sits down on the bed. Lisicky, P.
The **mother** who stayed. Furman, L.
MOTHERHOOD *See* Mothers
MOTHERS
See also Mothers and daughters; Mothers and sons; Mothers-in-law; Stepmothers
Bacigalupi, P. Pop squad
Baker, S. W. Poison, inside the walls
Barrett, N., Jr. Getting dark
Beattie, A. The rabbit hole as likely explanation
Brennan, M. An attack of hunger
Chau, A. Everything forbidden
Davis, L. Glenn Gould
Davis, L. What you learn about the baby
Drabble, M. A day in the life of a smiling woman
Gottlieb, D. Somewhere, over
Grossman, V. S. Mama
Hunter, L. Marie Noe, talks to you about her kids
Kozak, H. J. Lamborghini mommy
Lychack, W. Love is a temper
Nagai, M. Georgic
Phillips, H. The mothers
Pung, A. The shed
Ruocco, J. Marzipan lambs
Schappell, E. Elephant
Shapiro, J. In its place
Terry, G. P. The promise
Thon, M. R. Heavenly creatures: for wandering children and their delinquent mother
Trueblood, V. Invisible river
Ulysse, K. D. The last department
Wieland, L. At Wanship
Wieland, L. Slip, out, back, here

Mothers. Davis, L.
The **mothers**. Phillips, H.
MOTHERS AND DAUGHTERS
See also Parent and child
Allen, D. Goat on a hill
Baker, A. The persistence of memory
Beattie, A. Find and replace
Bergman, M. M. Housewifely arts
Bernheimer, K. A cageling tale
Binkley, P. Keepsakes
Boggs, B. Jonas
Breen, S. Triplet
Bynum, S. S.-L. The erlking
Cerat, M. L. Maloulou
Chau, A. Arcade games
Cooper, D. Breakin' down
Davis, L. The housemaid
Davis, L. Varieties of disturbance
Diab, F. The power of silence
Dib, M. La cuadra
Dixon, S. Piers
Eisenberg, D. All around Atlantis
Eisenberg, D. Under the 82nd Airborne
Emshwiller, C. The abominable child's tale
Evans, D. Snakes
Fallon, S. Remission
Fowler, K. J. Standing room only
Furman, L. The hospital room
Gautier, A. Afternoon tea
Gautier, A. Held
Goodberg, D. Disabled
Gorman, E. Such a good girl
Grossman, V. S. A young woman and an old woman
Grove, L. L. Three seasons
Hardwick, E. A season's romance
Heathcock, A. The daughter
Horrocks, C. This is not your city
Kelly, J. P. Going deep
Kim, C.-s. Crimson fruit
Kyle, A. Allegiance
Leidiger, L. Tell me
Lindholm, M. Cut
Lippman, L. Cougar
Loory, B. The little girl and the balloon
Manilla, M. Get ready
Mariotte, J. J. Janey in Amber
Matheson, R. Life size
McGarry, J. Family happiness
Nagai, M. Autobiography
Nagai, M. Confession
Nagai, M. Grafting
Nolan, W. F. Child's care
Nutting, A. Deliverywoman
Nutting, A. Knife thrower
Oates, J. C. Bonobo momma
Oates, J. C. Honor code
Oates, J. C. ID
Oates, J. C. Nowhere
Oates, J. C. Smother
O'Brien, E. Green Georgette
O'Brien, E. My two mother
Osondu, E. C. Janjaweed wife
Papernick, J. The miracle birth
Pearlman, E. Rules
Pearlman, E. Tess
Platana, J. Some of this is true
Plummer, T. M. Happy hour
Ray, S. Rodin's the hand of god

MOTION PICTURES—*Continued*

Emshwiller, C. Biography of an uncircumcised man (including interview)

Evans, M. A. Low-budget monster flick

Faherty, T. The second coming

Fitzgerald, F. S. Pat Hobby and Orson Welles

Gifford, B. The great failure

Gifford, B. Innamorata

Harland, R. The fear

Hodge, B. The passion of the beast

Hubbard, L. R. The automagic horse

McMahon, G. Strange scenes from an unfinished film

Nevins, F. M., Jr. Bagworms

Nevins, F. M., Jr. Filmflam

Novack, S. Attack of the pod people

Pera, B. Roman à clef

Prentiss, N. In the porches of my ears

Ryman, G. The film-makers of Mars

Sands, B. Jared Bruckheiny

Shepard, J. Gojira, king of the monsters

Sneed, C. You're so different

Tóibín, C. Two women

Trevor, W. Good news

Wheat, C. Love me for my yellow hair alone

MOTOR BUSES *See* Buses

MOTOR INNS *See* Motels

MOTORCYCLE DRIVERS

Daisne, J. Death on a motorbike

Harper, J. Red hair and black leather

Waters, D. Mormons in heat

MOTORCYCLES

Davis, L. The race of the patient motorcyclists

Jeter, K. W. Bones

Murphy, B. Who do I have to kill to get a little respect up in here?

Mounk, Yascha

The Other Jesus

The Antioch Review v69 no3 p435-439 Summ 2011

MOUNT HOOD NATIONAL FOREST (OR.)

Lake, J. Fat man

MOUNTAIN CLIMBING *See* Mountaineering

Mountain fire. Boland, J. C.

MOUNTAIN LIFE

McCrumb, S. Rattler and the Mothman

Terry, G. P. On Orly's border

Southern States

See also Appalachian highlanders

MOUNTAIN LIONS *See* Pumas

The **mountain** of fear. Riccardi, T.

The **mountain** of the living god. Le Clézio, J.-M. G.

MOUNTAIN WHITES (SOUTHERN STATES)

See Appalachian highlanders

MOUNTAINEERING

Gilley, T. Mountains of the moon

Shepard, J. Happy with crocodiles

Shepard, J. Poland is watching

Wells, H. G. Little mother up the Mörderberg

MOUNTAINS

See also Appalachian Mountains; Catskill Mountains (N.Y.)

Emshwiller, C. Living at the center

Le Clézio, J.-M. G. The mountain of the living god

Matheson, R. Mountains of the mind

Mountains of the mind. Matheson, R.

Mountains of the moon. Gilley, T.

The **mourners**. Naipaul, V. S.

MOURNING *See* Bereavement

The **mourning**. Trevor, W.

MOURNING CUSTOMS *See* Funeral rites and ceremonies

The **mouse**. Davis, L.

MOUSTAKIS, MELINDA

Miners and Trappers

The Kenyon Review v33 no4 p136-148 Fall 2011

What You Can Endure

New England Review v32 no1 p108-13 2011

The **Move**. Urbanski, D.

The **movement**. Gray, A.

MOVING (HOUSEHOLD GOODS)

Beattie, A. The confidence decoy

Gilley, T. Physical wisdom

Moving black objects. Hughes, C. P.

Moving In. Miner, V.

MOVING PICTURE INDUSTRY *See* Motion pictures

MOVING PICTURES *See* Motion pictures

Moving water. Beattie, A.

The **mower**. Kaplan, J.

A **mown** lawn. Davis, L.

Moxon's master. Bierce, A.

Mozzi, Giulio

The Apprentice

Agni no73 p14-34 2011

Mphahlele, Ezekiel

A ballad of Oyo

Mphahlele, E. In Corner B; [by] Es'kia Mphahlele; introduction by Peter N. Thuynsma.

The barber of Bariga

Mphahlele, E. In Corner B; [by] Es'kia Mphahlele; introduction by Peter N. Thuynsma.

Crossing over

Mphahlele, E. In Corner B; [by] Es'kia Mphahlele; introduction by Peter N. Thuynsma.

Down the quiet street

Mphahlele, E. In Corner B; [by] Es'kia Mphahlele; introduction by Peter N. Thuynsma.

Grieg on a stolen piano

Mphahlele, E. In Corner B; [by] Es'kia Mphahlele; introduction by Peter N. Thuynsma.

He and the cat

Mphahlele, E. In Corner B; [by] Es'kia Mphahlele; introduction by Peter N. Thuynsma.

In Corner B

Mphahlele, E. In Corner B; [by] Es'kia Mphahlele; introduction by Peter N. Thuynsma.

The living and the dead

Mphahlele, E. In Corner B; [by] Es'kia Mphahlele; introduction by Peter N. Thuynsma.

Man must live

Mphahlele, E. In Corner B; [by] Es'kia Mphahlele; introduction by Peter N. Thuynsma.

Mphahlele, Ezekiel—*Continued*

The master of Doornvlei
Mphahlele, E. In Corner B; [by] Es'kia Mphahlele; introduction by Peter N. Thuynsma.

Mrs. Plum
Mphahlele, E. In Corner B; [by] Es'kia Mphahlele; introduction by Peter N. Thuynsma.

Nigerian talking points
Mphahlele, E. In Corner B; [by] Es'kia Mphahlele; introduction by Peter N. Thuynsma.

A point of identity
Mphahlele, E. In Corner B; [by] Es'kia Mphahlele; introduction by Peter N. Thuynsma.

The suitcase
Mphahlele, E. In Corner B; [by] Es'kia Mphahlele; introduction by Peter N. Thuynsma.

Women and their men
Mphahlele, E. In Corner B; [by] Es'kia Mphahlele; introduction by Peter N. Thuynsma.

Mr. Brisher's treasure. Wells, H. G.

Mr. Burdoff's visit to Germany. Davis, L.

Mr. Fern, Freestyle. Boast, W.

Mr. Frisbie. Lardner, R.

Mr. Gray. Hampton, E.

Mr. Greene. Dixon, S.

Mr. Knockly. Davis, L.

Mr. Ledbetter's vacation. Wells, H. G.

Mr. Marshall's doppelganger. Wells, H. G.

Mr money-maker. Couture, K. A.

Mr. Murphy's wedding. Williamson, E. M.

Mr. Pigsny. Oliver, R.

Mr. President . . . Goytisolo, J.

Mr. Roux. Bayley, E.

Mr. Scary. Baxter, C.

Mr. Skelmersdale in Fairyland. Wells, H. G.

Mr. Spaceship. Dick, P. K.

Mr. Tall. Earley, T.

Mr. Universe. Gray, G.

Mr. Williams. Shepard, S.

Mr. Z. Vonnegut, K.

Mrs. Agnes's Bathroom [Part of special issue: Slovak Fiction] Kovalyk, U.

Mrs. D and her maids. Davis, L.

Mrs. Dennison's head. Bierce, A.

Mrs. F is a fortunate woman/the desirable life of Mr. F. Pirzad, Z.

Mrs. Jones. Emshwiller, C.

Mrs. Mühlenbeck in her house [excerpt]. Kronauer, B.

Mrs. Plum. Mphahlele, E.

Mrs. Secrest. Ray, S.

Ms. Muffet. Resnik, L. K.

Mu Xin

The boy next door
Mu Xin. An empty room; translated from the Chinese by Toming Jun Liu.

Eighteen passengers on a bus
Mu Xin. An empty room; translated from the Chinese by Toming Jun Liu.

An empty room
Mu Xin. An empty room; translated from the Chinese by Toming Jun Liu.

Fellow passengers
Mu Xin. An empty room; translated from the Chinese by Toming Jun Liu.

Fong Fong no. 4
Mu Xin. An empty room; translated from the Chinese by Toming Jun Liu.

Halo
Mu Xin. An empty room; translated from the Chinese by Toming Jun Liu.

The moment childhood vanished
Mu Xin. An empty room; translated from the Chinese by Toming Jun Liu.

Notes from underground
Mu Xin. An empty room; translated from the Chinese by Toming Jun Liu.

Quiet afternoon tea
Mu Xin. An empty room; translated from the Chinese by Toming Jun Liu.

Tomorrow, I'll stroll no more
Mu Xin. An empty room; translated from the Chinese by Toming Jun Liu.

Weimar in early spring
Mu Xin. An empty room; translated from the Chinese by Toming Jun Liu.

The Windsor cemetery diary
Mu Xin. An empty room; translated from the Chinese by Toming Jun Liu.

Xia Mingzhu: a bright pearl
Mu Xin. An empty room; translated from the Chinese by Toming Jun Liu.

Mudure, Mihaela

(jt. auth) See Cornea, Andrei

Mueenuddin, Daniyal

A spoiled man
The Pen/O.Henry Prize stories, 2010; edited and with an introduction by Laura Furman; with essays on the stories they admire most by jurors Junot Diaz, Paula Fox, Yiyun Li.

Mueller, Daniel

At night we play hearts
Iowa Review v40 no3 p131-45 Wint 2010/2011

Muessig, Chris

Bias
The Best American mystery stories 2010; edited and with an introduction by Lee Child; Otto Penzler, series editor

Muffins. Kurlansky, M.

MUGGING

Schirach, F. v. Self-defense

MÜHSAM, ERICH, 1878-1934

About

Kalechofsky, R. My poor prisoner

Muir, Sharona

Monumental City
Orion v30 no4 p38-41 Jl/Ag 2011

MULATTOES

Alcott, L. M. My contraband

Connell, R. The color of honor

Evans, D. Snakes

Lethem, J. View from a headlock

Senna, D. The land of Beulah

Senna, D. What's the matter with Helga and Dave?

Mulberry boys. Lanagan, M.

The **muldoon.** Hirshberg, G.

Mulford, Clarence Edward
Hopalong's hop
  The Big book of adventure stories; edited and
    with a introduction by Otto Penzler; fore-
    word by Douglas Preston.
Mulkerns, Val
Memory and desire
  The Granta book of the Irish short story; [ed-
    ited by] Anne Enright.
Mullane, Eileen
Confessions of a Teenage Cheerleading Ninja
    Wheelchairnapper
  StoryQuarterly v44 p347-50 2010
Mullen, Carolyn
Poetic justice
  Mystery Writers of America presents the rich
    and the dead; edited by Nelson DeMille.
Muller, Marcia
Final resting place
  The Shamus winners: America's best private
    eye stories, volume I: 1982-1995; collected
    and introduced by Robert J. Randisi; found-
    er, Private Eye Writers of America
Telegraphing
  By hook or by crook and 27 more of the best
    crime + mystery stories of the year; edited
    by Ed Gorman and Martin H. Greenberg.
Mullins, David Philip
Arboretum
  Mullins, D. P. Greetings from below; winner
    of the 2009 Mary McCarthy Prize in short
    fiction selected by David Means.
Crash site on a desert mountain outside Las Ve-
    gas
  Mullins, D. P. Greetings from below; winner
    of the 2009 Mary McCarthy Prize in short
    fiction selected by David Means.
Driving lessons
  Mullins, D. P. Greetings from below; winner
    of the 2009 Mary McCarthy Prize in short
    fiction selected by David Means.
A familiar place
  Mullins, D. P. Greetings from below; winner
    of the 2009 Mary McCarthy Prize in short
    fiction selected by David Means.
First sight
  Mullins, D. P. Greetings from below; winner
    of the 2009 Mary McCarthy Prize in short
    fiction selected by David Means.
Glitter Gulch
  Mullins, D. P. Greetings from below; winner
    of the 2009 Mary McCarthy Prize in short
    fiction selected by David Means.
Longing to love you
  Mullins, D. P. Greetings from below; winner
    of the 2009 Mary McCarthy Prize in short
    fiction selected by David Means.
This life or the next
  Mullins, D. P. Greetings from below; winner
    of the 2009 Mary McCarthy Prize in short
    fiction selected by David Means.
True love versus the cigar-store Indian
  Mullins, D. P. Greetings from below; winner
    of the 2009 Mary McCarthy Prize in short
    fiction selected by David Means.
MULTIPLE PERSONALITY
  See also Personality disorders
Villegas, H. The other side

MUMMIES
Châteaureynaud, G. O. The guardicci master-
    piece
Dowling, T. The shaddowwes box
Farkas, A. The colonization of room 313
Fowler, K. J. Private grave 9
Prichard, K. O. R. and Prichard, H. V. The sto-
    ry of Baelbrow
Mummy dust tea. Harris, L.
Mun, Nami
The anniversary
  Granta no114 p185-97 Wint 2011
Mun-Yol, Yi
An Anonymous Island
  The New Yorker v87 no27 p72-77 S 12 2011
Mundy, Talbot
The soul of a regiment
  The Big book of adventure stories; edited and
    with a introduction by Otto Penzler; fore-
    word by Douglas Preston.
MUNICH (GERMANY) *See* Germany—Munich
Munro, Alice
Axis
  The New Yorker v86 no46 p62-9 Ja 31 2011
Corrie
  The New Yorker v86 no31 p94-101 O 11
    2010
DEAR LIFE
  The New Yorker v87 no28 p40-47 S 19 2011
Gravel
  The New Yorker v87 no18 p64-70 Je 27 2011
Material
  I found this funny; my favorite pieces of hu-
    mor and some that may not be funny at all;
    edited by Judd Apatow.
Pride
  Harper's v322 no1931 p59-60, 62-7 Ap 2011
Some women
  Blue collar, white collar, no collar; stories of
    work; edited by Richard Ford.
  The Pen/O.Henry Prize stories, 2010; edited
    and with an introduction by Laura Furman;
    with essays on the stories they admire most
    by jurors Junot Diaz, Paula Fox, Yiyun Li.
Munro, H. H. *See* Saki, 1870-1916
Murakami, Haruki
Town of cats
  The New Yorker v87 no26 p62-70 S 5 2011
Murakami, Haruki and Rubin, Jay
U.F.O. in Kushiro [Reprint]
  The New Yorker v87 no6 p92-6, 98, 100-1 Mr
    28 2011
Murder for dummies. Goulart, R.
Murder from Crime and punishment. Dostoevsky,
    F.
Murder in Bohemia. Davis, L.
Murder in one syllable. MacDonald, J. D.
Murder in the ring. Whitfield, R.
Murder in the sixth. Goodrich, J.
Murder is bad luck. Blassingame, W.
Murder on the gayway. Babcock, D. V.
MURDER STORIES
  See also Assassination; Crime and crimi-
    nals; Filicide; Fratricide; Infanticide; Mur-
    derers; Mystery and detective stories; Parri-
    cide; Strangling; Violence
Abdullah, A. The soul of a turk
Abraham, P. Hasidic noir
Ahmad, O. Yesterday man

MURDER STORIES—*Continued*

Allan, S. You're gonna get yours
Allyn, D. An early Christmas
Allyn, D. The Valhalla verdict
Anthony, M. Fishtown odyssey
Ardai, C. Cold reading
Armstrong, K. A haunted house of her own
Atwell, M. S. Maynard
Ayau, K. J. The brick murder: a tragedy
Ayau, K. J. Official friend
Ayres, J. Mahogany and monogamy
Babcock, D. V. Murder on the gayway
Bailie, T. The druid's dance
Baker, L. Ghost story
Bal, H. S. Just another death
Balázs, B. The revenge of the chestnut tree
Barba, D. Sweet croquette
Barrett, L. When, he wondered
Baxt, G. Schemes and variations
Bell, M. Dredge
Bhattacharya, N. Hissing cobras
Bierce, A. An adventure at Brownville
Bierce, A. The haunted valley
Bierce, A. The moonlit road
Bierce, A. The thing at Nolan
Bill, F. All the awful
Bill, F. Amphetamine twitch
Bill, F. Beautiful even in death
Bill, F. Cold, hard love
Bill, F. A coon hunter's noir
Bill, F. Hill clan cross
Bill, F. The Need
Bill, F. The penance of Scoot McCutchen
Bill, F. These old bones
Black, H. and Clare, C. The Rowan gentleman
Blassingame, W. Murder is bad luck
Blatnik, A. Thirty years
Boland, J. C. Bears watching
Boland, J. C. Easy money
Boland, J. C. Evidence seen
Boland, J. C. Last island south
Boland, J. C. No crime in the hills
Boland, J. C. Out of her depth
Boland, J. C. The passenger
Boland, J. C. Past life
Boland, J. C. The return of Jasper Kohl
Boland, J. C. Reunion in Baineville
Boland, J. C. Sargasso Sea
Boland, J. C. Stand-in
Boland, J. C. Two hundred big ones
Bosch, L. In this world, and at the time Mercedes died
Bruen, K. She wails through the fair
Buchan, J. The green wildebeest
Cannon, T. Instant karma
Catalona, K. The Sadowsky manifesto
Chabon, M. The god of dark laughter
Chambers, W. The black bottle
Champion, D. L. Death stops payment
Clark, M. H. The tell-tale purr
Cleeves, A. Neastly pleasures
Cook, F. The gift
Corbett, D. and Urrea, L. A. Who stole my monkey?
Cortijos, A. Brawner's shadows
Crider, B. Pure pulp
Crumley, J. Luck
Dalembert, L.-P. Dangerous crossroads
Davis, F. C. Flaming angel

Davis, L. The house behind
Davis, L. Mr. Knockly
Delee, D. Bling, bling
DeMille, N. Death benefits
Dixon, S. The wild bird reserve
Doctorow, E. L. A house on the plains
Dostoevsky, F. Murder from Crime and punishment
Downum, A. Blue valentine
Drees, C. By hook or by crook
Ellis, K. The feather
Ely, S. The poisoned arrow
Emshwiller, C. Hands
Emshwiller, C. Murray is for murder
Emshwiller, C. The victim
Evans, M. A. Low-budget monster flick
Faherty, T. The caretaker
Farmer, P. J. Cats, dogs, and other creatures
Faulkner, W. A rose for Emily
Fischer, B. Middleman for murder
Fisher, S. Wait for me
Ford, J. The summer palace
Fowler, K. J. Always
Franc, I. The enigma of her voice
Garcia-Aguilera, C. Personal experience
Gault, W. C. The bloody Bokhara
Gifford, B. Force of evil
Gifford, B. The sudden demise of Sharkface Bensky
Gilbow, S. L. Red card
Gilley, T. Vanishing world
Gilman, K. Devil's pocket
Glaspell, S. A jury of her peers
Gold, H. L. I know suicide
Gold, H. L. Perfect murder
Gold, H. L. Problem in murder
Gomel, E. Going east
Goodrich, J. Murder in the sixth
Gorky, M. A strange murderer
Gorman, E. Comeback
Gorman, E. Favor and the princess
Gorman, E. The long way back
Gorman, E. Loose ends
Gorman, E. Such a good girl
Gorman, E. and Morrish, R. Rafferty's comeback
Goulart, R. Murder for dummies
Gray, G. Mr. Universe
Greenman, B. Viva Regina
Haines, C. The cypress dream
Hale, D. J. The precipice
Hall, T. M. Erratum: insert "r" in "transgressors"
Hannah, S. The asking price
Heathcock, A. The daughter
Heathcock, A. Peacekeeper
Heathcock, A. Smoke
Highsmith, P. The baby spoon
Highsmith, P. Not one of us
Highsmith, P. Oona, the jolly cave woman
Highsmith, P. There I was, struck with Bubsy
Hill, R. Where are all the naughty people?
Hoch, E. D. The theft of the rusty bookmark
Holm, G. When it's tough out there
Holmes, R. The long winter's nap
Hunt, M. The angel's share
Hunter, L. My brother
Hutchinson, D. The fortunate isles
Ibrāhim, H. Fathers and sons

MURDER STORIES—*Continued*

Jakubowski, M. A price to pay
Johnson, R. P. L. In apprehension, how like a god
Jones, G. A. Grazing the long acre
Kava, A. and Bremmer, P. A. A breath of hot air
Keene, D. Sauce for the gander
Kilworth, G. Hats off to Mary
King, D. Green Gables
King, S. 1922
Kitterman, B. Crazy people
Klavan, A. The killer Christian
Kozak, H. J. Lamborghini mommy
Kuhlken, K. Homes
Lahens, Y. Death in July
Lahens, Y. Petty corruption
L'Amour, L. Off the mangrove coast
Langan, J. The unbearable proximity of Mr. Dunn's balloons
Lawrence, M. C. Key witness
Lehane, D. Animal rescue
Leonard, E. Comfort to the enemy
Leonard, E. Louly and Pretty Boy
Levinson, R. S. Between sins
Lippman, L. Cougar
Lister, M. Ultima forsan
Loory, B. The hunter's head
Loory, B. The snake in the throat
Lovesey, P. Ghosted
Lupoff, R. A. Patterns
Lutz, J. Lily & men
MacDonald, J. D. Murder in one syllable
Maḥfūẓ, N. The seventh heaven
Malone, M. Christmas spirit
Marār, M. Windows
Mariotte, J. J. Gold shield blues
Matera, L. Dead drunk
McAllister, J. Bog man
McBain, E. I saw mommy killing Santa Claus
McCormack, U. The sea is not full
Mehrotra, P. K. Fit of rage
Mena, M. C. The vine-leaf
Moore, T. A. Red milk
Muessig, C. Bias
Mullen, C. Poetic justice
Murphy, W. Another day, another dollar
Nadel, B. Two stars
Nair, M. Small fry
Neville, S. Queen on the hill
Nevins, F. M., Jr. Bad bargain
Nevins, F. M., Jr. Because the constable blundered
Nevins, F. M., Jr. Buford's last case
Nevins, F. M., Jr. Doomchild
Nevins, F. M., Jr. Funeral music
Nevins, F. M., Jr. The last passenger
Nevins, F. M., Jr. Leap day
Nevins, F. M., Jr. Luck of the dead
Nevins, F. M., Jr. A nightcap of hemlock
Nevins, F. M., Jr. Puzzle for Scots
Nevins, F. M., Jr. The spark
Nevins, F. M., Jr. Toad cop
Ní Dhuibhne, E. Trespasses
Nikitas, D. Trauma dyke
Nolan, W. F. Vampire dollars
Oates, J. C. Bleed
Oates, J. C. The first husband
Oates, J. C. Honor code

Oates, J. C. ID
Oates, J. C. Smother
Oates, J. C. Split/brain
Oates, J. C. The story of the stabbing
Oates, J. C. Strip poker
Orozco, D. Officers weep
Orozco, D. Only connect
Ozaki, M. K. The corpse didn't kick
Packard, F. L. Shanghai Jim
Page, N. Those Catrini
Parker, T. J. Vic Primeval
Parrish, P. J. The tell-tale pacemaker
Phelan, T. Time will tell
Poulson, C. Fishy story
Proulx, A. 55 miles to the gas pump
Pulver, J. S. Just another desert night with blood
Read, C. Hungry enough
Rickert, M. The Christmas witch
Roberge, R. Border radio
Rodriguez-Milanes, C. El Loco
Rollins Jr., W. The ring on the hand of death
Rozan, S. J. Iterations
Sabatini, R. Intelligence
Saintcrow, L. Monsters
Santlofer, J. The 74th tale
Santlofer, J. Richie and the rich bitch
Sawhney, H. Gautam under a tree
Schirach, F. v. Bliss
Schirach, F. v. The cello
Schirach, F. v. Fähner
Schirach, F. v. Self-defense
Schmitt, E.-E. Perfect crime
Schweitzer, D. The dead kid
Seabrook, T. When Robin Hood fell with an arrow through his heart
Seamans, S. Survival instincts
Sikka, M. The railway aunty
Silverberg, R. How they pass the time in Pelpel
Smith, C. A. Strange shadows
Sokoloff, B. The crime of Dr. Garine
Somerville, P. The mother
Somerville, P. The son
Somerville, P. Vaara in the woods
Spagnoli, L. A cut above
Stanley, G. E. The shrieking skeleton
Sublett, J. Moral hazard
Theodore-Pharel, M. K. Mercy at the gate
Tremblay, P. Nineteen snapshots of Dennisport
Trevor, W. Bravado
Trueblood, V. Amends
Tucher, A. Bismarck rules
Turtledove, H. Farmers' law
Ulysse, K. D. The last department
Unger, L. Wild Card
Vaughn, C. Il est ne
Victor, G. The finger
Victor, M. Blues for Irène
Vincent, R. Hunt
Vonnegut, K. Ed Luby's key club
Vukcevich, R. The wages of syntax
Walsh, T. Diamonds mean death
Warsh, L. The Russians
Wells, H. G. The cone
Whitfield, R. Murder in the ring
Wiecek, M. The shipbreaker
Wieland, L. Vision
Williams, S. The Jade Woman of the Luminous Star
Wilson, L. Precious things

MURDER STORIES—_Continued_
    Winslow, D. After thirty
    Wolfe, G. Why I was hanged
    Wolven, S. News about yourself
    Woodrell, D. The echo of neighborly bones
    Woodrell, D. Uncle
    Woollcott, A. Moonlight sonata
    Woolrich, C. Borrowed crime
    Zeltserman, D. When death shines bright
    Zeman, A. Daphne, unrequited
    Zhang Kangkang. White poppies
MURDER TRIALS _See_ Trials
MURDERERS
    See also Murder stories
    Barron, L. The siphon
    Baxter, C. The old murderer
    Bierce, A. An arrest
    Bierce, A. My favorite murder
    Boland, J. C. Deep water
    Boland, J. C. Mad hare
    Cohen, P. Designer justice
    Dufresne, J. Iffy
    Falk, M. R. The Apalachicola night
    Gash, J. The life business
    Gorman, E. Killing Kate
    King, J. Quiet
    Lake, J. Dogs in the moonlight
    Leland, C. T. Swim
    Oates, J. C. Bounty hunter
    Oates, J. C. High lonesome
    Olsen, L. May
    Pickard, N. Dark chocolate
    Trevor, W. Gilbert's mother
    Trevor, W. Lost ground
Murfree, Mary Noailles _See_ Craddock, Charles
    Egbert, 1850-1922
Murphy, Brian
  Who do I have to kill to get a little respect up
    in here?
      Blood, guts, & whiskey; edited by Todd Rob-
      inson; introduction by Max Allan Collins.
MURPHY, DEVIN
  A FINE MEMORY WHILE IN DETOX
    Michigan Quarterly Review v50 no3 p446-
    448 Summ 2011
  The Olean Football Roster
    Confrontation no109 p133-41 Spr 2011
Murphy, Warren
  Another day, another dollar
    Randisi, R. J. The Shamus winners: Ameri-
    ca's best private eye stories, volume II,
    1996-2009; collected and introduced by
    Robert J. Randisi; founder, Private Eye
    Writers of America
Murphy, Yannick
  The good word
    The best American nonrequired reading 2009;
    edited by Dave Eggers; introduction by
    Marjane Satrapi; managing editor, Jesse
    Nathan
Murphy's Hall. Anderson, P.
Murray, Joan
  Niagara Street
    The Hudson Review v64 no2 p277-89 Summ
    2011
Murray, Sabina
  His Actual Mark
    Southwest Review v96 no2 p181-99 2011

Periplus
    The Massachusetts Review v52 no1 p16-28
    Spr 2011
Murray and the Holy Ghost. Ayau, K. J.
Murray is for murder. Emshwiller, C.
MUSEUMS
    See also Waxworks
    Abraham, D. Baljour and Meriwether in the ad-
      venture of the emperor's vengeance
    Châteaureynaud, G. O. The bronze schoolboy
    Châteaureynaud, G. O. A city of museums
    Drakulic, S. A guided tour through the museum
      of communism
    Kiernan, C. R. The Colliers' Venus (1893)
    Latiolais, M. Pink
    Loory, B. The shield
    Miéville, C. Pulvadmonitor: the dust's warning
    Millhauser, S. The Barnum Museum
    Schirach, F. v. The thorn
MUSHROOMS
    Laidlaw, M. Leng
MUSIC
    Dick, P. K. The preserving machine
    McGarry, T. God of exile
    Monk, D. Singing down the sun
Music at Annahullion. McCabe, E.
MUSIC CRITICS
    Baxter, C. Harmony of the world
MUSIC HALL ENTERTAINERS _See_ Entertain-
  ers
MUSIC LESSONS
    Goss, T. The wings of Meister Wilhelm
MUSIC TEACHERS
    Engel, P. Refuge
Music, when soft voices die. Beagle, P. S.
MUSICAL INSTRUMENTS
    Sprenger, S. Dust
MUSICIANS
    See also Drummers; Flutists; Pianists;
    Saxophonists; Violinists
    Calhoun, K. Nightblooming
    Châteaureynaud, G. O. The dolceola player
    Châteaureynaud, G. O. The excursion
    Corbett, D. and Urrea, L. A. Who stole my
      monkey?
    De Lint, C. Ten for the devil
    Delee, D. Bling, bling
    Doctorow, E. L. Liner notes: the songs of Billy
      Bathgate
    Gifford, B. Bad night at the Del Prado
    Lemberg, R. Geddarien
    Lindholm, M. Drum machine
    Lukasik-Foss, T. Band names
    Neugeboren, J. The Turetzky Trio
    Pitts, J. A. Three chords and the truth
    Robinson, K. S. In Pierson's orchestra
    Sabar, A. Collision
    Vukcevich, R. The button
MUSLIM WOMEN
    Atta, S. Hailstones on Zamfara
    Riahi, K. From the novel The scalpel
MUSLIMS
    See also Islam; Muslim women
    Abdullah, A. The soul of a turk
    Fatima, A. Do you suppose it's the east winds?
    Howard, R. E. Hawks over Egypt
    Marãr, M. S.P.Y.
    Saeed, M. Warriors of the sky

MYSTERY AND DETECTIVE STORIES—
United States—*Continued*

Davis, N. Don't you cry for me
De Noux, O. The heart has reasons
Decolta, R. Rainbow diamonds
Deming, R. The man who chose the devil
Dent, L. Luck
Douglas, C. N. Monster mash
DuBois, B. The dark island
Estleman, L. D. The anniversary waltz
Estleman, L. D. Blond and blue
Estleman, L. D. Bloody July
Estleman, L. D. Bodyguards shoot second
Estleman, L. D. Cigarette stop
Estleman, L. D. The crooked way
Estleman, L. D. Dead soldier
Estleman, L. D. Deadly force
Estleman, L. D. Dogs
Estleman, L. D. Eight Mile & Dequindre
Estleman, L. D. Eight Mile and Dequindre
Estleman, L. D. Fast burn
Estleman, L. D. Greektown
Estleman, L. D. I'm in the book
Estleman, L. D. Kill the cat
Estleman, L. D. Lady on ice
Estleman, L. D. Major crimes
Estleman, L. D. The man who loved noir
Estleman, L. D. Necessary evil
Estleman, L. D. Needle
Estleman, L. D. People who kill
Estleman, L. D. Pickups and shotguns
Estleman, L. D. The prettiest dead girl in Detroit
Estleman, L. D. Redneck
Estleman, L. D. Robber's roost
Estleman, L. D. Rumble strip
Estleman, L. D. Safe house
Estleman, L. D. Slipstream
Estleman, L. D. Snow angels
Estleman, L. D. Sometimes a hyena
Estleman, L. D. Square one
Estleman, L. D. Sunday
Estleman, L. D. Trust me
Estleman, L. D. The Woodward Plan
Faherty, T. The second coming
Faye, L. The case of Colonel Warburton's madness
Gardner, E. S. Come and get it
Grafton, S. A little missionary work
Gruber, F. Ask me another
Halliday, B. A taste for cognac
Hammett, D. The maltese falcon
Haywood, G. A. And pray nobody sees you
Healy, J. F. Aftermath
Healy, J. F. The holiday fairy
Kornbluth, C. M. Beer-bottle polka
Linscott, G. The case of Colonel Crockett's violin
Long, J. Merely murder
Lutz, J. Second story sunlight
Lutz, J. What you don't know can hurt you
McCoy, H. Dirty work
Muller, M. Final resting place
Muller, M. Telegraphing
Nebel, F. Doors in the dark
Nelscott, K. Family affair a Smokey Dalton story
Nethercott, M. O'Nelligan's glory
Nevins, F. M., Jr. Black spider
Nevins, F. M., Jr. Chance pattern
Nevins, F. M., Jr. Consultation in the dark
Nevins, F. M., Jr. Counterplot
Nevins, F. M., Jr. The kumquats affair
Nevins, F. M., Jr. Night of silken snow
Nevins, F. M., Jr. The possibility of termites
Pickard, N. Dust devil
Powell, T. Her dagger before me
Pronzini, B. Cat's-paw
Randisi, R. J. Black & white memories
Randisi, R. J. Cowards die many times
Randisi, R. J. The disappearance of Penny
Randisi, R. J. The equine theft
Randisi, R. J. The final nail
Randisi, R. J. The final nail: a Val O'Farrel story
Randisi, R. J. The girl who talked to horses
Randisi, R. J. The goodly race
Randisi, R. J. Green legs and glam
Randisi, R. J. The guilt edge
Randisi, R. J. The hook
Randisi, R. J. The listening room
Randisi, R. J. Midnight pass
Randisi, R. J. The nickel derby
Randisi, R. J. So beautiful, so dead
Reeves, R. Blood, sweat and biers
Riccardi, T. The mountain of fear
Rozan, S. J. Seeing the moon
Sale, R. The dancing rats
Schutz, B. M. Mary, Mary, shut the door
Searls, H. Drop dead twice
Spillane, M. The killing man
Spillane, M. and Collins, M. A. The big switch: a Mike Hammer story
Stabenow, D. Siren song
Stinson, H. H. Three apes from the east
Tinsley, T. A. Body snatcher
Zeltserman, D. Julius Katz

MYTHICAL ANIMALS
See also Dragons; Unicorns; Vampires; Werewolves

Anthony, P. Possible to rue
Wells, H. G. The sea raiders

MYTHOLOGY
See also Mythical animals; Sirens (Mythology)

Monk, D. Singing down the sun
Parks, R. On the banks of the River of Heaven

N

Nabokov, Vladimir Vladimirovich
Revenge
The greatest Russian stories of crime and suspense; edited by Otto Penzler.

Nádas, Péter
Le nu féminin en mouvement
The Paris Review v52 no195 p85-129 Wint 2010

Nadel, Barbara
Two stars
Original sins; a Crime Writer's Association anthology; edited by Martin Edwards.

Nadjarian, Nora
Exhibition
Best European fiction 2011; edited by Aleksandr Hemon; preface by Colum McCann

Nadzam, Bonnie
  The Devil's Circle
    StoryQuarterly v44 p231-44 2010
  The Losing End
    Harper's v323 no1935 p69-72 Ag 2011
Naëma disappeared. Dib, M.
Nagai, Mariko
  Autobiography
    Nagai, M. Georgic; stories
  Bitter fruit
    Nagai, M. Georgic; stories
  Confession
    Nagai, M. Georgic; stories
    New Letters v76 no4 p9-22 2010
  Drowning land
    Nagai, M. Georgic; stories
  Fugue
    Nagai, M. Georgic; stories
  Georgic
    Nagai, M. Georgic; stories
  Grafting
    Nagai, M. Georgic; stories
  How we touch the ground, how we touch
    Nagai, M. Georgic; stories
  Love story
    Nagai, M. Georgic; stories
  Song
    Nagai, M. Georgic; stories
Naima. Matar, H.
Naimon, David
  Genetic Drift
    StoryQuarterly v44 p133-55 2010
Naipaul, V. S. (Vidiadhar Surajprasad)
  B. Wordsworth
    Naipaul, V. S. Collected short fiction; with an
      introduction by the author
  The baker's story
    Naipaul, V. S. Collected short fiction; with an
      introduction by the author
  The blue cart
    Naipaul, V. S. Collected short fiction; with an
      introduction by the author
  Bogart
    Naipaul, V. S. Collected short fiction; with an
      introduction by the author
  Caution
    Naipaul, V. S. Collected short fiction; with an
      introduction by the author
  A Christmas story
    Naipaul, V. S. Collected short fiction; with an
      introduction by the author
  The coward
    Naipaul, V. S. Collected short fiction; with an
      introduction by the author
  The enemy
    Naipaul, V. S. Collected short fiction; with an
      introduction by the author
  A flag on the island
    Naipaul, V. S. Collected short fiction; with an
      introduction by the author
  George and the pink house
    Naipaul, V. S. Collected short fiction; with an
      introduction by the author
  Greenie and yellow
    Naipaul, V. S. Collected short fiction; with an
      introduction by the author
  Hat
    Naipaul, V. S. Collected short fiction; with an
      introduction by the author

  The heart
    Naipaul, V. S. Collected short fiction; with an
      introduction by the author
  His chosen calling
    Naipaul, V. S. Collected short fiction; with an
      introduction by the author
  How I left Miguel Street
    Naipaul, V. S. Collected short fiction; with an
      introduction by the author
  Love, love, love, alone
    Naipaul, V. S. Collected short fiction; with an
      introduction by the author
  Man-man
    Naipaul, V. S. Collected short fiction; with an
      introduction by the author
  The maternal instinct
    Naipaul, V. S. Collected short fiction; with an
      introduction by the author
  The mechanical genius
    Naipaul, V. S. Collected short fiction; with an
      introduction by the author
  The mourners
    Naipaul, V. S. Collected short fiction; with an
      introduction by the author
  My aunt Gold Teeth
    Naipaul, V. S. Collected short fiction; with an
      introduction by the author
  The nightwatchman's occurance book
    Naipaul, V. S. Collected short fiction; with an
      introduction by the author
  One out of many
    Naipaul, V. S. Collected short fiction; with an
      introduction by the author
  The perfect tenants
    Naipaul, V. S. Collected short fiction; with an
      introduction by the author
  The pyrotechnicist
    Naipaul, V. S. Collected short fiction; with an
      introduction by the author
  The raffle
    Naipaul, V. S. Collected short fiction; with an
      introduction by the author
  Tell me who to kill
    Naipaul, V. S. Collected short fiction; with an
      introduction by the author
  The thing without a name
    Naipaul, V. S. Collected short fiction; with an
      introduction by the author
  Titus Hoyt, I. A.
    Naipaul, V. S. Collected short fiction; with an
      introduction by the author
  Until the soldiers came
    Naipaul, V. S. Collected short fiction; with an
      introduction by the author
Naipaul, Vidiadhar Surajprasad *See* Naipaul, V.
    S. (Vidiadhar Surajprasad), 1932-
Nair, Meera
  Small fry
    Delhi noir; edited by Hirsh Sawhney
The **Name** Changer. Clayton, J. J.
The **name** on the stone. Hearn, L.
NAMES, PERSONAL *See* Personal names
Names for water. Johnson, K.
The **Names** of All Things. FAULKNER, G.
The **names** of Yanils. Davis, C.
Naming of parts. Lebbon, T.
Naming the names. Devlin, A.
NANNIES *See* Governesses; Nursemaids
Nanny. Dick, P. K.

NANOTECHNOLOGY
   Cooper, S. Confliction
NANTUCKET ISLAND (MASS.)
   Adrian, C. The black square
   Bingham, S. Rachel's island
The Napoleon difference. Campbell-Such, J.
Napoleon's Eyes. Farnsworth, V.
Naranbhai, Anand Odhav
   George and Priti
      Nature v468 p340 N 11 2010
Narayan, Shweta
   The mechanical aviary of emperor Jalal-ud-din
      Muhammad Akbar
      Steampunk II: steampunk reloaded; edited by
         Ann & Jeff VanderMeer.
   Pishaach
      The beastly bride; tales of the animal people;
         edited by Ellen Datlow & Terri Windling;
         introduction by Terri Windling; selected
         decorations by Charles Vess.
Narayanan, Kalpana
   Aviator on the prowl
      Boston Review v36 no4 p36-40 Jl/Ag 2011
NARCOTIC HABIT See Drug addiction
NARCOTICS, CONTROL OF See Drug traffic
NARCOTICS AGENTS See Drug traffic
Nastenka. Solzhenitsyn, A.
Nathan, Micah
   One Act
      Gettysburg Review v24 no3 p467-476 S 2011
The national city reparation society. Urrea, L. A.
NATIONAL FRONT (FRANCE) See Front National (France)
NATIONAL SOCIALISM
      See also Germany—1918-1945
   Gomel, E. Going east
   Grossman, V. S. In Kislavodsk
   Lemberg, R. Geddarien
   Sullivan, J. Niels Bohr and the sleeping Dane
   Wieland, L. La fenêtre
A natural disaster. Davis, L.
 Natural selection. Schabas, M.
Natural Wonder. Kaplan, H.
The naturalist. McHugh, M.
NATURALISTS
      See also Paleontologists
NATURE
   Kronauer, B. A sort of achievement like nature's
Nauvoo, Illinois. Shepard, S.
NAVAL BATTLES
      See also Sea stories; World War, 1939-
      1945—Naval operations
Navigation. Sabar, A.
Naylor, Heidi
   Revolver
      New Letters v77 no2 p59-66 2011
NAZIS See National socialism
NAZISM See National socialism
NEANDERTHAL RACE
      See also Prehistoric man
NEAR-DEATH EXPERIENCES
   Cardinale, J. Action at a distance
   Lahens, Y. Who is that man?
NEAR EAST See Middle East
Near-extinct birds of the central cordillera. Fountain, B.
Neastly pleasures. Cleeves, A.

Nebel, Frederick
   Doors in the dark
      The Black Lizard big book of Black Mask
         stories; edited and with a foreword by Otto
         Penzler; introduction by Keith Alan
         Deutsch.
NEBRASKA
   Crane, S. The blue hotel
   Monk, D. When the train calls lonely
                Farm life
         See Farm life—Nebraska
Necessary angels. Thon, M. R.
The necessary brother. DuBois, B.
Necessary evil. Estleman, L. D.
Necromancy in Naat. Smith, C. A.
The Need. Bill, F.
Needle. Estleman, L. D.
Needle in a timestack. Silverberg, R.
Needles. Bear, E.
NEEDLEWORK
   Terry, G. P. The Holy Sisters of Shedir
Negarestani, Reza
   The gallows-horse
      The Thackery T. Lambshead cabinet of curi-
         osities; edited by Ann & Jeff VanderMeer.
Negative space. Gallari, A.
NEGROES See African Americans
The neighbor. Bayley, E.
The Neighbor. Bayley, E.
The Neighbor on Rue de Jarente. Fleischman, C.
The neighborhood, the ravine, and the old
   Peugeot. Lahens, Y.
NEIGHBORS
   Allen, D. Among the missing
   Allen, D. End of his tether
   Allen, D. Goat on a hill
   Archer, J. Politically correct
   Ayres, D. Seeing nothing
   Baker, L. Ghost story
   Balázs, B. The clumsy god
   Bardsley, G. Crazy Larry smells bacon
   Baxter, C. The old murderer
   Binkley, P. Keepsakes
   Davis, L. The house behind
   Davis, L. My neighbors in a foreign place
   Dixon, S. Evening
   Dixon, S. The neighbors
   Earley, T. Mr. Tall
   Eisenberg, D. The robbery
   Elliott, J. The Wilds
   Ellis, K. The feather
   Fallon, S. You know when the men are gone
   Ginsberg, D. The new girl
   Gray, A. Waste
   Hardwick, E. Cross-town
   Hemmingson, M. What happened?
   Hemmingson, M. Why don't you use your park-
      ing space?
   Hodge, B. Just outside our windows, deep inside
      our walls
   'Izz al-Dīn, M. The path to madness
   Johnston, B. A. Soldier of fortune
   Kurlansky, M. Margaret
   Laken, V. Remedies
   Matheson, R. Red is the color of desire
   Monzó, Q. Centripetal force
   Mosley, W. The trial
   Mphahlele, E. A point of identity
   Naipaul, V. S. Love, love, love, alone

Neugeboren, Jay—*Continued*

The Turetzky Trio

Neugeboren, J. You are my heart and other stories

You are my heart

Neugeboren, J. You are my heart and other stories

Neuman, Andrés

After Helena

Granta no113 p123-33 Wint 2010

NEURASTHENIA *See* Nervous breakdown

NEUROLOGISTS

Levine, S. The wolf

NEUROSES

Cather, W. Paul's case: a study in temperament

Davis, L. The fears of Mrs. Orlando

Davis, L. Five signs of disturbance

Davis, L. The housemaid

Davis, L. Sketches for a life of Wassilly

Emshwiller, C. Omens

NEUROTICS *See* Neuroses

Neutron star. Niven, L.

NEVADA

Krautkramer, K. Nevada

Mullins, D. P. Crash site on a desert mountain outside Las Vegas

Watkins, C. V. The last thing we need

Las Vegas

Bear, E. And the deep blue sea

Bear, E. King pole, gallows pole, bottle tree

Campbell, F. 4/18

Esposito, B. Kirby and the portal to Hell

Greenspon, J. Mirrors and infinity

Kiraly, A. Your recent acquisitions in the neonesque (microfables)

Kostival, B. Islanders

Kozlowski, L. Nuclear wasted love song

Magliocco, P. Monsieur Dombo in glitter town

Moss, P. Time machine

Mullins, D. P. Arboretum

Mullins, D. P. Driving lessons

Mullins, D. P. A familiar place

Mullins, D. P. First sight

Mullins, D. P. Glitter Gulch

Mullins, D. P. This life or the next

Niles, C. Sin's last stand

Shapiro, J. Bummer

Tran, V. Kubla Khan

Nevada. Krautkramer, K.

Nevarez, Daniel

(jt. auth) See Torres, David

Never come back. Tallent, E.

(Never) fade away. Barahona, F.

Nevermore. Cook, T. H.

Neville, Stuart

The last dance

Blood, guts, & whiskey; edited by Todd Robinson; introduction by Max Allan Collins.

Queen on the hill

Requiems for the departed; edited by Gerard Brennan & Mike Stone.

Nevins, Francis M., Jr.

Bad bargain

Nevins, F. M., Jr. Night forms; short stories; with an introduction and afterwords by the author.

Bagworms

Nevins, F. M., Jr. Night forms; short stories; with an introduction and afterwords by the author.

Because the constable blundered

Nevins, F. M., Jr. Night forms; short stories; with an introduction and afterwords by the author.

Black spider

Nevins, F. M., Jr. Night forms; short stories; with an introduction and afterwords by the author.

Buford's last case

Nevins, F. M., Jr. Night forms; short stories; with an introduction and afterwords by the author.

Chance pattern

Nevins, F. M., Jr. Night forms; short stories; with an introduction and afterwords by the author.

Consultation in the dark

Nevins, F. M., Jr. Night forms; short stories; with an introduction and afterwords by the author.

Counterplot

Nevins, F. M., Jr. Night forms; short stories; with an introduction and afterwords by the author.

Dogsbody

Nevins, F. M., Jr. Night forms; short stories; with an introduction and afterwords by the author.

Doomchild

Nevins, F. M., Jr. Night forms; short stories; with an introduction and afterwords by the author.

Evensong

Nevins, F. M., Jr. Night forms; short stories; with an introduction and afterwords by the author.

Fair game

Nevins, F. M., Jr. Night forms; short stories; with an introduction and afterwords by the author.

Filmflam

Nevins, F. M., Jr. Night forms; short stories; with an introduction and afterwords by the author.

Funeral music

Nevins, F. M., Jr. Night forms; short stories; with an introduction and afterwords by the author.

The kumquats affair

Nevins, F. M., Jr. Night forms; short stories; with an introduction and afterwords by the author.

The last passenger

Nevins, F. M., Jr. Night forms; short stories; with an introduction and afterwords by the author.

Leap day

Nevins, F. M., Jr. Night forms; short stories; with an introduction and afterwords by the author.

Luck of the dead

Nevins, F. M., Jr. Night forms; short stories; with an introduction and afterwords by the author.

Nevins, Francis M., Jr.—*Continued*
Night of silken snow
    Nevins, F. M., Jr. Night forms; short stories;
    with an introduction and afterwords by the
    author.
A nightcap of hemlock
    Nevins, F. M., Jr. Night forms; short stories;
    with an introduction and afterwords by the
    author.
Open letter to survivors
    Nevins, F. M., Jr. Night forms; short stories;
    with an introduction and afterwords by the
    author.
The other man in the pinstripe
    Nevins, F. M., Jr. Night forms; short stories;
    with an introduction and afterwords by the
    author.
The possibility of termites
    Nevins, F. M., Jr. Night forms; short stories;
    with an introduction and afterwords by the
    author.
Puzzle for Scots
    Nevins, F. M., Jr. Night forms; short stories;
    with an introduction and afterwords by the
    author.
The skull of the stuttering gunfighter
    Nevins, F. M., Jr. Night forms; short stories;
    with an introduction and afterwords by the
    author.
The spark
    Nevins, F. M., Jr. Night forms; short stories;
    with an introduction and afterwords by the
    author.
Superscam
    Nevins, F. M., Jr. Night forms; short stories;
    with an introduction and afterwords by the
    author.
Toad cop
    Nevins, F. M., Jr. Night forms; short stories;
    with an introduction and afterwords by the
    author.
Nevins, Jess
Lost pages from the Encyclopedia of Fantastic
    Victoriana
    Steampunk II: steampunk reloaded; edited by
    Ann & Jeff VanderMeer.
The **new** accelerator. Wells, H. G.
The **New** Baby. Holden, M.
NEW ENGLAND
Baker, L. Ghost story
Cooke, R. T. Odd Miss Todd
Fisher, D. C. The bedquilt
Freeman, M. E. W. A New England nun
Jewett, S. O. A white heron
Stowe, H. B. The village do-nothing from
    Oldtown folks
19th century
Buckell, T. S. Trinkets
A **New** England nun. Freeman, M. E. W.
A **New** Examiner. Wallace, D. F.
The **new** generation. Solzhenitsyn, A.
The **new** girl. Ginsberg, D.
NEW HAMPSHIRE
Perabo, S. Shelter
NEW JERSEY
Díaz, J. Edison, New Jersey
Engel, P. Lucho
Fusilli, J. Digby, attorney at law
Oates, J. C. ID

Oates, J. C. Tetanus
Sands, B. Terror in the haunted house
Tucher, A. Bismarck rules
Trenton
Oates, J. C. Probate
NEW MEXICO
Abbott, L. K. A great piece of elephant
Dillman, D. Cloudcroft
Los Alamos
Shepard, J. Minotaur
NEW ORLEANS (LA.) *See* Louisiana—New Or-
    leans
NEW SPAIN
Vaughn, C. Conquistador de la noche
The **new** Spain. Tóibín, C.
The **new** world. Goodberg, D.
NEW YEAR
Black, A. That of which we cannot speak
Vaughn, C. Kitty's zombie New Year
New Year's resolution. Davis, L.
NEW YORK (N.Y.)
Alenyikov, M. Barrel of laughs
Alenyikov, M. It takes all kinds
Alenyikov, M. Ivan and Misha
Alenyikov, M. Whirling dervish
Alenyikov, M. Who did what to whom?
Allio, K. Clothed, female figure
Black, A. Mollusk makes
Cameron, P. The end of my life in New York
Crowley, J. And go like this
Gallari, A. Reading Rilke
Jemison, N. K. Non-zero probabilities
Leland, C. T. Wonderful town
McCray, C. Double dead
McElroy, J. Silk, or the woman with the bike
Mehta, R. A better life
Mehta, R. Yours
Sabar, A. Depths
Segal, L. G. Making good
Sherman, D. How the pooka came to New York
    City
Willis, M. S. Elvissa and the rabbi
Zeman, A. Daphne, unrequited
Bronx
Beagle, P. S. The rock in the Park
Dixon, S. Pale cheeks of a butcher's boy
Gold, H. L. Problem in murder
Tuten, F. Self portrait with Sicily
Brooklyn
Abraham, P. Hasidic noir
Lethem, J. View from a headlock
McElroy, J. No man's land
Neugeboren, J. Lakewood, New Jersey
Neugeboren, J. Overseas
Neugeboren, J. You are my heart
Papernick, J. My darling sweetheart baby
Price-Thompson, T. Brotherly love
Central Park
Sabar, A. Green
Coney Island
McDonald, S. Bluebeard by the sea
Greenwich Village
Ikstena, N. Elza Kuga's old-age dementia
Page, N. Those Catrini
Sabar, A. Sightlines
Warsh, L. Harry Cray
Warsh, L. Mysterioso
Harlem
Evans, D. Jellyfish

NEW YORK (N.Y.)—*Continued*
Lower East Side
Stern, S. Avigdor of the Apes
Manhattan
Allen, D. The green suit
Baxt, G. Schemes and variations
Bingham, S. Mending
Dixon, S. Shoelaces
Egan, J. Out of body
Eisenberg, D. A cautionary tale
Eisenberg, D. Twilight of the superheroes
Emshwiller, C. Omens
Grodstein, L. Homewrecker
Hardwick, E. Back issues
Hardwick, E. Cross-town
Hardwick, E. The oak and the axe
Hardwick, E. On the eve
Hardwick, E. The purchase
Hardwick, E. A season's romance
Hardwick, E. Shot: a New York story
Havazelet, E. Gurov in Manhattan
Highsmith, P. Where the door is always open
  and the welcome mat is out
Hoch, E. D. The theft of the rusty bookmark
Kiernan, C. R. The pearl diver
Klavan, A. The killer Christian
Malone, M. Christmas spirit
Matheson, R. Man with a club
Melville, H. Bartleby the scrivener
Millet, L. Sir Henry
Neugeboren, J. The debt
Nolan, W. F. What love is this?
Novik, N. Priced to sell
O'Brien, E. Manhattan medley
Reed, K. Weston walks
Sabar, A. Collision
Sabar, A. Crossroads
Self, W. Caring, sharing
Slesinger, T. Missis Flinders
Tuten, F. The bar on Tompkins Square Park
Tuten, F. The park in winter
Queens
Davidson, H. Son of so many tears
Lychack, W. Love is a temper
Mu Xin. Tomorrow, I'll stroll no more
NEW YORK (N.Y.). GRAND CENTRAL TER-
MINAL *See* Grand Central Terminal (New
York, N.Y.)
NEW YORK (N.Y.). STATUE OF LIBERTY
See Statue of Liberty (New York, N.Y.)
NEW YORK (STATE)
    See also Long Island (N.Y.)
Boland, J. C. Evocation of evil
Kirshenbaum, B. The lunatic
Oates, J. C. Bounty hunter
Oates, J. C. Death certificate
Oates, J. C. Honor code
Oates, J. C. Nowhere
Oates, J. C. The Spill
Wolff, T. The deposition
Albany
Langan, J. City of the dog
New York City
    See New York (N.Y.)
Newman, Kim
  Castle in the desert: anno Dracula 1977
    Vampires; the recent undead; edited by Paula
    Guran.
News about yourself. Wolven, S.

News from home. Atta, S.
News from the front. Turtledove, H.
NEWSPAPER PUBLISHERS *See* Publishers and
  publishing
NEWSPAPERMEN *See* Journalists
NEWSPAPERS
  Davis, L. Alvin the typesetter
  Eidus, J. A bisel this, a bisel that
  Wells, H. G. The queer story of Brownlow's
    newspaper
The **next** best thing. Vukcevich, R.
The **next** building I plan to bomb. Baxter, C.
The **next** thing. Millhauser, S.
Next to nothing. Dixon, S.
Nguyen, Quang Lap
  The goat horn bell
    Family of fallen leaves; stories of Agent Or-
    ange by Vietnamese writers; edited by
    Charles Waugh and Huy Lien.
Nguyen, Thi Ngoc Ha
  The spirit pond
    Family of fallen leaves; stories of Agent Or-
    ange by Vietnamese writers; edited by
    Charles Waugh and Huy Lien.
Ni Dhuibhne, Eilis
  Midwife to the fairies
    The Granta book of the Irish short story; [ed-
    ited by] Anne Enright.
  Trespasses
    Best European fiction 2011; edited by Alek-
    sandr Hemon; preface by Colum McCann
Niagara Street. Murray, J.
Nicholson, Scott
  You'll never walk alone
    Z: zombie stories; edited by J. M. Lassen
Nick. Robinson, R.
The **nickel** derby. Randisi, R. J.
NIECES
  Black, A. Someday is today
  Grover, L. L. The dance boots
  Skurnick, L. Spectacle Pond
  Wieland, L. Resolution Trust
  Yamauchi, W. Onna
Niedzviecki, Hal
  The colorist
    Niedzviecki, H. Look down, this is where it
    must have happened
  Displacement
    Niedzviecki, H. Look down, this is where it
    must have happened
  Doing God's work
    Niedzviecki, H. Look down, this is where it
    must have happened
  Holiday
    Niedzviecki, H. Look down, this is where it
    must have happened
  Look down, this is where it must have happened
    Niedzviecki, H. Look down, this is where it
    must have happened
  Prenatal
    Niedzviecki, H. Look down, this is where it
    must have happened
  Punk rock role model
    Niedzviecki, H. Look down, this is where it
    must have happened
  Real estate
    Niedzviecki, H. Look down, this is where it
    must have happened

Nuila, Ricardo
  Dog bites
    The Best American short stories, 2011; select-
      ed from U.S. and Canadian magazines by
      Geraldine Brooks with Heidi Pitlor; with an
      introduction by Geraldine Brooks.
Null, Matthew Neill
  Something you can't live without
    The Pen/O.Henry Prize stories 2011; chosen
      and with an introduction by Laura Furman;
      with essays on the stories thety admire
      most by jurors A. M. Homes, Manuel Mu-
      ñoz, Christine Schutt
Number of the bus. Lake, J.
Nunez, Sigrid
  It's All Good
    Agni no73 p188-202 2011
NUNS
      See also Ex-nuns
  McLaverty, M. The road to the shore
  Terry, G. P. The Holy Sisters of Shedir
  Wieland, L. Some churches
The **nurse** and the black lagoon. Treadway, J.
NURSEMAIDS
  Chekhov, A. P. Sleepy
NURSES AND NURSING
  Archer, J. Where there's a will
  Boggs, B. Imperial Chrysanthemum
  Breen, S. Triplet
  Highsmith, P. The trouble with Mrs. Blynn, the
    trouble with the world
  Jones, S. G. Captain's lament
  Marley, L. Night shift
  Qiu Xiaolong. Return of pow 1
  Row, J. The call of blood
  Schmitt, E.-E. Getting better
  Swirsky, R. The debt of the innocent
  Willis, M. S. Pie Knob
NURSING HOMES
  Binkley, P. A convenient place to wait
  Franco, J. April in three parts: part II, Wasting
  Moore, L. M. Final dispositions
  Penkov, M. Makedonija
  Tóibín, C. The colour of shadows
Nutt, David
  The Corporate Body [Part of a special issue:
    Thresholds]
    DisClosure no15 p107-25 2006
Nutting, Alissa
  Alcoholic
    Nutting, A. Unclean jobs for women and girls
  Ant colony
    Nutting, A. Unclean jobs for women and girls
  Bandleader's girlfriend
    Nutting, A. Unclean jobs for women and girls
  Cat owner
    Nutting, A. Unclean jobs for women and girls
  Corpse smoker
    Nutting, A. Unclean jobs for women and girls
  Dancing rat
    Nutting, A. Unclean jobs for women and girls
  Deliverywoman
    Nutting, A. Unclean jobs for women and girls
  Dinner
    Nutting, A. Unclean jobs for women and girls
  Dying Is All I Think About
    Bomb no113 p supp6-supp9 Fall 2010
  Gardener
    Nutting, A. Unclean jobs for women and girls

Hellion
    Nutting, A. Unclean jobs for women and girls
Hot, fast, and sad
    Fantastic women; 18 tales of the surreal and
      the sublime from Tin House; introduction
      by Joy Williams; edited by Rob Spillman.
Ice melter
    Nutting, A. Unclean jobs for women and girls
Knife thrower
    Nutting, A. Unclean jobs for women and girls
Magician
    Nutting, A. Unclean jobs for women and girls
Model's assistant
    Nutting, A. Unclean jobs for women and girls
Porn star
    Nutting, A. Unclean jobs for women and girls
She-man
    Nutting, A. Unclean jobs for women and girls
Teenager
    Nutting, A. Unclean jobs for women and girls
Zookeeper
    Nutting, A. Unclean jobs for women and girls
Nwokolo, Chuma
  Sentencing for Six
    Agni no72 p171-8 2010

O

O, Thiam Chin
  Eyes and Ears
    World Literature Today v85 no4 p12-15 Jl/Ag
      2011
The **oak** and the axe. Hardwick, E.
OAKLAND (CALIF.) *See* California—Oakland
Oakland dragon blues. Beagle, P. S.
Oates, Joyce Carol
  Amputee
    Oates, J. C. Sourland; stories
  Babysitter
    Oates, J. C. Sourland; stories
  The barter
    Oates, J. C. Sourland; stories
  The beating
    Oates, J. C. Sourland; stories
  Bitch
    Oates, J. C. Sourland; stories
  Bleed
    Oates, J. C. Give me your heart; tales of mys-
      tery and suspense
  Bonobo momma
    Oates, J. C. Sourland; stories
  Bounty hunter
    Oates, J. C. Sourland; stories
  Death certificate
    Oates, J. C. Sourland; stories
  Donor organs
    Oates, J. C. Sourland; stories
  The first husband
    Oates, J. C. Give me your heart; tales of mys-
      tery and suspense
  Give me your heart
    Oates, J. C. Give me your heart; tales of mys-
      tery and suspense
  Golden gloves
    The vintage book of American women writ-
      ers; edited and with an introduction by
      Elaine Showalter.

Oates, Joyce Carol—*Continued*

High lonesome
  Blue collar, white collar, no collar; stories of work; edited by Richard Ford.
A Hole in the Head
  The Kenyon Review v32 no4 p30-64 Fall 2010
Honor code
  Oates, J. C. Sourland; stories
ID
  The Best American short stories, 2011; selected from U.S. and Canadian magazines by Geraldine Brooks with Heidi Pitlor; with an introduction by Geraldine Brooks.
Lost daddy
  Oates, J. C. Sourland; stories
Nowhere
  Oates, J. C. Give me your heart; tales of mystery and suspense
Papa at Ketchum, 1961
  Best of the West 2009; new stories from the wide side of the Missouri; edited by James Thomas and D. Seth Horton; foreword by Rick Bass.
Probate
  Oates, J. C. Sourland; stories
  Salmagundi no168/169 p158-91 Fall 2010/Wint 2011
Pumpkin-head
  Oates, J. C. Sourland; stories
Smother
  Oates, J. C. Give me your heart; tales of mystery and suspense
Sourland
  Oates, J. C. Sourland; stories
The Spill
  Oates, J. C. Give me your heart; tales of mystery and suspense
Split/brain
  Oates, J. C. Give me your heart; tales of mystery and suspense
The story of the stabbing
  Oates, J. C. Sourland; stories
Strip poker
  Oates, J. C. Give me your heart; tales of mystery and suspense
Tetanus
  Oates, J. C. Give me your heart; tales of mystery and suspense
  Freedom; stories celebrating the Universal Declaration of Human Rights; Amnesty International.
Three Girls
  The Georgia Review v65 no1 p225-33 Spr 2011
Uranus
  Oates, J. C. Sourland; stories
Vena cava
  Oates, J. C. Give me your heart; tales of mystery and suspense

Oates, Nathan

Famous for Crabs
  The Antioch Review v68 no3 p458-72 Summ 2010
Looking for Service
  The Antioch Review v69 no2 p293-309 Spr 2011

Obarrio, Juan

ER (...) Ellipses
  Social Text v29 no2 p121-7 Summ 2011
Obediently Yours. Melnick, M. A.

O'Berry, Tamsen Star

Homecoming
  Tribal College Journal of American Indian Higher Education v23 no1 p64-5 Fall 2011

OBESITY

Baxter, C. Mr. Scary
Hunter, L. Food luck
Orozco, D. Hunger tales
Stafford, J. The echo and the nemesis
Wells, H. G. The truth about Pyecraft
Wolff, T. Hunters in the snow

Psychological aspects

See also Anorexia nervosa

Obioma, Chigozie John

Fishermen
  The Virginia Quarterly Review v87 no3 p102-109 Summ 2011
Obit. Sanders, T.

OBITUARIES

Gray, A. Thoughts while strolling
Objects discovered in a novel under construction. Moore, A.
Oblivion by Calvin Klein. Fowler, C.

Obreht, Tea

Blue water djinn
  20 under 40; stories from the New Yorker; edited by Deborah Treisman.

O'Brien, Edna

Black flower
  O'Brien, E. Saints and sinners; stories
Green Georgette
  O'Brien, E. Saints and sinners; stories
Inner cowboy
  O'Brien, E. Saints and sinners; stories
Madame Cassandra
  O'Brien, E. Saints and sinners; stories
Manhattan medley
  O'Brien, E. Saints and sinners; stories
My two mother
  O'Brien, E. Saints and sinners; stories
Old wounds
  O'Brien, E. Saints and sinners; stories
Plunder
  O'Brien, E. Saints and sinners; stories
Send my roots rain
  O'Brien, E. Saints and sinners; stories
Shovel kings
  O'Brien, E. Saints and sinners; stories
Sinners
  O'Brien, E. Saints and sinners; stories
Sister Imelda
  The Granta book of the Irish short story; [edited by] Anne Enright.
The **obscure** bird. Royle, N.
Obsequy. Schoe, D. J.

OBSESSIONS

Blatnik, A. The man who didn't throw himself under a train speaks
Châteaureynaud, G. O. A life on paper
Gallari, A. Chasing Adonis
Hall, J. W. Overexposure
July, M. Majesty
Marías, J. While the women are sleeping
Matheson, R. Red is the color of desire
McOmber, A. Beneath us

OBSESSIONS—*Continued*
  Payne, M. Bullet
  Trevor, W. Old flame
  Tuttle, L. Shelf-life
  Villegas, H. His ghost
  Williamson, E. M. Rhoda's sack
OBSTETRICIANS *See* Physicians
The **obvious** candidate. Griffiths, R.
O'Callaghan, Billy
  Forty-One Is Not Old
    Confrontation no109 p32-43 Spr 2011
The **occidental** tourist. Jones, K.
OCCULTISM
        See also Fortune telling; Supernatural
        phenomena; Superstition; Witchcraft
  Worts, G. F. The master magician
Occupation duty. Turtledove, H.
Occupational Hazard. Pneuman, A.
Occupations, Settlements, Territories. Brownstein,
  G.
An **occurance** at Owl Creek Bridge. Bierce, A.
An **occurrence** at Owl Creek Bridge. Bierce, A.
OCEAN
  Archer, J. The undiplomatic diplomat
  Le Clézio, J.-M. G. Lullaby
  Loory, B. The house on the cliff and the sea
  Monk, D. Fishing the edge of the world
Ocean Avenue. Chabon, M.
Ocean state. McGarry, J.
OCEAN TRAVEL
  Bunin, I. A. The gentleman from San Francisco
OCEANIA *See* Islands of the Pacific
Ochsner, Gina
  Song of the selkie
    Fantastic women; 18 tales of the surreal and
      the sublime from Tin House; introduction
      by Joy Williams; edited by Rob Spillman.
Ockert, Jason
  Max
    Iowa Review v41 no1 p140-56 Spr 2011
O'Connell, Grace
  Noisemakers
    The Walrus v8 no5 p52-59 Je 2011
O'Connor, Flannery
  Good country people
    I found this funny; my favorite pieces of hu-
      mor and some that may not be funny at all;
      edited by Judd Apatow.
  Revelation
    The vintage book of American women writ-
      ers; edited and with an introduction by
      Elaine Showalter.
O'Connor, Frank
  The mad Lomasneys
    The Granta book of the Irish short story; [ed-
      ited by] Anne Enright.
O'Connor, Joseph
  Mothers were all the same
    The Granta book of the Irish short story; [ed-
      ited by] Anne Enright.
O'Connor, Mary Flannery *See* O'Connor,
  Flannery
O'Connor, Stephen
  All in good time
    O'Connor, S. Here comes another lesson; sto-
      ries
  Aunt Jules
    O'Connor, S. Here comes another lesson; sto-
      ries

Based on a true story
  O'Connor, S. Here comes another lesson; sto-
    ries
Bestiary
  O'Connor, S. Here comes another lesson; sto-
    ries
Disappearance and
  O'Connor, S. Here comes another lesson; sto-
    ries
Elodie
  O'Connor, S. Here comes another lesson; sto-
    ries
He will not see me stopping here
  O'Connor, S. Here comes another lesson; sto-
    ries
I think I'm happier
  O'Connor, S. Here comes another lesson; sto-
    ries
Love
  O'Connor, S. Here comes another lesson; sto-
    ries
Man in the moon
  O'Connor, S. Here comes another lesson; sto-
    ries
The professor of atheism: Department of refuta-
  tion
  O'Connor, S. Here comes another lesson; sto-
    ries
The professor of atheism: Glue factory bowling
  O'Connor, S. Here comes another lesson; sto-
    ries
The professor of atheism: Here comes another
  lesson
  O'Connor, S. Here comes another lesson; sto-
    ries
The professor of atheism: Magnum opus
  O'Connor, S. Here comes another lesson; sto-
    ries
The professor of atheism: Paradise
  O'Connor, S. Here comes another lesson; sto-
    ries
The professor of atheism: Stealing peaches from
  Sam Snnow
  O'Connor, S. Here comes another lesson; sto-
    ries
Sawed-in-half girl
  O'Connor, S. Here comes another lesson; sto-
    ries
White fire
  O'Connor, S. Here comes another lesson; sto-
    ries
Ziggurat
  O'Connor, S. Here comes another lesson; sto-
    ries
October. Olsen, L.
Octopi in the sky. Aiken, J.
OCTOPUS
  Aiken, J. Octopi in the sky
  Loory, B. The octopus
The **octopus.** Loory, B.
Odd behavior. Davis, L.
Odd Miss Todd. Cooke, R. T.
Odds on death. Mankiewicz, D. M.
Odette. Sylvain, P.
O'Donovan, Michael *See* O'Connor, Frank, 1903-
  1966
ODORS
  Vukcevich, R. A funny smell
Oedipus and the Sphinx. Cornea, A.

Of a sweet slow dance in the wake of temporary dogs. Castro, A.-T.
Of All His Good Life. Mills, R.
Of passage. Swirsky, R.
Of poetry. Bayley, E.
Of the cloth. Trevor, W.
Of wool. McOmber, A.
The **Off** Season. Adcox, J. T.
Off the mangrove coast. L'Amour, L.
The **offering**. McGarry, J.
The **offering**. Solana, T.
OFFICE WORKERS
  Comeau, J. Giraffes and everything
  Dixon, S. Overtime
  Kahaney, A. The temp
  McAdam, J. Inhuman resources
  Orozco, D. Orientation
  Orozco, D. Temporary stories
  Packer, A. Jump
  Self, W. Grey area
  Unferth, D. O. Wait till you see me dance
  Williamson, E. M. Rhoda's sack
Officer down (tweakers). Bill, F.
Officer Friendly. Robinson, L.
Officers' daughters. Blatnik, A.
Officers weep. Orozco, D.
Official friend. Ayau, K. J.
The **offspring**. Phillips, H.
Oh, death. Lasdun, J.
Oh I do like to be beside the seaside. Fowler, C.
Oh if you knew how the fishes do. Kronauer, B.
Oh, Yoko. Brubaker, J.
OHIO
  Bierce, A. A fruitless assignment
  Horrocks, C. It looks like this
            Frontier and pioneer life
        See Frontier and pioneer life—Ohio
                    Cincinnati
  Levine, S. Pat Smash
Ohlin, Alix
  The Cruise
    World Literature Today v84 no5 p50-4 S/O 2010
  These Foolish Things (Remind Me of You)
    Southwest Review v96 no1 p142-53 2011
Oil of dog. Bierce, A.
OJIBWA INDIANS *See* Chippewa Indians
Ojibwe boys. Grover, L. L.
The **OK** End of Funny Town. Polanzak, M.
O'KANE, JOHN
  GRAVITY'S GOD
    AMASS v15 no40 p28-33 Ap 2011
The **O'Kane** and the corpse. Hyde, D.
OKLAHOMA
  Chuculate, E. D. Cheyenne Madonna
  Chuculate, E. D. Dear Shorty
  Chuculate, E. D. A famous Indian artist
  Chuculate, E. D. Under the red star of Mars
  Chuculate, E. D. Yoyo
  Couch, S. The dandelion clock
  Leonard, E. Comfort to the enemy
  Leonard, E. Showdown at checotah [variant title: How Carlos Webster changed his name to Carl and became a famous Oklahoma lawman]
Okorafor, Nnedi
  The go-slow
    The way of the wizard; edited by John Joseph Adams.

Wahala
  Life on Mars: tales from the new frontier; an original science fiction anthology; edited by Jonathan Strahan
OLD AGE
    See also Aging; Elderly
  Archer, J. The queen's birthday telegram
  Archer, J. Where there's a will
  Barnes, J. Sleeping with John Updike
  Baxter, C. Horace and Margaret's fifty-second
  Baxter, C. The would-be father
  Beattie, A. The rabbit hole as likely explanation
  Beattie, A. That last odd day in L. A.
  Bierce, A. The applicant
  Bingham, S. Benjamin
  Binkley, P. A convenient place to wait
  Boggs, B. Election day
  Braddon, M. E. Good Lady Ducayne
  Châteaureynaud, G. O. Come out, come out
  Cheever, J. The world of apples
  Cornell, J. C. The swing of things
  Davis, L. The cottages
  Davis, L. Helen and Vi: a study in health and vitality
  Davis, L. In a northern country
  Davis, L. Old Mother and the Grouch
  Davis, L. The silence of Mrs. Iln
  Davis, L. What an old woman will wear
  Eisenberg, D. Someone to talk to
  Emshwiller, C. The institute
  Emshwiller, C. There is no evil angel but love
  Furman, L. The blue wall
  Grace, P. Busy lines
  Groff, L. Rue
  Hall, T. M. This is a love story, too
  Hannah, B. High-water railers
  Hannah, B. Mother Rooney unscrolls the hurt
  Lychack, W. Griswald
  Marãr, M. Biar Adass
  Monso, I. The customer is always right
  Moore, L. M. Final dispositions
  Mphahlele, E. Crossing over
  Mueenuddin, D. A spoiled man
  Nolan, W. F. Getting along just fine
  Oates, J. C. High lonesome
  Parrish, P. J. The tell-tale pacemaker
  Pearlman, E. Allog
  Pearlman, E. Capers
  Pearlman, E. Fidelity
  Pearlman, E. Lineage
  Pearlman, E. Relic and type
  Penkov, M. Makedonija
  Rodoreda, M. The mirror
  Ryman, G. VAO
  Schmitt, E.-E. The dreamer from Ostend
  Terry, G. P. Precious hairpin
  Vonnegut, K. The man without no kiddleys
  Wildt, J. Like riding a bike
OLD AGE HOMES
    See also Nursing homes
  Chambers, G. (I thought my father looked like FDR)
The **old** and the lost. Blake, G.
The **old** bean. Shapiro, J.
The **old** child. Balázs, B.
The **old** dictionary. Davis, L.
The **old** die rich. Gold, H. L.
Old Dime's Last Show. DeGhett, S. C.
Old flame. Trevor, W.

Old Friends. Grogan, G.
The **Old** God. Pirandello, L.
Old hunchback Fang. Qiu Xiaolong
OLD LADIES *See* Old age
An **old** lady travels by bus. Bayley, E.
OLD MAIDS *See* Single women
Old man. Cannon, P.
The **old** man and the Martian sea. Reynolds, A.
The **old** mechanic. Bill, F.
OLD MEN *See* Old age
The **old** mill. Scanlan, K.
Old Mother and the Grouch. Davis, L.
The **old** murderer. Baxter, C.
Old testament wisdom. Bill, F.
The **Old-Timers**. Makanin, V.
Old Wives' Mail: a short story [Part of a special issue: Stirrings: Journeys through emotion] Lewis, T.
The **old** woman and her thief. Lychack, W.
Old Woman Magoun. Freeman, M. E. W.
OLD WOMEN *See* Old age
Old wounds. O'Brien, E.
Oldblade. Monk, D.
The **oldest** man in Mississippi. Ely, S.
Oldshue, Robert
The Receiving Line
New England Review v31 no4 p70-80 2010/2011
The **Olean** Football Roster. Murphy, D.
O'Leary, Gabriela
(jt. auth) *See* Samudio, Álvaro Cepeda and O'Leary, Gabriela
O'Leary, Patrick
23 Skidoo
Swenson, P. The Best of Talebones; edited by Patrick Swenson.
Olingiris. Schweblin, S.
Oliu, Brian
C\ping scopuli.com
Butler, B. 30 under 30; an anthology of innovative fiction by younger writers; Blake Butler & Lily Hoang, eds.
Oliver, Reggie
Baskervilles midgets
Blood and other cravings; edited by Ellen Datlow.
Mr. Pigsny
The Best horror of the year: volume three; edited by Ellen Datlow.
Olivia's roses. Plummer, T. M.
Oloixarac, Pola
Conditions for the revolution
Granta no113 p81-96, 97-8 Wint 2010
Olsen, Lance
April
Olsen, L. Calendar of regrets
August
Olsen, L. Calendar of regrets
December
Olsen, L. Calendar of regrets
February
Olsen, L. Calendar of regrets
January
Olsen, L. Calendar of regrets
July
Olsen, L. Calendar of regrets
June
Olsen, L. Calendar of regrets

March
Olsen, L. Calendar of regrets
May
Olsen, L. Calendar of regrets
November
Olsen, L. Calendar of regrets
October
Olsen, L. Calendar of regrets
September
Olsen, L. Calendar of regrets
Omens. Emshwiller, C.
Omnisexual. Ryman, G.
On a dark night. Rodoreda, M.
On Chryse Plain. Baxter, S.
On Friendship. Mitchell, E.
On Junius Bridge. Pearlman, E.
On Orly's border. Terry, G. P.
On paper. Blatnik, A.
On the banks of the River of Heaven. Parks, R.
On the eve. Hardwick, E.
On the house of honor. Blatnik, A.
On the human plan. Lake, J.
On the road to New Egypt. Ford, J.
On the road with C. T. Savage. Willis, M. S.
On the sighting of other islands. MacLeod, I.
On the slide. Bowes, R.
On the streets. Trevor, W.
On the train. Rodoreda, M.
On the way down: a story for Ray Bradbury. Loory, B.
On the wheel. Parks, R.
O'Nan, Stewart
Monsters
The Year's best dark fantasy & horror; edited by Paula Guran
Once a very stupid man. Davis, L.
Once Removed. Francis, D.
Once upon a time. Gordimer, N.
Once Upon a Time a King . . . Marchis, V.
One. Blatnik, A.
O **one**. Roberson, C.
One Act. Nathan, M.
One character in search of her love story role. Cowie, F.
One-click banishment. Tolbert, J.
One day. Beattie, A.
One Dead Chicken. Heynen, J.
One every minute. Tillinghast, A. W.
One for all. Goodberg, D.
One good reason why not. Albert, E.
One hippopotamus. Barrett, L.
One Hundred Names for the Sea. Bell, C. D.
One Hundred Percent Cotton. Poissant, D. J.
One kind of officer. Bierce, A.
One kiss on the mouth in Mombasa. Keret, E.
One last meal. Goodberg, D.
One little life in Kenya (a 55-word story). Cayley, W. E.
One minus one. Tóibín, C.
One minute: Dumbo's death. Arsenijević, V.
One night in the long-ago. Shepard, S.
One night of love. Marías, J.
One night of love [Excerpt from While the Women Are Sleeping] Marías, J.
One of Sandy's dreams. Jones, G. A.
One of the missing. Bierce, A.
One of the rough ones. Bengtsson, J. T.
One of twins. Bierce, A.
One officer, one man. Bierce, A.

One out of many. Naipaul, V. S.
One part of the self is always tall and dark. Emshwiller, C.
One shot. Booth, C. G.
One stone. Shepard, S.
One summer night. Bierce, A.
One thin dime. Moore, S.
One thing. Dixon, S.
One time. Carey, E.
One united. Woodrell, D.
One version of the story. Sterling, P.
O'Nelligan's glory. Nethercott, M.
The ones who got away. Jones, S. G.
The ones who walk away from Omelas. Le Guin, U. H.
Only connect. Orozco, D.
The only mortal. Châteaureynaud, G. O.
The only way out is through. Black, A.
Onna. Yamauchi, W.
Oona, the jolly cave woman. Highsmith, P.
Open house. Gordimer, N.
Open letter to survivors. Nevins, F. M., Jr.
Open Mic. Frisch, S.
OPERA
    Kitterman, B. A place in the opera
Operation changeling. Anderson, P.
OPERATIONS, SURGICAL *See* Surgery
OPIUM
    Balázs, B. The opium smokers
    Moles, D. Seven cities of gold
The **opium** smokers. Balázs, B.
Opportunity. Boggs, B.
An **opportunity** of a lifetime. Goodberg, D.
Opposition in all things. Vestal, S.
Or else. Nelson, A.
The **oracle** of the dog. Chesterton, G. K.
Oral history. Gordimer, N.
Oral history (with hiccups). Davis, L.
Orange grove in my past. Shepard, S.
The **orange** tree. Marãr, M.
The **orange-tree** sacrifice. Kaftan, V.
Oranges. July, M.
Oranges and angel. Schulze, I.
Orangina. Kurlansky, M.
ORANIENBERG (GERMANY: CONCENTRATION CAMP)
    Kalechofsky, R. My poor prisoner
ORCHARDS
    Marãr, M. Planting the cacti
    Marãr, M. The wall of cacti
ORCHESTRA
    Robinson, K. S. In Pierson's orchestra
ORCHIDS
    Wells, H. G. The flowering of the strange orchild
Orczy, Baroness
    A question of passports
        The Big book of adventure stories; edited and with a introduction by Otto Penzler; foreword by Douglas Preston.
Order. Davis, L.
OREGON
    Kittredge, W. Stone boat
    Nolan, W. F. Getting along just fine
    Percy, B. Refresh, refresh
    Vukcevich, R. Tongues
                Eugene
    Packer, A. Her firstborn

                Portland
    Lake, J. A different way into the life
    Lake, J. Green grass blues
    Lake, J. Number of the bus
    Simmons, D. Letters
Oregon. Treadway, J.
O'Reilly, Sean
    Curfew
        The Granta book of the Irish short story; [edited by] Anne Enright.
ORIENT AND OCCIDENT *See* East and West
ORIENTALS *See* Asians
Orientation. Orozco, D.
The **original** impulse. Tillman, L.
Original sin. Shepard, S.
Orléans, three kilometers. Rodoreda, M.
ORNITHOLOGISTS
    Fountain, B. Near-extinct birds of the central cordillera
Orozco, Daniel
    The bridge
        Orozco, D. Orientation; and other stories
    Hunger tales
        Orozco, D. Orientation; and other stories
    I run every day
        Orozco, D. Orientation; and other stories
    Officers weep
        Orozco, D. Orientation; and other stories
    Only connect
        Orozco, D. Orientation; and other stories
        Best of the West 2010; new stories from the wide side of the Missouri; edited by James Thomas and D. Seth Horton; foreword by Kent Meyers.
    Orientation
        Orozco, D. Orientation; and other stories
    Shakers
        Orozco, D. Orientation; and other stories
    Somoza's dream
        Orozco, D. Orientation; and other stories
    Temporary stories
        Orozco, D. Orientation; and other stories
ORPHANS
    Baxter, C. The would-be father
    Bierce, A. A baby tramp
    Doerr, A. The river nemunas
    Gilley, T. The end zone
    Gordimer, N. The ultimate safari
    Grossman, V. S. Mama
    Le Clézio, J.-M. G. Hazaran
    Maberry, J. Saint John
    Niles, C. Sin's last stand
    Osondu, E. C. Waiting
    Priest, C. Addison Howell and the clockroach
    Russell, K. The dredgeman's revelation
Orphans of Holy Week. Goedjen, T.
Ortuño, Antonio
    Small mouth, thin lips
        Granta no113 p217-32 Wint 2010
OSAMA BIN LADEN
                About
    Turtledove, H. Bedfellows
Osetra. Kurlansky, M.
Osondu, E. C.
    Bar Beach show
        Osondu, E. C. Voice of America; stories
    Going back west
        Osondu, E. C. Voice of America; stories

Osondu, E. C.—*Continued*

I will lend you my wife
    Osondu, E. C. Voice of America; stories

An incident at Pat's Bar
    Osondu, E. C. Voice of America; stories

Janjaweed wife
    Osondu, E. C. Voice of America; stories

Jimmy Carter's eyes
    Osondu, E. C. Voice of America; stories

A letter from home
    Osondu, E. C. Voice of America; stories

The men they married
    Osondu, E. C. Voice of America; stories

Miracle baby
    Osondu, E. C. Voice of America; stories

Nigerians in America
    Osondu, E. C. Voice of America; stories

Our first American
    Osondu, E. C. Voice of America; stories

Pilgrimage
    Osondu, E. C. Voice of America; stories

A simple case
    Osondu, E. C. Voice of America; stories

Stars in my mother's eyes, stripes on my back
    Osondu, E. C. Voice of America; stories

Teeth
    Osondu, E. C. Voice of America; stories

Voice of America
    Osondu, E. C. Voice of America; stories

Waiting
    Osondu, E. C. Voice of America; stories

Welcome to America
    Osondu, E. C. Voice of America; stories

Ostaijen, Paul van

The lost house key: the reason why, or I told you so
    The Dedalus book of Flemish fantasy; edited by Eric Dickens and translated by Paul Vincent.

Ostlund, Lori

Bed death
    The Pen/O.Henry Prize stories 2011; chosen and with an introduction by Laura Furman; with essays on the stories thety admire most by jurors A. M. Homes, Manuel Muñoz, Christine Schutt

OSTRICHES

Wells, H. G. A deal in ostriches

O'Sullivan, Colin

Pick's place
    Blood, guts, & whiskey; edited by Todd Robinson; introduction by Max Allan Collins.

O'Sullivan, Patrick

Maddy Dune's first and only spelling bee
    L. Ron Hubbard presents Writers of the Future volume XXVII; the year's thirteen best tales from the Writers of the Future international writers' program; illustrated by winners in the Illustrators of the Future international illustrators' program; with essays on writing & illustration by L. Ron Hubbard / Mike Resnick / Robert Cadtillo; edited by K. D. Wentworth

The **other**. Davis, L.

The **other** box. Houarner, G.

The **other** door. Villegas, H.

The **Other** Girls. Haynsworth, L.

The **Other** Jesus. Mounk, Y.

The **other** lodgers. Bierce, A.

The **other** man in the pinstripe. Nevins, F. M., Jr.

The **other** one. Smith, M. M.

Other paths. Blatnik, A.

The **other** place. Gaitskill, M.

The **other** side. Villegas, H.

The **others**. Goodberg, D.

An **ounce** of prevention is worth a pound of flesh. Hodge, B.

Our dwelling is but a wandering. Shepard, S.

Our first American. Osondu, E. C.

Our kindness. Davis, L.

Our Lady of the Sauropods. Silverberg, R.

Our Last-Minute Christmas Tree. Sellars, J. W.

Our little neighbour. Wells, H. G.

Our stars, our selves. Pratt, T.

Our Time with the Pirates. Cohen, R.

Our trip. Davis, L.

Our turn too will one day come. Hodge, B.

Ours is the prettiest. Hopkinson, N.

Out, brief candle. Vonnegut, K.

Out in the garden. Dick, P. K.

Out of body. Egan, J.

Out of her depth. Boland, J. C.

Out of Order. Polanzak, M.

Out of phase. Haldeman, J.

Out of the blue. Slim, M. A.

Out of the blue and into the black. Schappell, E.

Out of the garden. Wieland, L.

Out of time. Counihan, E.

Out there. Hunter, L.

OUTDOOR LIFE
    See also Country life; Wilderness survival

OUTER SPACE
    See also Space flight
        Exploration

Anderson, P. Gypsy

Anderson, P. Kyrie

Anderson, P. Lodestar

Baxter, S. Return to Titan

Dick, P. K. Colony

Niven, L. The coldest place

Niven, L. Neutron star

Outfangthief. Williams, C.

The **outing**. Davis, L.

An **outing**. Dixon, S.

OUTLAWS
    See also Brigands and robbers
    Haydar Haydar. The dance of the savage prairies

Outside. Sands, B.

Outside the gates of Troy. Monzó, Q.

The **Outskirts** of Nowhere. McGuill, R.

Outsourcing. Ayau, K. J.

Over here. Vukcevich, R.

The **overcoat**. Gogol, N.

Overexposure. Hall, J. W.

OVERLAND JOURNEYS

Chuculate, E. D. Galveston Bay, 1826

Overload. Blatnik, A.

Overlocked. Clayton, L.

Overseas. Neugeboren, J.

Overtime. Allen, D.

Overtime. Dixon, S.

OVID, 43 B.C.-17 OR 18
        About
    Baxter, C. The cures for love

Owens, Victoria
Jane Austen over the Styx
Dancing with Mr. Darcy; stories inspired by Jane Austen and Chawton House Library; compiled by Sarah Waters.
Owl and Mouse. Hoffman, A.
Own stories. Blatnik, A.
The **Oxfam** dress. Randall, P.
OXFORD (ENGLAND) *See* England—Oxford
Oyeyemi, Helen
The very shoe
The Thackery T. Lambshead cabinet of curiosities; edited by Ann & Jeff VanderMeer.
Oz, Amos
The King of Norway
The New Yorker v86 no44 p66-9 Ja 17 2011
Ozaki, Milton K.
The corpse didn't kick
The Black Lizard big book of Black Mask stories; edited and with a foreword by Otto Penzler; introduction by Keith Alan Deutsch.
OZARK MOUNTAINS REGION
Bradbury, R. Is that you, Bert?
Watkins, M. Two midnights in a jug
Woodrell, D. Black step
Woodrell, D. The echo of neighborly bones
Woodrell, D. Florianne
Woodrell, D. The horse in our history
Woodrell, D. One united
Woodrell, D. Returning the river
Woodrell, D. Twin Forks
Woodrell, D. Uncle
Ozturk, Seyit
The booster station
Copenhagen noir; edited by Bo Tao Michaëlis; translated by Mark Kline.

P

P. Dixon, S.
PACIFIC NORTHWEST
Orozco, D. Only connect
Simmons, D. In the garden
Packard, Frank Lucius
Shanghai Jim
The Big book of adventure stories; edited and with a introduction by Otto Penzler; foreword by Douglas Preston.
Packer, Ann
Dwell time
Packer, A. Swim back to me
Her firstborn
Packer, A. Swim back to me
Jump
Packer, A. Swim back to me
Molten
Packer, A. Swim back to me
Things said or done
Packer, A. Swim back to me
Walk for Mankind
Packer, A. Swim back to me
Packer, Nancy Huddleston
Dust catchers
The Sewanee Review v119 no1 p18-29 Wint 2011

Packer, ZZ
Brownies
Best of times, worst of times; contemporary American short stories from the new Gilded Age; edited by Wendy Martin and Cecelia Tichi.
Dayward
20 under 40; stories from the New Yorker; edited by Deborah Treisman.
Geese
Blue collar, white collar, no collar; stories of work; edited by Richard Ford.
Pacquing, Mykelle
Finding Love, Sex and Gender [Part of a special issue: XYZ Transformations of Urban Space: Transgendered and Transsexual Experiences of the City]
Women & Environments International Magazine no78/79 p19-21 Fall/Wint 2009
Padmanabhan, Manjula
Cull
Delhi noir; edited by Hirsh Sawhney
Padua, Sydney
Lovelace & babbage; origins, with salamander
Steampunk II: steampunk reloaded; edited by Ann & Jeff VanderMeer.
PAGANISM
Wells, H. G. Jimmy Goggles the god
Page, Norvell
Those Catrini
The Black Lizard big book of Black Mask stories; edited and with a foreword by Otto Penzler; introduction by Keith Alan Deutsch.
Page, Norvell W.
The wings of Kali
The Big book of adventure stories; edited and with a introduction by Otto Penzler; foreword by Douglas Preston.
Pain and stuff. Yamauchi, W.
PAINTERS
See also Women painters
Barnes, J. The limner
Gogol, N. The portrait
Wells, H. G. The devotee of art
Wells, H. G. The temptation of Harringay
PAINTERS, INDUSTRIAL *See* Industrial painters
PAINTINGS
Aiken, J. The monkey's wedding
Archer, J. A good eye
Hodge, B. Brushed in blackest silence
Pearlman, E. Girl in blue with brown bag
Santlofer, J. Richie and the rich bitch
Thu, T. The quiet poplar
El **paisano** is a bird of omen. Anzaldúa, G.
PAKISTAN
Fatima, A. Do you suppose it's the east winds?
Mueenuddin, D. A spoiled man
PAKISTANIS
Spain
Tóibín, C. The street
The **palace** at midnight. Silverberg, R.
Pale cheeks of a butcher's boy. Dixon, S.
PALEONTOLOGISTS
Kiernan, C. R. The Colliers' Venus (1893)
Palermo, Lynn E.
(tr.) See Fleischman, Cyrille

PALESTINE
See also Israel; Jerusalem
Marār, M. The Arabs' battle
Marār, M. Hard work
Marār, M. I want a rifle!
Marār, M. The slaves' revolution
PALESTINIAN ARABS
Abu Lail, S. A letter to a betrayer
Abu Lail, S. My neighbor is a whore!
Abu Lail, S. A stranger at the bus stop!
Assadi, M. An apartment to let!
Assadi, M. Forbidden talk
Assadi, M. The nightmare of a summer night
Assadi, M. Tea, biscuits and sugar
Bakriyya, R. Leave this world for me . . . for a woman . . . who seems to be the hope
Bakriyya, R. The story of perfume to you in the beginning of the year at the end of the story . . . . . .
Burbara, R. An attempt at persuasion
Burbara, R. The last stop: Street of the Prophets
Burbara, R. A shelter, drizzle and a tempest
Burbara, R. Until the green blossom opens . . .
Burbara, R. Wipe your tears away, oh pine trees!
Diab, F. An added fraction
Diab, F. The power of silence
Diab, F. Thoughts of a sterile woman
Gribbons, D. A short story
Hlehel, A. Coexistence
Ibrāhim, H. As-Sayyed's space
Ibrāhim, H Family re-union
Ibrāhim, H Fathers and sons
Ibrāhim, H. A holy site
Ibrāhim, H. The informer
Ibrāhim, H. Intruders?!
Ibrāhim, H. My young friend
Kadish, R. Come on Zion put your hands together
Khalaylah, A. About spring, Marwah and the feast
Khalaylah, A. In the company of Jamal the trouble-maker
Khalaylah, A. The scabby woman's son
Khalaylah, A. Wafiyyah
Marār, M. Al-Qatāryz
Marār, M. And we used to squeeze the olives for oil
Marār, M. The Arabs' battle
Marār, M. Biar Adass
Marār, M. The birds
Marār, M. The court is convening!
Marār, M. The craving woman
Marār, M. The day of the calf
Marār, M. From the bag of others!
Marār, M. Ghanem's watermelon
Marār, M. Hard work
Marār, M. Hello, nations!
Marār, M. The home-coming guy!
Marār, M. I want a rifle!
Marār, M. May nobody save anything!
Marār, M. Planting the cacti
Marār, M. S.P.Y.
Marār, M. The sleeping person is dead!
Marjiyyah, R. A blessed whore: a story from life
Marjiyyah, R. The burning of a soul
Muwasi, E. Sin and eggs
Muwasi, E. The study hall monitor
Muwasi, E. Your love is soreness
Sa'īd, M. A. Ahmad and Mordekhai
Sa'īd, M. A. The delivery
Shibli, A. At the post office
Sirhan, A. Close to the bridge's edge
Sirhan, A. I will ask for a divorce
Sirhan, A. The wedding's night and the sacrifice
Uruq, S. The brightness of his eyes
Uruq, S. The path of deceit
Uruq, S. The student and the teacher
Palisades. Kamlani, B.
PALM BEACH (FLA.) *See* Florida—Palm Beach
Palm Springs, 1985. Johnson, D.
Palma, Ricardo
La camisa de Margarita
　　Callaloo v34 no2 p492-4 Spr 2011
Margarita's shirt
　　Callaloo v34 no2 p279-81 Spr 2011
Paloma. Engel, P.
Pamatesēw. Boyd, R.
Pamuk, Orhan
The black book
Tablet & pen; literary landscapes from the modern Middle East, a words without borders anthology; edited by Reza Asian.
Pan is dead. Gautier, A.
PANDAS
Nutting, A. Zookeeper
Pangea. Somerville, P.
PANTHERS
Bierce, A. The eyes of the panther
Frumkin, R. Monster
Panties. Kearney, G.
Paolo's Turn. Laws, K.
Papa at Ketchum, 1961. Oates, J. C.
PAPACY *See* Catholic faith
Paparazzo. Togneri, E.
Paper. Pascoe, J.
The **Paper** Queen. Aiken, J.
Papernick, Jon
The engines of Sodom
Papernick, J. There is no other; [by] Jonathan Papernick
A kiss for Mrs. Fisch
Papernick, J. There is no other; [by] Jonathan Papernick
The last five-year plan
Papernick, J. There is no other; [by] Jonathan Papernick
The Madonna of Temple Beth Elohim
Papernick, J. There is no other; [by] Jonathan Papernick
The miracle birth
Papernick, J. There is no other; [by] Jonathan Papernick
My darling sweetheart baby
Papernick, J. There is no other; [by] Jonathan Papernick
Skin for skin
Papernick, J. There is no other; [by] Jonathan Papernick
There is no other
Papernick, J. There is no other; [by] Jonathan Papernick
What is it then, between us?
Papernick, J. There is no other; [by] Jonathan Papernick
PAPERS *See* Manuscripts
The **parable** of Satan's adversary. Cady, J.

PARABLES
See also Allegories
Doctorow, E. L. Wakefield
Self, W. Conversation with Ord
Parade. Gordon, S.
PARADES
Gordon, S. Parade
Paradise. Guterson, D.
Paradise Inn. Mars, K.
PARAKEETS
Bernheimer, K. A cageling tale
The **parallel** (A blade of grass). Bradbury, R.
Parallel lines. Powers, T.
Paralysis. Rodoreda, M.
PARANOIA
Lake, J. Lehr, Rex
Paranoia. Sayrafiezadeh, S.
The **parasols**. Balázs, B.
PARENT AND CHILD
See also Fathers and daughters; Fathers and sons; Mothers and daughters; Mothers and sons
Beattie, A. The Cinderella waltz
Beattie, A. Wanda's
Bradbury, R. The small assassin
Call, R. Somewhere ahead smoked the wreckage of my evening
Doctorow, E. L. Willi
Doyle, R. Funerals
Doyle, R. The plate
Eisenberg, D. The flaw in the design
Gordimer, N. The generation gap
Gorman, E. The baby store
Heathcock, A. Lazarus
Hoang, M. T. Grace
Horrocks, C. In the Gulf of Aden, past the Cape of Guardafui
Johnston, T. Two years
Kennedy, A. L. What becomes
Lindholm, M. Drum machine
McHugh, M. Vic
Naipaul, V. S. The mourners
Packer, A. Dwell time
Pearlman, E. ToyFolk
Row, J. Sheep may safely graze
Saunders, G. Commcomm
Senna, D. Admission
Swirsky, R. Again and again and again
Trevor, W. Marrying Damian
Trevor, W. Solitude
Trevor, W. Timothy's birthday
Parikh, Ankur
Three Stories
The Literary Review (Madison, N.J.) v54 no1 p125-35 Fall 2010
PARIS (FRANCE) *See* France—Paris
Park, Paul
Mysteries of the Old Quarter
Ghosts by gaslight; stories of steampunk and supernatural suspense; [edited by] Jack Dann [and] Nick Gevers
The **park** in winter. Tuten, F.
The **park** near Marienbad. Tuten, F.
The **park** on fire. Tuten, F.
PARK RANGERS
Rash, R. Into the gorge

Parke, Graham
Amsterdam at midnight
Can'tLit; fearless fiction from Broken pencil magazine; edited by Richard Rosenbaum.
Parker, Bonnie, 1910-1934 *See* Bonnie, 1910-1934
Parker, Dorothy
Big blonde
The vintage book of American women writers; edited and with an introduction by Elaine Showalter.
Parker, I. J.
Akitada's first case
Randisi, R. J. The Shamus winners: America's best private eye stories, volume II, 1996-2009; collected and introduced by Robert J. Randisi; founder, Private Eye Writers of America
Parker, K. J. (Kenneth John)
Amor vincit omnia
The Best science fiction and fantasy of the year: volume five; edited by Jonathan Strahan.
Parker, Kenneth John *See* Parker, K. J. (Kenneth John)
Parker, T. Jefferson
Vic Primeval
San Diego noir; edited by Maryelizabeth Hart.
Parker Adderson, philosopher. Bierce, A.
Parking. Joshi, R.
Parking her car in Michigan Theatre. Kennedy, J.
Parking Tax. Gordimer, N.
PARKINSONISM
Dixon, S. Reinsertion
Parkison, Aimee
Harassment [Part of special issue: Sex and Surveillance]
Feminist Studies v36 no3 p618-28 Fall 2010
Parks, Richard
Brillig
Parks, R. On the banks of the river of heaven
Courting the Lady Scythe
Parks, R. On the banks of the river of heaven
The feather cloak
Parks, R. On the banks of the river of heaven
The finer points of destruction
Parks, R. On the banks of the river of heaven
A garden in Hell
Parks, R. On the banks of the river of heaven
Lord Goji's wedding
Parks, R. On the banks of the river of heaven
The man who carved skulls
Parks, R. On the banks of the river of heaven
Mooning viewing at Shijo Bridge
Parks, R. On the banks of the river of heaven
On the banks of the River of Heaven
Parks, R. On the banks of the river of heaven
On the wheel
Parks, R. On the banks of the river of heaven
A pinch of salt
Parks, R. On the banks of the river of heaven
Skin deep
Parks, R. On the banks of the river of heaven
Soft as spider silk
Parks, R. On the banks of the river of heaven
The twa corbies, revisited
Parks, R. On the banks of the river of heaven

PARKS

See also Amusement parks; Wilderness areas; Zoos

Beagle, P. S. The rock in the Park

Dixon, S. The wild bird reserve

McElroy, J. The man with the bagful of boomerangs in the Bois de Boulogne

Tuten, F. The park on fire

PAROCHIAL SCHOOLS See Church schools

PARODIES

See also names of prominent authors with the subdivision Parodies, imitations, etc.

Millhauser, S. The eighth voyage of Sinbad

Sands, B. Croatan (from the encyclopedia orangutannicas)

Sands, B. The two-toed sapsucker (from the encyclopedia orangutannicas)

PARRICIDE

Idol, K. Coyotes

Parrish, P. J.

The tell-tale pacemaker

On a raven's wing; new tales in honor of Edgar Allan Poe; edited by Stuart M. Kaminsky

The **Parrot**. Heynen, J.

The **parrot** that wouldn't talk. Brown, W. C.

PARROTS

Bergman, M. M. Housewifely arts

Brown, W. C. The parrot that wouldn't talk

Chaon, D. I demand to know where you're taking me

Drakulic, S. A communist with style

Naipaul, V. S. Greenie and yellow

Vukcevich, R. The button

Parry, Leslie

The vanishing American

The Pen/O.Henry Prize stories 2011; chosen and with an introduction by Laura Furman; with essays on the stories thety admire most by jurors A. M. Homes, Manuel Muñoz, Christine Schutt

The **Part-Time** Job. James, P. D.

Parthenogenetic grandmother. Levine, S.

Particle of difference. McElroy, J.

PARTIES

See also Dinners

Anthony, M. Fishtown odyssey

Beattie, A. Home to Marie

Beattie, A. Lofty

Bingham, S. Benjamin

Black, A. That of which we cannot speak

Drabble, M. Les liaisons dangereuses

Drabble, M. A success story

Emshwiller, C. Eclipse

Ferris, J. The pilot

Franco, J. Lockheed

Kozak, H. J. Lamborghini mommy

Levine, S. Believing it was George Harrison

Oates, J. C. Uranus

Sa'id, M. A. A cup of tea

Sterling, P. Impaired

Vaughn, C. Kitty's zombie New Year

PARTINGS (FAREWELLS) See Farewells

PARTISANS See Guerrillas

The **Partner**. Fraser, B.

Partridge, Norman

Lesser demons

The Best horror of the year: volume three; edited by Ellen Datlow.

Party Animal: The Strange and Savage Case of a Once Erudite and Eloquent Young Man. Scott, R. A.

Party time. Bryant, C.

Pascoe, Jim

Paper

Florida heat wave; [edited and with an] introduction by Michael Lister.

Passarella, John

Blood alone

The stories (in) between; edited by Greg Schauer, Jeanne B. Benzel, and W. H. Horner.

The **passenger**. Boland, J. C.

The **passenger**. Silver, M.

Passing wind. Davis, L.

The **passion** of the beast. Hodge, B.

PASSION WEEK See Holy Week

PASSPORTS

Blatnik, A. On paper

Past life. Boland, J. C.

Pasternak, Simon

(jt. auth) See Dorph, Christian and Pasternak, Simon

PASTEUR, LOUIS, 1822-1895

About

Lafferty, M. 1963: the argument against Louis Pasteur

Pastoral. Ramuz, C. F.

PASTORS See Clergy

Pastor's Elaine's newsletter. Davis, L.

Pat Hobby and Orson Welles. Fitzgerald, F. S.

Pat Smash. Levine, S.

PATENT MEDICINES See Medicines, Patent, proprietary, etc.

The **path**. Loory, B.

The **path** of deceit. Uruq, S.

The **path** to madness. 'Izz al-Din, M.

PATHOLOGISTS See Physicians

The **patient**. Davis, L.

The **Patient's** Patients. Redig, A. J.

Patriot girls. Sisson, A.

Patterns. Lupoff, R. A.

Patterson, Glenn

The Mill For Grinding Old People Young

Five Points v13 no2 p57-63 2010

Paul. Shepard, S.

Paul's case: a study in temperament. Cather, W.

The **pavilion** and the linden. Châteaureynaud, G. O.

Paycheck. Dick, P. K.

Payne, Marshall

Bullet

End of an Aeon; edited by Bridgett McKenna & Marti McKenna

Pea Ridge Battlefield, Arkansas. Shepard, S.

Peace waits at Marokee. Bedford-Jones, H.

Peacekeeper. Heathcock, A.

The **peacemaker**. Dozois, G. R.

The **peach**. Somerville, P.

Peach Festival. Villegas, H.

Peach Queen. Leland, C. T.

The **peacock** cloak. Beckett, C.

PEACOCKS

Châteaureynaud, G. O. The peacocks

The **peacocks**. Châteaureynaud, G. O.
Pearce, Nicole
 Contents May Have Shifted
  StoryQuarterly v44 p30-42 2010
The **pearl** diver. Kiernan, C. R.
The **pearl** fishers. Tóibín, C.
The **pearl** of love. Wells, H. G.
Pearlman, Edith
 Allog
  Pearlman, E. Binocular vision; new & select-
   ed stories
 Aunt telephone
  Pearlman, E. Binocular vision; new & select-
   ed stories
 Binocular vision
  Pearlman, E. Binocular vision; new & select-
   ed stories
 Capers
  Pearlman, E. Binocular vision; new & select-
   ed stories
 Chance
  Pearlman, E. Binocular vision; new & select-
   ed stories
 The coat
  Pearlman, E. Binocular vision; new & select-
   ed stories
 Day of awe
  Pearlman, E. Binocular vision; new & select-
   ed stories
 Elder Jinks
  Pearlman, E. Binocular vision; new & select-
   ed stories
 Fidelity
  Pearlman, E. Binocular vision; new & select-
   ed stories
 Girl in blue with brown bag
  Pearlman, E. Binocular vision; new & select-
   ed stories
 Granski
  Pearlman, E. Binocular vision; new & select-
   ed stories
 Hanging fire
  Pearlman, E. Binocular vision; new & select-
   ed stories
 Home schooling
  Pearlman, E. Binocular vision; new & select-
   ed stories
 HONEYDEW
  Orion v30 no5 p42-49 S/O 2011
 How to fall
  Pearlman, E. Binocular vision; new & select-
   ed stories
 If love were all
  Pearlman, E. Binocular vision; new & select-
   ed stories
 Inbound
  Pearlman, E. Binocular vision; new & select-
   ed stories
 Jan Term
  Pearlman, E. Binocular vision; new & select-
   ed stories
 Lineage
  Pearlman, E. Binocular vision; new & select-
   ed stories
 The little wife
  Pearlman, E. Binocular vision; new & select-
   ed stories

 Mates
  Pearlman, E. Binocular vision; new & select-
   ed stories
 The ministry of restraint
  Pearlman, E. Binocular vision; new & select-
   ed stories
 The noncombatant
  Pearlman, E. Binocular vision; new & select-
   ed stories
 On Junius Bridge
  Pearlman, E. Binocular vision; new & select-
   ed stories
 Purim night
  Pearlman, E. Binocular vision; new & select-
   ed stories
 Relic and type
  Pearlman, E. Binocular vision; new & select-
   ed stories
 Rules
  Pearlman, E. Binocular vision; new & select-
   ed stories
 Self-reliance
  Pearlman, E. Binocular vision; new & select-
   ed stories
 Settlers
  Pearlman, E. Binocular vision; new & select-
   ed stories
 The story
  Pearlman, E. Binocular vision; new & select-
   ed stories
 Tess
  Pearlman, E. Binocular vision; new & select-
   ed stories
 ToyFolk
  Pearlman, E. Binocular vision; new & select-
   ed stories
 Unravished bride
  Pearlman, E. Binocular vision; new & select-
   ed stories
 Vallies
  Pearlman, E. Binocular vision; new & select-
   ed stories
 Vaquita
  Pearlman, E. Binocular vision; new & select-
   ed stories
PEARLS
 Brown, W. C. The parrot that wouldn't talk
PEASANT LIFE
 Dib, M. The end
                    Russia
 Solzhenitsyn, A. Apricot jam
 Solzhenitsyn, A. Ego
                    Turkey
 Yaşar Kemal. Memed, my hawk
PEDDLERS AND PEDDLING
 Balázs, B. The parasols
The **pedestrian**. Bradbury, R.
PEDIATRICIANS *See* Physicians
PEDOPHILIA
 Davidson, H. Son of so many tears
 Dufresne, J. The cross-eyed bear
 Self, W. The Nonce prize
 Trevor, W. An afternoon
 Tucher, A. Bismarck rules
Peels for Salt. Luo, X.
Peggy's brother. Hunter, L.
PEKING (CHINA) *See* China—Beijing
The **Pelican** Bar. Fowler, K. J.
The **Pelican's** brother. Nolan, W. F.

PELOPONNESIAN WAR, 431-404 B.C. *See*
    Greece—Peloponnesian War, 431-404 B.C.
Pelt. Emshwiller, C.
Peltoniemi, Kip
    The Virkkala E-flat
        Journal of American Folklore v124 no491
        p74-83 Wint 2011
The **penance** of Scoot McCutchen. Bill, F.
Pendulum. Bradbury, R. and Hasse, H.
The **pendulum** (first version). Bradbury, R.
PENGUINS
    Gray, A. The darkness
Peninsula. Emshwiller, C.
PENIS
    Ruocco, J. Dolphins
Penkov, Miroslav
    Buying Lenin
        Penkov, M. East of the West; a country in
        stories
    Cross thieves
        Penkov, M. East of the West; a country in
        stories
    Devshirmeh
        Penkov, M. East of the West; a country in
        stories
    East of the West
        Penkov, M. East of the West; a country in
        stories
        Orion v30 no3 p56-71 My/Je 2011
    The letter
        Penkov, M. East of the West; a country in
        stories
    Makedonija
        Penkov, M. East of the West; a country in
        stories
    The night horizon
        Penkov, M. East of the West; a country in
        stories
    A picture with Yuki
        Penkov, M. East of the West; a country in
        stories
Penncavage, Michael
    The cost of doing business
        Blood, guts, & whiskey; edited by Todd Rob-
        inson; introduction by Max Allan Collins.
PENNSYLVANIA
                    Philadelphia
    Anthony, M. Fishtown odyssey
    Ayres, D. Seeing nothing
    Biddle, C. F. Reality
    Dozois, G. R. The hanging curve
    Gilman, K. Devil's pocket
    Holladay, C. Ghost walk
    Kolpan, G. The ratcatcher
    LaBrie, A. Princess
    Romano, C. "Cannot easy normal die"
    Swierczynski, D. Lonergan's girl
    Tafoya, D. Above the Imperial
    Zervanos, J. Your brother, who loves you
Penuel, John
    (tr.) See Ribeyro, Julio Ramón
PENZLER, OTTO, 1942-
                    About
    Healy, J. F. The holiday fairy
    Perry, A. My object all sublime
    Rozan, S. J. The grift of the magi
People Are Like That Only. SANGA, J.
People like me. Somerville, P.
People of leaf and branch. Lake, J.

People of the Book. Millhauser, S.
People of the sky. Le Clézio, J.-M. G.
People who kill. Estleman, L. D.
The **people** who live near me. Tremblay, P.
Pera, Brian
    Roman à clef
        Life as we show it; writing on film; co-edited
        by Masha Tupitsyn & Brian Pera; introduc-
        tion by Masha Tupitsyn
Perabo, Susan
    Shelter
        Pushcart Prize XXXV: best of the small
        presses 2011; edited by Bill Henderson
        with the Pushcart Prize editors.
Percy, Benjamin
    The Roof People
        World Literature Today v84 no5 p44-6 S/O
        2010

    The Red Balloon
        Ploughshares v36 no4 p98-113 Wint
        2010/2011
    Refresh, refresh
        Best of times, worst of times; contemporary
        American short stories from the new Gilded
        Age; edited by Wendy Martin and Cecelia
        Tichi.
    The Rubber-Band Gun
        Iowa Review v40 no2 p147-8 Fall 2010
    Writs of Possession
        The Virginia Quarterly Review v87 no2 p114-
        123 Spr 2011
The **perfect** age. Moffett, K.
The **perfect** angler. Bayley, E.
Perfect crime. Schmitt, E.-E.
A **perfect** gentleman on wheels. Wells, H. G.
Perfect murder. Gold, H. L.
Perfect Practice Makes Perfect. Goldberg, M.
A **perfect** relationship. Trevor, W.
The **perfect** tenants. Naipaul, V. S.
The **perfectionist.** Goodberg, D.
Performance. Doughtie, E.
A **performance.** Sands, B.
PERFORMANCE ART
    Blatnik, A. Save your kisses for me
PERFORMERS *See* Entertainers
PERGOLESI, GIOVANNI BATTISTA, 1710-
    1736
                    About
    Silverberg, R. Gianni
Peri. Emshwiller, C.
The **perils** of twilight. Smith, P. A.
Perin, Adam
    Medic!
        L. Ron Hubbard presents Writers of the Fu-
        ture volume XXVII; the year's thirteen best
        tales from the Writers of the Future inter-
        national writers' program; illustrated by
        winners in the Illustrators of the Future in-
        ternational illustrators' program; with es-
        says on writing & illustration by L. Ron
        Hubbard / Mike Resnick / Robert Cadtillo;
        edited by K. D. Wentworth
The **Period** in which We Live [Part of special is-
        sue: Slovak Fiction] Rankov, P.
Periplus. Murray, S.

Perlman, Edith
    Someday you'll find me: A plan B essay
        Ploughshares v36 no4 p184-7 Wint
        2010/2011
Perpetua in Glory. Johns, R.
Perpetual Warrior. Shepard, S.
Perpetuity. Drabble, M.
Perry, Anne
    My object all sublime
        Christmas at the Mysterious Bookshop; 'tis
        the season to be deadly; stories of mistletoe
        and mayhem from 17 masters of suspense;
        edited by Otto Penzler.
PERSECUTION
        See also Martyrs
The **persecution** machine. Lee, T.
PERSIA *See* Iran
Persian is sugar. Jamalzadeh, M. A.
The **persistence** of memory. Baker, A.
Person to person. Matheson, R.
PERSONAL BEAUTY
    Kronauer, B. The diva and her tricks
Personal experience. Garcia-Aguilera, C.
PERSONAL NAMES
    Leland, C. T. How the Coe boys got their
        names
    McGarry, J. The sweetness of her name
    Wells, H. G. Miss Winchelsea's heart
PERSONALITY
    Silverberg, R. The changeling
    Wells, H. G. The sad story of a dramatic critic
PERSONALITY DISORDERS
        See also Hallucinations and illusions; In-
        sane, Criminal and dangerous; Multiple per-
        sonality
    Bell, M. S. Barking man
    Highsmith, P. The terrors of basket-weaving
    Hunter, L. Unpreparing
    Stafford, J. The echo and the nemesis
PERU
                        Lima
    Alarcón, D. The bridge
PERUVIANS
                        Spain
    Taylor-Aragon, E. Epiphany
Pervert. Finlay, C. C.
Peshkov, Alexei Maximovich *See* Gorky,
    Maksim, 1868-1936
The **pest.** Châteaureynaud, G. O.
PESTS
                        Control
    Roberge, R. The exterminator
Pests. Ruocco, J.
Pet. Unferth, D. O.
PETER PAN (FICTITIOUS CHARACTER)
    Brennan, S. R. The spy who never grew up
Peter Shilling. Irvine, A.
Peter Torrelli, falling apart. Makkai, R.
Peterfreund, Diana
    The care and feeding of your baby killer uni-
        corn
        The Best science fiction and fantasy of the
        year: volume five; edited by Jonathan
        Strahan.
Peters, Kyle B.
    THE WALKING BIRD
        Dalhousie Review v91 no1 p37-41 Spr 2011

Petersen, Kate
    Construction bid for poets [Love letter]
        New England Review v32 no2 p19-23 Spr
        2011
Peterson, Adam
    The Cowboy
        StoryQuarterly v44 p56-9 2010
Petitions to Saint Chronic. Hill, M.
Petrushevskaya, Ludmilla and Summers, Anna
    A withered branch
        The New Yorker v87 no9 p108-9, 111 Ap 18
        2011
Petrushevskaya, Ludmilla and others
    Medea
        Harper's v322 no1933 p68-70 Je 2011
Petry, Ann Lane
    The migraine workers
        The vintage book of American women writ-
        ers; edited and with an introduction by
        Elaine Showalter.
Petry, Yves
    The straggler
        The Dedalus book of Flemish fantasy; edited
        by Eric Dickens and translated by Paul
        Vincent.
PETS
        See also names of individual pets
    Doyle, R. Animals
A **petting** zoo tale. Bernheimer, K.
Petty corruption. Lahens, Y.
Pevear, Richard
    (tr.) *See* Leskov, Nikolai
Phan, Ngoc Tien
    A dream
        Family of fallen leaves; stories of Agent Or-
        ange by Vietnamese writers; edited by
        Charles Waugh and Huy Lien.
Phantom father. Trueblood, V.
Phantoms. Millhauser, S.
PHARMACISTS
        See also Medicines, Patent, proprietary,
        etc.
    Strout, E. Pharmacy
Pharmacy. Strout, E.
Phelan, Twist
    Happine$$
        Mystery Writers of America presents the rich
        and the dead; edited by Nelson DeMille.
    Time will tell
        By hook or by crook and 27 more of the best
        crime + mystery stories of the year; edited
        by Ed Gorman and Martin H. Greenberg.
Phelan's first case. Sandlin, L.
Phelps, Elizabeth Stuart
    The angel over the right shoulder, or, the begin-
        ning of a new year
        The vintage book of American women writ-
        ers; edited and with an introduction by
        Elaine Showalter.
    The tenth of January
        The vintage book of American women writ-
        ers; edited and with an introduction by
        Elaine Showalter.
PHILADELPHIA (PA.) *See* Pennsylvania—Phila-
    delphia
PHILANTHROPY *See* Endowments
Philip, South Dakota (Highway 73). Shepard, S.
PHILISTINES
    Turtledove, H. Occupation duty

Phillips, Charles Lamar
Estranged
The Massachusetts Review v52 no2 p195-229
Summ 2011
Prairie Symposium
New England Review v32 no2 p55-65 Spr
2011
Phillips, Helen
The apocalypses
Phillips, H. And yet they were happy
The brides
Phillips, H. And yet they were happy
The droughts
Phillips, H. And yet they were happy
The envies
Phillips, H. And yet they were happy
The failures
Phillips, H. And yet they were happy
The far-flung families
Phillips, H. And yet they were happy
The fights
Phillips, H. And yet they were happy
The floods
Phillips, H. And yet they were happy
The hauntings
Phillips, H. And yet they were happy
The Helens
Phillips, H. And yet they were happy
The mistakes
Phillips, H. And yet they were happy
The monsters
Phillips, H. And yet they were happy
The mothers
Phillips, H. And yet they were happy
The offspring
Phillips, H. And yet they were happy
The punishments
Phillips, H. And yet they were happy
The regimes
Phillips, H. And yet they were happy
We?
Phillips, H. And yet they were happy
The weddings
Phillips, H. And yet they were happy
The wives
Phillips, H. And yet they were happy
Phillips, Holly
The long, cold goodbye
The Year's best dark fantasy & horror; edited
by Paula Guran
PHILOSOPHERS
MacLaverty, B. Language, truth and lockjaw
PHILOSOPHY OF LIFE *See* Life (Philosophy of
life)
Philosophy Seminar: The Carnivore. Grebowicz,
M.
PHOENIX (ARIZ.) *See* Arizona—Phoenix
Phoenix. Smith, C. A.
The **phone**. Dixon, S.
The **photograph**. Doyle, R.
PHOTOGRAPHERS
Baker, L. Still life
Gifford, B. El Carterista
Hodge, B. With acknowledgements to Sun Tzu
Kenyon, N. Breeding the demons
Sharp, Z. Rules of engagement
Shepard, L. The skinny girl
Sneed, C. A million dollars
Tillman, L. The original impulse

Togneri, E. Paparazzo
Trevor, W. An evening out
PHOTOGRAPHS
El Souwaim, M. From the novel The threshold
of ashes
Ely, S. 84 Avenue Foch
Hall, J. W. Overexposure
Loory, B. Photographs
Mu Xin. The boy next door
Tremblay, P. Nineteen snapshots of Dennisport
Photographs. Loory, B.
Phrases and philosophies for the use of the young.
Williamson, E. M.
PHYSICAL FITNESS
Gallari, A. Chasing Adonis
Physical wisdom. Gilley, T.
PHYSICALLY HANDICAPPED
See also Blind; Deaf; Hunchbacks; Phys-
ically handicapped children; Quadriplegics
Bernheimer, K. Whitework
Hoang, M. T. Grace
Laken, V. Separate kingdoms
McGarry, J. Welcome wherever he went
Oates, J. C. Golden gloves
Schmitt, E.-E. Getting better
Trevor, W. The woman of the house
Trueblood, V. Taken
Willis, D. Sky theatre
PHYSICALLY HANDICAPPED CHILDREN
Goodberg, D. Disabled
PHYSICIANS
See also Psychiatrists; Veterinarians;
Women physicians
Ahmed, S. Hooves and the hovel of Abdel
Jameela
Aiken, J. Girl in a whirl
Barry, K. Doctor Sot
Beattie, A. Coping stones
Bierce, A. A diagnosis of death
Bierce, A. Staley Fleming's hallucination
Bierce, A. A watcher by the dead
Bingham, S. Mending
Châteaureynaud, G. O. The styx
Châteaureynaud, G. O. La tete
Davis, L. The bone
Dib, M. Little Cousin
Dick, P. K. Piper in the woods
Emshwiller, C. Methapyrilene hydrochloride
sometimes helps
Farmer, P. J. Crossing the dark river
Farmer, P. J. The Sumerian oath
Farmer, P. J. Up the bright river
Farmer, P. J. Voice of the sonar in my vermi-
form appendix
Ford, J. Dr. Lash remembers
Grossman, V. S. In Kislavodsk
Matheson, R. The house of the dead
Mena, M. C. The vine-leaf
Neugeboren, J. Comfort
Neugeboren, J. Here or there
Neugeboren, J. Make-a-wish
Neugeboren, J. The state of Israel
Neugeboren, J. The Turetzky Trio
Pearlman, E. Lineage
Pearlman, E. The noncombatant
Pearlman, E. Self-reliance
Roberge, R. Border radio
Rodoreda, M. Paralysis
Sale, R. The dancing rats

PHYSICIANS—*Continued*
  Schirach, F. v. Fähner
  Sokoloff, B. The crime of Dr. Garine
  Somerville, P. Easy love
PHYSICISTS
  Kosmatka, T. Divining light
  Prindle, J. Einstein's proof
  Shepard, J. Low-hanging fruit
  Sullivan, J. Niels Bohr and the sleeping Dane
PHYSICS
  McElroy, J. Particle of difference
PIANISTS
  Barnes, J. Harmony
  Baxter, C. Harmony of the world
  Boland, J. C. Marley's ghost
  Eisenberg, D. Someone to talk to
  Matheson, R. Red is the color of desire
  Shehadeh, R. The unbecoming of Virgil Smythe
PIANO
  McCabe, E. Music at Annahullion
  Tan, A. Two kinds
The **Piano** Lesson. Cherry, K.
The **piano** tuner's wives. Trevor, W.
Picard, John
  Souvenir de Paris, 2002
    New England Review v31 no3 p22-30 2010
PICARESQUE STORIES
        See also Adventure; Rogues and vaga-
        bonds
Piccirilli, Tom
  Blood sacrifices and the Catatonic Kid
    By hook or by crook and 27 more of the best
      crime + mystery stories of the year; edited
      by Ed Gorman and Martin H. Greenberg.
  Caucasus
    Swenson, P. The Best of Talebones; edited by
      Patrick Swenson.
  The cruel thief of rosy infants
    The monster's corner; stories through inhu-
      man eyes; edited by Christopher Golden
  The return of inspiration
    Blood, guts, & whiskey; edited by Todd Rob-
      inson; introduction by Max Allan Collins.
Pickard, Nancy
  Dark chocolate
    By hook or by crook and 27 more of the best
      crime + mystery stories of the year; edited
      by Ed Gorman and Martin H. Greenberg.
  Dust devil
    The Shamus winners: America's best private
      eye stories, volume I: 1982-1995; collected
      and introduced by Robert J. Randisi; found-
      er, Private Eye Writers of America
Picking up the pieces. Cadigan, P.
PICKPOCKETS *See* Thieves
Pick's place. O'Sullivan, C.
Pickups and shotguns. Estleman, L. D.
Picnic. Villegas, H.
PICNICS
  Emshwiller, C. Day at the beach
  Fried, S. Frost mountain picnic massacre
  Villegas, H. Picnic
The **picture** window. Gray, A.
A **picture** with Yuki. Penkov, M.
Pictures of houses with water damage.
    Hemmingson, M.
Pie Knob. Willis, M. S.
Pie of the month. Thompson, J.
The **piece** thing. Emshwiller, C.

Pierce, Greg
  Later That Night
    New England Review v32 no2 p173-182 Spr
    2011
Piers. Dixon, S.
PIES
  Thompson, J. Pie of the month
Pigeon, Margeurite
  THE WOMAN ON THE MOVE (AFTER KAF-
    KA)
    Dalhousie Review v91 no1 p109-114 Spr
    2011
PIGEONS
  Highsmith, P. Two disagreeable pigeons
PIGS
  Bierce, A. The coup de grâce
  Drakulic, S. From gulag to goulash: the intro-
    duction to Ms. Piggy's Hungarian cook-
    book
  Leahy, K. H. Too fatal a poison
  McOmber, A. Of wool
Pigs is pigs. Butler, E. P.
Pilgrimage. Osondu, E. C.
PILGRIMAGES *See* Pilgrims and pilgrimages
PILGRIMS AND PILGRIMAGES
  Osondu, E. C. Pilgrimage
Pill and picture. Qiu Xiaolong
The **pilot**. Ferris, J.
PILOTS, AIRPLANE *See* Air pilots
PIMPS
        See also Prostitutes
  Marãr, M. It means ... : a pimp
  Nikitas, D. Trauma dyke
Pinborough, Sarah
  The nowhere man
    The Year's best dark fantasy & horror; edited
      by Paula Guran
  The screaming room
    The monster's corner; stories through inhu-
      man eyes; edited by Christopher Golden
A **pinch** of salt. Parks, R.
Pinede, Nadine
  Department lounge
    Haiti noir; edited by Edwidge Danticat
Ping, Wang
  Morning Cloud, Evening Rain
    Women's Studies Quarterly v38 no1/2 p49-57
    Spr/Summ 2010
Pink. Latiolais, M.
Pink Ribbon Days. Kwon, Y.-S.
PIONEER LIFE *See* Frontier and pioneer life
Pioneers. Alsup, A.
The **piper**. Bradbury, R.
The **piper** (first version). Bradbury, R.
Piper in the woods. Dick, P. K.
Pirandello, Luigi
  The Old God
    New England Review v32 no1 p173-7 2011
The **pirate** of Palm Beach. Bell, T.
PIRATES
  Finlay, C. C. Life so dear or peace so sweet
  Horrocks, C. In the Gulf of Aden, past the Cape
    of Guardafui
  Howard, R. E. The road of the eagles
  Sands, B. The anals of piracy
  Tuten, F. The ship at anchor

Pirzad, Zoya
  Mrs. F is a fortunate woman/the desirable life of
    Mr. F
      Tablet & pen; literary landscapes from the
        modern Middle East, a words without bor-
        ders anthology; edited by Reza Asian.
Pishaach. Narayan, S.
The **pit**. Gray, A.
Pitts, J. A.
  Three chords and the truth
    Swenson, P. The Best of Talebones; edited by
      Patrick Swenson.
Pity the poor mercenary. Shepard, S.
PIXIES *See* Fairies
Place. Latiolais, M.
A **place** in the opera. Kitterman, B.
PLACE IN THE SUN (MOTION PICTURE)
  Warsh, L. A place in the sun
A **place** in the sun. Warsh, L.
The **place** of losses. Hasbún, R.
PLAGIARISM
  McElroy, J. Annals of plagiary
PLAGUE
        See also Disasters
  Fowler, K. J. The dark
  McOmber, A. This new and poisonous air
  Sale, R. The dancing rats
  Tremblay, P. Figure 5
Planet Canada. Kalenda, J.
PLANETS, MINOR *See* Asteroids
PLANTATION LIFE
  Stephenson, C. Leiningen versus the ants
Planting the cacti. Marãr, M.
PLANTS
  Dowling, T. The lagan fishers
PLASTIC SURGERY
  Updike, J. Metamorphosis
Platana, Janette
  Some of this is true
    Can'tLit; fearless fiction from Broken pencil
      magazine; edited by Richard Rosenbaum.
The **plate**. Doyle, R.
PLATONIC LOVE *See* Love
A **platonic** relationship. Beattie, A.
The **plattner** story. Wells, H. G.
PLAYGROUNDS
  Niven, L. Cloak of anarchy
  Self, W. The five-swing wlak
The **playhouse**. Danishvar, S.
PLAYING CARDS *See* Cards
Playing hurt. Tillman, L.
PLAYWRIGHTS *See* Dramatists
Please come back to me. Treadway, J.
Please, if you love me, you should know what to
    do. Novack, S.
Please take me with you. Zhang Kangkang
PLEASURE *See* Happiness
The **pleasure** of your company. Sterling, P.
Plum Creek. Furman, L.
Plumbers. Popov, A.
Plummer, Toni Margarita
  All the sex is west
    Plummer, T. M. The bolero of Andi Rowe;
      stories
  The body
    Plummer, T. M. The bolero of Andi Rowe;
      stories

The bolero of Andi Rowe
  Plummer, T. M. The bolero of Andi Rowe;
    stories
The desert in green
  Plummer, T. M. The bolero of Andi Rowe;
    stories
Forces
  Plummer, T. M. The bolero of Andi Rowe;
    stories
Happy hour
  Plummer, T. M. The bolero of Andi Rowe;
    stories
Olivia's roses
  Plummer, T. M. The bolero of Andi Rowe;
    stories
To visit the cemetery
  Plummer, T. M. The bolero of Andi Rowe;
    stories
What would Mary do: a Christmas story
  Plummer, T. M. The bolero of Andi Rowe;
    stories
Yard work
  Plummer, T. M. The bolero of Andi Rowe;
    stories
Plunder. O'Brien, E.
Plus or minus. Kelly, J. P.
Pneuman, Angela
  Occupational Hazard
    Ploughshares v37 no1 p111-32 Spr 2011
POACHING
        See also Hunting
Poe, Edgar Allan
  The facts of M. Valdemar's case
    The book of the living dead; edited by John
      Richard Stephens.
  The purloined letter
    21 essential American short stories; edited by
      Leslie M. Pockell
POE, EDGAR ALLAN, 1809-1849
                About
  Allyn, D. Israfel
  Hoch, E. D. The Poe collector
  Lovesey, P. The deadliest tale of all
  Lutz, J. Poe, Poe, Poe
  Winslow, D. Poe, Jo, and I
  Zeman, A. Rue Morgue noir: the possible--
    probable--struggles Edgar Allan Poe might
    have faced while seeking success as a tal-
    ented new writer in the world of today
                Influence
  Breen, J. L. William Allan Wilson
The **Poe** collector. Hoch, E. D.
Poe, Jo, and I. Winslow, D.
Poe, Poe, Poe. Lutz, J.
The **poet.** Loory, B.
Poetic justice. Mullen, C.
POETRY
  Fowler, K. J. The last worders
  Riippi, J. Something about someone else's poem
  Woodrell, D. Two things
POETS
        See also Women poets
  Aiken, J. The Magnesia Tree
  Aiken, J. Water of youth
  Balázs, B. Li-Tai-Pe and springtime
  Balázs, B. Li-Tai-Pe and the thief
  Châteaureynaud, G. O. The bronze schoolboy
  Cheever, J. The world of apples
  Doctorow, E. L. Edgemont Drive

POETS—*Continued*
    Emmanuel, F. Lou dancing
    Emshwiller, C. Acceptance speech
    Emshwiller, C. Biography of an uncircumcised
        man (including interview)
    Harwood, J. Face to face
    Highsmith, P. The baby spoon
    Link, K. The wrong grave
    Loory, B. The poet
    Marăr, M. The internal pages
    McElroy, J. No man's land
    McOmber, A. Egyptomania
    Naipaul, V. S. B. Wordsworth
    O'Brien, E. Send my roots rain
    Qiu Xiaolong. (Tofu) Worker poet Bao 1
    Qiu Xiaolong. (Tofu) Worker poet Bao II
    Rajaniemi, H. Elegy for a young elk
    Riippi, J. Something about drinking in Baton
        Rouge
    Salter, J. My lord you
    Smith, C. A. Morthylla
    Wieland, L. At Wanship
    Wilson, J. The liars
    Woestijne, K. v. d. The saint of number
Poge, N. Wooten *See* Page, Norvell W., 1904-
    1961
A **point** of identity. Mphahlele, E.
Poison, inside the walls. Baker, S. W.
POISON PEN LETTERS *See* Letters (Stories
    about)
The **poisoned** arrow. Ely, S.
POISONING
    Allan, S. You're gonna get yours
    Cannon, T. Instant karma
    Ellis, K. The feather
    Fabra, J. S. I. A high-end neighborhood
    Fowler, C. Bryant and May in the soup
    Kurlansky, M. Crème brûlée
    Moore, T. A. Red milk
    Penncavage, M. The cost of doing business
    Todd, C. Yesterday
    Zeman, A. Daphne, unrequited
POISONOUS SNAKES *See* Snakes
POISONS
    See also Poisoning
Poissant, David James
    One Hundred Percent Cotton
        The Southern Review (Baton Rouge, La.) v47
        no3 p458-61 Summ 2011
POKER (GAME)
    Bond, J. Trapped
    Burton, M. T. Cherry Coke
    Link, K. Lull
    Oates, J. C. Strip poker
    Pearlman, E. Chance
    Tran, V. Kubla Khan
Pol Pot's beautiful daughter. Ryman, G.
POLAND
    Jones, G. A. Grazing the long acre
    Kalechofsky, R. Father Woytzski leads a Jewish
        youth group to the Holocaust memorial in
        Oswiecim, Poland
            Warsaw
    Drakulic, S. The cat-keeper in Warsaw (Letter
        to the state prosecutor)
Poland is watching. Shepard, J.
POLANSKI, ROMAN
            About
    Pera, B. Roman à clef

Polanzak, Mark
    The OK End of Funny Town
        The Southern Review (Baton Rouge, La.) v46
        no4 p651-6 Aut 2010
    Out of Order
        The American Scholar v80 no1 p97-101 Wint
        2011
POLAR BEAR
    Shipp, J. C. Agape walrus
POLAR REGIONS *See* Antarctic regions; Arctic
    regions
Pole, pole. Minot, S.
POLES
            Ireland
    Doyle, R. The pram
POLICE
    Boland, J. C. Last island south
    Boland, J. C. Reunion in Baineville
    Boland, J. C. Tequila
    Brown, W. C. The parrot that wouldn't talk
    Dixon, S. Burglars
    Duncan, H. The death of a love
    Gorman, E. Aftermath
    Gorman, E. and Morrish, R. Rafferty's come-
        back
    Jones, S. Black kids in lemon trees
    Jones, S. G. Teeth
    Kozlowski, J. First love never dies
    Lychack, W. Stolpestad
    Malone, M. Christmas spirit
    Monk, D. Sugar 'n' spice
    Muessig, C. Bias
    Orozco, D. Officers weep
    Robinson, L. Officer Friendly
    Somerville, P. The cop
    Stanley, G. E. The shrieking skeleton
    Taylor, A. Little Russia
    Vonnegut, K. Hundred-dollar kisses
    Warsh, L. The Russians
    Winchell, P. Ten carats of lead
            Barcelona (Spain)
    Gonzalez Ledesma, F. The police inspector who
        loved books
            California
        See also Police—Los Angeles (Calif.)
    Lawrence, M. C. Key witness
            England
        See also Police—London (England)
            Florida
    Bond, J. Trapped
    Jackson, A. A Tampa man
            Haiti
    Dalembert, L.-P. Dangerous crossroads
    Mars, K. Paradise Inn
            Hollywood (Calif.)
        See Police—Los Angeles (Calif.)
            India
    Joshi, R. Parking
            Indiana
    Bill, F. Officer down (tweakers)
            Ireland
    Bailie, T. The druid's dance
    Hutchinson, D. The fortunate isles
    Kilworth, G. Hats off to Mary
    McKinty, A. Diarmaid and Grainne
            London (England)
    Simms, C. Tick-tock
            Los Angeles (Calif.)
    Adams, C. F. The key

POLICE—Los Angeles (Calif.)—*Continued*
Levinson, R. S. Between sins
Mexico
Boland, J. C. Out of her depth
Michigan
Allyn, D. An early Christmas
New Jersey
Oates, J. C. ID
New York (N.Y.)
Baxt, G. Schemes and variations
Nevins, F. M., Jr. Because the constable blundered
Page, N. Those Catrini
Thomas, P. Short fuse
Warsh, L. Harry Cray
Oakland (Calif.)
Beagle, P. S. Oakland dragon blues
Pennsylvania
Anthony, M. Fishtown odyssey
Philadelphia (Pa.)
Swierczynski, D. Lonergan's girl
Singapore
MacLean, A. MacHinery and the cauliflowers
South Africa
Mphahlele, E. Man must live
Texas
Lansdale, J. R. Torn away
United States
Oates, J. C. High lonesome
West Virginia
Willis, M. S. On the road with C. T. Savage
The **police** inspector who loved books. Gonzalez Ledesma, F.
POLICEWOMEN
Margolin, P. The house on Pine Terrace
Nevins, F. M., Jr. Luck of the dead
Nevins, F. M., Jr. A nightcap of hemlock
Nevins, F. M., Jr. Puzzle for Scots
Nevins, F. M., Jr. The spark
Nevins, F. M., Jr. Toad cop
POLITICAL CAMPAIGNS *See* Politics
POLITICAL CRIMES AND OFFENSES
   See also Assassination; Political prisoners; Terrorism
Ahmad, O. Yesterday man
POLITICAL DEFECTORS *See* Defectors
POLITICAL INTRIGUE *See* Politics
The **political** poet. Bayley, E.
POLITICAL PRISONERS
Bakopoulos, N. Fresco, Byzantine
Dib, M. The companion
Grossman, V. S. Living space
Makkai, R. The briefcase
Qiu Xiaolong. A Jing Dynasty goat
Politically correct. Archer, J.
POLITICIANS *See* Politics
POLITICS
   See also Utopias
El Souwaim, M. From the novel The threshold of ashes
Phillips, H. The regimes
Africa
Gordimer, N. At the rendezvous of victory
Gordimer, N. A soldier's embrace
England
Wells, H. G. Wayde's essence
South Africa
Gordimer, N. Some Monday for sure

United States
McElroy, J. The campaign trail
Pollack, Rachel
Burning beard: the dreams and visions of Joseph ben Jacob, Lord Viceroy of Egypt
People of the book; a decade of Jewish science fiction & fantasy; edited by Rachel Swirsky & Sean Wallace.
Pollen road of life. Sloan, B.
Pollexfen, Muriel
Monsieur Fly-by-Night
The dreaming sex; early tales of scientific imagination by women; edited by Mike Ashley.
Pollock and the Porroh man. Wells, H. G.
POLLUTION
Self, W. Chest
POLYGAMY
   See also Mormons and Mormonism
The **pomegranate** seed. Wharton, E.
The **Pool**. Dowd, A.
The **pools** and the piano. Binshatwan, N.
Poolside musings in sunny L.A. Shepard, S.
POOR *See* Poverty
Poor devil. Baxter, C.
Poor me. LaValle, V.
Pop squad. Bacigalupi, P.
Pope, Robert
American Boy
The Kenyon Review v33 no3 p139-46 Summ 2011
The **Pope** of the chimps. Silverberg, R.
Popkes, Steven
Jackie's boy
The Year's best science fiction: twenty-eighth annual collection; edited by Gardner Dozois.
Popov, Alek
Plumbers
Best European fiction 2011; edited by Aleksandr Hemon; preface by Colum McCann
POPULATION
Ballard, J. G. Billennium
Vaughn, C. Amaryllis
The **Porchies**. Wilson, A.
Porlock's demise. Riccardi, T.
Porn star. Nutting, A.
PORNOGRAPHY
Barry, K. See the tree, how big it's grown
Bengtsson, J. T. One of the rough ones
Dubé, P. Echo
Dwyer, J. Biography of a porn star in three parts
Nutting, A. Porn star
Wallace, J. Custom sets
PORT-AU-PRINCE (HAITI) *See* Haiti—Port-au-Prince
PORT OF SPAIN (TRINIDAD AND TOBAGO)
   See Trinidad and Tobago—Port of Spain
Porter, Justin
'Demption road
Blood, guts, & whiskey; edited by Todd Robinson; introduction by Max Allan Collins.
Porter, Katherine Anne
The circus
The vintage book of American women writers; edited and with an introduction by Elaine Showalter.

Porter, William Sydney *See* Henry, O., 1862-1910

PORTLAND (OR.) *See* Oregon—Portland

The **portrait**. Gogol, N.

Portrait. Matheson, R.

Portrait of My Mother, Who Posed Nude in Wartime. Sandor, M.

Portrait of the artist with four other guys. Gifford, B.

PORTRAITS
  Gogol, N. The portrait

Portraits of a few of the people I've made cry. Sneed, C.

PORTUGAL
  Tavares, G. M. Six tales

A **position** at the university. Davis, L.

POSSESSION, DEMONIAC *See* Demoniac possession

The **possibility** of termites. Nevins, F. M., Jr.

A **possible** episode in the picaresque adventures of Mr. J. H. B. Monstrosee. Emshwiller, C.

Possible to rue. Anthony, P.

Post Production. Hadley, T.

POSTAL SERVICE
  Shibli, A. At the post office
  Vestal, S. Opposition in all things

Postmortem. Kumar, A.

The **potato** dealer. Trevor, W.

POTATO FAMINE *See* Famines

Potatoes. Mirvis, T.

Poulson, Christine
  Fishy story
    Original sins; a Crime Writer's Association anthology; edited by Martin Edwards.

POULTRY
    See also Guinea fowl
  Gruber, F. Ask me another

POUND, EZRA, 1885-1972
                About
  Wieland, L. The girl with radium eyes
  Wieland, L. Pound in Venice

The **Pound** Game. Cochrane, M.

Pound in Venice. Wieland, L.

Pourciau, Glen
  Zero Sum
    New England Review v32 no1 p181-3 2011

POVERTY
  Atta, S. The miracle worker
  Bell, M. S. Twenty dollars
  Bukowski, C. A day
  Dib, M. At the café
  Dib, M. Little Cousin
  Dixon, S. Contac
  Gordimer, N. Parking Tax
  Gordimer, N. The ultimate safari
  Hemmingson, M. Branches
  Keegan, C. Foster
  Lahens, Y. A commonplace disaster
  Le Clézio, J.-M. G. Hazaran
  Lindholm, M. A touch of lavender
  Marär, M. The loaf
  Thon, M. R. Confession for Raymond Good Bird
  Watkins, M. Two midnights in a jug

Powell, Talmage
  Her dagger before me
    The Black Lizard big book of Black Mask stories; edited and with a foreword by Otto Penzler; introduction by Keith Alan Deutsch.

The **power** of silence. Diab, F.

The **power** of speech. Babbitt, N.

The **power** of words. Blatnik, A.

The **power** of words. Monzó, Q.

Powers, J. F. (James Farl)
  The valiant woman
    Blue collar, white collar, no collar; stories of work; edited by Richard Ford.

Powers, James Farl *See* Powers, J. F. (James Farl), 1917-1999

Powers, Jessica
  Preacher's kid
    Lone Star noir; edited by Bobby Byrd & Johnny Byrd.

Powers, Richard
  To the measures fall
    The Best American short stories, 2011; selected from U.S. and Canadian magazines by Geraldine Brooks with Heidi Pitlor; with an introduction by Geraldine Brooks.
    The New Yorker v86 no32 p72-7 O 18 2010

Powers, Tim
  The Bible repairman
    Powers, T. The Bible repairman and other stories
  The hour of Babel
    Powers, T. The Bible repairman and other stories
  A journey of only two paces
    Powers, T. The Bible repairman and other stories
  Parallel lines
    Powers, T. The Bible repairman and other stories
  A soul in a bottle
    Powers, T. The Bible repairman and other stories
  A time to cast away stones
    Powers, T. The Bible repairman and other stories

PRACTICAL JOKES
  Marär, M. The internal pages
  Riippi, J. Something about a joke
  Vonnegut, K. Bomar

Practice. Lancelotta, V.

Prairie Symposium. Phillips, C. L.

Prakash, Uday
  The walls of Delhi
    Delhi noir; edited by Hirsh Sawhney

The **pram**. Doyle, R.

PRANKS *See* Practical jokes

Pratt, T. A.
  Mommy issues of the dead
    The way of the wizard; edited by John Joseph Adams.

Pratt, Tim
  Our stars, our selves
    Welcome to Bordertown; new stories and poems of the Borderlands; edited by Holly Black and Ellen Kushner; introduction by Terri Windling.

PRAYERS
  Marär, M. S.P.Y.

PRAYERS—*Continued*
Riippi, J. Something about the orange suitcase
Terry, G. P. The Holy Sisters of Shedir
Wells, H. G. Answer to prayer
Preacher's kid. Powers, J.
Precautions. Goodberg, D.
Precious Door. Goyen, W.
Precious hairpin. Terry, G. P.
Precious things. Wilson, L.
The **precipice**. Hale, D. J.
PRECOGNITIONS *See* Premonitions
Predation. Shapiro, J.
The **predator**. Roncagliolo, S.
PREGNANCY
    See also Abortion
Atwell, M. S. Maynard
Beattie, A. Girl talk
Bezmozgis, D. The train of their departure
Bissell, T. A bridge under water
Blake, G. When the gods want to punish you
Blatnik, A. Coming
Boggs, B. Good news for a hard time
Dixon, S. The baby
Ely, S. Mississippi rules
Evans, D. Harvest
Fallaras, C. The story of a scar
Fowler, K. J. Familiar birds
Gordimer, N. For dear life
Gray, A. Babies
Grossman, V. S. In the town of Berdichev
Haines, J. P. Ten with a flag
Hall, T. M. Visitations
Hemmingson, M. Forbidden scenes of affection
Hemmingson, M. Solid memories have the life-
    span of tulips and sunflowers
Hemmingson, M. Why don't you use your park-
    ing space?
Hodge, B. If I should wake before I die
Johnston, B. A. Soldier of fortune
Lamrabet, R. Ammetis the sleeper
Le Sueur, M. Annunciation
Leland, C. T. How the Coe boys got their
    names
Leland, C. T. What it came to
Lychack, W. Chickens
Marãr, M. And we used to squeeze the olives
    for oil
Mullins, D. P. This life or the next
Nagai, M. Bitter fruit
Nagai, M. Song
Niedzviecki, H. Prenatal
Niles, C. Sin's last stand
Oates, J. C. Golden gloves
Papernick, J. The miracle birth
Quade, K. V. The five wounds
Rodoreda, M. Nocturnal
Samardzic, G. Varneesh
Schappell, E. A dog story
Shapiro, J. Bummer
Shapiro, J. Maternity
Sisson, A. Patriot girls
Somerville, P. Vaara in the woods
Spahić, O. Raymond is no longer with us—Car-
    ver is dead
Tremblay, P. Feeding the machine
Trevor, W. The potato dealer
Vaughn, C. Amaryllis
Vonnegut, K. Ruth
Wieland, L. Quickening

Yared, H. Layla's belly
PREHISTORIC MAN
    See also Prehistoric times
Highsmith, P. Oona, the jolly cave woman
Matheson, R. Man with a club
Ruckley, B. Flint
PREHISTORIC TIMES
Emshwiller, C. Vilcabamba
Wells, H. G. The grisly folk
Wells, H. G. A story of the stone age
PREJUDICES
    See also Antisemitism; Race relations
Bierce, A. The haunted valley
Chaudhuri, A. Aniruddha: the latest installment
Kim, T.-s. In the shadow of Mount Fuji
Neugeboren, J. Summer afternoon
O'Connor, F. Revelation
Okorafor, N. Wahala
PREMATURE BURIAL
Bierce, A. A bottomless grave
Bierce, A. One summer night
PREMONITIONS
Koryta, M. The cypress house
Prenatal. Niedzviecki, H.
Prentiss, Norman
  In the porches of my ears
    The Year's best dark fantasy & horror; edited
      by Paula Guran
The **presence** by the fire. Wells, H. G.
Present at a hanging. Bierce, A.
Presents. Eisenberg, D.
The **preservation** society. Goodberg, D.
The **preserving** machine. Dick, P. K.
PRESIDENTS
Ajvaz, M. The wire book
Goytisolo, J. Mr. President . . .
          United States
Qiu Xiaolong. When President Nixon first visit-
    ed China
Tillman, L. Madame Realism's conscience
PRESLEY, GLADYS
          About
Hannah, B. Mother mouth
The **prettiest** dead girl in Detroit. Estleman, L. D.
The **Prettiest** Girls. Sneed, C.
Pretty Citadel. HOWLEY, K.
The **price**. Gaiman, N.
The **price** of silver. Glass, J.
Price-Thompson, Tracy
  Brotherly love
    Price-Thompson, T. My blue suede shoes;
      four novellas; [edited by] Tracy Price-
      Thompson and Taressa Stovall.
A **price** to pay. Jakubowski, M.
Priced to sell. Novik, N.
Prichard, Hesketh Vernon
  (jt. auth) See Prichard, Kate O'Brien Ryall and
    Prichard, Hesketh Vernon
Prichard, Kate O'Brien Ryall and Prichard,
    Hesketh Vernon
  The story of Baelbrow
    The book of the living dead; edited by John
      Richard Stephens.
Pride. Matheson, R.
Pride. Munro, A.
PRIDE AND VANITY
Bierce, A. One kind of officer
Drabble, M. A success story

Priest, Cherie
  Addison Howell and the clockroach
    The Thackery T. Lambshead cabinet of curi-
    osities; edited by Ann & Jeff VanderMeer.
  Tanglefoot (a clockwork century story)
    Steampunk II: steampunk reloaded; edited by
    Ann & Jeff VanderMeer.
A **priest** in the family. Tóibín, C.
PRIESTS *See* Anglican and Episcopal clergy;
    Catholic priests; Clergy
PRIESTS, CATHOLIC *See* Catholic priests
Prill, David
  Dating secrets of the dead
    Zombies: the recent dead; edited by Paula
    Guran.
The **primal** city. Smith, C. A.
PRIMATOLOGISTS
  Baker, L. The coming of age of Jane
PRIMITIVE RELIGION *See* Religion
Prince, Adam
  Action Figure
    The Southern Review (Baton Rouge, La.) v47
    no1 p101-15 Wint 2011
A **prince** of thirteen days. Johnson, A. D.
PRINCES
    See also Princesses
  Garner, A. Gray Wolf, Prince Jack, and the
    Firebird
Princess. LaBrie, A.
A **princess** of Spain. Vaughn, C.
PRINCESSES
  Balázs, B. The victor
  Smith, C. A. The witchcraft of Ulua
Prindle, Joseph
  Einstein's compass
    Prindle, J. Einstein's tears; a touch of genius
  Einstein's cross
    Prindle, J. Einstein's tears; a touch of genius
  Einstein's dreidel
    Prindle, J. Einstein's tears; a touch of genius
  Einstein's proof
    Prindle, J. Einstein's tears; a touch of genius
  Einstein's socks
    Prindle, J. Einstein's tears; a touch of genius
  Einstein's tears
    Prindle, J. Einstein's tears; a touch of genius
  Einstein's violin
    Prindle, J. Einstein's tears; a touch of genius
  Einstein's watch
    Prindle, J. Einstein's tears; a touch of genius
Prineas, Sarah
  The dog prince
    Swenson, P. The Best of Talebones; edited by
    Patrick Swenson.
Priority. Davis, L.
PRISON CAMPS *See* Korean War, 1950-1953—
    Prisoners and prisons; World War, 1939-
    1945—Prisoners and prisons
PRISON ESCAPES *See* Escapes
The **prison** of kronos. Terry, G. P.
The **prisoner.** Matheson, R.
PRISONERS, CONDEMNED *See* Condemned
    prisoners
PRISONERS, POLITICAL *See* Political prison-
    ers
PRISONERS AND PRISONS
    See also Ex-convicts; Political prisoners;
    Prisoners of war
  Al Ahdal, W. A crime in Mataeem Street

Archer, J. Double-cross
Bunker, E. Death of a rat
Gordimer, N. Amnesty
Jamalzadeh, M. A. Persian is sugar
Jones, S. G. The sons of Billy Clay
Lake, J. Journal of an inmate
Loory, B. Hadley
Marãr, M. The birds
Matheson, R. The prisoner
Meek, J. The kind of neighbor you used to have
Osondu, E. C. A simple case
Saunders, G. Escape from Spiderhead
Terry, G. P. The prison of kronos
Tolstoy, L., graf. Too dear
Trueblood, V. Amends
Vaughn, C. Long time waiting
                    Canada
Mofina, R. The last pursuit
                    China
Dixon, S. China
                    England
Self, W. The Nonce prize
                    Russia
Tolstoy, L., graf. God sees the truth, but waits
                United States
Chaon, D. I demand to know where you're tak-
    ing me
Chuculate, E. D. Dear Shorty
Shepard, S. Normal (Highway 39 South)
Straight, S. Mines
Vonnegut, K. Mr. Z
Woodrell, D. Two things
PRISONERS OF WAR
    See also Concentration camps; World
    War, 1939-1945—Prisoners and prisons
Chau, A. Taps
Qiu Xiaolong. Return of pow 1
Qiu Xiaolong. Return of pow II
PRISONS *See* Prisoners and prisons
PRIVATE DETECTIVES *See* Detectives, Private
Private Exploration. McCarthy, T. C.
PRIVATE EYE STORIES *See* Detectives, Pri-
    vate; Mystery and detective stories
Private grave 9. Fowler, K. J.
PRIVATE SCHOOLS *See* School life
The **prize** of peril. Sheckley, R.
Prize ship. Dick, P. K.
PRIZES *See* Rewards (Prizes, etc.)
Probate. Oates, J. C.
Probe. Monk, D.
Problem. Davis, L.
Problem in murder. Gold, H. L.
The **problem** of pain. Anderson, P.
The **problem** of Susan. Gaiman, N.
The **procession.** Sa'id, M. A.
PROCESSIONS
  Sa'id, M. A. The procession
PROCURERS *See* Pimps
Produce. Dixon, S.
Professional behavior. Uldes, E.
The **professionals.** Roberts, W. O.
The **professor.** Davis, L.
The **professor** asks his students if they agree with
    the conclusion: the table is an imitation and
    therefore not real. Williamson, E. M.
Professor Fritz and the runaway house. Matheson,
    R.
The **professor** of atheism: Department of refuta-
    tion. O'Connor, S.

The **professor** of atheism: Glue factory bowling. O'Connor, S.

The **professor** of atheism: Here comes another lesson. O'Connor, S.

The **professor** of atheism: Magnum opus. O'Connor, S.

The **professor** of atheism: Paradise. O'Connor, S.

The **professor** of atheism: Stealing peaches from Sam Snnow. O'Connor, S.

PROFESSORS *See* Teachers

The **professor's** teddy bear. Sturgeon, T.

The **Project**. Emshwiller, C.

The **projected** girl. Tidhar, L.

PROMISCUITY

Hannah, B. Coming close to Donna

The **promise**. Terry, G. P.

The **promise** of undying love. Emshwiller, C.

Promises. Lake, J.

Promising two-year-old. Shepard, S.

Promotion to satellite. Bradbury, R.

Pron, Patricio

A few words on the life cycle of frogs
Granta no113 p301-15 Wint 2010

Pronzini, Bill

Cat's-paw

The Shamus winners: America's best private eye stories, volume I: 1982-1995; collected and introduced by Robert J. Randisi; founder, Private Eye Writers of America

Pronzini, Bill and Malzberg, Barry N.

Caius

Blood and other cravings; edited by Ellen Datlow.

Proof of love. Black, A.

The **prop** master. Brieschke, P.

PROPAGANDA

Valentine, G. Is this your day to join revolution?

PROPERTY

See also Real estate

Property. McCracken, E.

The **prophecy**. Jančar, D.

PROPHETS

Monzó, Q. The lives of the prophets

Sparber, M. Eliyahu-ha-Navi

Proportions for the human figure. Cardinale, J.

Prosthesis, or The Metamorphosis. Marchis, V.

PROSTITUTES

See also Pimps

Abbas, G. The room with the blue light

Baker, K. The women of Nell Gwynne's

Byrd, B. The dead man's wife

Dixon, S. Fired

Dixon, S. The leader

Dorph, C. and Pasternak, S. Australia

Firth, M. Some kind of betrayal

Gorman, E. A little something to believe in

Hellenes, M. M. The Jesus

Hemmingson, M. You will not believe what happens to me, but does it matter? it only matters that I know what happens

Hoffman, N. K. The third dead boy

Krasznahorkai, L. The bill

Lahens, Y. And all this unease

Lutz, J. Lily & men

Marjiyyah, R. A blessed whore: a story from life

Mullins, D. P. Longing to love you

Nagai, M. Bitter fruit

Osondu, E. C. An incident at Pat's Bar

Osondu, E. C. Our first American

Osondu, E. C. A simple case

Papernick, J. My darling sweetheart baby

Rodoreda, M. Ada Liz

Schirach, F. v. Bliss

Schirach, F. v. Summertime

Shepard, L. Rose Street attractors

Sikka, M. The railway aunty

Tucher, A. Bismarck rules

Williamson, E. M. Hangman

PROSTITUTION

See also Prostitutes

Engel, P. Vida

Holm, G. When it's tough out there

July, M. Something that needs nothing

Matheson, R. Counterfeit bills

Nikitas, D. Trauma dyke

Rodoreda, M. The thousand franc bill

A **protest** against the sun. Millhauser, S.

Proulx, Annie

55 miles to the gas pump

The vintage book of American women writers; edited and with an introduction by Elaine Showalter.

Job history

Blue collar, white collar, no collar; stories of work; edited by Richard Ford.

The sagebrush kid

Best of the West 2009; new stories from the wide side of the Missouri; edited by James Thomas and D. Seth Horton; foreword by Rick Bass.

Them old cowboy songs

The Pen/O.Henry Prize stories, 2010; edited and with an introduction by Laura Furman; with essays on the stories they admire most by jurors Junot Diaz, Paula Fox, Yiyun Li.

Proverbs of hell. Valente, C. M.

PROVINCETOWN (MASS.) *See* Massachusetts—Provincetown

The **proving** of Smollett Standforth. Lanagan, M.

PSYCHIATRISTS

See also Mentally ill—Care and treatment

Broderick, D. Under the moons of Venus

Davis, L. Therapy

Marcus, H. Swimming

McGarry, J. Transference

Pearlman, E. Aunt telephone

Roberts, W. O. The professionals

Self, W. Design faults in the Volvo 760 Turbo: a manual

Self, W. Tough, tough toys for tough, tough boys

Smith, C. A. Schizoid creator

PSYCHIC PHENOMENA *See* Extrasensory perception; Occultism; Spiritualism; Supernatural phenomena

PSYCHOANALYSIS

Gash, J. The life business

A **psychological** shipwreck. Bierce, A.

PSYCHOLOGISTS

Fowler, K. J. King Rat

Kyle, A. Take care

Mehta, R. The cure

Self, W. The quantity theory of insanity

Silverberg, R. A thousand paces along the Via Dolorosa

PSYCHOPATHS *See* Insane, Criminal and dangerous; Personality disorders
PSYCHOTHERAPISTS *See* Psychotherapy
PSYCHOTHERAPY
Meno, J. Children are the only ones who blush
PUBLIC HOUSING
Mosley, W. The trial
PUBLIC RELATIONS
Saunders, G. Commcomm
PUBLIC SCHOOLS *See* School life
PUBLICITY
Blatnik, A. Experts
PUBLISHERS AND PUBLISHING
    See also Newspapers
Eugenides, J. Great experiment
Falksen, G. D. The strange case of Mr. Salad Monday
Lupoff, R. A. Patterns
Trevor, W. A friend in the tade
PUBS *See* Hotels, taverns, etc.
Puenzo, Lucía
Cohiba
    Granta no113 p11-28 Wint 2010
PUGILISM *See* Boxing
The **pugilist**. Anderson, P.
Puglsey, Alex
CRISIS ON EARTH-X
    Dalhousie Review v91 no1 p9-32 Spr 2011
Pugno, Laura
Iceland
    Chicago Review v56 no1 p24-31 Spr 2011
Pull. Hodge, B.
Pulse. Barnes, J.
Pulvadmonitor: the dust's warning. Miéville, C.
Pulver, Joseph S.
Just another desert night with blood
    The Best horror of the year: volume three; edited by Ellen Datlow.
PUMAS
Jablokov, A. Blind cat dance
Lee, T. The puma's daughter
Spofford, H. E. P. Circumstance
The **puma's** daughter. Lee, T.
Pumpkin-head. Oates, J. C.
Punchline. MCGRAW, E.
Pung, Alice
The shed
    Freedom; stories celebrating the Universal Declaration of Human Rights; Amnesty International.
PUNIC WAR, 2D, 218-201 B.C.
Anderson, P. Delenda est
PUNISHMENT
Phillips, H. The punishments
Punishment. Smith, G. B.
Punishment. Thon, M. R.
The **punishments**. Phillips, H.
Punk rock role model. Niedzviecki, H.
The **Punks**. Crownover, D.
PUNNU'S JIHAD. Aslam, N.
PUNS
Matheson, R. Counterfeit bills
Puppies. Bonfiglio, T.
The **purchase**. Hardwick, E.
Pure pulp. Crider, B.
Pure water. Ely, S.
Purge among peanuts. Matheson, R.
PURIM
Papernick, J. There is no other

Purim night. Pearlman, E.
Puritan planet. Emshwiller, C.
The **purloined** letter. Poe, E. A.
The **purple** pileus. Wells, H. G.
Push. Gautier, A.
Pushing. Erby, S.
Pushkin, Alexander
The queen of spades
    The greatest Russian stories of crime and suspense; edited by Otto Penzler.
Pushkin, Alexander Ivanovich
The coffin-maker
    The book of the living dead; edited by John Richard Stephens.
The **pussycats**. Chau, A.
Puzzle for Scots. Nevins, F. M., Jr.
The **pyrotechnicist**. Naipaul, V. S.
A **Pyrrhic** victory. Drabble, M.
The **python** pit. Worts, G. F.

Q

Qed. Blatnik, A.
Qiu Xiaolong
Big bowl and firecracker
    Qiu Xiaolong. Years of Red Dust; stories of Shanghai
Chinese chess
    Qiu Xiaolong. Years of Red Dust; stories of Shanghai
A confidence cap
    Qiu Xiaolong. Years of Red Dust; stories of Shanghai
Confucius and crab
    Qiu Xiaolong. Years of Red Dust; stories of Shanghai
Cricket fighting
    Qiu Xiaolong. Years of Red Dust; stories of Shanghai
Eating and drinking salesman
    Qiu Xiaolong. Years of Red Dust; stories of Shanghai
Father and son
    Qiu Xiaolong. Years of Red Dust; stories of Shanghai
Foot masseur
    Qiu Xiaolong. Years of Red Dust; stories of Shanghai
Housing assignment
    Qiu Xiaolong. Years of Red Dust; stories of Shanghai
Iron rice bowl
    Qiu Xiaolong. Years of Red Dust; stories of Shanghai
A Jing Dynasty goat
    Qiu Xiaolong. Years of Red Dust; stories of Shanghai
Lottery
    Qiu Xiaolong. Years of Red Dust; stories of Shanghai
Old hunchback Fang
    Qiu Xiaolong. Years of Red Dust; stories of Shanghai
Pill and picture
    Qiu Xiaolong. Years of Red Dust; stories of Shanghai

Qiu Xiaolong—*Continued*
  Return of pow 1
    Qiu Xiaolong. Years of Red Dust; stories of
      Shanghai
  Return of pow II
    Qiu Xiaolong. Years of Red Dust; stories of
      Shanghai
  Shoes of the cultural revolution
    Qiu Xiaolong. Years of Red Dust; stories of
      Shanghai
  (Tofu) Worker poet Bao 1
    Qiu Xiaolong. Years of Red Dust; stories of
      Shanghai
  (Tofu) Worker poet Bao II
    Qiu Xiaolong. Years of Red Dust; stories of
      Shanghai
  Uniform
    Qiu Xiaolong. Years of Red Dust; stories of
      Shanghai
  Welcome to Red Dust Lane
    Qiu Xiaolong. Years of Red Dust; stories of
      Shanghai
  When I was conceived
    Qiu Xiaolong. Years of Red Dust; stories of
      Shanghai
  When President Nixon first visited China
    Qiu Xiaolong. Years of Red Dust; stories of
      Shanghai
Quade, Kirsti Valdez
  The five wounds
    Best of the West 2010; new stories from the
      wide side of the Missouri; edited by James
      Thomas and D. Seth Horton; foreword by
      Kent Meyers.
QUADRIPLEGICS
  Keene, B. Captive hearts
QUADROONS *See* Mulattoes
Quake, Memory. Taugher, M.
Quality of life. Sneed, C.
Quanah, Texas. Shepard, S.
The **quantity** theory of insanity. Self, W.
Quarantine. Mehta, R.
QUARRELING
  Davis, L. Old Mother and the Grouch
  Davis, L. Story
  Dixon, S. The argument
  Rodoreda, M. Afternoon at the cinema
  Wolff, T. Hunters in the snow
Quarry, Justin
  Home Schooling
    New England Review v31 no3 p68-82 2010
Quatro, Jamie
  1.7 to Tennessee
    The Antioch Review v69 no3 p502-514 Summ
      2011
  Imperfections
    Agni no73 p128-9 2011
  Relatives of God
    Agni no73 p132-3 2011
  You Look Like Jesus
    Agni no73 p130-1 2011
QUÉBEC (PROVINCE) *See* Canada—Québec
  (Province)
Queen. De Coster, S.
Queen kong. Emshwiller, C.
Queen of hell. Stanton, M.
The **queen** of sleep. Emshwiller, C.
The **queen** of spades. Pushkin, A.
Queen on the hill. Neville, S.

QUEENS
        See also Courts and courtiers names of
      queens
  Monk, D. Bearing life
  Smith, C. A. The death of Ilalotha
  Terry, G. P. The Queen's instructions
QUEENS (NEW YORK, N.Y.) *See* New York
  (N.Y.)—Queens
The **queen's** birthday telegram. Archer, J.
The **Queen's** instructions. Terry, G. P.
The **queer** story of Brownlow's newspaper. Wells,
  H. G.
Question. Dixon, S.
A **question** of passports. Orczy, B.
Quickening. Wieland, L.
Quiet. King, J.
Quiet afternoon tea. Mu Xin
Quiet as they come. Chau, A.
Quiet night. Highsmith, P.
The **quiet** poplar. Thu, T.
The **quilt.** Chughtai, I.
QUILTS
  Horrocks, C. It looks like this
Quintana Roo, Mexico. Shepard, S.
Quixote and the windmill. Anderson, P.
QURAN *See* Koran

R

RABBIS
  Ayau, K. J. Outsourcing
  Beagle, P. S. The rabbi's hobby
  Cook, T. H. Nevermore
  Fintushel, E. How the little rabbi grew
  Papernick, J. The Madonna of Temple Beth Elo-
    him
The **rabbi's** hobby. Beagle, P. S.
The **rabbit** hole as likely explanation. Beattie, A.
A **rabbit** in the lettuce patch. Bill, F.
Rabbit in the trap. Hong, P.
RABBITS
  Goodberg, D. Mercy blow
  Harris, J. C. Brer Rabbit and the Tar-Baby
  Hong, P. Rabbit in the trap
  Kitterman, B. The man who raised rabbits
  Kronauer, B. Martens and rabbits
  Riippi, J. Something about Maxine
  Slouka, M. The hare's mask
The **race** of the patient motorcyclists. Davis, L.
RACE PROBLEMS *See* Race relations
RACE RELATIONS
        See also African Americans;
      Antisemitism; Culture conflict; Miscegena-
      tion; Prejudices
  Naipaul, V. S. The baker's story
            South Africa
        See South Africa—Race relations
            United States
        See United States—Race relations
RACEHORSES *See* Horses
Rachel's island. Bingham, S.
RACING
        See also Horse racing
RACISM *See* Antisemitism; Prejudices; Race rela-
    tions
RACKETEERS *See* Crime and criminals; Gang-
    sters; Mafia
RACKETS *See* Gambling

RADIATION
Dick, P. K. The infinites
Physiological effect
Bryant, E. Jody after the war
Moody, D. Big man
RADICALS AND RADICALISM
See also Anarchism and anarchists
RADIO BROADCASTING
Olsen, L. April
Pronzini, B. and Malzberg, B. N. Caius
Roberge, R. Border radio
RADIUM
Twain, M. Sold to Satan
Wieland, L. The girl with radium eyes
Raes, Hugo
The smell of fresh linen
The Dedalus book of Flemish fantasy; edited
by Eric Dickens and translated by Paul
Vincent.
Rafe's coat. Eisenberg, D.
Rafferty's comeback. Gorman, E. and Morrish, R.
The **raffle**. Naipaul, V. S.
RAILROAD ACCIDENTS
Staalesen, G. Last train from central station
RAILROADS
See also Subways
Budnitz, J. Aboard
Employees
McPherson, J. A. A solo song: for Doc
Ray, S. The great divide
Models
Vonnegut, K. With his hand on the throttle
Stations
Ḥaqqī, Y. The first lesson
Rodoreda, M. Departure
Schmitt, E.-E. The woman with the bouquet
Simms, C. Tick-tock
Trains
Blatnik, A. In passing
Dozois, G. R. Counterfactual
Drabble, M. A voyage to Cythera
Koryta, M. The cypress house
Leland, C. T. Peach Queen
Mphahlele, E. Man must live
Shehadeh, R. The unbecoming of Virgil Smythe
Tidhar, L. The night train
Tuten, F. Self portrait with Sicily
Wells, H. G. A tale of the twentieth century for
advanced thinkers
Travel
Bloch, R. That hell-bound train
Delbanco, N. The writers' trade
Rodoreda, M. On the train
Swierczynski, D. Lonergan's girl
The **railway** aunty. Sikka, M.
Rain. McCall Smith, A.
Rain in the distance. Gifford, B.
Rain-queen. Gordimer, N.
Rainbow diamonds. Decolta, R.
The **rainbow** goblins. See Franco, J. April in three
parts: part 1, The rainbow goblins
The **rainbow's** end. Fievre, M. J.
RAIS, GILLES DE, 1404-1440
About
Shepard, J. Classical scenes of farewell
The **Rajah's** treasure. Wells, H. G.

Rajaniemi, Hannu
Elegy for a young elk
The Best science fiction and fantasy of the
year: volume five; edited by Jonathan
Strahan.
The Year's best science fiction: twenty-eighth
annual collection; edited by Gardner
Dozois.
Rakha, Youssef
Suicide 20, or the Hakimi Maqama
Beirut 39; new writing from the Arab world;
edited by Samuel Shimon; with a preface
by Hanan al-Shaykh
Rakshasi. Armstrong, K.
RAMADAN
Marār, M. May nobody save anything!
Ramirez, Steven
Five Movie Endings (I Would Banish from This
World if I Were Ruler Supreme of Holly-
wood)
The North American Review v295 no3 p32-6
Summ 2010
Rammer. Niven, L.
Ramuz, C. F.
Pastoral
The Kenyon Review v33 no1 p131-6 Wint
2011
RANCH LIFE
See also Cowboys
Anzaldúa, G. El paisano is a bird of omen
Anzaldúa, G. Reading LP
Johnston, T. Two years
McGuane, T. Cowboy
Rancor. Madrid, F. M.
Rand, Ken
Song of mother jungle
Swenson, P. The Best of Talebones; edited by
Patrick Swenson.
Randall, Penelope
The Oxfam dress
Dancing with Mr. Darcy; stories inspired by
Jane Austen and Chawton House Library;
compiled by Sarah Waters.
Randall, Scott
THE SIX
Dalhousie Review v91 no1 p119-129 Spr
2011
Randisi, Robert J.
Black & white memories
Randisi, R. J. The guilt edge and other stories
Cowards die many times
Randisi, R. J. The guilt edge and other stories
The disappearance of Penny
Randisi, R. J. The guilt edge and other stories
The equine theft
Randisi, R. J. The guilt edge and other stories
The final nail
Randisi, R. J. The guilt edge and other stories
The final nail: a Val O'Farrel story
By hook or by crook and 27 more of the best
crime + mystery stories of the year; edited
by Ed Gorman and Martin H. Greenberg.
The girl who talked to horses
Randisi, R. J. The guilt edge and other stories
The goodly race
Randisi, R. J. The guilt edge and other stories
Green legs and glam
Randisi, R. J. The guilt edge and other stories

REVOLUTIONISTS
Dib, M. The end
Fountain, B. Near-extinct birds of the central
  cordillera
Gordimer, N. Amnesty
Gordimer, N. Something out there
Grossman, V. S. The elk
Qiu Xiaolong. Cricket fighting
REVOLUTIONS
  See also Revolutionists
Dozois, G. R. Dinner party
Gordimer, N. A soldier's embrace
Kurlansky, M. Espresso
Ryman, G. O Happy day !
Solzhenitsyn, A. Ego
Taraqqi, G. The grand lady of my soul
Revolver. Naylor, H.
REWARDS (PRIZES, ETC.)
Healy, J. F. In my ancestor's image: a Rory
  Calhoun short story
Woolrich, C. Borrowed crime
Reynolds, Alastair
The old man and the Martian sea
  Life on Mars: tales from the new frontier; an
  original science fiction anthology; edited by
  Jonathan Strahan
Sleepover
  The Year's best science fiction: twenty-eighth
  annual collection; edited by Gardner
  Dozois.
Reza Says. Webb, I.
Rhoda's sack. Williamson, E. M.
RHODESIA
Greene, L. P. Fire
RHODESIA, NORTHERN *See* Zambia
RHODESIA, SOUTHERN *See* Zimbabwe
Rhymes with Jew. Tremblay, P.
Riahi, Kamel
From the novel The scalpel
  Beirut 39; new writing from the Arab world;
  edited by Samuel Shimon; with a preface
  by Hanan al-Shaykh
Ribeyro, Julio Ramón
Butterflies and Bugles
  The Antioch Review v69 no2 p286-92 Spr
  2011
Riccardi, Ted
An affair in Ravello
  Riccardi, T. Between the Thames and the Ti-
  ber; the further adventures of Sherlock
  Holmes in Britain and the Italian Peninsula
A case of criminal madness
  Riccardi, T. Between the Thames and the Ti-
  ber; the further adventures of Sherlock
  Holmes in Britain and the Italian Peninsula
The case of Isadora Persano
  Riccardi, T. Between the Thames and the Ti-
  ber; the further adventures of Sherlock
  Holmes in Britain and the Italian Peninsula
The case of the missing lodger
  Riccardi, T. Between the Thames and the Ti-
  ber; the further adventures of Sherlock
  Holmes in Britain and the Italian Peninsula
The case of the plangent colonel
  Riccardi, T. Between the Thames and the Ti-
  ber; the further adventures of Sherlock
  Holmes in Britain and the Italian Peninsula

The case of the two Bohemes
  Riccardi, T. Between the Thames and the Ti-
  ber; the further adventures of Sherlock
  Holmes in Britain and the Italian Peninsula
The case of the vermillion face
  Riccardi, T. Between the Thames and the Ti-
  ber; the further adventures of Sherlock
  Holmes in Britain and the Italian Peninsula
A death in Venice
  Riccardi, T. Between the Thames and the Ti-
  ber; the further adventures of Sherlock
  Holmes in Britain and the Italian Peninsula
The death of Mycroft Holmes
  Riccardi, T. Between the Thames and the Ti-
  ber; the further adventures of Sherlock
  Holmes in Britain and the Italian Peninsula
The mountain of fear
  Riccardi, T. Between the Thames and the Ti-
  ber; the further adventures of Sherlock
  Holmes in Britain and the Italian Peninsula
Porlock's demise
  Riccardi, T. Between the Thames and the Ti-
  ber; the further adventures of Sherlock
  Holmes in Britain and the Italian Peninsula
A singular event in Tranquebar
  Riccardi, T. Between the Thames and the Ti-
  ber; the further adventures of Sherlock
  Holmes in Britain and the Italian Peninsula
Riccion, Catherine
(tr.) *See* Ringelnatz, Joachim
Rich, Mark
Zothique mi amor
  Swenson, P. The Best of Talebones; edited by
  Patrick Swenson.
RICH PEOPLE *See* Wealth
Richerson, Carrie
. . . With [ord crossed out] by good intentions
  Sympathy for the devil; edited by Tim Pratt.
Richie and the rich bitch. Santlofer, J.
Richter, Stacey
The doll awakens
  Fantastic women; 18 tales of the surreal and
  the sublime from Tin House; introduction
  by Joy Williams; edited by Rob Spillman.
Rickert, M.
The Christmas witch
  Rickert, M. Holiday
Don't ask
  Rickert, M. Holiday
Evidence of love in a case of abandonment; one
  daughter's personal account
  Brave new worlds; edited by John Joseph Ad-
  ams.
Evidence of love in a case of abandonment: one
  daughter's personal account
  Rickert, M. Holiday
Holiday
  Rickert, M. Holiday
Journey into the kingdom
  Rickert, M. Holiday
The machine
  Rickert, M. Holiday
Memoir of a deer woman
  Rickert, M. Holiday
Traitor
  Rickert, M. Holiday
War is beautiful
  Rickert, M. Holiday

Rickert, M.—*Continued*
Was she wicked? was she good?
    Rickert, M. Holiday
    The Best horror of the year: volume three;
        edited by Ellen Datlow.
You have never been here
    Rickert, M. Holiday
Rickert, Mary *See* Rickert, M., 1959-
RICKSHAW MEN
    Sealy, I. A. Last in, first out
Ricoh Gerbl. Gerbl, R.
Ride, fly, penetrate, loiter. Hannah, B.
Ridgway, Keith
Goo Book
    The New Yorker v87 no8 p62-71 Ap 11 2011
Shame
    The Granta book of the Irish short story; [ed-
        ited by] Anne Enright.
Rifbjerg, Klaus
Debt of honor
    Copenhagen noir; edited by Bo Tao
        Michaëlis; translated by Mark Kline.
Right and wrong. Davis, L.
Riippi, Joseph
An exchange
    Riippi, J. The orange suitcase; stories
Something about a finger
    Riippi, J. The orange suitcase; stories
Something about a joke
    Riippi, J. The orange suitcase; stories
Something about a nail
    Riippi, J. The orange suitcase; stories
Something about a painter
    Riippi, J. The orange suitcase; stories
Something about a promise
    Riippi, J. The orange suitcase; stories
Something about a Valentine's Day
    Riippi, J. The orange suitcase; stories
Something about Ben Jensen
    Riippi, J. The orange suitcase; stories
Something about birthdays
    Riippi, J. The orange suitcase; stories
Something about Borges and the blind Chelsea
    Riippi, J. The orange suitcase; stories
Something about drinking in Baton Rouge
    Riippi, J. The orange suitcase; stories
Something about ipek (on a Valentine's Day)
    Riippi, J. The orange suitcase; stories
Something about L—
    Riippi, J. The orange suitcase; stories
Something about last time at the Cedar Tavern
    Riippi, J. The orange suitcase; stories
Something about marriage, part I
    Riippi, J. The orange suitcase; stories
Something about marriage, pt 2
    Riippi, J. The orange suitcase; stories
Something about marriage, pt 3
    Riippi, J. The orange suitcase; stories
Something about Maxine
    Riippi, J. The orange suitcase; stories
Something about Moby Dick
    Riippi, J. The orange suitcase; stories
Something about my blood and yours
    Riippi, J. The orange suitcase; stories
Something about my book
    Riippi, J. The orange suitcase; stories
Something about New York City
    Riippi, J. The orange suitcase; stories

Something about perfecting a love
    Riippi, J. The orange suitcase; stories
Something about remembering a couch or a per-
    son
    Riippi, J. The orange suitcase; stories
Something about rings
    Riippi, J. The orange suitcase; stories
Something about someone else's poem
    Riippi, J. The orange suitcase; stories
Something about swimming with sea turtles
    Riippi, J. The orange suitcase; stories
Something about the orange suitcase
    Riippi, J. The orange suitcase; stories
Something about the rest
    Riippi, J. The orange suitcase; stories
Something about the unpublished and unfinished
    novels
    Riippi, J. The orange suitcase; stories
Something about the Zombies
    Riippi, J. The orange suitcase; stories
Something about Vegas: a note on the second
    edition of a first novel
    Riippi, J. The orange suitcase; stories
Something (entirely true) about your grandfather
    Riippi, J. The orange suitcase; stories
Rikki *See* Ducornet, Rikki
Riley, Regina
Undying love
    Hungry for your love; an anthology of
        zombie romance; edited by Lori Perkins.
Rilke. Novack, S.
Rilly, Ethan
What Sara tells me
    Can'tLit; fearless fiction from Broken pencil
        magazine; edited by Richard Rosenbaum.
Rinaldi, Nicholas
The Gods Wear Funny Hats
    Confrontation no109 p44-56 Spr 2011
The **ring** on the hand of death. Rollins Jr., W.
Ringelnatz, Joachim
The Wild Gal from Ohio
    New England Review v32 no2 p151-153 Spr
        2011
RINGS
    Gordimer, N. A find
Ríos, Alberto Álvaro
The Asterisk Company
    Orion v30 no2 p34-9 Mr/Ap 2011
RIOTS
    Ayau, K. J. At a loss for words
    Lahens, Y. Madness had come with the rain
    Niven, L. Flash crowd
Rip off the wings of dragonflies; virus; on loca-
        tion; still life with grapes; four art pieces;
        a Chinese folk tale, and the culture of pop
        art; anonymous anonymous. Cohen, J.
Rip Van Winkle. Irving, W.
Rise. Dent, C. Z.
The **rise** of Maud Martha. Brooks, G.
Ristow, Ben
Saint Jerome and the Dumpster Girls
    Bomb no114 p Supp7-Supp11 Wint 2010
Rita Münster [excerpt]. Kronauer, B.
Rites. Villegas, H.
RITES AND CEREMONIES
    Davis, C. The names of Yanils
    Mamatas, N. Summon, bind, banish
    Muwasi, E. Sin and eggs
The **river** came; fragmented recall. Tidhar, L.

The **river** nemunas. Doerr, A.
RIVERBOATS *See* Steamboats
The **Rivermutts** of Pig's Eye. Rapacz, M.
RIVERS
McCann, C. Everything in this country must
Slouka, M. Crossing
Rivers of wood. Kitterman, B.
The **road**. Grossman, V. S.
The **road** of Azrael. Howard, R. E.
The **road** of the eagles. Howard, R. E.
Road to nowhere. Terry, J.
The **road** to the shore. McLaverty, M.
The **roads**. Barillas, G. R.
The **road's** end. DuBois, B.
ROBBERS *See* Brigands and robbers; Robbery
The **robbers** of divine power. Balázs, B.
Robber's roost. Estleman, L. D.
ROBBERY
      See also Bank robbers; Theft
Eisenberg, D. The robbery
Hansen, P. Community property
Lister, M. Ultima forsan
Orozco, D. Only connect
Schirach, F. v. The hedgehog
Schirach, F. v. Tanata's tea bowl
Smith, C. A. The theft of the thirty-nine girdles
Swierczynski, D. Lonergan's girl
Watkins, C. V. The last thing we need
Wells, H. G. The Hammerpond Park burglary
The **robbery**. Eisenberg, D.
Robbie. Glass, J. C.
Roberge, Rob
Beano's deal
   Roberge, R. Working backwards from the
     worst moment of my life; stories
Border radio
   Roberge, R. Working backwards from the
     worst moment of my life; stories
Burn ward
   Roberge, R. Working backwards from the
     worst moment of my life; stories
Do not concern yourself with things Lee Nading
   has left out
   Roberge, R. Working backwards from the
     worst moment of my life; stories
Earthquake
   Roberge, R. Working backwards from the
     worst moment of my life; stories
The exterminator
   Roberge, R. Working backwards from the
     worst moment of my life; stories
A headache from Barstow to Salt Lake
   Roberge, R. Working backwards from the
     worst moment of my life; stories
Love and hope and sex and dreams
   Roberge, R. Working backwards from the
     worst moment of my life; stories
Swiss engineering
   Roberge, R. Working backwards from the
     worst moment of my life; stories
Whatever happened to Billy Brody?
   Roberge, R. Working backwards from the
     worst moment of my life; stories
Working backward from the worst moment of
   my life
   Roberge, R. Working backwards from the
     worst moment of my life; stories

Roberson, Chris
Larp of Mars
   Life on Mars: tales from the new frontier; an
     original science fiction anthology; edited by
     Jonathan Strahan
O one
   Steampunk II: steampunk reloaded; edited by
     Ann & Jeff VanderMeer.
Robert E. Lee dead. Evans, D.
Robertis, Carolina de
(tr.) *See* Hasbún, Rodrigo
Roberts, Ben
Marans
   Harvard Review (1992) no40 p110-19 2011
Roberts, Peter
Renewal
   Nature v471 no7339 p542 Mr 24 2011
Roberts, Wiliam Owen
The professionals
   Best European fiction 2011; edited by Alek-
     sandr Hemon; preface by Colum McCann
Robeson, Kenneth *See* Dent, Lester, 1904-1959
Robin. Bauer, T.
ROBIN HOOD (LEGENDARY CHARACTER)
Monzó, Q. A hunger and thirst for justice
Seabrook, T. When Robin Hood fell with an ar-
   row through his heart
The **Robin's** Nest. Heynen, J.
Robinson, Eden
Minnows
   The Walrus v7 no8 p64-5, 67 O 2010
Robinson, Kim Stanley
Discovering life
   Life on Mars: tales from the new frontier; an
     original science fiction anthology; edited by
     Jonathan Strahan
In Pierson's orchestra
   Before they were giants; edited by James L.
     Sutter; cover illustration by Kieran Yanner.
The lunatics
   Brave new worlds; edited by John Joseph Ad-
     ams.
Robinson, Lewis
Officer Friendly
   Blue collar, white collar, no collar; stories of
     work; edited by Richard Ford.
Robinson, Ron
Nick
   South Dakota Magazine v26 no5 p80-3 Ja/F
     2011
Robinson, Spider
The guy with the eyes
   Before they were giants; edited by James L.
     Sutter; cover illustration by Kieran Yanner.
ROBOTS
Abraham, D. Baljour and Meriwether in the ad-
   venture of the emperor's vengeance
Anderson, P. Quixote and the windmill
Bierce, A. Moxon's master
Black, A. Lisa with child
Bradbury, R. The parallel (A blade of grass)
Chiang, T. Dacey's patent Automatic Nanny
Colston, A. Not in the flesh
Dick, P. K. The defenders
Dick, P. K. The little movement
Dick, P. K. Nanny
Dick, P. K. Roog
Emshwiller, C. Baby
Emshwiller, C. Built for pleasure

ROBOTS—*Continued*

Emshwiller, C. But soft what light..

Emshwiller, C. Murray is for murder

Fuller, A. W. A wife manufactured to order

Grant, J. L. and Mantchev, L. As recorded on brass cylinders

Grossman, L. Sir Ranulph Wykeham-Rackham, GBE, a.k.a. Roboticus the All-Knowing

Hubbard, L. R. The automagic horse

Kiernan, C. R. The steam dancer

Lanagan, M. Machine maid

McDonald, S. Seven sexy cowboy robots

McOmber, A. The automatic garden

Monk, D. Probe

Niven, L. Becalmed in hell

Priest, C. Tanglefoot (a clockwork century story)

Ryman, G. Warmth

Sands, B. Outside

Smith, C. A. Monsters in the night

Swirsky, R. The taste of promises

Tiptree, J. The girl who was plugged in

Vonnegut, K. Jenny

Roche, Thomas S.

Deepwater miracle

Z: zombie stories; edited by J. M. Lassen

The **rock** in the Park. Beagle, P. S.

ROCK MUSIC

Allyn, D. Israfel

Black, H. Noble rot

Cadigan, P. Rock on

Nutting, A. Bandleader's girlfriend

Packer, A. Molten

Pratt, T. Our stars, our selves

Sands, B. Gen Papa-Georgio

Spinrad, N. The big flash

Vaughn, C. Kitty and the mosh pit of the damned

ROCK MUSICIANS *See* Rock music

Rock of ages. Lake, R.

The **rock** of crack as big as the Ritz. Self, W.

Rock on. Cadigan, P.

Rockaway. Conklin, L.

ROCKS

Ely, S. Rocks

Kiernan, C. R. The bone's prayer

Rocks. Ely, S.

Roden, Barbara

The brink of eternity

The Year's best dark fantasy & horror; edited by Paula Guran

Endless night

Vampires; the recent undead; edited by Paula Guran.

Sweet sorrow

Blood and other cravings; edited by Ellen Datlow.

RODEOS

Ray, S. The great divide

Rodgers, Susan Jackson

This Other Alan

The North American Review v296 no1 p8-11 Wint 2011

Rodin's the hand of god. Ray, S.

Rodoreda, Mercè

Ada Liz

Rodoreda, M. The selected stories of Merce Rodoreda; translated from the Catalan by Martha Tennent

Afternoon at the cinema

Rodoreda, M. The selected stories of Merce Rodoreda; translated from the Catalan by Martha Tennent

The bath

Rodoreda, M. The selected stories of Merce Rodoreda; translated from the Catalan by Martha Tennent

Before I die

Rodoreda, M. The selected stories of Merce Rodoreda; translated from the Catalan by Martha Tennent

The beginning

Rodoreda, M. The selected stories of Merce Rodoreda; translated from the Catalan by Martha Tennent

Blood

Rodoreda, M. The selected stories of Merce Rodoreda; translated from the Catalan by Martha Tennent

Carnival

Rodoreda, M. The selected stories of Merce Rodoreda; translated from the Catalan by Martha Tennent

Departure

Rodoreda, M. The selected stories of Merce Rodoreda; translated from the Catalan by Martha Tennent

Engaged

Rodoreda, M. The selected stories of Merce Rodoreda; translated from the Catalan by Martha Tennent

The fate of Lisa Sperling

Rodoreda, M. The selected stories of Merce Rodoreda; translated from the Catalan by Martha Tennent

Friday, June 8

Rodoreda, M. The selected stories of Merce Rodoreda; translated from the Catalan by Martha Tennent

Guinea fowls

Rodoreda, M. The selected stories of Merce Rodoreda; translated from the Catalan by Martha Tennent

Happiness

Rodoreda, M. The selected stories of Merce Rodoreda; translated from the Catalan by Martha Tennent

Ice cream

Rodoreda, M. The selected stories of Merce Rodoreda; translated from the Catalan by Martha Tennent

In a whisper

Rodoreda, M. The selected stories of Merce Rodoreda; translated from the Catalan by Martha Tennent

It seemed like silk

Rodoreda, M. The selected stories of Merce Rodoreda; translated from the Catalan by Martha Tennent

Love

Rodoreda, M. The selected stories of Merce Rodoreda; translated from the Catalan by Martha Tennent

The mirror

Rodoreda, M. The selected stories of Merce Rodoreda; translated from the Catalan by Martha Tennent

Rooney, Kathleen and Gabbert, Elisa
City walk IV, IX, XII, XIV
    Butler, B. 30 under 30; an anthology of innovative fiction by younger writers; Blake Butler & Lily Hoang, eds.
The **rope** and the sea. Loory, B.
Rosalind's Song. Cherry-Chandler, E.
Rosanna. Large, J.-R.
Roscoe, Patrick
LOVE, SWEET LOVE
    Dalhousie Review v91 no1 p91-98 Spr 2011
Roscoe, Theodore
Snake-head
    The Big book of adventure stories; edited and with a introduction by Otto Penzler; foreword by Douglas Preston.
A **rose** by any other name would still be red. Vaughan, E. A.
A **rose** for Emily. Faulkner, W.
Rose-Innes, Henrietta
Homing
    Agni no72 p139-50 2010
Rose Street attractors. Shepard, L.
Rose wept. Trevor, W.
Rosebud. Yamauchi, W.
Rosebud, South Dakota (Highway 83 North). Shepard, S.
Rosen, Jonathan
The true world
    Promised lands; new Jewish American fiction on longing and belonging; edited by Derek Rubin.
Rosenbaum, Benjamin
Biographical notes to "A discourse on the nature of causality, with air-planes" by Benjamin Rosenbaum
    People of the book; a decade of Jewish science fiction & fantasy; edited by Rachel Swirsky & Sean Wallace.
(jt. auth) See Ackert, David and Rosenbaum, Benjamin
Rosenbaum, Thane
The Yehuda triangle
    Promised lands; new Jewish American fiction on longing and belonging; edited by Derek Rubin.
Rosie gets a soul. Eisenberg, D.
Ross, Adam
Futures
    Ross, A. Ladies and gentlemen
In the basement
    Ross, A. Ladies and gentlemen
Ladies and gentlemen
    Ross, A. Ladies and gentlemen
Middleman
    Ross, A. Ladies and gentlemen
The rest of it
    Ross, A. Ladies and gentlemen
The suicide room
    Ross, A. Ladies and gentlemen
When in Rome
    Ross, A. Ladies and gentlemen
Roth, Philip
The conversion of the Jews
    I found this funny; my favorite pieces of humor and some that may not be funny at all; edited by Judd Apatow.

Rothenberg, Pir
Medusa's Daughter
    River Styx no83 p33-45 2010
Rough company. Bill, F.
Rough justice. Jordan, C.
Roundabouts. Lanigan, S.
The **route** of the crows. Kavukçu, C.
Row, Jess
The call of blood
    The Best American short stories, 2011; selected from U.S. and Canadian magazines by Geraldine Brooks with Heidi Pitlor; with an introduction by Geraldine Brooks.
    Harvard Review (1992) no38 p122-49 2010
Sheep may safely graze
    Pushcart Prize XXXV: best of the small presses 2011; edited by Bill Henderson with the Pushcart Prize editors.
    The Pen/O.Henry Prize stories, 2010; edited and with an introduction by Laura Furman; with essays on the stories they admire most by jurors Junot Diaz, Paula Fox, Yiyun Li.
The **Rowan** gentleman. Black, H. and Clare, C.
Rowson, Susanna Haswell
An intriguing teacher, from Charlotte Temple [excerpt]
    The vintage book of American women writers; edited and with an introduction by Elaine Showalter.
Royal blue. Baxter, C.
Royle, Nicholas
The obscure bird
    The Best horror of the year: volume three; edited by Ellen Datlow.
Roy's first car. Gifford, B.
Rozan, S. J.
The grift of the magi
    Christmas at the Mysterious Bookshop; 'tis the season to be deadly; stories of mistletoe and mayhem from 17 masters of suspense; edited by Otto Penzler.
Iterations
    Mystery Writers of America presents the rich and the dead; edited by Nelson DeMille.
Seeing the moon
    On a raven's wing; new tales in honor of Edgar Allan Poe; edited by Stuart M. Kaminsky
    By hook or by crook and 27 more of the best crime + mystery stories of the year; edited by Ed Gorman and Martin H. Greenberg.
The **Rubber-Band** Gun. Percy, B.
The **Rubber** Company Heiress. Brown, K.
Rubber reality. Goodberg, D.
Rubin, Jay
(jt. auth) See Murakami, Haruki and Rubin, Jay
Rubin, Joey
Toward Lithuania
    Promised lands; new Jewish American fiction on longing and belonging; edited by Derek Rubin.
Ruckley, Brian
Flint
    Speculative Horizons; edited by Patrick St-Denis.
Ruddick, Sam
Voyeur
    The North American Review v295 no4 p25-9 Fall 2010

Rudin, Phyllis
The Inside Scoop
The Massachusetts Review v51 no4 p693-7
Wint 2010
Rue. Groff, L.
Rue Morgue noir: the possible--probable--struggles
Edgar Allan Poe might have faced while
seeking success as a talented new writer in
the world of today. Zeman, A.
RUGS
McOmber, A. Of wool
Rules. Pearlman, E.
The **rules** are the rules. Foulds, A.
Rules of engagement. Sharp, Z.
The **Rules** of Engagement. Zentner, A.
RUMANIA *See* Romania
Rumble strip. Estleman, L. D.
The **rummy** affair of young Charlie. Cannon, P.
RUNAWAYS (CHILDREN)
McDonald, S. Bluebeard by the sea
Thon, M. R. Heavenly creatures: for wandering
children and their delinquent mother
RUNAWAYS (YOUTH)
Bender, A. Skinless
Black, H. Noble rot
July, M. Something that needs nothing
Reynolds, A. The old man and the Martian sea
Sabar, A. Green
Valente, C. M. A voice like a hole
Willis, M. S. Tara White
RUNNING
Doctorow, E. L. All the time in the world
Orozco, D. I run every day
Sands, B. Chase sequence
Running dreams. Beattie, A.
Ruocco, Joanna
Ants
Ruocco, J. Man's companions
Blood
Ruocco, J. Man's companions
Bobcat
Ruocco, J. Man's companions
Bones
Ruocco, J. Man's companions
Canary
Ruocco, J. Man's companions
Cat
Ruocco, J. Man's companions
Chipmunk
Ruocco, J. Man's companions
Dog
Ruocco, J. Man's companions
Dolphins
Ruocco, J. Man's companions
Endangered species
Ruocco, J. Man's companions
Flies
Ruocco, J. Man's companions
Flying monkeys
Ruocco, J. Man's companions
Frog
Ruocco, J. Man's companions
Butler, B. 30 under 30; an anthology of inno-
vative fiction by younger writers; Blake
Butler & Lily Hoang, eds.
Hart
Ruocco, J. Man's companions
Lemmings
Ruocco, J. Man's companions

Lighting bug
Ruocco, J. Man's companions
Marzipan lambs
Ruocco, J. Man's companions
Mice
Ruocco, J. Man's companions
Pests
Ruocco, J. Man's companions
Seabird
Ruocco, J. Man's companions
Small sharks
Ruocco, J. Man's companions
Snake
Ruocco, J. Man's companions
Strays
Ruocco, J. Man's companions
Swans
Ruocco, J. Man's companions
Three pigs
Ruocco, J. Man's companions
Turkey
Ruocco, J. Man's companions
Ugly ducks
Ruocco, J. Man's companions
Unicorns
Ruocco, J. Man's companions
White buffalo
Ruocco, J. Man's companions
White horses
Ruocco, J. Man's companions
Wolves
Ruocco, J. Man's companions
RURAL LIFE *See* Country life
Russell, Karen
The dredgeman's revelation
20 under 40; stories from the New Yorker;
edited by Deborah Treisman.
The seagull army descends on Strong Beach
Fantastic women; 18 tales of the surreal and
the sublime from Tin House; introduction
by Joy Williams; edited by Rob Spillman.
Vampires in the Lemon Grove
Vampires; the recent undead; edited by Paula
Guran.
Russell Now and Then. Chan, J. P.
RUSSIA
See also Lithuania
Bezmozgis, D. The train of their departure
Dobozy, T. The restoration of the villa where
Tibor Kalman once lived
Gelasimov, A. The evil eye
Gogol, N. The overcoat
Solzhenitsyn, A. Fracture points
Solzhenitsyn, A. Nastenka
Solzhenitsyn, A. The new generation
Solzhenitsyn, A. No matter what
Swanwick, M. Libertarian Russia
Vila-Matas, E. Far from here
Yolen, J. and Stemple, A. The tsar's dragon
19th century
Chekhov, A. P. Kashtanka
Lyeskov, N. The sentry
Pushkin, A. The queen of spades
1917-1945
Grossman, V. S. The elk
Grossman, V. S. In the town of Berdichev
Grossman, V. S. Mama
Grossman, V. S. A small life

RUSSIA—1917-1945—*Continued*
Grossman, V. S. A young woman and an old
woman
1945-
Grossman, V. S. The dog
Grossman, V. S. Living space
Grossman, V. S. The road
Army
Lyeskov, N. The sentry
Communism
See Communism—Russia
Peasant life
See Peasant life—Russia
Prisoners and prisons
See Prisoners and prisons—Russia
Revolution of 1917
See Russia—1917-1945
Rural life
Chekhov, A. P. The Swedish match
Tolstoy, L., graf. God sees the truth, but waits
Leningrad
See Russia—St. Petersburg
Moscow
Laken, V. Family planning
Laken, V. Map of the city
St. Petersburg
Gogol, N. The portrait
Lyeskov, N. The sentry
Meade, L. T. The Blue laboratory
RUSSIAN REVOLUTION, 1917-1921 *See* Rus-
sia—1917-1945
RUSSIAN SOLDIERS *See* Soldiers—Russia
RUSSIANS
United States
Alenyikov, M. Barrel of laughs
Alenyikov, M. It takes all kinds
Alenyikov, M. Ivan and Misha
Alenyikov, M. Whirling dervish
Alenyikov, M. Who did what to whom?
Allio, K. Clothed, female figure
Boland, J. C. Marley's ghost
Doctorow, E. L. Assimilation
Vapnyar, L. Things that are not yours
Wallace, J. Custom sets
Warsh, L. Harry Cray
Warsh, L. The Russians
The **Russians**. Warsh, L.
Russo, Patricia
Swoop
Swenson, P. The Best of Talebones; edited by
Patrick Swenson.
Ruta, Domenica
For Fact
Indiana Review v32 no2 p47-56,154 Wint
2010
Ruth. Vonnegut, K.
Rutherford, Ethan
John, for Christmas
Ploughshares v36 no2/3 p101-25 Fall 2010
Ruyslinck, Ward
The slugs
The Dedalus book of Flemish fantasy; edited
by Eric Dickens and translated by Paul
Vincent.

Ryan, Sara
Fair trade
Welcome to Bordertown; new stories and po-
ems of the Borderlands; edited by Holly
Black and Ellen Kushner; introduction by
Terri Windling.
Ryman, Geoff
Birth days
Ryman, G. Paradise tales
Blocked
Ryman, G. Paradise tales
Days of wonder
Ryman, G. Paradise tales
Dead space for the unexpected
Brave new worlds; edited by John Joseph Ad-
ams.
Everywhere
Ryman, G. Paradise tales
The film-makers of Mars
Ryman, G. Paradise tales
The future of science fiction
Ryman, G. Paradise tales
O Happy day !
Brave new worlds; edited by John Joseph Ad-
ams.
Home
Ryman, G. Paradise tales
K is for Kosovo (or, Massimo's career)
Ryman, G. Paradise tales
The last ten years in the life of hero Kai
Ryman, G. Paradise tales
No bad thing
Ryman, G. Paradise tales
Omnisexual
Ryman, G. Paradise tales
Pol Pot's beautiful daughter
Ryman, G. Paradise tales
Talk is cheap
Ryman, G. Paradise tales
VAO
Ryman, G. Paradise tales
Warmth
Ryman, G. Paradise tales
You
Ryman, G. Paradise tales
Ryu, Sukhee
Buddha Jumps over the Wall
Gettysburg Review v24 no2 p299-312 Summ
2011

S

S.P.Y.. Marär, M.
Saadawi, Ahmad
From the novel Frankenstein in Baghdad
Beirut 39; new writing from the Arab world;
edited by Samuel Shimon; with a preface
by Hanan al-Shaykh
Saare, Jaime
I heart brains
Hungry for your love; an anthology of
zombie romance; edited by Lori Perkins.
Sabar, Ariel
Collision
Sabar, A. Heart of the city; nine stories of
love and serendipity on the streets of New
York

SATIRE—*Continued*
  Emshwiller, C. The institute
  Farmer, P. J. The Sumerian oath
  Farmer, P. J. Voice of the sonar in my vermi-
    form appendix
  Ford, J. On the road to New Egypt
  Ford, J. The summer palace
  Fowler, C. Oblivion by Calvin Klein
  Hodge, B. The passion of the beast
  Hodge, B. Re: your application of 5/5
  Horrocks, C. The sleep
  McElroy, J. The campaign trail
  Morrow, J. Auspicious eggs
  Niedzviecki, H. The colorist
  Orozco, D. Officers weep
  Ostaijen, P. v. The lost house key: the reason
    why, or I told you so
  Powers, R. To the measures fall
  Sands, B. Gen Papa-Georgio
  Sands, B. How to write a short story!
  Sands, B. Jared Bruckheiny
  Schmitt, E.-E. Trashy reading
  Self, W. Caring, sharing
  Self, W. Chest
  Self, W. The North London book of the dead
  Self, W. The quantity theory of insanity
  Self, W. Understanding the Ur-Bororo
  Self, W. Ward 9
  Snoek, P. Apostle of artillery
  Sterling, B. The exterminator's want ad
  Tolstoy, L., graf. Too dear
  Turtledove, H. Bedfellows
  Turtledove, H. News from the front
  Wells, H. G. The loyalty of Esau Common a
    fragment
Saturday teatime. Kennedy, A. L.
Sauce for the gander. Keene, D.
Sauerkraut soup. Dybek, S.
Saunders, George
  Commcomm
    Best of times, worst of times; contemporary
      American short stories from the new Gilded
      Age; edited by Wendy Martin and Cecelia
      Tichi.
  Escape from Spiderhead
    The Best American short stories, 2011; select-
      ed from U.S. and Canadian magazines by
      Geraldine Brooks with Heidi Pitlor; with an
      introduction by Geraldine Brooks.
    The New Yorker v86 no41 p110-19 D 20-27
      2010
  Home [Part of the Summer Fiction Issue]
    The New Yorker v87 no17 p64, 67-70, 72,
      74-5 Je 13-20 2011
  MY CHIVALRIC FIASCO
    Harper's v323 no1936 p69-72 S 2011
Saunders, Nancy
  Tears fall on Orkney
    Dancing with Mr. Darcy; stories inspired by
      Jane Austen and Chawton House Library;
      compiled by Sarah Waters.
Saus, Steven
  Kicking the habit
    Hungry for your love; an anthology of
      zombie romance; edited by Lori Perkins.
Sausage. Levine, S.
Savage city, cruel city. Lundberg, K.
Save me from the pious and the vengeful. Tillman,
    L.

Save my soul. Novack, S.
Save your kisses for me. Blatnik, A.
Saving Agu's Wife. Enigwe, C.
Saving Fats. Shepard, S.
Saw Kler and Naw Kler: A Fairy Tale. Yost, D.
Sawed-in-half girl. O'Connor, S.
Sawhney, Hirsh
  Gautam under a tree
    Delhi noir; edited by Hirsh Sawhney
SAXOPHONISTS
  Hannah, B. Testimony of pilot
Say that. Blatnik, A.
Sayrafiezadeh, Saïd
  Paranoia
    The New Yorker v87 no2 p60-7 F 28 2011
The **scabby** woman's son. Khalaylah, A.
Scale. Self, W.
Scales. Erdrich, L.
Scales. Hunter, L.
Scandale d'estime. Hannah, B.
Scandalous Roy Critchfield. Willis, M. S.
Scanlan, Kathryn
  The old mill
    Iowa Review v40 no3 p39-41 Wint 2010/2011
Scar Tissue. Heynen, J.
The **Scarf** Dancers. Hamilton, J.
Scarlatina!. McCormack, D.
The **scarlet** band. Turtledove, H.
Scarred. Jones, S.
SCARS
  Fallaras, C. The story of a scar
  Novack, S. A good woman's love
Scavengers. Laken, V.
SCENT ADDICT. Jacobsen, R.
A **scent** of death. Lima, M.
Schabas, Martha
  Natural selection
    Can'tLit; fearless fiction from Broken pencil
      magazine; edited by Richard Rosenbaum.
Schaefer, C. A.
  Trespass
    Western Humanities Review v65 no1 p99-104
      Wint 2011
Schappell, Elissa
  Are you comfortable?
    Schappell, E. Blueprints for building better
      girls; fiction
  Aren't you dead yet?
    Schappell, E. Blueprints for building better
      girls; fiction
  A dog story
    Schappell, E. Blueprints for building better
      girls; fiction
  Elephant
    Schappell, E. Blueprints for building better
      girls; fiction
  I'm only going to tell you this once
    Schappell, E. Blueprints for building better
      girls; fiction
  The joy of cooking
    Schappell, E. Blueprints for building better
      girls; fiction
  Monsters of the deep
    Schappell, E. Blueprints for building better
      girls; fiction
    Bomb no116 p XIV-XXI Summ 2011
  Out of the blue and into the black
    Schappell, E. Blueprints for building better
      girls; fiction

Schemes and variations. Baxt, G.
Scherrer, Robert
  Inculturation
    Nature v469 no7331 p574 Ja 27 2011
Schirach, Ferdinand von
  Bliss
    Schirach, F. v. Crime; stories; translated by
      Carol Brown Janeway
  The cello
    Schirach, F. v. Crime; stories; translated by
      Carol Brown Janeway
  The Ethiopian
    Schirach, F. v. Crime; stories; translated by
      Carol Brown Janeway
  Fähner
    Schirach, F. v. Crime; stories; translated by
      Carol Brown Janeway
  Green
    Schirach, F. v. Crime; stories; translated by
      Carol Brown Janeway
  The hedgehog
    Schirach, F. v. Crime; stories; translated by
      Carol Brown Janeway
  Love
    Schirach, F. v. Crime; stories; translated by
      Carol Brown Janeway
  Self-defense
    Schirach, F. v. Crime; stories; translated by
      Carol Brown Janeway
  Summertime
    Schirach, F. v. Crime; stories; translated by
      Carol Brown Janeway
  Tanata's tea bowl
    Schirach, F. v. Crime; stories; translated by
      Carol Brown Janeway
  The thorn
    Schirach, F. v. Crime; stories; translated by
      Carol Brown Janeway
Schirmer, Robert
  The Woman Across the Table
    Confrontation no108 p147-64 Fall 2010
Schizoid creator. Smith, C. A.
SCHIZOPHRENIA
      See also Personality disorders
  Gilley, T. House of prayer
  Novack, S. Memphis
  Schirach, F. v. Green
Schmidt, Matthew
  The taker
    Arizona Attorney v47 no9 p30-3 My 2011
Schmitt, Eric-Emmanuel
  The dreamer from Ostend
    Schmitt, E.-E. The woman with the bouquet;
      translated from the French by Alison An-
      derson
  Getting better
    Schmitt, E.-E. The woman with the bouquet;
      translated from the French by Alison An-
      derson
  Perfect crime
    Schmitt, E.-E. The woman with the bouquet;
      translated from the French by Alison An-
      derson
  Trashy reading
    Schmitt, E.-E. The woman with the bouquet;
      translated from the French by Alison An-
      derson

The woman with the bouquet
    Schmitt, E.-E. The woman with the bouquet;
      translated from the French by Alison An-
      derson
Schnee, Samantha
  (tr.) See Hernández, Sònia
Schneier, Joel
  Dandruff
    Can'tLit; fearless fiction from Broken pencil
      magazine; edited by Richard Rosenbaum.
Schoe, David J.
  Obsequy
    Zombies: the recent dead; edited by Paula
      Guran.
Schoen, Lawrence M.
  The wrestler and the spear fisher
    The stories (in) between; edited by Greg
      Schauer, Jeanne B. Benzel, and W. H.
      Horner.
SCHOLARS
  Adichie, C. N. The headstrong historian
  Goldstein, R. The afterlife of skeptics
  Harvey, R. An acolyte of black spires
  Mu Xin. Halo
  Nabokov, V. V. Revenge
  Sneed, C. Interview with the second wife
Scholes, Ken
  Edward Bear and the very long walk
    Swenson, P. The Best of Talebones; edited by
      Patrick Swenson.
  (jt. auth) See Lake, Jay and Scholes, Ken
SCHOOL LIFE
  Binshatwan, N. The pools and the piano
  Evans, D. Robert E. Lee dead
  Frumkin, R. Monster
  Healey, E. Last winter here
  Houser, N. First kisses from beyond the grave
  Le Clézio, J.-M. G. Lullaby
  Sebold, G. Inspection day
  Trevor, W. Traditions
  Winslow, D. Poe, Jo, and I
              England
  Hazell, J. The school trip
              Germany
  Kronauer, B. Mrs. Mühlenbeck in her house
    [excerpt]
              Ireland
  O'Brien, E. Sister Imelda
              Japan
  Kim, S.-r. Into the light
         Trinidad and Tobago
  Naipaul, V. S. The raffle
            United States
  Baxter, C. Gryphon
  Boggs, B. Dear season
  Dozois, G. R. Chains of the sea
  Eisenberg, D. The girl who left her sock on the
    floor
  Gautier, A. Dance for me
  Grover, L. L. The dance boots
  Grover, L. L. Maggie and Louis, 1914
  Kyle, A. Allegiance
  Kyle, A. Brides
**SCHOOL SUPERINTENDENTS AND PRINCI-
    PALS**
  Boggs, B. Opportunity
  Kitterman, B. In dog years
SCHOOL TEACHERS *See* Teachers
The **school** trip. Hazell, J.

SCHOOLS *See* School life
Schottenfeld, Stephen
  Summer Avenue
    Gettysburg Review v23 no4 p521-74 Wint
      2010
Schrauwen, Olivier
  Best American hair analysis narrative
    The best American nonrequired reading 2009;
      edited by Dave Eggers; introduction by
      Marjane Satrapi; managing editor, Jesse
      Nathan
Schultz, Katey
  Grimshaw on the Ice
    River Styx no83 p82-3 2010
  My Father Calls Me Pequeña
    Calyx v26 no2 p10-15 Wint 2011
Schulze, Ingo
  Oranges and angel
    Best European fiction 2011; edited by Alek-
      sandr Hemon; preface by Colum McCann
Schutz, Benjamin M.
  Mary, Mary, shut the door
    The Shamus winners: America's best private
      eye stories, volume I: 1982-1995; collected
      and introduced by Robert J. Randisi; found-
      er, Private Eye Writers of America
Schutz, Greg
  Joyriders
    Ploughshares v36 no2/3 p126-41 Fall 2010
Schwartz, David J.
  Mike's place
    Sympathy for the devil; edited by Tim Pratt.
Schwarzschild, Edward
  Midhusband
    Promised lands; new Jewish American fiction
      on longing and belonging; edited by Derek
      Rubin.
    Commentary v130 no3 p59-66 O 2010
Schweblin, Samanta
  The Digger
    The Virginia Quarterly Review v86 no4 p90-3
      Fall 2010
  Olingiris
    Granta no113 p273-85 Wint 2010
Schweitzer, Darrell
  The dead kid
    Z: zombie stories; edited by J. M. Lassen
Scibona, Salvatore
  The kid
    20 under 40; stories from the New Yorker;
      edited by Deborah Treisman.
SCIENCE FICTION
    See also End of the world; Extrasensory
      perception; Fantasies; Future; Interplanetary
      visitors; Interplanetary voyages; Interplane-
      tary wars; Life on other planets; Robots;
      Space colonies; Space flight; Space ships;
      Time travel
  Ackley-McPhail, D. The devil you don't
  Allan, N. Flying in the face of god
  Anderson, P. Admiralty
  Anderson, P. Eutopia
  Anderson, P. Flight to forever
  Anderson, P. Home
  Anderson, P. Horse trader
  Anderson, P. Marius
  Anderson, P. The problem of pain
  Anderson, P. Sister planet
  Anderson, P. The star beast

  Baker, K. The books
  Baker, K. The women of Nell Gwynne's
  Baker, S. W. Poison, inside the walls
  Baxter, S. The unblinking eye
  Bear, E. And the deep blue sea
  Bear, G. Destroyers
  Benford, G. To the storming gulf
  Bergsoe, V. Flying fish "prometheus" (a fantasy
    of the future)
  Bishop, M. Vinegar Peace (or, The Wrong-Way,
    Used-Adult Orphanage)
  Black, A. Lisa with child
  Bova, B. A long way back
  Bowes, R. I needs must part, the policeman said
  Bradbury, R. Chrysalis
  Bradbury, R. Don't get technatal
  Bradbury, R. Fahrenheit 451 [excerpt]
  Bradbury, R. The monster maker
  Bradbury, R. Promotion to satellite
  Bradbury, R. The secret
  Bradbury, R. and Hasse, H. Final victim
  Bradbury, R. and Hasse, H. Gabriel's horn
  Bradley, M. Z. The secret of the Blue Star
  Brin, D. Just a hint
  Broderick, D. Under the moons of Venus
  Burnstein, M. A. I remember the future
  Cadigan, P. The taste of night
  Card, O. S. Geriatric ward
  Castro, A.-T. Of a sweet slow dance in the
    wake of temporary dogs
  Connelly, T. Silverfin harbour
  Cooper, B. My father's singularity
  Cooper, S. Confliction
  Crosshill, T. Seeing double
  Cummings, R. The girl in the golden atom
  D'Amico, D. A. Vector Victoria
  Davis, C. It walks in beauty
  Davis, C. The Statistomat pitch
  DeNiro, A. Comachrome
  Dick, P. K. Beyond lies the wub
  Dick, P. K. The Great C.
  Dick, P. K. The gun
  Dick, P. K. The indefatigable frog
  Dick, P. K. The infinites
  Dick, P. K. Menace react
  Dick, P. K. The monority report
  Dick, P. K. Paycheck
  Dick, P. K. Piper in the woods
  Dick, P. K. The preserving machine
  Dick, P. K. The short happy life of the brown
    oxford
  Dick, P. K. The variable man
  Dietrich, B. D. Gray matters
  Doctorow, C. Chicken little
  Doctorow, C. Makers [excerpt]
  Dowling, T. He tried to catch the light
  Dowling, T. The lagan fishers
  Dozois, G. R. Chains of the sea
  Dozois, G. R. Recidivist
  Dozois, G. R. Solace
  Edge, T. D. Repairs
  Emshwiller, C. Abominable
  Emshwiller, C. Acceptance speech
  Emshwiller, C. Bingo and Bongo
  Emshwiller, C. Built for pleasure
  Emshwiller, C. The coming
  Emshwiller, C. Creature
  Emshwiller, C. Foster mother
  Emshwiller, C. Grandma

SCIENCE FICTION—*Continued*

Emshwiller, C. Hunting machine
Emshwiller, C. Idol's eye
Emshwiller, C. If the word was to the wise
Emshwiller, C. Love me again
Emshwiller, C. Methapyrilene hydrochloride sometimes helps
Emshwiller, C. Moon songs
Emshwiller, C. Pelt
Emshwiller, C. The piece thing
Emshwiller, C. A possible episode in the picaresque adventures of Mr. J. H. B. Monstrosee
Emshwiller, C. Puritan planet
Emshwiller, C. This thing called love
Emshwiller, C. Two-step for six legs
Farmer, P. J. Attitudes
Farmer, P. J. Coda
Farmer, P. J. Crossing the dark river
Farmer, P. J. Skinburn
Farmer, P. J. Toward the beloved city
Farmer, P. J. The two-edged gift
Farmer, P. J. Up the bright river
Farmer, P. J. Voice of the sonar in my vermiform appendix
Foster, E. Sinner, baker, fabulist, priest; red mask, gentleman, beast
Fuller, A. W. A wife manufactured to order
Genge, S. Sins of the father
Gibson, W. Fragments of a hologram rose
Gold, H. L. A matter of form
Goodberg, D. Abandoned
Goodberg, D. Amnesia
Goodberg, D. Disabled
Goodberg, D. One for all
Goodberg, D. Weather channels
Gray, A. The pit
Greenspon, J. Mirrors and infinity
Haldeman, J. Fantasy for six electrodes and one adrenaline drip (a play in the form of a feelie script)
Haldeman, J. Out of phase
Haldeman, J. Sleeping dogs
Harvey, R. An acolyte of black spires
Henderson, C. J. The wonderous boundless thought
Hodge, B. With acknowledgements to Sun Tzu
Hubbard, L. R. The automagic horse
Hubbard, L. R. Final enemy
Hubbard, L. R. Greed
Idol, K. Coyotes
Irvine, A. Peter Shilling
Johnson, K. Names for water
Johnson, K. Spar
Johnson, R. P. L. In apprehension, how like a god
Jones, G. A. Blue clay blues
Jones, G. A. Collision
Jones, G. A. The Eastern succession
Jones, G. A. Identifying the object
Jones, G. A. Total internal reflection
Kehrli, K. R. M. Bonehouse
Kelly, J. P. Feel the zaz
Kelly, J. P. Going deep
Kelly, J. P. Plus or minus
Kessel, J. Iteration
Kiraly, A. Your recent acquisitions in the neonesque (microfables)
Knapp, A. The earth slept: a vision

Kosmatka, T. Divining light
Kozlowski, L. Nuclear wasted love song
Kressel, M. The history within us
Lake, J. Chain of fools
Lake, J. Lehr, Rex
Lake, J. The man with one bright eye
Lake, J. Skinhorse goes to Mars
Lake, J. To raise a mutiny betwixt yourselves
Lake, J. To this their late escape
Landis, G. A. The sultan of the clouds
Lanesskog, G. Sailing the sky sea
Lee, T. The persecution machine
Lee, Y. H. Flower, mercy, needle, chain
Levine, D. D. The true story of Merganther's run
Lindholm, M. Cut
Lindholm, M. Drum machine
London, J. A thousand deaths
Lyman, J. The unreachable voices of ghosts
Mann, B. Unfamiliar territory
Martin, G. R. R. Dark, dark were the tunnels
McDonald, S. Seven sexy cowboy robots
McElroy, J. The last disarmament but one
McIntosh, W. Bridesicle
McPhail, M. Beyond imagine
Meade, L. T. The Blue laboratory
Melko, P. Ten sigmas
Monk, D. Falling with wings
Morris, E. Rejection letter
Morrow, J. Bible stories for adults, no. 31: the covenant
Nesbit, E. The five senses
Niles, C. Sin's last stand
Niven, L. All the myriad ways
Niven, L. Bordered in black
Niven, L. The borderland of Sol
Niven, L. Flatlander
Niven, L. Limits
Niven, L. The missing mass
Niven, L. The return of William Proxmire
Niven, L. Smut talk
Niven, L. The soft weapon
Niven, L. A teardrop falls
Nolan, W. F. The underdweller
Nowlan, P. F. Armageddon-2419 A.D.
Nutting, A. Deliverywoman
Padmanabhan, M. Cull
Payne, M. Bullet
Popkes, S. Jackie's boy
Rajaniemi, H. Elegy for a young elk
Rand, K. Song of mother jungle
Reed, R. Alone
Regier, G. T. Glonze
Reynolds, A. Sleepover
Rickert, M. Evidence of love in a case of abandonment
Rickert, M. Evidence of love in a case of abandonment: one daughter's personal account
Ryman, G. Blocked
Ryman, G. Dead space for the unexpected
Ryman, G. The film-makers of Mars
Ryman, G. The future of science fiction
Ryman, G. Omnisexual
Ryman, G. VAO
Salaets, L. The black side of memory
Sallis, J. Roofs and forgiveness in the early dawn
Sheckley, R. The prize of peril
Shelley, M. W. Frankenstein

Searls, Hank

Drop dead twice

The Black Lizard big book of Black Mask stories; edited and with a foreword by Otto Penzler; introduction by Keith Alan Deutsch.

SEASHORE

Emshwiller, C. Living at the center
Fowler, K. J. Halfway people
Millhauser, S. A protest against the sun
Tuten, F. Self portrait with beach

SEASIDE RESORTS

Fowler, C. Oh I do like to be beside the seaside
Gordimer, N. A find
Kronauer, B. Desire for music and mountains [excerpt]
Marías, J. While the women are sleeping

SEASONS

Sa'id, M. A. The street
A **season's** romance. Hardwick, E.
SEATTLE (WASH.) See Washington (State)—Seattle

Sebold, Gaie

Inspection day

End of an Aeon; edited by Bridgett McKenna & Marti McKenna

A **second** chance. Davis, L.
Second chance. East, E.
The **second** coming. Faherty, T.
Second coming. Gordimer, N.
Second fruits. Tillotson, S.
Second journey of the magus. MacLeod, I.
Second lives. Alarcón, D.
Second question. Beattie, A.
SECOND SIGHT See Clairvoyance; Extrasensory perception
Second story sunlight. Lutz, J.
Second thoughts. Aiken, J.
Second thoughts. Solender, E. A.
Secondhand Wife. Kamoche, K. N.
The **secret**. Bradbury, R.
Secret. Warsh, L.
SECRET AGENTS See Secret service; Spies
The **secret** life of Walter Mitty. Thurber, J.
The **secret** of calling rabbits. Wagner, W. N.
The **secret** of Macarger's Gulch. Bierce, A.
The **secret** of the Blue Star. Bradley, M. Z.
Secret pool. Solomon, A.

SECRET SERVICE

Boland, J. C. Marley's ghost
Sabatini, R. Intelligence
The **Secret** Sits in the Middle. FREEMAN, C.

SECRETARIES

Atta, S. A temporary position
Kitterman, B. In dog years
Sa'id, M. A. The job
Sandlin, L. Phelan's first case
Vonnegut, K. Girl pool
Secrets and surprises. Beattie, A.
The **Secrets** of a Client Are Inviolate. Law, J.
Secrets of the native tongue. Emshwiller, C.
The **secrets** of the universe. Gifford, B.
Section 8. Díaz, J.

SECURITY GUARDS

Blatnik, A. Own stories
Mariotte, J. J. Gold shield blues
Schirach, F. v. The thorn

Sedgwick, Catharine Maria

Cacoethes scribendi

The vintage book of American women writers; edited and with an introduction by Elaine Showalter.

Sedia, Ekaterina

1972: the lichenologist's visit

The Thackery T. Lambshead cabinet of curiosities; edited by Ann & Jeff VanderMeer.

Cherrystone and shards of ice

The Year's best dark fantasy & horror; edited by Paula Guran

SEDUCTION

Blatnik, A. Melting point
McIlveen, J. Succumb
Vaughn, C. Life is the teacher
See **the tree, how big it's grown.** Barry, K.
The **seed** from the sepulcher. Smith, C. A.
Seeing double. Crosshill, T.
Seeing eye. Watson, B.
Seeing nothing. Ayres, D.
Seeing the moon. Rozan, S. J.
Seepage. Macleod, C.

Segal, Lore Groszmann

Making good

The Pen/O.Henry Prize stories, 2010; edited and with an introduction by Laura Furman; with essays on the stories they admire most by jurors Junot Diaz, Paula Fox, Yiyun Li.

SEGREGATION See Race relations

Selasi, Taiye

The sex lives of African girls

Granta no115 p127-62 Spr 2011

Selecky, Sarah

The Cat

The Walrus v8 no6 p52-54 Jl 2011

Selected scenes from the end of the world: three stories from the universe of The rising. Keene, B.

Selected shorts. Goodberg, D.

Self, Will

Birdy num num

Self, W. The undivided self; selected stories; introduction by Rick Moody.

Caring, sharing

Self, W. The undivided self; selected stories; introduction by Rick Moody.

Chest

Self, W. The undivided self; selected stories; introduction by Rick Moody.

Conversation with Ord

Self, W. The undivided self; selected stories; introduction by Rick Moody.

Design faults in the Volvo 760 Turbo: a manual

Self, W. The undivided self; selected stories; introduction by Rick Moody.

The five-swing wlak

Self, W. The undivided self; selected stories; introduction by Rick Moody.

Flytopia

Self, W. The undivided self; selected stories; introduction by Rick Moody.

Grey area

Self, W. The undivided self; selected stories; introduction by Rick Moody.

The minor character

Self, W. The undivided self; selected stories; introduction by Rick Moody.

Seven brains, ten minutes. Atkins, M.
Seven cities of gold. Moles, D.
The **seven** geases. Smith, C. A.
Seven sexy cowboy robots. McDonald, S.
The **seven** stages of camping with the poet. Gabel, A.
Seven years from home. Novik, N.
Seventeen syllables. Yamamoto, H.
The **seventh** heaven. Maḥfūẓ, N.
The **Seventy-Fourth** Virgin. Armstrong, M. C.

SEWERS AND SEWAGE
  Byer, J. Rats, homosex, saunas, and Simon
SEX
  Adnan, Y. Two stories
  Barnes, J. Carcassonne
  Blatnik, A. Discourse
  Blatnik, A. Do it quickly, she said,
  Breen, S. Triplet
  Ceallaigh, P. O. Walking away
  Cheever, J. The world of apples
  Chowdhury, S. Hostel
  Coldwell, E. Everyone I love is dead
  Dixon, S. Sex
  Finlay, C. C. Pervert
  Franco, J. Chinatown in three parts
  Fredsti, D. First date
  Gautier, A. Girl of wisdom
  Gordimer, N. The diamond mine
  Gorman, E. Such a good girl
  Guerrero, L. A memory
  Gwyn, A. Drive
  Hannah, B. Get some young
  Harper, J. Red hair and black leather
  Hodge, B. Where the black stars fall
  Hunter, L. The fence
  Hunter, L. Loofah
  Hunter, L. Sex armageddon
  Hunter, L. This one
  Jones, G. A. Red Sonja and Lessingham in Dreamland
  July, M. Majesty
  Kennedy, A. L. Sympathy
  Kilpatrick, K. Last times at Ridgemont High
  Kyle, A. Brides
  Lake, J. The American dead
  Lake, J. The daughters of desire
  Lewycka, M. Business philosophy
  Lezhava, Z. Sex for fridge
  Mamatas, N. Summon, bind, banish
  Marías, J. One night of love
  Matheson, R. 1984 1/2
  McDonald, S. Seven sexy cowboy robots
  McIlveen, J. Succumb
  Mullins, D. P. Driving lessons
  Munro, A. Some women
  Niedzviecki, H. Real estate
  Niven, L. Man of steel, woman of Kleenex
  Nutting, A. Dancing rat
  Nutting, A. Teenager
  Pearlman, E. Granski
  Plummer, T. M. All the sex is west
  Popov, A. Plumbers
  Prakash, U. The walls of Delhi
  Rilly, E. What Sara tells me
  Ruocco, J. Dog
  Ryman, G. Omnisexual
  Salter, J. Foreign shores
  Schappell, E. Monsters of the deep
  Sernotti, C. Another young lust story

Shapiro, J. Ennui
Shawl, N. To the moment
Sikka, M. The railway aunty
Swirsky, R. Of passage
Swirsky, R. Those who wait through the drowsy dark
Tillman, L. More sex
Waters, D. Mormons in heat
Willis, D. Remember, relive
Sex. Dixon, S.
Sex and/or Mr. Morrison. Emshwiller, C.
Sex armageddon. Hunter, L.
Sex for fridge. Lezhava, Z.
The **sex** lives of African girls. Selasi, T.
SEX PROBLEMS
      See also Hermaphroditism; Incest; Marriage problems; Promiscuity; Sexual perversion; Transsexuals; Transvestism; Voyeurs
SEX ROLE
  Davis, C. It walks in beauty
  Kronauer, B. A successful effort for Miss Block
Sex scenes from a chain bookstore. Kyle, A.
SEXUAL DEVIATION
  Anders, C. Yes man
  Leland, C. T. What do you do with your nights?
SEXUAL HARASSMENT
  Bausch, R. Unjust
  Keene, B. Captive hearts
  Wolff, T. The deposition
SEXUAL INSTINCT
  Chuculate, E. D. Yoyo
  Hunter, L. Peggy's brother
  Hunter, L. Us
  Jordan, N. Night in Tunisia
  Laken, V. Before long
  Mullins, D. P. Arboretum
  Packer, A. Walk for Mankind
  Swirsky, R. Defiled imagination
  Trevor, W. Traditions
SEXUAL PERVERSION
  Read, C. Hungry enough
SEXUALLY TRANSMITTED DISEASES
  Ostaijen, P. v. The lost house key: the reason why, or I told you so
  Silverberg, R. The trouble with Sempoanga
The **shaddowwes** box. Dowling, T.
SHADES AND SHADOWS
  Lansdale, J. R. Torn away
  Loory, B. The shadow
The **shadow.** Loory, B.
The **shadow** of a doubt. Tillman, L.
The **shadow** of the vulture. Howard, R. E.
The **Shaggiest** Dog. Brown, R.
Shahla's Daughter. Walsh, C.
Shakers. Orozco, D.
Shamalung (the diminutions). Moorcock, M.
Shame. Ridgway, K.
Shame. Shepard, S.
Shami, Janset Berkok
  Tangled Dreams
    Confrontation no108 p195-211 Fall 2010
SHANGHAI (CHINA) *See* China—Shanghai
Shanghai Jim. Packard, F. L.
Shannon, Ray *See* Haywood, Gar Anthony
Shannon the Cannon. Fleischmann, R.
Shannon's law. Doctorow, C.
Shapiro, Janice
  1966
    Shapiro, J. Bummer and other stories

Silverberg, Robert—*Continued*

Our Lady of the Sauropods

Silverberg, R. The palace at midnight, 1980-82

The palace at midnight

Silverberg, R. The palace at midnight, 1980-82

The Pope of the chimps

Silverberg, R. The palace at midnight, 1980-82

The regulars

Silverberg, R. The palace at midnight, 1980-82

Smithers and the ghosts of the Thar

Ghosts by gaslight; stories of steampunk and supernatural suspense; [edited by] Jack Dann [and] Nick Gevers

Snake and ocean, ocean and snake

Silverberg, R. The palace at midnight, 1980-82

The sorcerer's apprentice

The way of the wizard; edited by John Joseph Adams.

Thesme and the Ghayrog

Silverberg, R. The palace at midnight, 1980-82

A thousand paces along the Via Dolorosa

Silverberg, R. The palace at midnight, 1980-82

The trouble with Sempoanga

Silverberg, R. The palace at midnight, 1980-82

Waiting for the earthquake

Silverberg, R. The palace at midnight, 1980-82

When we went to see the end of the world

The end of the world; stories of the apocalypse; edited by Martin H. Greenberg.

Silverfin harbour. Connelly, T.

Silverston, Sondra

(tr.) See Oz, Amos

Simić, Mima

My girlfriend

Best European fiction 2011; edited by Aleksandr Hemon; preface by Colum McCann

Šimko, Dušan

Excursion to Dubrovnik [Part of special issue: Slovak Fiction]

The Review of Contemporary Fiction v30 no2 p106-16 Summ 2010

Simmons, Diane

Holy sisters

Simmons, D. Little America

In the garden

Simmons, D. Little America

Letters

Simmons, D. Little America

Little America

Simmons, D. Little America

Roll

Simmons, D. Little America

Suitcase

Simmons, D. Little America

Ticket

Simmons, D. Little America

Yukon River

Simmons, D. Little America

Simms, C. N.

Silent Evolution

Nature v474 no7351 p412 Je 16 2011

Simms, Chris

Tick-tock

Original sins; a Crime Writer's Association anthology; edited by Martin Edwards.

Simms, Laura

Krishna and Radha [With commentary]

Parabola v35 no3 p51-4 Fall 2010

Simms, Paul

For immediate release

I found this funny; my favorite pieces of humor and some that may not be funny at all; edited by Judd Apatow.

Simner, Janni Lee

Crossings

Welcome to Bordertown; new stories and poems of the Borderlands; edited by Holly Black and Ellen Kushner; introduction by Terri Windling.

Simon, Norman

ESPN

The Literary Review (Madison, N.J.) v53 no4 p87-100 Summ 2010

A **simple** case. Osondu, E. C.

A **simple** idea. Tillman, L.

Simpson, Helen

Diary of an interesting year

The Pen/O.Henry Prize stories 2011; chosen and with an introduction by Laura Furman; with essays on the stories thety admire most by jurors A. M. Homes, Manuel Muñoz, Christine Schutt

Night thoughts

Granta no115 p115-25 Spr 2011 [Excerpt from Night Thoughts]

Ms. v21 no3 p50-53 Summ 2011

SIN

Hodge, B. Hate the sinner, love the sin

Sin and eggs. Muwasi, E.

SINBAD THE SAILOR (LEGENDARY CHARACTER)

Millhauser, S. The eighth voyage of Sinbad

SINGERS

Baxter, C. Harmony of the world

Blatnik, A. Save your kisses for me

Doctorow, E. L. Liner notes: the songs of Billy Bathgate

Singing down the sun. Monk, D.

The **singing** fish. El-Mohtar, A.

SINGLE MEN

See also Widowers

Aiken, J. Red-hot favourite

Allen, D. The green suit

Barnes, J. East wind

Barnes, J. Trespass

Barron, L. The siphon

Blatnik, A. Crossing the horizon

Bowen, E. Summer night

Burke, D. Beaverland

Daugherty, T. The inhalatorium

Dixon, S. Ass

Dixon, S. The good fellow

Emshwiller, C. Omens

Faulds, J. Sickness

Gallari, A. No cause for concern

Gordon, S. The worst of us

Gray, A. There will be sense

Sistla, Amber D.
  Unglued
    Nature v470 no7335 p568 F 24 2011
Sittin' Up With Uncle John. Webber, C. R.
Sitting with the dead. Trevor, W.
Six dead cabbies. Tingle, T.
Six feet of the country. Gordimer, N.
Six-finger Jack. Lansdale, J. R.
Six million and one. Gifford, B.
Six tales. Tavares, G. M.
Sizemore, Susan
  Dancing with the star
    Vampires; the recent undead; edited by Paula
    Guran.
Sizemore, Vic
  Hush Little Baby
    Southern Humanities Review v44 no3 p342-55
    Summ 2010
  What Really Happened to PFC Quinos
    StoryQuarterly v44 p176-94 2010
SKATEBOARDING
  Benvie, R. Into collapses
Skaters. Williamson, E. M.
Skein of sunlight. Monk, D.
Skeletons. Beattie, A.
Sketches for a life of Wassilly. Davis, L.
Skillingstead, Jack
  Two
    Swenson, P. The Best of Talebones; edited by
    Patrick Swenson.
SKIN
  Parks, R. Skin deep
Skin deep. Parks, R.
Skin for skin. Papernick, J.
Skinburn. Farmer, P. J.
Skinhorse goes to Mars. Lake, J.
Skinless. Bender, A.
The **skinny** girl. Shepard, L.
Skinny girls' constitution and bylaws. Hall, T. M.
SKIS AND SKIING
  Martel, Y. The moon above his head
The **skull**. Dick, P. K.
The **skull-faced** boy. Kirtley, D. B.
The **skull** of the stuttering gunfighter. Nevins, F.
  M., Jr.
Skurnick, Lizzie
  Spectacle Pond
    Cape Cod noir; edited by David L. Ulin.
The **sky** that wraps the world round, past the blue
  and into the black. Lake, J.
Sky theatre. Willis, D.
SKYDIVING
  Loory, B. The man and the moose
The **slap**. Millhauser, S.
**SLAUGHTERING AND SLAUGHTER-
HOUSES**
  Dozois, G. R. A kingdom by the sea
The **slave**. Doyle, R.
The **slave** brand of Sleman Bin Ali. Buck, J.
SLAVE TRADE
  Lewycka, M. Business philosophy
  Woolrich, C. Black cargo
SLAVERY
    See also African Americans; Slave trade
  MacLeod, I. The hob carpet
  Marār, M. The slaves' revolution
  Monk, D. Menders
  Packer, Z. Dayward
  Robinson, K. S. The lunatics

  Thon, M. R. Punishment
SLAVES *See* Slavery
The **slaves'** revolution. Marār, M.
Slavin, Julia
  Drive-through hosue
    Fantastic women; 18 tales of the surreal and
    the sublime from Tin House; introduction
    by Joy Williams; edited by Rob Spillman.
Slávko [Part of special issue: Slovak Fiction]
    Kompaníková, M.
SLEEP
  Emshwiller, C. The queen of sleep
  Horrocks, C. The sleep
  Marār, M. The sleeping person is dead!
Sleep. Doyle, R.
The **sleep**. Horrocks, C.
Sleeping dogs. Haldeman, J.
The **sleeping** person is dead!. Marār, M.
Sleeping with John Updike. Barnes, J.
Sleepover. Reynolds, A.
Sleepy. Chekhov, A. P.
Sleight of hand. Beagle, P. S.
Sleipner's assignment. Ursin, G.
The **slender** charm of Chinese women. Argemi, R.
Slesinger, Tess
  Missis Flinders
    The vintage book of American women writ-
    ers; edited and with an introduction by
    Elaine Showalter.
Sliabh Ban. Hunt, A.
Slim, Mohamad Atif
  Out of the blue
    Nature v476 no7361 p482 Ag 25 2011
Slimer. Crimmins, M.
Slip, out, back, here. Wieland, L.
A **slip** under the microscope. Wells, H. G.
Slipstream. Estleman, L. D.
Sloan, Brian
  Pollen road of life
    *Tribal College Journal of American Indian
    Higher Education* v23 no1 p62-3 Fall 2011
Slouka, Mark
  1963
    Agni no73 p122-7 2011
  Crossing
    The Pen/O.Henry Prize stories 2011; chosen
    and with an introduction by Laura Furman;
    with essays on the stories thety admire
    most by jurors A. M. Homes, Manuel Mu-
    ñoz, Christine Schutt
  Half-Life
    Bomb no113 p supp12-supp14 Fall 2010
  The hare's mask
    The Best American short stories, 2011; select-
    ed from U.S. and Canadian magazines by
    Geraldine Brooks with Heidi Pitlor; with an
    introduction by Geraldine Brooks.
Slowdown in Paxville. Terry, G. P.
Slowly bubbling in the void. Emshwiller, C.
The **slugs**. Ruyslinck, W.
Small. Shapiro, J.
The **small** assassin. Bradbury, R.
The **small** bridge. Sterling, P.
Small fry. Nair, M.
Small game hunter. Katelnikoff, J.
A **small** life. Grossman, V. S.
Small mouth, thin lips. Ortuño, A.
Small sharks. Ruocco, J.

SMALL TOWN LIFE
Aiken, J. Water of youth
Dowling, T. The fooly
Faulkner, W. A rose for Emily
Heathcock, A. The daughter
Heathcock, A. Fort Apache
Heathcock, A. Furlough
Heathcock, A. Peacekeeper
Heathcock, A. Volt
Horrocks, C. The sleep
Millhauser, S. The next thing
Munro, A. Some women
Sneed, C. For once in your life
Strout, E. Pharmacy
Smart Cows. Halvorsen, C.
The **smell** of death and flowers. Gordimer, N.
The **smell** of fresh linen. Raes, H.
Smith, Ali
After life
Critical Quarterly v52 no2 p84-91 Jl 2010
The go-between
Freedom; stories celebrating the Universal Declaration of Human Rights; Amnesty International.
Smith, C. W.
Caustic
Southwest Review v95 no3 p391-417 2010
Smith, Clark Ashton
The black abbot of puthuum
Smith, C. A. The last hieroglyph; edited by Scott Connors and Ron Hilger; with an introduction by Richard A. Lupoff.
The chain of Aforgomon
Smith, C. A. The last hieroglyph; edited by Scott Connors and Ron Hilger; with an introduction by Richard A. Lupoff.
The coming of the white worm
Smith, C. A. The last hieroglyph; edited by Scott Connors and Ron Hilger; with an introduction by Richard A. Lupoff.
The dark age
Smith, C. A. The last hieroglyph; edited by Scott Connors and Ron Hilger; with an introduction by Richard A. Lupoff.
The dart of Rasasfa
Smith, C. A. The last hieroglyph; edited by Scott Connors and Ron Hilger; with an introduction by Richard A. Lupoff.
The death of Ilalotha
Smith, C. A. The last hieroglyph; edited by Scott Connors and Ron Hilger; with an introduction by Richard A. Lupoff.
The death of Malygris
Smith, C. A. The last hieroglyph; edited by Scott Connors and Ron Hilger; with an introduction by Richard A. Lupoff.
Double cosmos
Smith, C. A. The last hieroglyph; edited by Scott Connors and Ron Hilger; with an introduction by Richard A. Lupoff.
The garden of Adompha
Smith, C. A. The last hieroglyph; edited by Scott Connors and Ron Hilger; with an introduction by Richard A. Lupoff.
The great god Awto
Smith, C. A. The last hieroglyph; edited by Scott Connors and Ron Hilger; with an introduction by Richard A. Lupoff.

The last hieroglyph
Smith, C. A. The last hieroglyph; edited by Scott Connors and Ron Hilger; with an introduction by Richard A. Lupoff.
The master of the crabs
Smith, C. A. The last hieroglyph; edited by Scott Connors and Ron Hilger; with an introduction by Richard A. Lupoff.
Monsters in the night
Smith, C. A. The last hieroglyph; edited by Scott Connors and Ron Hilger; with an introduction by Richard A. Lupoff.
Morthylla
Smith, C. A. The last hieroglyph; edited by Scott Connors and Ron Hilger; with an introduction by Richard A. Lupoff.
Mother of toads
Smith, C. A. The last hieroglyph; edited by Scott Connors and Ron Hilger; with an introduction by Richard A. Lupoff.
Necromancy in Naat
Smith, C. A. The last hieroglyph; edited by Scott Connors and Ron Hilger; with an introduction by Richard A. Lupoff.
Nemesis of the unfinished
Smith, C. A. The last hieroglyph; edited by Scott Connors and Ron Hilger; with an introduction by Richard A. Lupoff.
Phoenix
Smith, C. A. The last hieroglyph; edited by Scott Connors and Ron Hilger; with an introduction by Richard A. Lupoff.
The primal city
Smith, C. A. The last hieroglyph; edited by Scott Connors and Ron Hilger; with an introduction by Richard A. Lupoff.
Schizoid creator
Smith, C. A. The last hieroglyph; edited by Scott Connors and Ron Hilger; with an introduction by Richard A. Lupoff.
The seed from the sepulcher
The Big book of adventure stories; edited and with a introduction by Otto Penzler; foreword by Douglas Preston.
The seven geases
Smith, C. A. The last hieroglyph; edited by Scott Connors and Ron Hilger; with an introduction by Richard A. Lupoff.
Strange shadows
Smith, C. A. The last hieroglyph; edited by Scott Connors and Ron Hilger; with an introduction by Richard A. Lupoff.
Symposium of the Gorgon
Smith, C. A. The last hieroglyph; edited by Scott Connors and Ron Hilger; with an introduction by Richard A. Lupoff.
Th enchantress of Sylaire
Smith, C. A. The last hieroglyph; edited by Scott Connors and Ron Hilger; with an introduction by Richard A. Lupoff.
The theft of the thirty-nine girdles
Smith, C. A. The last hieroglyph; edited by Scott Connors and Ron Hilger; with an introduction by Richard A. Lupoff.
The tomb-spawn
Smith, C. A. The last hieroglyph; edited by Scott Connors and Ron Hilger; with an introduction by Richard A. Lupoff.

Smith, Clark Ashton—_Continued_
The treader of the dust
  Smith, C. A. The last hieroglyph; edited by
    Scott Connors and Ron Hilger; with an in-
    troduction by Richard A. Lupoff.
The witchcraft of Ulua
  Smith, C. A. The last hieroglyph; edited by
    Scott Connors and Ron Hilger; with an in-
    troduction by Richard A. Lupoff.
Xeethra
  Smith, C. A. The last hieroglyph; edited by
    Scott Connors and Ron Hilger; with an in-
    troduction by Richard A. Lupoff.
Smith, Claudia
Catgirl
  Lone Star noir; edited by Bobby Byrd &
    Johnny Byrd.
SMITH, CORDWAINER, 1913-1966
      Parodies, imitations, etc.
Lake, J. The man with one bright eye
Smith, Gregory Blake
Punishment
  Prairie Schooner v85 no1 p106-20 Spr 2011
Smith, Matthew Sanborn
Steve Sepp, tasty! tasty!
  Nature v472 no7342 p254 Ap 14 2011
Smith, Michael Marshall
Later
  Hungry for your love; an anthology of
    zombie romance; edited by Lori Perkins.
The other one
  The monster's corner; stories through inhu-
    man eyes; edited by Christopher Golden
The things he said
  Zombies: the recent dead; edited by Paula
    Guran.
This is now
  Vampires; the recent undead; edited by Paula
    Guran.
What happens when you wake up in the night
  The Year's best dark fantasy & horror; edited
    by Paula Guran
Smith, Peter Andrew
The perils of twilight
  Blood & devotion; tales of epic fantasy; ed-
    ited by W.H. Horner; illustrated by Nicole
    Cardiff
Smith, Rob McClure
A Glasgow Rose
  Gettysburg Review v23 no3 p443-55 Aut
    2010
Smith, Rosamond, 1938-
      See also Oates, Joyce Carol, 1938-
Smithers and the ghosts of the Thar. Silverberg,
  R.
Smoke. Davis, L.
Smoke. Heathcock, A.
Smoke in your eyes. Cave, H. B.
SMOKING
Willis, M. S. On the road with C. T. Savage
Smorgasbord. Wolff, T.
Smother. Oates, J. C.
Smut talk. Niven, L.
Snake. Ruocco, J.
Snake and ocean, ocean and snake. Silverberg, R.
The **Snake-Bit** Irishman [1867] Harris, G. W.
Snake-head. Roscoe, T.
The **snake** in the throat. Loory, B.

The **Snake** Story [With introduction by James
  Trilling] TRILLING, L.
SNAKES
Bierce, A. The man and the snake
Emshwiller, C. After shock
Gray, A. Code of operation: snake farm
Narayan, S. Pishaach
Snakes. Evans, D.
Snakes' shoes. Beattie, A.
Sneaking on. McGrath, C.
Sneed, Christine
Alex Rice Inc.
  Sneed, C. Portraits of a few of the people
    I've made cry; stories
Beach Vacation
  The Southern Review (Baton Rouge, La.) v47
    no3 p391-403 Summ 2011
By the way
  Sneed, C. Portraits of a few of the people
    I've made cry; stories
The First Wife
  New England Review v31 no4 p84-96
    2010/2011
For once in your life
  Sneed, C. Portraits of a few of the people
    I've made cry; stories
Interview with the second wife
  Sneed, C. Portraits of a few of the people
    I've made cry; stories
Litany: Four Men
  The Massachusetts Review v52 no2 p234-248
    Summ 2011
A million dollars
  Sneed, C. Portraits of a few of the people
    I've made cry; stories
Portraits of a few of the people I've made cry
  Sneed, C. Portraits of a few of the people
    I've made cry; stories
The Prettiest Girls
  Ploughshares v36 no4 p136-54 Wint
    2010/2011
Quality of life
  Sneed, C. Portraits of a few of the people
    I've made cry; stories
Roger Weber Would Like To Stay
  The Literary Review (Madison, N.J.) v54 no3
    p42-55 Spr 2011
Twelve + Twelve
  Sneed, C. Portraits of a few of the people
    I've made cry; stories
Walled city
  Sneed, C. Portraits of a few of the people
    I've made cry; stories
You're so different
  Sneed, C. Portraits of a few of the people
    I've made cry; stories
SNOBS AND SNOBBISHNESS
Hardwick, E. The classless society
Wells, H. G. A perfect gentleman on wheels
Snoek, Paul
Apostle of artillery
  The Dedalus book of Flemish fantasy; edited
    by Eric Dickens and translated by Paul
    Vincent.
SNOW
      See also Avalanches
Snow. Baxter, C.
Snow angels. Estleman, L. D.
Snow on snow. Hoffman, N. K.

SNOW STORMS *See* Storms
Snow white, rose red. Millet, L.
Snowball's chance. Stross, C.
Snowmelt. Ashfeldt, L.
Snowmen. Millhauser, S.
SNOWSTORMS *See* Storms
Snyder, Maria V.
Dr. Time
The stories (in) between; edited by Greg Schauer, Jeanne B. Benzel, and W. H. Horner.
Snyder, Midori
The monkey bride
The beastly bride; tales of the animal people; edited by Ellen Datlow & Terri Windling; introduction by Terri Windling; selected decorations by Charles Vess.
So beautiful, so dead. Randisi, R. J.
So deep that the bottom could not be seen. Valentine, G.
So perfect. Jones, S. G.
SOCCER
Downey, G. First to score
SOCIAL CLASSES
See also Class distinction
SOCIAL CONDITIONS *See* Social problems
SOCIAL ISOLATION
Goto, H. The hikikomori
SOCIAL PROBLEMS
See also Child labor; Crime and criminals; Divorce; Drug abuse; Drug addiction; Homeless persons; Juvenile delinquency; Poverty; Prejudices; Prostitution; Race relations; Suicide; Technology and civilization; Unemployed; Violence
Kaftan, V. Civilization
SOCIAL SATIRE *See* Satire
SOCIAL WORKERS
Bender, A. Skinless
Leland, C. T. What it came to
Oates, J. C. Tetanus
Price-Thompson, T. Brotherly love
Tremblay, P. Rhymes with Jew
SOCIALISM
Qiu Xiaolong. Iron rice bowl
Qiu Xiaolong. When I was conceived
SOCIETY STORIES
See also Aristocracy
The sock. Davis, L.
SOCRATES
About
Turtledove, H. The daimon
SOFIA (BULGARIA) *See* Bulgaria—Sofia
Sofia. Mankell, H.
Soft as spider silk. Parks, R.
The soft voice of the serpent. Gordimer, N.
The soft weapon. Niven, L.
Sokoloff, Boris
The crime of Dr. Garine
The greatest Russian stories of crime and suspense; edited by Otto Penzler.
Sola. Adichie, C. N.
Solace. Dozois, G. R.
Solana, Teresa
The offering
Barcelona noir; edited by Adriana V. Lopez & Cartmen Ospina; translated by Achy Obejas.
Sold to Satan. Twain, M.

Soldier of fortune. Johnston, B. A.
SOLDIERS
See also Women soldiers
Aiken, J. Reading in bed
Anderson, P. Among thieves
Argemi, R. The slender charm of Chinese women
Bierce, A. Two military executions
Châteaureynaud, G. O. The only mortal
Dick, P. K. Piper in the woods
Dobozy, T. The restoration of the villa where Tibor Kalman once lived
Dozois, G. R. Recidivist
Gordimer, N. The diamond mine
Gordon, S. The worst of us
Grossman, L. Sir Ranulph Wykeham-Rackham, GBE, a.k.a. Roboticus the All-Knowing
Haldeman, J. Sleeping dogs
Jančar, D. The prophecy
Jones, S. Scarred
Kipling, R. Garm - a hostage
Leland, C. T. Fellatio
Leland, C. T. Traveler
McPhail, M. Beyond imagine
Mitchell, D. Character development
Monk, D. Last tour of duty
Monk, D. When the train calls lonely
Mundy, T. The soul of a regiment
Niven, L. Night on Mispec Moor
Novik, N. Lord Dunsany's teapot
O'Connor, S. White fire
Papernick, J. The Madonna of Temple Beth Elohim
Rodoreda, M. On a dark night
Salaets, L. The black side of memory
Scibona, S. The kid
Todd, C. Yesterday
Verhelst, P. Swarm 10
Wells, H. G. The loyalty of Esau Common a fragment
Williams, T. And ministers of grace
Willis, M. S. Nineteen sixty-nine
Great Britain
Marãr, M. Hard work
Russia
See also Cossacks
Grossman, V. S. In the town of Berdichev
Pushkin, A. The queen of spades
Solzhenitsyn, A. Adlig Schwenkitten
Solzhenitsyn, A. No matter what
Solzhenitsyn, A. Zhelyabuga village
United States
Bierce, A. Killed at Resaca
Bierce, A. A son of the gods
Bierce, A. A tough tussle
Chambers, W. The black bottle
Dozois, G. R. Dinner party
Ely, S. Mississippi rules
Ely, S. Pure water
Evans, D. Someone ought to tell her there's nowhere to go
Fallon, S. Camp Liberty
Fallon, S. Leave
Gifford, B. War and peace
Hannah, B. Bats Out of Hell Division
Hannah, B. Midnight and I'm not famous yet
Heathcock, A. Furlough
Jaber, R. From the novel America
King, D. Green Gables

SOLDIERS—United States—*Continued*
Koryta, M. The cypress house
Langan, J. The wide, carnivorous sky
Rickert, M. War is beautiful
Shepard, J. Happy with crocodiles
Shepard, L. Salvador
Willis, M. S. Evenings with Dotson
Winslow, D. After thirty
A **soldier's** embrace. Gordimer, N.
SOLDIERS OF FORTUNE
Somerville, P. People like me
Solender, Elsa A.
Second thoughts
Dancing with Mr. Darcy; stories inspired by Jane Austen and Chawton House Library; compiled by Sarah Waters.
SOLICITORS *See* Law and lawyers
Solid memories have the life-span of tulips and sunflowers. Hemmingson, M.
SOLITUDE
Chekhov, A. P. The bet
Solitude. Trevor, W.
Solitude. Valente, M.
Solitude City. Yune, R.
A **solo** song: for Doc. McPherson, J. A.
Solomon, Asali
Secret pool
Philadelphia noir; edited by Carlin Romano.
SOLOMON ISLANDS
See also World War, 1939-1945—Solomon Islands
Black, M. A. The golden bug
Solzhenitsyn, Aleksandr
Adlig Schwenkitten
Solzhenitsyn, A. Apricot jam, and other stories; translated by Kenneth Lantz and Stephan Solzhenitsyn
Apricot jam
Solzhenitsyn, A. Apricot jam, and other stories; translated by Kenneth Lantz and Stephan Solzhenitsyn
Ego
Solzhenitsyn, A. Apricot jam, and other stories; translated by Kenneth Lantz and Stephan Solzhenitsyn
Fracture points
Solzhenitsyn, A. Apricot jam, and other stories; translated by Kenneth Lantz and Stephan Solzhenitsyn
Nastenka
Solzhenitsyn, A. Apricot jam, and other stories; translated by Kenneth Lantz and Stephan Solzhenitsyn
The new generation
Solzhenitsyn, A. Apricot jam, and other stories; translated by Kenneth Lantz and Stephan Solzhenitsyn
No matter what
Solzhenitsyn, A. Apricot jam, and other stories; translated by Kenneth Lantz and Stephan Solzhenitsyn
Times of crisis
Solzhenitsyn, A. Apricot jam, and other stories; translated by Kenneth Lantz and Stephan Solzhenitsyn
Zhelyabuga village
Solzhenitsyn, A. Apricot jam, and other stories; translated by Kenneth Lantz and Stephan Solzhenitsyn

Some churches. Wieland, L.
Some dead guys. Hazzan, D.
Some kind of betrayal. Firth, M.
Some Monday for sure. Gordimer, N.
Some new blood. Vaughn, V.
Some of this is true. Platana, J.
Some other, better Otto. Eisenberg, D.
Some other kind of happiness. Gautier, A.
Some other time. Vukcevich, R.
Some roses for the bonestell man. Dowling, T.
Some women. Munro, A.
Somebody for Everybody. FLANN, K.
Someday is today. Black, A.
Someday you'll find me: A plan B essay. Perlman, E.
Someone is stealing the great throne rooms of the galaxy. Turtledove, H.
Someone like me. Kitterman, B.
Someone ought to tell her there's nowhere to go. Evans, D.
Someone to talk to. Eisenberg, D.
Somers, Jane *See* Lessing, Doris May, 1919-
SOMERSET (ENGLAND) *See* England—Somerset
Somerville, Kristine
Inside Joan Crawford's Closet
The North American Review v295 no3 p24 Summ 2010
Somerville, Patrick
The abacus
Somerville, P. The universe in miniature in miniature
Confused aliens
Somerville, P. The universe in miniature in miniature
The cop
Somerville, P. The universe in miniature in miniature
Easy love
Somerville, P. The universe in miniature in miniature
Hair university
Somerville, P. The universe in miniature in miniature
The machine of understanding other people
Somerville, P. The universe in miniature in miniature
The mother
Somerville, P. The universe in miniature in miniature
No sun
Somerville, P. The universe in miniature in miniature
Pangea
Somerville, P. The universe in miniature in miniature
The peach
Somerville, P. The universe in miniature in miniature
People like me
Somerville, P. The universe in miniature in miniature
The son
Somerville, P. The universe in miniature in miniature
The universe in miniature in miniature
Somerville, P. The universe in miniature in miniature

Somerville, Patrick—*Continued*
    Vaara in the woods
        Somerville, P. The universe in miniature in
            miniature
    The wildlife biologist
        Somerville, P. The universe in miniature in
            miniature
Something about a finger. Riippi, J.
Something about a joke. Riippi, J.
Something about a nail. Riippi, J.
Something about a painter. Riippi, J.
Something about a promise. Riippi, J.
Something about a Valentine's Day. Riippi, J.
Something about Ben Jensen. Riippi, J.
Something about birthdays. Riippi, J.
Something about Borges and the blind Chelsea.
    Riippi, J.
Something about drinking in Baton Rouge. Riippi,
    J.
Something about ipek (on a Valentine's Day).
    Riippi, J.
Something about L—. Riippi, J.
Something about last time at the Cedar Tavern.
    Riippi, J.
Something about marriage, part I. Riippi, J.
Something about marriage, pt 2. Riippi, J.
Something about marriage, pt 3. Riippi, J.
Something about Maxine. Riippi, J.
Something about Moby Dick. Riippi, J.
Something about my blood and yours. Riippi, J.
Something about my book. Riippi, J.
Something about New York City. Riippi, J.
Something about perfecting a love. Riippi, J.
Something about remembering a couch or a per-
    son. Riippi, J.
Something about rings. Riippi, J.
Something about someone else's poem. Riippi, J.
Something about swimming with sea turtles.
    Riippi, J.
Something about the orange suitcase. Riippi, J.
Something about the rest. Riippi, J.
Something about the unpublished and unfinished
    novels. Riippi, J.
Something about the Zombies. Riippi, J.
Something about Vegas: a note on the second edi-
    tion of a first novel. Riippi, J.
Something borrowed. Butcher, J.
Something (entirely true) about your grandfather.
    Riippi, J.
Something foetid. Cannon, P.
Something out there. Gordimer, N.
Something Pretty, Something Beautiful. Barnes, E.
Something Sweet. Haigh, J.
Something that needs nothing. July, M.
Something you can't live without. Null, M. N.
Sometime next sunrise. Niedzviecki, H.
Sometimes a hyena. Estleman, L. D.
Somewhere. Brendel, K.
Somewhere ahead smoked the wreckage of my
    evening. Call, R.
Somewhere Close to the Start of the Game
    (Foosball). Waberi, A. A.
Somewhere Near the Beginning of the Match.
    Waberi, A. A.
Somewhere, over. Gottlieb, D.
SOMOZA, ANASTASIO, 1925-1980
                    About
    Orozco, D. Somoza's dream
Somoza's dream. Orozco, D.

The **son**. Somerville, P.
Son of Azathoth. Cannon, P.
The **Son** of Chung Wo. SUI SIN FAR
Son of so many tears. Davidson, H.
A **son** of the gods. Bierce, A.
Sonde, Susan
    Down Time
        Confrontation no109 p142-53 Spr 2011
Song. Nagai, M.
Song of mother jungle. Rand, K.
The **song** of Roe Náld. Womack, C.
The **Song** of the Railroad Crossing Barrier.
    Dovzhenko, O.
Song of the selkie. Ochsner, G.
SONGS
    Riippi, J. Something about the Zombies
SONGWRITERS *See* Composers
SONS *See* Fathers and sons; Mothers and sons;
    Stepsons
The **sons** of Billy Clay. Jones, S. G.
SONTAG, SUSAN, 1933-2004
                    About
    Gordimer, N. Dreaming of the dead
Soporific. Browne, L.
The **sorcerer** Minus. Ford, J.
The **sorcerer's** apprentice. Silverberg, R.
SORCERY *See* Witchcraft
Sorrentino, Christopher
    Unhappy Families
        The Literary Review (Madison, N.J.) v54 no2
            p105-21 Wint 2011
A **sort** of achievement like nature's. Kronauer, B.
SOUL
        See also Transmigration
    Kehrli, K. R. M. Bonehouse
    McIlveen, J. Succumb
    Morrow, J. The iron shroud
    Powers, T. The Bible repairman
A **soul** in a bottle. Powers, T.
Soul mate. Friedman. C. S.
The **soul** of a regiment. Mundy, T.
The **soul** of a turk. Abdullah, A.
SOUND
    Hautala, R. The hum
    Hodge, B. The firebrand symphony
    Hodge, B. If I should wake before I die
The **sound** and the fungi. Cannon, P.
The **sound** of the shot. Clark, D.
The **soup**. Kurlansky, M.
Sourland. Oates, J. C.
Soursop, orange, and lemongrass. Lahens, Y.
SOUTH (U.S.) *See* Southern States
South. Manning, K.
SOUTH AFRICA
        See also Africa
    Gordimer, N. Through time and distance
    Mphahlele, E. Down the quiet street
    Mphahlele, E. He and the cat
    Mphahlele, E. The suitcase
    Mphahlele, E. Women and their men
    Tidhar, L. The river came; fragmented recall
                    Farm life
        See Farm life—South Africa
                    Native peoples
    Gordimer, N. The bridegroom
    Gordimer, N. Not for publication
    Gordimer, N. Six feet of the country
    Gordimer, N. Which new era would that be?
    Mphahlele, E. In Corner B

Spinrad, Norman
The big flash
The end of the world; stories of the apocalypse; edited by Martin H. Greenberg.
Bug Jack Barron [excerpt]
Future media; [edited by Rick Wilber]
SPINSTERS *See* Single women
The **spirit** bird. Nelson, K.
Spirit gobs. Terry, G. P.
The **spirit** pond. Nguyen, T. N. H.
SPIRITUALISM
Langan, J. The unbearable proximity of Mr. Dunn's balloons
Spit Out What Is in Your Mouth. Abbas, L. H.
Split/brain. Oates, J. C.
Spofford, Harriet Elizabeth Prescott
Circumstance
The vintage book of American women writers; edited and with an introduction by Elaine Showalter.
The moonstone mass
The dreaming sex; early tales of scientific imagination by women; edited by Mike Ashley.
A **spoiled** man. Mueenuddin, D.
Spoils. Atta, S.
The **spontaneous** knotting of an agitated string. Tidhar, L.
The **spook** house. Bierce, A.
SPORTS
    See also Athletes; Coaching (Athletics); Games; Swimming
Sprenger, Stefan
Dust
Best European fiction 2011; edited by Aleksandr Hemon; preface by Colum McCann
SPRING
Mu Xin. Weimar in early spring
Spring spleen. Davis, L.
Spur of the moment. Aiken, J.
The **spy** who never grew up. Brennan, S. R.
Square one. Estleman, L. D.
Squeeze me. Bethman, D.
Squires & Morley. Fraser, B.
SQUIRRELS
Hall, T. M. Visitations
Sredni Vashtar. Saki
St. Brendan's shank. Barnhill, K.
St. Francis kisses his ass goodbye. Farmer, P. J.
St. Germain, Justin
Tortolita
Best of the West 2010; new stories from the wide side of the Missouri; edited by James Thomas and D. Seth Horton; foreword by Kent Meyers.
St. John, Nick
Further notes on my unfortunate condition
The best American nonrequired reading 2009; edited by Dave Eggers; introduction by Marjane Satrapi; managing editor, Jesse Nathan
St. Martin. Davis, L.
ST. PETERSBURG (RUSSIA) *See* Russia—St. Petersburg
Staalesen, Gunnar
Last train from central station
Copenhagen noir; edited by Bo Tao Michaëlis; translated by Mark Kline.
Stabbed by Rob. Nolan, W. F.

Stabenow, Dana
Siren song
The monster's corner; stories through inhuman eyes; edited by Christopher Golden
Stability. Dick, P. K.
Staff recruitment. Bayley, E.
Stafford, Jean
The echo and the nemesis
The vintage book of American women writers; edited and with an introduction by Elaine Showalter.
STAGE LIFE *See* Theater life
Staging a scene. Goodberg, D.
Stains. Blatnik, A.
Staley Fleming's hallucination. Bierce, A.
STALKERS
Campbell, R. Respects
STALKING
Blatnik, A. The man who didn't throw himself under a train speaks
Stand by me. Berry, W.
Stand-in. Boland, J. C.
A **stand** of fables. Lychack, W.
Standing room only. Fowler, K. J.
Stanger, Vaughan
The eye patch protocol
End of an Aeon; edited by Bridgett McKenna & Marti McKenna
Stanley, Garner Erle
The shrieking skeleton
The Black Lizard big book of Black Mask stories; edited and with a foreword by Otto Penzler; introduction by Keith Alan Deutsch.
Stansel, Ian
Dukes and Duchesses of Park Ridge
Ploughshares v36 no2/3 p142-59 Fall 2010
Stanton, Maura
Queen of hell
River Styx no85 p39-50 2011
Stanzas for an observation. Kronauer, B.
The **star**. Wells, H. G.
The **star** beast. Anderson, P.
STAR WARS FILMS
Bernheimer, K. A Star Wars tale
A **Star** Wars tale. Bernheimer, K.
STARK, FREYA, 1893-1993
    About
Shepard, J. The track of the Assassins
Stark, Richard
For works written by this author under other names see Westlake, Donald E.
Starkey, Laura
Eating potato salad on the lawn of the damned
Iowa Review v41 no1 p122-31 Spr 2011
STARLIGHT. Beattie, A.
STARS
Wells, H. G. The star
Stars and stripes. Roncagliolo, S.
Stars in my mother's eyes, stripes on my back. Osondu, E. C.
The **starship** mechanic. Lake, J. and Scholes, K.
The **start** of the end of it all. Emshwiller, C.
Starting again. Dixon, S.
STARVATION
Solzhenitsyn, A. Apricot jam
STARVE A RAT. Torres, J.
The **starving** dogs of Little Croatia. Gifford, B.

Stashower, Daniel
  Challenger
    On a raven's wing; new tales in honor of Edgar Allan Poe; edited by Stuart M. Kaminsky
The **State** Bird of Minnesota. McLeod, C.
The **state** of Israel. Neugeboren, J.
The **Statistomat** pitch. Davis, C.
The **statue**. Sa'īd, M. A.
STATUE OF LIBERTY (NEW YORK, N.Y.)
  Sabar, A. Freestanding
STATUES
  Beagle, P. S. Underbridge
  Emshwiller, C. White dove
  Johnson, A. D. A prince of thirteen days
  Nutting, A. Gardener
  Sa'īd, M. A. The statue
  Terry, G. P. The MacGuffin
  Trevor, W. Sacred statues
STATUETTES *See* Statues
Staun, Susanne
  All I want is my baby, woah woah, woah woah woah woah
    Copenhagen noir; edited by Bo Tao Michaëlis; translated by Mark Kline.
Stay special. Lanigan, S.
The **staying** freight. Heathcock, A.
Steal small. Horrocks, C.
STEAM
  Nevins, J. Lost pages from the Encyclopedia of Fantastic Victoriana
The **steam** dancer. Kiernan, C. R.
STEAMBOATS
  King, G. E. The little convent girl
STEEL INDUSTRY
  Wells, H. G. The cone
Steele, Allen M.
  The emperor of Mars
    The Year's best science fiction: twenty-eighth annual collection; edited by Gardner Dozois.
STEEPLECHASING *See* Horse racing
Stefan, Verena
  Doe a deer
    Best European fiction 2011; edited by Aleksandr Hemon; preface by Colum McCann
Stein, Gertrude
  Miss Furr and Miss Skeene
    The vintage book of American women writers; edited and with an introduction by Elaine Showalter.
Stein, Jeanne C.
  The ghost of Leadville
    Vampires; the recent undead; edited by Paula Guran.
  Superman
    Chicks kick butt; edited by Rachel Caine and Kerrie L. Hughes.
Steinberg, Susan
  Spectator
    Western Humanities Review v65 no1 p10-13 Wint 2011
Stemple, Adam
  (jt. auth) See Yolen, Jane and Stemple, Adam
Stemple, Jane H. Yolen *See* Yolen, Jane
STEPBROTHERS
  Levine, S. The fields
STEPCHILDREN
  See also Stepsons

STEPFATHERS
  Beattie, A. The women of this world
  Gifford, B. Bad night at the Del Prado
  Hemmingson, M. Daddy
  St. Germain, J. Tortolita
Stephenson, Carl
  Leiningen versus the ants
    21 essential American short stories; edited by Leslie M. Pockell
    The Big book of adventure stories; edited and with a introduction by Otto Penzler; foreword by Douglas Preston.
STEPMOTHERS
  Ma, V. K. A child, a man
Stepping westward: a topographical tale. Drabble, M.
STEPSONS
  Cortez, S. Montgomery Cleft
Sterling, Bruce
  The exterminator's want ad
    The Best science fiction and fantasy of the year: volume five; edited by Jonathan Strahan.
Sterling, Phillip
  An account in her name
    Sterling, P. In which brief stories are told
  Coda
    Sterling, P. In which brief stories are told
  Deja vu
    Sterling, P. In which brief stories are told
  Empty nest
    Sterling, P. In which brief stories are told
  First response
    Sterling, P. In which brief stories are told
  The good life
    Sterling, P. In which brief stories are told
  Housekeeping
    Sterling, P. In which brief stories are told
  Impaired
    Sterling, P. In which brief stories are told
  The last swim of the season
    Sterling, P. In which brief stories are told
  One version of the story
    Sterling, P. In which brief stories are told
  The pleasure of your company
    Sterling, P. In which brief stories are told
  A real deal
    Sterling, P. In which brief stories are told
  The small bridge
    Sterling, P. In which brief stories are told
  Within an inch of the burnished knob
    Sterling, P. In which brief stories are told
Sterling, Stewart *See* Winchell, Prentice, 1895-
Stern, Philip Van Doren
  The Greatest Gift
    Good Housekeeping v251 no6 p205-11 D 2010
Stern, Steve
  Avigdor of the Apes
    Promised lands; new Jewish American fiction on longing and belonging; edited by Derek Rubin.
  Heaven Is Full of Windows
    Studies in American Jewish Literature v29 p154-6 2010
  Little Woman
    Salmagundi no170/171 p74-91 Spr/Summ 2011

STEROIDS
Gray, G. Mr. Universe
Steve Sepp, tasty! tasty!. Smith, M. S.
Stevens, Angi Becker
Blood not sap
Butler, B. 30 under 30; an anthology of inno-
vative fiction by younger writers; Blake
Butler & Lily Hoang, eds.
Stevens, Francis
The curious experience of Thomas Dunbar
The dreaming sex; early tales of scientific
imagination by women; edited by Mike
Ashley.
Stevens, R. L. See Hoch, Edward D., 1930-2008
Stevenson, Robert Louis
The bottle imp
Sympathy for the devil; edited by Tim Pratt.
STEVENSON, ROBERT LOUIS, 1850-1894
About
Nolan, W. F. The man who stalked Hyde
Stewart, Michael
Sister
Butler, B. 30 under 30; an anthology of inno-
vative fiction by younger writers; Blake
Butler & Lily Hoang, eds.
Sticko. Ambrosio, G.
Still life. Baker, L.
Still life (a sexagesimal fairy tale). Tregillis, I.
Still life with boobs. Harris, A. L.
Still life with plums. Manilla, M.
The **still** point of the turning world. Highsmith, P.
Stillwater. Shepard, S.
Stinson, H. H.
Three apes from the east
The Black Lizard big book of Black Mask
stories; edited and with a foreword by Otto
Penzler; introduction by Keith Alan
Deutsch.
Stirbt der Mensch als Künstler (Teil 5). Müller,
A. and Dany, H.-C.
Stitchery. Monk, D.
STOCK EXCHANGE
Boland, J. C. Bears watching
Boland, J. C. Easy money
Stockbridge, Grant See Page, Norvell W., 1904-
1961
Stockton, Frank
The lady or the tiger?
21 essential American short stories; edited by
Leslie M. Pockell
STOCKYARDS See Meat industry
STOKER, BRAM, 1847-1912
Parodies, imitations, etc.
Hodge, B. Brushed in blackest silence
Konrath, J. A. The screaming
Stoklosa, Tony
Super intelligence
Nature v467 p878 O 14 2010
The **stolen** bacillus. Wells, H. G.
The **stolen** body. Wells, H. G.
Stolpestad. Lychack, W.
Stoltz, Kristina
The elephant's tusks
Copenhagen noir; edited by Bo Tao
Michaëlis; translated by Mark Kline.
Stone, Eric James
The greatest science-fiction story ever written
Nature v467 p1146 O 28 2010

Stone, Leslie F.
Men with Wings
Femspec v11 no1 p86-155 2011
Stone boat. Kittredge, W.
The **stone** inscription. Dib, M.
STONING
Atta, S. Hailstones on Zamfara
Ibrāhīm, H. The informer
The **store**. Jones, E. P.
The **store** of the worlds. Sheckley, R.
STORES
Horn, D. Shtetl World
Monso, I. The customer is always right
Riippi, J. Something about New York City
Stories. Dixon, S.
STORIES ABOUT DIARIES See Diaries (Stories
about)
STORIES ABOUT LETTERS See Letters (Sto-
ries about)
STORIES IN DIARY FORM See Diaries (Sto-
ries in diary form)
STORIES OF THE FUTURE See Future
Stories Under the Stars. Gildner, G.
The **storm**. Chopin, K.
Storm. Dixon, S.
STORMS
See also Hurricanes; Tornadoes
Ayau, K. J. Sand castle
Barrett, L. One hippopotamus
Loory, B. The girl in the storm
O'Connor, S. He will not see me stopping here
Shepard, S. Indianapolis (Highway 74)
Wells, H. G. The thing in no. 7
Story, Kate
Flame retarded
Can'tLit; fearless fiction from Broken pencil
magazine; edited by Richard Rosenbaum.
Story. Davis, L.
The **story**. Pearlman, E.
The **story** of a conscience. Bierce, A.
The **story** of a family. Hoang, M. T.
The **story** of a scar. Fallaras, C.
The **story** of an hour. Chopin, K.
The **story** of Baelbrow. Prichard, K. O. R. and
Prichard, H. V.
The **story** of my building (after Isaac Babel's
"Story of my dovecote"). Jarrar, R.
Story of my life. Kennedy, A. L.
The **story** of perfume to you in the beginning of
the year at the end of the story . . . . . .
Bakriyya, R.
A **story** of the days to come. Wells, H. G.
The **Story** of the Father. Selver-Kassell, A.
The **story** of the Last Trump. Wells, H. G.
The **story** of the late Mr. Elvesham. Wells, H. G.
The **story** of the stabbing. Oates, J. C.
A **story** of the stone age. Wells, H. G.
The **story** of two dogs. Lessing, D. M.
STORY WITHIN A STORY
Aiken, J. The sale of midsummer
Anderson, P. The problem of pain
Bass, R. The hermit's story
Chekhov, A. P. The head-gardener's story
Crawford, F. M. For the blood is the life
Gordimer, N. Once upon a time
Gribbons, D. A short story
Hughes, S. C. Broken words
Lake, J. The daughters of desire
Landon, P. Thurnley Abbey

STORY WITHIN A STORY—*Continued*
  Lansdale, J. R. Torn away
  Nevins, F. M., Jr. Fair game
  Penkov, M. Devshirmeh
  Rickert, M. Journey into the kingdom
  Santlofer, J. The 74th tale
  Twain, M. The celebrated jumping frog of
    Calaveras County
  Wells, H. G. The apple
The **Storyteller's** Tale. Lee, S.-U.
STORYTELLING
  Arnason, E. Mammoths of the great plains
  Beattie, A. The working girl
  Blatnik, A. Words matter
  Dixon, S. Stories
  Doyle, R. The pram
  McElroy, J. Character
  Millhauser, S. The eighth voyage of Sinbad
  Parks, R. Courting the Lady Scythe
  Ross, A. In the basement
  Yamauchi, W. A Christmas orange story
  Yellin, T. Reuben
Stovall, TaRessa
  Breakin' dishes
    Price-Thompson, T. My blue suede shoes;
    four novellas; [edited by] Tracy Price-
    Thompson and Taressa Stovall.
Stowe, Harriet Beecher
  The village do-nothing from Oldtown folks
  The vintage book of American women writ-
    ers; edited and with an introduction by
    Elaine Showalter.
Stowe, Harriet Elizabeth *See* Stowe, Harriet Bee-
  cher, 1811-1896
The **straggler**. Petry, Y.
Straight, Susan
  Mines
    Best of times, worst of times; contemporary
    American short stories from the new Gilded
    Age; edited by Wendy Martin and Cecelia
    Tichi.
Strand, Jeff
  Specimen 313
    The monster's corner; stories through inhu-
    man eyes; edited by Christopher Golden
The **strange** case of Mr. Salad Monday. Falksen,
  G. D.
The **strange** case of Nicholas Thomas: an excerpt
  from a history of the Longesian Library.
  Tremblay, P.
A **strange** impulse. Davis, L.
A **strange** murderer. Gorky, M.
Strange scenes from an unfinished film.
  McMahon, G.
Strange shadows. Smith, C. A.
The **stranger**. Bierce, A.
The **stranger**. Modesitt, L. E., Jr.
A **stranger** at the bus stop!. Abu Lail, S.
The **strangers**. Davis, L.
Strangers. Emshwiller, C.
The **strangler**. Nikitin, P.
STRANGLING
  Poulson, C. Fishy story
Strategies. Monzó, Q.
Straub, Peter
  Variations on a theme from Seinfeld
    The Year's best dark fantasy & horror; edited
    by Paula Guran
Strays. Lindholm, M.

Strays. Ruocco, J.
STREAM OF CONSCIOUSNESS
  Emshwiller, C. Omens
  Emshwiller, C. The queen of sleep
  Golshiri, H. My China doll
  Gordimer, N. For dear life
The **street**. Sa'id, M. A.
The **street**. Tóibín, C.
Street wizard. Green, S. R.
Streets. He, Q.
Stringing tomorrow. Monk, D.
Strip poker. Oates, J. C.
STRIPTEASERS
  Bernheimer, K. A cageling tale
  Gifford, B. Sad stories of the death of kings
  Hemmingson, M. You will not believe what
    happens to me, but does it matter? it only
    matters that I know what happens
  Latiolais, M. Boys
  Mullins, D. P. Glitter Gulch
  Turner, A. Fool in search of a country song
STROKE *See* Cerebrovascular disease
Strong suits. Vukcevich, R.
Stross, Charles
  The boys
    Before they were giants; edited by James L.
    Sutter; cover illustration by Kieran Yanner.
  Snowball's chance
    Sympathy for the devil; edited by Tim Pratt.
Stroud, Ben
  The Moor
    Boston Review v35 no5 p48-54 S/O 2010
Strout, Elizabeth
  Pharmacy
    Blue collar, white collar, no collar; stories of
    work; edited by Richard Ford.
Stuart, Ian, 1922-1987 *See* MacLean, Alistair,
  1922-1987
Stuart, J. E. B. *See* Stuart, Jeb, 1833-1864
Stuart, James Ewell Brown *See* Stuart, Jeb,
  1833-1864
STUART, JEB, 1833-1864
  About
  Hannah, B. Knowing he was not my kind yet I
    followed
Stuck on you. Archer, J.
The **student** and the teacher. Uruq, S.
STUDENT EXCHANGE PROGRAMS
  Frumkin, R. Monster
  Leebron, F. G. The exchange student
  Wieland, L. Pound in Venice
STUDENTS
    See also College life; College students;
    School life; Youth
  Barthelme, D. Me and Miss Mandible
  Binshatwan, N. The pools and the piano
  Emshwiller, C. The institute
  Glaser, R. B. Infections
  Hatoum, M. Torn
  Kilpatrick, K. Last times at Ridgemont High
  O'Brien, E. Sister Imelda
  Tingle, T. Six dead cabbies
  Tremblay, P. The teacher
  Villegas, H. His ghost
  Williams, T. A short history of Dunkelblau's
    Meistergarten
  Willis, D. Rely
  Wolff, T. Smorgasbord
  Zeltserman, D. When death shines bright

The **study** hall monitor. Muwasi, E.

STUNT MEN
Cornell, J. C. The swing of things

Sturgeon, Theodore
The professor's teddy bear
Sympathy for the devil; edited by Tim Pratt.

Sturtevant, Adam
How Do I Explain?
Boston Review v35 no4 p33-4 Jl/Ag 2010

STUTTERING
Kim, H.-y. Frozen mouth [(1966), chapters one and two]

The **styx**. Châteaureynaud, G. O.

Suárez Cobián, Armando
Born on October Fourth
Bomb no114 p Supp14-Supp20 Wint 2010

Sublett, Jesse
Moral hazard
Lone Star noir; edited by Bobby Byrd & Johnny Byrd.

SUBMARINES
Fowler, K. J. The Marianas Islands

The **substitute**. Boland, J. C.

The **substitute**. Tillman, L.

Subterfuge. Bradbury, R.

SUBURBAN LIFE
See also Commuters
Doctorow, E. L. Edgemont Drive
Doctorow, E. L. Wakefield
Eisenberg, D. Mermaids
Kirshenbaum, B. The lunatic
Millhauser, S. Flying carpets
Millhauser, S. The slap
Orozco, D. Officers weep
Villegas, H. Meadowdene Estates

SUBURBS *See* Suburban life

SUBVERSIVE ACTIVITIES
See also Terrorism

SUBWAYS
McElroy, J. Silk, or the woman with the bike
Sabar, A. Depths

SUCCESS
See also Ambition; Self-made men
Baxter, C. The winner
Goodberg, D. Precautions
Vonnegut, K. $10,000 a year, easy
Wells, H. G. Wayde's essence

A **success** story. Drabble, M.

A **successful** effort for Miss Block. Kronauer, B.

SUCCESSION *See* Inheritance and succession

Successor to the throne. Van den Broeck, W.

Succor. Allen, D.

Succumb. McIlveen, J.

Such a good girl. Gorman, E.

Such a story. Abasiyanik, S. F.

Suchow, Jordan
NPG's policy on authorship
Nature v477 no7363 p244 S 8 2011

The **sudden** demise of Sharkface Bensky. Gifford, B.

SUDDEN INFANT DEATH SYNDROME
Packer, A. Her firstborn

Suddenly. Shepard, S.

Suddenly afraid. Davis, L.

Suddenly speaking. Vukcevich, R.

SUFFERING
See also Good and evil

SUFFOLK (ENGLAND) *See* England—Suffolk

SUGAR
Child, L. Addicted to sweetness

Sugar 'n' spice. Monk, D.

Sui Sin Far
The inferior woman
The vintage book of American women writers; edited and with an introduction by Elaine Showalter.

SUI SIN FAR
The Son of Chung Wo
Legacy v28 no1 p126-135 My 2011

SUICIDE
Abbott, L. K. A great piece of elephant
Allyn, D. Israfel
Bierce, A. One officer, one man
Bill, F. The penance of Scoot McCutchen
Bradbury, R. Luana the living
Cather, W. Paul's case: a study in temperament
Danticat, E. Claire of the sea light
Delbanco, N. The writers' trade
Dixon, S. The killer
Ely, S. The oldest man in Mississippi
Evans, D. Snakes
Gifford, B. Call of the wild
Gordimer, N. Oral history
Grossman, V. S. In Kislavodsk
Hannah, B. Drummer down
Hodge, B. If I should wake before I die
Hoffman, N. K. Snow on snow
Kim, H.-y. Frozen mouth [(1966), chapters one and two]
Knox, J. H. Wake not the dead
Kowal, M. R. Death comes but twice
Laken, V. Scavengers
Latiolais, M. Damned spot
Leland, C. T. The congregation of love
Leland, C. T. Traveler
Marcus, H. Swimming
McGuane, T. Flight
Mihas, P. This is not a barren place
Monk, D. Fishing the edge of the world
Mu Xin. Eighteen passengers on a bus
Niven, L. All the myriad ways
Oates, J. C. Papa at Ketchum, 1961
Pearlman, E. Binocular vision
Rakha, Y. Suicide 20, or the Hakimi Maqama
Roberge, R. Working backward from the worst moment of my life
Rodoreda, M. Before I die
Rodoreda, M. The fate of Lisa Sperling
Schappell, E. Are you comfortable?
Senna, D. There, there
Shapiro, J. The old bean
Solana, T. The offering
Trueblood, V. Phantom father
Trueblood, V. Taken
Vonnegut, K. The epizootic
Willis, M. S. Speak well of the dead
Yezierska, A. Wild winter love
Yiyun Li. Alone

Suicide 20, or the Hakimi Maqama. Rakha, Y.

Suicide patrol. Surdez, G.

The **suicide** room. Ross, A.

The **suitcase**. Gray, A.

The **suitcase**. Mphahlele, E.

Suitcase. Simmons, D.

Suitors. Trueblood, V.

The **suits** at Auderlene. Dowling, T.

Sullins, Jacob
  12 Rounds
    The Georgia Review v65 no2 p432-445
    Summ 2011
Sullivan, Jonathon
  Niels Bohr and the sleeping Dane
    People of the book; a decade of Jewish sci-
    ence fiction & fantasy; edited by Rachel
    Swirsky & Sean Wallace.
Sullivan, Laura L.
  Louring Age
    StoryQuarterly v44 p266-76 2010
The **Sultan**. Gifford, B.
The **sultan** of the clouds. Landis, G. A.
The **sultana's** dream. Hossein, R. S.
The **Sumerian** oath. Farmer, P. J.
SUMMER
  Byer, J. Rats, homosex, saunas, and Simon
  Fowler, K. J. Familiar birds
  Furman, L. The eye
  Shapiro, J. 1966
  Shapiro, J. Small
Summer. Fried, G.
Summer. Rodoreda, M.
Summer afternoon. Neugeboren, J.
Summer Avenue. Schottenfeld, S.
The **summer** before. Black, A.
SUMMER CAMPS
  Franco, J. Camp
  Packer, Z. Brownies
SUMMER HOMES
  Beattie, A. Summer people
Summer night. Bowen, E.
The **summer** palace. Ford, J.
Summer people. Beattie, A.
SUMMER RESORTS
  Bingham, S. Rachel's island
SUMMER VACATIONS *See* Vacations
Summer voices. Banville, J.
Summers, Anna
  (jt. auth) See Petrushevskaya, Ludmilla and
    Summers, Anna
Summertime. Schirach, F. v.
Summon, bind, banish. Mamatas, N.
Sumner, Melanie
  Emergence
    Five Points v12 no2 p61-9 2008
Sumner-Smith, Karina
  When the zombies win
    The Best horror of the year: volume three;
    edited by Ellen Datlow.
SUN
  Niven, L. Inconstant moon
  Smith, C. A. Phoenix
  Somerville, P. No sun
The **sun** never rises in the big city. Shipp, J. C.
Sunday. Estleman, L. D.
Sunday dinners. Blatnik, A.
The **sunflower** state. Baker, M.
Sunshine. Freed, L.
Sunshine 320 Days a Year. Watterson, K.
Suong, Nguyet Minh
  Thirteen harbors
    Family of fallen leaves; stories of Agent Or-
    ange by Vietnamese writers; edited by
    Charles Waugh and Huy Lien.
Super intelligence. Stoklosa, T.
Superboy. Hong, P.

SUPERMAN
  Niven, L. Man of steel, woman of Kleenex
Superman. Stein, J. C.
SUPERNATURAL PHENOMENA
    See also Demoniac possession; Ghost
    stories; Horror stories
  Bierce, A. A baby tramp
  Bierce, A. The damed thing
  Bierce, A. The death of Halpin Frayser
  Bierce, A. The hight-doings at "Deadman's"
  Bierce, A. A holy terror
  Bierce, A. John Bartine's watch
  Bierce, A. A man with two lives
  Bierce, A. The middle toe of the right foot
  Bierce, A. One of twins
  Bierce, A. A psychological shipwreck
  Bierce, A. Staley Fleming's hallucination
  Bierce, A. The thing at Nolan
  Bierce, A. A vine on a house
  Boland, J. C. Evidence seen
  Butcher, J. Heorot
  Cannon, P. Azathoth in analysis
  Cannon, P. Azathoth in Arkham
  Cannon, P. Bride of Azathoth
  Cannon, P. The house of Azathoth
  Cannon, P. The revenge of Azathoth
  Cannon, P. Son of Azathoth
  Chabon, M. The god of dark laughter
  Douglas, C. N. Monster mash
  Dowling, T. The fooly
  Dowling, T. Toother
  Fenn, J. Twilight at the change house
  Freeman, M. E. W. The hall bedroom
  Frost, G. The comeuppance of Creegus Maxin
  Gaiman, N. "The truth is a cave in the Black
    Mountains. . . ."
  Hannah, B. Evening of the Yarp
  Kressel, M. The bricks of Gelecek
  Lake, J. Tall spirits, blocking the night
  Lima, M. A scent of death
  Lindholm, M. The fifth squashed cat
  Passarella, J. Blood alone
  Rickert, M. The Christmas witch
  Roden, B. The brink of eternity
  Ruckley, B. Flint
  Russo, P. Swoop
  Shepard, L. The skinny girl
  Sherman, D. How the pooka came to New York
    City
  Smith, C. A. The chain of Aforgomon
  Smith, C. A. Nemesis of the unfinished
  Smith, M. M. The other one
  Vaughn, C. Long time waiting
  Vaughn, C. The temptation of Robin Green
  Wells, H. G. The inexperienced ghost
  Wells, H. G. The stolen body
Superpowers. Vukcevich, R.
Superscam. Nevins, F. M., Jr.
SUPERSTITION
    See also Occultism; Talismans; Vam-
    pires; Voodooism; Werewolves
  Anderson, P. Eutopia
  Bierce, A. The man and the snake
  Bierce, A. The suitable surroundings [y]
  Naipaul, V. S. My aunt Gold Teeth
The **supremacy** of grief. Hamilton, H.

Surdez, Georges
Suicide patrol
The Big book of adventure stories; edited and with a introduction by Otto Penzler; foreword by Douglas Preston.
SURFERS
Hemmingson, M. It's very cold down here
SURGEONS
See also Physicians; Women physicians
SURGERY
See also Amputation; Plastic surgery; Transplantation of organs, tissues, etc.
Campbell-Such, J. The Napoleon difference
Gold, H. L. A matter of form
Laken, V. God of fire
Neugeboren, J. The state of Israel
Wells, H. G. Under the knife
SURPRISE ENDINGS
Archer, J. Politically correct
Hannah, B. Behold the husband in his perfect agony
Hautala, R. The hum
Surprised by joy. Baxter, C.
SURRATT, MARY E., 1820-1865
About
Fowler, K. J. Standing room only
SURREALISM
Abasıyanik, S. F. Such a story
Ballingrud, N. The way station
Budnitz, J. Aboard
Bulkin, N. Everything dies, baby
Châteaureynaud, G. O. Come out, come out
Châteaureynaud, G. O. Unlivable
Corin, L. The entire predicament
Davies, R. Bruise for bruise
Ehrenreich, B. Everything you see is real
El-Mohtar, A. The singing fish
Gray, A. The cube
Hidāyat, . The blind owl [excerpt]
Hunt, S. Beast
Idris, Y. The aorta
Jones, S. G. Teeth
Link, K. Light
Loory, B. The fish in the teapot
Loory, B. Hadley
Loory, B. The house on the cliff and the sea
Loory, B. The man and the moose
Loory, B. The octopus
Loory, B. Photographs
Loory, B. The rope and the sea
Loory, B. The snake in the throat
Loory, B. The walk that replaced understanding
Marías, J. Gualta
Marías, J. The life and death of Marcelino Iturriaga
Marías, J. Lord Rendall's song
McOmber, A. The automatic garden
McOmber, A. A memory of his rising
McOmber, A. Of wool
Michiels, I. It will end in tears
Millet, L. Snow white, rose red
Nutting, A. Ant colony
Nutting, A. Dinner
Nutting, A. Hot, fast, and sad
Richter, S. The doll awakens
Ross, A. Futures
Sands, B. Abridged version
Sands, B. The anals of piracy
Sands, B. Chase sequence

Sands, B. The walri republic of Sea World
Self, W. Flytopia
Shepard, S. Haskell, Arkansas (Highway 70)
Shipp, J. C. Agape walrus
Shipp, J. C. Ticketyboo
Shipp, J. C. Ula Morales
Slavin, J. Drive-through hosue
Somerville, P. The universe in miniature in miniature
Tuten, F. The bar on Tompkins Square Park
Tuten, F. The park on fire
Tuten, F. Self portrait with cheese
Tuten, F. Self portrait with icebergs
Young, M. The age of the tire boat
Zucker, G. Big people
Surveillance. Tang, J.
SURVIVAL (AFTER AIRPLANE ACCIDENTS, SHIPWRECKS, ETC.)
See also Wilderness survival
Aiken, J. Honeymaroon
Bass, R. The hermit's story
Bedford-Jones, H. Peace waits at Marokee
Benford, G. To the storming gulf
Bierce, A. A psychological shipwreck
Davis, C. Last year's grave undug
Emshwiller, C. Al
Martin, G. R. R. Dark, dark were the tunnels
Nolan, W. F. The underdweller
Ruocco, J. Frog
Survival instincts. Seamans, S.
The **survivor**. Hernández, S.
SURVIVORS, HOLOCAUST See Holocaust survivors
The **survivors**. Lahens, Y.
SUSPENSE STORIES
See also Adventure; Conspiracies; Horror stories; Kidnapping; Murder stories; Mystery and detective stories; Secret service; Spies; Terrorism
Sussman, Susana
Khunta
Femspec v10 no2 p70-4 2010
Swamp beast. Boland, J. C.
SWAMPS
Boland, J. C. Swamp beast
Le Clézio, J.-M. G. Hazaran
Swan, Gladys
The house on the lake
The Sewanee Review v118 no4 p465-79 Fall 2010
Swan Song. Dineen, F.
SWANS
Berman, S. Thimbleriggery and fledgling
Foster, E. Black swan, white swan
Swans. Ruocco, J.
Swanwick, Michael
The feast of Saint Janis
The end of the world; stories of the apocalypse; edited by Martin H. Greenberg.
Ginungagap
Before they were giants; edited by James L. Sutter; cover illustration by Kieran Yanner.
Libertarian Russia
The Year's best science fiction: twenty-eighth annual collection; edited by Gardner Dozois.
(jt. auth) See Dozois, Gardner R. and Swanwick, Michael
Swarm 10. Verhelst, P.

Sweat. Hurston, Z. N.
SWEDEN
    See also Lapland
SWEDES
    See also Vikings
        United States
    Baxter, C. The disappeared
The **Swedish** bakery. Gifford, B.
The **Swedish** match. Chekhov, A. P.
Sween, Gretchen S.
    Grounding the Tutu Girl
       Texas Bar Journal v74 no6 p482-4 Je 2011
Sweet croquette. Barba, D.
Sweet peas. Bingham, S.
The **sweet** shot. Bentley, E. C.
Sweet sorrow. Roden, B.
Sweet street. Châteaureynaud, G. O.
The **sweet** taste of slavery. Meyer, C.
The **sweetness** of her name. McGarry, J.
Swierczynski, Duane
    Lonergan's girl
       Philadelphia noir; edited by Carlin Romano.
Swift, Margaret *See* Drabble, Margaret, 1939-
Swift decline. Frost, G.
Swim. Leland, C. T.
SWIMMING
    Arsenijević, V. One minute: Dumbo's death
    Kitterman, B. The window
    Murphy, Y. The good word
Swimming. Brown, K.
Swimming. Marcus, H.
The **swimming** pool. Loory, B.
SWINDLERS AND SWINDLING
    Gaiman, N. How to sell the Ponti Bridge
    Nevins, F. M., Jr. Bagworms
    Nevins, F. M., Jr. Dogsbody
    Nevins, F. M., Jr. Doomchild
    Nevins, F. M., Jr. Filmflam
    Nevins, F. M., Jr. Superscam
The **swing** of things. Cornell, J. C.
Swirsky, Rachel
    1943: a brief note pertaining to the absence of
      one olivaceous cormorant, stuffed
      The Thackery T. Lambshead cabinet of curi-
        osities; edited by Ann & Jeff VanderMeer.
    Again and again and again
      The Year's best science fiction: twenty-eighth
        annual collection; edited by Gardner
        Dozois.
    The black angel's kiss
      Swirsky, R. Through the drowsy dark; short
        fiction and poetry
    The debt of the innocent
      Swirsky, R. Through the drowsy dark; short
        fiction and poetry
    Defiled imagination
      Swirsky, R. Through the drowsy dark; short
        fiction and poetry
    Detours on the way to nothing
      Swirsky, R. Through the drowsy dark; short
        fiction and poetry
    Heartstrung
      Swirsky, R. Through the drowsy dark; short
        fiction and poetry
    Heat engine
      Swirsky, R. Through the drowsy dark; short
        fiction and poetry

    The lady who plucked red flowers beneath the
      queen's window
      The Best science fiction and fantasy of the
        year: volume five; edited by Jonathan
        Strahan.
    A memory of wind
      The Nebula Awards showcase; edited by Kev-
        in J. Anderson.
    Mirror images
      Swirsky, R. Through the drowsy dark; short
        fiction and poetry
    No longer you
      Swirsky, R. Through the drowsy dark; short
        fiction and poetry
    Of passage
      Swirsky, R. Through the drowsy dark; short
        fiction and poetry
    The taste of promises
      Life on Mars: tales from the new frontier; an
        original science fiction anthology; edited by
        Jonathan Strahan
    Those who wait through the drowsy dark
      Swirsky, R. Through the drowsy dark; short
        fiction and poetry
Swiss engineering. Roberge, R.
SWITZERLAND
    Shepard, J. Your fate hurtles down at you
        Geneva
    Rodoreda, M. Paralysis
        Zurich
    Schmitt, E.-E. The woman with the bouquet
Swoop. Russo, P.
Sword woman. Howard, R. E.
SWORDS
    Lee, Y. H. Counting the shapes
    Monk, D. Oldblade
Sylvain, Patrick
    Odette
      Haiti noir; edited by Edwidge Danticat
SYMBOLISM
    See also Allegories; Parables
    Gordimer, N. A lion on the freeway
SYMPATHY
    See also Empathy
Sympathy. Kennedy, A. L.
Symposium of the Gorgon. Smith, C. A.
SYNAGOGUES
    Pearlman, E. Chance
Synecdoche. Goodberg, D.
SYRIA
        Damascus
    Wannous, D. Two stories

            T

T. McGuirk steals a diamond. Cummings, R.
Taaffe, Sonya
    The dybbuk in love
      People of the book; a decade of Jewish sci-
        ence fiction & fantasy; edited by Rachel
        Swirsky & Sean Wallace.
Table talk, 1882. Akunin, B.
TABOO *See* Superstition
Taboo. Martinovich, V.
Taengja. Yoon, D.-n.
Tafoya, Dennis
    Above the Imperial
      Philadelphia noir; edited by Carlin Romano.

TAXIDERMY
Cleeves, A. Neastly pleasures
Wells, H. G. The triumphs of a taxidermist
Taxidermy. Fall, T.
Taylor, Andrew
Little Russia
Original sins; a Crime Writer's Association anthology; edited by Martin Edwards.
Taylor, Bruce
Spiders
Swenson, P. The Best of Talebones; edited by Patrick Swenson.
TAYLOR, ELIZABETH, 1932-2011
About
Warsh, L. A place in the sun
Taylor, John Robert *See* Taylor, Andrew, 1951-
Taylor, Ruth
The Virgin of Candelaria
The Massachusetts Review v52 no2 p280-284 Summ 2011
Taylor-Aragon, Eric
Epiphany
Barcelona noir; edited by Adriana V. Lopez & Cartmen Ospina; translated by Achy Obejas.
TEA
Gautier, A. Afternoon tea
Mu Xin. Quiet afternoon tea
Novik, N. Lord Dunsany's teapot
Sa'id, M. A. A cup of tea
Tea, biscuits and sugar. Assadi, M.
The **Tea** Guy. Gabel-Hartman, L.
The **teacher.** Tremblay, P.
TEACHERS
See also Students; Tutors
Allen, D. A bed of ice
Ayau, K. J. Official friend
Barthelme, D. Me and Miss Mandible
Baxter, C. The cures for love
Baxter, C. Gryphon
Beagle, P. S. Underbridge
Beattie, A. A platonic relationship
Black, A. Good in a crisis
Blatnik, A. Discourse
Blatnik, A. Learning
Davis, L. The professor
Davis, L. Special chair
Delury, J. Nothing of consequence
Dixon, S. The good fellow
Doctorow, E. L. The hunter
Downum, A. Blue valentine
Doyle, R. Teaching
Drabble, M. Stepping westward: a topographical tale
Due, T. The lake
Gautier, A. Push
Gordimer, N. Beethoven one-sixteeth black
Havazelet, E. Gurov in Manhattan
Highsmith, P. The baby spoon
Horrocks, C. Zero conditional
Jazzār, ; From the novel Secret pleasures
Keene, D. Sauce for the gander
Kim, S.-r. Into the light
Knezevic, O. The classroom
Kronauer, B. Mrs. Mühlenbeck in her house [excerpt]
Kronauer, B. A successful effort for Miss Block
Kyle, A. Brides
Kyle, A. A lot like fun

Lovecraft, H. P. The call of Cthulhu
MacLaverty, B. Language, truth and lockjaw
Makkai, R. The briefcase
Manilla, M. Still life with plums
Marías, J. The resignation letter of Senor de Santiesteban
Matheson, R. Mountains of the mind
McOmber, A. A memory of his rising
Naipaul, V. S. A Christmas story
Naipaul, V. S. The raffle
Naipaul, V. S. Titus Hoyt, I. A.
Neugeboren, J. The debt
Oates, J. C. The beating
O'Connor, S. The professor of atheism: Here comes another lesson
Ostlund, L. Bed death
Papernick, J. There is no other
Pearlman, E. Settlers
Powers, R. To the measures fall
Qiu Xiaolong. A confidence cap
Ross, A. The rest of it
Royle, N. The obscure bird
Ruocco, J. White buffalo
Schmitt, E.-E. Trashy reading
Shapiro, J. Ennui
Sheinin, L. The hunting knife
Sneed, C. Alex Rice Inc.
Solzhenitsyn, A. Nastenka
Solzhenitsyn, A. The new generation
Somerville, P. The wildlife biologist
Tremblay, P. The teacher
Trevor, W. Death of a professor
Trevor, W. A perfect relationship
Trueblood, V. Taken
Turtledove, H. The genetics lecture
Tuttle, S. Amanuensis
Uruq, S. The student and the teacher
Vukcevich, R. The wages of syntax
Warsh, L. Mysterioso
Wells, H. G. The apple
Wells, H. G. Mr. Ledbetter's vacation
Wilhelm, K. The funeral
Williamson, E. M. The professor asks his students if they agree with the conclusion: the table is an imitation and therefore not real
Willis, D. Caught
Willis, D. The fiancée
Winslow, D. Poe, Jo, and I
Zhang Kangkang. Are birds better at walking or flying?
Teaching. Doyle, R.
The **teaching** of Don B. Williamson, E. M.
A **teardrop** falls. Niven, L.
Tearful gaze. Balázs, B.
Tears fall on Orkney. Saunders, N.
TECHNOLOGY AND CIVILIZATION
Valente, C. M. The anachronist's cookbook
Ted Agonistes. Kanakia, R.
TEDDY BEARS
Scholes, K. Edward Bear and the very long walk
Teenager. Nutting, A.
TEENAGERS *See* Adolescence; Youth
Tees and teens. Jenkins, D.
TEETH
Kaminsky, S. M. Rattle, rattle, rattle
Tremblay, P. Headstone in your pocket
Teeth. Jones, S. G.
Teeth. Osondu, E. C.

TEL AVIV (ISRAEL) *See* Israel—Tel Aviv
TELECOMMUNICATION
    See also Telephone; Television
Telegraphing. Muller, M.
TELEPATHY
  Anderson, P. Kyrie
  Beagle, P. S. Music, when soft voices die
  Crosshill, T. Seeing double
  Silverberg, R. Snake and ocean, ocean and snake
  Vaughn, C. The girl with the pre-Raphaelite hair
TELEPHONE
  Dixon, S. Biff
  Dixon, S. The phone
  Hemmingson, M. You can call and ask a question
  Johnson, K. Names for water
  Kennedy, A. L. Whole family with young children devastated
  Marār, M. Hello, nations!
  Matheson, R. Person to person
  Pearlman, E. Aunt telephone
  Vukcevich, R. Cold comfort
The **telephone** game. Trevor, W.
The **Telephone** of the Dead. Goldbloom, G.
TELEVISION
  Bowes, R. On the slide
  Davis, L. Television
  Loory, B. The tv and Winston Churchill
  Mulkerns, V. Memory and desire
  Reed, K. At central
  Spinrad, N. Bug Jack Barron [excerpt]
Television. Beattie, A.
Television. Davis, L.
TELEVISION PRODUCERS AND DIRECTORS
  Ferris, J. The pilot
  Wilhelm, K. Baby, you were great
TELEVISION PROGRAMS
  Bengal, R. Captioning for the blind
  Ciocan, I. Auntie Frosea
  Dixon, S. The talk show
  Emshwiller, C. A possible episode in the picaresque adventures of Mr. J. H. B. Monstrosee
  Nutting, A. Dancing rat
  Nutting, A. Porn star
  Pearlman, E. How to fall
  Sheckley, R. The prize of peril
  Spinrad, N. The big flash
  Willard, C. Little wite squirel angel
Tell me. Leidiger, L.
Tell Me the Truth About Love. Gilchrist, E.
Tell me who to kill. Naipaul, V. S.
The **tell-tale** pacemaker. Parrish, P. J.
The **tell-tale** purr. Clark, M. H.
Tem, Melanie
  Keeping Corky
    Blood and other cravings; edited by Ellen Datlow.
Tem, Steve Rasnic
  The cabinet child
    The Year's best dark fantasy & horror; edited by Paula Guran
  Miri
    Blood and other cravings; edited by Ellen Datlow.
The **temp**. Kahaney, A.
TEMPERATURES, LOW *See* Low temperatures

TEMPLES
  Mu Xin. An empty room
  Smith, C. A. The theft of the thirty-nine girdles
A **temporary** matter. Lahiri, J.
A **temporary** position. Atta, S.
Temporary stories. Orozco, D.
The **temptation** of Harringay. Wells, H. G.
The **temptation** of Robin Green. Vaughn, C.
Ten carats of lead. Winchell, P.
Ten for the devil. De Lint, C.
Ten sigmas. Melko, P.
Ten Stories from Flaubert. Davis, L.
Ten thousand years. Mehta, R.
Ten with a flag. Haines, J. P.
Ten-year plan. Hastings, W.
TENANT FARMING
  Marār, M. From the bag of others!
Tender is the night-gaunt. Cannon, P.
Teneem. Marār, M.
TENNESSEE
  Bierce, A. Three and one are one
  Craddock, C. E. The "harnt" that walks Chilhowee
  Shipp, J. C. Agape walrus
           Memphis
  Ely, S. The fishpond
  Mirvis, T. Potatoes
TENNIS
  Tillman, L. The unconscious is also ridiculous
The **tenth** of January. Phelps, E. S.
Teodorovici, Lucian Dan
  Goose chase
    Best European fiction 2011; edited by Aleksandr Hemon; preface by Colum McCann
Teper, Igor
  A sentence to life
    Nature v477 no7362 p126 S 1 2011
Tequila. Boland, J. C.
TERMINAL ILLNESS
  Cannon, T. Instant karma
  Goodberg, D. The doctor
  Gorman, E. Flying solo
  Gottlieb, D. Somewhere, over
  Grossman, V. S. The elk
  Highsmith, P. The trouble with Mrs. Blynn, the trouble with the world
  Holm, B. Q. The great actor
  Kuhlken, K. Homes
  Langan, J. The unbearable proximity of Mr. Dunn's balloons
  Mullins, D. P. Arboretum
  Novack, S. Ants
  Oates, J. C. Bitch
  Pearlman, E. The little wife
Terminal talk. Akalis, S.
Terrin, Peter
  Clean-up; or, The adventures of Abdullah and me
    The Dedalus book of Flemish fantasy; edited by Eric Dickens and translated by Paul Vincent.
Terror in the haunted house. Sands, B.
TERRORISM
    See also Violence
  Archer, J. Politically correct
  Burgis, B. Dark coffee, bright light and the paradoxes of omnipotence
  Caine, R. Shiny

TERRORISM—*Continued*

Castro, A.-T. Of a sweet slow dance in the wake of temporary dogs

Crosshill, T. Seeing double

Hlehel, A. Coexistence

Ibrāhīm, H. My young friend

Niedzviecki, H. Special topic: terrorism

Olsen, L. January

Thabit, A. The twentieth terrorist

Verhelst, P. Swarm 10

TERRORISTS *See* Terrorism

The **terrors** of basket-weaving. Highsmith, P.

Terry, Gay Partington

The Backward Man

Terry, G. P. Meeting the Dog Girls; stories

Barbara Hutton Toujours

Terry, G. P. Meeting the Dog Girls; stories

Breakthrough

Terry, G. P. Meeting the Dog Girls; stories

Douglas Dhubhagain

Terry, G. P. Meeting the Dog Girls; stories

Episcatory

Terry, G. P. Meeting the Dog Girls; stories

The general's tears

Terry, G. P. Meeting the Dog Girls; stories

The Goddess of Outen

Terry, G. P. Meeting the Dog Girls; stories

Grasping the bird's tail

Terry, G. P. Meeting the Dog Girls; stories

A gray matter

Terry, G. P. Meeting the Dog Girls; stories

The Holy Sisters of Shedir

Terry, G. P. Meeting the Dog Girls; stories

Icon

Terry, G. P. Meeting the Dog Girls; stories

The importance of cheese

Terry, G. P. Meeting the Dog Girls; stories

It takes a universe

Terry, G. P. Meeting the Dog Girls; stories

The line

Terry, G. P. Meeting the Dog Girls; stories

The MacGuffin

Terry, G. P. Meeting the Dog Girls; stories

Meeting the Dog Girls

Terry, G. P. Meeting the Dog Girls; stories

Now you see it ...

Terry, G. P. Meeting the Dog Girls; stories

On Orly's border

Terry, G. P. Meeting the Dog Girls; stories

Precious hairpin

Terry, G. P. Meeting the Dog Girls; stories

The prison of kronos

Terry, G. P. Meeting the Dog Girls; stories

The promise

Terry, G. P. Meeting the Dog Girls; stories

The Queen's instructions

Terry, G. P. Meeting the Dog Girls; stories

Slowdown in Paxville

Terry, G. P. Meeting the Dog Girls; stories

Spirit gobs

Terry, G. P. Meeting the Dog Girls; stories

The tale of the glass man

Terry, G. P. Meeting the Dog Girls; stories

There's always a monkey

Terry, G. P. Meeting the Dog Girls; stories

This is not a pipe

Terry, G. P. Meeting the Dog Girls; stories

Timepiece

Terry, G. P. Meeting the Dog Girls; stories

Unto others

Terry, G. P. Meeting the Dog Girls; stories

The Ustek Cloudy

Terry, G. P. Meeting the Dog Girls; stories

Terry, James

Road to nowhere

Iowa Review v41 no1 p165-90 Spr 2011

Terwilliger, Cam

Cherry Town

The Literary Review (Madison, N.J.) v54 no3 p89-98 Spr 2011

TESLA, NIKOLA, 1856-1943

About

Faust, M. Y. The electrical neurheographiton

Tess. Pearlman, E.

Test of faith. Frank, B. P.

TEST PILOTS *See* Air pilots

Testimony of a private. Almond, S.

Testimony of pilot. Hannah, B.

Testomony. Treadway, J.

Tet Offensive. Shepard, S.

Tetanus. Oates, J. C.

La **tete**. Châteaureynaud, G. O.

TETRAPLEGICS *See* Quadriplegics

Texaco on Biscayne. Barrett, L.

TEXAS

Blake, G. Degüello

Blake, G. The old and the lost

Blake, G. Return fire

Burton, M. T. Cherry Coke

Caine, R. Dead man stalking: a Morganville Vampires story

Cook, K. L. Bonnie and Clyde in the backyard

Crumley, J. Luck

Daugherty, T. The inhalatorium

Downum, A. Blue valentine

Henry, O. The caballero's way

Lake, J. Dogs in the moonlight

Lake, J. Tall spirits, blocking the night

Lansdale, J. R. Six-finger Jack

Lansdale, J. R. Torn away

Penkov, M. Devshirmeh

Powers, J. Preacher's kid

Sandlin, L. Phelan's first case

Tingle, T. Six dead cabbies

Wier, G. Duckweed

Williamson, E. M. Hope, among other vices and virtues

19th century

Brandon, J. A jury of his peers

Austin

Sublett, J. Moral hazard

Corpus Christi

Johnston, B. A. Soldier of fortune

Dallas

James, D. Bottomed out

El Paso

Byrd, B. The dead man's wife

Fort Worth

Bass, R. Fish story

Galveston

Smith, C. Catgirl

Houston

Cortez, S. Montgomery Cleft

Port Arthur

Corbett, D. and Urrea, L. A. Who stole my monkey?

San Antonio

Brandon, J. A jury of his peers

The **thing** itself. Black, A.

The **thing** without a name. Naipaul, V. S.

The **things**. Watts, P.

The **things** he said. Smith, M. M.

Things I don't remember. Alland, S.

Things said or done. Packer, A.

Things that are not yours. Vapnyar, L.

The **things** that make me weak and strange get engineered away. Doctorow, C.

Things we'll need for the coming difficulties. Vogrin, V.

Things you learn from others. Shepard, S.

Think. Wallace, D. F.

The **third** always beside you. Langan, J.

The **third** dead boy. Hoffman, N. K.

Third person on a bed built for five. Williamson, E. M.

The **Third** Reich: Part 2. Bolaño, R.

The **Third** World Is Just around the Corner. Spargo, R. C.

Thirteen harbors. Suong, N. M.

The **thirteen** texts of Arthyria. Fultz, J. R.

The **thirteenth** woman. Davis, L.

THIRTY SECONDS FROM NOW. Chu, J.

Thirty years. Blatnik, A.

This condition. Davis, L.

This is a love story, too. Hall, T. M.

"**This** Is Earl Sandt". Butler, R. O.

This is not a barren place. Mihas, P.

This is not a pipe. Terry, G. P.

This is not your city. Horrocks, C.

This is now. Smith, M. M.

This life or the next. Mullins, D. P.

This new and poisonous air. McOmber, A.

This one. Hunter, L.

This Other Alan. Rodgers, S. J.

This other us. Willis, D.

This peaceful state of war. Jansen, P.

This quiet complex. Gray, A.

This thing called love. Emshwiller, C.

THOMAS, CLARENCE
About
Tillman, L. Give us some dirt

Thomas, Donald
The case of a boy's honour
  Thomas, D. Sherlock Holmes and the ghosts of Bly and other new adventures of the great detective
The case of the ghosts at Bly
  Thomas, D. Sherlock Holmes and the ghosts of Bly and other new adventures of the great detective
The case of the matinee idol
  Thomas, D. Sherlock Holmes and the ghosts of Bly and other new adventures of the great detective
Sherlock Holmes the actor
  Thomas, D. Sherlock Holmes and the ghosts of Bly and other new adventures of the great detective

Thomas, Patrick
Short fuse
  The stories (in) between; edited by Greg Schauer, Jeanne B. Benzel, and W. H. Horner.

Thompson, Jean
Pie of the month
  Best of times, worst of times; contemporary American short stories from the new Gilded Age; edited by Wendy Martin and Cecelia Tichi.

Thompson, Neville
The children of gear
  Requiems for the departed; edited by Gerard Brennan & Mike Stone.

Thon, Melanie Rae
The Companionship of Stone
  The Antioch Review v69 no3 p409-423 Summ 2011
Confession for Raymond Good Bird
  Thon, M. R. In this light; new and selected stories
Father, lover, deadman, dreamer
  Thon, M. R. In this light; new and selected stories
First, body
  Thon, M. R. In this light; new and selected stories
Heavenly creatures: for wandering children and their delinquent mother
  Thon, M. R. In this light; new and selected stories
Home
  Thon, M. R. In this light; new and selected stories
In these woods
  Thon, M. R. In this light; new and selected stories
Iona Moon
  Thon, M. R. In this light; new and selected stories
Necessary angels
  Thon, M. R. In this light; new and selected stories
Punishment
  Thon, M. R. In this light; new and selected stories
Retreating Light
  Five Points v12 no3 p81-9 2009
Tu B'Shvat: for the drowned and the saved
  Thon, M. R. In this light; new and selected stories
Xmas, Jamaica Plain
  Thon, M. R. In this light; new and selected stories

The **thorn**. Schirach, F. v.

Thorne, Todd
The fisherman
  Nature v474 no7353 p672 Je 30 2011

Thorns. Latiolais, M.

Thor's Day (Highway 81 North, Staunton, Virginia). Shepard, S.

Those Catrini. Page, N.

Those who wait through the drowsy dark. Swirsky, R.

Though birdsong fills the air. Dib, M.

THOUGHT TRANSFERENCE See Telepathy

Thoughts of a sterile woman. Diab, F.

Thoughts while strolling. Gray, A.

THOUSAND AND ONE NIGHTS See Arabian nights

A **thousand** deaths. London, J.

The **thousand** franc bill. Rodoreda, M.

Today you are a man. Reiter, J.
Todd, Caroline
    See also Todd, Charles
Todd, Charles
  Yesterday
    Original sins; a Crime Writer's Association
    anthology; edited by Martin Edwards.
Toder, Emily
  (tr.) See Bayley, Edgar
(Tofu) Worker poet Bao 1. Qiu Xiaolong
(Tofu) Worker poet Bao II. Qiu Xiaolong
Togneri, Elaine
  Paparazzo
    Mystery Writers of America presents the rich
    and the dead; edited by Nelson DeMille.
Tóibín, Colm
  Barcelona, 1975
    Tóibín, C. The empty family; stories
  The colour of shadows
    Tóibín, C. The empty family; stories
  The empty family
    Tóibín, C. The empty family; stories
  The new Spain
    Tóibín, C. The empty family; stories
  One minus one
    Tóibín, C. The empty family; stories
  The pearl fishers
    Tóibín, C. The empty family; stories
  A priest in the family
    The Granta book of the Irish short story; [ed-
    ited by] Anne Enright.
  Silence
    Tóibín, C. The empty family; stories
  The street
    Tóibín, C. The empty family; stories
  Two women
    Tóibín, C. The empty family; stories
Tokarczuk, Olga
  The ugliest woman in the world
    Best European fiction 2011; edited by Alek-
    sandr Hemon; preface by Colum McCann
Tolbert, Jeremiah
  Arties aren't stupid
    Brave new worlds; edited by John Joseph Ad-
    ams.
  One-click banishment
    The way of the wizard; edited by John Joseph
    Adams.
Tolstoy, Leo, graf
  God sees the truth, but waits
    The greatest Russian stories of crime and sus-
    pense; edited by Otto Penzler.
  Too dear
    The greatest Russian stories of crime and sus-
    pense; edited by Otto Penzler.
Tom, Laurie
  Living rooms
    L. Ron Hubbard presents Writers of the Fu-
    ture volume XXVI; the year's twelve best
    tales from the Writers of the Future inter-
    national writers' program; illustrated by
    winners in the Illustrators of the Future in-
    ternational illustrators' program; with es-
    says on writing & illustration by L. Ron
    Hubbard/Dean Wesley Smith/ Stephen
    Youll; edited by K. D. Wentworth
Tom Clancy's "Brain-Dead or Alive". Clancy, T.
Tom Thumb wedding. Trueblood, V.

Tomasula, Steve
  Endurance
    Bomb no113 p supp22-supp23 Fall 2010
The **tomb** of Sarah. Loring, F. G.
The **tomb-spawn**. Smith, C. A.
Tomorrow and tomorrow. Bradbury, R.
Tomorrow, I'll stroll no more. Mu Xin
Tomorrow People. Hrbek, G.
Tongues. Vukcevich, R.
Too dear. Tolstoy, L., graf
Too fatal a poison. Leahy, K. H.
Too much mean me. Brown, G.
Toother. Dowling, T.
Topping off the spire. MacLeod, I.
Tops. Shepard, S.
Torgersen, Brad R.
  Exanastasis
    L. Ron Hubbard presents Writers of the Fu-
    ture volume XXVI; the year's twelve best
    tales from the Writers of the Future inter-
    national writers' program; illustrated by
    winners in the Illustrators of the Future in-
    ternational illustrators' program; with es-
    says on writing & illustration by L. Ron
    Hubbard/Dean Wesley Smith/ Stephen
    Youll; edited by K. D. Wentworth
Torn. Hatoum, M.
Torn away. Lansdale, J. R.
Torn stitches, shattered glass. Anderson, K. J.
TORNADOES
  Furman, L. Plum Creek
TORONTO (ONT.) *See* Canada—Toronto
Torres, David
  Grozny
    The Massachusetts Review v52 no2 p298-299
    Summ 2011
Torres, Justin
  Reverting to a wild state
    The New Yorker v87 no22 p58-61 Ag 1 2011
  STARVE A RAT
    Harper's v323 no1937 p69-74 O 2011
The **tortoise** and the hare. Gray, A.
Tortolita. St. Germain, J.
TORTURE
  Ambrosio, G. Sticko
  Argemi, R. The slender charm of Chinese wom-
    en
  Eliot, G. F. The copper bowl
  Mitchell, D. Character development
Total internal reflection. Jones, G. A.
TOTALITARIANISM
    See also Communism; Dictators; Nation-
    al socialism
  Anderson, P. The pugilist
  Dib, M. Naëma disappeared
  Eisenberg, D. Someone to talk to
  Lahens, Y. The survivors
  Lahens, Y. Wash your memory with lots of wa-
    ter
  Solzhenitsyn, A. The new generation
Touch and Go. Ferarro, S. L.
A **touch** of lavender. Lindholm, M.
Tough, tough toys for tough, tough boys. Self, W.
A **tough** tussle. Bierce, A.
Toujours. Koja, K.
TOURIST COURTS *See* Motels
TOURIST TRADE
  Budnitz, J. Aboard
  Eisenberg, D. Across the lake

Treadway, Jessica
  Dear Nicole
    Treadway, J. Please come back to me; stories
  Deprivation
    Treadway, J. Please come back to me; stories
  The nurse and the black lagoon
    Treadway, J. Please come back to me; stories
  Oregon
    Treadway, J. Please come back to me; stories
  Please come back to me
    Treadway, J. Please come back to me; stories
  Revelation
    Treadway, J. Please come back to me; stories
  Shirley wants her nickel back
    Treadway, J. Please come back to me; stories
  Testomony
    Treadway, J. Please come back to me; stories
TREASON
      See also Defectors; Spies
  Jones, S. Scarred
The **Treasonable** Parrot. Ifowodo, O.
Treasure. Hoffman, A.
The **treasure** in the forest. Wells, H. G.
TREASURE-TROVE *See* Buried treasure
The **tree**. Levine, S.
The **tree**. Loory, B.
The **tree** line, Kansas, 1934. Means, D.
The **tree** of life. McGarry, J.
TREES
  Aiken, J. The Magnesia Tree
  Davis, L. The cedar trees
  Loory, B. The tree
  Stevens, A. B. Blood not sap
  Thu, T. The quiet poplar
Tregillis, Ian
  Still life (a sexagesimal fairy tale)
    The Best science fiction and fantasy of the
      year: volume five; edited by Jonathan
      Strahan.
Trek. Hannah, B.
TRELAWNY, EDWARD JOHN, 1792-1881
                About
  Powers, T. A time to cast away stones
Tremblay, Paul
  The blog at the end of the world
    Tremblay, P. In the mean time
  Feeding the machine
    Tremblay, P. In the mean time
  Figure 5
    Tremblay, P. In the mean time
  Growing things
    Tremblay, P. In the mean time
  Harold the spider man
    Tremblay, P. In the mean time
  Headstone in your pocket
    Tremblay, P. In the mean time
    The Year's best dark fantasy & horror; edited
      by Paula Guran
  It's against the law to feed the ducks
    Tremblay, P. In the mean time
  The Marlborough man meets the end
    Tremblay, P. In the mean time
  Nineteen snapshots of Dennisport
    Cape Cod noir; edited by David L. Ulin.
  The people who live near me
    Tremblay, P. In the mean time
  Rhymes with Jew
    Tremblay, P. In the mean time

  The strange case of Nicholas Thomas: an ex-
    cerpt from a history of the Longesian Li-
    brary
    Tremblay, P. In the mean time
  The teacher
    Tremblay, P. In the mean time
  There's no light between floors
    Tremblay, P. In the mean time
  The two-headed girl
    Tremblay, P. In the mean time
  We will never live in the castle
    Tremblay, P. In the mean time
TRENTON (N.J.) *See* New Jersey—Trenton
TRESPASS
  Shapiro, J. In its place
Trespass. Barnes, J.
Trespass. Schaefer, C. A.
Trespass. Trueblood, V.
Trespasses. Ní Dhuibhne, E.
Trespassing between heaven and hell. Bill, F.
Trevor, Douglas
  The Librarian
    Michigan Quarterly Review v49 no3 p349-64
      Summ 2010
Trevor, William
  After rain
    Trevor, W. Selected stories
  An afternoon
    Trevor, W. Selected stories
  Against the odds
    Trevor, W. Selected stories
  At Olivehill
    Trevor, W. Selected stories
  Big bucks
    Trevor, W. Selected stories
  A bit of business
    Trevor, W. Selected stories
  A bit on the side
    Trevor, W. Selected stories
  Bravado
    Trevor, W. Selected stories
  The children
    Trevor, W. Selected stories
  Child's play
    Trevor, W. Selected stories
  The dancing-master's music
    Trevor, W. Selected stories
  A day
    Trevor, W. Selected stories
  Death of a professor
    Trevor, W. Selected stories
  The dressmaker's child
    Trevor, W. Selected stories
    The Granta book of the Irish short story; [ed-
      ited by] Anne Enright.
  An evening out
    Trevor, W. Selected stories
  Faith
    Trevor, W. Selected stories
  Folie à deux
    Trevor, W. Selected stories
  A friend in the tade
    Trevor, W. Selected stories
  A friendship
    Trevor, W. Selected stories
  Gilbert's mother
    Trevor, W. Selected stories
  Good news
    Trevor, W. Selected stories

TROY (ANCIENT CITY)
See also Trojan War
TRUCK DRIVERS
Matheson, R. C. Transfiguration
TRUCKS
Accidents
See Traffic accidents
True love versus the cigar-store Indian. Mullins, D. P.
The **true** story of Merganther's run. Levine, D. D.
The **true** world. Rosen, J.
Trueblood, Valerie
Amends
    Trueblood, V. Marry or burn; stories
Beloved, you looked into space
    Trueblood, V. Marry or burn; stories
Choice in dreams
    Trueblood, V. Marry or burn; stories
Invisible river
    Trueblood, V. Marry or burn; stories
Luck
    Trueblood, V. Marry or burn; stories
Mance Lipscomb
    Trueblood, V. Marry or burn; stories
Phantom father
    Trueblood, V. Marry or burn; stories
She had coarsened
    Trueblood, V. Marry or burn; stories
Suitors
    Trueblood, V. Marry or burn; stories
Taken
    Trueblood, V. Marry or burn; stories
Tom Thumb wedding
    Trueblood, V. Marry or burn; stories
Trespass
    Trueblood, V. Marry or burn; stories
Trung, Trung Dinh
Love forest
    Family of fallen leaves; stories of Agent Orange by Vietnamese writers; edited by Charles Waugh and Huy Lien.
Trust me. Estleman, L. D.
Trusta, H. *See* Phelps, Elizabeth Stuart, 1815-1852
The **trusty.** Rash, R.
The **truth** about Pyecraft. Wells, H. G.
The **truth,** from a lie of convenience. Harvey, B.
"The **truth** is a cave in the Black Mountains. . . .". Gaiman, N.
Truth or Dare. Czepiel, K. L.
Truth window: a tale of the bedlam rose. Dowling, T.
TRUTHFULNESS AND FALSEHOOD
See also Honesty
Evans, D. Someone ought to tell her there's nowhere to go
Kyle, A. Nine
Try the girl. Chandler, R.
Trying to learn. Davis, L.
Tsai, Nancy
(tr.) *See* Tang, Xuehua
The **tsar's** dragon. Yolen, J. and Stemple, A.
TSUBURAYA, EIJI, 1901-1970
About
Shepard, J. Gojira, king of the monsters
Tu B'Shvat: for the drowned and the saved. Thon, M. R.
TUAMOTU ISLANDS *See* Islands of the Pacific

TUBERCULOSIS
Dib, M. Little Cousin
Tubs. Vukcevich, R.
Tucher, Albert
Bismarck rules
    The Best American mystery stories 2010; edited and with an introduction by Lee Child; Otto Penzler, series editor
Tuck, Lily
Ice
    The Pen/O.Henry Prize stories 2011; chosen and with an introduction by Laura Furman; with essays on the stories thety admire most by jurors A. M. Homes, Manuel Muñoz, Christine Schutt
Tuesday. Hunter, L.
Tuesday night. Beattie, A.
TULIPS
Bernheimer, K. A tulip's tale
A **tulip's** tale. Bernheimer, K.
Tulum, Mexico. Shepard, S.
The **tunnel.** Loory, B.
TUNNELS
Martin, G. R. R. Dark, dark were the tunnels
Tunney, Deborah-Anne
The yellow purse
    South Carolina Review v43 no2 p105-12 Spr 2011
The **Turetzky** Trio. Neugeboren, J.
TURKEY
Tanpinar, A. H. A mind at peace
Uldes, E. Professional behavior
Peasant life
See Peasant life—Turkey
Rural life
Karay, R. H. The gray donkey
Yaşar Kemal. Memed, my hawk
Istanbul
Pamuk, O. The black book
Vukcevich, R. Chain
Turkey. Ruocco, J.
TURKS
Abdullah, A. The soul of a turk
Turn away. Gorman, E.
TURNCOATS *See* Defectors
Turner, Andy
Fool in search of a country song
    Blood, guts, & whiskey; edited by Todd Robinson; introduction by Max Allan Collins.
Turtledove, Harry
Audubon in Atlantis
    Turtledove, H. Atlantis, and other places
Bedfellows
    Turtledove, H. Atlantis, and other places
The catcher in the Rhine
    Turtledove, H. Atlantis, and other places
The daimon
    Turtledove, H. Atlantis, and other places
Farmers' law
    Turtledove, H. Atlantis, and other places
The genetics lecture
    Turtledove, H. Atlantis, and other places
The horse of bronze
    Turtledove, H. Atlantis, and other places
News from the front
    Turtledove, H. Atlantis, and other places
Occupation duty
    Turtledove, H. Atlantis, and other places

UNMARRIED COUPLES—*Continued*
Beattie, A. Girl talk
Beattie, A. Weekend
Bingham, S. The hunt
Bingham, S. Sweet peas
Eisenberg, D. Holy Week
Ely, S. Dream fishing
Ely, S. Mississippi rules
Ely, S. The poisoned arrow
Engel, P. Refuge
Fallon, S. Camp Liberty
Gray, A. The suitcase
Gwyn, A. Drive
Horrocks, C. World Champion Cow of the Insane
Lukasik-Foss, T. Band names
Mullins, D. P. This life or the next
Novack, S. Attack of the pod people
Nutting, A. Dancing rat
O'Connor, J. Mothers were all the same
O'Connor, S. Love
Pearlman, E. Mates
Phillips, H. We?
Samardzic, G. Varneesh
Schabas, M. Natural selection
Simić, M. My girlfriend
Simmons, D. In the garden
Smith, M. M. Later
Sneed, C. Interview with the second wife
Somerville, P. No sun
Villegas, H. Picnic
Vogrin, V. Things we'll need for the coming difficulties
Vukcevich, R. Dead girlfriend
Vukcevich, R. Magic makeup
Willis, D. Frank
Woodrell, D. Dream spot
UNMARRIED MOTHERS
Baxter, C. Ghosts
Hobb, R. Cat's meat
Leland, C. T. Reprise
Naipaul, V. S. The maternal instinct
Shapiro, J. Predation
Tremblay, P. Rhymes with Jew
Unpreparing. Hunter, L.
Unravished bride. Pearlman, E.
The **unreachable** voices of ghosts. Lyman, J.
Unsolved mystery. Gray, A.
Until the green blossom opens . . . Burbara, R.
Until the soldiers came. Naipaul, V. S.
Unto others. Terry, G. P.
The **unusual** case of the psychotic raven. Drakulic, S.
UNWED MOTHERS *See* Unmarried mothers
Up and down the Drosselgasse. Dixon, S.
Up the bright river. Farmer, P. J.
Up the down beanstalk: a wife remembers. Beagle, P. S.
Updike, John
Farrell's caddie
Golf stories; edited by Charles McGrath.
Metamorphosis
Best of times, worst of times; contemporary American short stories from the new Gilded Age; edited by Wendy Martin and Cecelia Tichi.

Uphoff, Manon
Desire
Best European fiction 2011; edited by Aleksandr Hemon; preface by Colum McCann
Uppsala. Levine, S.
Uranus. Oates, J. C.
Urbanski, Debbie
The Move
New England Review v32 no1 p117-25 2011
Ureta, Tito
An evanescent book
Nature v475 no7354 p134 Jl 7 2011
Urrea, Luis Alberto
Amapola
By hook or by crook and 27 more of the best crime + mystery stories of the year; edited by Ed Gorman and Martin H. Greenberg.
The national city reparation society
San Diego noir; edited by Maryelizabeth Hart.
The Southside Raza Image Federation Corps of Discovery
Orion v30 no1 p30-5 Ja/F 2011
(jt. auth) See Corbett, David and Urrea, Luis Alberto
Ursin, Georg
Sleipner's assignment
Copenhagen noir; edited by Bo Tao Michaëlis; translated by Mark Kline.
Ursus Arctos Horribilis. Trunkey, L.
Uruq, Shuqiyyah
The brightness of his eyes
Loud sounds from the Holy Land; short fiction by Palestinian women; edited and translated by Jamal Assadi with assistance from Martha Moody.
The path of deceit
Loud sounds from the Holy Land; short fiction by Palestinian women; edited and translated by Jamal Assadi with assistance from Martha Moody.
The student and the teacher
Loud sounds from the Holy Land; short fiction by Palestinian women; edited and translated by Jamal Assadi with assistance from Martha Moody.
Us. Hunter, L.
USAF *See* United States. Air Force
The **useless**. Niedzviecki, H.
Ussama bin Laden *See* Osama bin Laden
The **Ustek** Cloudy. Terry, G. P.
UTAH
Chapman, J. Great Salt Lake
                Salt Lake City
Chapman, J. Great Salt Lake
Thon, M. R. Tu B'Shvat: for the drowned and the saved
UTOPIAS
Anderson, P. Eutopia
Buckell, T. S. Resistance
Kaftan, V. Civilization
Le Guin, U. H. The ones who walk away from Omelas
O'Connor, S. The professor of atheism: Paradise
Ryman, G. Everywhere

V

Vaara in the woods. Somerville, P.

Van Den Berg, Laura
I Looked For You, I Called Your Name
Ploughshares v37 no2/3 p170-186 Fall 2011
Van den Broeck, Walter
Successor to the throne
The Dedalus book of Flemish fantasy; edited
by Eric Dickens and translated by Paul
Vincent.
Van der Veer, K. L.
Hammer song
Blood & devotion; tales of epic fantasy; ed-
ited by W.H. Horner; illustrated by Nicole
Cardiff
Van Horn, Texas (Highway 10). Shepard, S.
Van Ostaijen, Paul *See* Ostaijen, Paul van, 1896-
1928
Van Pelt, James
The yard god
Swenson, P. The Best of Talebones; edited by
Patrick Swenson.
VanBuren, Kelly
Hired by a Witch
Femspec v11 no1 p82-5 2011
VANDALISM
Gilley, T. White
Vandiver, E. B.
Forcing Bowl
The Kenyon Review v33 no3 p70-89 Summ
2011
VanDonkelaar, Curtis
Matilda, or, A Man of Maxims
Western Humanities Review v65 no2 p91-109
Summ 2011
Vanish. Kennedy, A. L.
The **vanished**. Gray, A.
Vanished Girls. Reisman, N.
Vanishing. Beagle, P. S.
Vanishing. Willis, D.
The **vanishing** American. Parry, L.
Vanishing world. Gilley, T.
Vannatta, Dennis
All the Bums in Rockaway
The Antioch Review v69 no2 p325-34 Spr
2011
VAO. Ryman, G.
Vapnyar, Lara
Things that are not yours
Promised lands; new Jewish American fiction
on longing and belonging; edited by Derek
Rubin.
Vaquita. Pearlman, E.
The **variable** man. Dick, P. K.
Variations on a fifty-pound bale. Mansbach, A.
Variations on a theme from Seinfeld. Straub, P.
Varieties of disturbance. Davis, L.
Varneesh. Samardzic, G.
Vasta, Giorgio
Bites
Chicago Review v56 no1 p62-70 Spr 2011
Vaughan, Elizabeth A.
A rose by any other name would still be red
Chicks kick butt; edited by Rachel Caine and
Kerrie L. Hughes.
Vaughn, Carrie
Amaryllis
Brave new worlds; edited by John Joseph Ad-
ams.

The Year's best science fiction: twenty-eighth
annual collection; edited by Gardner
Dozois.
The book of Daniel
Vaughn, C. Kitty's greatest hits
Conquistador de la noche
Vampires; the recent undead; edited by Paula
Guran.
Vaughn, C. Kitty's greatest hits
Il est ne
Vaughn, C. Kitty's greatest hits
The girl with the pre-Raphaelite hair
Swenson, P. The Best of Talebones; edited by
Patrick Swenson.
God's creatures
Vaughn, C. Kitty's greatest hits
Kitty and the mosh pit of the damned
Vaughn, C. Kitty's greatest hits
Kitty's zombie New Year
Vaughn, C. Kitty's greatest hits
Life is the teacher
Vaughn, C. Kitty's greatest hits
Long time waiting
Vaughn, C. Kitty's greatest hits
Looking after family
Vaughn, C. Kitty's greatest hits
A princess of Spain
Vaughn, C. Kitty's greatest hits
The temptation of Robin Green
Vaughn, C. Kitty's greatest hits
Threads
The Thackery T. Lambshead cabinet of curi-
osities; edited by Ann & Jeff VanderMeer.
Wild ride
Vaughn, C. Kitty's greatest hits
Winnowing the herd
Vaughn, C. Kitty's greatest hits
You're on the air
Vaughn, C. Kitty's greatest hits
Vaughn, Vanessa
Some new blood
Hungry for your love; an anthology of
zombie romance; edited by Lori Perkins.
VAULTING
Dillman, D. Cloudcroft
Veale, Kevin
Twisted
Zombies: the recent dead; edited by Paula
Guran.
Vector Victoria. D'Amico, D. A.
Vedran. Carroll, J.
Las **Vegas,** New Mexico. Shepard, S.
VEGETARIANS
Blatnik, A. The power of words
Kurlansky, M. Bean curd
Velocity of mass. Chacón, D.
Vena cava. Oates, J. C.
VENDETTA *See* Revenge
VENEREAL DISEASES *See* Sexually transmitted
diseases
VENGEANCE *See* Revenge
VENICE (ITALY) *See* Italy—Venice
VENUS (PLANET)
Anderson, P. Sister planet
Bradbury, R. Eat, drink and be wary
Broderick, D. Under the moons of Venus
Landis, G. A. The sultan of the clouds
Venus rising. Emshwiller, C.

A **vision** of judgment. Wells, H. G.
VISIONS

> *See also* Dreams; Hallucinations and illusions

Atta, S. The miracle worker
Gray, A. The picture window
O'Connor, S. The professor of atheism: Here comes another lesson
Vukcevich, R. Tongues
Visit. Donovan, G.
A **visit**. Millhauser, S.
Visit to her husband. Davis, L.
Visitation. Watson, B.
Visitations. Hall, T. M.
Le **visiteur**. Trevor, W.
VISITING

Engel, P. Dia
Trevor, W. Le visiteur
Villegas, H. Meadowdene Estates
The **Visitor**. Serizawa, A.
VISITORS, FOREIGN *See* Foreign visitors
Visitors. Mogelson, L.
VISITORS FROM OUTER SPACE *See* Interplanetary visitors
A **visitor's** guide to lawn guyland. Sands, B.
La **vita** nuova. Goodman, A.
VIVA!. McReynolds, E.
Viva Regina. Greenman, B.
VIVISECTION *See* Medicine—Research
Vo, Thi Hao

The blood of leaves
Family of fallen leaves; stories of Agent Orange by Vietnamese writers; edited by Charles Waugh and Huy Lien.
Vogrin, Valerie

Things we'll need for the coming difficulties
Pushcart Prize XXXV: best of the small presses 2011; edited by Bill Henderson with the Pushcart Prize editors.
A **voice** like a hole. Valente, C. M.
Voice of America. Osondu, E. C.
Voice of the sonar in my vermiform appendix. Farmer, P. J.
Volokhonsky, Larissa

(tr.) *See* Leskov, Nikolai
Volt. Heathcock, A.
Voltolini, Dario

Beatrixpark: An Illumination
Chicago Review v56 no1 p50-4 Spr 2011
Voltolini, Dario and Appel, Anne Milano

BEATRIXPARK: AN ILLUMINATION
Harper's v323 no1937 p27-31 O 2011
VOLUNTEER WORKERS

Pearlman, E. Rules
Von Goethe, Johann Wolfgang *See* Goethe, Johann Wolfgang von, 1749-1832
Vonnegut, Kurt

$10,000 a year, easy
Vonnegut, K. While mortals sleep; unpublished short fiction
Bomar
Vonnegut, K. While mortals sleep; unpublished short fiction
Ed Luby's key club
The Best American mystery stories 2010; edited and with an introduction by Lee Child; Otto Penzler, series editor

The epizootic
Vonnegut, K. While mortals sleep; unpublished short fiction
Girl pool
Vonnegut, K. While mortals sleep; unpublished short fiction
Guardian of the person
Vonnegut, K. While mortals sleep; unpublished short fiction
Harrison Bergeron
Brave new worlds; edited by John Joseph Adams.
The humbugs
Vonnegut, K. While mortals sleep; unpublished short fiction
Hundred-dollar kisses
Vonnegut, K. While mortals sleep; unpublished short fiction
Jenny
Vonnegut, K. While mortals sleep; unpublished short fiction
The man without no kiddleys
Vonnegut, K. While mortals sleep; unpublished short fiction
Money talks
Vonnegut, K. While mortals sleep; unpublished short fiction
Mr. Z
Vonnegut, K. While mortals sleep; unpublished short fiction
The No-Talent Kid
The Saturday Evening Post v283 no2 p42-50 Mr/Ap 2011
Out, brief candle
Vonnegut, K. While mortals sleep; unpublished short fiction
Ruth
Vonnegut, K. While mortals sleep; unpublished short fiction
Tango
Vonnegut, K. While mortals sleep; unpublished short fiction
While mortals sleep
Vonnegut, K. While mortals sleep; unpublished short fiction
With his hand on the throttle
Vonnegut, K. While mortals sleep; unpublished short fiction
VOODOOISM

> *See also* Zombies

Kurlansky, M. The leopard of Ti Morne
Lahens, Y. Aunt Résia and the spirits
Park, P. Mysteries of the Old Quarter
VOTING

Boggs, B. Election day
Buckell, T. S. Resistance
A **voyage** to Cythera. Drabble, M.
Voyagers. Tuten, F.
VOYAGES AND TRAVELS

> *See also* Adventure; Air travel; Railroads—Travel; Sea stories; Tourist trade; Travelers

Atta, S. Twilight trek
Bierce, A. The man overboard
Terry, G. P. Grasping the bird's tail
Voyeur. Blatnik, A.
Voyeur. Ruddick, S.
VOYEURS

July, M. Something that needs nothing

Vukcevich, Ray
The button
    Vukcevich, R. Boarding instructions; stories
Chain
    Vukcevich, R. Boarding instructions; stories
Cold comfort
    Vukcevich, R. Boarding instructions; stories
Dead girlfriend
    Vukcevich, R. Boarding instructions; stories
Duck
    Vukcevich, R. Boarding instructions; stories
Fired
    Vukcevich, R. Boarding instructions; stories
A funny smell
    Vukcevich, R. Boarding instructions; stories
Gas
    Vukcevich, R. Boarding instructions; stories
Glinky
    Vukcevich, R. Boarding instructions; stories
Grocery list
    Vukcevich, R. Boarding instructions; stories
Human subjects
    Vukcevich, R. Boarding instructions; stories
In the flesh
    Vukcevich, R. Boarding instructions; stories
Intercontinental Ballistic Missle Boy
    Vukcevich, R. Boarding instructions; stories
Jumping
    Vukcevich, R. Boarding instructions; stories
The library of pi
    Vukcevich, R. Boarding instructions; stories
Love leans in from the left
    Vukcevich, R. Boarding instructions; stories
Love story
    Vukcevich, R. Boarding instructions; stories
Magic makeup
    Vukcevich, R. Boarding instructions; stories
Morning meditation
    Vukcevich, R. Boarding instructions; stories
My eyes, your ears
    Vukcevich, R. Boarding instructions; stories
My shoes
    Vukcevich, R. Boarding instructions; stories
The next best thing
    Swenson, P. The Best of Talebones; edited by
        Patrick Swenson.
Over here
    Vukcevich, R. Boarding instructions; stories
The rescue
    Vukcevich, R. Boarding instructions; stories
Some other time
    Vukcevich, R. Boarding instructions; stories
Strong suits
    Vukcevich, R. Boarding instructions; stories
Suddenly speaking
    Vukcevich, R. Boarding instructions; stories
Superpowers
    Vukcevich, R. Boarding instructions; stories
Take the stairs
    Vukcevich, R. Boarding instructions; stories
Tongues
    Vukcevich, R. Boarding instructions; stories
Tubs
    Vukcevich, R. Boarding instructions; stories
The two of me
    Vukcevich, R. Boarding instructions; stories
The wages of syntax
    Vukcevich, R. Boarding instructions; stories

VULTURES
    Gray, A. Vultures
Vultures. Gray, A.

W

Waberi, Abdourahman A.
Somewhere Close to the Start of the Game
    (Foosball)
    Agni no72 p204-8 2010
Somewhere Near the Beginning of the Match
    The Massachusetts Review v51 no4 p636-40
    Wint 2010
Wading. Cruz, A.
Wafiyyah. Khalaylah, A.
WAGERS
Rankin, I. Graduation day
Twain, M. The celebrated jumping frog of
    Calaveras County
The **wages** of syntax. Vukcevich, R.
Waggoner, Tim
Disarmed and dangerous
    Zombies: the recent dead; edited by Paula
        Guran.
Wagner, Jeremy
Romance ain't dead
    Hungry for your love; an anthology of
        zombie romance; edited by Lori Perkins.
WAGNER, RICHARD, 1813-1883
                    About
Riccardi, T. A death in Venice
Wagner, Wendy N.
The secret of calling rabbits
    The way of the wizard; edited by John Joseph
        Adams.
Wagstaff, Mark
'Footnotes and Footlights'
    The Writer v124 no2 p23-5 F 2011
Wahala. Okorafor, N.
The **wait**. Bayley, E.
Wait for me. Fisher, S.
Wait till you see me dance. Unferth, D. O.
Waite, Urban
Don't look away
    Best of the West 2009; new stories from the
        wide side of the Missouri; edited by James
        Thomas and D. Seth Horton; foreword by
        Rick Bass.
The Republic of Curtis
    The Massachusetts Review v52 no2 p289-297
    Summ 2011
WAITERS
McPherson, J. A. A solo song: for Doc
Waiting. Beattie, A.
Waiting. Osondu, E. C.
Waiting for Rusty. Cole, W.
Waiting for the earthquake. Silverberg, R.
WAITRESSES
Gray, A. Love, mortar
Gray, A. There will be sense
Kim, C.-s. Crimson fruit
Mullins, D. P. Longing to love you
Shepard, S. Esmeralda and the flipping hammer
    (Highway 152, continued)
Sneed, C. A million dollars
Terry, G. P. Meeting the Dog Girls
Unger, L. Wild Card
Wake not the dead. Knox, J. H.

Wakefield. Doctorow, E. L.

Walbert, Kate
M&M World
The New Yorker v87 no15 p66-71 My 30 2011

Walcote. Wells, H. G.

WALES
Roberts, W. O. The professionals

The **walk**. Davis, L.

Walk for Mankind. Packer, A.

The **walk** that replaced understanding. Loory, B.

Walker, Bernadette
(tr.) See Meruane, Lina

Walker, Deborah
Green future
Nature v471 no7336 p130 Mr 3 2011

WALKING
Bradbury, R. The pedestrian
Loory, B. The walk that replaced understanding
Mu Xin. Tomorrow, I'll stroll no more

Walking away. Ceallaigh, P. O.

The **Walking** Woman. Austin, M. H.

The **wall** of cacti. Marār, M.

WALL STREET (NEW YORK, N.Y.)
See also Stock exchange

Wallace, Daniel
The End
Five Points v12 no1 p51-63 2008

Wallace, David Foster
Backbone
The New Yorker v87 no3 p66-71 Mr 7 2011
A New Examiner
Harper's v321 p23-5 S 2010
Think
Best of times, worst of times; contemporary American short stories from the new Gilded Age; edited by Wendy Martin and Cecelia Tichi.

Wallace, Edgar
Bosambo of Monrovia
The Big book of adventure stories; edited and with a introduction by Otto Penzler; foreword by Douglas Preston.

Wallace, Joseph
Custom sets
The Best American mystery stories 2010; edited and with an introduction by Lee Child; Otto Penzler, series editor

Walled city. Sneed, C.

WALLPAPER
Gilman, C. P. The yellow wall-paper

WALLS
Gordimer, N. Once upon a time
Prakash, U. The walls of Delhi

The **walls** of Delhi. Prakash, U.

The **walri** republic of Sea World. Sands, B.

WALRUS
Shipp, J. C. Agape walrus

The **Walrus** and the Tub. Shaw, K. L.

Walser, Robert
Cowshed
Agni no73 p216-17 2011
Do You Know Meier?
Agni no73 p210-12 2011
Kutsch
Agni no73 p213-15 2011

Walsh, Courtney
Shahla's Daughter
Callaloo v33 no3 p792-806 Summ 2010

Walsh, Thomas
Diamonds mean death
The Black Lizard big book of Black Mask stories; edited and with a foreword by Otto Penzler; introduction by Keith Alan Deutsch.

Walt. Dixon, S.

Walter John Harmon. Doctorow, E. L.

The **waltz**. Bayley, E.

Wamsutter in Dali vision. Williamson, E. M.

Wanda's. Beattie, A.

Wang Village and the World [With biographical note] Bi, F.

Wannous, Dima
Two stories
Beirut 39; new writing from the Arab world; edited by Samuel Shimon; with a preface by Hanan al-Shaykh

Wanted: dead or alive. Banks, L. E.

Wanting Only to Be Heard. Driscoll, J.

WAR
See also Armaments; Imaginary wars and battles; Interplanetary wars; Nuclear warfare names of individual wars
Arsenijević, V. One minute: Dumbo's death
Blatnik, A. Experts
Blatnik, A. I think
Dib, M. He who bestows all worldly goods
Dib, M. Naëma disappeared
Dick, P. K. The defenders
Dozois, G. R. Morning child
Dozois, G. R. Recidivist
Finlay, C. C. Hail, conductor
Harris, C. Dahlia underground
Hodge, B. With acknowledgements to Sun Tzu
Moles, D. Seven cities of gold
Monk, D. Bearing life
Monk, D. Last tour of duty
Monzó, Q. During the war
Novik, N. Seven years from home
Rodoreda, M. On a dark night
Ryman, G. K is for Kosovo (or, Massimo's career)
Schoen, L. M. The wrestler and the spear fisher
Shepard, L. Salvador
Shipp, J. C. Spider house
Sisson, A. Patriot girls
Stefan, V. Doe a deer
Thompson, J. Pie of the month
Casualties
Bierce, A. Chickamauga
Dozois, G. R. A dream at noonday

WAR AND CHILDREN
O'Brien, E. Plunder

War and peace. Gifford, B.

The **War** Between the Men and the Women. Lambert, S.

WAR CORRESPONDENTS *See* Journalists

WAR CRIME TRIALS
Wieland, L. La fenêtre

WAR CRIMINALS
Nagai, M. Confession

War is beautiful. Rickert, M.

The **war** on women. Atkinson, K.

War Wounds. Sirisena, H.

Ward, Arthur Sarsfield *See* Rohmer, Sax

Ward, Elizabeth Stuart Phelps *See* Phelps, Elizabeth Stuart, 1844-1911

Ward 9. Self, W.

WARLOCKS *See* Witchcraft

The **warm** fuzzies. Adrian, C.

Warmth. Ryman, G.

Warren, Kaaron
  All you can do is breathe
    Blood and other cravings; edited by Ellen
    Datlow.

The **warrior**. Butcher, J.

A **warrior's** daughter. Zitkala-Sa

Warriors of the sky. Saeed, M.

WARSAW (POLAND) *See* Poland—Warsaw

Warsh, Lewis
  Endless embrace
    Warsh, L. A place in the sun
  Harry Cray
    Warsh, L. A place in the sun
  Mysterioso
    Warsh, L. A place in the sun
  A place in the sun
    Warsh, L. A place in the sun
  The Russians
    Warsh, L. A place in the sun
  Secret
    Warsh, L. A place in the sun

Warwick Damon. Gallari, A.

Was I? Blatnik, A.

Was she wicked? was she good? Rickert, M.

WASATCH RANGE (UTAH AND IDAHO)
  Tuttle, S. Amanuensis

Wash your memory with lots of water. Lahens, Y.

WASHINGTON (D.C.)
  Dixon, S. Meet the natives
  Griffiths, R. The obvious candidate
  Naipaul, V. S. One out of many
  Row, J. Sheep may safely graze

WASHINGTON (STATE)
  Barron, L. Blackwood's baby
  Knickerbocker, A. Same as it was when you left
  Waite, U. Don't look away
          Seattle
  Beagle, P. S. Underbridge
  Kurlansky, M. Margaret
  Phelan, T. Time will tell
  Ray, S. The miracles of Vincent Van Gogh
  Sui Sin Far. The inferior woman

Wasps. Ely, S.

Wasps. Kennedy, A. L.

Waste. Gray, A.

Waste land. Dedman, S.

Wasting. See Franco, J. April in three parts: part
  II, Wasting

A **watcher** by the dead. Bierce, A.

WATCHMEN
  Naipaul, V. S. The nightwatchman's occurance
  book

WATER
     See also Wells
  Johnson, K. Names for water

The **water**. Levine, S.

Water liars. Hannah, B.

A **water** matter. Lake, J.

Water of youth. Aiken, J.

Water Running on the Moon. Hill, L. S.

The **water** tower. Mantooth, J.

The **waterfall** and the linguist. Bayley, E.

The **Waterfall** and the Linguist. Bayley, E.

WATERMELONS
  Marār, M. Ghanem's watermelon

Waters, Don
  Last Rites
    The Antioch Review v69 no3 p478-501 Summ
    2011
  Mormons in heat
    Best of the West 2009; new stories from the
    wide side of the Missouri; edited by James
    Thomas and D. Seth Horton; foreword by
    Rick Bass.

Waters, Jesse
  Year of the Demon Tree
    StoryQuarterly v44 p223-30 2010

The **watershed**. Shields, S.

The **waterwheel**. Le Clézio, J.-M. G.

Watkins, Claire Vaye
  Gold Mine
    The Paris Review v52 no195 p189-204 Wint
    2010
  The last thing we need
    Best of the West 2011; new stories from the
    wild side of the Missouri; edited by James
    Thomas and D. Seth Horton; foreword by
    Ana Castillo.
    Granta no111 p81-96 Summ 2010

Watkins, Marc
  Two midnights in a jug
    Pushcart Prize XXXV: best of the small
    presses 2011; edited by Bill Henderson
    with the Pushcart Prize editors.
  A Wooden Nickel Life
    StoryQuarterly v44 p216-22 2010

Watsmore, Andrea
  Bina
    Dancing with Mr. Darcy; stories inspired by
    Jane Austen and Chawton House Library;
    compiled by Sarah Waters.

Watson, Brad
  Alamo Plaza
    The Pen/O.Henry Prize stories 2011; chosen
    and with an introduction by Laura Furman;
    with essays on the stories thety admire
    most by jurors A. M. Homes, Manuel Mu-
    ñoz, Christine Schutt
  Seeing eye
  Visitation
    The Pen/O.Henry Prize stories, 2010; edited
    and with an introduction by Laura Furman;
    with essays on the stories they admire most
    by jurors Junot Diaz, Paula Fox, Yiyun Li.

Watterson, Kathryn
  Sunshine 320 Days a Year
    TriQuarterly v138 53473 bytes Summ/Fall
    2010

Watts, Peter
  The things
    The Best science fiction and fantasy of the
    year: volume five; edited by Jonathan
    Strahan.
    The Year's best science fiction: twenty-eighth
    annual collection; edited by Gardner
    Dozois.

WAXWORKS
  Highsmith, P. Woodrow, Wilson's necktie
  McOmber, A. There are no bodies such as this

The **way** he laughs. Sands, B.

The **way** home. Ray, S.

The **way** station. Ballingrud, N.

The **way** they limp. Howard, C.

The **way** to perfection. Davis, L.

The **way** we are. Tillman, L.
WAY WE WERE (MOTION PICTURE)
   Tillman, L. The way we are
Wayde's essence. Wells, H. G.
We. Hunter, L.
We?. Phillips, H.
We Are Family. Melnyczuk, A.
We can get them for you wholesale. Gaiman, N.
We Come in Peace. Gartner, Z.
We do not come in peace. Barzak, C.
We Don't Deserve This. Leong, S.
We miss you: a study of get-well letters from a
   class of fourth graders. Davis, L.
We need to talk about Mr Collins. Howell, M.
We Once Were Slaves. Koretzky, M.
We others. Millhauser, S.
We sat around in rosy candlelight. Shepard, S.
We was. Hunter, L.
We Whistled While We Worked. Amdahl, G.
We will never live in the castle. Tremblay, P.
We Will Win the World Cup 2010. Mabanckou,
   A.
WEALTH
   See also Millionaires
   Baxter, C. The winner
   Bell, T. The pirate of Palm Beach
   Boggs, B. Imperial Chrysanthemum
   Châteaureynaud, G. O. Another story
   Doctorow, C. Chicken little
   Fitzgerald, F. S. The diamond as big as the Ritz
   Goodberg, D. Flying cars
   Goodberg, D. Precautions
   Large, J.-R. Rosanna
   MacLeod, I. Re-crossing the Styx
   Morrell, D. The controller
   Packer, A. Jump
   Rozan, S. J. Iterations
   Shapiro, J. Night and day
   Vonnegut, K. Tango
WEAPONS *See* Armaments; Arms and armor;
   Nuclear weapons
WEATHER
   See also Storms
The **weather**. Willis, D.
Weather channels. Goodberg, D.
Weaver, Rachel
   What Remains
     Gettysburg Review v24 no1 p69-75 Spr 2011
Webb, Igor
   Reza Says
     The Hudson Review v63 no4 p575-91 Wint
     2011
Webber, Clyde Ray
   Computers, VCR's & Football
     Southern Quarterly v48 no2 p121-2 Wint
     2011
   Sittin' Up With Uncle John
     Southern Quarterly v48 no2 p120-1 Wint
     2011
The **wedding**. Bayley, E.
The **wedding**. Bingham, S.
The **wedding**. Levine, S.
WEDDING ANNIVERSARIES
   Allen, D. Overtime
   Baxter, C. Horace and Margaret's fifty-second
Wedding day. Kitterman, B.
The **wedding** gowns. McGarry, J.
Wedding of the Week. Brown, R.

WEDDINGS
   Anzaldúa, G. El paisano is a bird of omen
   Atkins, E. The wrong side of Mr. Right
   Bingham, S. The wedding
   Butcher, J. Something borrowed
   Dib, M. A fine wedding
   Freudenberger, N. An arranged marriage
   Kitterman, B. Wedding day
   Latiolais, M. The long table
   Levine, S. The wedding
   McGarry, J. The wedding gowns
   Packer, A. Things said or done
   Phillips, H. The brides
   Phillips, H. The weddings
   Qiu Xiaolong. Big bowl and firecracker
   Riippi, J. Something about marriage, part I
   Sharp, Z. Rules of engagement
   Trevor, W. The telephone game
   Trueblood, V. Beloved, you looked into space
   Trueblood, V. Invisible river
   Trueblood, V. Taken
   Villegas, H. Rites
   Willis, D. Remember, relive
The **weddings**. Phillips, H.
The **wedding's** night and the sacrifice. Sirhan, A.
Wee Robin. Aiken, J.
Weekend. Beattie, A.
The **Weeper**. Gifford, B.
Weepers. Fincke, G.
The **Weeping** Yangtze. He, Q.
The **Weight** of the Internet. Adcox, J. T.
The **weight** of the night. Lahens, Y.
Weil, Josh
   I Want You to Know That I Know That He
     Loved You
     Agni no73 p85-104 2011
Weimar in early spring. Mu Xin
Welcome, Lost Dogs. Blakeslee, V.
Welcome to America. Osondu, E. C.
Welcome to Bordertown. Kushner, E. and
   Windling, T.
Welcome to Red Dust Lane. Qiu Xiaolong
Welcome wherever he went. McGarry, J.
The **well**. Loory, B.
Wellington, David
   Dead man's land
     Zombies: the recent dead; edited by Paula
     Guran.
Wells, H. G. (Herbert George)
   Aepyornis Island
     Wells, H. G. Complete short story omnibus
   Answer to prayer
     Wells, H. G. Complete short story omnibus
   The apple
     Wells, H. G. Complete short story omnibus
   The argonauts of the air
     Wells, H. G. Complete short story omnibus
   The beautiful suit
     Wells, H. G. Complete short story omnibus
   A catastrophe
     Wells, H. G. Complete short story omnibus
   The cone
     Wells, H. G. Complete short story omnibus
   The country of the blind
     Wells, H. G. Complete short story omnibus
   The country of the blind (revised version)
     Wells, H. G. Complete short story omnibus
   The crystal egg
     Wells, H. G. Complete short story omnibus

Wells, H. G. (Herbert George)—*Continued*

A deal in ostriches
   Wells, H. G. Complete short story omnibus
The devotee of art
   Wells, H. G. Complete short story omnibus
The diamond maker
   Wells, H. G. Complete short story omnibus
The door in the wall
   Wells, H. G. Complete short story omnibus
A dream of Armageddon
   Wells, H. G. Complete short story omnibus
The empire of the ants
   Wells, H. G. Complete short story omnibus
A family elopement
   Wells, H. G. Complete short story omnibus
Filmer
   Wells, H. G. Complete short story omnibus
The flowering of the strange orchid
   Wells, H. G. Complete short story omnibus
The flying man
   Wells, H. G. Complete short story omnibus
The grisly folk
   Wells, H. G. Complete short story omnibus
The Hammerpond Park burglary
   Wells, H. G. Complete short story omnibus
How Gabriel became Thompson
   Wells, H. G. Complete short story omnibus
How Pingwill was routed
   Wells, H. G. Complete short story omnibus
In the abyss
   Wells, H. G. Complete short story omnibus
In the Avu observatory
   Wells, H. G. Complete short story omnibus
In the modern vein: an unsympathetic love story
   Wells, H. G. Complete short story omnibus
The inexperienced ghost
   Wells, H. G. Complete short story omnibus
The jilting of Jane
   Wells, H. G. Complete short story omnibus
Jimmy Goggles the god
   Wells, H. G. Complete short story omnibus
The land ironclads
   Wells, H. G. Complete short story omnibus
Little mother up the Mörderberg
   Wells, H. G. Complete short story omnibus
The Lord of the Dynamos
   Wells, H. G. Complete short story omnibus
The lost inheritance
   Wells, H. G. Complete short story omnibus
The loyalty of Esau Common a fragment
   Wells, H. G. Complete short story omnibus
The magic shop
   Wells, H. G. Complete short story omnibus
The man who could work miracles
   Wells, H. G. Complete short story omnibus
The man with a nose
   Wells, H. G. Complete short story omnibus
Le mari terrible
   Wells, H. G. Complete short story omnibus
Miss Winchelsea's heart
   Wells, H. G. Complete short story omnibus
A misunderstood artist
   Wells, H. G. Complete short story omnibus
The moth
   Wells, H. G. Complete short story omnibus
Mr. Brisher's treasure
   Wells, H. G. Complete short story omnibus
Mr. Ledbetter's vacation
   Wells, H. G. Complete short story omnibus

Mr. Marshall's doppelganger
   Wells, H. G. Complete short story omnibus
Mr. Skelmersdale in Fairyland
   Wells, H. G. Complete short story omnibus
My first aeroplane
   Wells, H. G. Complete short story omnibus
The new accelerator
   Wells, H. G. Complete short story omnibus
Our little neighbour
   Wells, H. G. Complete short story omnibus
The pearl of love
   Wells, H. G. Complete short story omnibus
A perfect gentleman on wheels
   Wells, H. G. Complete short story omnibus
The plattner story
   Wells, H. G. Complete short story omnibus
Pollock and the Porroh man
   Wells, H. G. Complete short story omnibus
The presence by the fire
   Wells, H. G. Complete short story omnibus
The purple pileus
   Wells, H. G. Complete short story omnibus
The queer story of Brownlow's newspaper
   Wells, H. G. Complete short story omnibus
The Rajah's treasure
   Wells, H. G. Complete short story omnibus
The reconciliation
   Wells, H. G. Complete short story omnibus
The red room
   Wells, H. G. Complete short story omnibus
The remarkable case of Davidson's eyes
   Wells, H. G. Complete short story omnibus
The sad story of a dramatic critic
   Wells, H. G. Complete short story omnibus
The sea raiders
   The Big book of adventure stories; edited and
     with a introduction by Otto Penzler; fore-
     word by Douglas Preston.
   Wells, H. G. Complete short story omnibus
A slip under the microscope
   Wells, H. G. Complete short story omnibus
The star
   Wells, H. G. Complete short story omnibus
The stolen bacillus
   Wells, H. G. Complete short story omnibus
The stolen body
   Wells, H. G. Complete short story omnibus
A story of the days to come
   Wells, H. G. Complete short story omnibus
The story of the Last Trump
   Wells, H. G. Complete short story omnibus
The story of the late Mr. Elvesham
   Wells, H. G. Complete short story omnibus
A story of the stone age
   Wells, H. G. Complete short story omnibus
A tale of the twentieth century for advanced
   thinkers
   Wells, H. G. Complete short story omnibus
The temptation of Harringay
   Wells, H. G. Complete short story omnibus
The thing in no. 7
   Wells, H. G. Complete short story omnibus
Through a window
   Wells, H. G. Complete short story omnibus
The thumbmark
   Wells, H. G. Complete short story omnibus
The treasure in the forest
   Wells, H. G. Complete short story omnibus

Wells, H. G. (Herbert George)—*Continued*
The triumphs of a taxidermist
  Wells, H. G. Complete short story omnibus
The truth about Pyecraft
  Wells, H. G. Complete short story omnibus
Under the knife
  Wells, H. G. Complete short story omnibus
The valley of spiders
  Wells, H. G. Complete short story omnibus
A vision of judgment
  Wells, H. G. Complete short story omnibus
Walcote
  Wells, H. G. Complete short story omnibus
Wayde's essence
  Wells, H. G. Complete short story omnibus
The wild asses of the devil
  Wells, H. G. Complete short story omnibus
Wells, Herbert George *See* Wells, H. G. (Herbert
  George), 1866-1946
WELLS
Carlson, R. Escape from prison
Carpenter, S. S. Elk medicine
Loory, B. The well
Welsch, Gabriel
A Country of Shoes
  New Letters v77 no2 p11-28 2011
Groundscratchers
  The Southern Review (Baton Rouge, La.) v47
  no1 p65-81 Wint 2011
Welty, Eudora
Death of a traveling salesman
  Blue collar, white collar, no collar; stories of
  work; edited by Richard Ford.
WEREWOLVES
Anderson, P. Operation changeling
Beagle, P. S. La lune t' attend
Black, H. The Aarne-Thompson Classification
  Revue
Butcher, J. Something borrowed
Douglas, C. N. Monster mash
Elliott, J. The Wilds
Jones, S. G. Wolf Island
Langan, J. The revel
Martin, G. R. R. In the lost lands
Nolan, W. F. Wolf song
Saintcrow, L. Monsters
Shetterly, W. The sages of elsewhere
Simner, J. L. Crossings
Smith, C. A. Monsters in the night
Smith, C. A. Th enchantress of Sylaire
Vaughn, C. Il est ne
Vaughn, C. God's creatures
Vaughn, C. Kitty and the mosh pit of the
  damned
Vaughn, C. Kitty's zombie New Year
Vaughn, C. Long time waiting
Vaughn, C. Looking after family
Vaughn, C. Wild ride
Vaughn, C. Winnowing the herd
Vaughn, C. You're on the air
Werlin, Stan Lee
In the summer of the big bass, forever and ever
  Southern Humanities Review v45 no1 p67-82
  Wint 2011
WERWOLVES *See* Werewolves
WEST (U.S.) *See* Western States
WEST INDIES
  See also Trinidad and Tobago
WEST INDIES REGION *See* Caribbean region

WEST VIRGINIA
Bierce, A. The mocking-bird
Bierce, A. A tough tussle
Frost, G. Swift decline
McCrumb, S. Rattler and the Mothman
Mehta, R. Quarantine
Willis, M. S. Big boss is back
Willis, M. S. Pie Knob
Willis, M. S. Scandalous Roy Critchfield
Westerfeld, Scott
Non-disclosure agreement
  Sympathy for the devil; edited by Tim Pratt.
WESTERN STATES
Carlson, R. Escape from prison
Ehrenreich, B. Everything you see is real
Glass, J. The price of silver
Johnston, T. Two years
Kiernan, C. R. The Colliers' Venus (1893)
MacLeod, M. Horn hunter
Shepard, S. Five shorts
WESTERN STORIES
  See also Adventure; Cowboys; Ranch
  life; Western States
Jones, S. G. Lonegan's luck
Lansdale, J. R. The crawling sky
Lansdale, J. R. The dark down there
Lansdale, J. R. Deadman's road
Lansdale, J. R. The gentleman's hotel
McCulley, J. Zorro deals with treason
Mulford, C. E. Hopalong's hop
Stein, J. C. The ghost of Leadville
Westlake, Donald E.
Give till it hurts
  Christmas at the Mysterious Bookshop; 'tis
  the season to be deadly; stories of mistletoe
  and mayhem from 17 masters of suspense;
  edited by Otto Penzler.
Westland. Baxter, C.
Weston walks. Reed, K.
We've got a great future behind us. Black, A.
Whalen, Tom
My Father's Coat
  Agni no73 p105-13 2011
WHALES
Jones, S. G. Wolf Island
Wharton, Edith
The pomegranate seed
  21 essential American short stories; edited by
  Leslie M. Pockell
The Valley of Childish Things
  The vintage book of American women writ-
  ers; edited and with an introduction by
  Elaine Showalter.
What American is. Johnson, D.
What an old woman will wear. Davis, L.
What animal are you? Keret, E. and Shlesinger,
  M.
What becomes. Kennedy, A. L.
What do you do with your nights? Leland, C. T.
What every woman knows. Emshwiller, C.
What happened? Hemmingson, M.
What happens when my wife's ex-boyfriend, back
  from Iraq, pays us a visit. Hemmingson, M.
What happens when you wake up in the night.
  Smith, M. M.
What Have You Done? Marcus, B.
What I didn't see. Fowler, K. J.
What I feel. Davis, L.
What If. Heynen, J.

What is all this? Dixon, S.
What is it then, between us? Papernick, J.
What it came to. Leland, C. T.
What it was like, seeing Chris. Eisenberg, D.
What love is this? Nolan, W. F.
What Really Happened to PFC Quinos. Sizemore, V.
What Remains. Weaver, R.
What retired engineer Roger Mudge thinks upon his son Patrick's announcement of his engagement. Almond, S.
What Rises. Arnegard, I.
What Sara tells me. Rilly, E.
What separates us from the animals. Boyle, T. C.
What she knew. Davis, L.
What Some Other Guys Can Call The Byron Story: Miami, 1996. Crucet, J. C.
What the butler said. Marías, J.
What There Was. Campbell, B. J.
What tune the enchantress plays. Beagle, P. S.
What was interesting. Davis, L.
What Was There Long Ago. LIN-GREENBERG, K.
What we mean. Mehta, R.
What would Mary do: a Christmas story. Plummer, T. M.
What You Can Endure. Moustakis, M.
What you do out here, when you're alone. Meyer, P.
What you don't know. Novack, S.
What you don't know can hurt you. Lutz, J.
What you learn about the baby. Davis, L.
Whatever happened to Billy Brody? Roberge, R.
What's in a name? Clark, M. H.
What's the matter with Helga and Dave? Senna, D.
Wheat, Carolyn
    Love me for my yellow hair alone
        Randisi, R. J. The Shamus winners: America's best private eye stories, volume II, 1996-2009; collected and introduced by Robert J. Randisi; founder, Private Eye Writers of America
The wheel. Wyndham, J.
Wheeler, Theodore
    How to Die Young in a Nebraska Winter
        The Kenyon Review v33 no2 p70-82 Spr 2011
WHEELS
    Wyndham, J. The wheel
Wheels within wheels. Sapper
When death shines bright. Zeltserman, D.
When Gretchen was human. Turzillo, M. A.
When, he wondered. Barrett, L.
When I was conceived. Qiu Xiaolong
When in Rome. Ross, A.
When it's tough out there. Holm, G.
When President Nixon first visited China. Qiu Xiaolong
When Robin Hood fell with an arrow through his heart. Seabrook, T.
When the bough doesn't break. Hodge, B.
When the gods want to punish you. Blake, G.
When the great days come. Dozois, G. R.
When the immigrant is hot. Hopkins, T. I.
When the silence gets too loud. Hodge, B.
When the time came. Kaaberbol, L. and Friis, A.
When the train calls lonely. Monk, D.
When the zombies win. Sumner-Smith, K.
When we rise. Ray, S.

When we went to see the end of the world. Silverberg, R.
Where are all the naughty people? Hill, R.
Where are we now? Shepard, S.
Where Do You Go? Fitzgerald, S. F.
Where He Went Under. Spilman, R.
Where I Am Now. Day, R.
Where I keep my faith. Dunmore, H.
Where the black stars fall. Hodge, B.
Where the door is always open and the welcome mat is out. Highsmith, P.
Where there's a will. Archer, J.
Where there's a will. Matheson, R. and Matheson, R. C.
Where you'll find me. Beattie, A.
Wherever you go, there you are. Evans, D.
Which new era would that be? Gordimer, N.
Which one? Trouillot, E.
Which Rocks We Choose. Singleton, G.
While he sleeps. Villegas, H.
While mortals sleep. Vonnegut, K.
While the women are sleeping. Marías, J.
While waiting for the verdict. Sa'id, M. A.
Whirling dervish. Alenyikov, M.
Whisper Hill. Birdsall, J.
White, Eva Roa
    Back to Galicia [Part of a special issue: Roots and routes]
        DisClosure no17 p6-12 2008
White, Michael J.
    Fukuoka and the Way to Be Free
        Chicago Review v55 no3/4 p126-46 Aut 2010
White. Gilley, T.
White buffalo. Ruocco, J.
White Charles. Monette, S.
White dove. Emshwiller, C.
White fire. O'Connor, S.
White geranium. Rodoreda, M.
A white heron. Jewett, S. O.
White horses. Ruocco, J.
White night, black horse. Loomis, M.
White poppies. Zhang Kangkang
The white silence. London, J.
WHITE SOX (BASEBALL TEAM) *See* Chicago White Sox (Baseball team)
White trees in summer. Novack, S.
The white tribe. Davis, L.
The white vase. Timmermans, F.
Whitework. Bernheimer, K.
Whitfield, Raoul
    Murder in the ring
        The Black Lizard big book of Black Mask stories; edited and with a foreword by Otto Penzler; introduction by Keith Alan Deutsch.
Whittall, Zoe
    Check mate
        Can'tLit; fearless fiction from Broken pencil magazine; edited by Richard Rosenbaum.
WHITTLING *See* Wood carving
Who did what to whom? Alenyikov, M.
Who do I have to kill to get a little respect up in here? Murphy, B.
Who Gets the Dog? Specht, M. H.
Who he? Dixon, S.
Who Is Danny Pendergast? Nelson, K.
Who is that man? Lahens, Y.
Who stole my monkey? Corbett, D. and Urrea, L. A.

WHODUNITS *See* Mystery and detective stories

Whole family with young children devastated. Kennedy, A. L.

Why don't you use your parking space? Hemmingson, M.

Why haven't you written? Gordimer, N.

Why I was hanged. Wolfe, G.

Why the World Is Not my Oyster. Braun, R.

Wichita, Kansas (Highway 35 North). Shepard, S.

Wicked be. Graham, H.

Wickersham, Joan
The Boys' School, *or* The News from Spain
Agni no72 p20-36 2010

The **wide,** carnivorous sky. Langan, J.

Wideman, John Edgar
Always raining somewhere, said Jim Johnson
Harper's v322 no1929 p65-8 F 2011
Microstories
The Pen/O.Henry Prize stories, 2010; edited and with an introduction by Laura Furman; with essays on the stories they admire most by jurors Junot Diaz, Paula Fox, Yiyun Li.

Widow. Latiolais, M.

WIDOWERS
Abbas, G. The room with the blue light
Aiken, J. Hair
Barnes, J. Marriage lines
Beattie, A. Coping stones
Berry, W. Stand by me
Bill, F. The penance of Scoot McCutchen
Byrd, B. The dead man's wife
Cardinale, J. May I not seem to have lived
Carroll, J. Vedran
Châteaureynaud, G. O. A life on paper
Danticat, E. Claire of the sea light
Dixon, S. In memoriam
Ely, S. Lovers of hurricanes
Gorman, E. Flying solo
Hamilton, H. The supremacy of grief
Matheson, R. Red is the color of desire
McCracken, E. Property
Neugeboren, J. The debt
Nolan, W. F. Descent
Novack, S. White trees in summer
Papernick, J. The last five-year plan
Priest, C. Addison Howell and the clockroach
Rash, R. Into the gorge
Skurnick, L. Spectacle Pond
Trevor, W. Against the odds
Trevor, W. The children
Trevor, W. Graillis's legacy
Trueblood, V. Beloved, you looked into space
Tuten, F. The park near Marienbad
Vila-Matas, E. Far from here
Wells, H. G. The presence by the fire
Willis, D. And the living is easy
Willis, D. Escape
Wolff, T. Her dog
Yiyun Li. Alone

WIDOWS
Abu Lail, S. My neighbor is a whore!
Adichie, C. N. The headstrong historian
Allen, D. Goat on a hill
Beattie, A. Find and replace
Binkley, P. Keepsakes
Black, A. Someday is today
Cameron, D. Ardent
Chopin, K. The story of an hour
Drabble, M. The merry widow

Fallon, S. Gold star
Furman, L. The mother who stayed
Furman, L. A thousand words
Hughes, M.-B. Double happiness
Ibrāhīm, H. A holy site
Kennedy, A. L. Another
Latiolais, M. Caduceus
Latiolais, M. Damned spot
Latiolais, M. Hoarding
Latiolais, M. Place
Latiolais, M. Widow
Lindholm, M. Finis
Lychack, W. The architect of flowers
Lychack, W. To the farm
Manilla, M. Amnesty
Marías, J. A kind of nostalgia perhaps
Matheson, R. The house of the dead
Mihas, P. This is not a barren place
Mphahlele, E. Crossing over
Mullen, C. Poetic justice
Mullins, D. P. A familiar place
Neugeboren, J. The debt
Neugeboren, J. Make-a-wish
Neugeboren, J. The Turetzky Trio
Oates, J. C. Probate
Oates, J. C. Pumpkin-head
Oates, J. C. Sourland
O'Connor, S. Aunt Jules
Osondu, E. C. Janjaweed wife
Rodoreda, M. The fate of Lisa Sperling
Sterling, P. Empty nest
Terry, G. P. Barbara Hutton Toujours
Thompson, J. Pie of the month
Tóibín, C. Two women
Treadway, J. Please come back to me
Trevor, W. At Olivehill
Trevor, W. Sitting with the dead
Trevor, W. Widows
Trueblood, V. Suitors
Vonnegut, K. Out, brief candle
Vonnegut, K. Ruth
Willis, M. S. Big boss is back
Willis, M. S. Scandalous Roy Critchfield

Widows. Trevor, W.

Wiecek, Mike
A death in Ueno
Randisi, R. J. The Shamus winners: America's best private eye stories, volume II, 1996-2009; collected and introduced by Robert J. Randisi; founder, Private Eye Writers of America
The shipbreaker
The Best American mystery stories 2010; edited and with an introduction by Lee Child; Otto Penzler, series editor

Wieland, Liza
At Wanship
Wieland, L. Quickening; stories
Body and engine
Wieland, L. Quickening; stories
The Columbus School for Girls
The Georgia Review v65 no1 p264-75 Spr 2011
La fenêtre
Wieland, L. Quickening; stories
First, marriage
Wieland, L. Quickening; stories
The girl with radium eyes
Wieland, L. Quickening; stories

Wieland, Liza—*Continued*
Out of the garden
　Wieland, L. Quickening; stories
Pound in Venice
　Wieland, L. Quickening; stories
Quickening
　Wieland, L. Quickening; stories
Resolution Trust
　Wieland, L. Quickening; stories
Slip, out, back, here
　Wieland, L. Quickening; stories
Some churches
　Wieland, L. Quickening; stories
Vision
　Wieland, L. Quickening; stories
Wieland, Mitch
The bones of hagerman
　Best of the West 2009; new stories from the
　wide side of the Missouri; edited by James
　Thomas and D. Seth Horton; foreword by
　Rick Bass.
Wier, George
Duckweed
　Lone Star noir; edited by Bobby Byrd &
　Johnny Byrd.
WIFE ABUSE
Ayau, K. J. Spawning
Bill, F. The old mechanic
Cameron, D. Femme sole
Gorman, E. That day at Eagle's Point
Grove, L. L. Three seasons
Kennedy, A. L. Marriage
Kennedy, A. L. Saturday teatime
Simmons, D. Roll
WIFE AND HUSBAND *See* Husband and wife
WIFE BEATING *See* Wife abuse
Wife Leaves Left. Buckbee, B.
A **wife** manufactured to order. Fuller, A. W.
The **Wife** of R. Kilito, A.
Wife one in country. Davis, L.
WIFE SWAPPING *See* Marriage problems
The **wife** you wanted. Manilla, M.
Wight, James Alfred *See* Herriot, James
Wilbur, Eileen
Depression
　Harvard Review (1992) no39 p58-9 2010
Wilbur, Ellen
Fifteen
　The Yale Review v98 no4 p127-33 O 2010
Listening and Speaking
　The Georgia Review v64 no3 p536-43 Fall
　2010
The Sinner
　Ploughshares v37 no2/3 p187-192 Fall 2011
Wild About Harry. Epstein, J.
The **wild** asses of the devil. Wells, H. G.
Wild berry blue. Galchen, R.
The **wild** bird reserve. Dixon, S.
Wild Card. Unger, L.
WILD CHILDREN
Fowler, K. J. The dark
Freed, L. Sunshine
Wild copper. Henderson, S.
The **Wild** Gal from Ohio. Ringelnatz, J.
Wild ride. Vaughn, C.
Wild winter love. Yezierska, A.
The **Wilderness**. Ducker, M.
WILDERNESS AREAS
Shepard, S. Wisconsin wilderness

WILDERNESS SURVIVAL
Jones, S. G. Father, son, holy rabbit
The **wildlife** biologist. Somerville, P.
The **Wilds**. Elliott, J.
Wildt, Jan
Like riding a bike
　Sympathy for the devil; edited by Tim Pratt.
**WILE E. COYOTE (CARTOON CHARAC-
　TER)**
Frazier, I. Coyote v. Acme
Wilhelm, Kate
Baby, you were great
　Future media; [edited by Rick Wilber]
The funeral
　Brave new worlds; edited by John Joseph Ad-
　ams.
Wilkins, Mary Eleanor, 1852-1930 *See* Freeman,
　Mary Eleanor Wilkins, 1852-1930
Willard, Christopher
Little wite squirrel angel
　Can'tLit; fearless fiction from Broken pencil
　magazine; edited by Richard Rosenbaum.
Willey, Brenden
Far Woods
　The Antioch Review v69 no1 p140-50 Wint
　2011
Willi. Doctorow, E. L.
**WILLIAM, PRINCE OF GREAT BRITAIN,
　1982-**
About
July, M. Majesty
William Allan Wilson. Breen, J. L.
William Wei. Barrodale, A.
Williams, Conrad
Outfangthief
　Vampires; the recent undead; edited by Paula
　Guran.
Williams, Liz
Shift
　Nature v472 no7341 p130 Ap 7 2011
Williams, Sean
The Jade Woman of the Luminous Star
　Ghosts by gaslight; stories of steampunk and
　supernatural suspense; [edited by] Jack
　Dann [and] Nick Gevers
Williams, Tad
And ministers of grace
　The Year's best science fiction: twenty-eighth
　annual collection; edited by Gardner
　Dozois.
A short history of Dunkelblau's Meistergarten
　The Thackery T. Lambshead cabinet of curi-
　osities; edited by Ann & Jeff VanderMeer.
Williams, Arizona (Highway 40 West). Shepard,
　S.
Williamson, Eric Miles
The Cow Island Open
　Williamson, E. M. 14 fictional positions;
　short fictions
Creusa
　Williamson, E. M. 14 fictional positions;
　short fictions
Hangman
　Williamson, E. M. 14 fictional positions;
　short fictions
Hope, among other vices and virtues
　Williamson, E. M. 14 fictional positions;
　short fictions

Williamson, Eric Miles—*Continued*

Kickshaws

Williamson, E. M. 14 fictional positions; short fictions

Mr. Murphy's wedding

Williamson, E. M. 14 fictional positions; short fictions

Phrases and philosophies for the use of the young

Williamson, E. M. 14 fictional positions; short fictions

The professor asks his students if they agree with the conclusion: the table is an imitation and therefore not real

Williamson, E. M. 14 fictional positions; short fictions

Rhoda's sack

Williamson, E. M. 14 fictional positions; short fictions

Skaters

Williamson, E. M. 14 fictional positions; ·short fictions

The teaching of Don B.

Williamson, E. M. 14 fictional positions; short fictions

Third person on a bed built for five

Williamson, E. M. 14 fictional positions; short fictions

Wamsutter in Dali vision

Williamson, E. M. 14 fictional positions; short fictions

A wise man is known by his laughter

Williamson, E. M. 14 fictional positions; short fictions

Williamson, Matt

Sacrament

Brave new worlds; edited by John Joseph Adams.

Willis, Deborah

And the living is easy

Willis, D. Vanishing and other stories

Caught

Willis, D. Vanishing and other stories

Escape

Willis, D. Vanishing and other stories

The fiancée

Willis, D. Vanishing and other stories

Frank

Willis, D. Vanishing and other stories

Hard currency

The Walrus v7 no10 p50-7, 59-60 D 2010

Rely

Willis, D. Vanishing and other stories

Remember, relive

Willis, D. Vanishing and other stories

Romance languages

Willis, D. Vanishing and other stories

The separation

Willis, D. Vanishing and other stories

Sky theatre

Willis, D. Vanishing and other stories

This other us

Willis, D. Vanishing and other stories

Traces

Willis, D. Vanishing and other stories

Vanishing

Willis, D. Vanishing and other stories

The weather

Willis, D. Vanishing and other stories

Willis, Meredith Sue

Big boss is back

Willis, M. S. Out of the mountains; Appalachian stories

Elvissa and the rabbi

Willis, M. S. Out of the mountains; Appalachian stories

Evenings with Dotson

Willis, M. S. Out of the mountains; Appalachian stories

Fellowship of kindred minds

Willis, M. S. Out of the mountains; Appalachian stories

The little harlots

Willis, M. S. Out of the mountains; Appalachian stories

Nineteen sixty-nine

Willis, M. S. Out of the mountains; Appalachian stories

On the road with C. T. Savage

Willis, M. S. Out of the mountains; Appalachian stories

Pie Knob

Willis, M. S. Out of the mountains; Appalachian stories

Scandalous Roy Critchfield

Willis, M. S. Out of the mountains; Appalachian stories

Speak well of the dead

Willis, M. S. Out of the mountains; Appalachian stories

Tara White

Willis, M. S. Out of the mountains; Appalachian stories

Triangulation

Willis, M. S. Out of the mountains; Appalachian stories

Willows village. Gilb, D.

WILLS

Archer, J. Where there's a will

Bierce, A. The famous Gilson bequest

Ely, S. Rocks

Nevins, F. M., Jr. A nightcap of hemlock

Nevins, F. M., Jr. The skull of the stuttering gunfighter

Powers, T. A journey of only two paces

Wells, H. G. The lost inheritance

Wilson, Adam

The Porchies

Promised lands; new Jewish American fiction on longing and belonging; edited by Derek Rubin.

Wilson, Jonathan

The liars

Promised lands; new Jewish American fiction on longing and belonging; edited by Derek Rubin.

Wilson, Laura

Precious things

Original sins; a Crime Writer's Association anthology; edited by Martin Edwards.

Wilson, Marion Jackel

Hospice on ice

Nursing v41 no1 p45 Ja 2011

Wimmer, Natasha

(tr.) See Bolaño, Roberto

Winchell, Prentice
Ten carats of lead
The Black Lizard big book of Black Mask stories; edited and with a foreword by Otto Penzler; introduction by Keith Alan Deutsch.

Wind, Herbert Warren
Harry Sprague meets the masters
Golf stories; edited by Charles McGrath.
The **wind**. Bradbury, R.

Windeye. Evenson, B.

Windling, Terri
(jt. auth) See Kushner, Ellen and Windling, Terri

WINDMILLS
Alexie, S. Green world

Window. Eisenberg, D.
The **window**. Kitterman, B.

WINDOWS
O'Brien, E. Sinners

Windows. Marãr, M.

WINDS
Bradbury, R. The wind
Couch, S. The dandelion clock
MacLeod, I. The master Miller's tale
The **winds** of Brennan Marcher. Hendee, B.

The **Windsor** cemetery diary. Mu Xin

Wing, Chrystal
Ariadne Sees Dr. Frank
Calyx v26 no3 p98-107 Summ 2011

Wingfield, Andrew
Air Space
Prairie Schooner v84 no3 p158-84 Fall 2010

The **wings** of Kali. Page, N. W.
The **wings** of Meister Wilhelm. Goss, T.
The **winner**. Baxter, C.

Winnowing the herd. Vaughn, C.

Winslow, Don
After thirty
San Diego noir; edited by Maryelizabeth Hart.
Poe, Jo, and I
On a raven's wing; new tales in honor of Edgar Allan Poe; edited by Stuart M. Kaminsky

Winter, Kathleen
Madame Poirer's Dog
The Walrus v8 no6 p58-60 Jl 2011

Winter. Villegas, H.

Winter, 1979. Chuculate, E. D.

Winter dreams. Fitzgerald, F. S.

Winter journey. Baxter, C.

Winter solstice. Resnick, M.

Winter term. Bingham, S.

Winterson, Jeanette
All I know about Gertrude Stein
Granta no115 p255-65 Spr 2011

Wipe your tears away, oh pine trees!. Burbara, R.

The **wire** book. Ajvaz, M.

A **wireless** message. Bierce, A.

WISCONSIN
Shepard, S. Wisconsin wilderness
Milwaukee
Gault, W. C. The bloody Bokhara

Wisconsin wilderness. Shepard, S.

A **wise** man is known by his laughter. Williamson, E. M.

WISHES
Ackert, D. and Rosenbaum, B. The king of the djinn

Jacobs, W. W. The monkey's paw
Nolan, W. F. To be with Amy
Stevenson, R. L. The bottle imp
Vukcevich, R. The next best thing

The **wishing** time. Monk, D.

Wishing Well. Nesset, K.

Wisniewski, Mark
Zoom
The Antioch Review v69 no3 p449-458 Summ 2011

WIT *See* Humor

WITCHCRAFT
See also Demoniac possession; Exorcism; Voodooism
Beagle, P. S. El regalo
Châteaureynaud, G. O. The beautiful coalwoman
Finlay, C. C. Life so dear or peace so sweet
Graham, H. Wicked be
Hawthorne, N. Young Goodman Brown
Niven, L. Not long before the end
Pratt, T. A. Mommy issues of the dead
Rickert, M. The Christmas witch
Riley, R. Undying love
Rodoreda, M. The salamander
Smith, C. A. Mother of toads
Smith, C. A. Necromancy in Naat
Smith, C. A. Th enchantress of Sylaire
Smith, C. A. The witchcraft of Ulua
Terry, G. P. There's always a monkey
Valente, C. M. A delicate architecture
Wells, H. G. Pollock and the Porroh man

The **witchcraft** of Ulua. Smith, C. A.

WITCHES *See* Witchcraft

With acknowledgements to Sun Tzu. Hodge, B.

With his hand on the throttle. Vonnegut, K.

. . . **With** [ord crossed out] by good intentions. Richerson, C.

A **withered** branch. Petrushevskaya, L. and Summers, A.

Within an inch of the burnished knob. Sterling, P.

Witness to the fall. Lake, J.

WITNESSES
Bunker, E. Death of a rat

Witte, Francine
Husband weight
River Styx no85 p87 2011

The **wives**. Phillips, H.

WIZARD OF OZ (MOTION PICTURE)
Gottlieb, D. Somewhere, over

The **wizard** of West Orange. Millhauser, S.

WIZARDS *See* Magicians

Wizard's apprentice. Sherman, D.

The **wizards** of Perfil. Link, K.

Wodehouse, P. G. (Pelham Grenville)
The mixer
The salvation of George Mackintosh
Golf stories; edited by Charles McGrath.

WODEHOUSE, P. G. (PELHAM GRENVILLE), 1881-1975
Parodies, imitations, etc.
Cannon, P. Cats, rats, and Bertie Wooster
Cannon, P. The rummy affair of young Charlie
Cannon, P. Something foetid

Wodehouse, Pelham Grenville *See* Wodehouse, P. G. (Pelham Grenville), 1881-1975

Woe to live on. Woodrell, D.

Woestijne, Karel van de
The saint of number
The Dedalus book of Flemish fantasy; edited by Eric Dickens and translated by Paul Vincent.
Wolf. duBois, J.
The **wolf**. Levine, S.
Wolf dreams. Beattie, A.
Wolf Island. Jones, S. G.
Wolf river. Hunter, L.
Wolf song. Nolan, W. F.
Wolfe, Gene
Why I was hanged
Ghosts by gaslight; stories of steampunk and supernatural suspense; [edited by] Jack Dann [and] Nick Gevers
Wolff, Tobias
The deposition
Blue collar, white collar, no collar; stories of work; edited by Richard Ford.
Her dog
Hunters in the snow
I found this funny; my favorite pieces of humor and some that may not be funny at all; edited by Judd Apatow.
Smorgasbord
Best of times, worst of times; contemporary American short stories from the new Gilded Age; edited by Wendy Martin and Cecelia Tichi.
Wolven, Scott
News about yourself
Blood, guts, & whiskey; edited by Todd Robinson; introduction by Max Allan Collins.
WOLVES
Rickert, M. Don't ask
Vaughan, E. A. A rose by any other name would still be red
Wolves. Ruocco, J.
Wolves of the Atlantic. Diome, F.
Womack, Craig
Sappho's round dance
Womack, C. Art as performance, story as criticism; reflections on native literary aesthetics
The song of Roe Náld
Womack, C. Art as performance, story as criticism; reflections on native literary aesthetics
Uncle Jimmy's personal emissary
Womack, C. Art as performance, story as criticism; reflections on native literary aesthetics
A **woman**. Dammaj, Z. M.
The **Woman** Across the Table. Schirmer, R.
The **woman** and the basement. Loory, B.
The **Woman** at the Grave. Sanders, S. R.
The **Woman** at the Pond. Rash, R.
Woman in love. Household, G.
The **woman** in the pillows [excerpt]. Kronauer, B.
The **woman** of the house. Trevor, W.
Woman waiting. Emshwiller, C.
The **woman** who fell in love with a meteorologist and stopped the rain. Hall, T. M.
The **woman** who loved Claude Rains. Leland, C. T.
The **woman** who married the man in the moon. Beagle, P. S.
The **woman** with the bouquet. Schmitt, E.-E.

WOMEN
See also African American women; Jewish women; Muslim women; Single women
Beattie, A. The women of this world
Bernheimer, K. Whitework
Bierce, A. Killed at Resaca
Dammaj, Z. M. A woman
Davis, L. Helen and Vi: a study in health and vitality
Davis, L. Thyroid diary
Davis, L. What an old woman will wear
Doctorow, E. L. Jolene: a life
Drabble, M. Homework
Dunmore, H. Where I keep my faith
Emshwiller, C. Abominable
Emshwiller, C. After shock
Emshwiller, C. Draculalucard
Emshwiller, C. Maybe another long march across China 80,000 strong
Emshwiller, C. Methapyrilene hydrochloride sometimes helps
Fried, G. Summer
Grace, P. Busy lines
Hall, T. M. This is a love story, too
Humphries, C. The Jane Austen hen weekend
Kennedy, A. L. Story of my life
Krinard, S. Mist
Kronauer, B. The diva and her tricks
Kronauer, B. Rita Münster [excerpt]
Kronauer, B. The woman in the pillows [excerpt]
Lahens, Y. Moon bathing
Lahens, Y. Soursop, orange, and lemongrass
Latiolais, M. Breathe
Latiolais, M. Involution
Levine, S. The cat
Levine, S. Tippy flowery
Manilla, M. Childproof
Manilla, M. Counting backwards
Mu Xin. Fong Fong no. 4
Osondu, E. C. The men they married
Phillips, H. The Helens
Rodoreda, M. Paralysis
Ruocco, J. Swans
Schmitt, E.-E. The woman with the bouquet
Solzhenitsyn, A. Nastenka
Stefan, V. Doe a deer
Terry, G. P. The line
Tillman, L. The original impulse
Trueblood, V. Tom Thumb wedding
Vint, T. Beyond the window a park is dimming
Yamauchi, W. Annie Hall, Annie Hall
Yamauchi, W. Dogs I owe to
Yamauchi, W. McNisei
Yamauchi, W. Onna
Employment
Drabble, M. A day in the life of a smiling woman
Psychology
Barrett, N., Jr. Getting dark
Baxter, C. Ghosts
Beattie, A. Like glass
Bingham, S. Heaven
Carpenter, S. S. Elk medicine
Davis, L. What you learn about the baby
Drabble, M. A day in the life of a smiling woman
Drabble, M. A Pyrrhic victory
Drabble, M. A success story

Woodrell, Daniel—*Continued*
Dream spot
Woodrell, D. The outlaw album; stories
The echo of neighborly bones
Woodrell, D. The outlaw album; stories
Florianne
Woodrell, D. The outlaw album; stories
The horse in our history
Woodrell, D. The outlaw album; stories
Night stand
Woodrell, D. The outlaw album; stories
One united
Woodrell, D. The outlaw album; stories
Returning the river
Woodrell, D. The outlaw album; stories
Twin Forks
Woodrell, D. The outlaw album; stories
Esquire v155 no4 p134-6, 137, 140 Ap 2011
Two things
Woodrell, D. The outlaw album; stories
Uncle
Woodrell, D. The outlaw album; stories
Woe to live on
Woodrell, D. The outlaw album; stories
Woodrow, Wilson's necktie. Highsmith, P.
A **woods** encounter. Nolan, W. F.
The **Woodward** Plan. Estleman, L. D.
Woolford, Linda
The Space Between
Calyx v26 no2 p104-17 Wint 2011
Woollcott, Alexander
Moonlight sonata
The Big book of adventure stories; edited and
with a introduction by Otto Penzler; fore-
word by Douglas Preston.
Woolrich, Cornell
Black cargo
The Big book of adventure stories; edited and
with a introduction by Otto Penzler; fore-
word by Douglas Preston.
Borrowed crime
The Black Lizard big book of Black Mask
stories; edited and with a foreword by Otto
Penzler; introduction by Keith Alan
Deutsch.
Woolson, Constance Fenimore
Miss Grief
The vintage book of American women writ-
ers; edited and with an introduction by
Elaine Showalter.
The **word** of unbinding. Le Guin, U. K.
Words matter. Blatnik, A.
WORK
Bravo, É. Best American comic by a French art-
ist
Bukowski, C. A day
Keith, E. My lips are sealed
Kyle, A. Economics
A **Work** of Fiction. Bloom, S.
Working backward from the worst moment of my
life. Roberge, R.
The **working** girl. Beattie, A.
Workingmen. Davis, L.
World at war. Goodberg, D.
The **World** Began with Charlie Chan. Busch, F.
World Champion Cow of the Insane. Horrocks, C.
The **world** of apples. Cheever, J.
The **world** of Barry. Levine, S.
The **world,** the words, this man. Downey, R.

WORLD WAR, 1914-1918
United States
Jaber, R. From the novel America
WORLD WAR, 1939-1945
Châteaureynaud, G. O. The gulf of the years
Gordimer, N. The diamond mine
Turtledove, H. News from the front
Atrocities
See also Holocaust, Jewish (1933-1945)
Casualties
Berry, W. Stand by me
Jews
See also Holocaust, Jewish (1933-1945)
Naval operations
Bradbury, R. Undersea guardians
Prisoners and prisons
See also Concentration camps
Leonard, E. Comfort to the enemy
England
Pearlman, E. If love were all
Germany
Hodge, B. And they will come in the hour of
our greatest need
New Guinea
Shepard, J. Happy with crocodiles
Russia
Grossman, V. S. In Kislavodsk
Grossman, V. S. The road
Solzhenitsyn, A. Adlig Schwenkitten
Solzhenitsyn, A. Times of crisis
Solzhenitsyn, A. Zhelyabuga village
Solomon Islands
Black, M. A. The golden bug
United States
Leonard, E. Comfort to the enemy
Love, Y. G. Lonely, lonely, lonely is the Lord
of Hosts
Pearlman, E. The noncombatant
World Wire Web. Jones, G. D.
The **Worm** in Philly. Lipsyte, S.
The **worst** of us. Gordon, S.
Worth more dead. Boland, J. C.
Worts, George Frank
The master magician
The Big book of adventure stories; edited and
with a introduction by Otto Penzler; fore-
word by Douglas Preston.
The python pit
The Big book of adventure stories; edited and
with a introduction by Otto Penzler; fore-
word by Douglas Preston.
The **would-be** father. Baxter, C.
Wounded Knee, Pine Ridge Reservation. Shepard,
S.
WOUNDED MAN (MOTION PICTURE) *See*
Homme blessé (Motion picture)
The **wounded** man. Taia, A.
WOUNDS AND INJURIES
Roberge, R. Love and hope and sex and dreams
Wren, P. C. (Percival Christopher)
A gentleman of color
The Big book of adventure stories; edited and
with a introduction by Otto Penzler; fore-
word by Douglas Preston.
Wren, Percival Christopher *See* Wren, P. C.
(Percival Christopher), 1885-1941
The **wrestler** and the spear fisher. Schoen, L. M.
Wretchedness. Zobal, S. D.

YEMEN
   Al Ahdal, W. A crime in Mataeem Street
Yes and no. Hardwick, E.
Yes man. Anders, C.
Yes, Virginia. Emshwiller, C.
Yesterday. Todd, C.
Yesterday man. Ahmad, O.
Yezbek, Samar
   From the novel The scent of cinnamon
      Beirut 39; new writing from the Arab world;
      edited by Samuel Shimon; with a preface
      by Hanan al-Shaykh
Yezierska, Anzia
   Wild winter love
      The vintage book of American women writ-
      ers; edited and with an introduction by
      Elaine Showalter.
Yi-Yang-ji
   Koku
      Into the light; an anthology of literature by
      Koreans in Japan; edited by Melissa L.
      Wender.
Yiyun Li
   Alone
      Best of the West 2011; new stories from the
      wild side of the Missouri; edited by James
      Thomas and D. Seth Horton; foreword by
      Ana Castillo.
   The science of flight
      20 under 40; stories from the New Yorker;
      edited by Deborah Treisman.
Yo-yo. Dixon, S.
YOGURT
   Apple, M. Business talk
Yolen, Jane and Stemple, Adam
   The tsar's dragon
      People of the book; a decade of Jewish sci-
      ence fiction & fantasy; edited by Rachel
      Swirsky & Sean Wallace.
YOM KIPPUR
   Bernheimer, K. A cuckoo tale
   Pearlman, E. Day of awe
YORKSHIRE (ENGLAND) *See* England—York-
   shire
Yoshimoto, Banana
   A special boy
      Freedom; stories celebrating the Universal
      Declaration of Human Rights; Amnesty In-
      ternational.
Yost, David
   Mautam
      The Massachusetts Review v51 no4 p738-9
      Wint 2010
   Saw Kler and Naw Kler: A Fairy Tale
      The Southern Review (Baton Rouge, La.) v47
      no3 p427-9 Summ 2011
You. Ryman, G.
You are free. Senna, D.
You are my heart. Neugeboren, J.
You Are the Heirs of All My Terrors. Menéndez,
   A.
You can call and ask a question. Hemmingson, M.
You Can Do This in a Sentence. Browne, L.
You don't need a place to sleep if you don't plan
   on sleeping; or, 5 shorts. Yeh, J.
You have never been here. Rickert, M.
You know when the men are gone. Fallon, S.
You Look Like Jesus. Quatro, J.

You survived the war, now survive the homecom-
   ing. Fallon, S.
You will not believe what happens to me, but
   does it matter? it only matters that I know
   what happens. Hemmingson, M.
You'll feel better... Emshwiller, C.
You'll never walk alone. Nicholson, S.
Youmans, Marly
   The grave reflection
      Ghosts by gaslight; stories of steampunk and
      supernatural suspense; [edited by] Jack
      Dann [and] Nick Gevers
   The salamander fire
      The beastly bride; tales of the animal people;
      edited by Ellen Datlow & Terri Windling;
      introduction by Terri Windling; selected
      decorations by Charles Vess.
Young, G. C.
   After Office
      New Letters v76 no3 p51-60 2010
Young, Jeff
   Written in light
      L. Ron Hubbard presents Writers of the Fu-
      ture volume XXVI; the year's twelve best
      tales from the Writers of the Future inter-
      national writers' program; illustrated by
      winners in the Illustrators of the Future in-
      ternational illustrators' program; with es-
      says on writing & illustration by L. Ron
      Hubbard/Dean Wesley Smith/ Stephen
      Youll; edited by K. D. Wentworth
Young, Mike
   The age of the tire boat
      Butler, B. 30 under 30; an anthology of inno-
      vative fiction by younger writers; Blake
      Butler & Lily Hoang, eds.
Young, Ronder Thomas
   Exit 19-A
      The Georgia Review v65 no1 p276-87 Spr
      2011
Young and poor. Davis, L.
Young Goodman Brown. Hawthorne, N.
The **young** man who read brilliant books. Dixon,
   S.
The **young** painters. Krauss, N.
Young Thing. Farah, N.
The **young** wife's tale. Bynum, S. S.-L.
A **young** woman and an old woman. Grossman, V.
   S.
Youngest daughter. Boggs, B.
Your brother, who loves you. Zervanos, J.
Your Children and Mine. McCoy, M.
Your fate hurtles down at you. Shepard, J.
Your life, fifteen minutes from now. Mamatas, N.
Your love is soreness. Muwasi, E.
Your mother and I. Eggers, D.
Your recent acquisitions in the neonesque
   (microfables). Kiraly, A.
You're gonna get yours. Allan, S.
You're on the air. Vaughn, C.
You're so different. Sneed, C.
Yours. Mehta, R.
YOUTH
      See also Adolescence; Boys; Girls; Stu-
      dents
   Allen, D. Deferment
   Benvie, R. Into collapses
   Bingham, S. The banks of the Ohio
   Franco, J. Camp

Zhelyabuga village. Solzhenitsyn, A.

Zhima. Zhang Kangkang

ZHUKOV, GEORGIĬ KONSTANTINOVICH, 1896-1974

About

Solzhenitsyn, A. Times of crisis

Zig Zag Lane. Grimes, S.

Ziggurat. O'Connor, S.

ZIMBABWE

Gappah, P. An incident at lunchtime

Zimmer, Paul

Brief Lives

Gettysburg Review v23 no3 p377-87 Aut 2010

Zimmerman, Joanne

Carolyn Came to Visit

The North American Review v295 no3 p9-14 Summ 2010

Zimmerman, Ryan

Blood and dirt

The Best American mystery stories 2010; edited and with an introduction by Lee Child; Otto Penzler, series editor

Zitkala-Sa

A warrior's daughter

The vintage book of American women writers; edited and with an introduction by Elaine Showalter.

Zlatka. Hrgovic, M.

Zobal, Silas Dent

Wretchedness

The North American Review v295 no3 p15-20 Summ 2010

Zoboi, Ibi Aanu

The harem

Haiti noir; edited by Edwidge Danticat

Zolaria. Horrocks, C.

The **zombie** prince. Reed, K.

ZOMBIES

Atkins, M. Seven brains, ten minutes

Block, F. L. Farewell, my zombie

Block, F. L. Revenants anonymous

Braunbeck, G. A. Glorietta

Brooks, M. The Great Wall: a story from the zombie war

Brown, S. The magician's apprentice

Buckell, T. S. Trinkets

Burke, T. The hollow man

Coldwell, E. Everyone I love is dead

Cross, S. M. Through death to love

Duffy, S. Lie, still, sleep becalmed

Duncan, A. Zora and the zombie

Edelman, S. The human race

Edelman, S. The last supper

Fredsti, D. First date

Gaiman, N. Bitter grounds

Graham, S. Eye of the beholder

Gresh, L. H. Julia Brainchild

Hart, R. G. My partner the zombie

Hoffman, N. K. The third dead boy

Howard, J. L. The Ereshkigal working

Hutter, G. W. Salt is not for slaves

Jones, S. G. Lonegan's luck

Keene, B. Captive hearts

Keene, B. Selected scenes from the end of the world: three stories from the universe of The rising

Kilpatrick, K. Last times at Ridgemont High

Kim, A. S. Beautiful white bodies

Kirtley, D. B. The skull-faced boy

Kozlowski, J. First love never dies

Lebbon, T. Naming of parts

Link, K. The hortlak

Loomis, M. White night, black horse

Maberry, J. Family business

McAdam, J. Inhuman resources

McHugh, M. The naturalist

McMahon, G. Dead to the world

McQueen, G. Apolcalypse as foreplay

Monk, D. That Saturday

Morgan, C. The barrow maid

Nicholson, S. You'll never walk alone

Partridge, N. Lesser demons

Prill, D. Dating secrets of the dead

Reed, K. The zombie prince

Reed, R. Dead man's run

Riley, R. Undying love

Roche, T. S. Deepwater miracle

Roman, I. Zombified

Saare, J. I heart brains

Saus, S. Kicking the habit

Schoe, D. J. Obsequy

Schweitzer, D. The dead kid

Shipp, J. C. Agape walrus

Smith, M. M. Later

Smith, M. M. The things he said

Sumner-Smith, K. When the zombies win

Valente, C. M. The days of flaming motorcycles

Vaughn, C. Kitty's zombie New Year

Vaughn, V. Some new blood

Veale, K. Twisted

Waggoner, T. Disarmed and dangerous

Wagner, J. Romance ain't dead

ZOMBIES (MUSICAL GROUP)

Riippi, J. Something about the Zombies

Zombified. Roman, I.

Zookeeper. Nutting, A.

ZOOLOGICAL GARDENS *See* Zoos

Zoom. Wisniewski, M.

ZOOS

Baxter, C. Westland

Horrocks, C. At the zoo

Kronauer, B. Oh if you knew how the fishes do

Kronauer, B. The woman in the pillows [excerpt]

Matheson, R. Purge among peanuts

Pronzini, B. Cat's-paw

Vaughn, C. The temptation of Robin Green

Zora and the zombie. Duncan, A.

Zorro deals with treason. McCulley, J.

Zothique mi amor. Rich, M.

Zouhira. Isaacs, H.

Zucker, Gina

Big people

Fantastic women; 18 tales of the surreal and the sublime from Tin House; introduction by Joy Williams; edited by Rob Spillman.

ZUÑI INDIANS

Vaughn, C. Conquistador de la noche

ZURICH (SWITZERLAND) *See* Switzerland—Zurich

PART II

List of Collections Indexed

14 fictional positions. Williamson, E. M.
20 under 40; stories from the New Yorker; edited by Deborah Treisman. Farrar, Straus and Giroux 2010 431p ISBN 978-0-374-53287-1 LC 2010-32677
21 essential American short stories; edited by Leslie M. Pockell. Thomas Dunne Books/St. Martin's Press 2011 300p ISBN 978-0-312-64803-9
30 under 30; an anthology of innovative fiction by younger writers; Blake Butler & Lily Hoang, eds. Starcherone Books 2011 299p ISBN 978-0-9842133-3-7 LC 2011-19019
30 years in the pulps. Boland, J. C.

A

Adams, John Joseph, 1976-
(ed) Brave new worlds. *See* Brave new worlds
(ed) The way of the wizard. *See* The way of the wizard
Admiralty. Anderson, P.
Aiken, Joan, 1924-2004
The monkey's wedding, and other stories. Small Beer Press 2011 203p ISBN 978-1-93152074-4 LC 2011-04625
Alenyikov, Michael
Ivan and Misha; stories. TriQuarterly Books 2010 199p ISBN 978-0-8101-2718-0 LC 2010-24016
All the time in the world. Doctorow, E. L.
Allen, Dwight, 1951-
The green suit; stories. [New ed.] Terrace Books 2011 300p ISBN 978-0-299-28364-3 (pa); 978-0-299-28363-6 (e-book) LC 2011-18268
First published 2000 by Algonquin Books of Chapel Hill; this edition includes an additional story
Amberjack. Dowling, T.
American masculine. Ray, S.
Amnesty International
Freedom. *See* Freedom
Amos Walker. Estleman, L. D.
And thereby hangs a tale. Archer, J.
And yet they were happy. Phillips, H.
Anderson, Alison
(tr) Mondo and other stories = Mondo et autres histoires. *See* Le Clézio, J.-M. G. (Jean-Marie Gustave), 1940-. Mondo and other stories = Mondo et autres histoires
Anderson, Kevin J., 1962-
(ed) The Nebula Awards showcase. *See* The Nebula Awards showcase
Anderson, Poul, 1926-2001
Admiralty; edited by Rick Katze. NESFA Press 2011 v4 508p (the collected short works of Poul Anderson) ISBN 978-1-886778-94-8; 1-886778-94-9
Anzaldúa, Gloria, 1942-2004
The Gloria Anzaldúa reader; AnaLouise Keating, editor. Duke University Press 2009 361p bibl (Latin America otherwise) ISBN 978-0-8223-4555-8; 978-0-8223-4564-0 (pa) LC 2009-29299
Apatow, Judd
(ed) I found this funny. *See* I found this funny
Apricot jam, and other stories. Solzhenitsyn, A.
Archer, Jeffrey, 1940-
And thereby hangs a tale. St. Martin's Press 2010 301p ISBN 978-0-312-53953-5; 0-312-53953-3 LC 2010-21666
The **architect** of flowers. Lychack, W.

Art as performance, story as criticism. Womack, C.
Ashley, Mike, 1948-
(ed) The dreaming sex. *See* The dreaming sex
Aslan, Reza
(ed) Tablet & pen. *See* Tablet & pen
Assadi, Jamal, 1960-
(ed) Father and son. *See* Ibrāhīm, Ḥannā, 1927-, and Sa'īd, Muḥammad 'Alī, 1950-. Father and son
(ed and tr) Loud sounds from the Holy Land. *See* Loud sounds from the Holy Land
At-risk. Gautier, A.
At the café & The talisman. Dib, M.
Atlantis, and other places. Turtledove, H.
Atta, Sefi, 1964-
News from home; stories. Interlink Books 2010 293p ISBN 978-1-56656-803-6; 1-56656-803-X LC 2009-48648
Aunt Resia and the spirits and other stories. Lahens, Y.
Ayau, Kurt Jose
The brick murder: a tragedy and other stories. Livingstone Press/University of West Alabama 2011 189p ISBN 978-1-60489-068-6; 978-1-60489-060-3 (pa) LC 2011-920336

B

Baker, Lori, 1962-
Crash & tell; stories. Louisiana State University Press 2011 133p ISBN 978-0-8071-4206-6 LC 2011-11951
Balázs, Béla, 1884-1949
The cloak of dreams; Chinese fairy tales; translated and introduced by Jack Zipes; illustrated by Mariette Lydis. Princeton University Press 2010 177p il ISBN 978-0-691-14711-6 LC 2009-47839
Barcelona noir; edited by Adriana V. Lopez & Cartmen Ospina; translated by Achy Obejas. Akashic Books 2011 241p ISBN 978-1-936070-95-4 LC 2010-939099
Barnes, Julian, 1946-
Pulse. Alfred A. Knopf 2011 227p il ISBN 978-0-307-59526-3; 0-307-59526-9; 978-0-307-59599-7 (ebook); 0-307-59599-4 (ebook) LC 2011-02736
Barrett, Lynne
Magpies. Carnegie Mellon University Press 2011 119p ISBN 978-0-88748-543-5 LC 2011-926143
Baxter, Charles
Gryphon; new and selected stories. Pantheon Books 2011 400p ISBN 978-0-307-37921-4; 0-307-37921-3 LC 2010-13785
Bayley, E., 1919-1990
The life and memoirs of Dr. Pi and other stories; by Edgar Bayley; translated by Emily Toder. Clockroot Books 2011 86p ISBN 978-1-56656-837-1 LC 2010-22646
Original Spanish edition, 1983
Beagle, Peter S.
Sleight of hand. Tachyon Publications 2011 287p ISBN 9781-61696-004-9
The **beastly** bride; tales of the animal people; edited by Ellen Datlow & Terri Windling; introduction by Terri Windling; selected decorations by Charles Vess. Viking 2010 500p ISBN 978-0-670-01145-2; 0-670-01145-2 LC 2009-14317
Analyzed for short stories only
Beattie, Ann
The New Yorker stories. Scribner 2010 514p ISBN 978-1-4391-6874-5; 1-4391-6874-1 LC 2010-32933
Before; short stories about pregnancy from our top writers; edited by Emily Franklin and Heather Swain. Overlook Press 2006 318p ISBN 1-58567-740-X
Before they were giants; edited by James L. Sutter; cover illustration by Kieran Yanner. Paizo Publishing 2010 227p (Planet stories, #28) ISBN 978-1-60125-266-1
Before you suffocate your own fool self. Evans, D.

Beirut 39; new writing from the Arab world; edited by Samuel Shimon; with a preface by Hanan al-Shaykh. Bloomsbury 2010 304p ISBN 978-1-60819-202-1 LC 2009-52486

Chiefly translated from Arabic; collection of new writing from the Arab world, by thirty-nine writers under thirty-nine

Benzel, Jeanne B.

(ed) The stories (in) between. *See* The stories (in) between

Bernheimer, Kate

Horse, flower, bird; stories. Coffee House Press 2010 185p il ISBN 978-1-56689-247-6; 1-56689-247-3 LC 2010-16257

The **Best** American mystery stories 2010; edited and with an introduction by Lee Child; Otto Penzler, series editor. Houghton Mifflin Harcourt 2010 400p ISBN 978-0-547-23746-6 ISSN 1094-8384

"A Mariner original"

The **best** American nonrequired reading 2009; edited by Dave Eggers; introduction by Marjane Satrapi; managing editor, Jesse Nathan. Houghton Mifflin Harcourt 2009 413p il (Best American series) ISBN 978-0-547-24160-9 ISSN 1539-316X LC 2002-213163

"A Mariner original."

The **Best** American short stories, 2011; selected from U.S. and Canadian magazines by Geraldine Brooks with Heidi Pitlor; with an introduction by Geraldine Brooks. Houghton Mifflin Harcourt 2011 363p ISBN 978-0-547-24208-8; 0-547-24208-5; 978-0-547-24216-3 (pa); 0-547-24216-6 (pa)

Best European fiction 2011; edited by Aleksandr Hemon; preface by Colum McCann. Dalkey Archive Press 2010 511p ISBN 978-1-56478-600-5 ISSN 2152-6672

The **Best** horror of the year: volume three; edited by Ellen Datlow. Night Shade Books 2011 361p ISBN 978-1-59780-217-8

The **Best** of Larry Niven. Niven, L.

The **Best** of Talebones; edited by Patrick Swenson. Fairwood Press 2010 346p il ISBN 978-1-933846-24-8

Best of the West 2009; new stories from the wide side of the Missouri; edited by James Thomas and D. Seth Horton; foreword by Rick Bass. University of Texas Press 2009 268p ISBN 978-0-292-72122-7 LC 2009-21566

Best of the West 2010; new stories from the wide side of the Missouri; edited by James Thomas and D. Seth Horton; foreword by Kent Meyers. University of Texas Press 2010 246p ISBN 978-0-292-72298-9 LC 2010-17403

Best of the West 2011; new stories from the wild side of the Missouri; edited by James Thomas and D. Seth Horton; foreword by Ana Castillo. University of Texas Press 2011 277p ISBN 978-0-292-72879-0 LC 2011-19072

Best of times, worst of times; contemporary American short stories from the new Gilded Age; edited by Wendy Martin and Cecelia Tichi. New York University Press 2011 357p ISBN 978-0-8147-9627-6; 978-0-8147-9628-3 (pa); 978-0-8147-6147-2 (ebook) LC 2010-33746

The **Best** science fiction and fantasy of the year: volume five; edited by Jonathan Strahan. Night Shade Books 2011 536p ISBN 978-1-59780-172-0

Between the Thames and the Tiber. Riccardi, T.

The **Bible** repairman and other stories. Powers, T.

Bierce, Ambrose, 1842-1914?

The devil's dictionary, tales, & memoirs; S. T. Joshi, editor. Library of America 2011 880p ISBN 987-1-59853-102-2 LC 2010-942020

Analyzed for short stories only

The **Big** book of adventure stories; edited and with a introduction by Otto Penzler; foreword by Douglas Preston. Vintage Crime/Black Lizard 2011 874p ISBN 978-0-307-47450-6; 0-307-47450-X LC 2011-02226

Bill, Frank, 1974-

Crimes in southern Indiana; stories. Farrar, Straus and Giroux 2011 272p ISBN 978-0-374-53288-8 LC 2011-756

Bingham, Sallie
  Mending; new and selected stories. Sarabande Books 2011 260p ISBN 978-1-936747-00-9; 1-936747-00-6; 978-1-936747-01-6 (pa); 1-936747-01-4 (pa) LC 2011-06208

Binkley, Phyllis, 1928-
  Up from the marsh; stories and poems. Fithian Press 2011 124p ISBN 978-1-56474-512-5 LC 2010-51826
    Analyzed for short stories only

Binocular vision. Pearlman, E.

Black, Alethea
  I knew you'd be lovely; stories. Broadway Paperbacks 2011 238p il ISBN 978-0-307-88603-3 (pa); 978-0-307-88604-0 (ebook) LC 2010-33120

Black, Holly, 1971-
  (ed) Welcome to Bordertown. *See* Welcome to Bordertown

The **Black** Lizard big book of Black Mask stories; edited and with a foreword by Otto Penzler; introduction by Keith Alan Deutsch. Vintage Crime/Black Lizard 2010 1116p ISBN 978-0-307-45543-7 LC 2010-24508

Blake, Glenn
  Return fire; stories. Johns Hopkins University Press 2010 96p (Johns Hopkins, poetry and fiction) ISBN 978-0-8018-9431-2; 0-8018-9431-X LC 2009-23831

Blatnik, Andrej, 1963-
  You do understand; translated by Tamara M. Soban. Dalkey Archive Press 2010 94p ISBN 978-1-56478-599-2 LC 2010-11886
    Original Slovenian edition, 2009

Bliss and other short stories. Gilley, T.

Blood & devotion; tales of epic fantasy; edited by W.H. Horner; illustrated by Nicole Cardiff. Fantasist Enterprises 2010 253p ISBN 978-1-934571-02-6; 1-934571-02-4

Blood and other cravings; edited by Ellen Datlow. Tor 2011 317p ISBN 978-0-7653-2828-1 LC 2011-19917
    "A Tom Doherty Associates book"

Blood, guts, & whiskey; edited by Todd Robinson; introduction by Max Allan Collins. Kensington Books 2010 321p ISBN 978-0-7582-2268-8

Blue collar, white collar, no collar; stories of work; edited by Richard Ford. Harper Perennial 2011 607p ISBN 978-0-06-202041-3

Blueprints for building better girls. Schappell, E.

Boarding instructions. Vukcevich, R.

Boggs, Belle
  Mattaponi queen; stories. Graywolf Press 2010 225p ISBN 978-1-55597-558-6

Boland, John C.
  30 years in the pulps; stories of mystery & suspense. Perfect Crime Books 2009 345p ISBN 978-0-9825157-2-3 LC 2009-928564

The **bolero** of Andi Rowe. Plummer, T. M.

The **book** of the living dead; edited by John Richard Stephens. Berkley Books 2010 399p ISBN 978-0-425-23706-9 LC 2010-22755
    Analyzed for short stories only

Boys and girls like you and me. Kyle, A.

Bradbury, Ray, 1920-
  The collected stories of Ray Bradbury: volume I: 1938-1943; a critical edition; William F. Touponce, general editor; Jonathan R. Eller, textual editor. Kent State University Press 2010 498p ISBN 978-1-60635-071-3 LC 2010-23893

Brave new worlds; edited by John Joseph Adams. Night Shade Books 2011 481p ISBN 978-1-59780-221-5

Brennan, Gerard
  (ed) Requiems for the departed. *See* Requiems for the departed

The **brick** murder: a tragedy and other stories. Ayau, K. J.

Brooks, Geraldine
  (ed) The Best American short stories, 2011. *See* The Best American short stories, 2011

Bullfighting and other stories. Doyle, R.

Bummer and other stories. Shapiro, J.

Bush, Peter R., 1946-
  (tr) Guadalajara. *See* Monzó, Quim, 1952-. Guadalajara

Butcher, Jim, 1971-
  Side jobs; stories from the Dresden files. Roc 2010 418p ISBN
    978-0-451-46365-4; 0-451-46365-X LC 2010-28768
By hook or by crook and 27 more of the best crime + mystery stories
    of the year; edited by Ed Gorman and Martin H. Greenberg. Tyrus
    Books 2010 677p ISBN 978-1-935562-31-3; 978-1-935562-32-0
    (pa)
Byrd, Bobby, 1942-
  (ed) Lone Star noir. *See* Lone Star noir
Byrd, John William, 1973-
  (ed) Lone Star noir. *See* Lone Star noir

C

Caine, Rachel
  (ed) Chicks kick butt. *See* Chicks kick butt
Calendar of regrets. Olsen, L.
Cannon, Peter, 1951-
  Forever Azathoth; parodies and pastiches. Subterranean Press 2011
    231p ISBN 978-1-59606-411-9
Can'tLit; fearless fiction from Broken pencil magazine; edited by
    Richard Rosenbaum. ECW Press 2009 218p ISBN
    978-1-55022-896-0
Cape Cod noir; edited by David L. Ulin. Akashic Books 2011 221p
    ISBN 978-1-936070-97-8 LC 2010-939098
Cardinale, Joseph
  The size of the universe. FC2 2010 121p ISBN 978-1-57366-158-4;
    978-1-57366-820-0 (ebook) LC 2009-47701
Chandler, Elizabeth, 1947-
  (ed. & tr) The road. *See* Grossman, Vasiliĭ Semenovich, 1905-1964.
    The road
Chandler, Robert, 1953-
  (ed. & tr) The road. *See* Grossman, Vasiliĭ Semenovich, 1905-1964.
    The road
Châteaureynaud, Georges Olivier
  A life on paper; stories; translated by Edward Gauvin. Small Beer
    Press 2010 231p ISBN 978-1-931520-62-1 LC 2009-54291
Chau, Angie
  Quiet as they come. Ig Publishing 2010 199p ISBN
    978-1-935439-18-9 LC 2010-23043
Chen, Zeping, 1953-
  (tr) White poppies and other stories. *See* Zhang Kangkang. White
    poppies and other stories
Cheyenne Madonna. Chuculate, E. D.
Chicks kick butt; edited by Rachel Caine and Kerrie L. Hughes. Tor
    2011 349p ISBN 978-0-7653-2577-8 LC 2011-11543
Child, Lee
  (ed) The Best American mystery stories 2010. *See* The Best American
    mystery stories 2010
Christmas at the Mysterious Bookshop; 'tis the season to be deadly;
    stories of mistletoe and mayhem from 17 masters of suspense;
    edited by Otto Penzler. Vanguard Press 2010 245p ISBN
    978-1-59315-617-6
Chuculate, Eddie D.
  Cheyenne Madonna; [by] Eddie Chuculate. David R. Godine 2010
    146p ISBN 978-1-57423-216-5 LC 2010-08780
    "A Black Sparrow book"
The **cloak** of dreams. Balázs, B.
Collected short fiction. Naipaul, V. S.
The **Collected** Stories of Carol Emshwiller. Emshwiller, C.
The **collected** stories of Deborah Eisenberg. Eisenberg, D.
The **collected** stories of Lydia Davis. Davis, L.
The **collected** stories of Philip K. Dick, volume one: The King of the
    Elves (1947-1952). Dick, P. K.
The **collected** stories of Ray Bradbury: volume I: 1938-1943. Bradbury,
    R.
Comfort to the enemy and other Carl Webster stories. Leonard, E.
Complete short story omnibus. Wells, H. G.

Constructs of desire. Kronauer, B.

Copenhagen noir; edited by Bo Tao Michaëlis; translated by Mark Kline. Akashic Books 2011 254p ISBN 978-1-936070-66-4 LC 2010-922712

Crash & tell. Baker, L.

Crime. Schirach, F. v.

Crimes in southern Indiana. Bill, F.

A **cup** of normal. Monk, D.

D

Daddy's. Hunter, L.

The **dance** boots. Grover, L. L.

Dancing with Mr. Darcy; stories inspired by Jane Austen and Chawton House Library; compiled by Sarah Waters. Harper 2010 244p ISBN 978-0-06-19906-2

Dann, Jack
(ed) Ghosts by gaslight. *See* Ghosts by gaslight

Danticat, Edwidge, 1969-
(ed) Haiti noir. *See* Haiti noir

Dark dimensions. Nolan, W. F.

Datlow, Ellen
(ed) The beastly bride. *See* The beastly bride
(ed) The Best horror of the year: volume three. *See* The Best horror of the year: volume three
(ed) Blood and other cravings. *See* Blood and other cravings
(ed) Naked city. *See* Naked city

Davis, Chandler, 1926-
It walks in beauty; selected prose of Chandler Davis; edited and with an introduction by Josh Lukin. Aqueduct Press 2010 359p il (Heirloom books, 1) ISBN 978-1-933500-37-9 LC 2010-904003
Analyzed for short stories only

Davis, Lydia
The collected stories of Lydia Davis. Farrar, Straus and Giroux 2010 733p ISBN 978-0-374-27060-5; 0-374-27060-0 LC 2009-25451

A **day** in the life of a smiling woman. Drabble, M.

Day out of days. Shepard, S.

Dead neon; tales of near-future Las Vegas; edited by Todd James Pierce and Jarret Keene. University of Nevada Press 2010 183p ISBN 978-0-87417-828-9 LC 2010-14698

Deadman's road. Lansdale, J. R.

The **Dedalus** book of Flemish fantasy; edited by Eric Dickens and translated by Paul Vincent. Dedalus 2010 325p ISBN 978-1-903517-93-2

Delhi noir; edited by Hirsh Sawhney. Akashic Books 2009 297p map ISBN 978-1-933354-78-1; 1-933354-78-X LC 2008-937355

DeMille, Nelson
(ed) Mystery Writers of America presents the rich and the dead. *See* Mystery Writers of America presents the rich and the dead

The **devil's** dictionary, tales, & memoirs. Bierce, A.

Dib, Mohammed, 1920-2003
At the café & The talisman; translated by C. Dickson; afterword by Mildred Mortimer. University of Virginia Press 2011 183p (CARAF books: Carribbean and African literature translated from French) ISBN 978-0-8139-3119-7; 978-0-8139-3120-3 (pa); 978-0-8139-3147-0 (ebook) LC 2010-45464

Dick, Philip K.
The collected stories of Philip K. Dick, volume one: The King of the Elves (1947-1952). Subterranean Press 2010 487p ISBN 978-1-59606-340-2

Dickens, Eric
(ed) The Dedalus book of Flemish fantasy. *See* The Dedalus book of Flemish fantasy

Dickson, C., 1951-
(tr) At the café & The talisman. *See* Dib, Mohammed, 1920-2003. At the café & The talisman

Dixon, Stephen, 1936-
What is all this?; uncollected stories. Fantagraphics Books 2010 563p
ISBN 978-1-60699-350-7
Doctorow, E. L., 1931-
All the time in the world; new and selected stories. Random House
2011 277p ISBN 978-1-4000-6963-7; 978-0-679-60462-4 (ebook)
LC 2010-42500
Dowling, Terry, 1947-
Amberjack; tales of fear and wonder. Subterranean Press 2010 361p
ISBN 978-1-59606-293-1
Analyzed for short stories only
Doyle, Roddy
Bullfighting and other stories. Viking 2011 214p ISBN
978-0-670-02287-8; 0-670-02287-X LC 2010-53424
Dozois, Gardner R.
When the great days come; [by] Gardner Dozois. Prime 2011 358p
ISBN 978-1-60701-278-8
(ed) The Year's best science fiction: twenty-eighth annual collection.
See The Year's best science fiction: twenty-eighth annual collection
Drabble, Margaret, 1939-
A day in the life of a smiling woman; complete short stories; edited
by José Francisco Fernández. Houghton Mifflin Harcourt 2011 227p
ISBN 978-0-547-55040-4 (Houghton Mifflin Harcourt);
0-547-55040-5 (Houghton Mifflin Harcourt); 978-0-14-119604-6
(Penguin Classics); 0-14-119604-1 (Penguin Classics)
LC 2010-49798
English edition has subtitle: the collected stories
Drakulić, Slavenka, 1949-
A guided tour through the museum of communism; fables from a
mouse, a parrot, a bear, a cat, a mole, a pig, a dog, and a raven.
Penguin Books 2011 192p ISBN 978-0-14-311863-3
LC 2010-38778
Dream fishing. Ely, S.
The **dreaming** sex; early tales of scientific imagination by women;
edited by Mike Ashley. Peter Owen 2010 252p il ISBN
978-0-7206-1354-4

E

East of the West. Penkov, M.
Edible stories. Kurlansky, M.
Edwards, Martin, 1955-
(ed) Original sins. *See* Original sins
Eggers, Dave, 1970-
(ed) The best American nonrequired reading 2009. *See* The best
American nonrequired reading 2009
Einstein's tears. Prindle, J.
Eisenberg, Deborah
The collected stories of Deborah Eisenberg. Picador/Farrar, Straus And
Giroux 2010 992p ISBN 978-0-312-42989-8; 0-312-42989-4
LC 2010-02081
Ely, Scott
Dream fishing. Livingston Press 2010 187p ISBN 978-1-60489-056-3;
978-1-60489-057-0 (pa) LC 2010-929242
The **empty** family. Tóibín, C.
An **empty** room. Mu Xin
Emshwiller, Carol
The Collected Stories of Carol Emshwiller. Nonstop Press 2011 576p
ISBN 978-1-933065-22-9 (v1)
End of an Aeon; edited by Bridgett McKenna & Marti McKenna.
Fairwood Press 2011 241p il ISBN 978-0-9820730-9-4
The **end** of the world; stories of the apocalypse; edited by Martin H.
Greenberg. Skyhorse Publishing 2010 328p ISBN
978-1-60239-967-9; 1-60239-967-0 LC 2010-06101
Engel, Patricia
Vida. Black Cat 2010 182p ISBN 978-0-8021-7078-1; 0-8021-7078-1

Estleman, Loren D.

Amos Walker; the complete story collection. Tyrus Books 2010 637p il ISBN 978-1-935562-24-5; 1-935562-24-X

Evans, Danielle

Before you suffocate your own fool self. Riverhead Books 2010 232p ISBN 978-1-59448-769-9; 1-59448-769-3 LC 2010-07179

Everyone but you. Novack, S.

F

Fallon, Siobhan

You know when the men are gone. G.P. Putnam's Sons 2011 226p ISBN 978-0-399-15720-2 LC 2010-029597

"Amy Einhorn books"

Family of fallen leaves; stories of Agent Orange by Vietnamese writers; edited by Charles Waugh and Huy Lien. University of Georgia Press 2010 181p ISBN 978-0-8203-3600-8; 0-8203-3600-9; 978-0-8203-3714-2 (pa); 0-8203-3714-5 (pa) LC 2010-5977

Fantastic women; 18 tales of the surreal and the sublime from Tin House; introduction by Joy Williams; edited by Rob Spillman. Tin House Books 2011 262p ISBN 978-1-935639-10-7 (pa); 978-1-935639-11-4 (ebook) LC 2011-09695

Farmer, Philip José, 1918-2009

Up the bright river; the worlds of Philip José Farmer; edited by Gary K. Wolfe. Subterranean Press 2010 333p ISBN 978-1-59606-329-7

Father and son. Ibrāhim, ; and Sa'īd, M. A.

Fernández, José Francisco

(ed) A day in the life of a smiling woman. *See* Drabble, Margaret, 1939-. A day in the life of a smiling woman

Florida heat wave; [edited and with an] introduction by Michael Lister. Tyrus Books 2010 363p ISBN 978-1-935562-17-7; 978-1-935562-16-0 (pa)

Ford, Richard, 1944-

(ed) Blue collar, white collar, no collar. *See* Blue collar, white collar, no collar

Forever Azathoth. Cannon, P.

Four women from Ravensbrück: five stories from the Shoa. Kalechofsky, R.

Fourteen fictional positions. *See* Williamson, E. M. 14 fictional positions

Fowler, Karen Joy

What I didn't see and other stories. Small Beer Press 2010 197p ISBN 978-1-932520-68-3; 1-931520-68-2 LC 2010-25911

Franco, James, 1978-

Palo Alto; stories. Scribner 2010 197p ISBN 978-1-4391-6314-6; 1-4391-6314-6 LC 2010-32932

Franklin, Emily

(ed) Before. *See* Before

Freedom; stories celebrating the Universal Declaration of Human Rights; Amnesty International. Three Rivers Press 2011 413p ISBN 978-0-307-58883-8; 978-307-58884-5 (ebook) LC 2010-10573

From the San Joaquin. Kitterman, B.

Full dark, no stars. King, S.

Fungus of the heart. Shipp, J. C.

Furman, Laura

The mother who stayed; stories. Free Press 2010 212p ISBN 978-1-4391-9465-2 LC 2010-12906

(ed) The Pen/O.Henry Prize stories, 2010. *See* The Pen/O.Henry Prize stories, 2010

(ed) The Pen/O.Henry Prize stories 2011. *See* The Pen/O.Henry Prize stories 2011

Future media; [edited by Rick Wilber] Tachyon Publications 2011 431p ISBN 978-1-61696-020-9; 1-61696-020-5

Analyzed for short stories only

G

Gallari, Adam
We are never as beautiful as we are now; stories. Ampersand Books
2009 138p ISBN 978-0-9841025-3-2
Gautier, Amina, 1977-
At-risk; stories. University of Georgia Press 2011 154p ISBN
978-0-8203-3888-0; 0-8203-3888-5 LC 2011-10454
Gauvin, Edward
(tr) A life on paper. *See* Châteaureynaud, Georges Olivier. A life on
paper
Georgic. Nagai, M.
Gernant, Karen
(tr) White poppies and other stories. *See* Zhang Kangkang. White
poppies and other stories
Gevers, Nick
(ed) Ghosts by gaslight. *See* Ghosts by gaslight
Ghosts by gaslight; stories of steampunk and supernatural suspense;
[edited by] Jack Dann [and] Nick Gevers. Harper Voyager 2011
400p ISBN 978-0-06-199971-0; 0-06-199971-7
Gifford, Barry, 1946-
Sad stories of the death of kings. Seven Stories Press 2010 201p il
ISBN 978-1-58322-922-4 LC 2010-35353
Gilley, Ted
Bliss and other short stories. University of Nebraska Press 2010 125p
ISBN 978-0-8032-3261-7 LC 2009-50224
The **girl** with brown fur. Levine, S.
Give me your heart. Oates, J. C.
The **Gloria** Anzaldúa reader. Anzaldúa, G.
Gold, E. J.
(ed) Perfect murders. *See* Gold, H. L., 1914-1996. Perfect murders
Gold, H. L., 1914-1996
Perfect murders; introduction to the Bison Books edition by E. J.
Gold. University of Nebraska Press 2010 343p (Bison frontiers of
the imagination series) ISBN 978-0-8032-3359-1 LC 2009-52458
Golden, Christopher
(ed) The monster's corner. *See* The monster's corner
Golf stories; edited by Charles McGrath. Everyman's Pocket Classics;
Alfred A. Knopf 2011 331p ISBN 978-0-307-59689-5
LC 2010-54259
Goodberg, David
Selected shorts and other methods of time travel. Blue World
Publications 2010 293p il ISBN 978-0-9827041-0-3
Gordimer, Nadine, 1923-
Life times; stories, 1952-2007. Farrar, Straus and Giroux 2010 549p
ISBN 978-0-374-27053-7; 0-374-27053-8 LC 2010-23403
Gorman, Edward
(ed) By hook or by crook and 27 more of the best crime + mystery
stories of the year. *See* By hook or by crook and 27 more of the
best crime + mystery stories of the year
Noir 13; [by] Ed Gorman. Perfect Crime Books 2010 237p ISBN
978-0-9825157-5-4
The **Granta** book of the Irish short story; [edited by] Anne Enright.
Granta Books 2010 442p ISBN 978-1-84708-097-4
Gray, Amelia, 1982-
Museum of the weird. FC2/University of Alabama Press 2010 171p
ISBN 978-1-57366-156-0; 1-57366-156-2 LC 2009-41859
The **greatest** Russian stories of crime and suspense; edited by Otto
Penzler. Pegasus Books 2010 354p ISBN 978-1-60598-135-2
Greed. Hubbard, L. R.
The **green** suit. Allen, D.
Greenberg, Martin Harry
(ed) By hook or by crook and 27 more of the best crime + mystery
stories of the year. *See* By hook or by crook and 27 more of the
best crime + mystery stories of the year
(ed) The end of the world. *See* The end of the world
Greetings from below. Mullins, D. P.

Grossman, Vasiliĭ Semenovich, 1905-1964
The road; stories, journalism, and essays; [by] Vasily Grossman; translated from the Russian by Robert and Elizabeth Chandler with Olga Mukovnikova; commentary and notes by Robert Chandler with Yury Bit-Yunan; afterword by Fyodor Guber. New York Review Books 2010 373p il ISBN 978-1-59017-361-9; 1-59017-361-9 LC 2010-23048
Analyzed for short stories only
Grover, Linda LeGarde
The dance boots. University of Georgia Press 2010 149p (Flannery O'Connor Award for short fiction) ISBN 978-0-8203-3580-3; 0-8203-3580-0 LC 2009-51211
Gryphon. Baxter, C.
Guadalajara. Monzó, Q.
A **guided** tour through the museum of communism. Drakulić, S.
The **guilt** edge and other stories. Randisi, R. J.
Guran, Paula
(ed) Vampires. *See* Vampires
(ed) The Year's best dark fantasy & horror. *See* The Year's best dark fantasy & horror
(ed) Zombies: the recent dead. *See* Zombies: the recent dead

H

The **hair** wreath and other stories. Villegas, H.
Haiti noir; edited by Edwidge Danticat. Akashic Books 2010 c2011 309p ISBN 9781617750137; 9781936070657 (pa)
Hall, Tina May
The physics of imaginary objects. University of Pittsburgh Press 2010 147p ISBN 978-0-8229-4398-3; 0-8229-4398-0 LC 2010-20938
"Drue Heinz Literature Prize 2010"
Hannah, Barry
Long, last, happy; new and selected stories. Grove Press 2010 459p ISBN 978-0-8021-1968-1; 0-8021-1968-9
Hardwick, Elizabeth
The New York stories of Elizabeth Hardwick; selected and with an introduction by Darryl Pinckney. New York Review Books 2010 224p ISBN 978-1-59017-287-2; 1-59017-287-6 LC 2009-41526
Hart, Maryelizabeth
(ed) San Diego noir. *See* San Diego noir
Heart of the city. Sabar, A.
Heathcock, Alan
Volt; stories. Graywolf Press 2011 207p ISBN 978-1-55597-577-7; 1-55597-577-1
Hemmingson, Michael
Pictures of houses with water damage; stories. Black Lawrence Press 2010 173p ISBN 978-0-98252-4-2-0
Hemon, Aleksandar, 1964-
(ed) Best European fiction 2011. *See* Best European fiction 2011
Henderson, Bill, 1941-
(ed) Pushcart Prize XXXV: best of the small presses 2011. *See* Pushcart Prize XXXV: best of the small presses 2011
Here comes another lesson. O'Connor, S.
Highsmith, Patricia, 1921-1995
Patricia Highsmith: selected novels and short stories; edited with an introduction by Joan Schenkar. W. W. Norton & Co. 2011 644p ISBN 978-0-393-08013-1; 0-393-08013-7 LC 2010-34589
Analyzed for short stories only
Hoang, Lily, 1981-
(ed) 30 under 30. *See* 30 under 30
Hobb, Robin
The inheritance and other stories. See Lindholm, Megan, and Hobb, Robin
Hodge, Brian, 1960-
Picking the bones. Cemetery Dance 2011 313p ISBN 978-1-58767-220-0
Holiday. Rickert, M.

Horner, W. H.
(ed) Blood & devotion. *See* Blood & devotion
(ed) The stories (in) between. *See* The stories (in) between
Horrocks, Caitlin, 1980-
This is not your city; stories. Sarabande Books 2011 169p ISBN
    978-1-932511-91-8 LC 2010-50304
Horse, flower, bird. Bernheimer, K.
Horton, D. Seth, 1976-
(ed) Best of the West 2009. *See* Best of the West 2009
(ed) Best of the West 2010. *See* Best of the West 2010
(ed) Best of the West 2011. *See* Best of the West 2011
Howan, Lillian
(ed) Rosebud and other stories. *See* Yamauchi, Wakako. Rosebud and
    other stories
Howard, Robert Ervin, 1906-1936
Sword woman and other historical adventures; [by] Robert E. Howard;
    fully illustrated by John Watkiss. Ballantine Books/Del Rey 2011
    547p ISBN 978-0-345-50546-0; 978-0-345-52432-4 (ebook)
    LC 2010-39976
Hubbard, L. Ron (La Fayette Ron), 1911-1986
Greed. Galaxy Press 2008 137p il ISBN 978-1-59212-369-8;
    1-59212-369-4 LC 2007-927677
Hughes, Kerrie L.
(ed) Chicks kick butt. *See* Chicks kick butt
Hungry for your love; an anthology of zombie romance; edited by Lori
    Perkins. St. Martin's Griffin 2010 368p ISBN 978-0-312-65079-7
    LC 2010-30187
Hunter, Lindsay
Daddy's; 24 fictions. Featherproof Books 2010 217p il ISBN
    978-0-9825808-0-6   (pa);   978-0-9825808-8-2   (ebook)
    LC 2009-944042

I

I found this funny; my favorite pieces of humor and some that may not
    be funny at all; edited by Judd Apatow. McSweeney's Books 2010
    476p il ISBN 978-1-934781-90-6
        Analyzed for short stories only
I knew you'd be lovely. Black, A.
Ibrāhīm, Ḥannā, 1927-, and Saʿīd, Muḥammad ʿAlī, 1950-
Father and son; selected short fiction; by Hanna Ibrahim Elias and
    Mohammad Ali Saeid; translated by Jamal Assadi. P. Lang 2009
    132p bibl f ISBN 978-1-4331-0638-5 LC 2009-05757
In Corner B. Mphahlele, E.
In the mean time. Tremblay, P.
In this light. Thon, M. R.
In which brief stories are told. Sterling, P.
The **inheritance** and other stories. Lindholm, M. and Hobb, R.
"The **internal** pages" and other stories. Mārar, M.
Into the light; an anthology of literature by Koreans in Japan; edited by
    Melissa L. Wender. University of Hawaii Press 2011 226p ISBN
    978-0-8248-3367-1; 978-0-8248-3490-6 (pa) LC 2010-12338
It walks in beauty. Davis, C.
Ittner, Jutta
(ed) Constructs of desire. *See* Kronauer, Brigitte, 1940-. Constructs of
    desire
Ivan and Misha. Alenyikov, M.

J

Jones, Gwyneth A., 1952-
The universe of things; short fiction; by Gwyneth Jones. Aqueduct
    press 2011 279p ISBN 978-1-933500-44-7 LC 2010-930273
Jones, Stephen Graham, 1972-
The ones that got away. Prime Books 2010 251p ISBN
    978-1-60701-235-1

Joshi, S. T., 1958-
(ed) The devil's dictionary, tales, & memoirs. *See* Bierce, Ambrose, 1842-1914? The devil's dictionary, tales, & memoirs
Journeys. MacLeod, I.

K

Kalechofsky, Roberta, 1931-
Four women from Ravensbrück: five stories from the Shoa. Micah Publications 2011 148p ISBN 978-0-916288-57-0
Kaminsky, Stuart M.
(ed) On a raven's wing. *See* On a raven's wing
Keating, AnaLouise, 1961-
(ed) The Gloria Anzaldúa reader. *See* Anzaldúa, Gloria, 1942-2004. The Gloria Anzaldúa reader
Keene, Jarret, 1973-
(ed) Dead neon. *See* Dead neon
Kennedy, A. L., 1965-
What becomes; stories. Alfred A. Knopf 2010 208p ISBN 978-0-307-27354-3; 0-307-27354-7 LC 2009-46507
First published 2009 in the United Kingdom
King, Stephen, 1947-
Full dark, no stars. Scribner 2010 368p ISBN 978-1-4391-9256-6; 1-4391-9256-1 LC 2010-32866
Kitterman, Barry
From the San Joaquin; stories. Southern Methodist University Press 2011 251p ISBN 978-0-87074-569-0 LC 2010-51608
Kitty's greatest hits. Vaughn, C.
Kronauer, Brigitte, 1940-
Constructs of desire; selections from Brigitte Kronauer; translated and edited by Jutta Ittner. Bucknell University Press 2009 347p ISBN 978-0-8387-5709-3; 0-8387-5709-X LC 2008-29852
Analyzed for short stories only
Kurlansky, Mark
Edible stories; a novel in 16 parts. Riverhead Books 2010 265p il ISBN 978-1-59448-488-9; 1-59448-488-0 LC 2010-17475
Kushner, Ellen, 1955-
(ed) Welcome to Bordertown. *See* Welcome to Bordertown
Kyle, Aryn
Boys and girls like you and me; stories. Scribner 2010 225p ISBN 978-1-4165-9480-2; 978-1-4165-9481-9 LC 2009-37972

L

L. Ron Hubbard presents Writers of the Future volume XXVI; the year's twelve best tales from the Writers of the Future international writers' program; illustrated by winners in the Illustrators of the Future international illustrators' program; with essays on writing & illustration by L. Ron Hubbard/Dean Wesley Smith/ Stephen Youll; edited by K. D. Wentworth. Galaxy Press 2010 463p il ISBN 978-1-59212-847-1; 1-59212-847-5 LC 2010-911254
L. Ron Hubbard presents Writers of the Future volume XXVII; the year's thirteen best tales from the Writers of the Future international writers' program; illustrated by winners in the Illustrators of the Future international illustrators' program; with essays on writing & illustration by L. Ron Hubbard / Mike Resnick / Robert Cadtillo; edited by K. D. Wentworth. Galaxy Press 2011 543p il ISBN 978-1-59212-870-9; 1-59212-870-X LC 2011-926124
Ladies and gentlemen. Ross, A.
Lahens, Yanick, 1953-
Aunt Resia and the spirits and other stories; translated by Betty Wilson; afterword by Marie-Agnes Sourieau. University of Virginia Press 2010 212p ISBN 978-0-8139-2900-2; 978-0-8139-2901-9 (pa); 978-0-8139-2959-0 (e-book) LC 2009-31102
Lake, Jay
The sky that wraps; collected short fiction. Subterranean Press 2010 406p ISBN 978-1-59606-266-5

Laken, Valerie
    Separate kingdoms; stories. Harper Perennial 2011 199, 14p ISBN
        978-0-06-084094-5 LC 2010-34615
Lansdale, Joe R., 1951-
    Deadman's road. Subterranean Press 2010 271p il ISBN
        978-1-59606-330-3
        Analyzed for short stories only
Lantz, K. A.
    (tr) Apricot jam, and other stories. *See* Solzhenitsyn, Aleksandr,
        1918-2008. Apricot jam, and other stories
Lassen, J. M.
    (ed) Z: zombie stories. *See* Z: zombie stories
The **last** hieroglyph. Smith, C. A.
Latiolais, Michelle
    Widow; stories. Bellevue Literary Press 2011 160p ISBN
        978-1-934137-30-7; 1-934137-30-8 LC 2010-53023
Le Clézio, J.-M. G. (Jean-Marie Gustave), 1940-
    Mondo and other stories = Mondo et autres histoires; translated [from
        the French] by Alison Anderson. University of Nebraska Press 2011
        236p ISBN 978-0-8032-2999-0; 978-0-8032-3000-2 (pa)
        LC 2010-32665
Leland, Christopher T.
    Love/imperfect; stories. Wayne State University Press 2011 176p
        ISBN 978-0-8143-3495-9 LC 2010-42159
Leonard, Elmore, 1925-
    Comfort to the enemy and other Carl Webster stories. Harper 2010
        c2009 197p ISBN 978-0-06-173515-8 LC 2010-10151
        First published 2009 in the United Kingdom
Levine, Stacey
    The girl with brown fur; tales & stories. Starcherone Books 2011 179p
        ISBN 978-0-9842133-4-4 LC 2010-53896
Lien, Huy
    (ed) Family of fallen leaves. *See* Family of fallen leaves
The **life** and memoirs of Dr. Pi and other stories. Bayley, E.
Life as we show it; writing on film; co-edited by Masha Tupitsyn &
    Brian Pera; introduction by Masha Tupitsyn. City Lights 2009 290p
    bibl f il ISBN 978-0-8728-6525-9 LC 2008-35720
        Analyzed for short stories only
Life on Mars: tales from the new frontier; an original science fiction
    anthology; edited by Jonathan Strahan. Viking 2011 333p ISBN
    978-0-670-01216-9; 0-670-01216-5 LC 2011-02998
A **life** on paper. Châteaureynaud, G. O.
Life times. Gordimer, N.
Lindholm, Megan, and Hobb, Robin
    The inheritance and other stories; [by] Megan Lindholm [and] Robin
    Hobb. Harper Voyager 2011 374p ISBN 978-0-06-156164-1
Lister, Michael
    (ed) Florida heat wave. *See* Florida heat wave
Little America. Simmons, D.
Liu, Toming Jun
    (tr) An empty room. *See* Mu Xin. An empty room
Lone Star noir; edited by Bobby Byrd & Johnny Byrd. Akashic Books
    2010 276p ISBN 978-1-936070-64-0 LC 2010-922717
Long, last, happy. Hannah, B.
Look down, this is where it must have happened. Niedzviecki, H.
Loory, Ben, 1971-
    Stories for nighttime and some for the day. Penguin Books 2011 210p
        ISBN 978-0-14-311950-0 LC 2011-12131
Lopez, Adriana
    (ed) Barcelona noir. *See* Barcelona noir
Loud sounds from the Holy Land; short fiction by Palestinian women;
    edited and translated by Jamal Assadi with assistance from Martha
    Moody. Peter Lang 2011 119p ISBN 978-1-4331-1317-8
    LC 2010-47708
Love/imperfect. Leland, C. T.
Lukin, Josh
    (ed) It walks in beauty. *See* Davis, Chandler, 1926-. It walks in beauty

Lychack, William
   The architect of flowers. Houghton Mifflin Harcourt 2011 161p ISBN
     978-0-618-30243-7 LC 2010-24953
Lydis, Mariette, 1894-1970
   The cloak of dreams. See Balázs, Béla, 1884-1949

M

MacLeod, Ian
   Journeys; stories; by Ian R. Macleod. Subterranean Press 2010 231p
     ISBN 978-1-59606-297-9
Magpies. Barrett, L.
Manilla, Marie
   Still life with plums; a collection of short stories. Vandalia Press 2010
     185p ISBN 978-1-933202-60-0; 1-933202-60-2 LC 2010-4710
Man's companions. Ruocco, J.
Mârar, Muṣṭafá
   "The internal pages" and other stories; [by] Mustafa Murrar; edited
     and translated by Janal Assadi; with assistance from Martha Moody.
     P. Lang 2010 139p ISBN 987-1-4331-1049-8 LC 2010-07059
Marías, Javier, 1951-
   While the women are sleeping; translated by Margaret Jull Costa. New
     Directions 2010 128p ISBN 978-0-8112-1663-0; 0-8112-1663-2
     LC 2010-21110
      Original Spanish edition, 1990
Marry or burn. Trueblood, V.
Martin, Chelsea, 1986-
   The really funny thing about apathy. Sunnyoutside 2010 68p ISBN
     978-1-934513-24-8
Martin, Wendy, 1940-
   (ed) Best of times, worst of times. *See* Best of times, worst of times
Matheson, Richard, 1926-
   Matheson uncollected: volume one. Gauntlet Publications 2008 266p
     ISBN 978-1-887368-97-1; 1-887368-97-3
      Analyzed for short stories only
   Matheson uncollected: volume two. Gauntlet Publications 2010 377p
     ISBN 978-1-934267-17-2; 1-934267-17-1
Matheson uncollected: volume one. Matheson, R.
Matheson uncollected: volume two. Matheson, R.
Mattaponi queen. Boggs, B.
McElroy, Joseph
   Night soul and other stories. Dalkey Archive Press 2010 293p ISBN
     978-1-56478-602-9; 1-56478-602-1 LC 2010-37602
McGarry, Jean
   Ocean state; stories. Johns Hopkins University Press 2010 214p (Johns
     Hopkins, poetry and fiction) ISBN 978-0-8018-9658-3;
     0-8018-9658-4 LC 2009-48413
McGrath, Charles
   (ed) Golf stories. *See* Golf stories
McKenna, Bridget
   (ed) End of an Aeon. *See* End of an Aeon
McKenna, Marti
   (ed) End of an Aeon. *See* End of an Aeon
McOmber, Adam
   This new & poisonous air; stories. BOA Editions 2011 179p
     (American Reader series, no. 15) ISBN 978-1-934414-51-4
     LC 2010-29669
Meeting the Dog Girls. Terry, G. P.
Mehta, Rahul
   Quarantine; stories. Harper Perennial 2011 214p ISBN
     978-0-06-202045-1; 0-06-202045-5 LC 2010-53604
Mending. Bingham, S.
Michaëlis, Bo Tao
   (ed) Copenhagen noir. *See* Copenhagen noir
Millhauser, Steven
   We others; new and selected stories. Alfred A. Knopf 2011 387p
     ISBN 978-0-307-59590-4; 0-307-59590-0 LC 2011-00078

Mondo and other stories = Mondo et autres histoires. Le Clézio, J.-M.
  G.
Monk, Devon
  A cup of normal. Fairwood Press 2010 260p ISBN 978-0-9820730-9-4
The **monkey's** wedding, and other stories. Aiken, J.
The **monster's** corner; stories through inhuman eyes; edited by
  Christopher Golden. St. Martin's Griffin 2011 388p ISBN
  978-0-312-64613-4 LC 2011-20407
Monzó, Quim, 1952-
  Guadalajara; stories; translated from the Catalan by Peter Bush. Open
  Letter 2011 125p ISBN 978-1-934824-19-1; 1-934824-19-4
  LC 2011-08812
    Original Catalan edition, 1996
Moody, Martha
  (ed and tr) Loud sounds from the Holy Land. *See* Loud sounds from
  the Holy Land
The **mother** who stayed. Furman, L.
Mphahlele, Ezekiel, 1919-2008
  In Corner B; [by] Es'kia Mphahlele; introduction by Peter N.
  Thuynsma. Penguin Books 2011 237p ISBN 978-0-14-310602-9
  LC 2010-43074
Mu Xin
  An empty room; translated from the Chinese by Toming Jun Liu. New
  Directions Book 2011 150p ISBN 978-0-8112-1922-8
  LC 2010-52844
Mullins, David Philip, 1974-
  Greetings from below; winner of the 2009 Mary McCarthy Prize in
  short fiction selected by David Means. Sarabande Books 2010 167p
  ISBN 978-1-932511-88-8 LC 2010-05123
Museum of the weird. Gray, A.
My blue suede shoes; four novellas; [edited by] Tracy Price-Thompson
  and Taressa Stovall. Atria Paperback 2011 307p ISBN
  978-1-4165-4208-7; 978-1-4391-8746-3 (ebook) LC 2010-31314
My heart said no, but the camera crew said yes! Sands, B.
Mystery Writers of America presents the rich and the dead; edited by
  Nelson DeMille. Grand Central Publishing 2011 370p ISBN
  978-0-446-55587-6; 0-446-55587-8; 978-0-446-55588-3 (pa);
  0-446-55588-6 (pa) LC 2010-34196

N

Nagai, Mariko
  Georgic; stories. BkMk Press 2010 163p ISBN 978-1-886157-76-7
  LC 2010-38966
    Winner of the G.S. Sharat Chandra Prize for Short Fiction.
Naipaul, V. S. (Vidiadhar Surajprasad), 1932-
  Collected short fiction; with an introduction by the author. Alfred A.
  Knopf 2011 xxiii, 409p (Everyman's Library) ISBN
  978-0-307-59402-0; 0-307-59402-5
Naked city; tales of urban fantasy; edited by Ellen Datlow. St. Martin's
  Griffin 2011 539p ISBN 978-0-312-60431-8; 978-0-312-38524-8
  (pa) LC 2011-08088
The **Nebula** Awards showcase; edited by Kevin J. Anderson. Tor 2011
  412p ISBN 978-0-7653-2842-7 LC 2011-07410
    "A tom Doherty Associates book"
    Analyzed for short stories only
Neugeboren, Jay, 1938-
  You are my heart and other stories. Two Dollar Radio 2011 180p
  ISBN 978-0-9826848-8-7 LC 2011-925178
Nevins, Francis M., Jr.
  Night forms; short stories; with an introduction and afterwords by the
  author. Perfect Crime Books 2010 357p ISBN 978-1-935797-00-5
The **New** York stories of Elizabeth Hardwick. Hardwick, E.
The **New** Yorker stories. Beattie, A.
News from home. Atta, S.
Niedzviecki, Hal, 1971-
  Look down, this is where it must have happened. City Lights Books
  2011 174p ISBN 978-0-87286-539-6 LC 2010-53211

Night forms. Nevins, F. M., Jr.
Night soul and other stories. McElroy, J.
Niven, Larry
 The Best of Larry Niven; edited by Jonathan Strahan. Subterranean
  2010 616p ISBN 978-1-59606-331-0; 1-59606-331-9
Noir 13. Gorman, E.
Nolan, William F., 1928-
 Dark dimensions; newly-collected shock fiction by a living legend in
  dark fantasy. Fairwood Press 2010 201p ISBN 978-0-9820730-6-3
Novack, Sandra
 Everyone but you; stories. Random House 2011 272p ISBN
  978-1-4000-6681-0; 1-4000-6681-6 LC 2010-53002
Nutting, Alissa
 Unclean jobs for women and girls. Starcherone Books 2010 184p
  ISBN 978-0-9842133-2-0

O

Oates, Joyce Carol, 1938-
 Give me your heart; tales of mystery and suspense. Houghton Mifflin
  Harcourt 2011 260p ISBN 978-0-547-38546-4; 0-547-38546-3
  LC 2010-05752
  "An Otto Penzler book"
 Sourland; stories. Ecco/HarperCollins 2010 373p ISBN
  978-0-06-199652-8; 0-06-199652-1
Obejas, Achy, 1956-
 (ed) Barcelona noir. *See* Barcelona noir
O'Brien, Edna
 Saints and sinners; stories. Back Bay Books/Little, Brown and Co.
  2011   245p   ISBN   978-0-316-12272-6;   0-316-12272-6
  LC 2010-31577
Ocean state. McGarry, J.
O'Connor, Stephen, 1952-
 Here comes another lesson; stories. Free Press 2010 305p ISBN
  978-1-4391-8199-7; 1-4391-8199-3 LC 2010-05545
Olsen, Lance, 1956-
 Calendar of regrets. FC2/University of Alabama Press 2010 445p
  ISBN 978-1-57366-157-7; 978-1-57366-819-4 LC 2009-41860
On a raven's wing; new tales in honor of Edgar Allan Poe; edited by
  Stuart M. Kaminsky. Harper 2008 393p ISBN 9780061690426
  LC 2008-26740
On the banks of the river of heaven. Parks, R.
The **ones** that got away. Jones, S. G.
The **orange** suitcase. Riippi, J.
Orientation. Orozco, D.
Original sins; a Crime Writer's Association anthology; edited by Martin
  Edwards. Severn House 2011 c2010 229p ISBN 978-1-84751-298-7
Orozco, Daniel, 1957-
 Orientation; and other stories. Faber and Faber, Inc. 2011 162p ISBN
  978-0-86547-853-4; 0-86547-853-8 LC 2010-38531
Osondu, E. C.
 Voice of America; stories. HarperCollins Publishers 2010 215p ISBN
  9780061990861; 0-06-199086-8 LC 2010-05729
Ospina, Carmen
 (ed) Barcelona noir. *See* Barcelona noir
Out of the mountains. Willis, M. S.
The **outlaw** album. Woodrell, D.

P

Packer, Ann, 1959-
 Swim back to me. Alfred A. Knopf 2011 225p ISBN
  978-1-4000-4404-7; 1-4000-4404-9 LC 2010-51792
The **palace** at midnight, 1980-82. Silverberg, R.
Palo Alto. Franco, J.

Papernick, Jon
   There is no other; [by] Jonathan Papernick. Exile Editions 2010 183p
      ISBN 978-1-55096-138-6 LC 2010-399455
Paradise tales. Ryman, G.
Parks, Richard, 1943-
   On the banks of the river of heaven. Prime 2010 254p ISBN
      978-1-60701-226-9
Patricia Highsmith: selected novels and short stories. Highsmith, P.
Pearlman, Edith
   Binocular vision; new & selected stories. Lookout Books/University of
      North Carolina Wilmington 2011 374p ISBN 978-0-9823382-9-2;
      0-9823382-9-5 LC 2010-33376
The **Pen/O.Henry** Prize stories, 2010; edited and with an introduction by
      Laura Furman; with essays on the stories they admire most by
      jurors Junot Diaz, Paula Fox, Yiyun Li. Anchor Books 2010 xxv,
      479p ISBN 978-0-307-47236-1
The **Pen/O.Henry** Prize stories 2011; chosen and with an introduction
      by Laura Furman; with essays on the stories thety admire most by
      jurors A. M. Homes, Manuel Muñoz, Christine Schutt. Anchor
      Books 2011 xxvi, 403p ISBN 978-0-307-47237-3
Penkov, Miroslav, 1982-
   East of the West; a country in stories. Farrar, Straus and Giroux 2011
      226p ISBN 978-0-374-11733-7 LC 2010-47602
Penzler, Otto, 1942-
   (ed) The Big book of adventure stories. *See* The Big book of
      adventure stories
   (ed) The Black Lizard big book of Black Mask stories. *See* The Black
      Lizard big book of Black Mask stories
   (ed) Christmas at the Mysterious Bookshop. *See* Christmas at the
      Mysterious Bookshop
   (ed) The greatest Russian stories of crime and suspense. *See* The
      greatest Russian stories of crime and suspense
People of the book; a decade of Jewish science fiction & fantasy; edited
      by Rachel Swirsky & Sean Wallace. Prime Books 2010 318p ISBN
      978-1-60701-238-2
Pera, Brian
   (ed) Life as we show it. *See* Life as we show it
Perfect murders. Gold, H. L.
Perkins, Lori
   (ed) Hungry for your love. *See* Hungry for your love
Philadelphia noir; edited by Carlin Romano. Akashic Books 2010 265p
      ISBN 978-1-936070-63-3 LC 2010-922722
Phillips, Helen, 1983-
   And yet they were happy. Leapfrog Press 2011 309p ISBN
      978-1-935248-18-7 LC 2011-03402
The **physics** of imaginary objects. Hall, T. M.
Picking the bones. Hodge, B.
Pictures of houses with water damage. Hemmingson, M.
Pierce, Todd James, 1965-
   (ed) Dead neon. *See* Dead neon
Pinckney, Darryl, 1953-
   (ed) The New York stories of Elizabeth Hardwick. *See* Hardwick,
      Elizabeth. The New York stories of Elizabeth Hardwick
Pitlor, Heidi
   (ed) The Best American short stories, 2011. *See* The Best American
      short stories, 2011
A **place** in the sun. Warsh, L.
Please come back to me. Treadway, J.
Plummer, Toni Margarita
   The bolero of Andi Rowe; stories. Northwestern University Press 2011
      119p ISBN 978-0-8101-2767-8; 0-8101-2767-9 LC 2010-52518
Pockell, Leslie
   (ed) 21 essential American short stories. *See* 21 essential American
      short stories
Portraits of a few of the people I've made cry. Sneed, C.
Powers, Tim
   The Bible repairman and other stories. Tachyon Publications 2011
      170p ISBN 978-1-61696-047-6; 1-61696-047-7

Pratt, Tim, 1976-
  (ed) Sympathy for the devil. *See* Sympathy for the devil
Prindle, Joseph
  Einstein's tears; a touch of genius. Roma J Press 2010 218p ISBN
    978-0-9823106-0-1 LC 2010-901941
Promised lands; new Jewish American fiction on longing and belonging;
    edited by Derek Rubin. University Press of New England 2010
    xxviii, 306p ISBN 978-1-58465-939-6; 1-58465-939-4;
    978-1-58465-920-4 (pa); 1-58465-920-3 (pa) LC 2010-29160
Pulse. Barnes, J.
Pushcart Prize XXXV: best of the small presses 2011; edited by Bill
    Henderson with the Pushcart Prize editors. Pushcart 2010 c2011
    598p ISBN 978-1-888889-59-8; 978-1-888889-60-4 (pa) ISSN
    0149-7863 LC 76-58675

Q

Qiu Xiaolong, 1953-
  Years of Red Dust; stories of Shanghai. St. Martin's Press 2010 227p
    ISBN 978-0-312-62809-3; 0-312-62809-9 LC 2010-29209
Quarantine. Mehta, R.
Quickening. Wieland, L.
Quiet as they come. Chau, A.

R

Randisi, Robert J.
  The guilt edge and other stories. Perfect Crime Books 2010 230p
    ISBN 978-0-9825157-3-0
  (ed) The Shamus winners: America's best private eye stories, volume
    I: 1982-1995. *See* The Shamus winners: America's best private eye
    stories, volume I: 1982-1995
Ray, Shann
  American masculine; stories. Graywolf 2011 185p ISBN
    978-1-55597-588-3 LC 2011-923187
The **really** funny thing about apathy. Martin, C.
Requiems for the departed; edited by Gerard Brennan & Mike Stone.
    Morrigan Books 2010 294p ISBN 978-1-451539-68-4
Return fire. Blake, G.
Riccardi, Ted, 1937-
  Between the Thames and the Tiber; the further adventures of Sherlock
    Holmes in Britain and the Italian Peninsula. Pegasus 2011 336p
    ISBN 978-1-60598-187-1
Rickert, M., 1959-
  Holiday. Golden Gryphon Press 2010 164p ISBN 978-1-930846-65-4;
    1-930846-65-7 LC 2010-26768
Riippi, Joseph
  The orange suitcase; stories. Ampersand Books 2011 87p il ISBN
    978-0-9841025-5-6
The **road.** Grossman, V. S.
Roberge, Rob
  Working backwards from the worst moment of my life; stories. Red
    Hen Press 2010 103p ISBN 978-1-59709-165-7; 1-59709-165-0
    LC 2010-26684
Robinson, Todd, 1972-
  (ed) Blood, guts, & whiskey. *See* Blood, guts, & whiskey
Rodoreda, Mercè, 1908-1983
  The selected stories of Merce Rodoreda; translated from the Catalan
    by Martha Tennent. Open Letter 2011 255p ISBN
    978-1-934824-31-3; 1-934824-31-3 LC 2010-38976
Romano, Carlin
  (ed) Philadelphia noir. *See* Philadelphia noir
Rosebud and other stories. Yamauchi, W.
Rosenbaum, Richard
  (ed) Can'tLit. *See* Can'tLit

S

Shapiro, Janice
  Bummer and other stories. Soft Skull Press 2010 195p ISBN
    978-1-59376-296-4; 1-59376-296-8 LC 2010-10919
Shepard, Jim
  You think that's bad; stories. Alfred A. Knopf 2011 225p ISBN
    978-0-307-59482-2; 0-307-59482-3 LC 2010-35998
Shepard, Sam, 1943-
  Day out of days; stories. Alfred A. Knopf 2010 282p ISBN
    978-0-307-26540-1; 0-307-26540-4 LC 2009-19578
Sherlock Holmes and the ghosts of Bly and other new adventures of the
    great detective. Thomas, D.
Shimon, Samuel, 1956-
  (ed) Beirut 39. *See* Beirut 39
Shipp, Jeremy C.
  Fungus of the heart; collected fiction. Raw Dog Screaming Press 2010
    158p ISBN 978-1-935738-01-5 LC 2010-933091
Showalter, Elaine
  (ed) The vintage book of American women writers. *See* The vintage
    book of American women writers
Side jobs. Butcher, J.
Silverberg, Robert
  The palace at midnight, 1980-82. Subterranean Press 2010 480p (The
    collected stories of Robert Silverberg, vol. 5) ISBN
    978-1-59606-321-1
Simmons, Diane, 1948-
  Little America. Ohio State University Press 2011 115p ISBN
    978-0-8142-5178-2; 978-0-8142-9258-7 (cd-rom) LC 2010-54476
The size of the universe. Cardinale, J.
The sky that wraps. Lake, J.
Sleight of hand. Beagle, P. S.
Smith, Clark Ashton, 1893-1961
  The last hieroglyph; edited by Scott Connors and Ron Hilger; with an
    introduction by Richard A. Lupoff. Night Shade Books 2010 360p
    (Collected fantasies of Clark Ashton Smith, v. 5) ISBN
    978-1-59780-032-7
Sneed, Christine, 1971-
  Portraits of a few of the people I've made cry; stories. University of
    Massachusetts Press 2010 154p ISBN 978-1-55849-858-7
    LC 2010-27928
      Winner of the 2009 Grace Paley Prize for Short Fiction
Soban, Tamara M.
  (tr) You do understand. *See* Blatnik, Andrej, 1963-. You do
    understand
Solzhenitsyn, Aleksandr, 1918-2008
  Apricot jam, and other stories; translated by Kenneth Lantz and
    Stephan Solzhenitsyn. Counterpoint 2011 375p ISBN
    978-1-58243-602-9; 1-58243-602-9 LC 2011-12332
Solzhenitsyn, Stephan
  (tr) Apricot jam, and other stories. *See* Solzhenitsyn, Aleksandr,
    1918-2008. Apricot jam, and other stories
Someday this will be funny. Tillman, L.
Somerville, Patrick, 1979-
  The universe in miniature in miniature. Featherproof Books 2010 307p
    il ISBN 978-0-9825808-1-3 LC 2009-944043
Sourland. Oates, J. C.
Speculative Horizons; edited by Patrick St-Denis. Subterranean Press
    2010 127p ISBN 978-1-59606-336-5
Spillman, Rob
  (ed) Fantastic women. *See* Fantastic women
St. Denis, Patrick
  (ed) Speculative Horizons. *See* Speculative Horizons
Steampunk II: steampunk reloaded; edited by Ann & Jeff VanderMeer.
    Tachyon 2010 426p il ISBN 978-1-61695-001-8; 978-1-61695-001-9
Stephens, John Richard
  (ed) The book of the living dead. *See* The book of the living dead
Sterling, Phillip
  In which brief stories are told. Wayne State University Press 2011
    134p (Made in Michigan writers series) ISBN 978-0-8143-3507-9
    LC 2010-31652

Still life with plums. Manilla, M.

Stone, Mike, 1966-

(ed) Requiems for the departed. *See* Requiems for the departed

Stories for nighttime and some for the day. Loory, B.

The **stories** (in) between; edited by Greg Schauer, Jeanne B. Benzel, and W. H. Horner. Fantasist Enterprises 2009 284p ISBN 978-0-9713608-8-4; 0-9713608-8-X

Strahan, Jonathan, 1964-

(ed) The Best of Larry Niven. *See* Niven, Larry. The Best of Larry Niven

(ed) The Best science fiction and fantasy of the year: volume five. *See* The Best science fiction and fantasy of the year: volume five

(ed) Life on Mars: tales from the new frontier. *See* Life on Mars: tales from the new frontier

Sutter, James L.

(ed) Before they were giants. *See* Before they were giants

Swain, Heather

(ed) Before. *See* Before

Swim back to me. Packer, A.

Swirsky, Rachel

(ed) People of the book. *See* People of the book

Through the drowsy dark; short fiction and poetry. Aqueduct Press 2010 145p (Conversation pieces, volume 27) ISBN 978-1-933500-38-6

Analyzed for short stories only

Sword woman and other historical adventures. Howard, R. E.

Sympathy for the devil; edited by Tim Pratt. Night Shade Books 2010 431p ISBN 978-1-59780-189-8

T

Tablet & pen; literary landscapes from the modern Middle East, a words without borders anthology; edited by Reza Asian. W. W. Norton & Company 2011 657p ISBN 978-0-393-06585-5; 0-393-06585-5 LC 2010-32679

Analyzed for short stories only

Tennent, Martha

(tr) The selected stories of Merce Rodoreda. *See* Rodoreda, Mercè, 1908-1983. The selected stories of Merce Rodoreda

Terry, Gay Partington

Meeting the Dog Girls; stories. Nonstop Press 2011 201p ISBN 987-1-933065-30-4

The **Thackery** T. Lambshead cabinet of curiosities; edited by Ann & Jeff VanderMeer. Harper Voyager 2011 320p il ISBN 978-0-06-200475-8

There is no other. Papernick, J.

This is not your city. Horrocks, C.

This new & poisonous air. McOmber, A.

Thomas, Donald, 1926-

Sherlock Holmes and the ghosts of Bly and other new adventures of the great detective. Pegasus Books 2010 364p ISBN 978-1-60598-134-5; 1-60598-134-6

Thomas, James, 1946-

(ed) Best of the West 2009. *See* Best of the West 2009

(ed) Best of the West 2010. *See* Best of the West 2010

(ed) Best of the West 2011. *See* Best of the West 2011

Thon, Melanie Rae

In this light; new and selected stories. Graywolf Press 2011 270p ISBN 978-1-55597-585-2

Through the drowsy dark. Swirsky, R.

Tichi, Cecelia, 1942-

(ed) Best of times, worst of times. *See* Best of times, worst of times

Tillman, Lynne

Someday this will be funny. Red Lemonade/Cursor 2011 159p ISBN 978-1-935869-00-9; 1-935869-00-0 LC 2010-941274

Toder, Emily

(tr) The life and memoirs of Dr. Pi and other stories. *See* Bayley, E., 1919-1990. The life and memoirs of Dr. Pi and other stories

Tóibín, Colm, 1955-
The empty family; stories. Scribner 2010 275p ISBN 978-1-4391-3832-8; 1-4391-3832-X LC 2010-32931
Treadway, Jessica, 1961-
Please come back to me; stories. University of Georgia Press 2010 238p (Flannery O'Connor Award for short fiction) ISBN 978-0-8203-3584-1; 0-8203-3584-3 LC 2010-05958
Treisman, Deborah
(ed) 20 under 40. *See* 20 under 40
Tremblay, Paul
In the mean time. ChiZine Publications 2010 214p ISBN 978-1-926851-06-8 LC 2010-903996-3
Trevor, William, 1928-
Selected stories. Viking 2010 c2009 567p ISBN 978-0-670-02206-9 LC 2010-19583
Trueblood, Valerie
Marry or burn; stories. Counterpoint 2010 294p ISBN 978-1-58243-598-5; 1-58243-598-7 LC 2010-17803
Tupitsyn, Masha
(ed) Life as we show it. *See* Life as we show it
Turtledove, Harry
Atlantis, and other places. ROC 2010 440p ISBN 978-0-451-46364-7 LC 2010-29373
    'A ROC book.'
Tuten, Frederic
Self portraits; fictions. W. W. Norton & Co. 2010 232p ISBN 978-0-393-07905-0 LC 2010-19761

U

Ulin, David L.
(ed) Cape Cod noir. *See* Cape Cod noir
Unclean jobs for women and girls. Nutting, A.
The **undivided** self. Self, W.
The **universe** in miniature in miniature. Somerville, P.
The **universe** of things. Jones, G. A.
Up from the marsh. Binkley, P.
Up the bright river. Farmer, P. J.

V

Vampires; the recent undead; edited by Paula Guran. Prime Books 2011 430p ISBN 978-1-60701-254-2
VanderMeer, Ann
(ed) Steampunk II: steampunk reloaded. *See* Steampunk II: steampunk reloaded
(ed) The Thackery T. Lambshead cabinet of curiosities. *See* The Thackery T. Lambshead cabinet of curiosities
VanderMeer, Jeff
(ed) Steampunk II: steampunk reloaded. *See* Steampunk II: steampunk reloaded
(ed) The Thackery T. Lambshead cabinet of curiosities. *See* The Thackery T. Lambshead cabinet of curiosities
Vanishing and other stories. Willis, D.
Vaughn, Carrie, 1973-
Kitty's greatest hits. Tor 2011 318p ISBN 978-0-7653-2696-6; 978-0-7653-2957-8 (pa) LC 2011-13448
    "A Tom Doherty Associates book"
Vida. Engel, P.
Villegas, Halli
The hair wreath and other stories. ChiZine Publications 2010 266p ISBN 978-1-926851-02-0
Vincent, Paul
(ed) The Dedalus book of Flemish fantasy. *See* The Dedalus book of Flemish fantasy

The **vintage** book of American women writers; edited and with an introduction by Elaine Showalter. Vintage Books 2011 822p ISBN 978-1-4000-3445-1 LC 2010-32691
   Analyzed for short stories only
Voice of America. Osondu, E. C.
Volt. Heathcock, A.
Vonnegut, Kurt, 1922-2007
   While mortals sleep; unpublished short fiction. Delacorte Press 2011 253p il ISBN 978-0-385-34373-2; 978-0-440-33987-8 (ebook) LC 2010-33817
Vukcevich, Ray
   Boarding instructions; stories. Fairwood Press 2010 219p ISBN 978-1-933846-23-1

W

Wallace, Sean, 1976-
   (ed) People of the book. *See* People of the book
Warsh, Lewis
   A place in the sun. Spuyten Duyvil 2010 217p ISBN 978-1-933132-71-6 LC 2009-26427
Waters, Sarah
   (ed) Dancing with Mr. Darcy. *See* Dancing with Mr. Darcy
Waugh, Charles, 1970-
   (ed) Family of fallen leaves. *See* Family of fallen leaves
The **way** of the wizard; edited by John Joseph Adams. Prime Books 2010 477p ISBN 978-1-60701-232-0
We are never as beautiful as we are now. Gallari, A.
We others. Millhauser, S.
Welcome to Bordertown; new stories and poems of the Borderlands; edited by Holly Black and Ellen Kushner; introduction by Terri Windling. Random House 2011 517p ISBN 978-0-375-86705-7; 0-375-86705-8; 978-0-375-96705-4 (lib bdg); 0-375-96705-2 (lib bdg); 978-0-375-89745-0 (e-book) LC 2010-35558
Wells, H. G. (Herbert George), 1866-1946
   Complete short story omnibus. Gollancz 2011 959p ISBN 978-0-575-09524-3; 0-575-09524-5 LC 2010-526130
Wender, Melissa L.
   (ed) Into the light. *See* Into the light
Wentworth, K. D., 1951
   (ed) L. Ron Hubbard presents Writers of the Future volume XXVI. *See* L. Ron Hubbard presents Writers of the Future volume XXVI
   (ed) L. Ron Hubbard presents Writers of the Future volume XXVII. *See* L. Ron Hubbard presents Writers of the Future volume XXVII
What becomes. Kennedy, A. L.
What I didn't see and other stories. Fowler, K. J.
What is all this? Dixon, S.
When the great days come. Dozois, G. R.
While mortals sleep. Vonnegut, K.
While the women are sleeping. Marías, J.
White poppies and other stories. Zhang Kangkang
Widow. Latiolais, M.
Wieland, Liza
   Quickening; stories. Southern Methodist University Press 2010 239p ISBN 978-0-87074-564-5 LC 2010-24681
Wilber, Rick, 1948-
   (ed) Future media. *See* Future media
Williamson, Eric Miles
   14 fictional positions; short fictions. Raw Dog Screaming Press 2010 148p ISBN 987-1-933293-97-4 LC 2010-928479
Willis, Deborah
   Vanishing and other stories. Harper Perennial 2010 288, 20p ISBN 978-0-06-200752-0 LC 2010-03362
      First published 2009 in Canada
Willis, Meredith Sue
   Out of the mountains; Appalachian stories. Ohio University Press 2010 170p ISBN 978-0-8214-1919-9; 978-0-8214-1920-5 (pa); 9780-8214-4331-6 (ebook) LC 2010-4382

Wilson, Betty, 1940-
(tr) Aunt Resia and the spirits and other stories. *See* Lahens, Yanick, 1953-. Aunt Resia and the spirits and other stories
Windling, Terri, 1958-
(ed) The beastly bride. *See* The beastly bride
Wolfe, Gary K., 1946-
(ed) Up the bright river. *See* Farmer, Philip José, 1918-2009. Up the bright river
Womack, Craig
Art as performance, story as criticism; reflections on native literary aesthetics. University of Oklahoma Press 2009 406p bibl f ISBN 978-0-8061-4064-3; 0-8061-4064-X; 978-0-8061-4065-0 (pa); 0-8061-4065-8 (pa) LC 2009-06876
The **woman** with the bouquet. Schmitt, E.-E.
Woodrell, Daniel
The outlaw album; stories. Little, Brown 2011 167p ISBN 978-0-316-05756=1 LC 2011-01107
Working backwards from the worst moment of my life. Roberge, R.

Y

Yamauchi, Wakako
Rosebud and other stories; edited by Lillian Howan. University of Hawaii Press in association with UCLA Asian American Studies Center 2011 127p ISBN 978-0-8248-3260-5 LC 2010-26340
The **Year's** best dark fantasy & horror; edited by Paula Guran. 2010 ed. Prime Books 2010 568p ISBN 978-1-60701-233-7
The **Year's** best science fiction: twenty-eighth annual collection; edited by Gardner Dozois. St. Martin's Griffin 2011 xli, 662p ISBN 978-0-312-54633-5; 978-0-312-56950-1 (pa)
Years of Red Dust. Qiu Xiaolong
You are free. Senna, D.
You are my heart and other stories. Neugeboren, J.
You do understand. Blatnik, A.
You know when the men are gone. Fallon, S.
You think that's bad. Shepard, J.

Z

Z: zombie stories; edited by J. M. Lassen. Night Shade Books 2011 296p il ISBN 978-1-59780-312-0; 978-1-59780-313-7 (e-book)
Zhang Kangkang
White poppies and other stories; translated by Karen Gernant and Chen Zeping. Cornell University East Asia Program 2011 164p (Cornell East Asia series) ISBN 978-1-933947-23-5; 978-1-933947-23-2 (pa) LC 2010-931924
Zipes, Jack David, 1937-
(tr) The cloak of dreams. *See* Balázs, Béla, 1884-1949. The cloak of dreams
Zombies: the recent dead; edited by Paula Guran. Prime Books 2010 473p ISBN 978-1-60701-234-4

PERIODICALS INDEXED

A

Abitare. 11 times a yr ISSN (0001-3218) Editrice Abitare, Segesta s.p.a., 15 Corso Monforte, 20122 Milan, Italy
Text in Italian and English; summaries in French, German, and Spanish

The Advocate (Vancouver, B.C.). 6 times a yr ISSN (0044-6416) Vancouver Bar Association, 4765 Pilot House Rd., West Vancouver, B.C. V7W 1J2, Canada

African American Review. q ISSN (1062-4783) African American Review, Arts & Sciences Administration, Saint Louis University, Ritter Hall 125, 220 N. Grand Blvd., St. Louis, MO 63103-2007

Afro-Hispanic Review. semi-ann ISSN (0278-8969) Vanderbilt University, Department of Spanish and Portuguese, Station B, PO Box 351617, Nashville, TN 37235 US

Agni. semi-ann ISSN (1046-218X) Agni, Boston University Writing Program, 236 Bay State Road, Boston, MA 02215

AMASS. irr Society For Popular Democracy, 10920 Wilshire Blvd, Ste 150, Los Angeles, CA 90024 US

Amerasia Journal. 3 times a yr ISSN (0044-7471) University of California, Los Angeles, Asian American Studies Center, 3230 Campbell Hall, Los Angeles, CA 90024-1546

The American Conservative. m ISSN (1540-966X) American Conservative LLC, 1300 Wilson Blvd., Ste. 120, Arlington, VA 22209 US

American Medical Association Journal. See JAMA

The American Scholar. q ISSN (0003-0937) The American Scholar, Editorial and Circulation Offices, 1606 New Hampshire Ave., NW, Washington, DC 20009

Américas. 6 times a yr ISSN (0379-0940) Americas, P.O. Box 3000, Denville, NJ 07834-3000

The Antioch Review. q ISSN (0003-5769) Antioch Review, Subscriptions, P.O. Box 148, Yellow Springs, OH 45387

Archipiélago. q Confluencia S.A. de C.V., Mexico

Arizona Attorney. m (Ag/S combined) ISSN (1040-4090) State Bar of Arizona, 111 W. Monroe St., Ste. 1800, Phoenix, AZ 85003-1742

Atlantic Monthly (1993). m (bi-m Ja/F and Jl/Ag) ISSN (1072-7825) Atlantic Subscription Processing Center, Box 52661, Boulder, CO 80322

B

Bomb. q ISSN (0743-3204) New Art Publications, Subscriptions Dept., P.O. Box 3000, Denville, NJ 07834

Border Crossings. q ISSN (0831-2559) Arts Manitoba Publications Inc., 500-70 Arthur St., Winnipeg, MB R3B 1G7, Canada

Boston Review. 6 times a yr ISSN (0734-2306) Boston Critic, Inc., 30 Wadsworth Street, Suite 407, Cambridge, Massachusetts, 02139

C

Callaloo. q ISSN (0161-2492) Johns Hopkins University Press, Journals Publishing Div., 2715 North Charles St., Baltimore, MD 21218-4363

Calyx. 3 times a yr ISSN (0147-1627) Calyx Inc., PO Box B, Corvallis, OR 97339-0539

Chicago Review. q ISSN (0009-3696) Chicago Review, 5801 S. Kenwood, Chicago, IL 60637

Chinese Literature Today. semi-ann ISSN (2151-4399) Board of Regents of the University of Oklahoma, 660 Parrington Oval, Norman, OK 73019-0390

Commentary. m ISSN (0010-2601) Commentary, Inc., 165 East 56th Street, New York, N.Y. 10022

Commonweal. bi-w (except Christmas/New Year's; m in Jl, Ag) ISSN (0010-3330) Commonweal Foundation, 475 Riverside Dr., Room 405, New York, NY 10115

Confrontation. semi-ann ISSN (0010-5716) Long Island University, C.W. Post College of Long Island University, Brookville, NY 11548

Critical Quarterly. q ISSN (0011-1562) Blackwell Publishers, Subscriber Services Coordinator, 238 Main St., Cambridge, MA 02142

D

Dalhousie Review. 3 times a yr ISSN (0011-5827) Dalhousie Review, Dalhousie University, Halifax, Nova Scotia, Canada B3H 4R2

DisClosure. ann ISSN (1055-6133) College of Arts and Sciences, University of Kentucky, 213 Patterson Office Tower, Lexington, KY 40503-002

E

Entertainment Weekly. w ISSN (1049-0434) Entertainment Weekly Inc., 1675 Broadway, 29th floor, New York, NY 10019

Esquire. m ISSN (0194-9535) Esquire Subscriptions, P.O. Box 7146, Red Oak, IA 51591

F

Feminist Studies. 3 times a yr ISSN (0046-3663) Women's Studies Program, University of Maryland, College Park, MD 20742

Femspec. semi-ann ISSN (1523-4002) Lexington Books, 4501 Forbes Boulevard, Suite 200, Lanham, Maryland 20706

Five Points. 3 times a yr ISSN (1088-8500) Board of Regents of the University System of Georgia, Georgia State University, Dept. of English, P.O. Box 3970, Atlanta, GA 30302-3970

Flying. m ISSN (0015-4806) Bonnier Corporation, 460 N. Orlando Ave., Suite 200, Winter Park, FL 32789

FS. See Feminist Studies

G

Georgia Bar Journal. 6 times a yr ISSN (1085-1437) State Bar of Georgia, 800 The Hurt Bldg., 50 Hurt Plz., Atlanta, GA 30303-2934

The Georgia Review. q ISSN (0016-8386) University of Georgia, Athens, GA 30602

Gettysburg Review. q ISSN (0898-4557) Gettysburg Review, Gettysburg College, Gettysburg, PA 17325-1491

Glamour. m ISSN (0017-0747) Glamour, P.O. Box 37690, Boone, IA 50037-0690
Incorporating: Mademoiselle

Good Housekeeping. m ISSN (0017-209X) Good Housekeeping, P.O. Box 7186, Red Oak, IA 51591-0186

Granta. q ISSN (0017-3231) Granta Publications, 12 Addison Avenue, London W11 4QR

H

Hali. q ISSN (0142-0798) Hali Publications, P.O. Box 1518, Champlain, NY 12919-1518

Hanging Loose. semi-ann ISSN (0440-2316) Hanging Loose Press, 231 Wyckoff Street, Brooklyn, N.Y. 11217

Harper's. m ISSN (0017-789X) Harper's Magazine, P.O. Box 7511, Red Oak, IA 51591-0511

Harvard Review. semi-ann ISSN (1077-2901) Houghton Library of the Harvard College Library, Lamont Library, Harvard University, Cambridge, MA 02138

The Hudson Review. q ISSN (0018-702X) The Hudson Review, 684 Park Ave., New York, NY 10021

The Humanist. bi-m ISSN (0018-7399) Humanist, 7 Harwood Dr., P.O. Box 1118, Amherst, NY 14226-7188

I

Iceland Review. q ISSN (0019-1094) Iceland Review, Borgartuni 23, Reykjavik 105, Iceland

Indiana Review. semi-ann ISSN (0738-386X) Indiana Review, Ballantine Hall 465, Indiana University, Bloomington, IN 47405 US

Indianapolis Monthly. 14 times a yr ISSN (0899-0328) Emmis Broadcasting Corp., 950 N. Meridian St., Ste. 1200, Indianapolis, IN 46204-3908

Intersections. semi-ann ISSN (1440-9151) Murdoch University, School of Asian Studies, Available from: http://wwwsshe.murdoch.edu.au/intersections/
Electronic resource

Iowa Review. 3 times a yr ISSN (0021-065X) The Iowa Review, The University of Iowa, 308 English-Philosophy Building, Iowa City, Iowa 52242

J

JAMA. 4 times a month ISSN (0098-7484) American Medical Association, Circulation and Fulfillment Division, 535 N. Dearborn St., Chicago, IL 60610

Journal of American Folklore. q ISSN (0021-8715) University of Illinois Press, 1325 S. Oak St., Champaign, IL 61820

Journal of Medical Ethics. m ISSN (0306-6800) British Medical Journal, P.O. Box 590A, Kennebunkport, ME 04046
Includes supplement: Medical Humanities

Journal of the American Medical Association. See JAMA

K

The Kenyon Review. q ISSN (0163-075X) The Kenyon Review, Kenyon College, Gambier, OH 43022

Koreana. q ISSN (1016-0744) Korea Foundation, 526 Namdaemunno 5-ga, Chung-gu, Seoul 100-095, S. Korea

Kunstforum International. semi-m ISSN (0177-3674) Kunstforum International, Nidegger Str. 21, D-5000 Koln 41, Germany

L

Lapham's Quarterly. q ISSN (1935-7494) American Agora Foundation, Inc., 33 Irving Place, Eighth Floor, New York, N.Y. 10003

Legacy. semi-ann ISSN (0748-4321) University of Nebraska Press, 1111 Lincoln Mall, Lincoln, NE 68588 US

The Literary Review (Madison, N.J.). q ISSN (0024-4589) Fairleigh Dickinson University, 285 Madison Ave., Madison, NJ 07940

M

The Massachusetts Review. q ISSN (0025-4878) University of Massachusetts, Memorial Hall, Amherst, MA 01002

Medical Humanities. See Journal of Medical Ethics

Michigan Quarterly Review. q ISSN (0026-2420) University of Michigan, 3032 Rackham Bldg., Ann Arbor, MI 48109

Ms. q ISSN (0047-8318) Ms. Magazine, P.O. Box 5299, Harlan, IA 51593

N

National Review. bi-w (except 1st issue in Ja) ISSN (0028-0038) National Review, P.O. Box 668, Mt. Morris, IL 61054-0668

Nature. w ISSN (0028-0836) Nature, Subscription Dept., P.O. Box 5055, Brentwood, TN 37024-5055

Nature Conservancy. q ISSN (0028-5200) Nature Conservancy, 1815 N. Lynn St., Arlington, VA 22209

Nebraska Life. bi-m ISSN (1091-2886) Nebraska Life Magazine, 202 Norfolk Avenue, P.O. Box 819, Norfolk, NE 68702

New England Review. q ISSN (1053-1297) New England Review, Univ. Press of New England, 23 S. Main St., Hanover, NH 03755-2048

New Letters. q ISSN (0146-4930) University of Missouri-Kansas City, 5100 Rockhill Rd., Kansas City, MO 64110

New Statesman (London, England: 1996). w ISSN (1364-7431) New Statesman & Society, C and C Mailers Int'l, 900 Lincoln Blvd., P.O. Box 177, Middlesex, NJ 08846

The New York Review of Books. bi-w (m Ja, Jl, Ag, S) ISSN (0028-7504) New York Review of Books, P.O. Box 420384, Palm Coast, FL 32142-0384

The New Yorker. w (except 6 combined issues) ISSN (0028-792X) The New Yorker, Box 56447, Boulder, CO 80328-6447

The North American Review. 4 times a yr ISSN (0029-2397) University of Northern Iowa, 1222 W. 27th St., Cedar Falls, IA 50614

Nursing. m ISSN (0360-4039) Lippincott Williams & Wilkins, 323 Norristown Rd., Suite 200, Ambler, PA 19002-2758

O

Orion. bi-m ISSN (1058-3130) Orion, Subscription Dept., 136 E. 64th St., New York, NY 10021

P

Parabola. q ISSN (0362-1596) Parabola, 656 Broadway, New York, NY 10012-2317

The Paris Review. q ISSN (0031-2037) The Paris Review, 45-39 171 Place, Flushing, NY 11358

Piecework. bi-m ISSN (1067-2249) Interweave Press, LLC, 201 E. Fourth St., Loveland, CO 80537

Ploughshares. 3 times a yr ISSN (0048-4474) Ploughshares, Inc., Emerson College, 120 Boylston St., Boston, MA 02116-4624

Prairie Schooner. q ISSN (0032-6682) University of Nebraska, 201 Andrews Hall, Lincoln, NE 68588

Public Management. m ISSN (0033-3611) International City Management Assn., 777 N. Capitol St. NE, Ste. 500, Washington, DC 20002-4201

R

Raritan. q ISSN (0275-1607) Rutgers University, 31 Mine St., New Brunswick, NJ 08903

The Review of Contemporary Fiction. 3 times a yr ISSN (0276-0045) Review of Contemporary Fiction, 1805 S. Wright St, MC-011, Champaign, IL 61820 US

River Styx. 3 times a yr ISSN (0149-8851) Big River Association, 634 North Grand Blvd, 12th Fl. Saint Louis, MI 63103

S

Salmagundi. q ISSN (0036-3529) Skidmore College, Saratoga Springs, NY 12866

The Saturday Evening Post. bi-m ISSN (0048-9239) Saturday Evening Post Subscription Offices, P.O. Box 420235, Palm Coast, FL 32142-1235

Seventeen. m ISSN (0037-301X) Seventeen Subscription Dept., Box 55195, Boulder, CO 80322-5195

The Sewanee Review. q ISSN (0037-3052) The Johns Hopkins University Press, 2715 North Charles Street, Baltimore, Maryland 21218-4363

Social Text. q ISSN (0164-2472) Duke University Press, 905 W. Main St., Suite 18B, Durham, NC 27701

South Carolina Review. semi-ann ISSN (0038-3163) Clemson University, Dept. of English, Box 341503, Clemson, SC 29634-1503

South Dakota Magazine. bi-m ISSN (0886-2680) South Dakota Magazine, 410 E Third St, Yankton, SD 57078-0175

Southern Humanities Review. q ISSN (0038-4186) Auburn University, 9088 Haley Center, Auburn, AL 36849

Southern Quarterly. q ISSN (0038-4496) University of Southern Mississippi, Box 5078, Southern Station, Hattiesburg, MS 39406

The Southern Review (Baton Rouge, La.). q ISSN (0038-4534) Southern Review, 43 Allen Hall, LSU, Baton Rouge, LA 70803-5005

Southwest Review. q ISSN (0038-4712) Southwest Review, 6410 Airline Rd., SMU, Dallas, TX 75275

SQ. See StoryQuarterly

StoryQuarterly. ann ISSN (1041-0708) Rutgers University, Camden, 303 Cooper St, Camden, NJ 08102

Studies in American Jewish Literature. ann ISSN (0271-9274) Purdue University Press, 504 West State Street, Stewart Center, Room 370, West Lafayette, Indiana 47907

T

Texas Bar Journal. m (except Ag) ISSN (0040-4187) Texas Bar Journal, Box 12487, Austin, TX 78711-2487

Tribal College Journal of American Indian Higher Education. q ISSN (1052-5505) American Indian Higher Education Consortium, 2509 Montgomery Way, Sacramento, CA 95818

> Earlier title: Tribal College, 1052-5505

TriQuarterly. 3 times a yr ISSN (0041-3097) TriQuarterly, Available from: http://triquarterly.org/

> Electronic resource

V

The Virginia Quarterly Review. q ISSN (0042-675X) The University of Virginia, One West Range, Charlottesville, VA 22903

> Suspended publication with Vol. 87, No. 1 (Winter 2011).

Voices from the Middle. q ISSN (1074-4762) Council of Teachers of English, 1111 W. Kenyon Rd., Urbana, IL 61801-1096

VQR. See The Virginia Quarterly Review

W

The Walrus. 10 times a yr ISSN (1708-4032) The Walrus Foundation, 19 Duncan St., Suite 101, Toronto, ON M5H 3H1, Canada

Western Humanities Review. 3 times a yr ISSN (0043-3845) Western Humanities Review, University of Utah, English Dept., 255 South Central Campus Dr., Rm. 3500, Salt Lake City, UT 84112-0494

Women & Environments International Magazine. semi-ann ISSN (1499-1993) Women & Environments International Magazine, Institute for Women's Studies & Gender Studies, New College, University of Toronto, 40 Willcocks St., Toronto, ON, Canada, M5S 1C6

> Formerly WE International; name changed with Spring/Summer 2001

Women's Review of Books. bi-m ISSN (0738-1433) Old City Publishing, Inc., 628 North 2nd Street, Philadelphia, PA 19123

> Temporarily suspended after Vol. 22, No. 3 (December 2004); resumed publication with Vol. 23, No. 1 (January/February 2006).

Women's Studies Quarterly. q ISSN (0732-1562) The Feminist Press at CUNY, The Graduate Center, 365 Fifth Avenue, Suite 5406, New York, NY 10016

> Continues: Women's Studies Newsletter with Vol. 9, No. 1 (Spring 1981).

World Literature Today. bi-m ISSN (0196-3570) University of Oklahoma Press, Editorial Office, 110 Monnet Hall, Univ. of Oklahoma, Norman, OK 73069

The Writer. m ISSN (0043-9517) The Writer, Inc., 120 Boylston St., Boston, MA 02116-4615

Y

The Yale Review. q ISSN (0044-0124) Blackwell Publishers, Yale Review, Subscriber Services Coordinator, 238 Main St., Cambridge, MA 02142